KU-019-579

CONVEYANCING PRACTICE IN SCOTLAND

Ann Stewart:

For my mother Jackie Stewart, for holding on with open hands
and in memory of my darling father, George (Tony) Stewart of Dalbuie.

Euan Sinclair:

In memory of JHS –

"I think I caught his spirit
Later that same year
I'm sure I heard his echo
In my baby's new born tears
I just wish I could have told him in the living years."

(Mike & The Mechanics)

CONVEYANCING PRACTICE IN SCOTLAND

Sixth Edition

Euan Fraser Fitzpatrick Sinclair LLB, MBA, LLM

Writer to the Signet, Solicitor in Scotland

Former member of the Conveyancing Committee of the Law Society of Scotland

Ann Eileen Atkinson Stewart WS, LLB, Signet Accredited (Commercial Property)

Associate and Senior Professional Support Lawyer at Shepherd+Wedderburn

Writer to the Signet, Solicitor in Scotland

Founding member of the Property Standardisation Group

Bloomsbury Professional

Bloomsbury Professional Limited, Maxwelton House, 41–43 Boltro Road, Haywards Heath, West Sussex, RH16 1BJ

© Bloomsbury Professional Limited 2011

Bloomsbury Professional, an imprint of Bloomsbury Publishing Plc

All rights reserved. No part of this publication may be reproduced in any material form (including photocopying or storing it in any medium by electronic means and whether or not transiently or incidentally to some other use of this publication) without the written permission of the copyright owner except in accordance with the provisions of the Copyright, Designs and Patents Act 1988 or under the terms of a licence issued by the Copyright Licensing Agency Ltd, Saffron House, 6–10 Kirby Street, London EC1N 8TS. Applications for the copyright owner's written permission to reproduce any part of this publication should be addressed to the publisher.

Whilst every care has been taken to ensure the accuracy of the content of this work, no responsibility for loss occasioned to any person acting or refraining from action as a result of the material in this publication can be accepted by the author or by the publisher.

Warning: The doing of an unauthorised act in relation to a copyright work may result in both a civil claim for damages and criminal prosecution.

Crown copyright material is reproduced with the permission of the Controller of HMSO and the Queen's Printer for Scotland. Any European material in this work which has been reproduced from EUR-lex, the official European Communities legislation website, is European Communities copyright.

A CIP Catalogue record for this book is available from the British Library.

ISBN: 978 184766 881 3

Typeset by Phoenix Photosetting, Chatham, Kent
Printed and bound in Great Britain by CPI Group (UK) Ltd, Croydon, CR0 4YY

Contents

Chapter 1 – The Legal Profession

Chapter 2 – The Framework

Chapter 3 – New Clients and New Instructions

Chapter 7 – Searches and Enquiries

Chapter 8 – Examination of and Reporting on Title

Chapter 9 – Conveying the Property: The Disposition and Other Deeds

Chapter 10 – Security

Contents

Table of Statutes

References are to paragraph number

Table of Orders, Rules and Regulations

Table of European Legislation

Table of Cases

References are to paragraph number

T

W

Introduction

This sixth edition marks a major restructuring and rewrite of the previous edition. However, the overall objective is the same as that consistently expressed by the original author, John Henderson Sinclair, in previous editions: to write a book in relatively straightforward English, explaining what the various steps were, from the time someone woke up and said 'I must move house urgently' until the final steps.

Sadly John H. Sinclair, my father and co-author, died suddenly in November 2009 before he and I had the opportunity to discuss the possibility of a sixth edition and the shape it might take. By the time I was over the shock of Dad's untimely death combined with the birth of our third child two months later, many of Dad's friends and colleagues began to ask me what would happen to the Conveyancing handbook. It is a well-regarded book, occupying a unique place on the conveyancer's bookshelf. So I am particularly grateful to Dad's dear friend Christine Lockhart, to Professor George Gretton, and to Paula O'Connell of Bloomsbury for their encouragement to embark on another edition.

It was, however, clear to me that that the fifth edition was due a major overhaul. If there was to be a sixth edition, there would be no half-measures or tinkering. I realised early on in the project that I neither had the capacity nor the will to write it myself – I needed a co-author. I was very pleased when Ann Stewart agreed to be that co-author. Ann brings her many years of transactional experience and her dedicated role in informing and shaping best practice in conveyancing for the lawyers at Shepherd +Wedderburn, one of Scotland's leading firms.

Both Ann and I recognised that a practitioner's handbook should encompass as many of the practical realities of working in a conveyancer's office as possible – and that the sixth edition should therefore not be exclusively thought of as a student text. We have tried to make it relevant to an experienced practitioner, too. Thanks to Ann's wide experience, we have expanded the content significantly to include examination of title and also to weave commercial conveyancing into the mainstream of the book.

Ann has worked like a Trojan to bring this edition together in a short space of time. In fact, Ann has written all of the 'stuff of conveyancing' pretty much straight off the bat. Any credit for this new edition must all go to Ann. Her sterling commitment to the project has been unwavering. At the same time as we were writing the book, I moved with my family to take up a new job in Vancouver and I have had to lean on Ann more than I wanted to, but she has never once complained. Ann and I have been able to keep in regular contact, thanks to Skype, and it is fair to say that, with the different time zones, this edition has been written 24 hours a day.

As ever, there are numerous contributions to acknowledge and be grateful for. Donald Reid of Mitchells Roberton for sense-checking an advanced manuscript, Ross MacKay of HBJ Gateley for the advance copy of the Combined Standard Clauses 2nd Edition, Gary Robertson and Andrew Hickie of Millar & Bryce for the search reports in the appendix, Struan Douglas of Purdie & Co for several styles, Ken Steele and Ruth Swanson at The Lints Partnership, Robert Pirrie at the WS Society, Douglas Hunter, Iain Macniven, and Rachel Oliphant of the Property Standardisation Group, and many friends at S+W for their support, encouragement and sense (and sanity) checking including: Amy Campbell, Gerald Carter, Joanna Clark, Elaine Colville, James Dobie, Anthea Duncan, Ian Gibson Jenny Keenan, Julia Kidd, Steven King, Sharon Martin and Anne Millar.

Writing a book like this takes an immense amount of time and effort on the parts of the authors, and that necessarily means that there are collateral effects for our home lives. So huge gratitude must be acknowledged for our respective spouses, Alexandra and Steve for keeping us both sane and in good humour whilst writing this book – and attending to our day jobs.

Euan Sinclair
Vancouver, 20 June 2011

Notes:

This text is correct as at 20 June 2011.

References to the 'Law Society' are to the Law Society of Scotland unless otherwise stated. Reference to 'the Journal' or 'JLSS' is to the Journal of the Law Society of Scotland, available at www.journalonline.co.uk and articles are retrievable from that website.

See website to accompany this book at
www.conveyancingpracticescotland.com

Chapter 1

The Legal Profession

CONVEYANCERS

1.01 First of all, let's establish the correct terminology for people engaged in conveyancing.

A **solicitor** is a person who is qualified and licensed to practise as such by having obtained a law degree (or passing equivalent examinations assessed by the Law Society), a Diploma in Legal Practice, and then having served a two-year traineeship in a solicitor's office, which incorporates trainee specific seminars, and from 2011 onwards, will also focus on achieving professional skills outcomes. This rigorous basic training occupies at the very least six years, which is the equivalent of the basic medical training. The aspiring Scottish solicitor must also be shown to be a fit and proper person to be admitted as a solicitor.

Solicitors have long enjoyed being considered as 'men of business', that is to say people who dealt with a wide variety of affairs—they used to be town clerks of small local government units, banking agents, land and estate agents, company secretaries and a variety of other engagements, as well as looking after what we now think of as legal business. Increased specialisation has closed many opportunities for solicitors, but equally it has opened other doors—employment law, pensions law, corporate finance law and many others, not mention the variety of 'in-house' legal jobs. Despite a requirement for increased commercialism, however, there remains a place for the key skills of the 'trusted adviser' in all aspects of the provision of legal services.

Solicitors are also often involved in the marketing of residential property, offering a co-ordinated selling service for the client. Local Solicitors' Property Centres eg the ESPC in Edinburgh and GSPC in Glasgow, have given even the smallest firm of solicitors a shop window for estate agency services, but there remains healthy competition among solicitors and estate agents.

A **lawyer** is anyone who practises law, which includes solicitors and also advocates and judges. Advocates are specialists in pleading before the supreme courts and are rarely conveyancers. Paralegals do not practise law in a technical sense and are not lawyers.

A **conveyancer** is a solicitor or the employee of a solicitor, who deals in practice mainly with the purchase and sale of heritable property. Conveyancers include paralegals.

A **paralegal** is a skilled employee of a solicitor or legal firm who carries out specific and less complex conveyancing. The first course in paralegal conveyancing was held in the University of Strathclyde in the 1980s and soon was extended to other cities, other methods (by distance learning) and in other subjects (executry, court work etc).

The paralegal, in conveyancing, executry, court work, debt collection etc is now a highly-valued part of the legal team, and the Scottish Paralegal Association ('**SPA**') is recognised by the Law Society (www. scottish-paralegal.org.uk). The SPA categorises paralegals according to three grades qualifications and experience and recommends salary scales accordingly. The paralegal's immense supporting role has now been recognised by the Law Society's Registered Paralegal Scheme.

However attractive delegation seems in terms of the business model, it should not be forgotten that the oversight of the conveyancing transaction is the responsibility of the solicitor. It is the solicitor who will have to account to the client and the Law Society and his or her partners for any shortcomings in the service provided and consequent complaint.

THE SOLICITORS' CONVEYANCING MONOPOLY

1.02 Having outlined how difficult it is to become a solicitor, and perhaps having indicated how expensive this is all going to be for the aspiring solicitor, it is now appropriate to consider the benefits of being a solicitor. Quite apart from the intangible benefits of the profession, which are many and depend on the perception of each individual, one of the most important privileges has been the so-called 'solicitors' monopoly' of conveyancing matters. This is contained in the Solicitors (Scotland) Act 1980, s 32, which states:

> 'Any unqualified person, including a body corporate who draws or prepares a writ relating to heritable or moveable estate.... shall be guilty of an offence.'

Section 32(3) then continues, to exclude from the definition of a writ: '(a) a will or other testamentary writing; (b) a document in re mercatoria (in business matters), missive or mandate; (c) a letter or power of attorney; and (d) a transfer of stock containing no trust or limitation thereof.'

Thus, of the four major steps of a property transaction: marketing, completing missives, completing title and drafting the deed, and settling up, it is only the third part that is protected by the conveyancing monopoly. A person who is not legally qualified, or employed by a solicitor, may market heritable property, and even complete missives on behalf of a purchaser or seller. When, however, it comes to drawing up the formal deeds (ie those deeds that are not excepted by s 32(3)) this work must be done by a solicitor (although advocates are also included in the conveyancing monopoly as well, but as a matter of tradition they do not handle conveyancing, except perhaps on a personal basis).

It tends to be the case that other peoples' monopolies are seen as oppressive, while one's own is of course 'in the public interest'. Statutory monopolies, like other kinds of anti-competitive arrangements, are not popular, and are gradually being dismantled. The Law Reform (Miscellaneous Provisions) (Scotland) Act 1990, created two new roles, that erode monopolies: the solicitor-advocate, a solicitor with coveted rights of audience in the upper courts (solicitors already have rights of audience in Sheriff Courts and other lower courts and tribunals), and the licensed conveyancer and executry practitioner, who might practise conveyancing although not qualified as a solicitor. The former concept has worked quite well, and solicitor advocates regularly appear in the upper courts, which were previously denied to them, and some have also been recognised with the dignity of QC.

The latter category did not enjoy similar success, as the Scottish Conveyancing and Executry Board, set up to oversee these practitioners, was abolished in 2003. In hindsight the trouble was that the bar was raised too high, and candidates would have been as well to qualify as solicitors. The former Board's responsibilities to the small group of conveyancing practitioners were transferred to the Law Society.

The categories of person entitled to participate in this 'monopoly' has expanded over the years through successive enactments, and, as well as conveyancing practitioners now includes registered foreign lawyers and is soon to include 'licensed legal services providers' under the Legal

Services (Scotland) Act 2010. The concept of the conveyancing monopoly is becoming increasingly illusory.

Nothing said above, however, limits the right of non-qualified parties selling or buying houses, to act on their own behalf in the matter. As a rough analogy, if you have a sore tooth, you may pull it out yourself with a doorknob and string, but do not even ask a non-dentally qualified person to do the job for you, as that will be an offence. Thus if the Smiths sell a house there is no reason why they should not do all the work themselves—sell the property on the internet or otherwise, complete missives and check the Disposition, prepare a discharge of any security over the property, and present it for registration. A solicitor need not be employed, but a non-solicitor may not be employed, at a fee, to draw up a writ covered by the monopoly. If that person is prepared to act gratuitously that is permitted. The only snag from the Smiths' point of view, is that they cannot grant a valid letter of obligation and may result in a trip to Register House for a personal settlement. If a bank were involved, they would also have to pay the bank's solicitors, negating any saving as their solicitor could act for the bank for around the same fee.

PROFESSIONAL RESPONSIBILITIES

1.03 The solicitors' profession was the last of the non-specialising professions, and a solicitor is still qualified to advise on a great number of matters, although, inevitably, with the greater complexity of matters, a degree of specialisation is becoming more prevalent and desirable. Thus we are seeing an increase in 'boutique' firms who handle only for example commercial conveyancing, employment law, corporate finance law etc It is very difficult for the individual to combine 'chamber' work with litigation, as attendance at court can take up so much of the working day, and at the other end of the scale, large firms are split into discrete practice areas, where specialised expertise is developed. Most solicitors these days will focus their practice on one or only a few areas of proficiency. The solicitor, like other agents, is bound by duties of agent to client imposed by the common law of agency, which although often woven into modern statutory duties, remain as clear duties and should not be forgotten:

   (a)   the agent must carry out the principal's instructions;

(b)   the agent is in a personal relationship with the principal, and must not delegate the duties of the principal to another, without the principal's instructions;

(c)   the agent must keep the money and property of the principal separate from the agent's own money and property, and keep accounts of dealings with it;

(d)   the agent must give the principal the full benefit of contracts made with third parties, and any secret commission must not be gained without the principal's consent.

In return for these duties, the agent is entitled to receive a reasonable remuneration, reimbursement of expenses, to be relieved of all liabilities incurred in the performance of the agency, and to the agent's lien over the property of the principal in the agent's hands in the course of the agency, until remuneration has been received.

To the law of agency there must now be added various regulatory controls, principally under the Law Society Regulations, and under Financial Services and Markets Act 2000 (generally known as '**FISMA**'), and various other statutes. These regulatory controls are designed to protect the general public from unscrupulous individuals, and are a feature of 21st century living.

The financial services provisions are particularly important, and are designed to protect investors from obtaining incompetent or dishonest advice from incompetent and dishonest advisers and dealers, who are, regrettably, more prevalent in our society than any of us would wish. While the Acts are framed on the basis that investors must accept responsibility for the risk involved in every investment to be made, and are thus not protected from the consequence of their own folly, they are nevertheless entitled to the benefit of sound and impartial advice, from someone who is skilled at giving such advice. This is known technically as 'best advice' and the concept is not greatly different from that laid down by the law of agency.

Best advice is therefore precisely what every competent solicitor, registered as a financial adviser under the Act, would, or should, have offered anyway. The Act is aimed at rather more 'colourful' figures on the financial spectrum. Nevertheless solicitors who give financial advice are inevitably brought into the regulatory net and, again, this involves the Law

Society which is the regulatory body for the profession under the umbrella of the **Financial Services Authority (FSA)**.

The solicitor who gives any form of financial advice must now be registered in one of three ways:

- FSA authorisation.

- An Incidental Financial Business (**IFB**) Licence from the Law Society.

- Acting as an introducer to an independent financial adviser - this option can be undertaken in connection with either of the first two options.

The giving of financial advice, without registration, is a criminal offence, punishable by up to two years in prison. Sales of heritable property are not covered by the Act, but sometimes the solicitor will be asked for financial advice by clients as part of a sale or purchase. The solicitor who is not registered should avoid even discussing certain stocks or shares, as a criminal offence might be committed.

Under the Solicitors (Scotland) (Incidental Investment Business) Practice Rules 2004, solicitors who give financial advice must comply with these rules, and submit to regular inspection to ensure compliance.

Thus, solicitors must be able to show that they have given 'best advice' taking into account the clients' means and needs, and that the product recommended is best suited to these circumstances, taking into account other products offered on the market. The clients' instructions must also be shown to have been followed through on the best basis—the 'best execution' rule. Records must be kept to prove compliance with the best advice and best execution rules, and these records are frequently inspected by the Law Society.

The FISMA and FSA requirements naturally are expensive and compliance is time consuming, and solicitors who do not do much financial business are therefore well advised to seek an IFB licence, act as an introducer or simply avoid offering any form of financial advice.

Other duties incumbent on the solicitor are:

(a)   To effect through the Law Society's nominated broker and its Master Policy, professional indemnity insurance covering the solicitor's clients against any loss caused by the solicitor's negligence (Solicitors (Scotland) Professional Indemnity Insurance Rules 2005). As a guideline, the maximum payment from the policy is £2 million per claim, unless an additional premium is paid, which may be justified for a large firm, or for a small firm with an exceptionally large transaction. The premium is calculated having regard to: the number of partners; the ratio of partner to staff; the fee income of the firm as a proportion of the whole profession; and the firm's claim experience in the last five years. Many solicitors may feel that they could reach a better bargain through their own broker, but this is doubtful, bearing in mind the Society's negotiating experience and formidable market presence. In fact, they have been able to negotiate reductions in the annual premiums in certain years.

(b)   To contribute to the Solicitors' Guarantee Fund, which reimburses persons who have been defrauded by their solicitors (Solicitors' (Scotland) Accounts, Account Certificates, Professional Practice and Guarantee Fund Rules 2001). The amount payable by each solicitor depends on the amounts paid out by the Fund in the previous period.

(c)   To observe the Solicitors' (Scotland) (Advertising and Promotion) Practice Rules 2006. Advertising was formerly strictly forbidden by the Law Society, but is now allowed in the interests of informing the general public of the contact details and specialities of the solicitors advertising. Such advertising is useful, but not, by and large, particularly entertaining. The former prohibition on claims of superiority and comparison of fees was removed in 2006, although the prohibition on inaccurate and misleading advertising, unsurprisingly, remains.

(d)   To observe the Accounts etc Rules mentioned above. The general reminder is merely given that each partner of a firm will be responsible for ensuring compliance by the firm with the provisions of these Rule. While the operation of this rule is slightly relaxed for junior partners who are not given responsibility in accounting matters (*Sharp v Council of the Law Society of Scotland* 1984 SLT 313 at 316), solicitors cannot wash their hands of accounting matters, and knowledge of, and compliance with the Accounts rules applies to solicitors of all levels.

Reliance on staff, or on computer programmes, without understanding them, is a theme of Discipline Tribunal cases. There was a particularly distressing case a few years ago of a solicitor who fell victim to one of the first email scams. Unfortunately he committed his firm's clients' account to a withdrawal of almost three million US dollars, for a scheme which promised untold riches, but was just too good to be true. Needless to say this was done without the knowledge of the other partners of the firm, who nevertheless were all declared bankrupt.

Some larger practices now employ accountants as their partnership accountants or secretaries, and they may employ other professional people, such as chartered surveyors, to deal with specialist functions within the firm. The names of such persons may be printed on the firm's stationery, provided that the public are not misled as to the status of the individual within the firm or to think that they are solicitors (Solicitors (Scotland) (Associates, Consultants and Employees) Practice Rules 2001) but this will no doubt change with the advent of Alternative Business Structures (see below). A smaller practice could not possibly justify having a chartered accountant in the practice, but might consider having access to the services of a competent bookkeeper, who will probably be trained by the excellent Society of Law Accountants in Scotland (**SOLAS**).

(e) To accept unlimited liability for the debts of the partnership, and even, in extreme cases, of the other partners. The financial obligations of this requirement are, however, to some extent mitigated by:

- The possibility of forming a limited liability partnership (LLP) under the provisions of the Limited Liability Partnership Act 2000 or a limited company in terms of the Companies Acts. An LLP is a corporate body and not a partnership, and the LLP limits the liability of the partners (styled 'members' in the Act). In return for limited liability, annual accounts have to be lodged with Companies House for public inspection, showing the income of the highest paid member of an LLP. Many firms of solicitors have taken advantage of these arrangements and are now incorporated as LLPs.

- The cover against defaulting partners offered by the compulsory professional indemnity policy (see *infra*).

(f) Not to act in the same matter for two parties who might have conflicting interests (Solicitors (Scotland) (Standards of Conduct) Practice Rules 2008). Many years ago a solicitor might have acted, and sometimes did, for both seller and purchaser in a house transaction. Where there was no substantial conflict of interest, the result was usually, somehow, satisfactory to both parties. But, you only need to consider how different the position would be in a court case, where the one solicitor acts for both parties, to realise how unrealistic it is to expect one person to represent both sides fairly. There is basically a conflict of interest where one person is buying and another selling—even when parties are married there can be a conflict of interest when one person acts for both husband and wife. The general principle against acting for clients when there is a conflict of interest was codified in 1986 and has been developed over the years in successive Practice Rules.

(g) To observe the code of conduct contained in Solicitors (Scotland) (Standards of Conduct) Practice Rules 2008, and the associated Standards of Conduct and Service, which have the following principles at their core:

- Competence;
- Diligence;
- Communication; and
- Respect.

(h) To observe the Anti-Money Laundering legislation. Briefly these Regulations are intended to prevent the placing of 'dirty' money acquired through drug dealing, terrorism or crime generally into a 'clean' investment, such as a bank account, bonds or house purchase. The investment is then realised and the proceeds emerge as 'clean' or 'laundered' money. See paras 3.01 and 3.02 for a more detailed consideration of Anti Money laundering requirements. There are five money laundering offences: assistance, concealment, acquisition, failure to disclose or tipping off.

It should be noted that a solicitor was jailed in 2002, for six months, for the offence of receiving a sum of money from a client to account of expenses, and then refunding it in a laundered condition, when the sums came to be re-imbursed when the transaction did not proceed.

(i) To maintain complete confidentiality and silence as to a client's affairs, (except Making a Suspicious Activity Report in terms of the Money Laundering Regulations). Solicitors should not reveal details, even names, of their clients, especially in cases where complete secrecy is required. A major difficulty can arise where solicitors are asked to act against a former client. The rule is that the knowledge they have gained of the former client's affairs should not be used in any way against the interest of the former client. That is a vague enough proposition, and really the only solution is for the solicitor to decline to act for the new client against the former client because suspicions of double dealing are bound to arise. The leading case in this respect concerns an accountancy firm (*Prince Jefri Bolkiah v KPMG* [1999] 1 All ER 517; see also *Koch Shipping Inc v Richards Butler* 2002 All ER (Comm) 957).

(j) The solicitor will also be subjected to occasional visits from the Law Society, as the profession's regulator, and the tax or VAT inspector, none of which are, even remotely, social in character. Regular and random inspections of this type are designed to help to ensure compliance and maintain standards throughout the profession, which is of benefit to all concerned, and should be prepared for and embraced in a spirit of full co-operation. Some firms even use retired regulators to do a 'dummy run' before the day, which is undoubtedly useful, as they may spot something that might cause embarrassment.

(k) It goes without saying, that a group of solicitors, like any other group, must resist the temptation to get together and fix agreed fees. This is anti-competitive behaviour prohibited by the

Competition Act 1998. The Law Society itself had to abandon its former table of fees and the rate for a unit of ten minutes in 2005, following worries that its practices might be breaking competition law, after the European Commission found the Belgian Architects' Association, another professional body, guilty of price fixing for adopting recommended minimum fees.

PRACTICE RULES CONSOLIDATION

1.04 With the increasing plethora of practice rules affecting the profession, often making it extremely difficult to ascertain what the current requirements are, the Law Society has undertaken a major project to rationalise and consolidate the rules. The Practice Rules Consolidation Project aims to help lawyers by creating a single document that will replace the current 35 individual sets of practice rules. The aim is to organise, rationalise and modernise all the practice rules which will greatly to improve accessibility and use. The consolidated rules will not, with a few exceptions, make any material changes to the substance of the existing rules, rather the changes concern structure and format and modification to some of the technology. The project will however made some changes to the accounts rules, and during the consultation on the consolidation project, a simultaneous consultation on the proposed changes to the accounts rules was run, those changes designed to improve firm operations and reduce some regulatory burdens, reduce risk and improve regulatory efficiency.

REGULATION AND COMPLIANCE

1.05 The solicitor is governed by the Solicitors (Scotland) Acts 1980 and 1988, which supersede the Legal Aid and Solicitors (Scotland) Act 1949, the foundation Act which set up the Law Society as the governing body for the profession. The S(S)A 1980 continues to empower the Council of the Law Society to make regulations, with the concurrence of the Lord President of the Court of Session and under the provisions of the Legal Services (Scotland) Act 2010, the regulatory functions of the Law Society will require to be exercised on their behalf by a regulatory committee, so that those functions are exercised independently and properly (for the purposes of achieving public confidence). Many of these regulations are printed in full in the *Parliament House Book* (W Green, looseleaf), or in the offprint known as the *Solicitors Compendium* (W Green), and are also available online. The Council is now permitted to delegate functions to committees, sub-committees or individuals in terms of the Council of the Law Society Act 2003.

To practise as a solicitor, the solicitor must hold a practising certificate under the S(S)A 1980, s 4 and is automatically a member of the Law Society (unlike English solicitors in England who need not be a member of their Law Society).

The Law Society, as part of the first object of its duty under the S(S)A 1980, is responsible, among other things, for the training and admission of solicitors, continuing professional development, legal education, practice development, maintaining links with other societies, publications, giving advice on numerous professional topics through a network of specialist committees and the secretariat, scrutinising proposed legislation and making representations as necessary, ensuring that accounting rules and the regulations under FISMA are observed, liaising with the Scottish Government and the Scottish Law Commission, corporate public relations and advertising, and negotiating professional indemnity insurance through the Society's block policy.

COMPLAINTS

1.06

'An error does not become a mistake until you refuse to correct it.'

(John F Kennedy)

The dread of every solicitor is a complaint. Even the threat of a complaint can make the solicitor feel vulnerable. But this threat can be neutralised by the firm having proper systems in place. Firstly, a firm should ideally have an office risk or quality management policy, so that the solicitor can be sure that best practice was followed. Secondly, a firm should have a robust complaints procedure so that a complaint can be escalated to the firm's Client Relations Partner and 'nipped in the bud'. Defending a claim is time-consuming and expensive business, therefore it is far preferable to put resources into ensuring client satisfaction. A badly handled complaint can also spin out of control very quickly, so that the firm's reputation can be damaged as well. Spreading news of bad service was bad enough with old fashioned word-of-mouth, but with the advent of social media, a complaint can 'go viral' within days, if not hours and is always recorded on the internet.

With a robust complaints procedure, the solicitor should be confident that the firm will support him or her in the defence or settlement of the claim. If there is a mistake by the solicitor (they do happen) then the firm should use this as a learning opportunity to ensure that it does not happen again.

There should not be a 'blame culture' or any recriminations, Such a culture is counter productive, because lawyers will be afraid to ventilate any problems at any early stage and may instead try to put things right themselves, which often compounds the problem.

Failing resolution within the firm (and some claims are irresolvable at the firm level), then the client can make a formal complaint to the Scottish Legal Complaints Commission (**SLCC**).

The SLCC was created by the Legal Profession and Legal Aid (Scotland) Act 2007 and started work in October 2008. This entailed the redeployment of some 40 Law Society complaints staff. The initial costs of establishment were borne by the Scottish Government, but the ongoing revenue costs are borne by the legal profession, collected by the Law Society. The creation of the SLCC sought to address concerns and the public's perception of the Law Society's system of self-regulation. The SLCC acts as a gateway for complaints. Service complaints are dealt with by the SLCC whilst conduct complaints continue to be referred to the Law Society for resolution.

Of course, not all complaints are justified, and many are dismissed, sometimes causing great ill-will against the profession, because justice has not been perceived to have been done, whether justified or not.

Equally, the SLCC complaints process can sometimes seem to be problematic to solicitors, as a Glasgow solicitor's letter to the Journal, published in August 2011, makes plain. When asked for fees that were overdue, the client complained that the solicitor did not show 'sufficient sympathy and understanding' towards him, when demanding the fees be paid, and complained to SLCC.

Far from sifting out the complaint, the SLCC warned that there would be a charge of £500 if the case investigator recommended that the complaint be upheld. The only way to challenge the sift decision would be to appeal to the Court of Session. The solicitor makes the point that there are no financial implications for the complainer should the complaint be dismissed or held as spurious.

Solicitors in private practice have to pay an annual levy (£209 in 2011) to fund the SLCC.

In serious cases of professional misconduct arising from complaints received, or from the investigations of the Society, principally under the Solicitors (Scotland) Accounts Rules, Accounts Certificate Rules, Professional Practice Rules, or the Guarantee Fund Rules, the Law Society may make a complaint to the Solicitors Discipline Tribunal. This body operates under the Scottish Discipline Tribunal Procedures Rules 2008 and its members are appointed by the Lord President of the Court of Session. The members are made up from lay people and lawyers who must not be members of the Law Society Council, lest the Law Society be thought to be both judge and prosecutor.

The tribunal has the power to order a solicitor's name to be struck off the roll of practising solicitors, or to suspend or restrict their practising certificates quite independently of any criminal prosecution there may be. A right of appeal exists against the decisions of the Tribunal to the Court of Session.

Although one might form a contrary conclusion, a very small proportion of the many transactions that must be carried out by solicitors every year in Scotland actually result in a complaint to the SLCC or the Law Society. It is a matter of pride that this is so, and the standard should be maintained and improved in the interests of the profession. The Law Society requires each firm to have a designated partner to handle all complaints. Many can be sorted out quite easily—often a statement of regret, or a modification of the fees charged. It should be remembered that there is a requirement for a high degree of regulation in the profession, and that the disciplinary functions of the Society and the SLCC are in the interests of the whole profession, however irksome they may seem, to ensure the preservation of the highest levels of integrity, honesty and ethical behaviour.

REPRESENTATION

1.07 The Law Society as regulator of the profession has to maintain an impartial role in resolving or adjudicating disputes. In terms of the Solicitors (Scotland) Act 1980, s 1(2), the objects of the Law Society include the promotion of:

(a)   the interests of the solicitors' profession in Scotland; and

(b)   the interests of the public in relation to that profession.

It seeks to support and represent the interests of solicitors at every stage of their careers, through provision of:

- Education: focusing on the education and training of solicitors in Scotland from the foundation (university) stage, through diploma and traineeship and into all levels of post qualifying practice;

- Continuing professional development (CPD); through Update, which organises post-qualification CPD events and training programmes for solicitors and other legal providers;

- A professional practice advice service: through its Professional Practice Department, which provides training, business information and other support, for example for solicitors wishing to become an accredited specialist or a solicitor advocate;

- Law reform: by working to improve the law in Scotland and the legal system for the benefit of the profession and the public, and representing the views of solicitors and their clients in response to legislative proposals; and

- Regulation liaison: by offering help, training and support on client complaints handling, including advice on how to avoid complaints.

If a solicitor finds himself in trouble, as well as approaching the Law Society for help, he can turn to various other bodies for assistance such as the Legal Defence Union (**LDU**), which is analogous to the well-established Medical and Dental Defence Union (**MDDU**), which represents the interest of doctors and dentists who are in trouble, and meets their costs.

The Society of Writers to Her Majesty's Signet (**WS Society**) is an independent association for lawyers and one of the oldest professional bodies in the world with over 500 years of history. It supports Scottish lawyers and legal businesses, with professional support lawyer and research services, highly regarded training seminars and programmes, an accreditation system, and networking and social events, as well as offering the facilities of a first class law library, located in the iconic Signet Library in Edinburgh.

The Scottish Law Agents Society (**SLAS**) was incorporated by Royal Charter in 1884 and membership is open to all Scottish solicitors and trainees. SLAS is concerned with all legal and practical matters affecting its members and endeavours to represent and promote their interests and standards. SLAS recently led a high-profile campaign against Alternative Business Structures (see para 1.09).

Additionally, local faculties, professional societies and bar associations can provide much advice and support for the solicitor.

CLIENT SERVICE DELIVERY

1.08

> 'There is only one boss. The customer. And he can fire everyone in the company from the chairman on down simply by spending his money elsewhere.'

> *(Sam Walton, founder of Wal-Mart Asda Supermarkets)*

As a conveyancer starting out, it is important to remember who is the boss. The original author of this handbook, John Sinclair, used to have a banner at his desk that said 'clients make pay day happen'. While the banner is long since lost, the maxim should not be forgotten.

Some lawyers are uncomfortable with the idea that clients are also customers. As a profession we pride our integrity and independence and these virtues are valued by clients. That said, law firms are businesses, and need new and repeat business to survive. So there is a line to be drawn between offering robust advice that will save clients from themselves and executing clients' instructions mechanically. Above all, one aim of working with clients is to form the relationship of trusted adviser, being someone who knows and understands their business and requirements and can add value to the client through experience and wisdom.

Since the last edition of this book was published in 2006, the world has changed quite remarkably. The economic situation worsened considerably. The property market almost went into freefall and is still recovering very gradually from the credit crunch and then the recession. Worsening balance sheets for law firms are likely to lead to consolidation. All of this has had an impact on clients, so that client loyalty has become a more scarce commodity and legal services are often now procured like any other service. To the extent that they cannot be taken for granted, solicitors need to nurture relationships and one of the best ways to do this is to ensure excellence in the delivery of your service.

Consider how best you can communicate with your clients. Do they know and understand the various stages that they will have to go through and what is expected of them? Are you bombarding them with letters or emails when they would prefer a short text? Are you following a checklist so that every stage is completed in the right order and in good time? Would the client like to see a Flow chart, with all the steps mapped out? How do you evaluate the client's feedback at the end of the transaction?

Accept no interruptions to meetings with clients, even 'very important' telephone calls. The client will think you have other things on your mind, and you should never give that impression. Do not constantly look at your mobile phone. Give your clients the impression that they are the only people that matter, for they are and they think that as well. Telephone messages should be carefully recorded and returned that day. Letters and emails should be speedily and helpfully answered.

Above all lawyers should remember that they are engaged to help people and businesses through some of the biggest financial events of their lives, and should give them a service that smoothes out the bumps and, as one client once put it, gives them 'a warm feeling inside' and leads to further recommendations. If you have done a good job and the client is delighted you should capitalise on that. Don't be afraid to ask them to recommend you to their friends or colleagues by word of mouth or even on LinkedIn or Twitter.

ALTERNATIVE BUSINESS STRUCTURES

1.09

'Legal advice will be "just like buying a tin of beans".'

(Headline in *Daily Telegraph*, 18 October 2005, after the
Lord Chancellor announced reforms to legal regulation
in England and Wales)

The 5th edition of this book broke with tradition in the introduction. Instead of the 'welcome to the profession(?)' title in the previous four editions, the title was changed to 'welcome to Tescolaw(?)' as a reflection of the despondency at that time about the introduction of Alternative Business Structures. It was clear then that the Scottish Government's preferred position was that solicitors firms should be able to be owned 100% by non-solicitors, which would change the face of the legal profession in an unknown way forever.

The ability for Scottish legal firms to establish as, or convert into, an 'alternative business structure' was introduced by the Legal Services (Scotland) Act 2010. What this means in practice is that solicitors firms no longer have to be owned exclusively by practising solicitors. After a long-running debate, a compromise between the 'Tescolaw' position of allowing any external investors to own 100% of a solicitors firm and the trenchant position against any dilution of the previous position was reached and accepted by the Parliament. In future, a Scottish solicitors' firm need only be 51% owned by Scottish solicitors and other regulated professionals, still to be defined by regulations.

The new structures are known in the LS(S)A 2010 as licensed legal services providers. They will hold a licence and be regulated by a regulator still to be appointed by the Scottish Ministers, possibly the Law Society. The non-professional owners of the remaining 49% of the firm will be subject to a 'fitness for involvement' test by the regulator. If the non-solicitor owner is subsequently found to be unfit for involvement, he or she may be disqualified from being involved in solicitors' firms in future.

This legislation represents a radical break from the past for the legal profession and, depending on the experience, the 51% rule may not rest as the final position. Although it remains to be seen how these structures will be used in practice, as a relatively commoditised service, domestic conveyancing is likely to become an active area for investment by companies involved in associated services. The day may yet come when conveyancing is indeed like buying a tin of beans, in one way or another.

FURTHER READING

Findings of the Scottish Solicitors' Discipline Tribunal
http://www.ssdt.org.uk/

Standards for Scottish Solicitors
http://www.lawscot.org.uk/members/regulation-and-standards/standards/standards-for-scottish-solicitors

Chapter 2

The Framework

1617 AND ALL THAT

2.01 Registration of title is a key driver of economic growth: one of the fundamentals of any developing economy is to have certainty in property rights for investment potential and granting security, and for ease of transacting for liquidity of investment. Such a system encourages banks and other lenders to lend in security of property and so the virtuous cycle of a flourishing market economy begins. That we have had such a system in Scotland for almost four hundred years should be a source of immense pride as it has enabled the Scottish economy to grow out of relative poverty to the prosperous, mercantile country that we are today.

In 1617, the General Register of Sasines was created, overseen by 'the Keeper'. The office of Keeper is a personal commission from the sovereign, distinct from government appointments, and endures to this day. The Keeper of the Registers of Scotland of course has a multitude of staff these days who diligently assist her to maintain 16 different registers and over half a million registration transactions every year. The Keeper's office is called the Registers of Scotland Executive Agency (it is a self financing agency of the Scottish Government), but is still referred to by conveyancers colloquially and, often formally, as the Keeper, as in the dread phrase 'the Keeper bounced my deed'.

The Register of Sasines and the Land Register that is succeeding it, are public registers. Therefore rights in property are there for everyone to see. Once a right to land is published in either Register, it gives the holder a 'real right' in the property, which is to say it is defensible against anyone on the basis of being preferred, as it was registered first. This contrasts with a personal right under a private contract, which could be challengeable by another party who has a competing right.

In essence the Register of Sasines is beautifully simple. In 1617, the majority of Scotland's landmass was owned by surprisingly few owners. Each property or estate was given a search sheet with a chronological number, which is categorised by (now historic) counties. Any subdivision is given a search sheet and new number but also recorded as a 'break-off' from the original estate it is recorded against. As a register of deeds rather than property, this entry only contains abstract details of the type of dealing eg disposition, servitude etc and the parties, consideration (price), date of execution, date of recording and the folio and fiche number. Each party will also have an index search sheet for each county recording their transactions, so that it is possible to search against individuals, not just properties.

So for example, the sale of an acre of land from the Inverlour estate by the estate owner Sir Murray Plaice to Harriet Roe would be recorded as a break off from the Inverlour Estate search sheet, numbered 238 in the county of Moray. This transaction would then trigger the creation of a new search sheet Moray 4536 for the new holding of land that Harriet Roe has acquired. Should Harriet Roe sell 0.23 hectare (measurements must now be metric) of her land for development to Hammerhead Properties Ltd a number of years later, this would be noted against the search sheet for the one acre, Moray 4536, and also trigger the creation of a further new search sheet Moray 73537. The land is then developed and once the roads have been adopted by the Local Authority they are given official names.

And this is a crucial limitation. As noted above, the searcher could either search against the property or the person. However, because Hammerhead Properties Ltd has not developed its land into housing at the time of sale, it remains categorised as 0.23 hectare in the Parish of Inverlour. The new address of Bream Avenue would not appear anywhere in the records until the road has been adopted and Hammerhead Properties start to sell their new homes with new addresses. A searcher can use some intuition to find out if this is the correct property. She could cross-refer the names index, but it is not uncommon for several deeds by the same parties to be recorded on the same day.

Further, because only abstract details are noted in the search sheets, you may know that Harriet Roe has sold 0.23 hectare but the only way to see where the boundaries are was to order a' quick copy' (as opposed to the more expensive, but no slower, Official Extract of the same deed, which can be used for evidential purposes) of the disposition by Sir Murray Plaice from the National Archives and await its arrival in several days' time. Although it was customary to annex a plan to a Sasine deed, as a register of deeds all that is required is that property is sufficiently described, so there might not even be a plan. Even if you were 'lucky' and a plan had been annexed, many plans presented to the Sasine Register were badly prepared and inaccurate. They followed no consistent pattern of scales, or even north points, and matching plans of adjoining lands is difficult. It is not unusual to have a 'floating rectangle' plan, which is a plan showing a rectangular area of land but, the utility of which is seriously limited without reference points to tie it into features on a map.

An even more terrible prospect is to try to establish the extent of the Inverlour Estate at any point in time. There will likely be an 'estate search' which was started many decades ago and is 'brought down' (updated) every time there is a break off. It may be the size of a book and will almost certainly be kept in a tin box within a trunk full of old titles (and maybe a few moths…).

On the first page, in copperplate handwriting, will be the original description of the estate 'ALL and WHOLE the lands and estate of Inverlour, in the Parish of Inverlour extending to one thousand two hundred and sixty acres or thereby as more particularly described in Conveyance by the Testamentary Trustees of Andrew Square to Sir Carlton Plaice recorded in the General Register of Sasines for the County of Moray on tenth November 1874'. Then the succeeding pages will list all the break off dispositions, any servitudes, statutory wayleaves and so on.

It can actually be an impossible job and there must be a number of landed estates that have an understanding of what they own, but that is more through good estate management than any official record keeping.

Carrying out a Sasine purchase and sale transaction was time consuming and repetitive, and potentially involved several people doing exactly the same work in a short space of time. Thus for example, solicitors would note title for their client Harriet Roe (if they hadn't already for her purchase) before she sells the land to ensure that she has good title. When missives are concluded and Harriet Roe is committed to sell to Hammerhead Developments Ltd, their solicitors then have to note title, and their bank's solicitors, too and so on, all down the ownership chain. This all added to the overall expense

Another limitation of the Sasines system was that once the sellers' solicitors handed over the title deeds at settlement in a Sasine transaction, the sellers' responsibility for the title ceased, unless a successful claim for warrandice (the sellers' warranty against ejection from the property, granted in the disposition) was established.

LAND REGISTRATION: A BETTER WAY

2.02 From the late nineteenth century and throughout the twentieth century a different way of recording titles to land emerged in other Commonwealth jurisdictions, such as the 'Torrens' system, named after a premier of the State of South Australia who introduced it to the then colony in 1858. It is similar to the Sasine system in that each new grant is given a unique folio number but, crucially, this number relates to a map. In England a plan based system of Registration of Tile was made compulsory in 1925.

These systems of registration of title offer three significant advantages over the Sasines:

(i) **The 'mirror' principle** - the register reflects accurately and completely the current state of the title;

(ii) **The 'curtain' principle** - it is not necessary to go beyond the registered title, as it contains all the necessary information on the title; and

(iii) **The 'insurance' principle** - the validity of the title is guaranteed by the state registrar. In the event of any error, the injured party can claim compensation for any loss from the registrar. This principle ensures that registered titles can be relied upon.

These systems of registration of title (or interests) rather than deeds were catching the imagination in Scotland. Even as far back as 1903, Professor Wood wrote in his lectures on conveyancing: 'I am unable to see any real difficulty in the way of introducing registration of title into Scotland'.

In 1959 the Secretary of State for Scotland set up a committee under Lord Reid to investigate the introduction of registration of title into Scotland. This committee reported favourably (Scottish Home and Health Department, Registration of Title to Land in Scotland: 1963, Cmnd 2032) and recommended that another committee be set up to devise a scheme. This committee under Professor Henry reported in 1969 (Scottish Home and Health Department, Scheme for the Introduction and Operation of Registration of Title To Land in Scotland: 1969, Cmnd 4137) with a workable scheme, which after a trial in Register House, was introduced by the Land Registration (Scotland) Act 1979.

To set things in context, in 1959 there existed only a few huge main frame computers, and the electric typewriter was the latest luxury. There was no thought of personal computers, with the same, or greater, power than the main frame computer. The fact that the Reid Committee produced a scheme that fitted personal computers so perfectly was fortuitous, and it is hard to see how the concept of registration of title could work so well without the personal computer.

The scheme is based on the Ordnance Survey of Scotland using the scale 1:1250 for urban areas where modern house plots are small, 1:2,500 in villages and small towns where plots are rather larger, and 1:10,000 for farms and moorland areas. Ordnance Survey maps are extremely accurate, and are consistently updated. It should be noted, however, that they reflect boundaries as they actually exist on the ground, and not as they exist in title plans registered in the Sasine Register. This difficulty is met by asking the Keeper, in a form P16 (see para 7.08) to compare the title plan with the Ordnance Survey map.

The Land Register is based, like the General Register of Sasines, on the old Scottish county system, which was phased out for local government purposes in 1974. Thus regions and districts, introduced by the Local Government (Scotland) Act 1973 have no significance in land registration, and have in any event been superseded by Councils and City Councils, introduced by the Local Government etc (Scotland) Act 1994 in 1996. However, as a system of categorisation, the old county system was left untouched so far as the Land and Sasine Registers were concerned, as any change would have been too complicated and expensive.

The original intention was to make all Scotland operational in nine years, starting year one on 6 April 1981 with the County of Renfrew; then in year two—The City of Glasgow; year three—Lanark; year four—Midlothian; year five—Rest of Central Belt; year six—Angus, Kincardine, Aberdeen; year seven—Ayr, Dumfries and Galloway; year eight—Southern Rural Areas; year nine—Northern Rural Areas.

This programme however, proved wildly over-optimistic, and by 1990 only four counties were operational: Renfrew, Dumbarton, Lanark and Glasgow. It appeared at that time that the scheme was irretrievably stalled, for the Register was under-staffed, and could not keep pace with the applications pouring in, let alone the arrears that were building up. Long delays were commonplace, and the Keeper acknowledged this problem in his 1988 report, and explained that the backlogs on his shelves would generate a fee income of £9m, if only he could process them.

The property boom of the late eighties coupled with the success of the 'right to buy' legislation led to a soaring demand for the services of the Registers of Scotland at a time when the department was subject to both staffing and accommodation constraints. The situation was steadily deteriorating and invidious comparisons were being drawn with the English system, which had only covered 50–52% of the country after 63 years. Fortunately the position in both countries has since been rectified.

The Department of the Registers of Scotland was created Scotland's first (and only) executive agency in 1990 and the consequent removal of constraints enabled the agency to tackle its problems. In particular the land registration process picked up momentum, as shown by the extension of land registration to the counties of Clackmannan (1 October 1992); Stirling (1 April 1993); West Lothian (1 October 1993); Fife (1 April 1995); Aberdeen and Kincardine (1 April 1996); Ayr and Dumfries, Kirkcudbright and Wigtown (1 April 1997); Angus, Perth and Kinross (1 April 1999); Berwick, East Lothian, Peebles, Roxburgh and Selkirk (1 October 1999); Argyll and Bute (1 April 2000); Inverness and Nairn (1 April 2002); Banff, Caithness, Moray, Orkney and Zetland, Ross and Cromarty, and Sutherland (1 April 2003). Thus, the whole of Scotland is now on the land registration system. See Appendix VI for a map of the Registration Counties.

ONE SYSTEM, TWO REGISTERS

2.03 All transfers for value must now be registered in the Land Register. It would have been good to be able say to twenty first century conveyancers that there is no need for you to know about the Sasine Register, however, that register remains in operation for deeds 'without financial consideration'. This means land given as a gift or, more significantly, newly created securities over land held under a Sasine title, which would apply if a new mortgage is created on an old title. Without further reform, some land may never be registered (eg parks, landed estates remaining in the family and large tracts of land owned by public bodies such as the Forestry Commission) unless the owners apply to register the title voluntarily.

Thus, if Mr and Mrs Skate bought a house in the county of Renfrew in 1975, and lived there continuously, the deed in their favour, and the standard security to their building society, would have been registered in the Sasine Register. The reason for this is that in 1975 the Land Register was not yet established.

If Mr and Mrs Skate then sold their house to Mr Sturgeon in 1994, the necessary documentation would then be registered in the Land Register.

Supposing, however, Mr and Mrs Skate decided to transfer their house to their children as a gift (there are possible inheritance tax benefits in this action), the disposition would be recorded in the Sasine Register, as the transfer was not for valuable consideration. There are exceptions to general rule, though. Rather oddly, if Mr and Mrs Skate gave the house to a child as a gift in contemplation of marriage (this may also have possible inheritance tax benefits), that would then be treated as a transfer for valuable consideration, and the documentation would be registered in the Land Register.

If Mr and Mrs Skate decided that it was all too complex and they would rather stay put, but get another loan, the documentation would again be recorded in the Sasine Register, as the granting of a heritable security does not trigger registration.

It is worth noting that once the title is registered in the Land Register, all relevant documents are registered in that Register, irrespective of whether the consideration is valuable or not.

The Register of Sasines still operates in parallel with the Land Register, and will continue to do so until it is finally phased out. The Keeper reports that there are currently some 1.2 million titles on the Land Register, representing 19% of the landmass of Scotland and around 55% of titles. The remainder, being about 0.9 million titles amounting to 81% of landmass, is predominantly the subject of Sasine recorded titles (some titles, unbelievably, have not had a recordable transaction since 1617).

CAVEAT CUSTODIEN

2.04 There is nothing particularly tricky about land registration. The first registration does, however, require extra work as the seller's solicitors not only have to satisfy the purchaser's solicitors as to the seller's title, but the purchaser's solicitors have immediately to satisfy the Keeper of the Land Register that a sufficient title is being registered, and that no restriction of indemnity is called for. Whereas formerly the purchaser's solicitors may have been content to take a view on, for example, a copy deed without the recording stamp, the Keeper invariably will not and will requisition quick copies of the deed from the purchaser's solicitors. The purchaser's solicitors will in turn revert to the sellers' solicitors, demanding answers in terms of the obligation under missives.

Once the Keeper is satisfied, a comprehensive Land Certificate is issued, which contains all necessary information on the title (but not the planning or building or other information) and the Title Sheet which it reflects is conclusive evidence of ownership, the extent of the property, and the land obligations affecting the land.

Thus it may be said that while the Sasine system is one of *caveat emptor* (buyer beware), the land registration system might be said to be one of *caveat custodien* (Keeper beware), as once the title is registered in the Land Register, there is effectively a State guarantee of the title which provides indemnity against defects and third party challenge.

THE KEEPER'S INDEMNITY

2.05 Indemnity from the Keeper is available where a person has suffered loss through rectification of an inaccuracy or a refusal by the Keeper to rectify, or where the Keeper has lost documents or they have been destroyed while in his custody, or an error or omission has been made in the Land Certificate (s 12(1) of LR(S)A 1979).

However the right to claim compensation is heavily qualified by s 12(3) of LR(S)A 1979, which contains a long and miscellaneous list of exclusions where indemnity is not available. These include loss due to the existence of a prescriptive title acquired through an *a non domino* disposition, reduction of deeds under the Bankruptcy (Scotland) Act 1985 and certain other statutes; loss because the person was presumed dead; minor inaccuracies in boundaries due to the limitations of the Ordnance Survey map; loss arising due to an inability to enforce real burdens, or in relation to an interest in mines and minerals where the title sheet does not expressly state that the minerals are included in the title, or from any omission to mention any overriding interests (such as an unregistered servitude created by passage of time, or 'prescription'), or where the loss has been caused by the fraud or carelessness on the part of the claimant. See s 12(3) of LR(S)A 1979 for the full list of statutory exclusions. None of these exclusions will be noted on the Title Sheet of a property.

Similarly, the Keeper can expressly exclude indemnity, either against the whole title or in respect of particular aspects where it is thought likely that a claim may be made, such as where there is an obvious defect in the title, or there is apparent adverse possession. Any such exclusion will be stated on the face of the Land Certificate.

In any of these situations, there is no recourse against the Keeper for defects in title.

RECTIFICATION OF THE REGISTER

2.06 The Keeper largely depends on the terms of the application for accuracy. Sometimes there are errors and there exists a procedure for rectification of the register under LR(S)A 1979, s 9. This section allows the Keeper to rectify the title sheet where an error is brought to his notice, or if ordered to do so by the Lands Tribunal. This provision is, however, restricted by the terms of s 9(3), which does not allow rectification to the prejudice of the proprietor in possession, except in very limited circumstances:

(a)   to note an overriding interest, which does not prejudice the proprietor because an overriding interest is overriding, whether noted or not;

(b)   where all concerned consent;

(c)   where the error is caused by the fraud or carelessness of the proprietor in possession;

(d)   where rectification relates to something for which the Keeper has previously refused to indemnify the proprietor in possession. An example of this would be where the proprietor in possession has only an *a non domino* title, but this has now been perfected by positive prescription, and the proprietor wants the title to be rectified to the extent that the exclusion of indemnity is removed.

The Keeper asks to be cited in any action for rectification that is raised, although the action is not directed primarily against the Keeper. This is in order that she can enter an appearance if the integrity of the Register appears to be under threat in any way.

E-REGISTRATION

2.07 The Scottish e-registration system is called ARTL which stands for Automated Registration of Title to Land, (and is referred to by its abbreviation, pronounced 'ar-til'), and has been operating since August 2007. The system works well enough, with the right kind of deed and with a fair wind. Some difficulties and frustrations in using ARTL have been reported for whole conveyancing transactions that have completed using the system, but practitioners report that it works well for discharges of a security, which are in a standard form, Lenders, of course, love the cost savings that derive from the paperless transaction and recently one bank required all panel solicitors to use ARTL (where appropriate of course), or face removal from the panel.

At the moment however, the use of ARTL is limited to transactions that involve 'dealings of whole', by which is meant a disposition and/or standard security that transfers or secures the whole of a registered title. Discharges of securities over a registered title can, as already mentioned, be dealt with in this way, as well as some other simple conveyancing documents. Another current limitation is the fact that processing transactions involving limited companies through ARTL are problematic, as while it is perfectly possible for a discharge or a disposition by or in favour of a company to be processed, standard securities granted by companies cannot, because the charge created by the security also requires to be registered in the Register of Charges, and electronic communication between ARTL and Companies House is not, at present, possible. That has meant that there has not as yet been any significant take-up of ARTL for commercial property transactions.

The ARTL system effectively allows the solicitor to go online to submit deeds and populate Land Registration forms in real time on the Register. While it has long been the practice that solicitors conclude missives on behalf of clients, ARTL requires solicitors to sign deeds electronically on their behalf. The solicitor must have a mandate from clients to allow him or her to sign deeds in this way. The signature is adhibited by means of a secure e-signature using a chip and PIN card. The registration fees and

Stamp Duty Land Tax are collected by Registers of Scotland from the solicitor's account at the point of registration. The use of ARTL in practice is considered further at para 14.09.

The writer uses the term 'e-registration' quite deliberately, for it needs to be clear that ARTL is not an e-conveyancing system. Unfortunately, Scotland is still some distance from introducing e-conveyancing, but hopefully the Land Registration Bill, mentioned below, will remedy that.

BENEFITS OF E-CONVEYANCING

2.08 You may have heard that the Scottish Legal system is at its foundation a civilian legal system, but you just need to look at the case index to see that the common law theme is prevalent. Conveyancing practitioners have sometimes overlooked the ancient principles that underpin our law and over time often developed our own practices and tacit understandings. A sharp reminder that established principles take precedence came in August 2009 in the form of *Park, Petitioner* [2009] CSOH 122, in which case the current e-conveyancing solution of faxing missives (a fax is really just a secure scanner, transmitter and printer) was held by an Outer House judge to be ineffective. The case related to an inhibition (court order preventing the sale of property) which came into effect at a specific time and day. The solicitors relied on the fact that missives had been concluded by fax to defeat the inhibition. The judge said not. Referring to Erskine's Institutes, Book 3, Title 2, para 43, the case of *Stamfield's Creditors v Scott* (1696) Br.Supp.IV 344, and the fact that leading conveyancing academics were divided on the issue, the judge concluded that a binding contract in Scots Law requires delivery, not mere intimation (apart, that is, from the increasing absurd postal acceptance rule, which requires neither). This rule means that a contract in concluded when the acceptance is posted, regardless of when or whether it reaches its destination - qv *Carmarthan Developments Ltd v Pennington* [2008] CSOH 139). Delivery could be by fax, but that turns on the intention of the parties. There has to be an agreement between the parties that this form of delivery is final and irrevocable and intended to bind the parties. As there was no agreement that the faxed version would be binding, following up a fax with the 'pen and ink' missive suggested to the judge that it was not intended to be irrevocable.

The solution to the dilemma suggested by the Judge, Temporary Judge Thomson QC, was a form of 'constructive delivery'. For constructive delivery to be effective, both solicitors would seem to have to agree in writing to rely wholly on their faxed (or, more usually, emailed pdf) missives and hold the original documents, in a form of constructive trust. This practice would run contrary to the intuitive and traditional practice that missives are concluded by sending the original signed letters to the other solicitor. See para 6.05 for a more detailed consideration.

The trouble with the judge's comments on constructive delivery is that the writer uncovered an Inner House authority that would make them unsafe to rely upon. In *Life Association of Scotland v Douglas* (1886) 13R 910, the question was whether the placing of the signed deed with Mr Douglas's own agent, with an irrevocable mandate to deliver it, was sufficient to constitute constructive delivery before the actual delivery, which occurred after Mr Douglas's death. The court held that *de facto* the deed was undelivered, and the Lord President (Inglis) stated at 911:

'It must always be kept in mind, when considering such questions, that the delivery of a deed is a matter of fact and not a matter of law.'

This dictum is a clear and authoritative statement of the law. The correct statement of the law all along was that of Professors Gretton and Reid, whose passage at page 47 of the third edition of *Conveyancing* was cited in the Park case:

'We tentatively suggest that when the law requires that a contract be in writing that means that a piece of paper produced to the other party, and that an unsigned copy of such a document is insufficient. If that is right then missives cannot be concluded by fax.'

The long term solution is not a contrived legal fiction of constructive delivery, which will inevitably lead to uncertainties if the intention of the parties is critical to its efficacy, nor a return to the days of the horse and cart. There is a perfectly workable solution in e-conveyancing, described below. The authors have been vocal in calling for this to be brought forward in the Land Registration Bill, and we are to note that the government and the Scottish Law Commission have been listening.

LAND REGISTRATION REFORM

2.09 Although Land Registration has worked very well and coped with many subsequent changes to Scottish property law since its inception, it was becoming clear at the turn of the century that the system was beginning to creak in places and a review was needed to suggest improvements. In 2001, Registers of Scotland asked the Scottish Law Commission to review the system. The Commission published three discussion papers in 2004 and 2005 and the review culminated in the Commission's 'Report on Land Registration' in 2010, with a draft Bill annexed.

It's fair to say that many of the 150 proposals are not radical, more of a 'tidying up' exercise with experience of thirty years' practice of Land Registration. Or, as the Commission put it, 'pouring concrete into the foundations' where registration practice has evolved, but needs a legislative basis. The Bill also seeks to update the 1979 Act for technological advances and looks to adopt practices that have proven successful elsewhere.

SUMMARY OF PROPOSALS

The Commission's Report and the Draft Bill are very comprehensive proposals. A very brief summary of some of the relevant suggestions are as follows:

- A gradual closure of the Register of Sasines, so that it becomes an historical archive rather than an active register.
- The acceleration of the completion of the Land Register by removing the Keeper's discretion to reject voluntary registrations, compulsory first registrations for all transfers of unregistered land, and empowering the Keeper to register plots without any application being made.
- The introduction of advance notices. At present the gap in time between delivery of a deed at settlement and its presentation for registration is covered by the seller's solicitor issuing a letter of obligation to indemnify the title for 14 days. The advance notice would alert the Keeper that the seller intends to sell to a party and will give that party priority for the advance notice period (possibly 35 days). (See also para 11.04(e)).

- Electronic contracts and e-enablement. This is arguably the centrepiece of the proposals. The Bill proposes to allow solicitors to use electronic signatures to sign missives, currently outside the scope of both the Electronic Communications Act 2000 and the ARTL Regulations. E-enablement means that any type of deed could be electronically signed (not just the pro forma deeds currently available on ARTL) and submitted to the Keeper for registration.

- There will be a new principle of no registration without mapping. A practice had grown up of solicitors recording ancillary rights as a pertinent of the main property. The Keeper adopted a pragmatic stance, and registered the title with the ancillary rights noted, but not mapped. The proposal means any areas of land that are owned in common among different owners such as a shared driveway, will have its own Land Register title number and will be noted in the Property section of the Land Certificate of each owner. The only exception to this rule would be tenements.

- The problem with common areas highlighted by the Lands Tribunal case of *PMP Plus v The Keeper* LTS/LR/2007/02 is addressed. The case concerned a developer who was constructing blocks of flats with common areas on its site. Before the all the flats were completed and the titles transferred, the developer purported to transfer the title to a particular common area to another developer. When this was challenged, it was clear that the title remained with the developer to do with as it pleased. The scope of the common area had not been ascertained as it was to be the 'bit left over' after all the sales had taken place. The new proposal is that a developer would lodge a Provisional Shared Plot Title Sheet with the Keeper, which would become ascertained once completed. Should the developer fail to ascertain the Title Sheet, then the owners would be able to apply to the Keeper to do this. See also paras 9.10(f)(vi) to (vii) for detail.

- Rectification. Where the Land Register fails to reflect the true legal position, the Keeper will have a duty to rectify all demonstrable inaccuracies, regardless of whether or not it operates to prejudice the proprietor in possession.

● The Keeper's guarantee will be reformed to the extent that even if the Land Register is wrong, after a prescriptive period the rights in the Land Register will become the correct version so that the face of the title can absolutely be relied upon. There would be a short period of time for owners to rebut the version on the Land Register. After that, any dispossession after the confirmation of the Land Register would be compensated by the Keeper.

At the time of going to publication, the Scottish Government has announced its legislative programme for 2011–2012, which will include the introduction of the Land Registration (Scotland) Bill.

FURTHER READING

'Report on Land Registration', Scottish Law Commission 222, 2010

http://www.scotlawcom.gov.uk/law-reform-projects/completed-projects/land-registration/

Land Registration (Scotland) Bill micro-site:

http://www.ros.gov.uk/lrbillconsultation/index.html

Chapter 3

New Clients and New Instructions

NEW CLIENTS AND ANTI-MONEY LAUNDERING

3.01 However tempting it may be to start work on a new client matter immediately to show your (prospective) new client how efficient you are, that temptation must be resisted. There are important prospective client due diligence procedural hurdles that have to be cleared first.

An established solicitors' office will already have robust procedures for client clearance and you should always follow these to the letter. Of these procedures by far and away the most significant is the anti-money laundering check for a client. Nothing should be done and no money accepted until this is completed.

This is a super-important legal requirement that, once explained to the client, they should understand. Sophisticated clients will be used to this kind of due diligence, which is also required for banking and financial services. Do not allow yourself to be persuaded by the prospective client. In fact, be extra suspicious of those prospective clients who do try to persuade you to act for them before you are ready. Conveyancing is deemed to be high risk by the **Serious Organised Crimes Agency (SOCA)** so you must always be on your guard.

On no account should you disclose any of the firm's bank account details in advance of clearance, in case the prospective client deposits 'dirty' money in your firm's account without your knowledge. If this should happen and then has to be returned to the client before you have completed your checks, this money is 'clean' because it has been 'laundered' by your firm and the full weight of the criminal law will bear down upon you.

THE ANTI-MONEY LAUNDERING REGIME

3.02 The Money Laundering Regulations 2007 are the main instruments of the anti-money laundering regime. There are four key requirements under the Regulations, namely to:

- Verify the identity of the prospective client on the basis of documents, data or information obtained from an independent, credible source before carrying out any occasional transactions or establishing a business relationship;

- Understand the ownership and control structure of a legal person, trust or similar arrangement. Where there is a 'beneficial' owner under a trust or other arrangement, you should be satisfied as to the beneficial owner's identity as well as any trustees;

- Know your clients' business and obtain information on the nature and purpose of the intended business relationship; and

- Maintain vigilance through monitoring of the client and the transaction, being alert to any changes in behaviour during the course of the transaction.

(a) Verification

There are many types of independently issued documentation that can verify the prospective client's identity, and the prospective client will normally provide evidence such as original passports, driving licences etc. For companies and other legal persons, you can also check details electronically or obtain information from other bodies such as Companies House.

For a private individual, the MLR 2007 require at least two of the following original documents, one from each section, as proof of identity of an individual:

Section 1	*Section 2*
Full national passport	Gas, electricity or telephone bill, dated within the last three months
Full national driving licence with photograph	Mortgage statement, dated within last three months
Armed Forces ID card	Council Tax bill, dated within last three months
National ID card	Bank/Building Society/Credit Card statement
Signed photographic ID card of reputable employer	Copy of telephone entry from online directory enquiries

Section 1	Section 2
Reference from a partner of the firm stating that they have known the prospective client in a non-business context for at least five years	Visit to prospective client's home address

Two hard copies (preferably in colour for photographs) of the evidence should made in all cases: one for the firm's **Money Laundering Reporting Officer (MLRO)** and one to be retained in your file.

If a client cannot satisfy you as to the nature of the business and their identity, you should decline to act. You are not obliged to take on any particular client or piece of business. If in doubt, err on the side of caution.

You should complete a checklist for your file - usually completion of such a checklist will be a prerequisite of opening a new file for the prospective client.

VERIFICATION OF CLIENT IDENTITY CHECKLIST

FOR CLIENT

Name:_____

    A.   **Evidence not obtained – reasons:**

        1.   Client previously identified in Month…............. Year......

        2.   Client identified personally by – Name _____

                             Position _____

        3.   Other – state reason fully_____

        _____

    B.   **Evidence obtained to verify name and address**

        Full National Passport   –

        Full National Driving Licence   –

        Pension Book   –

        Armed Forces ID Card   –

        Signed ID Card of employer known to you   –

        Young person NI card (under 18 only)   –

        Pensioner's travel pass   –

        Building Society passbook   –

        Credit Reference agency search   –

National ID Card   –
Copy Company Certificate of Incorporation   –
Gas, electricity, telephone bill   –
Mortgage statement   –
Council tax demand   –
Bank/Building Society/credit card statement   –
Young persons medical card (under 18 only)   –
Home visit to applicants address*   –
Check of telephone directory*   –
Check voters roll*   –
Suitable for proof of address only

C.   **Evidence for unquoted company or partnership**

Certificate of Incorporation or equivalent   –
Certificate of Trade or equivalent   –
Latest report and audited accounts   –
Principal shareholder/partner   –
Principal director   –

I confirm that:

a) I have seen the originals of the documents indicated above and have identified the above Customer(s), or

b) In accordance with the Regulations, evidence is not required for the reasons stated.

Signed_____**Date**_____

Solicitors firms are permitted to take a risk based approach to anti money laundering. This means that firms will carry out enhanced due diligence where the prospective client has a higher risk profile, and reduced due diligence where the risk profile is lower than normal, such as acting for a clearing bank or local authority.

As the first line of defence, it falls to the individual conveyancers to determine whether the prospective client is in a higher or lower risk category. You need to be satisfied, therefore, that the documentary evidence provided by the prospective client is satisfactory for the purposes of identification. If there is a trust or other structure, you have to sure that you understand the nature of the structure and can identify the beneficial owner. It's an important responsibility and you can't rely on others in the firm or the MLRO to carry out all the diligence for you. You are the one in direct contact with the prospective client and you need to be vigilant and alert to any aspects of the instructions which could affect the risk profile.

(b) The 'Smell Test'

As the eyes and ears of the firm, you should have a feeling about a prospective client and whether they are being honest or evasive. The following 'smell test' provided by HM Treasury illustrates some of the questions you might ask yourself about the behaviour of the prospective client:

- Has there been any reluctance on behalf of the client to provide adequate ID?

  A common theme amongst money laundering problems is endless promises to provide ID, which is then produced at the last minute and given little or no scrutiny.

- Why has the client advised at a late stage that a third party will become involved in the transaction/provide the funds?

  Both of these should be a concern.

- Does the client appear to have a deep understanding of the money laundering regulations?

  This is beginning to appear as a concern, on the simple principle that some criminals are very good at being criminals.

- Is the client proposing a transaction that is unnecessarily complicated?

  The stock explanation for complexity is that it is for 'tax reasons'. Ask to see the tax advice upon which the whole proposal is based.

- Why have I been chosen for instructions on this particular matter?

  Another common thread with money laundering problem cases is a solicitor being engaged to do work outwith their normal sphere of expertise. Do not be flattered but consider the money laundering implications and also issues of general risk management.

- Why is a client so disinterested in the proposed level of fee?

  If a significant sum of money is being laundered, criminals tend to regard fees as irrelevant.

(c) Suspicion of money laundering

Section 328 of the Proceeds of Crime Act 2002 creates the offence. It says that 'a person commits an offence if he enters into or becomes concerned in an arrangement which he knows or suspects facilitates (by whatever means) the acquisition, retention, use or control of criminal property by or on behalf another person'. This is clearly dangerous for a law firm which could unwittingly become concerned in such an arrangement by holding 'dirty' funds.

The question of what suspicion means in this context has occurred in a number of cases. In the case of *Shah v HSBC Private Bank (UK) Ltd* [2009] EWHC 79(QB), a bank customer (Mr Shah) suffered considerable penalties because the bank delayed remitting his funds due to the suspicion of illegal activity. Mr Shah sought substantial damages from the bank. (Letters of engagement are considered below, but you should be aware that the Law Society 'strongly' recommends the use of robust clauses in letters of engagement to limit compensation payable in the case of disruption or delay caused by anti money laundering procedures).

The court confirmed the test of suspicion as set out in the cases of *R v Da Silva* [2006] EWCA Crim 1654 and *K Ltd v National Westminster Bank plc* [2006] EWCA Civ 1039. For the purposes of s 328 of the POCA 2002, a suspicion does not have to be firmly grounded and targeted on specific facts or on reasonable grounds, it just has to be 'more than fanciful'.

The key point to remember, however, is that the suspicion must be that *the person is engaging in money laundering*. It is not sufficient simply to suspect that the client is 'dodgy', poses a reputational risk to the firm, or that the transaction seems somehow 'fishy'.

(i) What to do if you are suspicious

If you realise something is not right during the course of the transaction, you should raise your concern in writing (including email) with your firm's MLRO. This effectively passes responsibility for reporting to your MLRO and it is now their responsibility to make a decision on whether to make a Suspicious Activity Report (SAR) to SOCA and to inform you how to proceed.

Section 328(2) of the POCA 2002 provides protection for solicitors in relation to money laundering offences. It says that an offence is not committed if the person makes a SAR, or intended to make a SAR but has reasonable excuse for not doing so, or if the act is done in carrying out enforcement of the POCA 2002 or any other similar Act.

The case of *R v Anwoir* [2008] EWCA Crim 1354 shows that there are two ways you may form a suspicion of existing criminal property:

- If you know or suspect that a specific type of criminal conduct, such as fraud, tax evasion, drug trafficking, is occurring and you suspect such conduct has generated property.

- If there are such a cluster of warning signs which cannot be satisfactorily explained so that the manner in which you are asked to handle the funds gives rise to an irresistible inference that the funds must be criminal in origin.

If the problem arises at the last possible moment, remember that professional money launderers often engineer this situation to put you under pressure. However, you must think rationally and do not put yourself or your firm in jeopardy out of misplaced loyalty to the client. If you have good grounds for suspicion, alert the MLRO as early as possible. If a transaction fails to settle on schedule despite heavy contractual penalties, it is likely to be due to failure on the client's part to comply with Money Laundering Regulations. It may even lead to a complaint or claim but if you have good grounds for suspicion of money laundering the firm will support you. In any event, a complaint is preferable to an accusation of criminal conduct.

(ii) 'Tipping off'

If you do have reasonable grounds to suspect that your prospective client is engaged in money laundering and you have reported it to the MLRO, generally speaking, you cannot 'tip off' the client or any other third party. In terms of s 333A of the POCA 2002 it would be an offence to disclose to a third party that a SAR has been made or that an investigation is contemplated or being carried out, if that disclosure is likely to prejudice the investigation. This offence can only be committed after the SAR has been made, but it is good practice that the 'shutters should come down' on the transaction as soon as the MLRO is alerted.

Although this will potentially result in awkwardness in dealing with your client, it is better to dodge calls and risk a complaint than prejudice the investigation. Sections 333B and C permit disclosures from a lawyer to another lawyer within the same firm or in a different (European) firm and this would avoid the frustration and confusion that the other side would experience when the otherwise smooth transaction suddenly stalls for no apparent reason.

TAKING INSTRUCTIONS

3.03 Whether you are taking instructions over the telephone or in person, be very meticulous in noting all the details. Although overly 'defensive lawyering' is not generally good practice, remember you may be called to produce evidence to support your actions or omissions some years later. There have been a number of professional negligence cases in the Court of Session recently where a file note has saved the day for the lawyer.

It is good practice to prepare for the initial meeting or call, so that you have all the bases covered. The Conveyancing Committee of the Law Society avoid pronouncements of best practice, which could rebound on solicitors, so how you record these instructions is up to you or your firm's practice. You may use a pro forma instruction form with a checklist, a file note or make your own notes. Marsh, the Law Society's Master Policy insurer suggest that it is good practice to use a checklist.

It is not uncommon these days to communicate with clients by e-mail. This is an excellent medium for recording instructions, since there will be evidence of the e-mail having been sent to the client and generally speaking, even if the e-mail has been accidentally deleted from the solicitor's own computer, there is a good chance it has been backed up on a cryoserver and can therefore be recovered relatively easily by those who know about these things.

Instructions will change according to circumstances. If you are talking to your client on the telephone or in person, at the end of the conversation, you should sum up your understanding of the position, the action points arising and any new instructions. Then confirm these points by sending the client a letter or an e-mail to recap the discussion and the instructions. E-mail may be preferable, simply because it is more immediate.

In the initial conference, you should glean some basic information from the purchasers. You clearly need to know all about your clients. You should note their full names, contact details, dates of birth and marital status. If a company, you need to understand who is authorised to give you instructions, the ownership of the company and where the company fits into any group structure.

If your clients are married, consider whether they will own the property jointly and also whether they require a survivorship destination. A survivorship destination is a clause in the title that will vest the survivor of the couple in the half share of the property belonging to the deceased automatically, without needing a will or executors. Many law firms advise against survivorship destinations in the strongest terms because of the difficulty in getting out of (or 'evacuating') them (but see para 9.04 for a detailed consideration of this issue).

If the purchasers are not married, you may also want to advise on the pitfalls of a joint purchase. It would certainly be in the purchasers' interests to set out the ground rules of their cohabitation in a minute of agreement to avoid or settle disputes at a later stage. If the purchasers are buying other than equal shares, you should make a careful note of the proportions to be reflected in the title at a later stage in the process.

You need to discuss the price, date of entry and any suspensive conditions (sometimes called 'conditions precedent') that need to be fulfilled before the deal will be binding.

Avoid being drawn into areas that are not within your expertise, such as how much the purchasers should offer. By all means provide some market data to help inform the purchasers but do not cross the line between advising and taking instructions (which is encouraged) and taking decisions (which oversteps the mark).

Use your expertise to guide the purchasers. If the address is, for example, 'Artillery Lane', you might want to flag up the possibility of a former use that could cause potential contamination and advise that the property be referred for further investigation as part of the initial due diligence.

CONFLICTS OF INTEREST

3.04 The principle of conflict of interests was originally laid out in Rule 3 of the Solicitors (Scotland) Practice Rules 1986 ('the Conflict of

Interest Rules'). The Rule states simply enough that a solicitor shall not act for two or more parties whose interests conflict. As usual, the devil is in the detail. What is meant by a conflict? The Law Society's guidance note suggests (somewhat unhelpfully for newer solicitors) that it is hard to define but that 'you know it when you see it'. Or perhaps not - the guidance note also refers to the concern expressed by the Discipline Tribunal in their Annual Reports about continuing failure of solicitors to recognise conflicts of interest.

The Law Society advise that there will be a conflict of interest if you find yourself agreeing with any of the three following statements:

1. You would give different advice to different clients about the same matter;

2. Your actings on behalf of one client would have an adverse impact on a matter you are dealing with for another client, even when the matters are unrelated; and

3. You are unable to disclose relevant information to one client because of a duty of confidentiality to another client.

The term 'solicitor' is broadly defined in the Conflict of Interest Rules so as to apply to firms of solicitors rather than just individuals.

Rule 5 of the Conflict of Interest Rules sets out some broad exceptions from the general principle. These are:

- Associated Companies (in the same group) or public bodies;

- Connected Bodies within the meaning of s 839 of the Income and Corporations Taxes Act 1988;

- Parties related by blood, adoption or marriage;

- Established client - a client for whom a solicitor or his firm has acted on at least one previous occasion; and

- Where there is no other solicitor in the vicinity who the client could reasonably be expected to consult.

Rule 5 also deals with the same solicitor acting for borrower and lender. It is permitted to act for both the borrower and the lender (in residential transactions, and for commercial loans of under £250,000), but the terms of the loan must have been agreed between the parties before the solicitor has been instructed by the lender and the granting of the security must only be to give effect to such agreement. You must always remember that, in these circumstances, the lender is also a client.

The Law Society has agreed to review the Conflict of Interest Rules following criticism from the Scottish Law Agents Society (SLAS) in particular. In an article in the Journal, Ian C Ferguson noted that the exemptions 'drive a coach and horses' through the clear and simple principle.

LETTER OF ENGAGEMENT AND FEES

3.05 Following the initial contact with the client, a terms of business letter and/or letter of engagement outlining the terms of the professional relationship should be sent to the client as soon as possible. The Letter of Engagement is usually a customised letter to the client, which outlines the details of the work undertaken, the day-to-day contact and the responsible partner and details of the proposed fee. This is usually a summary of the initial discussion where these matters are discussed. It can include the detailed terms of business but it is common for firms to have a separate Terms of Business Letter as a standard letter containing the 'small print'. It runs to around five or six pages (depending on the size of the print).

It is not usual to expect a reply or acknowledgement of the Letter of Engagement and the Terms of Business Letter - silence implies consent.

Style of a basic Letter of Engagement approved by the Law Society, as reported in the Journal (November 2003)

Dear [Name]

We refer to your recent meeting with [Name]

We are pleased to confirm that [the Firm] will be acting on your behalf in connection with [work to be carried out].

The solicitor who will be dealing with your work on a day to day basis is [Name].

We will advise you at regular intervals regarding the progress of your work and keep you informed of all significant developments. If you are uncertain about what is happening at any time, please ask.

We enclose an Estimate of our Fees and Outlays for this transaction. If the work turns out to be more complex than normal, we may require to increase our estimate to take account of this. We will inform you as soon as possible about any such increase.

The Money Laundering Regulations require us to be satisfied as to the identity of our clients and as to the source of any funds passing through our hands. In order to comply with these Regulations, we may need to ask you for proof of identity and other information in relation to these matters. We reserve the right to withdraw from acting for you if you fail to provide us with the information requested of you and required in connection with our Money Laundering Procedures.

Finally, our aim is to provide a service which is satisfactory in every respect. However, if you have any concerns about the manner in which work is being carried out on your behalf, please contact our Client Relations Partner [Name] who will be happy to discuss your concerns.

Yours faithfully,

[Name]

This letter should clearly outline the following:

1   The source of authorisation of the solicitor – the Law Society of Scotland.

2   The work to be carried out by the solicitor.

3   Method by which instructions should be given and received and any other aspects of communication, such as setting out the firm's normal office hours.

4   The requirement to identify for Anti Money Laundering purposes the client's identity and that of directors, partners, trustees, controllers of companies or firms and all of the connected shareholders. You should also notify the client that in some circumstances otherwise confidential information is required to be shared with authorities by law without their permission and that the firm will cease acting until clearance is received from those authorities.

5   Authority of the client to instruct (eg who is the authorised person if the client is a company or a partnership, husband/wife or other multiple clients.)

6   The fees and outgoings to be charged or the basis on which they are to be charged (including VAT).

7   Supervision of client business (ie name and status of person responsible for day-to-day conduct of matter and principal responsible for overall supervision if different).

8   Conflict of interest policy.

9   Requirement of confidentiality.

10   Procedures for resolving problems, including the identity of the person to whom the client should refer in the event of there being any dissatisfaction in relation to the work.

The following matters would normally be included in addition to those listed above:

1   Holding client money in a separate clients' account and the notification of rates of interest and where the rate will be displayed.

2   Timing of payment of fees and outlays, late payment provisions and the ability to pay fees and outlays from funds held on the client's behalf.

3   Timescale of the proposed transaction in general.

4   Provisions for the termination of the engagement.

5   Governing law - law of Scotland.

6   Any areas of advice that are specifically excluded. It cannot be assumed that it is implicitly understood by the client that although you are acting in a conveyancing matter, you will not be advising on, for example, taxation or environmental aspects - you should expressly exclude these in your letter of engagement.

In addition, it is good practice for the following matters also to be included:

1   Indemnity/liability for loss.

2   Client's right to taxation (independent audit of fee).

3   Document retention policy and any charges for storing deeds and documents.

4   Lien (claim in security) over titles and papers.

5   Level of service to be provided.

FURTHER READING

'Money Laundering', Alastair N Brown (W. Green)

Guidance from the Joint Money Laundering Steering Group available at http://www.jmlsg.org.uk/industry-guidance/article/part-i-part-ii-part-iii-and-treasury-ministal-approval

Anti-Money Laundering Section of the Law Society's website: http://www.lawscot.org.uk/members/member-services/a-to-z-rules—guidance/a—f/anti-money-laundering/anti-money-laundering

'Fraud alert! (and a cautionary tale)', John Scott (The Journal, January 2009)

'Knowledge is protection' Callcredit Direct (The Journal, April 2009)

'Lawyers in their sights', Elaine Morrison (The Journal, August 2009)

'Frauds and scams beware', Alistair Sim and Russell Lang (The Journal, March 2011)

'Time for a fresh look at conflict of interest', Ian C Ferguson (The Journal, March 2011)

Chapter 4

The Seller's Preparations

READINESS FOR SALE

4.01 The key to a smooth running conveyancing transaction from the seller's point of view, and that of his solicitor, is preparation. Most residential sale and purchase transactions start with houseowners deciding to move, and putting their property up for sale, although it is not unknown for the purchaser to initiate the process. Sellers will usually market their property through estate agents, or their solicitors, if the solicitors deal with this sort of business generally (residential property only). There are many firms of solicitors, particularly in the central belt, who, largely due to the success of solicitors' property centres (SPCs) conduct a large volume of residential property marketing. It should be made quite clear, however, that property marketing has become a separate skill, and if a solicitor is to market property it must be done professionally and properly. As we have seen (para 1.02) the marketing process is not part of the solicitors' monopoly, and may be done by anyone. The choice between solicitor and estate agent is for the houseowner to make, and to a large extent the answer to this question will depend on the services offered, and the part of the country in which the house is situated.

Conversely, solicitors are unlikely to be involved in the marketing of commercial property, unless it is to check some aspect of the draft sales particulars, such as the terms of a right of access or confirming that the plan conforms to the title extent. Marketing will usually be conducted through commercial estate agents, who will have considerable expertise in marketing the types of property being offered for sale although some firms with a large estate agency practice might also market the odd small commercial property, such as a shop, from time to time.

Where the seller's solicitors can assist the process is to assemble all of the necessary due diligence items, or to identify items that will need to be ordered when a purchaser emerges. This means that the title examination element of the transaction, and the inspection of reports and certificates can be conducted speedily and comprehensively, avoiding a back and forth exchange of communications seeking further items of information that the purchaser's solicitors need to complete their investigations.

The sellers should be encouraged to contact their solicitors at the earliest opportunity, so that preparations can be made in good time. Obviously there is nothing the solicitor can do to be organised in advance if the first intimation he receives of a sale is when an offer lands on his desk, or in his inbox, requiring urgent attention, but clients who sell property regularly can be encouraged to alert their solicitor in good time. Usually estate agents will ask who the seller's solicitor is and usually contact them direct, as they will want to put the relevant details of the purchaser's solicitor onto the sales particulars.

THE HOME REPORT

4.02 It is fair to say that the practice of conveyancing in Scotland usually evolves gradually and does not normally seek (or respond well to) radical change. From time to time however, significant changes are seen, and since the re-establishment of the Scottish Parliament, property has received what may seem to be more than a fair share of transformational legislation in the form of the Abolition of Feudal Tenure etc (Scotland) Act 2000, the Title Conditions (Scotland) Act 2004, and the Tenements (Scotland) Act 2004, to name only three.

The Housing (Scotland) Act 2006 introduced a revolutionary new arrangement for residential properties in the form of the Home Report. Following on the tails of, and similar in a number of respects to its English cousin, the Home Information Pack (HIP), the Home Report became compulsory in Scotland from 1 December 2008, it must be said, in the teeth of fierce opposition from the legal profession, and fundamentally changed the way that purchasers of residential property receive information on the condition of a residential property. Since that date, any home for sale has to be marketed with a Home Report. Ironically, the HIP has been abandoned, described as expensive and unnecessary. The Home Report prevails and there are no plans to scrap it.

The Home Report is the collective name for documentary information to help prospective purchasers make an informed decision about a property. It includes:

(i) a Single Survey Report by the seller's choice of surveyor detailing the condition of the property, accessibility for disabled people and a valuation;

(ii) an Energy Report, which consists of an Energy Performance Certificate (EPC), also compiled by the surveyor, detailing the house's grade of energy efficiency, including recommendations for improvement. The EPC is not a home grown initiative, but implements a European Union Directive on energy efficiency; and

(iii) a Property Questionnaire, in which the seller discloses some (quite a lot actually, if properly completed) information about the property in very general terms, such as their knowledge of services, septic tanks, common parts, replacement windows, and the Council tax banding for the property etc. This should be completed as fully as possible, but there may be gaps if the seller does not have knowledge of the information sought, for example if they have not lived at the property for very long, or if the sale is being instructed by an executor, who has never lived at the property.

A Home Report is required even if the property is being marketed privately by the seller himself, and also if the home is being sold by auction, but no Home Report is needed for a private deal off the market, (although an EPC will still be required), new build houses being sold for the first time, or for newly converted homes. A secure tenant purchasing his home under 'right to buy' legislation is not entitled to a Home Report either. Also exempt from the requirement are mixed sales where a house is sold along with, or forms a part of a non-residential property. Seasonal and holiday accommodation, but not holiday homes, do not require a Home Report, and sales of a portfolio of residential properties are considered to be commercial transactions and, as such, are exempt. Homes that are going to be demolished, or that are in such a state of disrepair that they are unfit for habitation, do not need a Home Report, since clearly there would be little point in obtaining either a survey or an energy report in such circumstances.

The penalty for not having a Home Report, once a property is put on the market, is £500 for every day that it remains on the market. This is quite a swingeing penalty, so clearly the obtaining of a Home Report is a priority matter.

The Home Report should be instructed as soon as instructions are received to put the property on the market. Timing of the Home Report is important however, as a property must not be put on the market with a Home Report that is more than 12 weeks old, although it is possible to take the property off the market again for up to four weeks without having to obtain a new Home Report. A survey commissioned at the outset of the marketing campaign will obviously date in a slow market. Although there is no formal shelf life on a Home Report, in practice the lender may insist on a refreshed Survey, if it accepts the Survey at all (it may have a preferred panel of surveyors, whose surveys and only whose surveys it will accept). The cut-off point in most cases will be a survey that is 12 weeks old, but there is no need for a seller to refresh a Home Report after 12 weeks, if the property has not been sold. The purchaser's lender may require the survey to be refreshed before it will accept it. This means that the surveyor is asked to confirm that the original terms of the survey, in particular the valuation, are still good, (or not – and if not, an amended valuation given). It is a matter for negotiation who pays for that refresh (which will normally be a lot less than the cost of the original survey). In a buyers' market, it is likely that the seller will be expected to meet the cost.

From a practical point of view, the estate agent or solicitor will normally organise the single survey and EPC inspection to coincide with the visit to measure up the property and take details (and photographs) for the sales brochure. Most SPCs offer a service through which the solicitor can commission a Home Report online, although they can also be, and often are, instructed in a more traditional way.

At the same time, the seller should be asked to fill out the Property Questionnaire, giving as much information as possible. In some cases the seller will simply be asked to complete this as far as possible and return it to the agent. Some solicitors or agents will help clients to complete the form, while others prefer, for a number of reasons, to leave it to the seller to deal with. It can be a time consuming process, which places an additional burden on the solicitor's or agent's workload, and if they are involved they may also be concerned about being liable for any mistakes or misleading information that it contains. That said, the more detailed and accurate the information in the Property Questionnaire, the less time the solicitor may need to spend during the marketing or during the sale transaction, dealing with queries and requests for information from prospective purchasers or their solicitors.

Once the property has been put on the market, the seller or his agents must provide a copy of the Home Report to a prospective purchaser within 9 days of receiving a request, and may make a reasonable charge to cover the costs of copying and postage, although in practice this does not usually happen. Most properties for sale will appear on the website of their selling agents, and /or the relevant SPC. The Home Report will usually be available through the particulars on the websites, as well as by request by phone or email. It is a good idea to make the Home Report readily available (ie not expect to charge for it), subject to taking some contact details for the person enquiring. It is good property marketing practice to keep a log of people expressing some interest in the property so that it can be followed up later, for example if a closing date is fixed, or to obtain feedback on what they thought about the property, which can be useful for the seller to know. This is best done through requiring people to provide an email address to be able to access the Home Report, but there is not generally speaking, any resistance to this.

MARKETING A RESIDENTIAL PROPERTY

4.03 If your clients are going to employ an estate agent, they should carefully consider the wording of the contract. They may consult their solicitor about this although often the seller will have already engaged an estate agent by the time they get in touch with their solicitor. The estate agents will seek sole selling rights, that is: they are entitled to commission if the property is sold during the agreed period, whoever finds the buyer— even if it is the clients themselves. As to commission, the law is quite clear on the subject: if the estate agent is instrumental in the sale of the house, the agent is entitled to claim commission at the standard rate (*Walker Fraser & Steele v Fraser's Trustees* 1910 SC 222). In practice, these days, terms and conditions are set out in detail in the terms of engagement.

In particular, the clients should not be panicked into employing two agencies. The dangers of this arrangement were highlighted in an unreported case in Paisley Sheriff Court: Mr and Mrs A decided to sell their house, and asked estate agents F to handle the sale. F duly advertised the sale, and several parties, including a Mr Q, inspected the property. No sale resulted. Mr and Mrs A then saw a property advertised by estate agents Z, and while negotiating with Z, they decided to entrust the sale of their own house to Z. They signed Z's standard sale contract, which required a commission to be paid on sale, whether they were instrumental in effecting a sale or not.

In the meantime, Mr Q returned from abroad, looked again at Mr and Mrs A's house, and bought it. Agents F claimed a commission as they had introduced Mr Q to the sellers. Agents Z also claimed a commission in terms of their contract, which granted them a sole selling agency. It was held that Mr and Mrs A had to pay both agents. (See also *Lordsgate Properties v Balcombe* [1985] 1 EGLR 20, (1985) 274 EG 493).

Marketing a property requires particular skills, and many of the firms who undertake significant volumes of property marketing, employ staff to perform this role exclusively. Presentation is all important, and so good quality photographs and brochures and clear appealing descriptions are essential. Particulars of the property now appear on the internet, and most prospective purchasers will pre-view the property by accessing those details and may decide, on the strength of what they see online, not to view the property at all. Armed with as much knowledge as possible, the solicitors who are marketing the property through their own firm will prepare property details and instruct advertising.

The solicitor who engages in selling houses will adopt a procedure broadly similar to that outlined here, although practice will obviously vary from firm to firm.

(a) Visit the house in question, and take measurements and details

Take photographs of the exterior and several interior shots. The dimensions of rooms are taken, so that prospective purchasers can have an indication of the size of the property. Measurements should be accurately given in metres. A lot of people, however, still think in imperial measurement, and subsidiary measurements in feet and inches, are often provided. The conversion should, however, be made accurately, as they can sometimes be relied on for ordering carpets and working out areas. Viewing arrangements should be discussed—the easiest arrangement is to have the owners show the property, at times that suit them. If the house is empty, the solicitor can arrange to show it, but the amount of remuneration sought for this service may be more. Some firms retain the services of retired persons who will conduct viewings on their behalf. It is advisable that, wherever possible, two people conduct the viewings, and a representative of your firm should not be alone in an empty house. Keep careful control of keys.

(b) Basic rules to make the property more attractive to buyers

The seller should try to make the house and garden appear attractive from the street; attend to essential repairs; don't spend money on expensive redecoration which may not be to potential buyers' tastes, but a fresh coat of paint in a neutral colour can assist with the all-important first impression; keep the house clean and tidy and well lit and as attractive as possible from the outside—so-called 'kerb appeal'; avoid cooking and other smells—even freshly ground coffee, which, contrary to legend, some viewers may not like; make sure that there is a parking space for buyers' cars if at all possible; be ready to show the house at short notice. While furnishing, decor and personal items are usually insignificant compared to structure and location, clearing clutter will make a good first impression on potential buyers.

(c) Evaluation and asking price

The single survey that forms part of the Home Report will provide a market valuation of the property. Solicitors who market properties regularly will have knowledge of the current market and be able to advise sellers on a suitable asking price to set for the property, although if the property does not sell quickly then this can be revised at any time. The SPC will provide details of recently achieved sale prices, or this information can be found on Registers Direct, although the SPC information is more up to date, as solicitors provide data once an offer is accepted. Registers of Scotland data is based on registration. The Registers of Scotland now offer a service that provides a free house price search on their website. Also, many websites conduct property price comparisons which can be checked. At the time of writing, the property market is suffering from the effects of the recent recession, and house prices and values have fallen dramatically, with a slow recovery expected. Selling techniques have to be adjusted to suit market conditions, and 'fixed price' asking prices are currently more popular than 'offers over' as they provide certainty for both the buyer and seller. However, sales at prices under the fixed price figure, or under the Home Report valuation, are not uncommon in current (2011) conditions. Both writers express the hope that a return to a healthy and not inflated housing market in Scotland, is not far away.

The idea of a fixed price offer is that the first offer of the price fixed by the seller is usually accepted. However, the Law Society guidance on fixed price offers is that a property advertised at a fixed price is an invitation to submit an offer at that price, but does not imply any obligation on the part of the solicitor that the first offer at that price will be accepted (see *Pharmaceutical Society of Great Britain v Boots Cash Chemists (Southern) Ltd* [1983] 1 QB 401, CA: the advertisement is only an offer to treat, and the bargain must be concluded by written offer and acceptance, as is the rule with heritable property generally). A fixed price offer that is stated to be subject to the purchaser's own property being sold for example would probably be unacceptable to a seller, and it is recommended that sales particulars should make it clear whether or not suspensive conditions (see para 6.09 (third) and also generally 6.14) of this type will be entertained.

(d) Prepare a schedule of particulars

These are made available via websites and through the SPC as well as being available at the property, to be handed out to reasonably interested enquirers. They serve as a preview to prospective purchasers to encourage them to come and view the property, and as a useful reminder once they have visited and may compare the advantages of various properties they have seen. The details in the sales particulars should give truthful and accurate details of the house, with photographs and floor plans and a location plan (if available). Moveable items included in the sale should be clearly specified. Bear in mind the Property Misdescriptions Act 1991 which makes it a criminal offence for an agent to misdescribe a property, or to 'touch up' a photograph to give a false impression. The Property Misdescriptions (Specified Matters) Order 1992 gives a list of specified matters that must be correctly stated in particulars of the property, and these include: the location or address; aspect, view, outlook or environment; availability and nature of services, facilities or amenities; proximity to any services, places, facilities or amenities; accommodation, measurements or sizes; fixtures and fittings; physical or structural characteristics, form of construction or condition; fitness for any purpose or strength of any buildings or other structures on land or of land itself; treatments, processes, repairs or improvements; history, including the age, ownership or use of land or any building or fixture. Prosecutions under this Act and its associated Regulations are relatively rare in Scotland, as breaches of the law are usually dealt with by compensation. There are, however, recorded instances in England of prosecutions where a house was described as 'south facing' when in fact it faced north, and did not accordingly enjoy the same amount of sun. The PMA 1991 would not apply to a misdescription by a person who sells the house personally.

There are proposals to repeal the PMA 1991 given that similar protections are now available for consumers under the Consumer Protection Unfair Trading Regulations 2008. This duplication is seen as unnecessary and placing an additional compliance burden on business. At the time of writing, the findings of a BIS consultation on the proposal are awaited.

(e) 'For Sale' board, SPC registration and advertising

Placing details of the property in the local SPC will give the property good exposure on the market by providing a high street display facility for all properties, and will publish an advertisement in its regular property list. Successful SPCs are often the first port of call for purchasers, who will check the listings that are produced each week for properties that are new on the market. SPCs generally charge a single registration fee, and will hold the property on their books until is sold. If the property has not sold after a certain period eg six months, then a re-insertion fee is usually required. The solicitor will supply the SPC with details of the property and a supply of property schedules. The SPC will put the details on its website, along with 'virtual tours' if required, and access to the Home Report, display the property in its centre, and publish details in its weekly newspaper. It will also make available to prospective purchasers copies of the property brochure or particulars, supplied by the solicitors.

Discuss advertising and an advertising budget with the seller and plan a suitable marketing campaign. Newspaper advertising is expensive but it is useful to highlight the availability of the property. Descriptions and advertisements should be concise and truthful, giving a summary description and a telephone number for further details and viewing arrangements. Over-elaborate advertisements are unnecessary. The solicitors will supply the For Sale board, which incidentally advertises their own services as estate agents too. The SPC's weekly lists of properties also raise the profile of the solicitors who are active in marketing property.

(f) Have main details available; record enquiries and interest

Every firm that is engaged in marketing property will have a system for keeping track of interest in each property. The seller will want to know how the marketing of the property is going, and useful feedback can be obtained from parties who view the property, even if they decide not to proceed further. They may point out some feature of the property that is off-putting, and steps can be taken to change or minimise that effect. Keep a list of all serious enquiries for future reference. In particular, all formal notifications of interest must be carefully and scrupulously recorded, so that in the event of a closing date, all relevant parties are given an opportunity to make an offer. There may be a fair amount of 'hand-holding' required, with the residential client, particularly if the marketing period is protracted, so that regular updates and a sympathetic ear are appreciated by a seller, for whom this can be a particularly stressful time.

CLOSING DATES

4.04 If several parties have indicated their interest in a property, then a closing date can be fixed. A 'closing date' is a date and time selected by the seller's agents by which any interested parties must submit their best offer. A good agent should have a feel of when there is sufficient serious interest to merit a closing date. Sometimes closing dates are fixed to try to galvanise potential purchasers into action, but a closing date at which no offers are received can be a demoralising experience for a seller.

Collect all offers, and arrange to discuss these with the sellers. Accept the offer most attractive to your clients and advise all unsuccessful offerors. There are clear guidelines issued by the Law Society about conduct before, during and after a closing date which are available to view on the Law

Society website at: http://www.lawscot.org.uk/members/member-services/ a-to-z-rules--guidance/a---f/closing-dates-guidelines. It is important to let your clients know what they can and cannot do, and that once they have instructed you to accept an offer, and you have done so, they should not seek to renege on that instruction. If they do, then you will have to cease from acting. It is also important to act scrupulously fairly and openly, to ensure that aggrieved unsuccessful purchasers can have no complaint as to the conduct of the closing date. In particular, the terms of one party's offer should never, under any circumstances, be made known to another offeror.

If there is a delay due to, for example, a client being abroad, or the terms of acceptance being subject to committee or board approval, then it is courteous, when setting the closing date, to let all offering solicitors know that there will be a delay, and suggest a timeframe for a decision.

Over the years, attempts have sometimes been made to circumvent the closing date system, but offers that constitute either referential bids or progressive bids should not be entertained. A referential bid is where a purchaser submits an offer of eg '£100 more than the highest offer received by you'. This would be a dangerous strategy for a purchaser in any event, as he has no way of knowing precisely what the highest offer will be (and see the case of *Harvela Investments Ltd v Canada Royal Trust Co Ltd* [1985] 2 All ER 966, [1985] 1 All ER 261, where a referential bid for a company's shares was briefly approved by the court, but the decision was reversed by the House of Lords). A progressive bid would be where a bidder frames a number of offers that are identical except that the price in each is progressively higher than the last. They are then put in numbered envelopes, and the sellers are told to open them in sequence, until a satisfactory price is reached. The snag from the bidder's point of view, is that the sellers must be tempted to open only the envelope last in the sequence. In practice offers of these types are rarely seen, and purchasers' solicitors will know to discourage this type of suggestion.

A seller is not obliged to accept the highest offer received, or any offer at all. A slightly lower offer may actually be preferable to a higher offer, if there is a significant difference in the dates of entry and the lower offeror is offering a date of entry suitable to the sellers, while the higher offeror is not. There have doubtless been many occasions on which a lower offer has been accepted for reasons that have nothing to do with price: eg 'they were such a nice young couple' is a very common syndrome.

This pleasure of accepting a lower offer from someone you like is not, however, open to persons acting in a fiduciary or representative capacity, such as trustees, heritable creditors, administrators etc

When missives are concluded, the SPC should be informed, any other advertisements cancelled and the For Sale board removed.

OTHER TYPES OF SALE METHOD

(a) Auction

4.05 Heritable property can be sold at auction, or to use the old Scots word, 'roup'. There is a fairly brisk market in auctions of unusual properties, such as railway and telecoms property, although sale by auction, being open and fair, and producing a fair market price, can be an attractive alternative for a seller. It is not much used in Scotland by the private seller, since the property is sold at the drop of the auctioneer's hammer. However a reserve price can be set, meaning that if a minimum amount is not reached, the property remains unsold.

The process of a sale by auction is:

(i) the Auctioneer will have advertised the properties for sale and usually publishes general auction conditions which will apply to all of the properties being sold. Key among these conditions is that the property is to be accepted by the purchaser *tantum et tale*. This means that the purchaser must take the property and its title 'as it stands', with all or any defects and problems. For a solicitor acting for a prospective purchaser, this means that unless specifically instructed not to by your client, you must examine the title before the auction takes place. This can be a time consuming process and of course you will not know until the day whether your client's bid will be the preferred one. You must obviously advise your client of the risks in not checking the title, and should also consider the need to instruct searches and obtain other reports such as a PEC in advance of the auction;

(ii) the seller's solicitor prepares Articles of Roup, which is effectively an open offer to sell. If there are any special conditions attaching to the property, these need to be advertised by the Auctioneer, and also contained in the Articles of Roup;

(iii)   the auction takes place, and when the hammer falls, the highest bidder is preferred;

(iv)   the successful bidder and the auctioneer then sign a Minute of Enactment and Preference, which is usually contained in the Articles of Roup, and has the effect of an acceptance of the offer, producing a binding contract, similar in effect to missives;

(v)   a deposit is usually taken from the purchaser on the day of the auction. This will be applied toward the price at settlement.

(b) Internet sales

Sales of heritable property by online auction appear from time to time on the internet. Details of the property are given on the seller's website, and bids are requested. The size of bids are publicised on the website, and interested parties are given a certain time to raise the bid. If this is not done, the highest bid received is the successful one. One difficulty here is that a signature to the documents must be given, which although possible electronically, is not widespread. The necessary framework for electronic signatures is contained in the Electronic Communications Act 2000 and the Electronic Signatures Regulations 2002. Heritable property crops up from time to time on eBay™. Originally conceived as an electronic noticeboard for pedlars of junk in the San Francisco Bay Area, it has grown to become a central part of our way of life. Although intended for unwanted items and collectibles it also has a section for residential property. eBay™ works like any other auction—the highest bid at the close secures—but for heritable property, e-Bay™ and similar online sites are generally used as a form of advertising, since an online contract would not be legally binding, given the provisions of s 1(2)(a)(i) of the Requirements of Writing (Scotland) Act 1995, which state that 'a written document shall be required for the constitution of a contract or unilateral obligation for the creation, transfer, variation or extinction of a real right in land'. Electronic documents currently only qualify as written documents for this purpose if they are created within the ARTL system (ss 2A and 2B of RoW(S)A 1995). For a description of ARTL see para 2.07.

The Scottish Law Commission's proposals on the reform of the Land Registration system (see chapter 2, and throughout) propose changes to these rules that could open up the way for electronic transacting in heritable property, but the arrangements will be carefully controlled to protect the individual from inadvertently entering into a contract that he does not intend.

ENERGY PERFORMANCE CERTIFICATES

4.06 An Energy Performance Certificate (EPC) is required whenever an existing building is sold or let. For residential properties, the EPC forms part of the Home Report, but for commercial buildings, the EPC is a standalone document that the seller must obtain, to be available to exhibit to prospective purchasers, in accordance with The Energy Performance of Buildings (Scotland) Regulations 2008 as amended (EPB Regulations). The requirement also applies to landlords and prospective tenants, but landlord/tenant issues are outwith the scope of this current work.

Note that for new buildings, an EPC is required as part of the building warrant procedure for construction of the building, where the application for a building warrant was made on or after 1 May 2007, before the Certificate of Completion can be issued.

The idea behind the requirement, which emanates originally from the EU Energy Performance of Buildings Directive, is that a certificate giving information about the energy performance and efficiency of a building will help a prospective purchaser to decide whether to buy the building. While the EPC is part of the Home Report and therefore available to prospective purchasers, it sometimes (often?) happens with commercial property, that an EPC is only ordered when a purchaser has already decided to buy the property. One reason for this may be cost. While a residential EPC can be produced for a comparatively modest sum, the cost of commercial EPCs can sometimes run to hundreds of pounds (and more), particularly for large complicated structures. The requirement to obtain an EPC is however something of which you should ensure your commercial client is aware. Once obtained, an EPC lasts for 10 years.

The EPB Regulations provide that the 'triggers' for the EPC requirement are when a prospective purchaser (or prospective tenant) requests information about the building from the owner or makes a request to view the building, or makes an offer, whether oral or written, to buy (or lease) the building, and the EPC has to be produced, free of charge to any prospective purchaser or tenant.

The EPC should be affixed to a building, but it doesn't need to be displayed in the building unless it is a public building (new build or existing) ie a building with a floor area of more than 1000 square metres, which is occupied by a public authority or by an institution providing public services and which can be visited by the public.

For multi occupancy buildings, (eg an office block that is let to several separate tenants) an EPC can be obtained for the whole building, or individual EPCs can be obtained for individual lettings within the building. In the case of a mixed use building of both residential and commercial properties however, separate EPCs are required for each type of use. An EPC would only be required for the common parts of the building alone if they are heated or conditioned. An EPC for the whole building will probably include the common parts unless the common parts were not heated or cooled mechanically, in which case the EPC would not be required to cover them. For multi occupancy developments however, where each unit is standalone or separated from other units in such a way that each unit would need to be separately rated, then separate EPCs are needed for each unit. A surveyor qualified in producing EPCs should be able to advise appropriately.

EPCs are not required for:

- temporary buildings with a planned time of use of two years or less, workshops and non-residential agricultural buildings with low energy demand

- small stand-alone buildings with a total useful floor area of less than 50 square metres which are not dwellings (A stand-alone building may be detached, or attached, but thermally separated from a main building)

- public buildings with a floor area of less than 1000 square metres

- buildings which do not use fuel or power for controlling the temperature of the internal environment

- conversions, alterations and extensions to buildings other than alterations and extensions to stand-alone buildings having an area less than 50 square metres that would increase the area to 50 square metres or more, or alterations to buildings involving the fit-out of the shell which is the subject of a 'continuing requirement' under standard 6.1 or 6.9 of building regulations.

- buildings that are subject to Sch 1 of the Building (Scotland) Regulations 2004, as amended, such as certain agricultural buildings or those not frequented by people or governed by other legislation such as nuclear of explosives legislation. For a full list see: http://www.legislation.gov.uk/ssi/2004/406/schedule/1/made

There are penalties for failing to produce an EPC, although there are some limited defences for not having an EPC at the point at which a prospective purchaser or tenant is entitled to see one. Local authorities are responsible for enforcing the EPB Regulations and can require an owner (in this case, the seller) to comply with its obligation to make an EPC available to a prospective purchaser or tenant, at any time up to 6 months from the date when it appears to the local authority that the EPC should have been produced. The owner has 7 days to comply, unless he has a 'reasonable excuse' defence for not complying, such as: that he had commissioned an EPC at least 14 days before the relevant time (ie when the prospective purchaser requested information, or asked to view, or made an offer) and despite all reasonable efforts and enquiries by the owner, he did not have possession or control of a valid EPC at the relevant time.

Where the local authority believes an owner to be in breach, it can give a Penalty Charge Notice to the owner. The amount of the penalty charge is (currently) £500 for dwellings and £1,000 in other cases.

It should be noted that there are separate EPC regulations that apply to property in England and Wales, which although similar contain some differences of detail.

GATHER INFORMATION EARLY

4.07 On the 'readiness for sale' principle, it is good practice for the seller's solicitor to obtain as much information and documentation as you can, as soon as you can. This means that the seller's solicitor should start gathering together all the documents that the purchaser's solicitors are likely to want to see, as soon as she is told that the property is to be sold.

A word here about getting really ahead of yourself in this connection: take some time, at the end of a purchase transaction, to properly organise and catalogue all the relevant purchase documents. If you are instructed in the sale some months or years later, these good housekeeping steps will make a significant difference to the speed with which you are able to react to offers and progress a transaction. More frequently than most solicitors would like, probably, instructions come in requiring them to complete a sale in a very short window of time. More common in commercial transactions, perhaps, but not unheard of in residential ones.

If your client is selling a portfolio of properties, or a retail park with dozens of units and occupational leases, then there can be a vast amount of documentation to go through, and having this available, with all documents listed, and sensibly assembled in bibles (bound or lever arch folders, or scanned copies loaded into a CD, of all the documents (or copies of them), that relate to a particular property or transaction) can give all parties a good, often essential, head start on the due diligence process which will help to keep the transaction on track.

If your client has used estate agents to sell his home, it might mean that you have little advance warning of an acceptable offer arriving with you for acceptance. If the title is unfamiliar to you, it is a wise move to have quick check before you conclude missives that there are no pre contract issues that need to be attended to, such as a right of pre-emption (see para 8.25(l)).

(a) Titles

If you acted for the clients when they purchased the property, then you will probably already have details of the whereabouts of the titles, and may in fact hold them on behalf of your client. If not, obtain the mortgage account details or other access information, and request the titles to be sent to you.

If the title is already registered, then the Land Certificate, or a new Office Copy Land Certificate and any relevant Charge Certificate is, strictly speaking, all that is required, but if the prior Sasine titles are still available do not throw them away, as often they can contain essential information or provide clarification that is not evident from the Title Sheet on the Land Register.

If the title is still in the Sasine Register, or if a Land Certificate has not yet been produced, then check through the title to ensure that everything that will be required is there (see Chapter 8 on Examination of Title). If the Land Certificate or the titles are missing, extracts, office copies or quick copies may be obtained from the appropriate Register. Search organisations, such as Millar & Bryce, can do this for you.

Checking the terms of the title at this stage is important, so that you can ascertain if there are any unusual conditions of title, such as rights of pre-emption, unusual servitude rights, or an exclusion of indemnity. If there is a weakness or flaw in the title, it is as well to know about it before entering into missives, and take a decision, in consultation with the seller, about how to deal to with it and whether to disclose it to the purchaser before missives are concluded. It may be better to reveal the difficulty before conclusion of missives, when it can be negotiated, than after conclusion, when the purchasers may prefer to use a breach of warranty as to good title, as an excuse to resile from the bargain. It is however a matter of judgement, depending on the nature of the issue, how best to deal with it. There is a school of thought, on the *caveat emptor* principle, that the purchaser may not notice a flaw, and that unless or until they do, the seller should not necessarily volunteer that information. Provided that you do not tip into misrepresenting the position or misleading a fellow solicitor, it is hard to argue against this approach.

(b) Certificates, Surveys, Records and Reports

It is also helpful at this stage to obtain a property enquiry certificate from the relevant local authority or from specialist PEC providers, planning and building warrant histories, planning permission, building warrants, completion certificates, a coal mining report (if required), any guarantees for damp proofing, timber or dry rot treatments, or double glazing, any site investigation or environmental reports that might be relevant or which might be able to be made available to a purchaser (subject to the person who produced the report being prepared to update it and/or readdress it to the purchaser, for which they may request a fee). Bear in mind however the time limits on the transitional 'shelf life' of such things as PECs (3 months for residential) and coal authority reports (90 days).

You should also obtain copies or principals of any other records or surveys that will be relevant to the purchaser, such as (in relation to commercial property) any asbestos register or reports or correspondence in connection with the Control of Asbestos at Work Regulations 2002 and the Control of Asbestos Regulations 2006 and fire risk assessments in terms of the Fire (Scotland) Act 2005 and the Fire Safety (Scotland) Regulations 2006.

In the case of a first registration, it is also important to receive a form 10A report, which is equivalent to a Sasine Register search, and form P16 report (a comparison of the title plan or description with the Ordnance Survey map) in case there is any major discrepancy in the boundaries. For registered properties, a Form 12A (search of the Land Register) should be ordered. Amongst other things a Form 10A or Form 12A report would disclose if any preservation notices had been registered in terms of AFT(S)A 2000 or TC(S)A 2003. For more detail on searches and reports see Chapter 7.

If your client doesn't know whether the title is registered or not, you can instruct a Form 14 report: 'application for a report to ascertain whether or not subjects have been registered'. This is not a form that is much used however, as usually the seller's solicitor will simply instruct a Form 10 report which will tell him the same thing.

(c) Plan

If the property is not yet registered in the Land Register, or if what is being sold is only part of the title (Sasine or Land Register) then an accurate taxative plan (ie an accurate plan that can be founded upon) of the property to be sold should be obtained as soon as possible. Ideally any sales particulars should contain a plan showing what is being offered for sale, (where appropriate) and it is also the opportunity for the seller's solicitor to compare that plan against the title to make sure that the seller (i) owns everything he plans to sell or (ii) will sell all the property that he owns (if that is the intention).

(d) Matrimonial Homes/Civil Partnership documentation

When selling residential property on behalf of the owner who is an individual, it is necessary to have regard to the provisions of the

Matrimonial Homes (Family Protection) (Scotland) Act 1981 and the Civil Partnership Act 2004. If the title to the home is in the joint names of husband and wife or of both civil partners, then neither Act is relevant. It is when the title is in the name of one spouse or one civil partner only that the provisions of the relevant Act applies, and as the name of the MH(FP)(S)A 1981 implies, the purpose of that legislation is to protect spouses and children from being excluded from the matrimonial home. The legislation was originally brought into being, principally to provide protection for victims of domestic abuse and violence (usually women), by giving them a statutory right to not to be excluded from, and to occupy (or to enter and occupy) the matrimonial home (defined in s 22 of MH(FP)(S)A 1981), even if the home was owned only by the husband. In extreme cases, the 'non-entitled spouse' can apply to the courts to have the 'entitled spouse' excluded from the home by obtaining an 'exclusion order' (s 3 of MH(FP)(S)A 1981). These statutory occupancy rights also apply when the home is rented rather than owned.

Similar rights were created for civil partners by s 101 of the CPA 2004, in the context of which the property is termed a 'family home' (defined in s 135 of the CPA 2004 and is in similar terms to the definition of matrimonial home). Both Acts provide for other subsidiary rights as well, such as paying rent or the mortgage, or carrying out repairs. The protection also extends to any children of the family, and of course applies to husbands, where the title to the home is in the wife's name.

Such is the importance of these rights that they have precedence over the rights of third parties (eg purchasers and lenders) in a dealing with the entitled spouse or civil partner. The effect of this is that, without the agreement of the non entitled spouse or civil partner, a third party would not be able to occupy the home even if they had otherwise validly contracted to do so with the entitled spouse or partner, paid the price and taken delivery of a disposition. In the case of a lender to the entitled spouse or partner, since one of their remedies on default is the right to sell the property (after due process) any rights of a non entitled spouse or partner could potentially prevent that.

Accordingly, s 6 of the MH(FP)(S)A 1981 and s 106 of the CPA 2004 provide a procedure that will protect third parties in dealings with the entitled spouse or civil partner, while also protecting the non entitled parties. The consent of the non entitled party must be obtained to the dealing, or as an alternative, they can renounce their occupancy rights. If a non entitled party is unreasonably refusing to consent to a dealing, or is incapable of consenting because of physical, mental or legal disability, or if their whereabouts are unknown, then application can be made to the court to dispense with their consent (and see also s 7 of the Family Law (Scotland) Act 2006).

So, you should establish the relationship status of the seller, and if they have a spouse or civil partner, who is not included in the title, the consent of that spouse or civil partner will be required. Usually, the non entitled party's agreement is denoted by obtaining their signed consent rather than by renunciation, but either is effective. The renunciation is a separate document that must be signed and notarised by a notary public, but the consent can be either a standalone document or incorporated into the body of the disposition. It is prudent to establish at this early stage that the non entitled party is ready and willing to consent, and if there is any doubt or any suggestion of coercion, then they must be advised to seek independent legal advice.

The terms of the documentation are the same for spouses and civil partners, and most firms will usually use a style that provides for both, and strike out the wording that does not apply in the circumstances.

The renunciation of occupancy rights is in the following style:

I, [   ], residing at [   ], [spouse][civil partner] of [   ] residing at [   ], HEREBY RENOUNCE THE Occupancy Rights to which I am or may become entitled in terms of the [Matrimonial Homes (Family Protection) (Scotland) Act 1981, as amended by Section 13 of the Law Reform (Miscellaneous Provisions) (Scotland) Act 1985] [Civil Partnership Act 2004], in the property known as [ ] being/intended to become a [Matrimonial][Family] Home as defined in the said Act [as amended]; And I hereby swear/affirm that this Renunciation is made by me freely and without coercion of any kind; And I declare that this renunciation is irrevocable.

Given under my hand at [   ] this [   ] day of [   ] Two Thousand and [   ] in the presence of [   ] Notary Public and in the presence of this witness:

The renunciation must be signed in the presence of a notary public. If it is signed outside Scotland, then this can be any person duly authorised by the law of that country to administer oaths or receive affirmation in that other country (eg a commissioner for oaths in England). It is recommended that if a renunciation is being obtained, the spouse should seek independent legal advice.

The form of consent as a separate document (which does not need to be signed before a notary public) is:

> I, [   ], residing at [   ], [spouse][civil partner] of
> [   ], residing at [   ], HEREBY CONSENT for the purposes
> of the [Matrimonial Homes (Family Protection) (Scotland) Act 1981]
> [Civil Partnership Act 2004], to the undernoted dealing of the said [   ]
> relating to [   ].
>
> Dealing referred to:
>
> Signed by the said [   ] at [   ] on the [   ] day of [   ]
> 20[   ] in the presence of the following witness:

And where the consent is incorporated into the body of the disposition which is being granted by the entitled spouse or civil partner:

> ...with the consent of [   ] residing at [   ], the [spouse]
> [civil partner] of the said [   ], for the purposes of the [Matrimonial
> Homes (Family Protection) (Scotland) Act 1981 as amended][Civil
> partnership Act 2004] ...

But what of the single person? There is no spouse or civil partner to consent or renounce rights, but there is the need to 'prove the negative' ie confirm that they have no non entitled spouse or civil partner. This is done by way of declaration, and the form of words varies according to whether the dealing referred to is a sale or a standard security:

> I, [   ] proprietor of the subjects known as [   ] 'the subjects
> of sale' HEREBY DECLARE as follows:
>
> With reference to the sale of the subjects of sale to [   ] the subjects
> of sale are neither a matrimonial home in relation to which a spouse
> of mine has occupancy rights, the expressions 'matrimonial home' and
> 'occupancy rights' having the meanings respectively ascribed to them
> by the Matrimonial Homes (Family Protection) (Scotland) Act 1981,
> as amended, nor a family home in relation to which a civil partner of
> mine has occupancy rights under the Civil Partnership Act 2004.

Declared by the above named [   ] at [   ] on the [   ] day of
[   ] 20[   ] in the presence of [   ]; or

I, [   ], residing at [   ] HEREBY DECLARE as follows:

With reference to the grant by me of a Standard Security over [   ]
('the security subjects') in favour of [   ] the security subjects
are neither a matrimonial home in relation to which a spouse of
mine has occupancy rights, the expressions 'matrimonial home' and
'occupancy rights' having the meanings respectively ascribed to them
by the Matrimonial Homes (Family Protection) (Scotland) Act 1981,
as amended, nor a family home in relation to which a civil partner of
mine has occupancy rights under the Civil Partnership Act 2004.

Declared by the above named [   ] at [   ] on the [   ] day of
[   ] 20[   ] in the presence of [   ]

Occupancy rights do not automatically apply in the case of co-habiting
couples but a 'non entitled co-habitee' may apply to the court for occupancy
rights, which may be granted for a period or successive periods of six months.

An exception to the rule applies where the 'entitled' spouse occupies a
matrimonial home which is jointly owned (or tenanted) along with another
individual who is not the other spouse. That other spouse is not a non
entitled spouse, unless the other individual has waived his or her right of
occupation in favour of the 'entitled' spouse. An example might be where
a mother and son jointly own and occupy a property, and the son and his
wife also live there. Unless the mother waives her right of occupation in
favour of the son's wife, the wife cannot be a 'non entitled spouse', and
would not benefit from statutory occupancy rights.

(e) Builders' Sale Packs

Selling plots for a builder requires a great deal of preliminary preparation.
Gone, (or going) are the days when unruly piles of copy title deeds
would be sent out to prospective purchasers' solicitors to examine, and
it is becoming more the norm for title and other key documents such as
Form 10A or Form 12A reports, planning consent and building warrants,
property enquiry certificates, the Deed of Conditions and title plans to
be scanned and loaded onto a compact disc, copies of which are then
sent out to the purchaser's solicitors. This allows them to access all of

the relevant title documents on screen and save them to file if they want. Setting up this arrangement within the solicitors firm does require some specialised equipment, but nothing that the average 13 year old couldn't competently handle these days. This process must be done carefully and methodically, but once the master copy is created, making additional copies is a lot quicker, more economic and more environmentally friendly than producing many sets of photocopies.

Plans of individual plots, and NHBC (or other home warranty provider) documents also need to be obtained from the builder and style missives and dispositions, letters of obligation and any other standard form documents, such as deeds of disburdenment of any standard security granted by the builder, should also be drafted and assembled well in advance of the first plot sales. It is also a good idea to organise some standard form letters or emails of routine correspondence that can be used during the conveyancing process. The procedures for the sales of plots or units by a builder or developer lend themselves well to systemisation.

(f) Leasehold Documentation

The sale of an investment property can involve a large amount of documentation. It is particularly useful to properly organise and inventorise all of the documents at the end of acting in the purchase of investment property, as these can often change hands every few years or so.

While the property is being marketed, the seller's solicitor should be taking the opportunity to assemble all of the titles, certificates and reports, and check for and assemble all letting documents, which will include the leases with coloured plans, and any back letters, guarantees, rent deposit agreements, licences for works, letters of consent, notices, subleases, rent review memoranda assignations and any management regulations.

The seller and the selling agents (who may also be the managing agents for the property, or if not, the managing agents) should be asked about any transactions that may have taken place since the purchase of the property (although if your firm has acted in respect of new leases, or consent to assignations, then you should have copies, which should be placed with the principal documents for the property). There may be some minor transactions that have taken place without your involvement, so you should always check, particularly to find out if there are any informal, undocumented arrangements in place, or applications for consents, or new lease negotiations that are ongoing. Information about rent collection, service charge and management issues should all be obtained from the managing agents. See also para 4.07(i) 'Using the Due Diligence Questionnaire'.

Where you act for the landlord in connection with the lettings, then it is also a good idea to provide the purchaser's solicitors with a disc containing copies of all the current management documentation, including the pro-forma lease, licences and any other documents used in connection with lettings of the property, so that there is continuity for the future lettings.

If the seller is a participant in the Carbon Reduction Commitment Energy Efficiency Scheme ('CRC') then you may want to obtain some basic information, such as whether the tenants have been charged for the cost of CRC allowances or any other CRC costs and expenses (such as administrative charges) incurred by the seller in relation to the energy supplied to the property, and whether these have been charged directly or indirectly (under the lease, service charge accounts or any informal arrangements). Obtain copies of any correspondence between the seller or its agents and the tenants or their agents in this connection. CRC issues will only be relevant if the purchaser is also a CRC participant.

(g) Construction and alterations documentation

When acting in the purchase of a new (ie less than 12 years old) commercial property, the purchaser's solicitor will require to inspect all of the original construction documentation, so this should also be carefully preserved and itemised with the other documentation relating to the property. This will also apply to any works that have been carried out to older properties, but which required planning consents and/or building warrants.

In the case of large developments, there can be massive amounts of documentation to exhibit, as well as the planning and building warrant permissions, including building/engineering contracts, appointment agreements, sub-contracts, collateral warranties, certificates of practical completion, snagging lists, 'as built' drawings for the buildings or the works, Health & Safety file, any service or maintenance contracts, tenant fit-out works, crane oversail agreements, evidence of contractors and consultants PI insurance etc. See also para 4.07(i) 'Using the Due Diligence Questionnaire'.

Less documentation is required in the case of new or altered residential properties, (for example you wouldn't normally expect to examine the contractor documentation), but again you should find out from the seller whether they have carried out any alterations and obtain from them the planning permission, building warrant, certificates of completion, or notice of acceptance of completion certificate and stamped warrant drawings (ie the copies of the drawings that have been stamped by the local authority's building standards department in connection with the application for building warrant). It is important to ask about and obtain this documentation as early in the transaction as possible, as the missives will contain a provision about these documents, and it is surprising how frequently (particularly with residential property) either no permissions at all have been obtained, or the seller has been unaware of the requirement for, and has done nothing about getting, a certificate of completion or notice of acceptance of completion certificate. If that is the case then steps will need to be taken either to obtain a letter of comfort from the local authority, or even apply for a retrospective building warrant. That can take many weeks, and so early identification of this issue is imperative. See the example transaction in Appendix 1 for how this is dealt with in practice.

(h) VAT

Not an issue when buying or selling a dwelling house, but the VAT status of commercial property should always be ascertained. If the land has been opted to tax and VAT applies in the transaction, or if it is a TOGC (see para 6.13(d)) then the seller will have to exhibit copies or certified copies of certain documents, which may include the seller's VAT Registration Certificate, documents evidencing an option to tax or real estate election given to HM Revenue & Customs, and any relevant notices and correspondence. See also para 4.07(i) 'Using the Due Diligence Questionnaire'.

(i) Using the Due Diligence Questionnaire

Although designed to be used by the solicitors for the commercial purchaser, as a list of their requirements to be able to conduct a full due diligence examination, the solicitor for the commercial seller will also find the Due Diligence Questionnaire (DDQ) a useful tool in helping to ensure that their pre sale preparations are thorough and effective, by using it as a checklist of items to identify, locate, order or ask the client or the selling agents about.

Produced by the Property Standardisation Group (PSG) and available to download from www.psglegal.co.uk, the DDQ provides a comprehensive list of the likely due diligence requirements of a purchaser and their solicitors, and is particularly appropriate to large transactions where there are a number of properties or units. The main body of the DDQ deals with fairly comprehensive commercial property enquiries relating to such matters as titles, property enquiries, fire certification, planning and building control matters, insurance and the like. The detail of more specialised areas which may not necessarily apply to all transactions, namely VAT treatment of the transaction, capital allowances, staff/TUPE matters, occupational leases and construction documentation, are dealt with in a detailed annexe on each of those topics. For the seller's solicitor therefore, acting in the sale of a two year old building, the annexe dealing with construction documents will be an essential checklist of items to assemble in readiness for the sale. The annexe on occupational leases, similarly will assist when preparing for the sale of a multi-let building or development (see also para 7.10)

SALES BY INSOLVENCY PRACTITIONER

4.08 As we will see elsewhere (paras 6.18, 8.18(g), (h) and (i), 9.10(o) and 11.04(d)), acting for an insolvency practitioner has its own specialities in conveyancing terms. You will require to exhibit the evidence of the IP's appointment or other entitlement to sell the property and convey the title, and so copies of these should be obtained to exhibit along with the titles and other documents. See para 8.18 (e) to (i) for details of the documentation required for each insolvency situation.

Each insolvency procedure allows for appointment of the IP by various different routes and the various documents constituting the appointment should be exhibited to the purchaser.

Often the option to tax documents is not with the company records and as such, whether VAT can be charged on the sale of the property is not known. In most cases the IP will try to obtain this information from HMRC prior to sale, or will seek an indemnity for any VAT that is found to be due upon the sale price subsequently. An IP may also apply to opt to tax.

IPs are not automatically immune from the application of statutory liability and the terms of each statutory notice and statutory regime affecting the property should be checked; eg a defective building notice requiring rectification of defects, as the notice may specify liability on an owner of a building arises under the Building (Scotland) Act 2003. If the owner does not take the necessary rectification steps required by the notice, the legislation provides that the owner is guilty of a criminal offence and that the local authority may carry out the work, recovering any expenses reasonably incurred from the owner. A Trustee in Sequestration or Liquidator would become an owner if they registered title but they are specifically carved out as an exception to the regime. Similarly, any notice of liability registered under the Tenements (Scotland) Act 2004 will affect an owner, but a Trustee in Sequestration will only be affected where they have registered title to the property. In any event these notices would still require to be dealt with on sale.

Prior Ranking Securities: Inhibitions and standard securities are treated differently under the different regimes, and you may require to obtain a discharge of the inhibition or standard security where there is no ability to deal with the property with the security in place eg a discharge of an inhibition will be required for a sale in Administration.

Searches may or may not be exhibited by the IP, depending on their funding arrangements, and instructions should be taken.

SALES BY HERITABLE CREDITORS IN POSSESSION

4.09 When a heritable creditor calls up its security and exercises its power of sale (see para 10.07) there are certain steps that it must follow when marketing the property, to ensure that it obtains the best price that could reasonably be obtained (see para 8.18 (c)). You should obtain the service copy calling up notice(s) and extract of any decree (both are required for sale of residential property, but a decree is not compulsory for the sale of commercial property). You should also obtain certificates of advertising to comply with the advertising requirement. These are usually obtained from the newspaper's publisher. The purchaser's solicitors will require to see these.

A sale by a heritable creditor provides the purchaser of the security subjects with as good a title as the debtor had. The property is disburdened of the security in favour of the creditor and also all other heritable securities and diligences (eg inhibitions) that rank *pari passu* with, or postponed to that security (s 26 of the CFR(S)A 1970). A prior ranking security holder's rights are not affected, but the enforcing creditor has the same rights to redeem that security as the debtor had. In practice, the enforcing creditor will pay the prior security holder from the sale proceeds, to redeem the prior security (or securities if more than one), so that a clear title can be given to the purchaser, who (obviously) is likely to insist on one. There exists the possibility that the whole of the sale proceeds could be taken up by the indebtedness due to the prior security holder, meaning that the enforcing creditor gets nothing. Clearly the amount of prior ranking indebtedness is a key piece of information for any creditor considering this route. When the sale has completed, the sale proceeds require to be distributed as follows:

(i)   in payment of all expenses that the creditor properly incurred in connection with the sale; then

(ii)   payment of the whole amount due under any prior ranking standard security; followed by

(iii)   payment of the whole amount due under the standard security being enforced and, if there are any other standard securities that rank equally with it, equal payment of the whole sums due under those standard securities, then

(iv)   payment of any amounts due under any postponed standard securities, according to their ranking; and finally

(v)   any balance left over is paid to the debtor or the owner of the security subjects (as appropriate).

THE 'SELLER'S DRAFTS'

4.10 Traditionally, the solicitors on each side of the transaction are responsible for preparing drafts of certain of the conveyancing documents, and providing then to the other side for checking, revisal or approval. Once the missives are complete (see Chapter 6) the seller's solicitors send to the purchaser's solicitors the following (at the same time as sending the titles and other documents for examination):

(a)   Draft letter of obligation (see para 11.04);

(b)   a form 10A report with a draft form 11, or a Form 12A report with a draft Form 13; and

(c)   a draft discharge or deed of restriction/deed of disburdenment of any security (see para 10.03(f)).

FURTHER READING

Home Reports: Guidance and information is available from the Scottish Government at www.scotland.gov.uk/Topics/Built-Environment/Housing/BuyingSelling/Home-Report

Energy Performance Certificates (domestic and commercial): Further information, FAQs and Guidance from the Scottish Government at www.scotland.gov.uk/Topics/Built-Environment/Building/Building-standards/publications/pubepc

Checklists

Due Diligence Questionnaire and accompanying Guidance Notes available at www.psglegal.co.uk

Chapter 5

The Purchaser's Overture

FINANCING THE RESIDENTIAL PURCHASE AND DEALING WITH LENDERS

5.01 It is absolutely imperative that you discuss with your purchasing clients their arrangements for financing their purchase and that they will have access to the full amount of money required to complete the purchase. It is very useful for this purpose to produce for them a statement showing how much money will be required. Many purchasers under-estimate the total costs, once all the outlays and taxes are added on. It may also have a material bearing on how much they will be prepared to offer for the property.

If the purchase requires to be financed with a loan, you need to know how much has been offered to the purchaser. With any luck, the purchaser will have organised funding ahead of consulting you, and will already have a written offer of loan or mortgage 'promise'. If so, he can tell his lender that you are acting for him in the purchase transaction and, in the majority of cases (in residential purchase transactions), the lender will want you to act for them as well. The lender will send you an instruction pack, with a pro-forma report on title form for you to complete, and a copy of the offer of loan with any conditions. You should also check if the lender is a member of the Council of Mortgage Lenders (CML), and if so, (most are) check that lender's requirements in the CML Handbook. For other third party lenders, or where the loan has not yet been agreed with the lender, consider the Conflict of Interest Rules carefully before thinking about acting.

Most lenders require purchasers to contribute some equity to the purchase price and you should find out from your clients where that will come from. It is important that the purchaser understands that these funds have to be fairly liquid (ie readily accessible) so that they can be applied to the purchase in good time.

If it becomes clear that the purchasers may not have access to liquid funds, for example it may transpire that he has to give many months' notice to uplift funds, or has to sell a property before he has all the funds they need, then you have to advise him that it is not prudent to pursue the particular property until the funding is in place. It is possible to offer without the finance being in place, but this needs to be made clear in the offer. That said, the seller would be entitled to treat an offer 'subject to satisfactory finance' or 'subject to the sale of the purchaser's property' as pretty worthless and she would be well advised to continue to market the property in the hope of achieving a more concrete result.

Similar considerations apply to the purchase of commercial property, although a lender's loan is summarised in a term sheet and detailed in facility letter. As commercial properties are generally higher in value, and therefore represent greater risk to the bank, it would be usual for a bank to instruct another firm of solicitors to protect its interest and ensure that sufficient security is in place for the bank. For commercial loans of £250,000 or more, solicitors are not permitted to act for both borrower and lender under the Conflict of Interest rules - see para 10.06.

ESTATE AGENTS AND SURVEYORS

5.02 Once you have advised your client and taken instructions, you will have to deal with other property professionals, including estate agents. The estate agent's job is to market the property effectively in order to achieve the best price for the seller in the shortest time.

If you are acting for a purchaser, you will probably contact an estate agent for the first time after the initial meeting with your client, to ask them for a copy of the marketing materials - generally known as the property particulars or the 'schedule' (see para 4.03) and the Home Report (see paras 4.02 and 5.03). This is also the opportunity to ask any questions about the property or the seller's position or arising from the Home Report. You may also 'note' your client's interest (see below) or intimate that an offer will be forthcoming, depending on your instructions from the purchaser.

As noted in Chapter 1, an estate agent could also encompass a solicitors' or surveyors' firm. There is no requirement for estate agents to be licensed or to follow an industry code of conduct unless they are governed by the Law Society or the Royal Institution of Charted Surveyors.

THE HOME REPORT

5.03 One of the principal problems perceived with Home Reports is that the seller can choose the surveyor who provides the Single Survey and valuation. This can lead to beauty parades, where the surveyor who inflates the value the most wins the appointment, although according to the Scottish Government's interim report on Home Reports, this is apparently not that common. At the time of writing, a random search brought up a house for sale in Prestonpans offered in the region of £249,950 but with a Home Report Valuation of £290,000. Therefore the usefulness of the valuation to the purchaser must sometimes be in doubt, particularly in times of financial fragility.

The traditional method that the Home Report replaced was far from perfect, either. In that system, the purchaser would make an offer based on his survey which he would commission from a chartered surveyor. Where there were multiple notes of interest, sometimes the purchaser's solicitor would ask the seller's solicitor whether any surveyors had already surveyed the property. Armed with this information, the purchaser's solicitor could then contact the surveyors direct for a copy of the survey, but addressed to the purchaser, so that a duty of care existed. There were also cases of multiple surveys from different surveyors being commissioned for the same property, leading to wasted expenditure for the purchasers (and hence the term 'Single Survey')

However, when the property market began to overheat, some offers were solely based on an assessment of the market, but made 'subject to survey'. Once the offer was found acceptable, then the seller would commission a survey and deduct the cost of remedying any defects highlighted by the survey. The problem with this practice is that the amount of money offered was perceived to be divorced from the value of the house, because without a survey the price was driven by emotion and market forces (cf the current example, above, where the valuation is likely to be divorced from the amount of money offered). In fact many solicitors and estate agents have compiled very sophisticated market data, fed by information gathered from recent sales marketed through the solicitors' property centres that offer an accurate and up-to-date picture of the market.

In this respect the Home Report may be a useful tool for the purchaser, who can get a good idea of any likely issues that affect the property, but if the conditions list shows a sufficient amount of category 1 and category 2 comments, then most purchasers will be happy enough. Lots of category 3 comments means the dilapidated condition of the property should be reflected in the valuation.

RESIDENTIAL SURVEYS

5.04 For residential purchasers there are three grades of survey:

- a brief valuation for mortgage purposes;
- a full conditional survey, which investigates most of the accessible 'nooks and crannies'; and
- a structural survey.

The third of these surveys is rare in residential property as it is usually only appropriate if there is some concern over the structural integrity of the building. Most residential purchasers – or, if not, their lenders – will be put off by an earlier survey that indicates structural problems. The conditional survey would normally recommend a specialist opinion, whether from a structural engineer or an infestation specialist.

The Home Report Survey contains a valuation and some comments on the condition, so is something of a hybrid.

COMMERCIAL SURVEYS

5.05 For commercial property, the traditional system endures, namely the purchaser commissions their own survey of the property. The commercial survey will give a detailed report on the condition of the property as well as the situation, location and any other relevant considerations, such as planning and environmental considerations, as well as a valuation.

COMMERCIAL PROPERTY - HEADS OF TERMS

5.06 In commercial property, clients are generally advised by surveyors, also sometimes called agents. It would be usual for the seller's and purchaser's respective surveyors to agree a document that reflects the broad terms of the consensus that they have reached. This is normally set out in one or two page document called the heads of terms. Although it reflects the *consensus ad idem*, it is stated that the parties' intention is that this document does not constitute a contract, because the actual terms of the contract will be agreed by the solicitors in the missives. The heads of terms will cover the main points such as parties, price, date of entry, the subjects, suspensive conditions, legal costs and any other conditions, such as option to purchase additional subjects.

The heads of terms are passed to both sets of solicitors to progress the conveyancing in accordance with the agreed terms.

FIXED PRICE

5.07 In a cooling market, marketing a property at a fixed price can be a useful way to entice offers. Even in a good market, fixed prices can be used to secure a quick sale or to differentiate your property from others.

It is a simple system, the first purchaser to make a satisfactory offer at the correct price secures the deal. However, it can be difficult to manage when multiple offers are received. The Law Society considers that marketing at a fixed price is an invitation to prospective purchasers, not an offer in itself. There is therefore no obligation on the seller to accept the first or any other offer.

Advice from the Law Society is that if marketing at a fixed price, you must make clear at the outset if there are any material conditions that need to apply to the offer. Also it is useful to set out whether any suspensive conditions will be entertained, such as being subject to finance or subject to the sale of the seller's house. There is clearly no need to note interest in these circumstances.

NOTING INTEREST

5.08 Assuming that the finance is in place, and the client is still keen, it is customary for the purchaser's solicitor to 'note' their client's interest with the seller's agent. A note of interest is sometimes intimated by a letter which is sent or faxed identifying the client and containing all your contact details as the prospective purchaser's solicitor, so that you will be informed should a closing date be set. It is an indication to the selling agent that your client is serious enough to speak to a solicitor about making an offer.

These days, interest can be noted by telephone, but it is best to follow up with an e-mail to be safe. Very often, this telephone conversation is an opportunity to gauge the interest received by asking about the number of other notes of interest. However, it's worth being cautious here. Although it is courteous to withdraw a note of interest if the purchaser's interest wanes, this is not always done in practice. It's not especially in the seller's interest to follow up on older notes of interest that might lead to withdrawal, as a higher number makes the property look more sought-after to prospective purchasers - although the agent may have a feel for their true weight.

Estate agents, and sometimes surveyors, can also treat an expression of interest by the prospective purchasers direct (such as requesting particulars) as a note of interest. There can often be doubt, therefore, as to what exactly is a 'note of interest'. Notes of interest have been developed in practice and are governed only by professional bodies. There is no statutory footing for notes of interest, so they can mean different things to different professions.

Once a critical mass of good quality, recent notes of interest have been received, the seller should have a good indication of the number of seriously interested parties who would be likely (but are not committed to) offer. Once satisfied, the seller will normally set a closing date, but this is again custom and practice, rather than a legal requirement. Clients interested in purchasing should therefore be advised that noting interest will not guarantee an opportunity to submit an offer. There is no obligation incumbent upon the seller's solicitors to set a closing date and the seller is at liberty to accept any offer from any party up till the point a closing date is set. This state of affairs may not be fully appreciated by prospective purchasers, who may be under the impression that noting interest 'guarantees' them an opportunity to make an offer.

CLOSING DATES

5.09 A closing date is a date and time set by the seller's solicitor or estate agent for the receipt of offers (akin to best and final offers or sealed bid procedure in England).

It can be a tricky balancing act between forcing prospective purchasers' hands too early and leaving it too late, by which time serious parties have drifted off and found somewhere else. It's the seller's call. Once the seller's solicitor or estate agent receives instructions to proceed, they will notify everyone who noted interest that a closing date has been set. Any new prospective purchasers enquiring about the property can be made aware of the position and any marketing materials updated (eg a 'Closing Date set' banner may appear in the last advertisements for the property) (See also para 4.04).

If acting for a purchaser, make sure that you have received full instructions in plenty of time. Draft your offer in advance and check the details with the client if in any doubt about your instructions. Make sure that you have inserted any special conditions that the purchaser instructed. Closing dates are drop-dead deadlines - if your offer is late it will not be considered. It is therefore of utmost importance that the date and time is recorded in a system. Most offices have a double diary system or linked computer calendars. Technology is fine, but it needs humans to act upon the information.

Mistakes can happen. See *Watts v Bell & Scott WS* CSOH [2007] 108 for a really simple mistake where the offer was accidentally faxed to the client (who was away on holiday) rather than the chartered surveyors to whom it ought to have been transmitted. The result was that what would have been the highest offer was never received and the client successfully sued the firm for damages.

There are occasions when clients instruct an offer but then try to renegotiate the price once the closing date has been 'won'. This practice has been largely halted by the introduction of Home Reports, since information on the condition of the property is now available upfront and offers are now less likely to be submitted 'subject to survey'. However, in instances where it is clear that the purchaser has got cold feet and wishes to reduce the price for no good reason, you must consider the client/solicitor relationship as at an end and not continue to act for that client.

Unsuccessful offeror's solicitors should be notified as soon as possible by the seller's solicitor. Purchaser's solicitors should try to gather some feedback for their clients as to how many offers were received, the highest price and where their offer was ranked. It can provide some solace but also will help to form a view as to the current state of the market for next time.

DUE DILIGENCE QUESTIONNAIRE

5.10 The PSG Due Diligence Questionnaire (DDQ) is specifically designed to help purchasers and their solicitors at the start of a commercial property transaction (although elements of it will be helpful to the residential purchaser's solicitors too, by way of checklist).

The original concept of the DDQ, is that it is sent to the seller's solicitors as a way of finding out and obtaining all the information that a commercial purchaser might need to conduct its due diligence processes. It is similar in some ways to the English Commercial Property Standard Enquiries (CPSEs) that are in common use, but is not intended to form part of any contract. Instead, it is supposed to elicit a full disclosure of all relevant information. If the document is actually marked up by the parties, it can form a record of what information has been exchanged and act as a road map for the transaction. It is used as a robust checklist of requirements that a purchaser's solicitor will seek to examine. It includes information similar to that contained in the Property Questionnaire part of the Home Report, as well as listing all title, searches, certificates and reports that the purchasers solicitors require to see, an information about tax matters, employees, tenants and construction documentation for new or recently constructed buildings (see also para 4.07(i)).

The Law Society's guidelines for closing dates: http://www.lawscot.org.uk/members/member-services/a-to-z-rules--guidance/a---f/closing-dates-guidelines

Due Diligence Questionnaire - available at www.psglegal.co.uk

Chapter 6

The Contract

'A verbal contract isn't worth the paper it's written on.'
(Samuel Goldwyn)

MODERN PRACTICE

6.01 In modern conveyancing practice, much more emphasis is placed on the preparation and content of the missives than used to be the case. Several decades ago, an offer consisted of only the bare essential clauses: property, price, date of entry and a requirement for a valid marketable title, for example, but now many of the matters formerly dealt with at the examination of title stage are dealt with in the contract, which can run to many pages, particularly in commercial purchases.

It also seems that there are many more regulatory and legal issues to take into account than ever before, and so it is important for the conveyancer to know their way round all the clauses and conditions in a modern offer for the purchase or sale of heritable property, their purpose and effect, and how they interact with the rest of the conveyancing process: the due diligence procedures of examination of title, searches, reports and other documents; the transfer of the property; the payment and settlement/completion arrangements and the perfecting of the purchaser's real right in the property through the registration stages.

WHAT ARE MISSIVES?

6.02 'Missives' is the name we give to the contract for the sale and purchase of heritable property in Scotland that is constituted by a series of formal letters entered into by or on behalf of a purchaser and a seller dealing with the conditions that are to apply to the purchase and sale. A contract for the purchase or sale of land must be in written form, and while that usually takes the form of missives, it can equally be effected by a Sale and Purchase Agreement between the parties themselves, although one of the advantages of the missives (which are signed by the respective solicitors on behalf of seller or purchaser) is that they can be concluded with more speed, particularly if the parties themselves are in different countries, or if execution formalities are subject to an approval process, which is not uncommon in a number of organisations. For the purposes of this Chapter we shall refer to missives only, although the terms apply equally to a Sale and Purchase Agreement, as the content is very similar, it is the format that is different. Incidentally, there might sometimes be a perception of some disadvantage from the client's point of view re loss of control. English clients buying property without a loan are often surprised that they don't actually need to sign any document or deed.

Traditionally, the missives take the form of an Offer to buy from the purchaser, which is accepted by either a *de plano* (without further procedure) outright acceptance from the seller, or may be met with a qualified acceptance if there are any elements of the purchaser's offer that the seller does not wish to accept, or wants to suggest an alternative. This can be something as simple as a change to the date of entry, or deleting a time limit for acceptance that has not been met, to more significant changes in relation to undertakings or warranties that the seller is being asked to give, or shifting the onus back to the purchaser, such as where the purchaser will be expected to 'satisfy himself' as to the position in relation to matters such as titles and condition of the property. The process is referred to as 'adjusting the Missives'. Once all matters are agreed between the parties, which may involve the back and forth exchange of a number of letters, the final letter of acceptance with no new conditions, 'concludes the bargain'.

While missives can be entered into directly between the contracting parties, invariably the missive letters are prepared by the solicitors on behalf of their respective clients and are signed by the solicitors. The missives need not necessarily be witnessed, but it is common practice for this to be done. It means then that they are self proving and can be registered in Books of Council and Session if required and thus provide for faster diligence, if it comes to that. By the missives the sellers bind themselves to sell, and the purchasers bind themselves to buy the property in question. The conclusion of Missives represents *consensus ad idem* and the formation of a binding contract.

It is becoming increasingly common in commercial property transactions, for an offer to sell to be issued by the seller's solicitors, once the essential terms of the deal have been agreed by the parties or their agents in Heads of Terms which consist of a document setting out the principal points agreed by the parties eg price, entry, suspensive conditions. It is also becoming common for offers to sell to be issued in transactions involving insolvency, as these circumstances generate specific requirement of the parties (see para 6.18).

The contract will describe the property, the price being paid, the date that the price is to be paid and all other conditions affecting the transaction. For both residential and commercial the missives will also contain a wide variety of additional conditions according to circumstances relating to such matters as: condition of the property and the systems in it, tax, title and title conditions, planning and building control and other construction matters, roads and services, and details regarding any occupational leases affecting the property.

Strictly speaking, there is no legal requirement for missives to be entered into. Parties can, and occasionally do, go straight to completion of the transaction without any prior contract at all, the documentation consisting only of the disposition to transfer the title, which will be delivered to the purchasers in return for payment of the price. This would be most unusual - not to mention risky - in an arms length transaction, but might take place if the property is being transferred between members of the same family, for example. However, missives not only bind the parties into the transaction, they also deal (as we shall see) with many other matters not normally dealt with in the disposition, but which are equally important to the purchaser of the property.

ADJUSTING MISSIVES

6.03 The 'formal offer and series of acceptance letters' model is becoming somewhat old fashioned however, with the increasing use, either of standardised offers (see paras 6.09, 6.10 and 6.13 below), or of treating the offer that has been submitted as a draft document, which the parties then adjust, as a single document, until its terms are agreed between the parties. It is rare these days that conveyancers need a set of coloured pens for this purpose: it is usual for changes to be marked up electronically.

The days of having to craft complicated sentences in the missives to express small changes in a previous letter are rapidly becoming a thing of the past. It is so much easier, not to mention less risky, to make a manuscript or on-screen change of words, replacing the previous words with your alternative provision, than having to produce tortuous sentences along the lines of: 'The words 'within three months' where they appear in lines four and five of clause ten of your qualified acceptance will be deleted and there will be substituted the words 'by not later than 31 August 2010', both in terms of drafting, and, later on, when reading and understanding the final basis of the agreement between the parties. It is not necessary to flip backwards and forwards between letters to work out what the final version actually says – it is set out in the final agreed version of the single document.

If you do have to exchange formal letters in this way for any reason, it is vital to ensure that your revisals are accurate, and to check that the new provision that results says what it is supposed to say. It is too easy to delete reference to a string of words, and substitute them with an alternative that no longer makes grammatical sense within the sentence. Each qualified acceptance is in effect a counter offer, and if a complex offer is followed by a complex acceptance, there is still no *consensus ad idem*, and the purchaser's solicitors will have to write again formally, accepting the qualifications made by the seller before a binding contract can exist. Theoretically this process could go on indefinitely. The more letters that are exchanged, the more complex the contract becomes, and the longer the missives remain unconcluded, the greater the uncertainty, and the possibility of the whole deal collapsing. The dire consequences of having too many letters can be seen in the case of *Rutterford Ltd v Allied Breweries Ltd* 1990 SLT 249, in which, after a series of qualified acceptances, Rutterford's solicitors acting in their client's purchase of the property, purported to withdraw the qualifications in their previous qualified acceptance to Allied Breweries' solicitors, and to hold the bargain as concluded. Unfortunately the effect of the earlier acceptance had been to cancel out the offer represented by the previous qualified acceptance, so that the final letter in the chain was not sufficient to conclude the contract, but should properly be regarded as a proposal that a contract be concluded on the basis of the earlier exchange of letters.

Clearly the practice of adjusting the draft single document is preferable.

The offer can stay in draft format for some time, particularly if there are complex issues to deal with, or some essential pieces of information are outstanding. It may be useful to insert drafting notes, either in bold type, or italics or square-bracketed, into the document to remind you to return to these points and resolve them before the final version is produced for signing. During the adjustment period, there may be a number of iterations of the draft offer that are passed between the solicitors. You must check the terms of each version you receive against the previous version produced by you. Sometimes the other solicitors will have used revision indicators (like 'Track changes' in Word) to show the changes they have made, and while this is an easy way to see only the changes that have been made, without having to re-read the whole document again, it is not entirely without risk. Some changes may have been made inadvertently without having the revision indicator function 'switched on', and so the best way to be sure that you are seeing all of the changes is to use a document comparison tool, like Workshare DeltaView™. Some solicitors will send you a comparison document to accompany their new version of the document but you may prefer to produce your own comparison. It is very easy to get out of sync with multiple versions of a document, and so careful version control procedures may be required.

At all times of course it is important to be alive to the effect that changes to one clause may have on another clause elsewhere in the document.

If the process of adjusting the offer is becoming protracted, (and even if it is not, for speed), often the best course of action is to have a meeting, or lengthy phone call with the other solicitors, to thrash out the differences, although often nowadays the negotiation takes place through exchange of emails.

CONCLUDING THE CONTRACT

6.04 A regrettable feature of modern conveyancing is (or has been) the long delay in conclusion of missives, sometimes until the date of settlement. While occasionally necessary due to protracted negotiations as to the terms of the missives, simply delaying the conclusion of the contract until the last minute is poor practice and it equates to the English system of the contract only being complete when contracts are exchanged, and runs the risk of the English features of gazumping, gazundering and contract chains to enter Scottish conveyancing. Sometimes the reason is that the lending institutions, which are taking longer and longer to issue loan papers means that the purchaser's solicitor does not want to run the risk of concluding the contract only to have his client unable to settle, if an offer of loan is not forthcoming. Sometimes, it is simply pressure of work that is to blame. I suspect also that some solicitors, faced by increasingly complex contracts, are quite happy not to conclude them. While solicitors must have regard to the interests of their clients and take their clients' instructions, they must also act professionally and not mislead other professionals. The Law Society issued a Practice Note urging conveyancers in residential transactions to conclude contracts at an early stage, to inform their clients of the requirement to do so, and advising of action that they should take if instructed by their client to delay concluding the bargain pending resolution of some other matter such as selling their own house or waiting confirmation of funding, which may include withdrawing from acting for that client. See http://www. lawscot.org.uk/members/member-services/a-to-z-rules--guidance/g---m/ missives/avoidance-of-delay-in-concluding-missives.

DELIVERY

6.05 There are differing views concerning the requirement for delivery of missives. Some commentators describe missives as a bilateral contract, which is effective as soon as it has been executed. Others consider that, to be effective, the writing must physically be delivered to the other party, because (*Erskine Institutes* at 3.2.43) as long as a writing remains in the granter's own custody, he is free to change his mind and to destroy it, or at least not to deliver it.

Now that it is possible using fairly simple and affordable technology to make a pdf document of the signed principals of documents, it is commonplace to send pdf versions of signed missives letters via email to the other party's solicitors during the course of the transaction. Solicitors who do not have the capability to create pdf documents can, and do, resort to sending facsimile versions of the letters via fax machine. Although the principals of the letters are then sent by post or DX or Legal Post, the parties had come to regard the missies as 'concluded' on the date on which they were signed and faxed or emailed. Where conclusion of the missives and completion were simultaneous or occurred close together, it would not be unusual for completion to take place and funds be transferred on the strength of faxed or emailed missives, particularly, apparently, in residential transactions.

This practice came into sharp relief following on the decision in the case of *Thomas Park and Another, Petitioners [2009] CSOH 122*, which concerned a petition for partial recall of an inhibition, to release from the ambit of the inhibition the petitioners' leasehold interest in The Grapevine Restaurant in Bothwell. The basis for the recall was that, before the inhibition was effective, missives had been concluded for the sale of the business and property.

It was agreed that the effective date of the inhibition was midnight on 31 August 2007, but earlier on that day, after an offer to purchase the lease of the property had been made in early August, the petitioners' solicitors had sent a fax with a signed qualified acceptance to the purchaser's solicitors, who faxed back a full acceptance, that same day. Both formal letters were then put in the post.

The point at issue was whether missives had effectively been concluded on 31 August. In support of their contention that they had, the petitioners sought to rely on the 'postal acceptance rule', and also on case law that indicated that communication by fax would be sufficient to constitute a contract. The postal acceptance rule provides that, while an offer is effective only when it is received, an acceptance is effective from the date of posting (*Thomson v James* [1855] 18 D 1*). This however assumes that the acceptance is a clear and complete acceptance of the offer and not a qualified acceptance setting out new terms. In *Park*, the judge decided that the inhibition **did** attach to the property, as actual delivery was necessary for offers and *qualified* acceptances. Although the letter concluding the contract was posted on 31 August, the qualified acceptance, or counter offer to which it referred had not been delivered, and so the contract could not be regarded as concluded until that acceptance actually arrived.

The decision in *Park* threw something of a judicial cat amongst the conveyancing pigeons. *Obiter* references in the case to the possibility of 'constructive delivery' set off the practice of giving undertakings not to withdraw a formal letter delivered electronically (by fax or email) and irrevocably undertaking to put it in the post.

There are, however, considerable doubts that 'constructive delivery' of missives letters is possible, given that the remarks made in *Park* were *obiter* and did not form part of the *ratio* or actual decision of the judge. It seems that while the undertakings that are given by solicitors in these cases, although forming a binding obligation upon the solicitor to do what is stated in the undertaking, do not necessarily have the effect of rendering the missives letters binding and enforceable. The timing of delivery issue may not be crucial, in the way that it was in *Park*, but if there are circumstances, for example a need to conclude a contract before the end of the financial year to benefit from a tax break, then until the position is unequivocally determined, the prudent course of action is to ensure physical delivery of the letters. On this point see also para 2.08.

Law Society guidance on electronic communications is that there is a duty on a solicitor to follow up a fax or email of a contractual document with the original as soon as possible. If the solicitor is instructed by the client not to send the hard copy, that fact must be communicated to the other solicitor immediately and the solicitor must withdraw from acting if the client cannot be persuaded to withdraw those instructions.

The proposals for electronic missives contained in the Scottish Law Commission's Report on Land Registration (see para 2.09) would of course resolve the issue.

OPTIONS

6.06 There are occasions when parties agree that property, or land, may be sold by the owner to a prospective purchaser, but not right now, or only if certain circumstances apply. For example, a party might want to obtain detailed planning permission for a proposed development of the property, conclude a contract with a third party to take a Lease of the site (conditional upon the purchase being completed), enter into a contract to purchase some adjoining land (again conditional upon the purchase being completed), and so on. Missives can be entered into on a conditional basis (see para 6.14), but another alternative is for the parties to enter into an option agreement, giving the prospective purchaser an exclusive option to buy the property in question at some future date. A well drafted option will contain details of the terms and conditions on which the purchase, if it goes ahead, will proceed, very similar to adjusted missives. Separate missives are not strictly speaking necessary, but it may sometimes be preferable to adjust missives at the time the option is exercised. One essential difference with an option is that, unless its terms provide otherwise, the party need not ever purchase the site and cannot be made to do so by the owner. An option can however contain a provision that the owner of the land can call upon the party to purchase the land at some point (known as a 'call option').

The option will ordinarily only be enforceable for a certain period of time, after which one or other of the parties will be entitled to bring the contract to an end. Obviously the owner of the land does not want to be tied into a contract for an unlimited period of time where there is no possibility of the sale ever taking place. The period of time for which the option is in place will depend upon the circumstances of the transaction, it could be months, or even years. In many instances the potential purchaser will pay a fee for the option, which will be retained by the seller even if the option is never exercised. Options are typical in situations where a developer might want to acquire an unzoned piece of land and then try to get a planning consent. Usually he will want an option with as long a duration as possible since obtaining the right planning consent can be a very long drawn out process.

It is common for the option holder's rights also to be protected by having the landowner grant a standard security over the land in favour of the option holder. That way, any attempted sale to a third party would be prevented, as the standard security would appear as a marker on the title, and of course would need to be discharged (by the option holder) for the landowner to be able to produce a clear title to a purchaser. This device is used in preference to imposing a condition in the title, which would not be enforceable in any event as a real burden, because if it attempted to prevent the landowner from selling, it would be repugnant with ownership.

Remember that a badly drafted suspensive condition can also amount to an option, in effect (see para 6.14(a)).

EXCLUSIVITY ARRANGEMENTS ('LOCK-OUT' OR 'LOCK-IN' AGREEMENTS)

6.07 From time to time in commercial transactions, the parties may agree that for a, usually short, period of time, a prospective purchaser may be given complete exclusivity to carry out due diligence and agree the terms of the contract with the seller, to the exclusion of any other parties. This arrangement should be distinguished from the process of 'noting interest' where, once parties have intimated their interest with a selling agent, they are entitled to an opportunity to offer for the property along with other interested parties (see para 5.08). Exclusivity agreements are not generally known in residential transactions, although they can happen – perhaps with a large estate, where a purchaser, having a clear run at offering for the property, wants to have the freedom to negotiate the terms of the purchase without other potential purchasers appearing on the scene, which would prompt the seller to set a closing date.

Exclusivity agreements, which are also sometimes called lock-out or lock-in agreements, will tie the parties into an arrangement in advance of entering into a legally binding contract and provide time to carry out all the investigations a purchaser needs to conduct. The seller cannot sell, or attempt to sell, the property to a third party for the duration of the agreement, in other words the parties have 'locked-out' third parties and 'locked-in' themselves. However, the arrangements within the exclusivity agreement do not need to be too prescriptive, for example neither party need necessarily be committed to proceed with a transaction.

The purchaser benefits from the comfort that the seller will not dispose of the property for a certain period of time, during which the buyer can carry out surveys, arrange funding, set up a tenant, discuss commercial terms with the seller in greater detail, and examine the title and any leases. In many agreements, the buyer will be under a positive obligation to take those steps which it needs to progress the transaction during the period the agreement is in force.

Often a seller may seek payment of a premium or fee, to compensate for the fact that it is unable to dispose of the property for a fixed period. The amount of premium will depend on the circumstances, however it is sometimes paid on the basis that if the sale does take place, then the price paid on completion will have that premium deducted from it.

STANDARDISED OFFERS – RESIDENTIAL STANDARD CLAUSES

6.08 As offers became progressively longer and more complex, each firm of solicitors developed its own style of offer (sometimes different solicitors in the same firm had their own individual preferred style of offer). This meant that the terms of the offer had to be carefully studied in each transaction, and a bespoke qualified acceptance prepared. Considerable time could be spent negotiating all the terms of the contract.

The Law Society tried to introduce a standard Scottish contract a number of years ago, but this was never really adopted by the profession at large, due to the lack of flexibility. More recently however, local faculties and associations of solicitors have produced standard clauses for residential missives, couched in terms that ought to be acceptable for many transactions. There are a number of regional variations to cater for, so currently we have standard clauses for Aberdeen, Ayr, Borders, Dumfries and Galloway, Dundee/Tayside, Highland, Inverclyde, Moray, Paisley and Combined Standard Clauses for Edinburgh and Glasgow. The Combined Standard missives are seen as a 'first step' towards greater standardisation among the various regional options, and it is hoped that other regions may also adopt these clauses or similar clauses. This last initiative is to be welcomed, as previously there were separate sets of Clauses for Edinburgh and Glasgow. Standardisation does not work so well if there are so many variations that the benefits of standardisation are diluted or even lost. Naturally, a solicitor acting in the relevant 'region' will be familiar with their own variation, but it is recommended that if you are acting for a purchaser of a property in one of the other 'regions' that you use the Standard Clauses for that area, and so it will be necessary to familiarise yourself with that version, for the purposes of advising your client. Although the differences are not substantial, there is not, as far as we know, any document that compares each of these missives and sets out the differences between them. However, the majority of the provisions will be the same or similar and the benefits to local solicitors dealing with other firms in the same area are enormous. The Standard Clauses are all available on the Law Society website at http://www.lawscot.org.uk/members/member-services/a-to-z-rules--guidance/s---z/standard-missives. The concept of the standard offer has proved to be successful and enjoys widespread use, although it is not mandatory to use it.

The idea is that you submit a short one page offer containing the essentials of price, property and date of entry and any conditions that are property- or client-specific, and then refer to the Standard Clauses that are regionally most appropriate to the property for which you are offering.

Each variation of the Clauses has been registered in the Books of Council and Session, and so are fixed and can easily be identified by reference to the dates of registration. They are also declared to be 'open source' documents that can be used without any restriction.

STANDARDISED OFFERS – THE RESIDENTIAL OFFER

6.09 The one page offer will look something like this, which is the version included with the Combined Standard Clauses (2011 Edition):

Dear Sirs

Seller

Purchaser

Property address

For the purposes of this offer and the Combined Standard Clauses (2011 Edition) aftermentioned:

The Purchaser means [   ] residing at [   ]

The Property means [   ] together with any garden, carport, garage, parking space and/or outbuildings pertaining thereto and all other parts and pertinents.

The Price is [   ] POUNDS STERLING (£[   ]), and

The Date of Entry shall be [   ] or such other date as may be mutually agreed in writing.

The Purchaser hereby offers to purchase from your client (hereinafter referred to as the 'Seller') the Property at the Price and upon the conditions contained in the Combined Standard Clauses (2011 Edition) specified in the Deed of Declaration by Ross Alexander MacKay and Others dated (   ) and registered in the Books of Council and Session for preservation on (   ) both 2011, and upon the following further conditions:

(First)   The Price will include the following additional items (if any): [
]

Note: When the purchasers of a house buy furniture and furnishings with that house, the purchasers' solicitors should ask the sellers to confirm that they own these effects, and that there are no outstanding hire purchase, credit sale, leasing or other debts, which would mean that the sellers do not own the moveables they have sold.

> (Second)   This offer unless earlier withdrawn is open for verbal acceptance by 5pm today with written acceptance reaching us no later than 5pm on the fifth working day following the date of this offer and if not so accepted shall be deemed to be withdrawn.

Note: The offer may also include a clause making the offer conditional on the purchaser obtaining a loan, or selling his own property. In the first case, the seller's response will probably be to delete this clause in any acceptance, and the purchaser should get on with getting the loan arrangements in place as soon as possible. The second case is of course more problematic, and is tantamount to no offer at all. If the purchaser has difficulty in selling, the seller could find himself tied into a contract indefinitely, and so at the very least, if this condition is to be accepted, a long stop date **must** be included in the acceptance, after which, if the purchaser has not sold, the seller is free to find another purchaser. It all depends on the circumstances, - eg the purchaser may be waiting for interested parties to offer for her property, at a closing date in a few days' time. The seller's solicitor should find out as much about the purchaser's circumstances to be able to advise the seller if this type of condition can be entertained.

> (Third)   This offer and any contract to follow hereon are entirely conditional upon (a) a satisfactory survey report and (b) a satisfactory valuation report being obtained by the Purchaser in respect of the Property. The Purchaser and his lenders shall be the sole judges as to what constitutes satisfactory reports.

> (Fourth)   If the transaction following on from this offer is ARTL compatible (and provided that the Seller's Solicitors are registered under ARTL) it will proceed under ARTL. Neither the Purchaser's Solicitors nor the Seller's Solicitor will withdraw from using ARTL during the progress of the transaction without good cause and without giving reasonable prior notice to that effect to the other Solicitor. The following definitions apply to this clause:

'ARTL' means the computer system provided by the Registers of Scotland to enable the creation of electronic documents and the electronic generation and communication of an application for registration of an interest in land in the Land Register of Scotland and the automated registration of that interest;

'ARTL compatible' means in respect of a transaction one which is capable of being processed under ARTL as being of a kind and falling within a geographical area approved by the Registers of Scotland for such processing.

Yours faithfully

NB: Optional clause (Fifth) for Edinburgh agents:

(Fifth)   In the event that any of the windows within the Property have been altered or replaced within ten years of the Date of Entry, written confirmation from a Local Authority, qualified architect or other approved third party will be delivered at settlement confirming that such replacement windows comply with building and planning regulations as at date of installation.

Note: The reference to the Combined Standard Clauses in this version would of course be altered to refer to the appropriate version that you wish to import into the offer.

While there might be a few qualifications to this offer because of specific circumstances of the transaction, the hope and expectation is that the seller's solicitors will be able to issue a *de plano* acceptance (see para 6.20).

STANDARDISED OFFERS – THE COMBINED STANDARD CLAUSES

6.10 Much of the content of the various regional variations of the Standards Missives is very similar and designed to cover the same issues. For the following clause by clause consideration, we look at the current version (2011) of the Combined Standard Clauses.

(a) 1. Fixtures, fittings & contents

The Property is sold with:

(a)   all heritable fittings and fixtures;

(b)   all items of whatever nature fixed or fitted to the Property the removal of which would materially damage the fabric or decoration of the Property;

(c)   all items stated to be included in the sales particulars or advertisements made available to the Purchaser; and

(d)   the following insofar as any were in the Property when viewed by the Purchaser: garden shed or hut, greenhouse, summerhouse; all growing plants, shrubs, trees (except those in plant pots); all types of blinds, pelmets, curtain rails and runners, curtain poles and rings thereon; a carpets and floorcoverings (but excluding loose rugs), stair carpet fixings; fitted bedroom furniture; all bathroom and cloakroom mirrors, bathroom and toilet fittings; kitchen units; all cookers, hobs, ovens, washing machines, dishwashers, fridges and freezers if integral' to or encased within matching units; extractor hoods, extractor fans, electric storage heaters, electric fires, electric light fittings (including all fluorescent lighting, .external lighting, wall lights, dimmer switches and bulbs and bulb holders but not shades); television aerials and associated cables and sockets, satellite dishes; loft ladders; rotary clothes driers; burglar alarm, other security systems and associated equipment; secondary glazing; shelving, fireplace surround units, fire grates, fenders and associated ironmongery.

The Seller warrants that at the Date of Settlement all items included in the Price are owned by the Seller, are or will be free of all debt, and are not the subject of any litigation.

The Seller undertakes that the Property will be left in a clean and tidy condition at settlement.

Note: The rule is all property that is heritable is included in the sale, and that moveable property is excluded. More and more the distinction between the two becomes blurred, and it is not unknown for sellers to strip the house, especially of bulbs—both light bulbs, which are moveable, and garden bulbs, which are heritable. This clause sets out that all heritable property is included in the purchase, but also items which might be either heritable or moveable, to avoid tiresome disputes. Any moveable items which are to be included in the sale should be specifically mentioned in the main offer.

(b) 2. Specialist reports

(a) Any guarantees in force at the Date of Entry in respect of (i) treatments which have been carried out to the Property (or to the larger subjects of which the Property forms part) for the eradication of timber infestation, dry rot, wet rot, rising damp or other such defects, and/or (ii) insulation and double glazing, together with all supporting estimates, survey reports and other papers relating thereto ('the Guarantees') will be exhibited on conclusion of the Missives and delivered at settlement.

(b) The Seller confirms that he is not aware of anything having been done or omitted to be done which might invalidate the Guarantees.

(c) If requested, and insofar as necessary and competent, the Guarantees will be assigned to the Purchaser at the Purchaser's expense.

Note: If there have been any specialist treatments carried out to the property, these are normally accompanied by a guarantee – sometimes for many years – against failure of the treatment, so the purchaser will want to have the benefit of those guarantees if they are still valid and enforceable. The existence of any such guarantees should have been flagged up in the Questionnaire section of the Home Report. The guarantees should be examined, in case of recurrence of the problem, and should be checked to identify the areas affected, and the status of the guarantor. If the company that originally gave the guarantee is no longer in existence and there is no insurance or industry back-up for the guarantee, then it is unfortunately worthless. Many of these guarantees do not require a formal assignation to the purchaser and transfer automatically, but you should check the terms of the documentation to be certain.

(c) 3. Central heating etc

(a) The Seller undertakes that any systems or appliances of a working nature (including central heating, water, drainage, electric and gas) forming part of the Property will be in working order commensurate with age as at the Date of Settlement.

(b) The Seller will make good any defect which prevents any system or appliance being in such order provided said defect is intimated in writing within 5 working days of settlement. Failing such intimation, the Purchaser will be deemed to be satisfied as to the position.

(c)   The Seller will only be responsible for carrying out any necessary repairs to put any system or appliance into such order and shall have no liability for any element of upgrading (except to the extent such upgrading is required to put any such system or appliance into such order).

(d)   The lack of any regular service or maintenance of any system or appliance or the fact that it may no longer comply with current installation regulations shall not, of itself, be deemed to be a defect.

(e)   The Purchaser shall be entitled to execute any necessary repairs at the expense of the Seller without reference to the Seller or the Seller's tradesmen (i) in the event of an emergency; (ii) in the event that the Seller's tradesmen do not inspect the alleged defects within 5 working days of intimation; or (iii) in the event that any necessary repairs are not carried out within five working days of inspection.

(f)   The Seller confirms that he has received no notice or intimation from any third party that any system (or any part thereof) is in an unsafe or dangerous condition.

Note: The Purchaser will have had the property valued on the basis that the systems and appliances included in the property are in good working order. Obviously if the central heating system was installed 12 years ago, then the property is clearly being sold with a 12-year old system and the purchaser is not entitled to seek works that would upgrade it to a current state of the art system, hence the reference to 'commensurate with age'. However, if any of these systems or appliances are found not to function upon taking entry, then it is entirely appropriate that the purchaser should seek recompense from the seller, always subject to the *de minimis* level of £200 in Clause 24: Limitation of Claims. Clause 3 provides for the purchaser to check immediately that all systems and appliances are working, and to formally (ie in writing) intimate any problems with them within a tight timescale of 5 days. Note: The Purchaser should get these systems checked by a qualified person at the date of entry, and submit any claim timeously. The seller does not want to be kept hanging on for a long time with the possibility of a claim by the purchaser, so when acting for the purchaser, you should be sure to remind him to check all the systems thoroughly as soon as he moves in.

From the point of view of the seller, if they have had the central heating system regularly serviced, for example, then they should be less concerned about this type of clause. Details of any maintenance contracts will show up in the Home Report. It makes sense of course, if there are any problems with any of the systems or appliances that these are disclosed during the contract stage so that liability can be excluded or limited, or repair work carried out before settlement.

If repairs are necessary then it is up to the seller to have them done as soon as possible. A five working day period is allowed, except in the case of emergency. Clearly the seller would prefer to be in control of instructing the work, as he is the one meeting the cost. You may find yourself involved in some of these arrangements immediately post settlement.

(d) 4. Development

The Seller warrants that he has not served or been served with nor received any neighbour notification notice issued in terms of planning legislation in respect of any development. This warranty shall not apply in respect of, (i) a development which has been completed, (ii) where any planning permission has lapsed, or (iii) where an application for planning consent has been refused or withdrawn. In the event of any such notice being served on or received by the Seller prior to the Date of Settlement the Seller will forward such notice to the Purchaser within 5 working days of receipt of such notice.

Note: the position regarding planning notices actually issued and affecting the property can be verified either by the planning department of the local council or by a Property Enquiry Certificate that specifically deals with planning matters. This clause only deals with matters that should be within the knowledge of the seller, and should have already been disclosed in the Home Report, although of course they might have been served after the questionnaire was completed. The seller's solicitor should already have checked whether the seller has received any notices (see para 4.07) and is therefore able to give this warranty. The clause also makes it clear that the seller's warranty doesn't extend to completed works or lapsed, refused or withdrawn permissions.

(e) 5. Statutory notices

(a)   Any Local Authority (or other public body) notices or orders calling for repairs or other works to the Property dated prior to or on the date of conclusion of the Missives (or any other work affecting the Property agreed to or authorised by the Seller outstanding at the Date of Entry) will be the responsibility of the Seller. Liability under this condition will subsist until met and will not be avoided by the issue of a replacement notice or order.

Note: This covers notices or orders issued prior to the date of conclusion of the missives, not the date of entry. This distinction used to be the subject of an east-west divide, with the west holding out for the date of entry when liability passed. It had long been felt in the alternative that if a statutory notice, for example, for repairs to the roof of a tenement in which a flat that was the subject of the purchase was located, was issued just after conclusion of missives, but before settlement, then it was unfair to expect the seller to have to be liable for that cost, particularly when the purchaser would have offered for the property on the basis of it in its unrepaired state, and presumably also at a valuation that reflected that state of repair. The existence of any such notices prior to the sale will be stated in the Home Report, and the PEC will disclose any that have been issued.

(b)   The Seller warrants that he has not received written notification of, approved, entered into or authorised any scheme of common repairs or improvement affecting any larger building of which the Property forms part. Where the Seller approves, enters into or authorises any such scheme or where any such scheme is instructed, the Seller shall remain liable for his share of the cost of such works. Details of any such scheme will be disclosed to the Purchaser prior to settlement. The Seller undertakes not to enter into, approve or otherwise authorise any such scheme prior to settlement without the consent of the Purchaser.

Note: This provision relates to tenements.

(c)   When any work in terms of clauses (a) or (b) above is incomplete or unpaid for at the Date of Settlement the Purchaser will be entitled to retain from the Price a sum equivalent to the estimated cost of the

Seller's share of such works (which estimate shall be augmented by 25%). Such retention shall be held in an interest bearing account by the Purchaser's solicitor pending settlement of the Seller's liability. The retention shall not be released or intromitted with without the written authority of the solicitors for both parties. Any shortfall will remain the liability of the Seller.

Note: Common repairs in tenements can be fraught with issues. The costs of major schemes can be huge, and the disruption significant. If there are common repairs ongoing in a tenement building, then full details need to be obtained and decisions made about respective liabilities of the seller and purchaser. This will usually mean that estimates of the remaining cost of repairs will have to be provided so that the purchaser can determine what sum to retain from the price until the repairs are finished (this is the usual arrangement, but other provision can be made if the parties want). The usual position is that the seller will bear the whole costs (which need to be vouched or verified) and an appropriate sum is retained from the price – not handed over to the seller, but reserved in some account until the works are finished. Usually, the purchaser's solicitors will arrange for consignation of the funds and will hold these until the works are finished and paid for (see (d)).

(d)   On issue of invoices for such works in terms of clauses (a) and/or (b) above by the Local Authority or other authorised party the retention shall be released to make payment of such invoices as soon as reasonably practical.

Note: If the purchaser has retained funds, then payment should be met from these.

(e)   Notwithstanding any other term within the Missives, this condition will remain in full force and effect without limit of time and may be founded upon until implemented.

(f)   Without prejudice to the above, the Purchaser may retain from the Price such sum as is reasonably required to meet any costs for which he may be contingently liable under s 10(2) of the Title Conditions (Scotland) Act 2003 or s 12(2) of the Tenements (Scotland) Act 2004. Such retention shall be held in an interest bearing account by the Purchaser's solicitor pending settlement of that liability. The retention shall not be released or intromitted with without the written authority of the solicitors for both parties. Any shortfall will remain the liability of the Seller.

(g)   Prior to the Date of Entry the Seller will provide full details of any common repairs in respect of which a notice of potential liability for costs has been or is to be registered.

Note: the arrangements under the TC(S)A 2003 s 12 and T(S)A 2004 s 10 provide for a notice to be registered against the title to a property where there is an obligation to pay a share of costs relating to maintenance or other work (but not local authority work) carried out before the property is sold. The notice must be registered at least 14 days before the purchaser's 'acquisition date' for the new owner to be liable for these costs. What this means in practice is that it gives a purchaser notification that costs are due, so that arrangements can be made for a suitable retention from the price. This clause provides an equitable agreed mechanism for retention of a sum to deal with notices served on the property, a situation which in the past has provided many problems through the default of sellers.

(f) 6. Property management and factors

Where the Property is part of a larger building or of a development, it is a condition that:

(a)   common charges will be apportioned between the Seller and the Purchaser as at the Date of Entry on the basis that the Seller will be responsible for all common repairs and improvements carried out, instructed or authorised on or prior to the Date of Entry;

(b)   there are no major repairs or improvements proposed, instructed, authorised or completed but not yet paid for in respect of the Property or the larger building or development of which it forms part;

(c)   evidence of any block insurance policy will be exhibited prior to the Date of Entry; and

(d)   all other outgoings and charges payable in respect of the Property will be apportioned as at the Date of Entry.

Note: This applies an equitable scheme of division between seller and purchaser of accounts for maintenance and repair of parts of a building which is in multiple ownership. If there is a factor or property manager, he will carry out an apportionment between the parties, and should be asked to do this by the seller's solicitor. It is up to the seller's solicitor, and obviously desirable, to inform the factor of the change in ownership so that the seller's responsibility for such accounts will cease as at the date of entry. The seller will remain liable for repairs authorised or instructed, or work undertaken but not yet completed, or completed but not yet paid for prior to the date of entry.

(g) 7. Alterations

(a)   Where there have been additions or alterations completed to the Property (or if the Property has been erected) within 20 years of the Date of Entry then the following documentation shall be exhibited before and delivered at the Date of Entry:

(i)   all necessary Listed Building Consents, Building Warrants (including stamped warrant drawings) and Certificates of Completion (or, if applicable, Notices of Acceptance of Completion Certificate); or

(ii)   an unqualified Local Authority Property Inspection Report, Letter of Comfort, or equivalent.

Note: The importance of this provision cannot be overstated. Any building work, with only very minor exceptions, carried out to the property after its construction requires building regulation consents (building warrant) from the local authority, to ensure that it is carried out safely and correctly. Although one could seek confirmation that *any* such works have been done with the appropriate authorisation from the local authority, in practice a cut-off period of 20 years has been agreed. Often information and assistance will be required from the surveyor to (a) point out in the first place if any works have been carried out and (b) when these works are likely to have been done. Equally as important is the completion certificate (pre Building (Scotland) Act 2003), or notice of acceptance of completion certificate (post B(S)A 2003 (date of commencement 1 May 2005)) - when the work is complete the building will be inspected, to ensure that the approved plans have been faithfully followed; and if so, a certificate will be issued. Prior to May 2005, this inspection was carried out by the local authority inspector who produced the certificate. Now the certificate is produced by a certifier, such as an architect, and sent to the local authority, which issues the notice of acceptance (following an inspection) to complete the documentation.

Listed building consent is only required for alterations to buildings that are listed as being of architectural or historic importance. The consent is obtained from the planning authority, and is strictly monitored.

Failure to obtain or comply with, planning or building consents can, at worst, entitle the local council to require that the property be restored to its original condition, even if this involves demolition. It is vital that the purchaser is satisfied of these consents, and form part of the purchaser's marketable title, and any lender will insist on these being available or obtained.

If work has been carried out without obtaining the necessary building warrant then it may be possible to apply to the local authority for a retrospective consent. Depending on when the work was carried out, and the type of work entailed, this may involve either an application for a completion certificate with no prior warrant being obtained, or the local authority may be prepared to carry out a property inspection (when the work pre-dates the B(S)A 2003) and, if it complies with the necessary buildings standards, issue a unqualified report or a 'letter of comfort' confirming that the local authority will take no enforcement action regarding the unauthorised works. Note however, that it is more difficult to obtain a letter of comfort for missing Listed Buildings Consent, as the local authority does not have the same opportunity for discretion, and a retrospective application may be required, with the prospect of remedial work being required if the alterations fail to comply. Not all types of alterations will be eligible for this service and it does not apply to commercial property.

(b)   All Planning Permissions necessary for additions or alterations completed to the Property (or if the Property has been erected) within 10 years of the Date of Entry shall be exhibited before and delivered at the Date of Entry.

Note: Any additions to or alterations to the external parts of a property must have planning permission from the local authority that certifies that it meets the requirements of planning legislation. Planning permission is also required for original construction. This applies not only to the dwellinghouse itself but also to some outbuildings such as garages. Again the surveyor should confirm in his report, whether there are any works that required planning permission, in his report. There are some exceptions for minor additions or alterations in terms of the Town and Country Planning (General Permitted Development) (Scotland) Order 1992, unless this has been suspended by an Article 4 Direction (in terms of the TCP(GPD)(S) Order 1992) for Conservation areas, eg Culross.

> (c)   The Seller warrants (i) that any building work carried out to the Property has been in a state of substantial completion for a period of not less than 12 weeks prior to the date of conclusion of the Missives; and (ii) that no valid objection to the work was made at any time by a person with title and interest to do so under a valid real burden.

Note: This is to take account of the acquiescence provisions in s 16 of TC(S)A 2003. They provide that where a burden is breached (eg erecting an extension in contravention of a prohibition against alterations) and there has been material expenditure, which would be substantially lost if the burden were to be enforced, then if no objection to the work is made within a period of 12 weeks after the work is substantially complete, the burden is extinguished to the extent of the breach. The persons entitled to enforce the burden must have either consented, or have had actual or constructive knowledge of the breach and did not object.

(h) 8. Family Law Act/Litigation

> The Seller warrants that neither the Property nor the Seller's title are affected by or are under consideration in any court proceedings or other litigation or are the subject of any dispute.

Note: The Family Law (Scotland) Act 1985, s 8(1)(aa), enables either party in an action of divorce, or dissolution of a civil partnership, to apply to the court for an order transferring property to him or her by the other party to the marriage or civil partnership. Such an order has to be registered but the purchaser's solicitor should be satisfied that no such order has been granted and not yet registered.

(i) 9. Access

> The Seller will after conclusion of the Missives and upon receipt of reasonable notice by the Purchaser give access to the Purchaser or his

agents to the Property at reasonable times for the purposes of inspection, measurement or the provision of quotations. This right of access however shall not be exercised on more than two occasions without the consent of the Seller.

(j) 10. Title disputes

There are no current disputes with neighbouring proprietors or occupiers or any other parties relating to access, title or common property.

Note: Clearly any serious disputes as to eg disputed ownership of part of the property or the right to use a road or way for access to the property must be fully disclosed by the seller. Any dispute that relates to the property or title should properly be disclosed. Neighbour disputes can often be very bitter, insoluble, expensive, and regrettably, sometimes often very petty. In fact sometimes, disputes can go away when one of the protagonists leaves, as a clash of personalities can add fuel to the flames of minor grievances.

(k) 11. Utilities and services

(a)   Prior to settlement the Seller will confirm the present suppliers of utility services (gas, electricity and telephone as applicable) to the Property. The Seller shall act reasonably in ensuring that such services are not terminated prior to the Date of Settlement and shall co-operate reasonably with the Purchaser in ensuring the transfer of such services to the Purchaser.

(b)   The Property is connected to mains services (that is: public water and drainage).

(c)   There is direct access to the Property from a road which has been adopted for maintenance by the local authority.

Note: Most, if not all of this information will be contained in the Home Report, and the usual Property Enquiry Certificates (PECs) will confirm the position regarding mains services and the status of the road giving access to the property. For rural properties and the appropriate contractual provisions to make concerning access, water and drainage see para 6.17(c)

(l) 12. Breach of contract by seller

If at the Date of Entry the Seller does not give vacant possession or otherwise fails to implement any material obligations due by the Seller in terms of the Missives, then the Purchaser will be entitled (provided the Purchaser is in a position to settle the transaction on the Date of Entry) to claim damages for any reasonable loss incurred by the Purchaser arising from such failure. In the event that the Seller's breach of contract continues for 14 days after the Date of Entry the Purchaser will be entitled to treat that breach as repudiation and to rescind the Missives on giving the Seller notice to that effect. This condition (i) shall apply without prejudice to any other rights or remedies available to the Purchaser, and (ii) shall not apply in the event of the Seller's failure to settle being attributable to the fault of the Purchaser.

Note: Thankfully, most missives are successfully implemented, but it is more common for the purchaser to fail to honour the contract, through financial or personal difficulties, than the seller. However it does occasionally happen that the seller has a change of mind and refuses to fulfil the contract. The remedy of the purchasers lies in the case of *Mackay v Campbell* (1967 SC (HL) 53).

The purchaser can ask the court: (1) for declarator that the seller has failed to implement missives; (2) for decree ordaining the seller to implement the missives and deliver a valid title in exchange for the price; and (3) failing such implement for the payment of a sum in damages.

This clause in missives entitles the purchaser merely to accept the seller's repudiation and rescind the contract and claim damages for loss thus caused ie cost of alternative accommodation, storage of furniture, etc.

If the seller refuses, or is unable, to sign a valid disposition the court may order the Deputy Principal Clerk of Session or the sheriff clerk to sign a disposition on the seller's behalf (see *Pennell's Trustee* 1928 SC 605).

(m) 13. Breach of contract by purchaser

(a)   The Price will paid in full on the due date.

(b)   The Seller will not be obliged to give vacant possession except as against payment of the Price and any interest or losses due as aftermentioned.

(c)   If the Price is paid after the due date, whether in whole or in part, the Seller will be entitled to payment from the Purchaser, at the Seller's option, of one (but not both) of:

   (i)   ordinary damages in respect of all proper and reasonable losses arising out of the late payment of the Price (which will include Wasted Expenditure); or

   (ii)   interest on the amount of the Price outstanding at the Prescribed Rate from the due date until the date when payment is made.

(d)   If the Price remains unpaid in whole or in part at any time more than two weeks after the due date, the Seller will be entitled to rescind the Missives, and to payment from the Purchaser, at the Seller's option, of one (but not both) of:

   (i)   ordinary damages in respect of all proper and reasonable losses arising out of the non payment of the Price and failure of the Missives (which will include Wasted Expenditure); or

   (ii)   liquidated damages, payable on the end date, calculated as the amount of interest which would have run on the amount of the Price outstanding at the Prescribed Rate from the due date until the end date (under deduction of any amount by which the Price obtained by the Seller on a re-sale of the Property exceeds the Price).

(e)   In this clause:

   (A)   The 'due date' means whichever is the later of:

      (i)   the Date of Entry; or

      (ii)   the date on which payment of the Price was due having regard to the circumstances of the case including any entitlement to withhold payment owing to non-performance by the Seller.

   (B)   The 'end date' means whichever is the earlier of:

      (i)   the date falling 12 months after the due date; or

      (ii)   where the Property is re-sold following rescission, the date of entry under the contract of re-sale.

115

(C)   'Wasted Expenditure' means the aggregate of:

    (i)   any capital loss sustained by the Seller on the resale of the Property being the difference between the Price under the Missives and the resale price under any such resale;

    (ii)   any estate agency, marketing and other advertising expenses properly incurred in connection with the resale;

    (iii)   any legal expenses properly incurred in connection with the resale;

    (iv)   any expenses in connection with the cancellation of removal of furniture, storage of furniture and transfer or retransfer of furniture properly incurred as a result of the Purchaser's breach of contract; and

    (v)   any bridging loan costs incurred by the' Seller in respect of any purchase transaction which they require to complete under concluded Missives.

(D)   'Prescribed Rate' means the rate of 4% above The Royal Bank of Scotland plc base rate from time to time in force.

Note: This clause deals with the usual provision in missives that if the purchaser delays or fails to pay the price on the due date, the seller is entitled to extract some compensation for that delay or failure. Following on the decisions in 2006 in the cases of *Black v McGregor* [2006] CSIH 45; [2007] SC 69 and *Wipfel Ltd v Auchlochan Developments Ltd* [2006] CSIH 183, the previous approach to 'penalty' clauses, by which a seller would make provision for entitlement both to interest on the price **and** all loss and damages that he may have incurred in the event of the purchaser's failure, is no longer followed. The approach now taken is that the seller is entitled to **either** interest or damages, but not both. This is also the approach taken by the PSG in the Offers to Sell (see commentary on Clause 2.4 of that offer in para 6.13).

Note however that if the seller opts for damages, in the Combined Standard Clauses, he has two choices: either ordinary damages based on his actual loss, or a 'liquidated damages' sum, based on the amount of interest that would have run on the amount of the price unpaid until the date of resale. There is however a longstop date of 12 months imposed on the second of these options, as it is generally considered that a liquidated damages amount based on a longer period might be regarded as more of a penalty, and potentially unenforceable, so the provision of an 'end date' in this option is intended to remove that risk.

For an explanation of liquidated damages clause see para 12.04(d).

Rate of Interest: Interest runs at the rate of 4% over bank base rate. This rate is now universally accepted for these purposes in both commercial and residential transactions. It is intended to compensate for the overdraft interest that the sellers might have to incur, or for the costs of their other borrowings or expenses.

These provisions are standard boilerplate in modern missives and are rarely, if ever, qualified. In the majority of transactions of course, there is never any need for these clauses to be applied.

(n) 14. New home warranty schemes

If the Property was constructed within ten years prior to the Date of Entry, there shall be delivered at settlement either (i) appropriate NHBC documentation or such equivalent new home warranty documentation as provided by any alternative warranty provider as approved by and acceptable to the Council of Mortgage Lenders, in which event, the Seller warrants that no claims have been made or reported or are pending under the relevant warranty scheme; or (ii) a Professional Consultant's Certificate with other necessary information all in compliance with the current edition of the CML Lenders' Handbook for Solicitors (Scotland).

Note: A house is treated as being 'new' for ten years from the date of its construction, in that it is covered for most defects for two years, and for major defects for up to ten years. The cover is a form of insurance provided either by the National House Builders Council (NHBC) or by some other company providing similar warranties, approved by the Council of Mortgage Lenders (CML), the organisation representing most mortgage lenders.

Not all builders are covered by these schemes, in which case they will require to produce a Professional Consultant's Certificate (PCC) certifying that a qualified person has supervised the building and that they certify that the work is satisfactory (see the style in para 6.11). The granter of the PCC should, of course, have professional indemnity insurance, and you should ask to see evidence of this. You must also check if the lender will accept a PCC and if so whether the lender has any other specific requirements of a provider of a PCC. For example some lenders will only accept PCC instead of NHBC or similar provided there are no more than 15 properties on the development.

(o) 15.1 Title conditions

(a)   Any part of the Property which is common or mutual with any adjoining property (including the roof and roof systems; rhones and downpipes; drains and boundary walls; fences or divisions) falls to be maintained, renewed and upheld by respective proprietors, on an equitable basis.

Note: the provisions of the Tenements (Scotland) Act 2003 should mean that even if the titles are silent, incomplete or inconsistent, the position with regard to maintenance etc of common parts of tenement buildings ought to be equitable (see para 8.27). The titles will need to be checked for arrangements applicable to such features as mutual walls and fences between houses, communal lanes and so on.

(b)   Any reservation of minerals will be subject to conditions as to adequate compensation and will not include any right to enter the Property or lower its surface. The minerals are included in so far as the Seller has right to same.

Note: This refers to the situation where the original sellers of the property (often a former feudal superior) reserved the minerals in their own ownership when the property was sold. This is quite common, and the mineral owner will also reserve certain rights to work the minerals. There should also be provisions for payment of compensation to the owner (see para 8.25(k)). Failure to mention the exclusion of the minerals from the sale can mean that there is not a proper contract, as there is no *consensus ad idem* ('agreement to the same thing'). See *Campbell v McCutcheon* (1963 SLT 290) in which, in missives the owner of a house undertook to give the purchaser vacant possession of the house together with a valid marketable title. There was no mention of the minerals in the missives, and it transpired that they were in fact reserved to the superior. The purchaser resiled from the contract and when the seller sued, the court held that the purchaser was entitled to resile from the contract because, as the missives made no reference to reservation of the minerals, that meant in effect that the seller had contracted that the purchaser would be entitled to the whole property, including the minerals.

(c)   The existing use of the Property is in conformity with the title deeds. There are no unusual, unduly onerous or restrictive burdens, conditions or servitudes affecting the Property.

Note: Section 28 of the LR(S)A 1979 sets out a number of restrictions to the free ownership of land, known as 'overriding interests' (see para 8.24). Burdens, conditions, and servitudes can also limit the use of property. The impact of some burdens has been somewhat lessened by the terms of AFT(S)A 2000 and the TC(S)A 2003, but many still exist (see para 8.25), and arguably TC(S)A 2003 creates as many issues as it solves. Normal burdens are acceptable, but if they are unduly onerous and restrictive, the purchaser may withdraw from the purchase (see para 8.03). This is part of the task of examining title, and satisfying the purchaser that the title is valid and marketable (ie readily resaleable). Although it doesn't happen all that often, if you act for a purchaser who has special requirements which would make normal burdens unacceptable to them (eg for cultural or religious reasons) then this would need to be taken into account – for example, provisions relating to common ownership.

(d)   There is no outstanding liability for any part of the cost of constructing walls, fences, roadways, footpaths or sewers adjoining or serving the Property.

Note: This paragraph is largely self-explanatory, but some mention must be made of roadways, footpaths and sewers. As a general rule these are taken over and maintained by the council, and this can be confirmed by the terms of the PEC. But, particularly in rural areas or certain urban areas where the roads have never been made up to council standards, the ownership remains in the adjoining proprietors and they maintain the roadway at their own expense in accordance with their respective frontages, or as otherwise provided in the titles. There are certain advantages in having the roadway private, in that access and third party parking can be restricted. Nevertheless, most homeowners opt for public ownership of these features and an ongoing liability for maintenance of roads is often perceived as unacceptable for a residential purchaser, due to the potential costs. It is obviously important to find out the status of any roads, footpaths and sewers, and to be sure that there is no inherited debt from the previous owner.

    (e)   The Property has the benefit of all such servitudes and wayleaves as are required for its proper and convenient use (including vehicular access rights).

Note: This is to ensure that the owner has all rights of access and egress to and from the property that are required for people and vehicles, and other servicing etc rights. In urban areas it is often the case that the road immediately opposite the property will be publicly adopted, meaning that access can be exercised over it without any specific rights being in the title. Likewise, water and drainage will come from a public supply. However, when that is not the case, adequate servitude or other rights will be needed, and this must always be carefully investigated (see paras 8.19 and 8.21).

If the title deeds disclose a position other than as stated above, the Purchaser (regardless of his previous state of knowledge) will be entitled to resile from the Missives without penalty to either party but only provided (i) the Purchaser intimates his intention to exercise this right within 10 working days of receipt of the Seller's titles; and (ii) such matters intimated as prejudicial are not rectified or clarified to the Purchaser's satisfaction (acting reasonably) by the Date of Entry or within 6 weeks from the date of such intimation whichever is earlier. The Purchaser's right to resile shall be his sole option in terms of the Missives. Failing the exercise of such right to resile, (i) the Purchaser shall be deemed satisfied as to the position, and (ii) the Seller shall be deemed not to be in breach.

Note: The built-in time limit in this clause and clauses similar to it is essential to assist the rapid conclusion of missives. If something unacceptable is found in the title exhibited, the purchaser must intimate that fact within ten working days. It is vital to look at the titles as soon as they arrive, if you have concluded missives on this basis, as, if the deadline is missed, the purchaser will have lost the right to get out of the contract if something is found in the title after that time. Obviously you must receive all of the titles before this clock starts to run. The Seller is to be given six weeks to sort the problem if he can, before the purchaser can withdraw completely - another good reason for preparedness (see para 4.01).

The final sentence of this Clause is new for the Second edition Combined Standard Clauses. A difficulty could arise because, even if the purchaser has not intimated anything unacceptable and therefore lost the right to resile, if there was some major flaw in the title, the sellers would be in breach of their obligation to deliver a good and marketable title in terms of Clause 16. This additional wording at (ii) resolves this conflict. Similar provisions now also appear in Clauses 19 and 20.

(o) 15.2 Awareness of servitudes

The Seller is not aware of servitudes or overriding interests (within the meaning of section 28(1) of the Land Registration (Scotland) Act 1979) affecting the Property which are not disclosed in the title deeds.

Note: This clause should elicit a disclosure from the seller of any matters of which he is aware, especially if there are any servitudes being exercised which have been acquired through prescription. The seller's solicitor should check this point with the seller. For commentary on overriding interests, see para 8.24.

(p) 16. Settlement/Registration of title

The Price will be payable on the Date of Entry in exchange for (i) a good and marketable title; (ii) a validly executed Disposition in favour of the Purchaser or his nominee(s); (iii) vacant possession of the Property; and (iv) the keys for the Property; together with:

(a)   If the provisions of the Land Registration (Scotland) Act 1979 ('the Act') relating to **a first registration** under the Act apply, (i) a Form 10 Report brought down to a date not more than 3 working days prior to the Date of Entry and showing no entries adverse 'to the Seller's interest in the Property (the cost of the said Report being the Seller's liability); and (ii) such documents and evidence, including a plan, as the Keeper may require to enable the Keeper to issue a Land

Certificate (in paper or electronic format) in the name of the Purchaser as the registered proprietor of the Property without exclusion of indemnity in terms of s 12(2) of the Act. Such documents will include (unless the Property comprises only part of a tenement or flatted building and does not include an area of ground specifically included in the title to that part) a plan or bounding description sufficient to enable the whole Property to be, identified on the ordnance survey map and evidence (such as a Form P16 report or equivalent) that the description of the whole Property as contained in the title deeds is *habile* to include the whole of the occupied extent.

(b)   If the title to the Property is **already registered** in terms of the Act, there will be delivered in exchange for the Price a Land Certificate (in paper or electronic format) containing no exclusion of indemnity in terms of s 12(2) of the Act with all necessary links in title evidencing the Seller's exclusive ownership of the Property together with (i) a Form 12 Report brought down to a date not more than three working days prior to the Date of Entry and showing no entries adverse to the Seller's interest in the Property (the cost of the said Report being the Seller's liability); and (ii) such documents and evidence as the Keeper may require to enable the interest of the Purchaser to be registered in the Land Register as registered proprietor of the Property without exclusion of indemnity under s 12(2).

(c)   Where clauses (a) or (b) apply the Land Certificate will disclose no entry, deed or diligence prejudicial to the Purchaser's interest other than such as have been created by or against the Purchaser or have been disclosed to and accepted in writing by the Purchaser prior to the Date of Settlement.

(d)   If an Application for First Registration of the title to the Property is still being processed by the Keeper, the Seller warrants (i) that no requisitions have been made by the Keeper but not implemented, and (ii) the Keeper has not· indicated any concern with the Application such as might result in any exclusion of indemnity or refusal to register.

(e)   Without prejudice to the above, the Seller warrants that the Property is not affected by any entry in the Register of Community Interests in Land.

(f)   Notwithstanding any other term with in the Missives, this condition shall remain in full force and effect without limit of time and may be founded upon until implemented.

Note: This clause sets out the obligations of the seller which are: (i) to provide a good and marketable title; (ii) to deliver a valid disposition (iii) to give vacant possession and (iv) to hand over the keys of the property. If it is a first registration the seller will show the purchaser a clear form 10A report and, nearer settlement, a clear form 11A report which continues the searching process almost up to the date of entry. It is thought that to leave obtaining the initial form 10A report until just before settlement is extremely risky, as it would allow no time to sort out any unexpected matters that might show up in the form 10A report, such as an inhibition against the seller. So it is common practice to obtain the 10A as soon as possible, and then follow it up with an 11 A continuation report just before completion.

Similarly, the seller should obtain and exhibit to the purchaser a form P16 or Property Definition Report (a comparison of boundaries) in good time so as to allow for any corrective action that might be required, if the P16 report discloses any discrepancy between the legal extent and the occupational extent of the property.

In a sale of land that is already registered, forms 12 and 13 take the places of, respectively, forms 10 and 11, and a form P16 is not required as the boundaries are clearly delineated on the title plan (see Chapter 7 for searches and reports generally).

(q) 17. Incorporated bodies

(a)   If the Seller is a limited company, then prior to the Date of Entry the Seller will exhibit searches in the Register of Charges and company file of the Seller brought down to a date not more than 3 working days prior to the Date of Entry which searches will confirm that there is no notice regarding the appointment of a receiver, administrator or liquidator, winding up, striking off or change of name affecting the Seller and the full names of the present directors and secretary of the Seller. In the event of such searches disclosing any floating charge affecting the Property at the Date of Entry, there will be delivered a certificate of non-crystallisation of such floating charge granted by the chargeholder, dated not more than 3 working days prior to the Date of Entry, confirming that no steps have been taken to crystallise such floating charge and releasing the Property from the floating charge. Within 3 months after the date of settlement such searches against the Seller will be delivered or exhibited brought down to a date 22 days after the date of registration of the Disposition in favour of the Purchaser or his nominees or 43 days after the Date of Entry whichever is the earlier disclosing no entries prejudicial to the registration of the said Disposition.

(b)   The Seller will exhibit or deliver clear searches in the Register of Charges and company files of all companies disclosed as owner or former owner of the Property, in the Land Certificate or Form 10, 11, 12 or 13 reports, brought down in each case to a date 22 days after registration in the Land Register of the deed divesting the relevant company of its interest, disclosing no entries prejudicial to the registration of the said deed.

Note: This clause deals with the possibility that the seller is a limited company, and the additional searches that should be made in the Register of Charges and in the company's file. For more detail on companies searches see para 7.04. Where there is a floating charge, it will be necessary to ensure that the floating charge holder has not taken any steps to crystallise it (see paras 10.06(e) and 11.05(i)).

(r) 18. Risk

(a)   The Seller will maintain the Property in its present condition, fair wear and tear excepted, until the time at which settlement takes place.

(b)   The risk of damage to or destruction of the Property howsoever caused will remain with the Seller until the time at which settlement takes place.

Note: Paradoxical as it may seem, at common law the risk of destruction of, or damage to, the property passes on the completion of missives according to the case of *Sloan's Dairies Ltd v Glasgow Corporation* (1979 SLT 17). In most areas of the country it has been standard practice to amend the common law position and provide that risk will not pass until the date of entry, or settlement if that is a different date. The reference to 'the time at which settlement takes place' is to avoid the possibility that risk passes immediately after midnight.

  (c)   In the event of the Property being destroyed or materially damaged prior to the time at which settlement takes place, either the Purchaser or the Seller shall have the right to rescind the Missives without penalty to the other.

Note: Although the eventuality of damage or destruction will presumably be covered by insurance – the seller should ensure that he maintains cover and does not cancel it until after settlement – clearly, if the property is substantially damaged or destroyed before the date of entry, the purchaser is unlikely to want to proceed with the purchase if the property is a burntout shell, and so will want the right to withdraw. Equally, the seller will probably not want the trouble that would be involved in restoring the property to its original condition for the benefit of the purchaser, and so this arrangement normally suits both parties.

(s) 19. Property enquiry certificate

  (a)   A Property Enquiry Certificate ('PEC') dated after the date of conclusion of the Missives but not earlier than 3 months prior to the Date of Entry will be exhibited at least 5 working days prior to the Date of Entry. The PEC shall require to report on all matters required for the Purchaser's solicitors to comply with the current Edition of the CML Lenders' Handbook for Solicitors (Scotland).

  (b)   If the PEC discloses any matter which is materially prejudicial to the Purchaser or the Property, the Purchaser shall be entitled to resile from the Missives and that without penalty to either party but only provided that (i) the Purchaser intimates his intention to exercise this right within 10 working days of receipt of the PEC; and (ii) such matters intimated as being prejudicial are not rectified or clarified to the Purchaser's satisfaction (acting reasonably) by the Date of Entry or within 6 weeks from the date of such intimation whichever is earlier. The Purchaser's right to resile shall be his sole option in terms of the Missives. Failing the exercise of such right to resile, (i) the Purchaser shall be deemed satisfied as to the position, and (ii) the Seller shall be deemed not to be in breach.

(c)   For the avoidance of doubt, should the Property be sited within a
        Conservation Area; form part of or be a Listed Building; be subject to
        the Local Authority Windows Policy or an Article 4 Direction; or be
        affected by a Tree Preservation Order, this shall not be deemed to be a
        prejudicial ground entitling the Purchaser to so resile.

Note: PECs can be obtained from the local authority or from specialist
agencies, on payment of a fee. (See para 7.02). A PEC should be obtained
as early as possible by the seller, in case it discloses any matter that might
present a difficulty, but it should be borne in mind that the information
contained can become out of date, hence the requirement for a PEC not
more than 3 months old. Some solicitors will insist on a PEC dated after
the conclusion of missives, so that it discloses the position regarding
statutory notices at the date of conclusion of missives, when the respective
responsibilities change (see Clause 5) For this reason Clause 19(a) states
that the PEC should be dated after the date of conclusion of missives.
The seller should know if there are any notices etc affecting the property,
but it is always possible that a PEC might show up something of which
the seller is unaware. The PEC should therefore be ordered straight away
on conclusion of missives, so that the position can be established with
certainty at the earliest opportunity.

The PEC gives details of any notices served upon the property
owners, such as a repairs notice, and so careful attention should be paid
to the matters it discloses, as further action may be required. Rather
more benevolent notices, such as a notice that the property lies within
a conservation area, although disclosed, are not generally regarded as
problematic, but all of the details should be notified to the purchaser
immediately on receipt of the PEC, as there may be circumstances where
a notice gives the purchaser cause for concern.

As with clause 15, there is a built-in time limit for intimating any issues
of ten working days.

(t) 20. Coal Authority Report

If the Coal Authority or similar statutory body recommends that a Coal
Mining Report is obtained for the Property, then such report shall be
exhibited prior to settlement. In the event that such report discloses a position
materially prejudicial to the Property or the Purchaser's proposed use of

same, then the Purchaser shall be entitled to resile from the Missives and that without penalty to either party only provided (i) the Purchaser intimates his intention to exercise this right in writing within 10 working days of receipt of the said report; and (ii) such matters intimated as being prejudicial are not rectified or clarified to the Purchaser's satisfaction (acting reasonably) by the Date of Entry or within 6 weeks from the date of such intimation whichever is earlier. The Purchaser's right to resile shall be his sole option in terms of the Missives. Failing the exercise of such rights to resile, (i) the Purchaser shall be deemed satisfied as to the position, and (ii) the Seller shall be deemed not to be in breach.

Note: Many parts of Scotland have been affected at some time by coal mining and there is a comprehensive list available of cities, towns and villages where, if you are purchasing a property in that location, you must also examine a coal authority report (see para 7.03). The position must be 'materially prejudicial' to the purchaser, and not something that is quite minor. If you are in any doubt about what is disclosed in the report then it may be necessary to make further investigation, which may include referring the terms of the report to the surveyor for comment.

(u) 21. Occupancy rights

At settlement the Property will not be affected by any occupancy rights as defined in the Matrimonial Homes (Family Protection) (Scotland) Act 1981 as amended or the Civil Partnership Act 2004.

Note: Any rights of non entitled spouses or civil partners under either of these two Acts must be dealt with in the course of the sale to ensure that there is no exclusion of indemnity on the purchaser's title sheet. No action is required if the title is held in the joint names of spouses or civil partners, or by legal persons other than individuals, but if not then you will need to see consent or a renunciation or a suitable declaration (see paras 4.07(d) and 8.33).

(v) 22. Supersession of missives

The Missives shall cease to be enforceable after a period of 2 years from the Date of Entry except insofar as (i) they are founded upon in any court proceedings which have commenced within the said period; or (ii) this provision is excluded in terms of any other condition of the Missives.

Note: The rule at common law was that the delivery of the disposition superseded the terms of the preceding contract (*Winston v Patrick* (1981 SLT 41). Following on that case 'non supersession' clauses appeared in missives to counteract the effect. The Contract (Scotland) Act 1997 brought relief by making it the law that a prior contract (ie missives) would not be superseded by a subsequent deed (ie disposition) but allowed parties to agree a date when the prior contract would no longer be enforceable. In this case the time agreed is two years, (which is the usual period specified) unless the dispute arises under clause 5 and 16. In the latter cases, the missives never go out of force (until of course, they prescribe (after 20 years)) (see also para 9.10 (i)).

(w) 23 Address details

All parties irrevocably authorise their agents to release their current address on demand.

Note: The previous version of this clause stated that the seller's new address could be disclosed to the purchaser's solicitors after settlement if it was needed in the event of any claim arising after settlement – obviously to make it quicker to raise an action against the seller if it was required. This version is obviously intended to be less inflammatory and more practical, as it applies before as well as after settlement.

(x) 24. Limitation of claims

Section 3 of the Contract (Scotland) Act 1997 will be qualified to the extent that any competent claim thereunder will not be available in respect of (i) matters disclosed to and accepted by the Purchaser prior to the Date of Entry or (ii) any item or claim amounting in value to less than £200.

Note: Section 3 of the C(S)A 1997 provided that the rule of Scots law, that the Purchaser could not claim damages for defective performance of a contract, but must reject the property and rescind the contract, would no longer be applicable. Prior to the C(S)A 1997, missives had started to incorporate a clause that permitted the *actio quanti minoris* – a remedy available under the Sale of Goods legislation, and developed from the

Roman Law, which would allow an action for damages to be raised to claim in respect of the amount by which the value of the property was diminished by some defect, for example.

This is infinitely preferable to both parties, compared to the sledgehammer of rescission, when the problem may have been comparatively minor. However, the seller will usually want to set some *de minimis* level so that very minor claims are not permitted. This clause sets the threshold at £200.

(y) 25. Entire agreement

The Missives will constitute the entire agreement and understanding between the Purchaser and the Seller with respect to all matters to which they refer and supersede and invalidate all other undertakings, representations, and warranties relating to the subject matter thereof which may have been made by the parties either orally or in writing prior to the date of conclusion of the Missives. Each party warrants to the other that he has not relied on any such undertaking, representation or warranty in entering into the Missives.

Note: An entire agreement provision is common in modern contracts, to prevent either of the parties disputing the terms of the basis of agreement between them, by reference to prior communings and claiming that pre-contractual statements made during negotiations but not included in the final contract are part of the arrangement. It is likely however that a clause of this type would not enable a party to escape liability for a misrepresentation that leads to the formation of the contract.

(z) 26. Minimum period of ownership

The Seller warrants that he has owned the Property for at least 6 months prior to the date of the Offer. This provision shall not apply where the Seller is a personal representative of the proprietor; or is an institutional heritable creditor exercising its power of sale; or is a receiver, trustee in sequestration or liquidator.

Note: This is a new clause that is intended to deal with the recent '6 month rule' introduced by the Council of Mortgage Lenders. Clause 5.1 in part 1 of the CML Handbook (see para 10.05(b)) which is entitled 'Surrounding circumstances' requires the lender's solicitors to report to them if the owner of the property (seller) has owned it for less than six months, unless the seller is acting in any of the three capacities mentioned in the clause above (personal representative; institutional heritable creditor; receiver, trustee in sequestration or liquidator). Clause 5.1 of the CML Handbook also excepts a sale by a developer or builder selling a property acquired under a part exchange scheme.

Lenders have introduced this requirement to prevent potential price rigging and mortgage fraud, and counteract the practice that was 'prevalent' (presumably in England) of properties being bought at below market value, for example on a distressed sale basis, financed through bridging and then immediately mortgaged on a market value basis at a higher valuation.

(aa) 27. Interpretation

In these Clauses:

(a) (i) The masculine includes the feminine; and (ii) words in the singular include the plural and vice versa;

(b) The phrase 'Date of Settlement' means the date on which settlement is actually effected whether that is the Date of Entry or not;

(c) 'the Missives' means the contract of purchase and sale concluded between the Purchaser and the Seller of which the Offer incorporating reference to these Clauses forms part;

(d) Any intimation shall be in writing (which shall include, for avoidance of doubt, faxes or emails);

(e) The terms 'the Purchaser', 'the Seller', ''the Property', 'the Price' and 'the Date of Entry' have the meanings set out in the Offer or other document incorporating reference to these Clauses; and

(f) Where any intimation must be given within a specified period, time will be of the essence.

Note: Interpretation provisions of this type are intended to clarify the terms of the document as well as cutting down unnecessary wording, such as having to specify the plural of things as well as the singular and so on, throughout the document, which could make for extremely tortuous provisions. It also provides some definitions of the meaning of certain expressions and applies an approach that should be taken for certain activities – in this case at (f): time being of the essence, without the need to state it every time the relevant situation applies throughout the document. As a matter of general practice you should always read the interpretation provisions of a document carefully, and not just assume that it is the usual boilerplate, as some specific interpretative provisions may have a significant effect on the terms of the clauses that appear elsewhere in the document, and it is important to be aware of the fact that the words in the clause itself may not give the whole picture.

BUYING A NEW HOUSE FROM A BUILDER

6.11 So far we have been looking at the procedures when acting in the purchase of a 'secondhand' residential property. When acting in the purchase of a new house, while much of the procedure is similar, there are some very important differences; especially at the missives stage. When purchasing a new property from a builder the accepted practice is, not to submit an offer to purchase, but for the builder either to produce an offer to sell, or provide standard missives for the purchaser to sign.

The terms of the builders' missives are usually stated to be not open for negotiation, and have come in for much criticism over the years. Helen Eadie MSP went as far as proposing a Missives for New-Build Houses (Scotland) Bill in 2007, but the proposal fell at dissolution of that particular parliament. There are normally tight time limits for conclusion of missives and builders' missives are one of the few occasions in Scotland where a deposit is routinely taken from the purchaser of heritable property.

Nowadays, and despite the assertion that the missives are not to be amended, it may still be worth asking for some adjustments that might be necessary or desirable from the purchaser's point of view, and if your qualifications are reasonable, some builders might be prepared to accommodate them. The purchaser generally enjoys more bargaining power in a weaker market. From the point of view of the purchaser's solicitor, it is no less important to ensure that you take clear instructions from your client, and check that the terms of the missives are acceptable from a legal standpoint.

(a) Environmental issues

Before entering into an agreement, one preliminary point that should be considered, is a check that the houses are not built on an environmentally unsound site. While this may sound rather dramatic, there have been a number of instances over the years of housing developments being built on sites which have some degree of contamination. The development of brownfield land is encouraged from a town planning perspective, and not just for residential purposes. A 'brownfield' site is not necessarily one that is contaminated, nor is it necessarily a site that is located in an urban area, but it will have been developed previously. Some sites can be contaminated by substances such as asbestos, petroleum, arsenic, explosives, creosote and radioactive substances, or have been subjected to mining or quarrying, or waste tipping. It is estimated, by Landmark Information Group, who provide information about contaminated sites, that 'approximately 40% of homes in Scotland are built on or near former industrial land which could potentially be contaminated'. Naturally, some more industrialised parts of the country will be more prone to this issue, than others.

Reputable builders acquiring sites will conduct extensive site investigations with a view to assessing the risks involved and determining the potential costs of development, which will include site remediation costs where this is necessary, and may even include abnormal development costs which will need to be factored in to the overall cost of the development and will affect the price the builder can pay to acquire the site. Environmental consultants will be employed to provide reports and warranties will be sought from them. Environmental issues will also be considered by the local planning authority at the planning stage.

Even when the site appears to be an attractive 'greenfield' site, it should be remembered that it may have been used for some other purpose in the past, particularly in wartime. The history of 'brownfield' sites—that is sites that have been previously occupied—should always be carefully checked. The builders should be able to provide sufficient evidence of the prior uses of the land, or treatment that has been done to the site, but if they do not, certain information as to past uses can be obtained from the local library, or online, or from asking a specialist surveyor or environmental consultant to investigate the history of the land. It may also be possible to shed some light on past uses from the title deeds, but an ironic aspect of land registration is that the title sheet does not provide the history of the title. Therefore, if you wish to find out who owned the site in previous years, investigations would have to be made in the old Sasine title.

It is possible to obtain comparatively inexpensive 'desktop' reports from a variety of providers, disclosing former uses, details of coal-mining and subsidence risks, as well as flood and other risks.

The current Law Society guidance on giving advice on contaminated land and environmental reports for both residential and commercial property is that due to the complexity of this area of law, if a solicitor does not feel qualified to comment on these issues, either in general terms or with particular reference to contaminated land matters, then, that solicitor may seek to exclude liability for environmental law and/or contaminated land matters in respect of a transaction. That exclusion must be made quite clear to the client in the solicitor's letter of engagement and terms of business. A lawyer should not 'dabble' in areas of law in which he is inexperienced (certainly not without proper supervision and support) and this area is clearly one of them. Equally clearly however, if contaminated land could be an issue, then this should be flagged to the client and possibly other specialist advice sought. This is an aspect of conveyancing that needs to be dealt with extremely carefully. It should also be borne in mind that it might be a requirement of a lender, in terms of its loan instructions or the CML Handbook that an environmental report be obtained.

See further reading at the end of the Chapter and also para 7.07.

(b) 'Off plan'

The average new house is often bought 'off plan', that is to say, before it is built, or only partially built. The surveyor's job is therefore somewhat different at this early stage, but a valuation will still need to be obtained for mortgage purposes, and a final inspection is normally required before funds will be released, as well as helping with matters of 'snagging'. The key thing here, is to make absolutely sure that your clients know exactly what they are buying, and that they have as much detailed information as possible about the site location and orientation, how close it will be to other properties, build specification and layout, quality standards and materials, and internal finishings and fittings.

(c) The builders' missives

The builder has to show a good marketable title, just as for any normal transaction and the missives will contain some familiar clauses of that nature, including the provision that the purchaser should be able to register his title without exclusion of indemnity, and that the Land Certificate to be issued in favour of the purchaser will disclose no adverse matters other than those that have been disclosed to and accepted by the purchaser prior to settlement. However there are a number of issues that are particular to the contracts for the purchase of new houses.

(i) Price

New properties are usually offered for sale by the builder at fixed prices, and so the process of noting interest, 'offers over' and closing dates would not apply. These days there are likely to be a variety of discounts and incentives available as well. The usual procedure will be for the purchaser to 'reserve' a 'plot' (which may be a house and garden, a flat, or some other unit in the builder's development) and pay a reservation fee (which should, in terms of the Consumer Code (see para (iii) below), be returnable under deduction of any expenses incurred by the builder). The prospective purchaser may be given missives at that time and should be advised to take them to a solicitor to obtain proper advice on the purchase. There will normally be a deadline by which the missives must be returned to the builder's solicitors, usually something like 14 days, failing which the reservation will fall. That 14 day period will allow time for the surveyor to produce a valuation, and for the lender to be lined up. If this timescale is too tight, it may be possible to negotiate a short extension.

There is also usually provision for a deposit to be paid by the purchaser on conclusion of the missives. Both the deposit and the reservation fee will count toward the purchase price of the plot. Once missives have been concluded, the deposit will often be non-returnable unless there are circumstances where the purchaser may be permitted to cancel the contract.

(ii) The plot

The property will usually be described in the builders' missive in general terms, probably by reference to a plot, and there should be a plan showing the location of that plot attached to the missives, so that the parties are clear where the property is situated in the development. The site plan needs to be as accurate as possible and in particular, the boundaries of the property should be clearly delineated. Difficulties have been caused to the Keeper by properties not being laid out as they were stated to be, in cases where estate plans have been submitted to the Keeper prior to sales. For this reason, issuing of land certificates for new houses can take some time, if the layout of the development is not finalised or does not yet appear on the Ordnance Survey map. Note that any illustrative estate plans are unlikely to be sufficient for attaching to the Disposition. The more information the purchaser can obtain from the builder about the property such as house type, ground and other pertinents like parking spaces or a garage, for the purposes of clear identification in the missives, the better.

(iii) Date of Entry

This can be a problematic provision for both parties. From the purchasers' point of view, they would like as much certainty as possible, particularly if they are selling another house, and are due to move out of that on a particular date. On the other hand, the builder, while clearly wanting to get to the point of sale as quickly as possible, has to build the house first and that can be subject to all sorts of variables, such as weather, availability of building materials, the contractor's building programme, labour issues and more. So there will be no fixed date of entry in a builders' missive (unless the house being purchased has already been completed), and instead settlement will be conditional upon the house being completed and passed as fit for habitation by the local authority. The builders may give a probable completion date, but they will not warrant this, nor pay any sort of damages if this date is not met. Thus a default or so-called 'penalty' clause and a *force majeure* clause, of the type seen in commercial development contracts, are not appropriate, which would force the builders to pay damages if the house is not ready by a certain date (default clause), but exempting the builders for any failure caused by certain events such as war or strikes (*force majeure* clause).

In many ways the problem is insoluble, since it is not economically viable for a builder to build all the houses speculatively, and the building programme will inevitably be dictated by sales and prospective sales. Attempts have been made however to provide purchasers with as much information as possible and with realistic estimates of when completion will be achieved. Since April 2010, any builder that is registered with the major home warranty providers – the National House-Building Council (NHBC), Premier Guarantee and LABC New Home Warranty – must comply with the Consumer Code for Home Builders (www.consumercodeforhomebuilders.com). Some builders who are registered with other home warranty providers nonetheless voluntarily comply with the Code.

The aim of the Code is to ensure that purchasers of new homes are treated fairly and know what levels of service to expect. They should get reliable information from the builder, before they purchase, to enable them to make appropriate decisions in connection with their purchase, including a written reservation agreement, explanation of the Home Warranty cover available, details of any management services and costs and reliable information about what the house will look like and the specification to which it will be built. The purchasers must also know how to get access to speedy, low-cost dispute resolution arrangements if they are dissatisfied.

The Code is a voluntary industry code but it takes account of OFT code criteria. However, for builders who are registered with NHBC, or Premier Guarantee and LABC, failure to comply with the Code could mean that they are struck off that home warranty providers register – which would be fairly disastrous for that builder. Amongst the obligations on the builder is the requirement to provide reliable and realistic information about when construction of the house may be finished, when settlement will take place and the date for handover. Although not mandatory, it is suggested that the builder provides estimates of completion dates at various stages during the construction, since the nearer the property is to completion the more able the builder should be to provide a definite date. For example, before completing the foundations and floor, the builder should indicate in which calendar quarter the house is likely to be ready; then when the roof is completed and the building is weatherproof, provide the month in which the house is likely to be ready, and when the house has been decorated and connected to the main services indicate what week the house is likely to be ready.

Purchasers should also be given clear termination rights to end the missives if there is an unreasonable delay in finishing the construction of the house.

(iv) Snagging

Inevitably with any builder work, there are bound to be items that require to be tidied up or rectified after completion, and the missives should contain provisions obliging the builder to attend to any such 'snagging' items. The builder will normally want to have their own surveyor or buildings inspector certify what needs to be done, but the purchaser will have the opportunity to look round the property, (probably with the builder's surveyor) and agree a list of works that need to be put right (the 'snagging list'). The purchaser may want to get their own surveyor to look at the property before they complete first, to check that it has been completed and advise on items of snagging that need to be done (although this is not routinely done if there is a properly organised inspection arranged with the builder). It is possible however, that the lender might need a reinspection to be conducted by the purchaser's surveyor, before releasing funds. The requirement should be checked, and may be specified in the loan instructions from the lender, or in the CML handbook. It is also a good idea for the purchasers to check round the property themselves, once they get the keys, and make a note of any further items of this nature that they think should be fixed by the builder, and pass on that information. A useful snagging checklist is provided by the NHBC at www.nhbc.co.uk/NHBCPublications/LiteratureLibrary/HomeownerDocuments/filedownload, 4,2392,en.pdf. Obviously the purchaser needs to be prepared to permit access to the builder's workmen to allow the snagging to be carried out. It is unlikely that the builder will entertain any retention from the price pending completion of the snagging work.

(v) Title Conditions

In most instances the builder will have arranged for his solicitor to prepare a Deed of Conditions for the whole development, containing arrangements for preservation of the amenity of the properties and for maintenance of common parts of the development (see para 9.10 (f)). This may contain arrangements for an annual maintenance charge to be paid by the owners in the development, and the missives may contain provisions for an initial maintenance deposit to be paid by the purchaser at the date of entry. If there is a manager or factor appointed for the development, additionally there might be a requirement to sign a management agreement or some other form of appointment. Purchasers will also be expected to join any residents association that is in existence (and will automatically be a member of any Owners' Association set up by the application of the Development Management Scheme to the development (see para 9.10 (g)).

(vi) Roads and services

The cost of constructing the roads and other services will be included in the price of the plot. The builder must have a roads construction consent and obtain a road bond in respect of completion of the roads to an adoptable standard (see para 8.20) and should exhibit copies of these, but will not therefore normally contemplate any retention from the price pending completion of the roads.

A feature of new housing developments is the creation of service strips which, if they are formed, are usually located between the road or pavement, and the garden of the houses affected. This is a dedicated strip of land into which service cables, pipes and other conduits are laid and to which statutory undertakers and other providers of services can have access. The strip will normally be included in the title to the plot, but must remain unbuilt on, although planting is sometimes permitted. The Local authority may adopt the service strips, although this will not be warranted.

(vii) Planning and Building consents

The builders will have applied for and obtained planning permission for the development and building warrant for construction of the houses. These days, the title pack that is produced for purchaser's solicitor to examine will usually include a copy of these consents. The missives should contain an obligation on the builder to deliver a completion certificate (or notice of acceptance where applicable) from the local authority, but settlement should not take place until the property has been inspected and passed as fit for habitation by the local authority, as it is not permitted to occupy a property until it has been certified. In some cases the plot may be passed as fit for habitation on a temporary basis, then the certificate will be granted for a limited period. In these circumstances the missives should contain an obligation the builder to update the temporary certificates as and when required until the final completion certificate is granted. It should also have been inspected and passed by NHBC or other home warranty provider, or the provider of the Professional Consultant Certificate if appropriate. Often, the practice is to advise the purchaser's solicitors by email or phone when the property has been passed, and it is recommended that the purchaser's solicitor should obtain the name of the relevant inspector and contact him or her to confirm, as it is usually a few days before the certificate itself is issued, and in the meantime steps will need to be taken to have the property inspected by the purchaser's surveyor, and requisition the mortgage and other funds, and the missives will normally provide for a tight window of time between intimation that the property has been passed, and settlement. Note that the system of 'verbal habitation' was judicially criticised in *FM Finneston v Ross* [2009] CSOH 48.

(viii) Variation of materials

The purchaser is entitled to have the property built more or less in accordance with what he expected and has contracted for, but the builder will usually reserve the right to make alterations and in particular to substitute materials, although these should be of an equivalent or better quality than those originally specified. The Consumer Code for Home Builders also provides that the purchaser should be entitled to terminate the contract where there is a substantial and significant change to the house.

(ix) Deeds and Searches

The prior titles that relate to the development will not be delivered, as of course they relate to the larger area that comprises the development, but will be exhibited for examination. If the title to the development is in the Sasine Register, often the builder may decide to do a voluntary registration of the title, so that examination of title is a lot more straightforward for purchaser's solicitor, although if the Land Certificate has not yet been issued, then the purchaser's solicitor may still need to see the title deeds. Well prepared builder's solicitors will have lending sets of the titles, or copies of the Land Certificate available for purchasers to examine.

However, while the builder's solicitor may have obtained a form 10A or Form 12 A report for the development, it is usual practice that they will not update searches or deliver reports, and it is therefore up to the purchaser's solicitor to instruct their own searches. Builders are usually limited companies and again, the missives will generally provide that no Companies searches will be exhibited. Reports such as PECs or Coal Authority reports are not usually provided, either. Letters of obligation are however usually given, but the builder's solicitors may require to see the up to date searches obtained by the purchaser's solicitors to be able to do so.

A disposition will of course be delivered in exchange for payment of the balance of the price (see *Gibson v Hunter Home Designs Ltd* 1976 SC 23 for a case when it was not, and the terrible consequences for the purchaser that flowed from this failure, who lost both the house and the money).

(x) Discounts and Incentives

As part of the marketing of new homes, builders have over the years used more and more inventive ways of encouraging prospective purchasers to buy one of their homes, and these can range from the financial, including discounts, cashbacks, mortgage subsidies, payment of SDLT, removal costs and legal and survey fees, to the non-financial such as appliances and equipment or even holidays or cars. Incentives can also be used by builders to encourage purchasers to settle on time. Such is the extent of these incentives and the effect that they have on the price and price to value ratio that lenders now require any incentives given to be fully disclosed. The CML now require the builder to complete a Disclosure of Incentives form (see the style forms on pages 141 to 144) providing full details, and give it to the purchaser's solicitor (or the lender's solicitor, if for any reason that is a different solicitor). Note that the lender will need to see a Disclosure of Incentives form even if there are no incentives being given. The purchaser/lender's solicitor should pass a copy of the form to the valuer so that the incentives will be reflected in the valuation.

(xi) NHBC or other Home Warranty provider

Most builders are members of the National House-Building Council, or one of the other Home Warranty providers, and as such offer a certificate (the NHBC certificate is branded as their 'Buildmark' Certificate) to cover the house against major defects arising over a ten-year period. The certificate

cml
Council of Mortgage Lenders

CML Disclosure of Incentives Form Version 2

(use from 1 October 2011)

This form must be completed by the seller(s) of any property that is to be occupied or purchased for the first time, or for the first time in its current form, i.e. a new build, renovated or converted property.

The completed form must be supplied to the solicitor/conveyancer acting on behalf of the lender providing the mortgage finance for the property. The form must be supplied to the valuer acting on behalf of the lender upon request.

This form is designed to ensure full disclosure of the financial aspects of the sale. It is not meant to be used to provide a valuation.

1. BUYER DETAILS

Name(s) of buyer(s)

....

2. NEW PROPERTY DETAILS

Plot Number ....

Dwelling type
(house, flat, maisonette etc) ....

Development Name and Address

....

Property Postal Address
(if allocated) ....

Postcode
(if allocated) ....

3. ASSISTED PURCHASE DETAILS

Please provide full details of any assisted purchase scheme utilised in this transaction
(e.g. shared ownership, shared equity or loan from seller)

IF SHARED EQUITY

Total of any 'equity loan(s)' held by seller, provided by government or by other third party
(usually in the legal form of a second charge)   .... **% (percent)**

Name of party or parties retaining/providing an equity loan   ....

Name of scheme   ....

IF SHARED OWNERSHIP

Ownership share purchased by the buyer   .... **% (percent)**

Ownership share retained by seller or purchased by third party   .... **% (percent)**

Name of party or parties retaining/purchasing an ownership share   ....

Name of scheme   ....

Please provide details of any resale restrictions included in the title   ....

LOAN FROM SELLER

Provide details of the loan including any interest and repayment terms, whether secured or unsecured   ....

141

4. NAME(S) AND ADDRESS(ES) OF THE SELLER(S)

List details of all organisations/individuals who will receive all or part of the sale consideration as a result of this transaction, including under any contract or agreement to sub-sell, assign contract, or through an option or agreement to purchase e.g. where a secondary buyer has entered into a sub-contract with the original buyer(s)
(continue on a separate sheet if necessary)

Name of firm/person   ....

Address   ....
(incl. postcode if known)

Telephone number   ....

Amount to be received   and/or

£ .... %

Name of firm/person   ....

Address   ....
(incl. postcode if known)

Telephone number   ....

Amount to be received   and/or

£ .... %

5. INTRODUCTORY/FINDERS FEES

List the details of any introductory/finders fees, however described, that have been agreed
(continue on a separate sheet if necessary)

Name of recipient(s)   ....

Address   ....
(incl. postcode if known)

Fee agreed   and/or

£ .... %

Name of recipient(s)   ....

Address   ....
(incl. postcode if known)

Fee agreed   and/or

£ .... %

6. NUMBER OF UNITS

Please complete (a) and, where appropriate, (b)

a) State the approximate number of constructed units on the seller's site

Units constructed in the   Units planned to be
last 12 months ....   constructed in the next 12 ....
                                            months

b) If the property is being sold by, or on behalf of, an investor/investment company or you have
identified an investor/investment company in question 4 above, please state the total number of ....
units on site in which the investor/investment company has ownership rights/an interest in the sale

7. GARAGE AND PARKING

Is an allocated garage, car port or parking space included   **YES** ☐   **NO** ☐
in the transaction?

If you have ticked Yes, is it, or will it be following first registration of the property:

Included in the same title as the property ☐   In a separate title but owned by the buyer ☐

A right to use a parking facility ☐

Physically adjoining the plot/property   **YES** ☐   **NO** ☐

8. SHARED AMENITIES

List full details of any shared amenities included in the transaction, e.g. access to gym facilities
(this should not include access to open spaces or use of communal stairwells, lifts or access points)

....

9. PRICE AND DISCOUNTS

Please provide the list price, any discounts and the agreed sales price
(this should not include any incentives as these will be detailed in question 10 below)

List price   Discount

£ ....   £ ....

Agreed sales price   Date sales price agreed

£ ....

Provide details where discount relates to
the sale of more than one property   ....

10. INCENTIVES

List the details of any incentives to be received by the purchaser either before or after completing the transaction
(continue on a separate sheet if necessary)

List full details of the value of all financial incentives to be received by the buyer(s):

Deposit

£ ....

Guaranteed rental income

£ .... Total (£.......... per month for .... months)

Mortgage subsidies

£ .... Total (£.......... per month for .... months)

(including payment of mortgage interest, subsidies of interest rate and mortgage payment subsidies)

Stamp Duty Land   Cashbacks
Tax payment   £ ....   £ ....

Moving costs   Legal fees

£ ....   £ ....

Valuer fees   Other financial
   £ ....   incentives not listed*   £ ....
         (give details below)

* Please provide full details of other financial incentives

....

Provide a list of all non-financial/in-kind incentives to be received by the buyer(s)

For example: white goods/kitchen appliances; furniture/furnishing; electrical equipment; garden furniture/landscaping; holidays; vehicles; buy-back guarantees; car-parking season tickets etc. This is NOT meant to be an exhaustive list.

Do not include any items provided as part of the standard specification of the property

....

11. PART EXCHANGE

If you have offered to purchase the buyer's property please list the agreed price. If the property is being purchased by a third party agent/property management company then please provide details of the fee paid. Please detail any price paid above/below the market valuation for the part exchanged property.

Agreed purchase price

£ ....

Price agreed above/below (if below express as a negative) market valuation (if any)

£ ....

Fee paid to seller's agent (if any) £ and % of price paid for part exchange property

£ .... / .... %

12. FORM PRESENTED TO VALUER

This form was presented to the valuer by:

Name

Company

Company registration number with the warranty provider
e.g. NHBC registration number

Date

13. SUSTAINABILITY

This property is built to the following recognised standard for sustainability (optional):

IMPORTANT INFORMATION ABOUT THIS FORM

The information provided in this form is a material consideration taken into account by any valuer valuing the property and any lender deciding how much to lend on the security of the property. The solicitor/conveyancer acting on behalf of the lender will assume that the information is accurate and complete to the best of the seller's belief and that there are no off-contract arrangements linked to this transaction.

After submitting this form the seller must inform the solicitor/conveyancer acting for the lender of any changes to the information provided as soon as is practicable, but in any event prior to exchange of contracts/missives. If the seller does not have the contact details for the lender's solicitor/conveyancer they must ensure that their solicitor/conveyancer passes this information on.

14. DETAILS OF PERSON COMPLETING THE FORM

Signature on behalf of the seller(s)

Print name

Organisation

Position

Date signed

is transferable to subsequent purchasers of the house, and so missives of 'secondhand' house will include a provision to this effect (see para 6.10 (n)).

In the first two years of the certificate the builder is bound to make good any defect arising from a breach of NHBC requirements. This does not include, however, fair wear and tear caused by neglect or failure to maintain, damage caused by shrinkage of plasterwork, cement and wood, provided it was not caused by a defect, or for anything caused by carrying out alterations. After two years and up to ten years, NHBC will make good any major defects in the structure or weather proofing.

The seller's solicitor will usually have the Buildmark documentation for all the plots in the development, and following conclusion of missives will send the documents for the plot in question to the purchaser's solicitors. The documents include an Acceptance Form which should be completed by or on behalf of the purchaser and returned to NHBC to ensure that the plot will benefit from the cover available. There is limited cover from conclusion of missives to settlement, but on completion of the house, the NHBC will inspect it and provided they are satisfied, issue their cover note, which is handed to the builder, and transferred to the purchaser's solicitor. Most lenders will not release funds until this cover note has been issued, and so timing of the inspection and transfer of documents is crucial. The final piece of paper is the Buildmark Insurance Certificate, which NHBC recommends be sent to the purchaser, although some solicitors might prefer, with their clients' permission, to retain it on their behalf, in case it gets lost.

A small builder may not be a registered with NHBC or one of the other Home Warranty providers, in which case a certificate of inspection will need to be produced from the independent architect who supervised the development, stating that the development is complete in accordance with the plans. The architect should possess full professional indemnity insurance cover, in the event that a mistake is made. In these cases, the lender will require a Professional Consultant's Certificate in terms of the example that follows. Note that not all lenders will accept this, so it is important to check at the very earliest opportunity, as soon as you know that the builder is not registered with an acceptable Home Warranty provider. This should be apparent from the missives. The CML website contains their style Professional Consultant's Certificate, which applies for a period of six years:

APPENDIX 1

PROFESSIONAL
CONSULTANT'S CERTIFICATE

Return To:_____

Name of Applicant(s) _____
_____
_____

Full address of property _____
_____
_____

I certify that:

1. I have visited the site at appropriate periods from the commencement of construction to the current stage to check generally:
(a) progress, and
(b) conformity with drawings approved under the building regulations, and
(c) conformity with drawings/instructions properly issued under the building contract.

2. At the stage of my last inspection on_____ ,
the property had reached the stage of _____
_____
_____
_____
_____

3. So far as could be determined by each periodic visual inspection, the property has been generally constructed:
(a) to a satisfactory standard, and
(b) in general compliance with the drawings approved under the building regulations.

4. I was originally retained by _____
_____
who is the applicant/builder/developer in this case. (Delete as appropriate)

5. I am aware this certificate is being relied upon by the first purchaser _____
_____
of the property and also by_____
(name of lender) when making a mortgage advance to that purchaser secured on this property.

6. I confirm that I will remain liable for a period of six years from the date of this certificate. Such liability shall be to the first purchasers and their lenders and upon each sale of the property the remaining period shall be transferred to the subsequent purchasers and their lenders.

7. I confirm that I have appropriate experience in the design and/or monitoring of the construction or conversion of residential buildings.

Name of Professional Consultant_____

Qualifications _____

Address _____
_____
_____

Telephone No._____Fax No. _____

Professional Indemnity Insurer _____
_____

8. The box below shows the minimum amount of professional indemnity insurance the consultant will keep in force to cover his liabilities under this certificate [£_____]
for any one claim or series of claims arising out of one event.

Signature _____

Date_____

BUYING COMMERCIAL PROPERTY

6.12 Commercial conveyancing is similar to domestic conveyancing in many ways, in that the same sort of basic sequence of events applies. There are the same four main stages: (1) negotiation; (2) missives; (3) examination of title and other materials (also referred to as 'due diligence'); and (4) settlement (referred to as 'completion'). There are some significant differences in the details, such as the types of parties involved and structures of transactions, different forms of documentation that are found exclusively in one discipline and not the other. Both types of conveyancing have their specialities. Within both types (if there can be said to be only two) are further specialities: eg dealing with the acquisition of a major shopping centre is quite different from the purchase of a small high street retail unit, just as buying a city centre tenement flat is quite different from the purchase of a large country estate. Often of course commercial transactions can involve extremely large amounts of money and therefore carry significant responsibility, but the basic building blocks of conveyancing are equally applicable to 'both' types of transaction.

It is at the missive stage where many of the specialities emerge, and the considerations when acting in the purchase of a commercial property for owner occupation are quite different from some of the key considerations that apply when negotiating the contract for the purchase of an investment property with occupational leases, and different again when dealing with the purchase of land for development.

Some of these issues are considered in the following paragraphs, which look at a commercial offer to sell an investment property, (ie one that is occupied by tenants, and is therefore being purchased, not for the purchaser's own occupation, but as an 'investment', with income from the property being generated from the rents payable under the leases).

Note that commercial offers to *purchase* will contain more clauses, similar to the residential offer to purchase, although many of the clauses will tend to be heavily qualified on a 'satisfy yourself' basis by the seller. However, although not referred to in the offer to sell, offers to purchase will often contain references to many of the 'due diligence' items that are referred to in the PSG Due Diligence Questionnaire, such as compliance with fire regulations, control of asbestos regulations, disability discrimination requirements under the Equality Act 2010, construction documentation in respect of original construction or extensions and alterations, Health and safety file and so on and on.

STANDARDISED OFFERS – THE PSG OFFER TO SELL INVESTMENT PROPERTY

6.13 Although commercial offers to purchase are often used, the use of the offer to sell, drafted by the seller's solicitors using the seller's existing knowledge of the property, as opposed to the offer to purchase which is often drafted in a state of ignorance about the property, is becoming more prevalent. It can be more targeted and specific – for example the seller knows what his VAT status is and that of the property, and so can provide the factual position in the initial offer, rather than the fishing expedition that an offer to purchase can often be. The traditional route of the offer to purchase is that the purchaser's solicitor sends out the offer often without knowing very much about the details of the property, and then gets the titles and all of the other materials he needs to find out what the offer should have said in the first place.

The PSG Offers to Sell are designed to be used for a variety of commercial property types and deal with commercial property being purchased with vacant possession, and a separate form for properties that are tenanted. There are different considerations for the purchaser in these two types of purchase – in many ways the terms of the leases are of more importance to the investor purchaser, as that is where the value in his investment lies.

The approach taken in the PSG Offers to Sell presupposes that (a) the seller accepts that it needs to provide a full package of titles and other due diligence information, and that some warranties/confirmations will need to be given by the seller to the purchaser and (b) the purchaser accepts that it will be expected to do full due diligence and satisfy itself as to title, planning etc from the documentation supplied to it by the seller. The content of the offers represents a reasonably balanced document, close to a negotiated end product, that purchasers and sellers alike will find reasonably acceptable to enable the parties to conclude missives more quickly and with less argument. It should be noted that some styles of offers to sell may not take such a balanced approach and instead seek to pass all of the requirements onto the purchaser, but with none of the confirmations that the seller gives in this more balanced approach.

In practice, however most reasonable sellers will not have too many difficulties with the balanced approach. Whereas the Combined Standard Clauses for residential purchases are intended to be adopted wholesale without amendment, there is no such constraint on the PSG Offers to Sell, although in practice there have been many commercial transactions where only minimal adjustments have been required. The PSG Offers to Sell are to be regarded as a balanced starting point, to help the parties to concentrate on the key commercial elements of the contract negotiation, although it is felt that most issues are addressed, and so the solicitors using the Offers should not feel under an obligation to make changes for change's sake. The PSG Offers are free for the parties to adapt as they see fit, but they should not then hold it out as being the PSG version of the offer.

The parties and their solicitors can if they wish use the PSG Due Diligence Questionnaire when conducting the transaction, either as a running record of information requested and received, or, as many users prefer to use it, as a list of requirements to check against and as an aide memoire for the various due diligence requirements of the transaction. Not everything in the DDQ will be relevant for every transaction; in fact there will be few transactions where all of the elements appear. However the Annexes to the DDQ can be useful when gathering information about tax, employees or construction documentation, or when obtaining tenancy information from the managing agents of the property.

Everything that is exhibited to the Purchaser by the Seller, which the Purchaser examines and satisfies itself on, then becomes 'Disclosed Documents' on which the Purchaser is deemed satisfied, and which are listed in the Schedule to the Offer.

It should be noted also that there are a number of optional clauses available in a separate document on the PSG website which provide drafting relating to other matters which need to be referred to in offers from time to time, but which are not necessarily always incorporated in every offer. These include provisions for payment of a deposit; a guarantee of the purchaser's obligations; imposition of burdens and servitudes; service contracts; construction documents; family law and occupancy rights, in case any part of the property is used for residential purposes and also provision for company searches when the title to the property is still in the Register of Sasines.

The structure of the Offer includes a Schedule of several parts at the end which incorporates lists of the Title Deeds and the Disclosed Documents and other information and style documentation. The Schedule can run to many pages and is a convenient way of assembling a number of pieces of information that are referred to in the Offer, and includes agreed form documents. For example, it is typical in commercial offers to agree the draft of the Disposition and other key documents at the missives stage and attach them to the offer. In the body of the offer these will be referred to as eg; 'the disposition of the Property in favour of the Purchaser in terms of the draft set out in Part 8 of the Schedule'. For the purposes of this consideration of the Offer to Sell, the Schedule has been omitted.

The Offer to Sell – Investment Property deals not only with the transfer of the property itself to the purchaser, but also the various issues that apply to the leases that are in place for the actual occupation of the property, including such matters as tenants' compliance with the provisions of the leases, apportionment of rent and service charges, how the parties will deal with any arrears of rent and notification of the change of ownership to the tenants. It should also be pointed out that with the sale of the property and the change of ownership, the new owner becomes the landlord under the leases, by virtue of his registered title, without any form of documentation being required in respect of the leases themselves ie no transfer or assignation of the lease is required for the landlord's part to vest in the new owner. This can be contrasted with the requirements when there is a change of tenant under a lease. In those circumstances an assignation by the outgoing tenant to the new tenant is required, and to be effective there must be intimation to the landlord, whose consent to the assignation is probably also required in terms of the lease.

The Offers to Sell and accompanying Guidance Notes can be accessed at www.psglegal.co.uk.

Offer to Sell Investment Property

Dear Sirs

[Seller's Name]

[Purchaser's Name]

[Postal Address of Property]

On behalf of and as instructed by the Seller, we offer to sell the Property to the Purchaser on the following conditions:

(a) 1 Definitions

1.1 In the Missives:

'[**Back Letters**' means the back letter(s) in terms of the draft(s) set out in Part [5] of the Schedule;]

'**Completion**' means the Date of Entry or, if later, the date when the Completion Payment is paid and the purchase of the Property is completed in terms of the Missives;

'**Completion Payment**' means the Price subject to all adjustments provided for in the Missives (including all rent and other apportionments);

'**Conclusion Date**' means the date of conclusion of the Missives;

['**Current Service Charge Year**' means the service charge year in which Completion falls;]

'**Date of Entry**' means [[   ] 20[ ]] [the first Working Day occurring [   ] [days] [weeks] after the Conclusion Date] or such other date as the Purchaser and the Seller may agree in writing with specific reference to the Missives;

'**Disclosed Documents**' means the documents listed in Part 1 of the Schedule;

'**Disposition**' means the disposition of the Property in favour of the Purchaser [(or its nominees)] [in terms of the draft set out in Part [8] of the Schedule];

'**Fixed Plant**' means such plant and machinery (within the meaning of the Capital Allowances Act 2001) as constitutes a fixture or fixtures and which is included in the sale of the Property;

'**HMRC**' means HM Revenue & Customs;

'**Interest**' means interest on the sum in question at 4% per annum above the base rate from time to time of [ ] from the date that such sum is due for payment or, if there is no such date specified, the date of demand for such sum until such sum is paid;

'**Landlords**' means the landlords under the Leases;

'**Leases**' means the lease(s) and other documentation listed in Part 3[A] of the Schedule;

'**Missives**' means the contract constituted by this offer and all duly executed letters following on it;

'**Moveables**' means the moveable items set out in Part [12] of the Schedule;

'**Plan**' means the [demonstrative] plan contained in Part [9] of the Schedule;

'**Price**' means [   ] POUNDS (£[   ]) Sterling exclusive of any VAT;

'**Property**' means **ALL** and **WHOLE** [   ] [shown edged red on the Plan]: Together with (i) the whole buildings and erections on it known as and forming [ ], (ii) the whole Landlords' fixtures and fittings in and on it, (iii) the whole rights, parts, privileges and pertinents, and (iv) the Landlords' interest in and under the Leases [and together also with [   ]], being the property [more particularly described in [the Disposition] [and disponed by [   ]] [registered in the Land Register of Scotland under Title Number [   ]];

'**Purchaser**' means [   ], incorporated under the Companies Acts (Registered Number [   ]) and having its Registered Office at [ ];

'**Purchaser's Bank**' means (a) the client account of the Purchaser's Solicitors and/or (b) the client account of the solicitors acting for the Purchaser's heritable creditor and/or (c) if it is a bank which is a shareholder in CHAPS Clearing Co Ltd, and the funds in question are loan funds from the bank for the purpose of acquiring the Property, the Purchaser's heritable creditor;

'**Purchaser's Solicitors**' means [   ] (Ref: [   ]) or such other solicitors as the Purchaser may appoint in their place from time to time and who have been notified in writing to the Seller's Solicitors;

'**Schedule**' means the schedule annexed to this offer;

'**Seller**' means [   ], incorporated under the Companies Acts (Registered Number [   ]) and having its Registered Office at [   ];

'**Seller's Bank Account**' means [Bank: [   ], Sort Code: [   ], Account Number: [   ], Account Name: [   ] or] such [other] UK clearing bank account as the Seller nominates (or the Seller's Solicitors on its behalf nominate) by written notice to that effect at least 3 Working Days prior to the Date of Entry;

'**Seller's Solicitors**' means [   ] (Ref: [   ]) or such other solicitors as the Seller may appoint in their place from time to time and who have been notified in writing to the Purchaser's Solicitors;

['**Service Contracts**' means the service, maintenance and other contracts entered into by or on behalf of the Seller (or its predecessors in title) in connection with the maintenance and management of the Property, brief details of which are set out in Part [14] of the Schedule;]

['**Subleases**' means the sublease(s) and other documentation listed in Part [3B] of the Schedule;]

'**Tenants**' means the current tenants (both collectively and individually) under the Leases;

'**Title Deeds**' means the title deeds of the Property [listed in Part 2 of the Schedule];

'**TOGC**' means a transfer of [part of] a business as a going concern for the purposes of section 49(1) of the VAT Act and Article 5 of the Value Added Tax (Special Provisions) Order 1995;

'**VAT**' means value added tax as provided for in the VAT Act and any tax similar or equivalent to value added tax or performing a similar fiscal function;

'**VAT Act**' means the Value Added Tax Act 1994;

'**VAT Group**' means two or more bodies corporate registered as a group for VAT purposes under s 43 of the VAT Act;

'**Working Day**' means any day on which clearing banks in
[Edinburgh, Glasgow and London] are open for normal business.

Note: Using defined terms in appropriate circumstances helps to streamline
the text of the clauses in the Offer. Ideally any terms which are defined
should appear in the Definitions section rather than within the body of the
deed or document. There is one exception to this approach, in the case of
the environmental and employment law definitions, which are specific to
those clauses only and which would otherwise clutter up the Definitions
section at the start.

Additional definitions can be incorporated to suit particular
circumstances, and equally, unnecessary definitions can be removed,
along with their corresponding clauses, if, for example, there are no
service contracts.

(b)   Interpretation

1.2   In the Missives, unless otherwise specified or the context
otherwise requires:

1.2.1   any reference to one gender includes all other
genders;

1.2.2   words in the singular only include the plural and
vice versa;

1.2.3   any reference to the whole is to be treated as
including reference to any part of the whole;

1.2.4   any reference to a person includes a natural person,
corporate or unincorporated body (whether or
not having separate legal personality) and words
importing individuals include corporations and *vice
versa*;

1.2.5   any reference to a Clause, Schedule or Part of the
Schedule is to the relevant Clause, Schedule or Part
of the Schedule of or to this offer;

1.2.6   any reference to a statute or statutory provision
includes any subordinate legislation which is
in force from time to time under that statute or
statutory provision;

1.2.7   any reference to any statute, statutory provision or subordinate legislation is a reference to it as it is in force from time to time taking account of any amendment or re-enactment;

1.2.8   any phrase introduced by the words 'including', 'include', 'in particular' or any similar expression is to be construed as illustrative only and is not to be construed as limiting the generality of any preceding words;

1.2.9   a document will be duly executed only if it is executed in such manner as meets the requirements of s 3 of the Requirements of Writing (Scotland) Act 1995;

1.2.10   where at any one time there are two or more persons included in the expression 'Purchaser' or 'Seller' obligations contained in the Missives which are expressed to be made by the Purchaser and/or the Seller are binding jointly and severally on them and their respective executors and representatives whomsoever without the necessity of discussing them in their order;

1.2.11   any reference to funds being cleared means that the funds are immediately available for withdrawal from the holder's bank account;

1.2.12   any reference to 'reasonable consent' means the prior written consent of the party in question, such consent not to be unreasonably withheld or delayed; and

1.2.13   where a Clause provides that Interest is payable and that the sum must be paid within a specified period, no Interest will accrue on the sum provided it is paid within that period.

1.3   The headings in the Missives are included for convenience only and are to be ignored in construing the Missives.

1.4   The Schedule forms part of the Missives.

Note: Much of this clause is standard interpretation boilerplate. Note however the terms of the two additional general interpretation provisions have been added in clauses 1.2.12 and 1.2.13 providing a definition of 'reasonable consent' and clarifying that Interest (on late payment) does not run if the principal sum to which it relates is paid within the specified period of grace. As with the interpretation provisions in the standard residential clauses, these provisions qualify some provisions that appear throughout the offer, and avoid constant repetitions.

(c) 2   Price

2.1   Payment

2.1.1   The Completion Payment will be paid by the Purchaser on the Date of Entry by instantaneous bank transfer of cleared funds from the Purchaser's Bank to the Seller's Bank Account in exchange for the Disposition and other items to be delivered by the Seller referred to in Clause [10].

2.1.2   A payment not made in accordance with Clause 2.1.1

Note: The Offer provides for the price to be paid by telegraphic transfer of funds. While this is the usual method for commercial property transactions, any alternative method of settlement that the parties decide on would need to be provided for. Clause 2.5 makes it clear that the funds are cleared and must be in the relevant bank account and available for use by the seller on the day of completion.

There is always concern, from an anti-money laundering point of view, when funds are sent to the seller's solicitor's Bank Account direct from a purchaser. If this is unexpected, then delays can result, while the seller's solicitors run anti money laundering checks, and there are often recriminations as a result. Property transactions are seen as a fertile source of money laundering activity. To address the practical issue, without adding further AML complications, it is made a contractual provision that funds must come either from a firm of solicitors, or direct from a lender who is a shareholder in CHAPS (the Clearing House Automated Payment System, or 'telegraphic transfer'), provided that the funds in question are loan funds for purchase of the property in question. Thus the purchaser and his solicitor is on notice to route the funds in the appropriate way and the seller's solicitors can legitimately decline to accept funds that do not come from the correct source.

2.2   [Apportionment

The Price will be apportioned as follows:

Property - £[   ]

Fixed Plant - £[   ]

Moveables - £[   ]].

2.3   Interest

If the Completion Payment (and any VAT which the Purchaser has agreed in terms of Clause 3 to pay to the Seller on the Date of Entry) or any part of it is not paid to the Seller on the Date of Entry then, notwithstanding consignation or that the Purchaser has not taken entry, the Purchaser will pay to the Seller Interest on the outstanding money.

2.4   Cancellation of Sale

If the Purchaser fails to pay the Completion Payment (and any VAT which the Purchaser has agreed in terms of Clause 3 to pay to the Seller on the Date of Entry) with Interest as set out in Clause 2.3 within [10] Working Days after the Date of Entry the Seller is entitled to rescind the Missives, to re-sell the Property to any third party and to claim damages from the Purchaser which may include:

2.4.1   all costs and expenses incurred in relation to the re-marketing of the Property and the re-sale of it;

2.4.2   any shortfall between:

(i)   the sale price rece

(ii)   the Price; and

2.4.3   financial losses including increased funding costs which the Seller would not have incurred had the Price been paid on the Date of Entry and interest which the Seller could have earned on the Price had it been paid on the Date of Entry.

If the Seller rescinds the Missives, no Interest will be due by the Purchaser in terms of Clause 2.3.

2.5 Receipt of Money

For the purposes of this Clause 2, money will not be deemed
paid to the Seller until such time as same day credit on it
is available to the holder of the Seller's Bank Account in
accordance with normal banking procedure.

2.6 Suspension

The provisions of Clauses 2.3 and 2.4 will not apply and the
Seller will not be entitled to the rents under the Leases in terms
of Clause 4.2 for any period(s) of time during which the delay
in payment by the Purchaser is due to any failure or breach by
or on behalf of the Seller to implement its obligations or duties
under the Missives on time.

Note: The Interest and Cancellation of Sale provisions reflect the change
in approach to penalty interest provisions following on the decisions in
2006 in the cases of *Black v McGregor* [2006] CSIH 45; [2007] SC 69 and
Wipfel Ltd v Auchlochan Developments Ltd [2006] CSIH 183.

The offer provides in the traditional way for interest (at the normally
agreed rate of 4% over base rate) to be payable on the price, if the purchaser
does not pay on the date of entry.

If, however, the seller decides that it wants to rescind the missives and
re-sell the property, on account of default by the purchaser, it would no
longer be entitled to any interest on the price. Instead, it would seek to
recover costs and losses actually incurred, which it is entitled to do at
common law. Several heads of loss are identified: re-marketing costs; any
shortfall in the price, and generally other financial losses that are actually
incurred because of the purchaser's failure to pay on the date of entry.
The list is not of course exhaustive, and there is a degree of flexibility at
common law. This is the approach also taken in the standard residential
clauses, which additionally provide for an alternative option to common
law damages, namely 'liquidated damages', but with a longstop date in
that case, of 12 months. See para 6.10(m) for commentary on liquidated
damages provisions).

In addition to interest, as the rents under the leases are apportioned at
completion (whether or not that is also the date of entry), the seller will be
entitled to the rents for any delayed completion (unless of course it is the

seller that is responsible for such a delay). This represents a fair balance of the seller's and the purchaser's respective interests.

(d) 3   VAT

3.1   [OPTION 1 - VAT Exempt

3.1   [OPTION 2 - TOGC relief applies and supply of Property would otherwise be exempt

3.1   [OPTION 3 – TOGC Non-exempt – option to tax made by the Seller and TOGC relief applies

3.1   [OPTION 4 - Non-exempt – supply of Property standard-rated within para (a) of the VAT Act Sch 9, Group 1, Item 1 and TOGC relief applies

3.1   [OPTION 5 - TOGC relief does not apply and VAT is payable

Note: The PSG offer to sell contains wording for five VAT options, which runs for several pages and so for the purposes of this commentary we have not replicated all of the wording. In fact, once you know which set of circumstances apply to the seller and the property it is really a question of selecting the relevant option and deleting the rest. The wording sets out the statutory basis for whichever option applies and the parties requirements of each other in relation to registration, opting to tax the property and so on. In addition the Guidance notes that accompany the PSG Offer to Sell on the website contain a detailed commentary on the purpose and effect of each option.

What is a TOGC?   Whether the transfer of a property constitutes a 'transfer of a going concern' ('TOGC') is of importance in relation to the VAT treatment of the transfer of that property. Whether the transfer of a commercial property constitutes a TOGC is a question of both fact and degree. However, if the circumstances of the transfer meet the criteria for a TOGC then the transfer has to be treated in that way. The effect of treating a transfer as a TOGC is to make what would have otherwise been a transfer that was liable to VAT fall outside the scope of VAT, meaning no VAT is payable on the transfer price.

The main element for the transfer to be a TOGC is that the transfer must be of a business. A property might be transferred as a business where, for example, it is leased and is held as an investment (a property rental business) or is being developed (a property development business). It is also essential that the same business being transferred (whether property rental or development) must be continued by the purchaser for a sufficient period of time after the transfer.

Before the transfer takes place, both the seller and the purchaser must be registered for VAT (or, in the case of the purchaser, be liable to become registered as a result of the transfer) and have opted to tax the property being transferred.

The five options of VAT clause are:

Option 1 – VAT Exempt: Where no option to tax or real estate election has been made which affects the property, and the sale of the property does not otherwise fall outside the exempt category of supply, and TOGC relief does **not** apply (eg the purchaser is not going to carry on the same kind of business as the seller), no VAT should be payable on the part of the price apportioned to the property and fixed plant; or

Option 2 – TOGC relief applies and supply of property would otherwise be exempt: Where no option to tax or real estate election has been made which affects the property and the sale of the property does not otherwise fall outside the exempt category of supply, if the purchaser is going to carry on the same type of business as the seller, the sale of the property should constitute a TOGC and no VAT should be payable; or

Option 3 – TOGC Non-exempt – option to tax made by the seller and TOGC relief applies where the seller has opted to tax the property or made a real estate election which affects the property and, in either case, the purchaser is going to carry on the same type of business as the seller, the purchaser should be able to obtain relief under the TOGC provisions from VAT which would otherwise have been payable; or

Option 4 – Non-exempt – supply of property standard-rated within para (a) of the VAT Act Sch 9, Group 1, Item 1 and TOGC relief applies: Where the property is a standard-rated supply within para (a) of the VAT Act 1994 Sch 9, Group 1, Item 1 (ie new commercial buildings) and the purchaser is going to carry on the same type of business as the seller, the purchaser should be able to obtain relief under the TOGC provisions from VAT which would otherwise have been payable; or

Option 5 – TOGC relief does not apply and VAT is payable: Where the seller has opted to tax the property or made a real estate election which affects the property or where the property falls outside the exempt category (eg new commercial buildings) and TOGC relief does **not** apply (eg the business to be carried out by the purchaser is different from that carried out by the seller), VAT will be payable.

> 3.2   [Capital Goods Scheme
>
> The Seller confirms to the Purchaser that none of the assets to be transferred to the Purchaser in terms of the Missives is a capital item to which the Capital Goods Scheme (per Regulation 112 to 116 of the Value Added Tax Regulations 1995 as amended) applies or will apply in the period up to Completion other than those assets specified in Part [11] of the Schedule.]

Note: This clause should only be included where the sale of the property constitutes a TOGC.

It broadly applies where VAT is incurred by an owner on capital property expenditure of £250,000 or more and provides a mechanism for adjusting input tax over a period of years to reflect any changes in the taxable use of a capital item. Where a property is disposed of as a TOGC, the purchaser will take over responsibility for operating the Capital Goods Scheme in respect of any of the remaining intervals in the adjustment period and will therefore need details of the Capital Goods Scheme history of the property.

In relation to the capital goods scheme, the seller confirms that the Capital Goods Scheme does not apply to any assets included in the transaction other than those listed in the specified part of the Schedule. The CGS rules are complex and specialist VAT advice should always be sought.

(e) 4   Entry and Apportionments

> 4.1   Entry
>
> Entry to the Property subject only to and with the benefit of the Leases [and the Subleases] will be given on the Date of Entry.
>
> **Entry:** Entry is granted by the Seller subject to (and with the benefit of) the Leases and any Subleases. Note therefore that the usual requirement for vacant possession is inappropriate.

4.2 Rent Apportionment

    4.2.1   The rents payable under the Leases will, subject to Clause 2.6, be apportioned (net of VAT) at Completion on the basis that the Purchaser will receive a 1/365th part of the rent for each day from (and including) Completion to (but not including) the next rent payment date(s) under the Leases.

    4.2.2   The rents will be apportioned on the assumption that the Seller has received payment of all sums due prior to Completion, whether or not that is in fact the case.

    4.2.3   In the case of any rent review under a Lease where the date of such review occurs prior to Completion but the reviewed rent has not been determined by Completion the rent will be apportioned on the basis of the passing rent.

4.3 Other apportionments

    4.3.1   All other payments under the Leases and all other outgoings for the Property (other than rates [and], insurance [and service charge]) will be apportioned as at Completion on an equitable basis.

    4.3.2   Within 5 Working Days after Completion, the Seller or the Seller's Solicitors will advise the local authority of the change of ownership of the Property so that any apportionment of rates can be carried out by the local authority.

Note: All apportionments of rent and other sums due under the lease are calculated with effect from completion, whether or not that is also the date of entry.

The standard approach to apportionment of rents is on a daily basis over a year (365 days). This irons out any imbalance which could result if the apportionments were carried out on a monthly or quarterly basis, where the periods may not be equal in number of days. This is particularly the case where the old Scottish quarter days (Whitsunday, Lammas, Martinmas and Candlemas) are referred to in the leases. In accordance with HMRC guidelines, any VAT on the rent is not apportioned. For an example of a Completion Statement showing an apportionment of rents see para 11.05(a).

It is also assumed that all rent has been paid up to date whether or not that is actually the case, so that the purchaser will receive from the seller the proportion of the rents due under the leases, counting from the date of completion to the next rent payment date under each of the leases. This means that if the Tenants have not paid the current quarter's rent or if there are any other arrears under the leases, they remain the seller's responsibility to recover. Clause 5.1 of the Offer deals with steps that the seller can take to recover these sums.

Naturally, the purchaser is only entitled to receive the rents under the leases for the actual date of completion, on condition that the seller receives the price on that day.

It is possible that there may be ongoing rent review negotiations when a let property is being sold. If there is an outstanding rent review under any of the leases, then an apportionment of the passing rent payable under that lease is calculated as at completion. Once the new rent is determined any uplift that applies to the period both before and after completion can be apportioned between the parties. Clause 5.4 of the Offer deals with the mechanism for this.

Other apportionments are dealt with in clause 5.2 (service charge), and clause 11(insurance). Apportionment of rates done by the local authority to whom notification of change of ownership is sent.

All other payments under the leases and any outgoings for the property which require apportionment are to be dealt with on an equitable basis.

(f) 5   Other Payments

5.1   Arrears

5.1.1   If any rents or other payments under the Leases are in arrears at Completion the Purchaser will use all reasonable endeavours to procure payment from the Tenants as soon as practicable after Completion provided that the Seller keeps the Purchaser free of expense.

5.1.2   The Purchaser will pay to the Seller all sums relating to such arrears (together with any interest paid by the Tenants in terms of the relevant Lease) within 5 Working Days of cleared funds being received from the relevant Tenant.

5.1.3   If the Seller or its agents receive any payments from the Tenants after Completion which do not relate to arrears due to the Seller it will pay them to the Purchaser within 5 Working Days of cleared funds being received from the relevant Tenant.

5.1.4   If requested by the other, the Seller and the Purchaser will each assign to the other such rights as are reasonably necessary to enable them to recover from the Tenants any sums due under the Leases to which they are entitled in terms of the Missives [but the Seller will not be entitled to take any proceedings against the Tenants other than actions for payment of debt and, except with the reasonable consent of the Purchaser, will not take any steps to sequestrate any Tenant or appoint a receiver or liquidator to any Tenant.]

Note: Since the seller retains responsibility for all arrears under any of the leases (see Clause 4 of the Offer), it is entitled to pursue the tenants for these arrears in the same way as any other debt. However, the purchaser will not want the seller to do anything which might adversely affect the solvency of what will now be the purchaser's tenants, and so, in recovering any arrears, the seller is not to be allowed to go to the extent of sequestrating or appointing a receiver/liquidator to the tenants, unless the purchaser agrees.

The purchaser should co-operate with the seller's attempts to recover any arrears.

(g) 5.2 [Service Charge

5.2.1   The Seller will take, and will ensure that its managing agents take, such action as the Purchaser may reasonably request in writing from time to time in relation to the transfer to the Purchaser on Completion of all service charge funds for the Property in accordance with the Missives.

5.2.2   The Seller will be responsible for all service charge expenditure properly incurred and invoiced prior to Completion, and will be entitled to apply any advance service charge monies received from the Tenants prior to Completion in respect of such expenditure.

5.2.3   The Seller will as soon as practicable and in any event within [10] Working Days after the Conclusion Date deliver to the Purchaser the service charge budget for the Property for the Current Service Charge Year and an interim service charge reconciliation showing, for the Current Service Charge Year:

(i)   the advance service charge payments invoiced to and paid by the Tenants and the sums attributable to unlet space;

(ii) the Landlords' service charge expenditure which has been properly incurred under the Leases and paid by the Seller; and

(iii) the service charge expenditure which it is anticipated will be incurred in the period up to the Date of Entry.

5.2.4   Except with the reasonable consent of the Purchaser the Seller will not after the Conclusion Date enter into any new contracts or commitments relative to the matters covered by service charge under the Leases unless they have already been taken into account in either the budget or interim reconciliation.

5.2.5   At Completion the Seller will deliver to the Purchaser an update of the interim service charge reconciliation disclosing the position as at Completion and containing (with copy invoices) details of all further service charge expenditure which has been properly incurred and invoiced but not paid at that time.

5.2.6   If the advance service charge payments shown in the update (including the sums attributable to unlet space) exceed the aggregate of the Landlords' service charge expenditure shown as having been paid and the further service charge expenditure, the Seller will pay or make over the excess to the Purchaser at Completion. For the avoidance of doubt, the Seller will, as soon as practicable [but in any event within [ ] Working Days] after Completion, pay all further service charge expenditure not paid at that time, but the Purchaser will be responsible for settling any service charge invoices received following Completion.

5.2.7   If the aggregate shown in the update exceeds the advance service charge payments, the Purchaser, who will be entitled to all service charge arrears, will pay and make over the excess once it has received the necessary funds to do so from the Tenants under the Leases.

5.2.8   The Seller confirms to the Purchaser that:

(i)   the Seller's expenditure on the Property for the Current Service Charge Year has been fully, properly and accurately kept and recorded in its accounts and records and will be reflected in the interim reconciliations which will not contain any material discrepancies or inaccuracies of any kind;

(ii) no repayment or credit is outstanding to any Tenant in respect of any overpayment by the Tenant arising from an excess of contributions towards estimated service expenditure over service expenditure actually incurred, in relation to any prior service charge year;

(iii) all sums received by the Seller from the Tenants by way of contribution towards insurance premiums have been duly applied to meet such premiums;

(iv) there are no outstanding claims from any current or former Tenant for reimbursement in relation to service expenditure in relation to any prior service charge year;

(v) no part of any common parts to which the service charge relates is currently rated.

5.2.9 The Seller will pay to the Purchaser any sum recovered at any time from any third party (whether by way of insurance proceeds, compensation or otherwise) to the extent that such sum ought properly to be taken into account in the calculation of the level of actual service expenditure for any service charge year.

5.2.10 Within [3] months after the end of the Current Service Charge Year, the Purchaser will prepare service charge accounts and deliver a copy of them to the Seller. The Seller's contribution to the service charge for the Current Service Charge Year in relation to unlet space will be re-calculated at that stage and any over or under-payment repaid within [10] Working Days of such recalculation and any Interest. The Seller will also bear the cost of any item incurred prior to Completion and attributed to the service charge which is not recoverable under the Leases.

5.2.11 The Seller will be liable for the service charge attributable to unlet space for the period up to Completion. The Seller's liability to contribute to the service charge for the Current Service Charge Year in relation to unlet space will be assessed on an equitable basis consistent with the provisions of the Leases for the Current Service Charge Year by being multiplied by the number of days between the expiry of the last service charge year and Completion and divided by 365 and, in the event of there being any dispute as to the amount of such contribution, the matter will be referred to the decision of an independent surveyor, who will act as an expert, appointed jointly or failing agreement, by the Chairman of the RICS in Scotland on the application of either party. The independent surveyor's decision will be binding on the parties. If the independent surveyor dies, delays or becomes unwilling or incapable of acting then either the Seller or the Purchaser may apply to the Chairman to discharge that independent surveyor and appoint a replacement. The fees and expenses of the independent surveyor and the cost of appointment are payable by the Seller and the Purchaser in the proportions which the independent surveyor directs and if no direction is made, equally.

5.2.12   [There is no sinking or similar fund held by or to the order of the Seller (or its agents) as Landlor[At Completion the Seller will:

(i)   pay to the Purchaser all sinking and similar funds held by the Seller (or its agents) as Landlords together with all interest earned on them;

(ii)   deliver to the Purchaser certified accounts detailing all intromissions with and all interest earned on such sinking funds.]

5.2.13   The Seller will, with effect from the Conclusion Date, allow the Purchaser and its authorised representatives to inspect, by prior arrangement, the Seller's accounts and other records relating to the service charge, rent collection and all matters relating to the management of the Property. Following Completion, the Seller and the Purchaser shall procure that their respective managing agents co-operate with each other in relation to the handover of all documentation and information in relation to service charge and management matters generally.

5.2.14   The Seller will provide details of any managing agents employed in respect of the Property together with a copy of their terms of appointment, immediately following the Conclusion Date. The Purchaser will have no obligations or liabilities in respect of the continuing employment of such agents except to the extent expressly undertaken by the Purchaser in the Missives.]

Note: Where the property is subject to a number of leases and with common parts, which each of the tenants is entitled to use, such as in a retail park, there are usually provisions in the leases for maintenance of these parts to be dealt with by the landlord. The landlord will then recover the costs through a service charge which the tenants are required to pay. The arrangements for dealing with service charge before and after the sale are set out at length in the Offer. The provisions reflect typical, well established procedure for ensuring that equitable arrangements are made, but these details should be discussed with the seller and purchaser to make sure that both parties (and their respective managing agents) are satisfied that it reflects the arrangements which they wish to apply, and also, to the extent necessary to comply with the RICS Code of Practice for Service Charges in Commercial Property (2011, 2nd edition).

The procedure will be for the seller to produce an interim reconciliation of the service charge for the current year, which is then updated at completion, and shows the service charge payments received from the tenants, and the service charge expenditure actually, or anticipated to be, incurred before the date of entry. Broadly speaking, if the payments received are more than the expenditure, then the difference between the two is the amount which should be handed over to the purchaser at completion. The purchaser needs to be satisfied the expenditure is properly incurred and thus recoverable from the tenants. The seller is responsible, prior to completion, for the amount of the service charge that applies to any unlet space in the property.

As a matter of practice, the purchaser should obtain, prior to completion, a copy of the service charge accounts for the last three years.

(**h**) 5.3 Rent Deposits

[There are no rent deposits paid by the Tenants and held by or to the order of the Seller (or their agents) as Landlords.]

5.3.1   [At Completion the Seller will:

(i)   pay to the Purchaser all rent deposits paid by the Tenants and held by or to the order of the Seller (or its agents) as Landlords together with all interest earned on them;

(ii) deliver to the Purchaser certified accounts detailing all intromissions with and all interest earned on the rent deposits.

5.3.2   The Seller will indemnify the Purchaser against all liability to the Tenants in relation to the rent deposits in respect of the period up to Completion and the Purchaser will indemnify the Seller in respect of the period from (and including) Completion.

5.3.3   In so far as the Seller can validly do so, the rent deposits will be assigned to the Purchaser in terms of the draft assignation of rent deposits forming Part [16] of the Schedule.

5.3.4   The Purchaser will:

(i)   within 15 Working Days after Completion duly execute the assignation of rent deposits delivered to the Purchaser at Completion; and

(ii) within 20 Working Days after Completion, intimate the assignation of rent deposits to the appropriate parties and deliver a copy of the intimation to the Seller.]

Note: Where the seller is holding any rent deposit sums from any of the tenants, provision should be made for the transfer of these sums to the purchaser at completion, along with any relevant financial details. The purchaser will then require to set up a deposit account to reflect the terms of the rent deposit agreement.

The rent deposit agreements themselves will also need to be assigned to the purchaser, and there is a style of assignation attached as part of the Schedule in the actual Offer. To be effective the assignation will need to be intimated to the tenant.

(i) 5.4 [Outstanding Rent Reviews

In the case of any rent review under a Lease where the date of such review occurs prior to Completion but the reviewed rent has not been agreed or determined by Completion:

5.4.1 subject to Clause 2.6, the reviewed rent will be apportioned (net of VAT) on the basis that the Seller will receive a 1/365th part of any increase in the rent for each day from (and including) the rent review date to (but not including) Completion assuming:

(i) that any increase in rent which is agreed or determined is payable by the Tenants under the Leases from the rent review date in each case in equal instalments without any undue weighting being afforded to any one period of time over another period of time; and

(ii) that, if the Purchaser has traded off any proposed or actual extension, variation or relaxation of enforcement of any terms of the Leases against any reduction in any uplift in rent otherwise achievable, that the rent to be apportioned is the rent so achievable as if there had been no such reduction;

5.4.2 the Purchaser will use all reasonable endeavours, at its own expense, to procure that any balancing payments due following settlement of any outstanding review are paid by the relevant Tenants as soon as practicable; and

171

> 5.4.3 the Purchaser will pay to the Seller the sums properly referable to the period prior to Completion together with any interest paid by the Tenants in terms of the relevant Lease up to Completion within 5 Working Days of cleared funds being received from the relevant Tenant.]

Note: When there are any outstanding rent reviews under any of the leases, the rent is apportioned on an interim basis at the passing rent, and there will be a further accounting of any uplift in the rent (assuming that the rent review provisions provide for upwards only review) once it has been determined. If the review is not upwards only, then drafting will be needed to take account of the possibility that a shortfall may have to be paid, if the reviewed rent turns out to be less than the passing rent.

(j) 6 Disclosed Documents

> 6.1 Subject to Clause[s 7 and [10]] the Purchaser is deemed to have examined the Disclosed Documents and accepts that it is purchasing the Property on the basis that it has satisfied itself on all matters disclosed in them and on the validity and marketability of the Seller's title to the Property.
>
> 6.2 Clause 6.1 will override any other provision of the Missives apparently to the contrary and any confirmation given by the Seller in the Missives is given subject to the Disclosed Documents whether or not that is expressly stated.

Note: The structure of the Offer and its interaction with the due diligence process is that, once documents, such as titles etc have been examined by the purchaser, they become 'disclosed documents'. The effect of this is that the purchaser is deemed to have accepted the content of all the disclosed documents and accepts that it is purchasing the property having satisfied itself on all matters disclosed in them. The disclosed documents (whatever they might be) are to be listed in the first part of the Schedule. In this way there is a clear record of what the purchaser has examined in case of any dispute at a later stage.

The purchaser has an agreed period in which to examine all the titles, leases and other documents that are exhibited, and if not satisfied, can raise queries or requisitions with the seller. Once the time limit has expired without any objections having been raised, the purchaser is deemed to be satisfied with the terms of the documents.

(k) 7 [Documents to be Disclosed

> 7.1 To the extent it has not already done so, the Seller will exhibit to the Purchaser as soon as reasonably practicable after the Conclusion Date:
>
> > 7.1.1   [the Title Deeds;]
> >
> > 7.1.2   [the Leases][and the Subleases];
> >
> > 7.1.3   [property enquiry certificate in respect of the Property which is dated not more than [sixty] days prior to the date of this offer;] and
> >
> > 7.1.4   [coal mining search from the Coal Authority in respect of the Property which is dated not more than ninety days prior to the date of this offer.]
>
> 7.2 The Purchaser will have [15] Working Days from receipt of each of the respective items referred to in Clause 7.1 to satisfy itself on their terms.
>
> 7.3 If any of the items referred to at Clauses 7.1.1, 7.1.3 or 7.1.4 disclose any matters materially prejudicial to the interest of the Purchaser or the Purchaser (at its sole discretion) is not satisfied with the terms of the Leases [or Subleases] the Purchaser will be entitled to resile from the Missives without penalty on delivery of written notice to that effect to the Seller's Solicitors within the [15] Working Days period, time being of the essence. Failing such notice, the Purchaser is deemed to be satisfied as to the terms of the items referred to in Clause 7.1 and each of such items will become a Disclosed Document for the purposes of the Missives.]

Note: A list of the documents that are typically disclosed is provided in the Offer, and can be added to or altered according to circumstances. They include the usual documents such as titles, leases, searches and property enquiry certificates (which are to be listed in full in the Schedule). These are exhibited to the purchaser as soon as possible after missives have been concluded.

The ninety day time limit for coal authority reports is based on current Law Society guidance. There is no equivalent guidance for PECs, but a sixty day expiry limit for PECs is a reasonable balance, since there are different risks associated with the information contained in PECs and coal authority reports. In all cases it will depend on the circumstances whether either expiry limit is appropriate, depending upon the nature of the property, the terms of the information contained in the report and the purchaser's plans for the property, and the parties should be prepared to be flexible. Contrast this with the three month period specified for PECs in the residential offer (see para 6.10(s)) which is a requirement of the Council of Mortgage Lenders.

A reasonable number of working days from receipt of each of the items should be provided for the purchaser to satisfy itself, depending on the nature and complexity of the property and its title. For example, if the title is not yet registered in the Land Register then more time will be needed in which to examine and report on title, particularly if it is complex.

Again there is a deemed provision that means that the purchaser is taken to be satisfied with what has been disclosed, unless objections are raised with in the specified period.

(l) 8   Title

8.1   Burdens

8.1.1   So far as the Seller is aware there are no servitudes, rights of way or similar rights affecting the Property other than as referred to in the Disclosed Documents.

8.1.2   The Property is sold with and under the real burdens, reservations, restrictions, servitudes, rights of way or similar rights, overriding interests, and other conditions affecting the Property whether specified or referred to in the Title Deeds or not.

8.2   Minerals

The minerals are included in the sale to the extent to which the Seller has any right to them.

8.3   Outstanding Disputes

During the period of the Seller's ownership of the Property, there have been no disputes which remain outstanding with neighbouring proprietors or third parties about items common to the Property and adjacent premises, access to or from the Property, the title to the Property or similar matters.

8.4   [Community Interests

The Seller has not received any notices in terms of s 37 of the Land Reform (Scotland) Act 2003 in respect of the Property.]

Note: The provisions in the commercial property offer concerning title, disputes and similar matters are similar to the equivalent provisions in residential missives. The seller is required to confirm that it is not aware of any servitudes or similar rights of way affecting the property which are not disclosed in the titles. It may not be possible to identify such rights from an inspection of the property either, but the seller ought to be able to confirm the position from its own knowledge.

(m) 8.5 [Occupancy Rights

The Seller warrants that no part of the Property is (or has within the prescriptive period been) used as a private residence and consequently that the provisions of none of the Matrimonial Homes (Family Protection) (Scotland) Act 1981 as amended, or the Family Law (Scotland) Act 1985, or the Civil Partnership Act 2004 apply to the Property or any part of it, or to the Seller's interest in the Property.]

Note: The provision confirming that none of the 'family law' legislation (ie Matrimonial Homes (Scotland) Act 1981; Family Law (Scotland) Act 1985 and Civil Partnership Act 2004) affects the property has been included as there may be occasions where the property incorporates some residential element such as a caretaker's flat. In this case the following alternative wording can be substituted

8.5   The Seller warrants that:

8.5.1   the Property is not and will not be affected by any Transfer of Property Order made in terms of the Family Law (Scotland) Act 1985 at Completion;

8.5.2   the Seller is not a party to any action in which any such Order is being or has been sought; and

8.5.3   at Completion the Property will not be affected by any occupancy rights as defined in the Matrimonial Homes (Family Protection) (Scotland) Act 1981 as amended or the Civil Partnership Act 2004.

(n) 8.6 Land Register Requisitions

8.6.1   The Seller will deliver to the Purchaser, on demand from time to time and at its expense, such documents and evidence as the Keeper may require to enable the Keeper to:

(i)   issue a Land Certificate in name of the Purchaser [(or its nominees)] and/or

(ii) update or create (as the case may be) the Title Sheet of the Property to disclose the Purchaser [(or its nominees)]

in each case as the registered proprietor of the whole of the Property and, provided that the Disposition presented for registration within fourteen days after Completion, containing no exclusion of indemnity in terms of s 12(2) of the Land Registration (Scotland) Act 1979. Such documents will include (unless the Property comprises part only of a building) a plan or bounding description sufficient to enable the Property to be identified on the Ordnance Survey Map and evidence (such as a Form P16 Report) that the description of the Property in the Title Deeds is habile to include the whole of the occupied extent.

8.6.2   Provided that the Disposition is presented for registration within fourteen days after Completion, the Seller warrants that the Land Certificate to be issued to the Purchaser [or its nominees] and/or the updated or newly created Title Sheet will disclose no entry, deed or diligence (including any notice of potential liability for costs registered under

the Tenements (Scotland) Act 2004 or the Title
Conditions (Scotland) Act 2003) prejudicial to the
interest of the Purchaser [or its nominees] other than
such as are created by or against the Purchaser [or its
nominees] or have been disclosed to, and accepted in
writing by, the Purchaser [or its nominees] prior to
Completion.

Note: The first part of this clause contains an unqualified undertaking by
the seller to deliver any additional documents and evidence that the Keeper
requires to register the purchaser's title. There is no time limit on that
undertaking. However a fourteen-day period is imposed in respect of the
seller's obligation that there will be no exclusion of indemnity in that title,
and in respect of the seller's obligation that the title sheet will be clear of
any item not either created by, or accepted by the purchaser. It is incumbent
on the purchaser (through his solicitor) to present his title for registration
as soon as possible after completion in any event, and the thinking behind
this time limit is that, without it, the seller could be expected to take steps
to remove anything that appeared in the title sheet at any time including
any entry or diligence over which he has no control, or which would not
have occurred had the purchaser registered his title expeditiously. It also
reflects the 14-day period allowed for registration and entitlement to clear
searches that is provided for in the seller's solicitors letter of obligation
(see para 11.04). Note that the Combined Standard Clauses for residential
property do not contain this time limit, although there is no less a duty
on the residential purchaser's solicitor to ensure that his client's title is
registered promptly, of course.

The parties to any conveyancing transaction may choose to dispense
with delivery of a physical Land Certificate and instead rest with the
updating or creation of the Title Sheet in the Land Register. This is known
as 'dematerialisation' and is part of the drive by the Registers of Scotland to
move away from paper based transactions towards electronic conveyancing.

(o) 9   Leases

9.1   Confirmations

The Seller confirms that, except as disclosed in Part [4] of the
Schedule:

9.1.1   The Leases accurately set out the whole terms of the letting or occupation of the Property [and the Subleases accurately set out the whole terms of the subletting or occupation of the Property].

9.1.2   The Leases [and the Subleases] have not been amended or varied in a manner which is binding on the Purchaser and they will not be so amended or varied, prior to Completion, except with the prior written consent of the Purchaser.

9.1.3   The information disclosed in the rent and service charge payment history (forming part of the Disclosed Documents) is complete and accurate in all respects.

9.1.4   The Seller is not aware of any material breach by the Tenants of any of their obligations under the Leases which would not be reasonably ascertainable from an inspection of the Property.

9.1.5   The Seller has not received written notification from any of the Tenants of claims or disputes under the Leases against the Landlords which are outstanding.

9.1.6   There are no notices issued by the Seller to any of the Tenants, or by any of the Tenants to the Seller, under the Leases which remain to be implemented.

9.1.7   No notices by or on behalf of any of the Tenants exercising any option to break or terminate any of the Leases have been served on the Seller or vice versa.

9.1.8   The Seller has not received written notification of the insolvency, liquidation, administration or receivership of any of the Tenants.

9.1.9   The Seller has not received written notification of the creation of any fixed or floating charges over the interest of any of the Tenants under the Leases.

Note: The leases are the key element in any investment purchase. An investment purchaser wants a property that will more or less pay for itself, in that as much of the repair, maintenance and insurance liabilities for the property (hence FRI – full repairing and insuring) or the obligation to pay for them, have been passed on to the tenants. Examination of the leases and other leasehold documentation, including assignations, rent review documents, licences for works, back letters and so on, is a major part of the due diligence process for the purchaser's solicitors, but there are some key pieces of information that a purchaser needs, that are not readily ascertainable from the documentation or otherwise verifiable by the purchaser, but ought to be in the knowledge of the seller, or its advisers.

Some careful consultation with the seller is needed before this provision can be finalised to ensure that the statements are accurate. Rather than start to alter and dilute the wording of the confirmations, the approach is to leave them as they are drafted, but, to the extent that the seller does not have the knowledge or information to make these statements, or to the extent that the position is, in any individual circumstances, different from these confirmations, then these matters are disclosed in the relevant part of the Schedule. So if for example there is an ongoing dispute about the amount of the service charge payment with one of the tenants, instead of deleting Clause 9.1.5, the details of that dispute are disclosed in the Schedule. This gives a much clearer indication of the actual situation, on which the purchaser is able to make a judgement or seek further details. The use of the expression 'so far as aware' is avoided as much as possible, because of the difficulty of establishing awareness, particularly where the seller is a corporate entity.

Traditionally, these statements would be couched in an offer to purchase as 'lease warranties'. Many offers still use this terminology, but it is often a sticking point with sellers, whose preferred approach is to sell the property with the minimum of liability, and the requirement to 'warrant' something is often perceived as unattractive to an investment seller, particularly when it is probably not directly involved in the day to day running of the property. However, while it appears that there is a distinction in English law between terms in a contract that are conditions or warranties, and thus the remedies that an aggrieved person is entitled to in the event of a breach of either, there does not appear to be any such distinction in Scots law. In the *Law of Contract in Scotland*, 3rd Edition (William McBryde: W Green) 'Scots law looks at the nature of the breach, and its concept of material breach does not depend on a classification of the term of the contract. There is no distinction in Scots law between a condition, a term and a warranty'

So, the materiality of the term can be determined according to its construction in the circumstances of each individual case, rather than on how the term itself is classified. The classification of these statements as 'confirmations' is conceptually more palatable to a seller, while still offering a suitable level of accountability to a purchaser, and should be pressed for, rather than reverting to the former 'warranty' method of dealing with such matters. Always remember that the object of the exercise is to streamline, simplify and accelerate the negotiations between the parties, so it would be counter productive for the solicitors to rack up hours of time arguing about semantics, tempting though that may be to some lawyers.

> 9.2 Period to Completion
>
> The Seller will take all necessary steps which a prudent landlord (acting reasonably) would take in the interests of good estate management to ensure that the confirmations given in Clause 9.1 apply at Completion.

Note: The confirmations are given at the date on which the offer is issued. From that date until completion, the seller is only required to disclose to the purchaser any changes to the confirmations which arise during that period – it is not required to take any further action.

> 9.3 Interim Management
>
> 9.3.1 In the period from the date of this offer until Completion, the Seller will:
>
> (i) implement its obligations under the Leases;
>
> (ii) continue to manage the Property and the Leases as a responsible landlord and in accordance with the principles of good estate management; and
>
> (iii) disclose in writing any changes to the confirmations given in Clause 9.1.
>
> 9.3.2 The Seller will not:
>
> (i) terminate or accept a renunciation of any Lease; or

(ii) grant any new lease; or

(iii) vary any Lease; or

(iv) settle any rent review under the Leases, propose or agree any reference to a third party for determination of any rent review or make or agree any proposal for a reviewed rent; or

(v) serve any notice under the Leases; or

(vi) carry out any alterations to the Property except with the prior written consent of the Purchaser.

9.3.3   [The Seller may complete the current management transactions set out in Part [6] of the Schedule.]

9.3.4   If any application to the Seller for its consent under the Leases is still outstanding, or if any such application is made prior to Completion, the Seller will not grant consent without the prior written approval of the Purchaser. In relation to each such application, the Purchaser will timeously comply with the obligations of the Seller, as Landlords, failing which the Purchaser will indemnify the Seller fully in respect of all liability incurred by the Tenants in relation to the relevant applications.

Note: The seller has continuing obligations for the management of the property between conclusion of missives and completion. While it is important that the position does not change significantly from that disclosed in the missives, the seller needs a reasonable degree of flexibility in the ongoing management of the property until it is handed over to the purchaser, but should continue to manage the property in accordance with the provisions of the leases and in accordance with the principles of good estate management. This is a standard catch-all phrase, although there is no published definition that can be pointed to, but guidance can be gleaned from codes such as the RICS Service Charge Code and the Code for Leasing Business Premises in England and Wales.

Consultation with the purchaser, who now has a vested interest in what happens at the property is required before the seller takes any action such as termination of a lease, or settlement of a rent review that could affect the value of the investment.

The seller should not however be able easily to irritate or terminate any lease since this is a critical component of the investment. Rent history reports of the tenants should be given to the purchaser, to assist him in assessing the financial covenant of the tenants.

However matters cannot grind to a halt during the interim period, so if the seller is approached by any tenant for consent for works for example, or even with a request to assign the tenant's interest under one of the leases, while the purchaser's agreement must be sought, it has to act as if it were the landlord under the relevant lease. In other words it should consider precisely the same issues as the seller has to, when looking at the request, and also be bound by any requirements in the lease, such as having to act reasonable and not unduly delay a decision.

9.4   Rent Reviews

[There are no outstanding rent reviews under any of the Leases.]

[In the case of any rent review under a Lease where the date of such review occurs prior to Completion but the reviewed rent has not been agreed or determined by Completion:

9.4.1   the Seller confirms that:

(i)   it has and will in the period up to Completion take all necessary action to preserve and safeguard the Landlords' rights to effect the outstanding reviews;

(ii)   no agreement has been reached in relation to the reviewed rent in any of the outstanding reviews and none of the outstanding reviews has been either waived or referred to a third party for determination.

9.4.2   The Seller will, immediately after the Conclusion Date (in so far as not already done) provide the Purchaser with a copy of all written material in its possession relative to the outstanding reviews.

9.4.3   In the period from the date of this offer until Completion, the Seller will, immediately after receipt, advise the Purchaser in writing of all written communications from the relevant Tenants or their advisers in connection with the outstanding reviews and will not take any action except as instructed in writing by the Purchaser (who will act reasonably in the matter and timeously comply with the obligations of the Seller, as Landlords, failing which the Purchaser will indemnify the Seller in respect of all liability incurred by the Tenants in relation to the outstanding reviews).

9.4.4   The Purchaser will take over the conduct of the outstanding reviews with effect from Completion and the Purchaser will have freedom at its discretion as to the manner in and level at which each of the outstanding reviews is settled.

9.4.5   For the avoidance of doubt, the Purchaser will have no liability or responsibility for the fees and costs of any agents or advisers appointed by the Seller in regard to the outstanding reviews.]

Note: There may be no outstanding rent reviews under any of the leases, but if there are, then the seller must conduct any discussions or negotiations in the best interests of the landlord of the building, which is, of course, soon to be the purchaser. In other words, the seller cannot take the view that the outcome of rent review negotiations no longer matters, just because it is soon to relinquish any interest in the property. Accordingly, the purchaser really runs the show through the seller, until the property changes hands, when it will pick up the negotiations direct with the tenant (usually through respective agents). Any portion of the increased rent due to the seller will be dealt with in accordance with Clause 5.4 of the offer.

(p) 10 Completion

10.1 At Completion, the Purchaser will:

10.1.1   pay the Completion Payment (and any VAT on the Price) to the Seller in terms of Clause 2.1.

10.1.2   [deliver to the Seller, duly executed by the
Purchaser, the Back Letters.]

10.2 In exchange for the items referred to in Clause 10.1, at
Completion the Seller will deliver to the Purchaser:

10.2.1   Disposition

the Disposition duly executed by the Seller.

10.2.2   Title Deeds

(i)   the Title Deeds; [and

(ii) all necessary links in title evidencing the
Seller's exclusive ownership of the Property].

10.2.3   Leases

the Leases [and the Subleases].

10.2.4   Disclosed Documents

the Disclosed Documents.

10.2.5   Property Searches

(i)   [Form 10/11 Reports brought down to a date as
near as practicable to Completion and showing
no entries adverse to the Seller's interest in the
Property]

(ii) [Form 12/13 Reports brought down to a date as
near as practicable to Completion and showing
no entries adverse to the Seller's interest in the
Property]

(iii) [Search in the Register of Community Interests
in Land brought down as near as practicable to
Completion showing nothing prejudicial to the
ability of the Seller validly to transfer title to
the Property to the Purchaser [or its
nominees]]

the cost of the Reports and Search being the
responsibility of the Seller.

10.2.6   Charges Searches

Searches in the Register of Charges and Company
File of the Seller [(including a Search to identify

the directors and the secretary of the Seller as at the date of signing the Disposition)] from the date of its incorporation or the date of inception of the Register (whichever is the later) brought down:

(i) as near as practicable to Completion; and

(ii) within 3 months following Completion, to a date at least thirty six days after Completion

in both cases disclosing no entry prejudicial to the Purchaser's [or its nominees] interest.

10.2.7 Letter of Obligation

a letter of obligation from the Seller's Solicitors in the appropriate form published by The Property Standardisation Group (www.psglegal.co.uk).

10.2.8 [VAT Invoice

a valid VAT invoice addressed to the Purchaser.]

10.2.9 [Discharge/Deed of Restriction

a discharge/deed of restriction duly executed by the heritable creditor in any standard security affecting the Property together with completed and signed application forms for recording/registration and payment for the correct amount of recording/registration dues.]

10.2.10 [Letter of Consent and Non-crystallisation

a letter of consent and non-crystallisation in the holder's usual form (releasing the Property from charge or otherwise in terms that confer a valid title on the Purchaser [or its nominees] subject to compliance with any time limit for registration of the Purchaser's title) in respect of the transaction envisaged by the Missives from each holder of a floating charge granted by the Seller.]

10.2.11 [Retrocession of Assignation of Rents]

a retrocession of assignation of rents duly executed by the creditor in terms of the draft forming Part [17] of the Schedule]

10.2.12 Change of Landlord

a notice of change of landlord in terms of the draft notice forming Part [7] of the Schedule addressed to each of the Tenants and signed by the Seller's Solicitors.

10.2.13 [Assignation of Guarantees

the assignation of guarantees in terms of the draft forming Part [13] of the Schedule duly executed by the Seller.]

10.2.14 [Assignation of Service Contracts

the assignation of service contracts in terms of the draft forming Part [15] of the Schedule duly executed by the Seller and, if required, by the Service Providers (as defined in it).]

10.2.15 [Assignation of Rent Deposits

the assignation of rent deposits in terms of the draft forming Part [16] of the Schedule duly executed by the Seller.]

10.2.16 Other Documents

any other deeds and documents to be delivered to the Purchaser on or before Completion in terms of the Missives.

Note: This clause lists all of the items which the seller and the purchaser are required to deliver to each other, and provides a useful checklist for both parties of the items that they are expected to deliver or receive. It is also recommended that the parties use a Completion Checklist (see Chapter 11) which not only helps to keep track of items and issues with which the parties have to deal by completion, but also identifies who is responsible for obtaining, completing or delivering each item. Last minute disasters because each party thought the other was dealing with some item are to be avoided at all costs.

Where the title to the property is still in the Sasine Register (meaning the transaction will induce a first registration) or where the property is still undergoing first registration and a Land Certificate has not yet been issued, it would be appropriate for the Purchaser's due diligence to include a check against any other corporate owners of the Property during the prescriptive period. Appropriate alternative wording in this situation is:

'Searches in the Register of Charges and Company File of every limited company having an interest in the Property in the prescriptive period (including, where appropriate, a search to identify the directors and secretary of the granter as at the date of signing of the disposition or other deed divesting such company of its interest in the Property) in each case from the date of their incorporation or the date of inception of the Register (whichever is the later) brought down to the date twenty-two days after the date of recording of the disposition or other deed divesting such company of its interest in the Property in each case disclosing no entry prejudicial to the Purchaser's interest.'

(q) 11 Insurance

11.1 From the Conclusion Date until Completion, the Seller will keep the Property insured in accordance with the Landlords' obligations under the Leases. As soon as reasonably practicable after the Conclusion Date, the Seller will make available to the Purchaser written details of such insurances, if it has not already provided this information.

11.2 Immediately following the Conclusion Date, the Seller will use its reasonable endeavours to have the Purchaser's interest in the Property (as purchaser, price unpaid) endorsed or noted on or otherwise (either specifically or generically) covered by its policies of insurance and will exhibit evidence to the Purchaser that it has done so.

11.3 The Seller will:

11.3.1 within 5 Working Days after Completion cancel such insurances (under reservation of all prior claims), and

11.3.2 provided that the insurance premiums have been paid in full by the Tenants in question, within 5 Working Days of receipt, refund to the relevant

> Tenants all repayments of premium due to them and
> exhibit evidence to the Purchaser of having done so.

Note: This provides what is fairly standard procedure in handover of commercial let property. Usually under an FRI lease, although the tenants pay for the cost of insurance, it is the landlord that actually arranges it (through the managing agents if there are any) and there will be obligations to do so in terms of the leases. Insurance companies will not always note a purchaser's interest on the policy, but this is usually a matter for the managing agents to deal with, and the solicitors do not normally get involved. There will be an adjustment to be done with the tenants once the property changes hands, as they are likely to have paid the insurance premium in advance. On cancellation of the policy there is likely to be some repayment of premium due, and the purchaser will need to set up his own insurance arrangements. Again this is usually a matter for the managing agents to attend to.

(r) 12 Damage or Destruction

12.1   Risk of damage to or destruction of the Property will not pass to the Purchaser until Completion.

12.2   If prior to Completion the Property sustains damage (whether insured or otherwise) which at common law would entitle a hypothetical tenant under a hypothetical lease of the Property to an abatement of rent of an amount exceeding [20%] of the rent, either party will be entitled to resile from the Missives without penalty on delivery of written notice to that effect to the other's solicitors no later than midday on the date on which Completion is due to take place, time being of the essence.

12.3   If there is any dispute as to whether the Property has suffered such damage, the matter will be referred to the decision of an independent surveyor, who will act as an expert, appointed, failing agreement, by the Chairman of the RICS in Scotland on application by either party. The independent surveyor's decision will be binding on the parties. If the independent surveyor dies, delays or becomes unwilling or incapable of acting then either the Seller or the Purchaser may apply to the

Chairman to discharge that independent surveyor and appoint a replacement. The fees and expenses of the independent surveyor and the cost of appointment are payable by the Seller and the Purchaser in the proportions which the independent surveyor directs and if no direction is made, equally.

12.4 Subject to Clause 12.2 if the Property is damaged or destroyed by an insured risk prior to Completion, the Seller's responsibility to the Purchaser, at Completion, will be:

12.4.1   to pay to the Purchaser the insurance proceeds received by the Seller to the extent that they have not been spent on reinstatement; and

12.4.2   to assign its rights in respect of the insurance proceeds specified in Clause 12.4.1 to the Purchaser.

Note: As with missives for residential properties, the common law rule (that the risk of damage or destruction of property passes to a purchaser on conclusion of missives) is also generally displaced in commercial property transactions. The seller will retain the risk until completion and maintain insurance until that time. The provisions about what is to happen if there is damage or destruction are a little bit more complicated, as the commercial property might be quite a large building, and even serious damage might not render it totally incapable of use. The rule of thumb concerning abatement (suspension) of rent is intended to be a reasonably objective test as to how much damage constitutes sufficient damage to entitle either party to resile. Even then the parties might not agree, particularly if the extent of the damage is borderline, and so reference to an independent third party expert is provided. If the purchaser decides to go ahead with the purchase anyway, then provision is made about transferring, or assigning rights to, the insurance proceeds to the purchaser.

It is also worth considering whether, even if the property were to be destroyed or seriously damaged, the purchaser might want to proceed anyway (eg where the Leases are about to expire and the Property is being purchased for re-development) in which case the purchaser would not necessarily want the seller to have a right to resile. The right of either party to resile is the standard starting off point, but in these circumstances the reference to 'either party' should then be amended.

(s) 13 Statutory Matters

13.1 Statute

[Subject to Clause 7,] the Purchaser is deemed to have satisfied itself on the application of all statute and statutory regulations and rules in so far as affecting or relating to the Property and, except as expressly provided for in the Missives, the Seller gives no warranties or assurances on such matters.

13.2 Statutory Repairs Notices

Any local authority statutory repairs notices (other than any notice or requirement of any Environmental Authority made pursuant to any Environmental Law (as such terms are defined in Clause [14])) affecting the Property which are issued prior to Completion will as between the Purchaser and the Seller be the responsibility of the Seller except to the extent that (i) they are instigated by or with the authority of the Purchaser or (ii) they are the responsibility of any of the Tenants in accordance with the Leases. Liability under this Clause will subsist until met and will not be avoided by the issue of a fresh notice.

13.3 Energy Performance Certificate

The Seller confirms that a valid current energy performance certificate (in terms of the Energy Performance of Buildings (Scotland) Regulations 2008) has been obtained for, and affixed to, the Property.

Note: The Seller will exhibit the usual PECs from which the purchaser will be deemed to have satisfied itself as to all statutory matters.

If the property is affected by any statutory repairs, this Offer provides that liability will remain with the seller. Practice varies in different parts of the country as to whether liability for statutory notices passes to the purchaser on conclusion of missives or at completion, and compare this with the option (conclusion of missives) that has been chosen in the Combined Standard Clauses for residential purchases (see para 6.10(e)). However the provision is qualified with reference to repairs notices instigated by the purchaser or which are the responsibility of the tenants under the leases.

Reference is made here to the requirement for an EPC for the property.

For multi occupancy buildings there might be several EPCs relating to different parts of the Property and the common parts, or a single EPC for the whole building.

(t) 14 Environmental

14.1 Definitions

In Clauses 13.2 and 14:

'**Environment**' means any and all organisms (including humans), ecosystems, natural or man-made buildings or structures, and the following media:

(i) air (including air within buildings or structures, whether above or below ground)

(ii) water (including surface and ground water and water in wells, boreholes, pipes, sewers and drains); and

(iii) land (including surface land and sub-surface strata and any land under seabeds or rivers, wetlands or flood plains);

'**Environmental Authority**' means any person or legal entity (whether statutory or non-statutory or governmental or non-governmental) having regulatory authority under Environmental Law and/or any court of law or tribunal or any other judicial or quasi-judicial body;

'**Environmental Law**' means all laws, regulations, directives, statutes, subordinate legislation, rules of common law and generally all international, EU, national and local laws and all judgments, orders, instructions, decisions, guidance awards, codes of practice and other lawful statements of any Environmental Authority applying from time to time in relation to the Property in respect of pollution of or protection of the Environment or the production, processing, treatment, storage, transport or disposal of Hazardous Substances, in each case insofar as having the force of law;

'**Hazardous Substances**' means any natural or artificial substance (whether in solid or liquid form or in the form of a gas or vapour and whether alone or in combination with any other substance) capable of causing harm to the Environment and/or harm to the health of living organisms or other interference with the ecological systems of which they form part and/or harm to property and/or in the case of humans, offence caused to any sense;

14.2 Agreement as to Environmental Liabilities

The Seller and the Purchaser agree that:

14.2.1 if any notice or requirement of any Environmental Authority made pursuant to Environmental Law is served on or made of either of them in respect of the Property or any Hazardous Substances attributable to the Property, then, as between the Seller and the Purchaser, the sole responsibility for complying with such notice or requirement is to rest with the Purchaser to the exclusion of the Seller; and

14.2.2 if any Environmental Authority wishes to recover costs incurred by it in carrying out any investigation, assessment, monitoring, removal, remedial or risk mitigation works under Environmental Law in respect of the Property or any Hazardous Substances attributable to the Property from either or both of the Seller and the Purchaser then, as between the Seller and the Purchaser, the sole responsibility for the payment of such costs\is to rest with the Purchaser to the exclusion of the Seller.

The agreements outlined under Clauses 14.2.1 and 14.2.2 are made with the intention that any Environmental Authority serving any notice or seeking to recover any costs should give effect to the agreements pursuant to the statutory guidance issued under Part IIA of the Environmental Protection Act 1990.

The Seller and the Purchaser agree that the appropriate Environmental Authority may be notified in writing of the provisions of Clause 14 if required to give effect to the agreements outlined under Clauses 14.2.1 and 14.2.2.

14.3 Sold with Information

14.3.1   The Purchaser acknowledges to the Seller that:

(i)   [it has been provided with the following reports, surveys and other environmental information prior to the date of this offer:

[   ];]

(ii) [it has carried out its own investigations of the Property for the purposes of ascertaining whether, and if so the extent to which, Hazardous Substances are present in, on, under or over the Property;]

(iii) such information [gathered through those investigations] is sufficient to make the Purchaser aware of the presence in, on, under or over the Property of any Hazardous Substances referred to in the reports;

(iv) it relies at its own risk on the contents of any report, plan and other written material and information either disclosed to it or orally communicated to it by or on behalf of the Seller both as to the condition of the Property and as to the nature and effect of any remedial works which may have been carried out [(including but not limited to the Report by [   ] dated [   ])] and no warranty is given or representation made by or on behalf of the Seller in this respect; and

(v)   it has satisfied itself as to the condition of the Property.

14.3.2   Both parties agree that:

(i)   [both the Purchaser and the Seller are [large commercial organisations] [public bodies]] [the Purchaser is a large commercial organisation and the Seller is a large public body] [the Seller is a large commercial organisation and the Purchaser is a large public body];

193

(ii) the Purchaser has been given permission and adequate opportunity to carry out its own investigations of the Property for the purpose of ascertaining whether, and if so the extent to which, Hazardous Substances are present in, on, under or over the Property;

(iii) the transfer of the Property pursuant to the Missives is an open market arm's length transaction; and

(iv) the Seller will not retain any interest in the Property or any rights to occupy or use the Property following Completion.

14.3.3   The acknowledgements in this Clause 14.3 are made in order to exclude the Seller from liability under Part IIA of the Environmental Protection Act 1990 so that the Seller is not an appropriate person, as defined therein.

14.4 Environmental Indemnity

The Purchaser will indemnify the Seller in respect of all and any actions, losses, damages, liabilities, charges, claims, costs and expenses which may be paid, incurred, suffered or sustained by the Seller arising (directly or indirectly) out of or in connection with the presence of any Hazardous Substances in, on or under the Property or migrating to or from the Property.

Note: This standardised clause is very much in favour of the seller, and assumes that if there are any environmental issues in respect of the property, there has already been agreement in principle between the parties, and that there will be a 'clean break' at completion, with liability transferring from the seller to the purchaser at that date. This approach is suitable for example when there are no environmental issues, but it is up to the purchaser to have conducted any necessary investigations and surveys to satisfy itself about the extent, if any, of environmental issues affecting the property.

Be aware however that in each transaction, the environmental provisions should be carefully considered to ensure that they reflect the parties' intentions, and if there are likely to be any issues, advice should be sought from environmental specialists, and alternative wording to reflect, for example, the 'polluter pays' principle may then have to be negotiated. It is beyond the scope of this work to consider such issues, however.

If environmental reports relating to the property have been previously obtained, the parties should consider whether these can be readdressed to the purchaser, to allow it to rely on the benefit of such reports.

(u) 15 [Moveables

The Moveables comprise all the moveable items owned by the Seller in connection with and located at the Property and will be included in the sale without further payment or other consideration. They will be handed over to the Purchaser at Completion in their then current condition free from any hire purchase, lease or credit agreements, licences, reservations, retention of title or other encumbrances whatsoever.]

Note: It will be a question of fact whether there are any moveables belonging to the seller that are included in the sale, and these should be listed in the Schedule. Such moveable items as are listed are included in the Price.

(v) 16 No Employees

16.1 As at the Conclusion Date and Completion, the Seller confirms that there are no persons to whom the provisions of the Transfer of Undertakings (Protection of Employment) Regulations 2006 (**'Employment Regulations'**) will apply in relation to:

16.1.1   the sale of the Property and

16.1.2   the creation or cessation of any contractual relationship consequent to such sale

with the effect of such person's employment (or liability for it and its termination) being deemed to transfer to the Purchaser [or any contractor of the Purchaser] at Completion.

16.2 If it is asserted or found by a court or tribunal that the Employment Regulations apply in relation to any person

('**Employee**'), the Purchaser [or any of its contractors] may terminate the employment of the Employee within 10 Working Days, where it has not already terminated, and if the Purchaser complies with its obligations under this Clause 16 (where applicable), the Seller undertakes to keep the Purchaser [and/ or its contractors] indemnified, on demand, against all costs, claims, liabilities and expenses (including reasonable legal expenses) of any nature arising out of the employment of the Employee prior to Completion or the termination of it (whether it is terminated by the Purchaser or any other person and whether before, on or after Completion).

16.3 [The Seller acknowledges and agrees that the Purchaser will grant an indemnity in favour of each and any of its contractors to the same extent that the Seller is undertaking to indemnify the Purchaser in terms of Clause 16 and agrees that in the event of a claim on any indemnity in terms of Clause 16 for loss incurred by the Purchaser, that loss will include the amount, if any, which the Purchaser has paid or is required to pay to any of its contractors by virtue of any indemnity granted by the Purchaser in accordance with the provisions of Clause 16.]

Note: This is another area where specialist advice may be necessary. If there are employment issues, then potentially the Transfer of Undertakings (Protection of Employment) Regulations 2006 (TUPE) could apply. A solicitor experienced in employment law should be consulted.

For the purposes of the Offer, it is assumed that there are no employees who are transferring from the Seller to the Purchaser and that therefore no TUPE issues arise. However, if there are employees and there are actual or potential TUPE issues, then advice should be taken from employment specialists, and specific provisions to cater for the actual circumstances will need to be drafted.

(w) 17 [Guarantees

17.1 In so far as the Seller can validly do so, the guarantees will be assigned to the Purchaser in terms of the draft assignation of guarantees forming Part [13] of the Schedule.

17.2 The Purchaser will:

17.2.1 within 15 Working Days after Completion duly execute the assignation of guarantees delivered to the Purchaser at Completion; and

17.2.2 within 20 Working Days after Completion, intimate the assignation of guarantees to the appropriate parties and deliver a copy of the intimation to the Seller.]

Note: It is quite common, particularly if the tenant is a subsidiary company in a larger group of companies, or is newly formed and so does not yet have a track record to show that it is a reliable (known as a tenant's 'covenant'), that the landlord will have sought a guarantee, usually from a parent company, which will provide that if the tenant defaults in any of its obligations under the lease, the parent company will step in and meet the obligations. Where such guarantees have been given, they need to be assigned to the purchaser, and you need to check whether the original guarantee is capable of being assigned. Note that the guarantee may appear in the body of the lease or in a separate document.

Although it is unlikely that the consent of the guarantor will be required to assignation of the guarantee, this should be checked. A style of Assignation of Guarantees is attached to the principle style Offer (part 13 of the Schedule).

(x) 18 [Service Contracts

18.1 Liability

With effect from Completion, the Purchaser will accept and take over liability for the Service Contracts and accordingly the Purchaser will, in respect of the period following Completion, keep the Seller indemnified from all liability arising under the Service Contracts.

18.2 Assignation

18.2.1 In so far as the Seller can validly do so, the Service Contracts will be assigned to the Purchaser in terms of the draft assignation of service contracts forming Part [15] of the Schedule.

18.2.2 The Purchaser will:

(i) within 15 Working Days after Completion duly execute the assignation of service contracts delivered to the Purchaser at Completion; and

(ii) within 20 Working Days after Completion, intimate the assignation of service contracts to the appropriate parties and deliver a copy of the intimation to the Seller.

18.3 Termination

The Purchaser will have no responsibility for any [other] service, maintenance, management or similar contracts relating to the Property entered into by the Seller (or its predecessors in title) prior to Completion and [(subject to Clause 18.1)] the Seller will, in respect of the period following Completion, indemnify the Purchaser from all liability arising under such contracts. The cancellation costs of any such contracts will be met by the Seller out of its own funds and will not, as between the Seller and the Purchaser, qualify as allowable expenditure for the purposes of any service charge calculations.]

Note: This clause contains practical arrangements for transferring any service, maintenance or management contracts to the purchaser, assuming they are transferable and/or assignable. The seller will be responsible for dealing with any existing service, management and/or maintenance contracts which the purchaser is not taking over, and for any termination costs that might be applied (which would not be allowable expenditure under the service charge provisions). Again a style of Assignation is attached in the Schedule to the principal style offer.

(y) 19 Capital Allowances

19.1 [The Seller confirms that it has not claimed or permitted any claim and that it will not claim or permit any claim for any capital allowances in respect of the Fixed Plant contained within the Property.]

19.2 [The Purchaser will make an election with the Seller under s
198 of the Capital Allowances Act 2001 in terms of the draft
contained in Part [10] of the Schedule, in which case:

    19.2.1 on Completion, the Seller and the Purchaser will
sign in duplicate the election agreeing the value of
Fixed Plant in accordance with the apportionment
set out in the election, being the disposal value for
the Fixed Plant required to be brought into account
by the Seller and falling to be treated as expenditure
incurred by the Purchaser on the provision of the
Fixed Plant and the Seller confirms that the amount
attributed to the Fixed Plant in the election is not
in excess of the aggregate amount treated for the
purposes of the Capital Allowances Act 2001 as
having been paid by the Seller for the Fixed Plant;

    19.2.2 both the Seller and the Purchaser will submit the
election to HMRC within the time limit prescribed
by law and take all reasonable steps to procure that
the value is accepted by HMRC.

    19.2.3 the Seller and the Purchaser agree to reflect such
value in their relevant tax computations and returns.]

19.3 The Seller will use reasonable endeavours to provide, or
procure that its agents provide:

    19.3.1 copies of all relevant information in its possession or
that of its agents, and

    19.3.2 such cooperation and assistance as the Purchaser
may reasonably require

to enable the Purchaser to make and substantiate claims under
the Capital Allowances Act 2001 in respect of the Property.

19.4 The Purchaser agrees that it will:

    19.4.1 use the information provided pursuant to Clause
19.3 only for the stated purpose; and

    19.4.2 not disclose, without the reasonable consent of
the Seller, any such information which the Seller
expressly provides on a confidential basis.

Note: This clause provides alternative wording depending upon the actual circumstances relating to claiming capital allowances. Where an election is to be made, Part 10 of the Schedule to the principal Offer contains a form of election notice for the parties to complete and sign. A distinction needs to be made between the property and fittings and fixtures. There are detailed notes attached to the style of Capital Allowances Election attached to the style Offer itself.

(z) 20 Access

Subject to the terms of the Leases access to the Property prior to the Date of Entry will be given to the Purchaser, its surveyors and other professional advisers [with machinery, plant and equipment] for all reasonable purposes (including examining the Property), provided that the Purchaser will ensure that in doing so they:

(i)   comply with the Seller's reasonable requirements,

(ii) comply with the access restrictions imposed on the Landlords under the Leases; and

(iii) exercise reasonable restraint and make good all loss, injury and damage caused to the Property.

(aa) 21 [Confidentiality

21.1 Pre-Completion

The Purchaser and the Seller will not disclose details of the Missives or the acquisition of the Property by the Purchaser to the press or otherwise prior to Completion except:

21.1.1   with the [prior written consent] [reasonable consent] of the other party;

21.1.2   to the Purchaser and the Seller's respective agents and professional advisers in connection with the acquisition/sale of the Property;

21.1.3   to the Purchaser's bankers or other providers of finance (and their professional advisers) in connection with the acquisition of the Property;

21.1.4   where required by law; and

21.1.5   where required to comply with the requirements of the Stock Exchange or any other regulatory or government authority.

21.2 [Post-Completion

Any press release after Completion relating to the acquisition/sale of the Property is to be agreed in writing between the Purchaser and the Seller prior to its publication (both parties acting reasonably).]

21.3 Agents

The Purchaser and the Seller will ensure that their respective agents and professional advisers

Note: There may be many reasons why the parties to a commercial transaction wish to keep the terms of the deal, or even the existence of the deal itself, confidential. Usually the parties will want to keep the transaction and other details confidential prior to completion and, if there is to be any press release, to control both its content and timing. Where confidentiality is required this should extend to agents and professional advisers as well, and they should be informed of this.

(bb) 22 Formal Documentation

22.1 Formal Documentation Required

Neither the Seller nor the Purchaser will be bound by any acceptance of this offer or any other letter purporting to form part of the Missives or any amendment or variation of the Missives unless it is duly executed.

22.2 Complete Agreement

The Missives (including the annexations) will represent and express the full and complete agreement between the Seller and the Purchaser relating to the sale of the Property at the Conclusion Date and will supersede any previous agreements between the Seller and the Purchaser relating to it. Neither the Seller nor the Purchaser has been induced to enter into the Missives on account of any prior warranties or representations.

Note: This provision ensures that the missives are to be properly executed to be effective, and that the Missives record the complete agreement between the parties in relation to the purchase and sale of the Property.

This clause serves the same purpose as the Entire Agreement clause in the Combined Standard Clauses in the Residential offer (see para 6.10(y)).

(cc) 23 Supersession

> The provisions of the Missives (other than Clauses [2.4, 8.6, 14, 16 and 19] which will remain in full force and effect until implemented) in so far as not implemented by the granting and delivery of the Disposition and others, will remain in full force and effect until:
>
> 23.1   in the case of the lease confirmations given in Clause [9] [six] years after the Date of Entry; and
>
> 23.2   in the case of all other provisions the earlier of:
>
> > 23.2.1   the date when such provisions have been implemented; and
> >
> > 23.2.2   [two years] after the Date of Entry except in so far as they are founded on in any court proceedings which have commenced within such [two year] period.

Note: As with the Combined Standard Clauses for residential offers, the commercial missives also provide for the contract to continue only for a period of two years (see commentary at para 6.10(v) and also para 8.10(i)), other than the clauses specified, and of course there is no reason why the supersession provisions cannot be tailored to suit the particulars of the transaction and a shorter or longer period specified.

However, specific provision has been made for the lease confirmations provided in clause 9 to remain in force for a period of six years. The reason for this significantly longer period is that, if any of the confirmations are incorrect, the time when that would be most likely to come to light would be when the next rent review negotiations with the tenants take place. A period of six years assumes a 5-year review cycle (which is typical) and an extra year to cover any delays in carrying out a review, so a shorter or longer period would be appropriate if the rent review cycle is different.

(dd) 24 Exclusion of Personal Liability

> 24.1   No personal liability will attach to the Purchaser's Solicitors by virtue of their entering into the Missives in their capacity as agents for the Purchaser.

24.2 No personal liability will attach to the Seller's Solicitors by virtue of their entering into the Missives in their capacity as agents for the Seller.

24.3 The Seller and the Purchaser will be solely liable to each other for compliance with, and fulfilment of, their respective obligations under the Missives.

Note: These provisions are to make it clear that both the purchaser's solicitors and the seller's solicitors are acting as agents only for their respective clients. It is principally relevant where either or both solicitors act for foreign parties such as offshore and foreign registered companies and nominees.

(ee) 25 [Assignation

The Purchaser may not (whether at common law or otherwise):

(i)   assign, transfer, grant any security interest over, hold on trust or deal in any other manner with the benefit of the whole or any part of its interest in the Missives;

(ii) sub-contract any or all of its obligations under the Missives; nor

(iii) purport to do any of the foregoing.]

Note: This is a default position, but can be changed if, in the particular circumstances of a transaction, there is no objection to assignation, although the parties would have to consider what requirements would be necessary in the event of assignation (eg consent of the other party). The seller cannot be constrained in the same way in respect of any possible dealings on his part, provided he does nothing to put him in breach of the conditions of the missives.

26   Proper Law and Prorogation

The Missives and the rights and obligations of the Seller and the Purchaser will be governed by and construed in accordance with the law of Scotland and the Seller and the Purchaser will be deemed to have agreed to submit to the non-exclusive jurisdiction of the Scottish courts.

27   Time Limit

This offer, if not previously withdrawn, will fall unless a binding written acceptance has been received by us by 5 pm on [   ] 20[ ].

Yours faithfully

THE SCHEDULE

The style offer contains a Schedule of 17 parts, which include style documents, or spaces for transactional documents to be inserted, once drafted and agreed. Accordingly, once it has been tailored to suit the transaction, the Offer to Sell and all the parts of the Schedule (to which of course more parts can be added, and those parts that are not applicable, removed) provides a comprehensive document for the transaction and recording the agreement between the parties, and also what the parties need to do at completion.

Part 1 of the Schedule is replicated below, showing the typical documents that will form the 'Disclosed Documents' for the purposes of the transaction (see Clauses 6, 7 and 10 of the Offer).

Part 1 – Disclosed Documents

1   Title Deeds
2   Leases
3   [Subleases]
4   Property enquiry certificate(s) dated [   ]
5   [Note: complete to include
    ● coal mining searches
    ● planning and building warrant documents
    ● VAT documents
    ● construction documents (appointments, building contract, collateral warranties, Health & Safety File etc)
    ● if either of the last two rent reviews under any of the Leases have been referred to third party for determination, all

submissions, counter submissions and determinations in connection with such reviews

- rent payment schedule
- service charge records for last [3] years (including payment history, estimates, reconciliations etc)
- details of any servitudes, rights of way or similar rights other than as disclosed in the Title Deeds
- other searches or documents]

Part 2 – Title Deeds

An inventory identifying the title deeds (together with a description of whether they are principals, Extracts, or quick/photo copies) relating to the Property should be listed in this Part of the Schedule.

Part 3 – Leases/Subleases

An inventory identifying the leases and subleases (together with a description of whether they are principals, Extracts or quick/photo copies) and any relevant documents to the letting of any part of the Property (eg outstanding applications for consent) should be listed in Parts 3A and 3B respectively of the Schedule.

Part 4 – Disclosures against Lease Confirmations

Full details of any disclosures which the Seller needs to make to any of the confirmations about the Leases should be provided here. If there are none, that should be stated.

Part 5 – Back Letters

The drafts of all of the current Back Letters which are to be granted by the Purchaser to the Tenants at Completion should be incorporated here.

Part 6 – Current Management Transactions

Full details of all management transactions (ie applications by tenants for consent to assign, carry out alterations, rent review discussions etc) which the Seller is entitled to complete should be provided here.

Part 7 – Notice of Change of Landlord

A Notice of Change of Landlord will need to be completed for each of the Tenants. Although not essential, you may want to consider sending it by Recorded Delivery as proof of postage. If there is no Retrocession of an Assignation of Rents then the third paragraph incorporating the intimation of it needs to be deleted. See also Chapter 11 for matters to be dealt with at and after completion.

Part 8 – Disposition

It is suggested that a copy of the proposed Disposition be attached to the Missives in this Part of the Schedule.

Part 9 - Plan

A clear plan of the Property should be included here, where required.

Part 10 – Capital Allowances Election

On the disposal of a property which contains fixtures on which the seller has claimed capital allowances, the seller is required to apportion part of the sale price to those fixtures. This apportionment will affect the amount of allowances available to the seller in the future and, in certain circumstances, could result in a tax change. Equally, the purchaser will be required to apportion part of the price to the fixtures to determine the capital allowances which the purchaser will be able to claim on the fixtures. The purpose of an election under s 198 of the Capital Allowances Act 2001 is to fix the apportionment to the fixtures. A style of Election is contained in Part 10 of the Schedule and the Guidance Notes that accompany the style Offer to Sell contain further details.

Part 11 – Capital Goods Scheme

The assets to be transferred to the Purchaser to which the Capital Goods Scheme applies should be listed in this part of the Schedule.

Part 12 – Moveables

Any moveable items included in the sale and included in the Price are to be listed here.

Part 13 – Assignation of Guarantees

This part of the Schedule contains a style Assignation of Guarantees, which, if it applies, should be completed incorporating details of the guarantees and any leases which incorporate guarantees.

Part 14 – Service Contracts

The existing service, maintenance and/or management contracts which the Purchaser is taking over should be listed here.

Part 15 – Assignation of Service Contracts

If there are service contracts to assign, this style document should be used.

Part 16 – Assignation of Rent Deposits

Likewise, where there are Rent Deposits to be assigned to the purchaser this style Assignation of Rent Deposits should be completed incorporating details of the existing rent deposits which are being taken over by the purchaser.

Part 17 - Retrocession of Assignation of Rents

The draft of the retrocession of assignation of rents referred to in clause 10.2.11 of the Offer should be inserted here, if applicable.

SUSPENSIVE CONDITIONS

6.14 (a) Conditionality

Properly completed missives which represent *consensus ad idem* ('complete agreement to the same thing') between the parties constitute a legally binding contract. It is, however, possible to conclude missives that are nonetheless conditional on some event or events happening, and which, if they do not happen, or do not happen in the way specified in the contract, will entitle one or both parties to withdraw from the contract. These are called conditional missives and they contain suspensive conditions – that is: conditions that suspend the final binding effect of the missives until the terms of the condition are met.

In fact, most missives for the purchase of property, both residential and commercial, contain some element of conditionality. There is a distinction to be made between suspensive conditions and resolutive conditions, and it is not always clear where the distinction lies (see K Reid and GL Gretton *Conveyancing* 3rd edn para 3-20). Sometimes in fact the terminology is conflated, and the contract will say that it is subject to 'the following suspensive and resolutive conditions'. From a practical point of view to the parties, the distinction may not matter. If the suspensive condition is not purified or if the resolutive condition does not come to pass, either the contract automatically falls or the parties can terminate it. Either way the matter does not proceed and the parties walk away from the arrangement.

(b) Subject to survey

The simplest and most common suspensive condition is the 'subject to survey' clause often found in both residential and commercial offers. The offer is submitted with price, date of entry and all the other conditions, but is declared to be suspensively conditional on a satisfactory survey being obtained. The effect of this is that even if the seller were to issue a *de plano* acceptance, the purchaser would not be bound to the contract until the survey clause had been satisfied, or 'purified', in the language of suspensive conditions.

The intention behind making an offer conditional on obtaining a satisfactory survey, is to find out first of all if the price and other conditions are acceptable to the seller, before spending money on getting the property surveyed. Although the availability of the single survey in the Home Report should mean that a purchaser of residential property has a clear idea of value and basic condition, there could be a number of reasons why the purchaser wants to have her own survey carried out: for example, it may not be clear if her lender will accept the single survey report, or the Home Report may have disclosed matters that require a more specialised survey to be conducted, and the purchaser wants to obtain more detail as to condition before definitely committing to the price or indeed the purchase. A typical survey clause in a residential offer will say:

> This offer and any contract to follow hereon are entirely conditional upon (a) a satisfactory survey report and (b) a satisfactory valuation report being obtained by the Purchaser in respect of the Property. The Purchaser and her lenders will be the sole judges as to what constitutes satisfactory reports.

Sometimes a time limit by which the satisfactory reports must be obtained will be stated, but more often than not, there will be none, and the usual procedure is for the seller's solicitors to indicate acceptance either by phone or informally by email, or if formally in writing, deleting the survey condition. The purchaser then needs to organise the survey as soon as possible and if all is well, confirms that the position is satisfactory and accepts deletion of the survey clause. Strictly speaking the condition is not purified – it is removed from the contract. It would be unusual, but not entirely unheard of, for residential missives to be concluded with a subject to survey clause still to be purified, since price and condition are such fundamental elements of whether the purchaser proceeds or not, the seller will prefer to know that these essentials are agreed before putting time and effort into tying the property into a contract, and equally the purchaser will not want time and effort to be put into other aspects of the purchase (the missives will also contain other time limits about satisfaction with title and searches), until it is clear that the property itself is acceptable.

For commercial purchasers, there is no equivalent to the Single Survey, and so all surveys as to value and condition have to be instructed by the prospective purchaser. Depending on the type of property, this may involve considerable cost which the purchaser will not want to incur until he knows that his offer is otherwise acceptable. The nature of the property might require types of survey that are extensive and involve, not just a valuation, but any of a full measured survey; structural reports; an environmental audit; ground condition and mineral stability assessments; geotechnical reports, site and soil condition examinations or even the requirement to make trial bores and sink pits to ascertain if the land is suitable for the development proposed, eg:

> It will be an essential and suspensive condition of the Missives that the Purchaser obtains reports in terms wholly satisfactory to it (as to which it will be the sole judge) on a full measured survey and structural survey in respect of the Property. The Seller will co-operate with the Purchaser and its surveyors and other agents in arranging such surveys and in securing unrestricted access to the Property. Such surveys will be carried out within [five] working days of the date of conclusion of the Missives [or as soon as reasonably practicable after that date].

Again the seller may prefer simply to allow the purchaser to get on with conducting its surveys before progressing the terms of the contract, but if the suspensive condition is accepted, then it would be usual for a reasonably (but realistically) short time limit to be imposed, with the provision that if the purchaser has not indicated by the expiry of the time limit that the survey is unsatisfactory and has withdrawn, it is deemed to be satisfied and the condition purified. The costs of carrying out site investigations can be considerable, and so the purchaser may not want to incur these costs until he has the protection of a signed contract. Bear in mind however that if site and soil surveys are required, purification can sometimes take three or four months.

(c) Subject to Planning Permission

The purchase of a property or land that is to be developed will invariably be made 'subject to planning'. The offer will contain a suspensive condition, often in considerable detail, that a satisfactory grant of planning permission (and other consents) must be obtained. At the very least, the type of planning permission should be specified – eg 'in principle' or detailed planning permission. Note that it is usual for the definitions section of the offer to contain definitions of a number of the terms that are used throughout the clauses:

1.1 It will be an essential and suspensive condition of the Missives that the Purchaser obtains in terms wholly satisfactory to it (as to which it will be the sole judge):

(i) Planning Permission in principle/detailed Planning Permission for the Development and including any consent to change of use of the Property required for the Development;

(ii) [any other consents required for Development will usually be specified as well, including building warrant, listed building consent etc];

1.2 The Purchaser will submit the Planning Application to the relevant Planning Authority seeking planning permission for the Development within [specify period] after conclusion of the Missives. In the event of such permission being refused or granted subject to conditions which are unacceptable to the Purchaser, the Purchaser will be entitled (but not bound) either (i) to terminate the Missives (without penalty) by written notice to the Seller to that effect or (ii) to appeal against such decision, including, if the Purchaser considers it desirable, by application to the Court of Session.

1.3 The Seller will not object to the Planning Application(s) or concur with or assist any other person in objecting to the Purchaser's Planning Application(s) or any other application for consents, warrants or authorisations made by the Purchaser in respect of the Property;

NB – (i) see below at paras (e) and (f) for further wording for this clause dealing with the essential time limits and long stops; (ii) an essential condition is one that would give rise to material breach.

Often the developer will have a particular type of consent in mind, on which he has based his costings and projections for the viability and profitability of the development, and the price that he is prepared to offer for the land is dependent on the terms of the planning permission that is granted, being in terms that will support the development proposal. This may involve density of units for example. The developer may have calculated the price offered on the basis of obtaining permission for one hundred dwellinghouses, so if planning permission is granted for only seventy five, this will make a considerable difference to the developer's profit and may make the proposal unviable. In these circumstances the offer may provide for the price to be reduced by £X per unit under the developer's optimum number of units, for which consent is actually given. Conversely of course the seller might want the price to be increased by £X per unit above the number of units specified, if consent is actually granted for a higher number.

The seller has an interest in the terms of the consent that is granted, as the price offered is usually dependent on the type of use to which the purchaser intends to put the property. If the seller agrees a price based on construction of a single house, but permission is obtained for ten houses, this considerably increases the value of the land to the purchaser. The seller will want to have clarity over what is to be obtained by way of planning, and the resultant price. However, the developer should be careful about being tied into requirements that are too prescriptive eg providing that planning must be obtained for an office building with a floor area of 3,000 square metres. Unless consent in these precise terms is obtained, the condition will be frustrated, whereas the parties might be equally as happy with a consent for 2,500 square metre offices. Accordingly, consideration should be given to providing sufficient flexibility, so that the respective parties' interests are considered, but the proposal is not frustrated by overly rigid requirements.

Other statutory and other consents may be required for the development and should be specified. This may include roads construction consent, demolition warrants, or consents from SEPA or Scottish Water. Note also that as part of the planning consent, particularly for large-scale developments, the local authority may require the developer to undertake certain planning obligations under s 75 of the Town and Country Planning (Scotland) Act 1997, which may include requirements regarding construction of roads, roundabouts or other infrastructure, for example, or restrictions on types of uses to which the development can be put. Planning obligations that are imposed by virtue of s 75 of TCP(S) A 1997 are an integral part of the planning permission and are usually embodied in a separate document known as a 'Section 75 Agreement', which is registered against the title of the development and the terms of which are effectively burdens on the title to the property. The Section 75 Agreement often needs to be in place before the planning consent is granted.

The Section 75 Agreement can only be granted by the landowner, and since planning permission will not be issued until the Agreement has been signed and registered, it is essential that the Missives bind the seller to sign such an agreement so that the consent can actually be issued. However, in the case of *Cala Management Ltd v Messrs A & E Sorrie* [2009] CSOH 79 an obligation on the landowner to enter into a Section 75 Agreement at the reasonable request of the prospective purchaser created a requirement for the terms of the Section 75 Agreement itself to be reasonable, rather than simply meaning that the request must be reasonable.

There are of course timing issues for the seller in signing a binding agreement affecting what can be done with the land while he still owns it, and the purchaser has not purified the conditions in the contract. The seller may, as a *quid pro quo*, look for confirmation that if the Agreement is signed, the developer will be deemed to be satisfied with the terms of the planning permission, or look for an indemnity against any costs or losses until the title transfer takes place.

The parties may also decide to specify what is to happen if planning permission is refused ie whether the purchaser is to appeal. Once the planning consent is granted, the developer will also want to be assured that it is valid and unchallengeable, and that the planning suspensive condition is not purified until this is established. When planning permission has been granted by the planning authority it may be open to a legal challenge by way of a judicial review. While there are no fixed timescales for when a judicial review can be lodged in Scotland, in England there is a statutory 12-week period in which to mount a challenge and the courts in Scotland broadly follow this timescale. See *CWS v Highland Council* [2008] CSOH 28. It is recommended therefore that at least 14 weeks is allowed for, following the grant of planning permission, before the suspensive planning condition in the missives is purified.

(d) Other conditions

In putting together a site for development, there might be a requirement to acquire other land, and if this is essential for the viability of the development – eg where it is needed to provide access perhaps, then the missives should be made suspensively conditional on acquiring that other land.

It should also be borne in mind that here might be consents or requirements that will be needed once the development has been built out such as an off sales licence for a new supermarket. Again the requirement for such essential components of the overall scheme should be incorporated where appropriate into the purchase contract.

(e) The benefit of the condition

Most suspensive clauses are drawn to allow the purchaser absolute discretion, to avoid arguments, and to allow the purchaser to withdraw a suspensive condition even though the condition has not yet been met. In *Manheath v H & J Banks Ltd* 1966 SLT 42 the contract was subject to a suspensive condition relating to the obtaining of planning permission which had not been obtained by the deadline stated in the condition. When the sellers sought to terminate the contract on that basis, the purchasers said that, as they had written to the sellers stating that the condition was purified, the contract had been concluded. However, whether a condition was for the sole benefit of a party seeking to waive it, was a question to be decided on the terms of the contract, and it was clear from the contract that both parties had an interest in the obtaining of planning permission, so that the purchasers' right to waive the condition was excluded.

In *Imry Property Holdings Ltd v Glasgow Young Men's Christian Association* 1979 SLT 261 the purchasers intimated that they were satisfied with the permissions and consents which had been obtained for the proposed development and accordingly held the relevant suspensive condition to be purified, whereas at the date of their intimation the necessary permissions and consents had not been obtained. The purported purification of the condition by the purchaser was incompetent because the condition required all the necessary permissions to have been actually obtained.

Accordingly suspensive conditions will normally contain wording specifying that the condition is for the benefit of the purchaser only and allowing them to waive the condition should they choose to do so, which will have the same effect as if the condition had in fact been purified:

'This clause will be construed solely for the benefit of the Purchaser and it will be in the sole option of the Purchaser at any time to intimate to the Seller in writing that any or all of the suspensive conditions contained in Clause [   ] is/are waived, in which case the Missives will be deemed purified to that extent.'

A condition that a condition is met 'to the purchaser's complete satisfaction' will be construed as excluding capriciousness and arbitrary actings and will imply a condition of reasonableness (*Gordon District Council v Wimpey Homes Holdings Ltd* 1989 SLT 141).

(f) Time limits

A prudent seller will want to put a time limit on the operation of the condition, so that the parties are not tied into the obligation indefinitely, and prevent giving the purchaser, in effect, a free option. Usually, a longstop date will be specified, by which time, if the condition has not been waived or purified, either or both parties will be entitled to terminate the contract. There might be several longstop dates for different conditions, or one date for all of them:

> In the event that all of the suspensive conditions contained in Clause [   ] have not been purified or waived by the Purchaser by **[insert here long-stop date]** (or by such later date as the parties may agree in writing) either party will be entitled (but not bound) at any time thereafter, provided this Clause remains unpurified, to resile from the Missives by written notice to that effect served on the other party, and that without penalty except in respect of any antecedent breach.

It is important to allow for a realistic timescale within which to purify conditions, although it is always open to the parties to try to negotiate an extension of time, but there may be reasons why one party is unwilling to extend the longstop period, or may only be prepared to do so in exchange for changes to the other terms of the contract, which may not be so attractive to the party seeking the extension.

PURCHASING PROPERTY FOR A BUSINESS

6.15 A business is simply a collection of assets, bound together by the goodwill of the business, and the sale of the business is really only a transfer of the various assets, with certain safeguards built in for the purchasers.

The assets of a business are generally regarded as: heritable property (whether owned or leased), stock-in-trade, trade fittings and fixtures, work-in-progress (although not particularly with retail businesses), money owing, vehicles, trade name, trade marks, copyrights, patents etc, domain name, website, knowhow, and any licences or franchises owned by the business. All of these assets are also wrapped up in the intangible goodwill of the business, which encompasses reputation and customer loyalty.

The liabilities of the business, which are deducted from the valuation of the assets, are basically money owing to suppliers, employees, pension fund, the taxman, and so on. And the people of the business, who are probably an asset in a good business and a liability in a bad business, but not always so.

The missives for the purchase of a business need to deal with the various issues that apply to these assets and liabilities. The sale agreement should, where necessary, call upon the sellers or their accountants to grant warranties that the situation is as they have stated. The purchasers will also conduct a thorough inspection of company records and other information provided by the sellers. Warranties need to be backed up by indemnities to cover them. For this reason agreements for the sale of large companies are very lengthy and complex, but that is outwith the scope of this work.

(a) Heritable property

The property of the business is valued by a surveyor, and the offer should make the usual stipulations for the purchase of heritage, that is: date of entry, clauses dealing with heritable and moveable property, clauses dealing with title, property enquiry certificates and outstanding notices, and so on. It should be remembered that there are certain statutory requirements for commercial property, particularly the Health and Safety at Work Acts, and the offer should stipulate that all requirements under these Acts have been met, along with compliance with fire regulations. When the missives are proceeding by way of an offer to sell, the purchaser's solicitor should use a tool such as the Due Diligence Questionnaire to make sure that all such requirements are checked

Where the property is leasehold, the lease will be valued taking a number of considerations into account, including: (a) the remaining duration of the lease; (b) the rent being charged; (c) the frequency of rent reviews and the terms of the rent review clause; (d) the use permitted by the lease; (e) the authorised planning use of the property; (f) restrictions on assigning, charging and subletting (alienation); (g) general fairness of the lease to the tenant; and (h) location and trading prospects of the site.

Transfer of a leasehold interest will take place by way of assignation by the outgoing tenant (the seller). Precaution should be taken that there are no outstanding liabilities to the landlord for, eg rent and dilapidations of the property (the cost of restoring the property to the condition it was in when it was first let), and if there are, the basis on which the purchaser takes over the property should take these into account, given the usual full repairing and insuring obligations that apply to tenants under most commercial leases.

As well as receiving permission from the landlord for the assignation of the lease or sublet, confirmation should also be sought from the landlord that there are no outstanding liabilities, and that the proposed use of the property by the purchaser is approved.

Check whether the purchaser has opted to tax the property for VAT purposes with HM Revenue and Customs (see para 6.13(d)), and ensure that the correct VAT provisions are included in the missives. How the VAT position affects your client's financial circumstances will usually be a matter for them to consult on with their accountant or finance director.

(b) Stock-in-trade

An ongoing business will need stock to continue to trade, and so generally stock remaining at the date the business changes hands is valued on (or as near as possible to) that date either by agreement between the parties, or by an independent valuer specialising in stocktaking. This is known as SAV, or Stock at Valuation. Depending on the nature of the business, or the purchaser's intentions for it, (for example they may plan to obtain different stock from a different supplier) it might be appropriate for the purchaser to provide that the seller must run down the stocks so that the amount of stock at handover is as low as possible. The valuer's fee will often be divided equally between the parties. A typical condition would be:

'The purchaser will take over the [non-perishable] stock of the business so far as of a usable and saleable nature commensurate with good business practice, as at the date of entry and transfer, at a price

[NB consider inserting provision regarding cost basis (eg wholesale price) according to customary practice for the type of business] to be agreed between the parties, and payment for such stock together with VAT thereon (if any) will be made within [14] days of the value being agreed or determined in accordance with this clause.

Failing agreement, the valuation of the stock will be referred to a single valuer to be mutually appointed by the parties, or in the absence of agreement as to appointment, by a single valuer appointed by the [Chairman of the Scottish Branch of the Incorporated Society of Valuers and Auctioneers] on the application of either party. The valuer's decision on the valuation of the stock and his determination on liability for the costs of his appointment will be final and binding on both parties. Failing a determination by the valuer, the costs of his appointment will be met equally by the seller and the purchaser.

(c) Trade fittings and fixtures

These include counters, shelving, cash registers etc. Some of these items are expensive to buy and may be on hire purchase or other credit arrangement. This should be clarified in the offer to buy, and if the item is owned by a finance company, arrangements for the transfer of the item should be made subject to the amounts still payable under the contract. Again the applicability of VAT on such items should be ascertained and provided for, including the requirement to obtain a VAT receipt from the Seller for any VAT paid on items (including the property itself).

The purchasers of a business relying largely on internet or telephone orders, will also want to acquire the website and telephone number(s), and to make sure that the telephone company has not withdrawn the number.

The offer should contain a fairly tight condition about the working order of any central heating, refrigeration, air-conditioning or other mechanical plant, and the liability of the sellers to pay for any repairs. The purchasers should inspect the mechanical equipment concerned, and arrange for the sellers to pay for any necessary repairs, before parting with any money. The contractual position should, however, also be preserved. See the provisions of Clause 3 of the Residential Combined Standard Clauses for suitable wording (para 6.10(c)).

To describe the business, the various component parts should be specified eg

'The 'Business' means

the shop premises at 44 Angus Avenue, Inverness together with all the heritable fittings and fixtures (the 'Property');

the goodwill of the business of Fishmonger and Poulterer carried on in the shop premises by the seller under the name 'Seafresh';

the Fittings and Equipment; and

the non-perishable stock-in-trade;'

Fittings and equipment should be set out clearly and provision made regarding outright ownership:

'Fittings and Equipment' means the whole trade fixtures and fittings, trade utensils and equipment including counters, refrigerators, cash registers and scales.

The Seller warrants that there are no hire-purchase or credit sale agreements, diligences, liens or charges of any kind affecting any of Fittings and Equipment, and that the title of the seller to them cannot be reduced or affected at the instance of third parties.

(d) Work-in-progress

This refers particularly to business people like solicitors or builders who do work and get paid at the end of that work. If the business is transferred while the work is continuing, a valuation needs to be made of the work done but not yet paid for, and that forms an asset of the business.

(e) Money owing to the business

The debts owing to the business are generally retained in the ownership of the sellers, who collect them as and when they can. If the sellers are emigrating or retiring, however, this may not be appropriate, and the purchasers may take these over. The purchasers should then pay the sellers for this asset, and it should be remembered that the debts should be assigned to the purchasers, and the assignation intimated to each debtor, both to satisfy the requirement that the right of a creditor in a debt is fully transferred by an assignation followed by an intimation, and to let the debtor know who the creditors are. The intimation can simply be printed on the account when it is rendered. A simple statement requesting the debtor to pay the account to the assignee should suffice.

Similarly the purchasers of a business, who take over the collection of the debts, can have the benefit (or liability) of any court actions in which their predecessors were engaged, or the benefit of any court decrees that they hold. The valuation of the debts of the business should reflect the likely outcome of the cases they have started.

(f) Vehicles

Vehicles being taken over are valued at date of sale, by reference to suitable trade values. Again care must be taken to ensure that there is no outstanding debt on these vehicles, or alternatively that the debt is allowed for in the price.

(g) Trade name

Some trade names form a very valuable part of the business; others may be of no or doubtful value, and may be changed on takeover. Requirements about company names and their disclosure and display are now contained in the Companies Act 2006.

(h) Intellectual property

A small retail business is unlikely to own any patents, designs, trade marks or copyrights, but a small electronics business, for example, might own all four, and be completely dependent on their existence. It is important, therefore, to check (a) that the sellers own the right to the particular intellectual property, (b) that the rights are validly registered, (c) any dates of renewal or re-registration required (d) that they are properly assigned and intimated, in the case of trade marks and patents, to the appropriate registrar. The specialist advice of a chartered patent agent should probably be sought, unless the firm has expertise in this area. Intellectual property rights in overseas countries should be protected as well.

(i) Licences and franchises

Many businesses depend almost entirely on a licence or franchise for their existence. There is little point in buying the business unless you can be sure the licence or franchise can be transferred to the purchaser. The purchasers should include a suspensive condition making the purchase dependent on getting a transfer of the licence or franchise. The commonest example of the former is a hotel or shop licensed to sell alcohol, and of the latter, a business which owns a franchise outlet of one of the franchise companies like McDonalds or Your Move estate agencies.

Liquor licensing is now dealt with under the Licensing (Scotland) Act 2005. A property where the sale of alcohol takes place needs a premises licence, applications for which must be accompanied by an operating plan, layout plan and certificates from Building Control, Environmental Health and Planning departments of the local authority in question. Once it is granted a premises licence remains in force for an indefinite period, subject to payment of an annual fee. The premises must be operated in accordance with the operating plan, and any changes require a variation of the operating plan. All premises are subject to mandatory conditions that are set out in the L(S)A 2005. The Licensing Board for an area can add local conditions. Every premises must have a premises manager ie the person named on the operating plan, who must hold a Personal Licence. An applicant for a personal licence must hold a licensing qualification. Premises Licences can be transferred at any time by application to the relevant Licensing Board.

The purchase of a business which depends on a franchise will depend on the consent of the franchisers, who will want to be satisfied as to the suitability of the purchasers to run the business, and ability to pay for the supplies. The reputation of the brand is an important element of franchises, and so it should not be assumed that it will be a foregone conclusion that the purchaser will be acceptable to the franchiser. Franchises are licences privately granted authorising the licensee to use the business style of the licensor.

Many other activities require a licence, eg road haulage, post offices, bookmakers, the operation of taxis and private hire-cars, secondhand dealing, boat hire, street trading, private markets, operation of places of entertainment, late-hours catering, window cleaning and many more.

Requirements vary widely and enquiries should be made of the appropriate council when acting in the acquisition of property involved in these and similar areas.

(j) Goodwill

Goodwill has been defined as 'the probability that the old customers will revert to the old place' (*Crutwell v Lye* (1810) 17 Ves 335 at 346 per Lord Eldon). But perhaps it is something more prosaic as suggested by Dr Samuel Johnson remarking on the sale of Thrale's Brewery in 1781: 'We are not here to sell a parcel of boilers and vats, but the potentiality of growing rich beyond the dreams of avarice.'

Goodwill is an asset that cannot be precisely valued, and its valuation will vary widely from case to case. To some extent it will also vary with the purchaser's opinion as to whether it is a good business that can be extended, or it is a poor business that will require an investment of time and money to bring it round. You must always be careful, especially in small businesses, of highly personal goodwill that will simply disappear when the sellers leave. Customers or clients of a business cannot be counted on not to take their business elsewhere. Advice on the appropriate basis of valuation of the goodwill of a business should be taken from the purchaser's accountant.

(k) People

A good business which is being sold will probably have high calibre employees whom the purchasers will wish to retain. A bad business may have been significantly affected by its employees, and the purchaser is unlikely to feel a great compulsion to inherit these liabilities.

Good employees may be hard to retain. They may feel upset at the business being sold over their heads, and the owner disappearing with a large sum, representing their unrewarded hard work. They may even decide that they could do the same thing better, and will leave to start up their own businesses. This is more of a personnel management exercise, than a legal one, in many respects.

The position of employees of a business that is changing hands is governed by the Transfer of Undertakings (Protection of Employment) Regulations 2006 (TUPE) which protects the employees' terms and conditions of employment on transfer to a new owner. It is not competent to provide in the sale agreement that the sellers are to dismiss employees before the business changes hands, if the sole reason is the transfer of the business. The matter was finally settled by the House of Lords in *Litster v Forth Dry Dock and Engineering Co Ltd* (1989 SLT 540) where it was ruled that employees, dismissed by the receivers of the company one hour before the receivership took effect, had continuity of employment, and, therefore, a claim for redundancy.

The complexities of employment law are such that specialist advice should be sought as soon as it is identified that employees are an element of any transaction. The PSG Offer to Sell provides wording that caters for the position where there are no employees (see para 6.13(v)). Where there are employees of a business, then TUPE compliant provisions will need to be drafted, and full details of each employee, and their terms and conditions of employment, including position, salary and benefits, hours of employment and holiday entitlement, as well as length of service, pension arrangements and other relevant information should be obtained from the sellers.

(l) Restrictive covenant

What of the departing sellers? Hopefully they will have made enough to enjoy a well-earned retirement, but whether they have or not, the attempt is sometimes made to impose a restrictive covenant (or non-competition clause) on them to prevent them from returning to business to compete with the purchasers. It should be borne in mind however that competition law is another area which has become increasingly complicated and prevalent, and especially with the Competition Act 1998 now applying to all land agreements by virtue of the Competition Act 1998 (Land Agreements Exclusion Revocation) Order 2010, great care should be exercised when drafting such clauses. The covenant should be neither too loose to prevent the sellers from competing unfairly, nor too tight to be declared unenforceable by the courts and fall foul of competition law. Any protection provided by a restrictive covenant must be limited both in time and area to what is necessary for a purchaser to take over the market position of the business to the same extent enjoyed by it when the seller was in control.

'The seller will not in any way carry on directly or indirectly (unless with the written consent of the purchaser) within [one year] after the date of transfer and within [one mile] of 44 Angus Avenue either on his own account or as a partner with, or in the name of, or as a servant or agent to any person or persons, firm or company, the business of Fishmonger or Poulterer.'

(m) Accounts and records. The books of account and financial, customer and other records relating to the business should be transferred to the purchaser on the date of transfer, but a period of time (eg six months) after transfer will need to be allowed for reasonable access for inspection by the seller or his agents for completing tax returns and the like.

SELLING PART OF A PROPERTY

6.16 When the property being sold is an area that is being split off from a larger title, there are several specific issues to bear in mind.

(a) Title conditions

The principal title of the larger area (or building of which the property being sold forms part) may be subject to a number of real burdens and servitudes. It may be necessary to specify in the missives whether, and the extent to which, existing burdens will affect the property and the extent to which it will (or can) benefit from existing servitudes (see para 9.09).

If new burdens or servitudes are required, then the missives should provide as clearly as possible what the terms of those are to be, and should also make provision regarding forms and payment of registration fees in respect of the dual registration requirement. When using the following suggested wording, a definition of 'Retained Property' will need to be added to the Definitions clause in the offer. Alternatively the burdens and servitudes can be added to the draft Disposition that is attached to the missives, in which case only clause 1.5 below suitably amended would be required

1.1   In the Disposition the following servitude rights will be imposed on the Property in favour of the Retained Property:

[Here list all new servitude rights in favour of the Retained Property]

1.2   In the Disposition the following servitude rights will be imposed on the Retained Property in favour of the Property:

[Here list all new servitude rights in favour of the Property]

1.3   In the Disposition the following real burdens will be imposed on the Property for the benefit of the Retained Property:

[Here list all new real burdens in favour of the Retained Property]

1.4   In the Disposition the following real burdens will be imposed on the Retained Property for the benefit of the Property

[Here list all new real burdens in favour of the Property]

1.5   [If the Disposition creates real burdens and/or servitudes affecting the Property, (whether as the burdened property or the benefited property), and dual registration is required:

(i)   the Seller will deliver a completed and signed SAF, or Form 2 in respect of the Seller's property which will benefit from or be burdened by the real burdens and/or servitudes, together with payment for the requisite amount of registration dues in respect of registration of the real burdens and/or servitudes against the Seller's property;

(ii)   the Purchaser will submit the Form 2 or 3 in respect of the registration of the real burdens and/or servitudes against the Seller's property contemporaneously with the Purchaser's application for registration of the Disposition, along with a Form 4 containing details of both applications, and will provide the Seller with a copy of the Keeper's letter acknowledging receipt of the application within 15 Working Days after Completion.]

Particular attention should be given to ensuring that all necessary rights of access are obtained, and rights to services, in, over or through common parts of a larger building and rights of access over adjoining land or properties for repairs, cleaning and other essential purposes are granted.

(b) Plan

Clear accurate plans are important in many aspects of conveyancing, and when identifying a piece of property for the first time, it is particularly important to have a plan that shows the precise extent, and this should be confirmed by the purchaser. Ideally, the plan should be taxative (such as an Ordnance Survey plan) and suitable for annexing to the Disposition of the Property (see para 9.08(g) for the Keeper's requirements).

(c) Reservations

The seller needs to make certain to reserve to himself any rights required to continue to use the remainder of the property retained by him. There have been instances where areas become landlocked or otherwise deprived of essential rights though a failure to make adequate reservations. While there may be essential servitudes implied by law, the practicalities of the configuration of the land might make these difficult to use, and so full consideration needs to be given not just to the property being sold, but the one being retained.

RURAL PROPERTY

6.17 When offering for property in the countryside, there are some specific issues that need to be borne in mind. Agricultural property and crofting have their own specialisations, and it is not the intention of this text to consider those, rather the more general matters that should be taken into account for rural property.

(a) The Property

When describing the property in the offer, especially if it comprises or includes land, it is prudent to include rights to woodlands, sporting rights and minerals, as these can be subject to leases or in some cases owned outright.

Salmon fishings are capable of being owned separately from the land in which the river or loch is situated, and the chances are if the property being purchased forms part of a larger estate, then the estate owner will be reserving salmon fishing rights, unless of course part of the benefit of the property being sold is that the salmon fishings are included. The purchases of rural property that includes salmon fishings, should be made aware that salmon beats, by their nature are often discontiguous from the rest of the property. Vigilence is required to ensure that sufficient rights of access to the river bank, and possibly for parking exist, or are granted.

Sporting rights, which include freshwater fishing and shooting of game are not generally held as a separate tenement in land except for such rights which had been held by a former feudal superior and which were capable of being preserved as a separate title by procedures under s 65A of AFT(S) A 2000 prior to feudal abolition. However leases of sporting rights are common and the existence of such rights needs to be identified and the terms on which they are held and exercised should be checked.

Accordingly, in addition to the property, which should be described as fully as possible (perhaps by reference to the schedule of sales particulars, and identified on a plan, the offer should also include:

(i)   all buildings and steadings, all heritable fixtures and fittings and fixed equipment including fencing and gates

(ii)   the whole shooting and other sporting rights, including the salmon and trout fishing in all rivers, lochs and streams lying within or *ex adverso* the Property so far as the seller has right to them;

(ii)   all plantations and all timber, standing, cut and fallen within the Property at the date of the offer;

(iii)   the whole mines, metals and minerals located in the Property including stone, sand and gravel (except coal and mines of coal) so far as the seller has right to them.

(iv)   all other pertinents of the Property including all servitude rights, rights of way, water, drainage and other rights and services.

The foreshore and seabed are traditionally Crown property. Therefore, if your client is proposing to purchase a coastal property bear in mind that rights to moorings jetties or using the seabed (eg for oyster farming) are likely to need to be separately negotiated with the Crown Estate.

In addition it should be specified that the Property is not subject to an agricultural tenancy or any other form of lease or tenancy agreement, nor affected by crofting tenure. Crofts may exist in the original crofting counties of Argyll, Caithness, Inverness, Orkney, Ross & Cromarty, Sutherland and Zetland and in the extended areas (since February 2010) of Arran, Bute, Greater and Little Cumbrae, Moray and parts of Highland that are not already covered within the traditional crofting counties.

Where the property is subject to agricultural holdings tenancies or crofting tenancies be aware that these may give rise to a tenant's right to buy, and expert advice should be sought. Grazing leases of less than a year's length should not pose a problem, so long as they have been properly terminated at the ish (end date).

(b) Roads and access

All property needs to be served by adequate access according to the nature of the property. In rural areas, often access roads and others are not publicly maintained and accordingly provision should be made in the Missives for adequate servitude rights to be available. For example:

(i)   The title to the Property contains a heritable and irredeemable servitude right of access for pedestrian and vehicular traffic, from the public road to the Property for all purposes [over the route(s) shown on the Plan]. Maintenance of the access route(s) is shared on an equitable basis, according to user. There are no outstanding maintenance, repair or renewal obligations in respect of the route(s).

In addition, depending on the use of the property, it might be necessary to check for the existence of local roads authority consents for uses such as agricultural and forestry purposes in relation to access off public roads. Confirmation should be sought that there are no road widening or road construction proposals which could adversely affect the Property or any part of it, and that there are no height, width or weight restrictions affecting roads, bridges, footpaths and verges providing access to the Property.

(c) Water and drainage

(i) Drainage

Very often drainage systems for rural properties will be private, rather than connected to the mains drainage system. This raises issues of access to systems, if they or parts of them are located in other land, and regulatory and environmental issues, if any part of the system discharges into a watercourse. Private drainage will be to a septic tank which may incorporate a soakaway and other pipes and connections. Other types of septic tank act as stores and require to be emptied from time to time and this is dealt with by the local authority. Since April 2006, septic tanks which discharge to land via a soakaway need to register under the Controlled Activities Regulations (CAR), the current version of which is the Water Environment (Controlled Activities) (Scotland) Regulations 2011, unless they were already registered under the Control of Pollution Act 1974. These regulations principally affect residential properties, but there may also be implications for developers if their activities involve water abstraction, engineering works or impoundment (see para 8.21(c)).

A suggested clause for missives is

If the drainage of the property is private, evidence will be produced to show that the septic tank, soakaway, tail pipe and other pipes and connections are in good working order, condition and repair and comply in all respects with the local authority and water authority standards and other relevant regulations, and in particular the Water Environment (Controlled Activities)(Scotland) Regulations 2011. Either (i) an existing valid authorisation from the Scottish Environmental Protection Agency, under the Control of Pollution Act 1974 or (ii) a Discharge Registration Certificate from SEPA under the Water Environment (Controlled Activities) (Scotland) Regulations 2011 will be exhibited prior to and delivered at the date of entry.

That wording will deal with the compliance aspects. If the septic tank has not been registered and needs to be, information on what to do can be obtained from the SEPA website www.sepa.org.uk. If the septic tank or any part of the system it uses is, or might be located outwith the land being purchased, then adequate servitude rights must be available:

If, to any extent the septic tank, soakaway, tail pipe and other pipes and connections are located outwith the Property, [there exists][the Purchaser will be granted] an unrestricted heritable and irredeemable servitude right to use, inspect, maintain, empty, repair and when necessary renew the same, with rights of access on all necessary occasions subject only to an obligation to make good all surface damage occasioned by the exercise of such rights. The location of the septic tank, soakaway and tail pipe will be indicated to the Purchaser on a plan accompanying your acceptance of this offer.

Provision should also be made in the missives if water supplies, drainage and sewerage are mutual:

> The liability to maintain any private water supplies, drainage and sewerage and other services which are mutual to the Property and any other subjects is shared on some equitable basis.

(ii) Water supply

Private water supplies are less common than private drainage systems, but more remote parts of the country may not have access to mains water, and require to take their supply of water from private reservoirs or water courses. It is estimated that over 150,000 people in Scotland rely on a private water supply, and many others, such as visitors and tourists will use them occasionally each year. Private water supplies are currently regulated by the Private Water Supplies (Scotland) Regulations 2006, which enable local authorities to monitor them to check they meet wholesomeness standards. The PWS(S)R 2006 also implement EU requirements in relation to drinking water quality to ensure the provision of clean and wholesome drinking water. Where the Property is served by a private water supply the Missives should provide:

> The Property is served by a private water supply. Evidence will be produced to show that the water supply is constant and sufficient in quality and quantity for the domestic and the other requirements of the Property and complies with The Private Water Supplies (Scotland) Regulations 2006, and all other regulations and requirements of the relevant Local Authority, the European Union and other relevant bodies. If, to any extent, the water supply or supplies and any tanks, pipes, connections and others relating to the supply lie outwith the Property, [there exists][the Purchaser will be granted] an unrestricted heritable and irredeemable servitude right to use, inspect, maintain, repair and when necessary renew the same, with rights of access on all necessary occasions subject only to an obligation to make good all surface damage occasioned by the exercise of such rights. The location of the source of the supply and all tanks, pipes, connections and others will be indicated to the Purchaser on a plan accompanying your acceptance of this offer.

It is also possible that the source of the water supply is in the Property being purchased by your client and so you should add:

'There are no water supplies emanating from within the Property and serving adjoining properties'.

If there are such water supplies, then this will elicit a response that should provide more information including particulars of the properties that benefit from this supply, and whether there are any requirements to guarantee quantity or quality of the water supplied.

(iii) Reservoirs

Proximity of a property to a large raised reservoir (ie with a capacity of more than 25,000 cubic meters of water above the natural level of the adjoining land) raises issues of risk of flooding, and therefore if there is a large raised reservoir in the vicinity the risks attendant with that will need to be assessed by the purchasers and their surveyor. The Reservoirs (Scotland) Act 2011 will repeal the Reservoirs Act 1975, and move from a capacity basis of assessment to one based on risk.

As far as the Seller is aware the Property is not affected by or situated *ex adverso* any large raised reservoir as defined for the purposes of the Reservoirs Act 1975 (*note this Act is prospectively repealed by the Reservoirs (Scotland) Act 2011*), nor is it within any water catchment area in relation to any public water supply.

(d) Walls and fences

Maintenance of boundary walls and fences can be a significant liability in large rural areas, and where they separate the Property from other subjects, the liability to maintain and repair should be borne equally:

'All boundary fences which separate the Property from adjoining subjects (other than those adjoining public roads which may belong solely to the Seller) are mutual between the seller and the adjoining proprietors, and the obligation to maintain, repair and renew them is shared equally. There are no outstanding obligations in respect of the boundary fences, and in particular, no obligation to erect or maintain deer-proof fences.'

(e) Rights of way and access rights

(i) Rights of Way

There are many rights of way across Scotland, some of which are well known. However a right of way can be established through use by the public for the prescriptive period of 20 years, for the purposes of getting from one public place to another, and not all rights of way are signposted, or marked as such. The Scottish Rights of Way and Access Society (SRWAS) maintains a record of all of the known rights of way in the National Catalogue of Rights of Way (CROW) and other routes. Sometimes the route of a right of way will be shown on plans of the property, or on the Ordnance Survey map, but you can also obtain information from CROW by contacting SRWAS, although it should be borne in mind that not all rights of way are logged with them, as many are only known about locally. Nor does it mean if nothing is shown on a plan that no rights exist. Only a small percentage of rights of way have been formally identified as such, or 'vindicated', and the vast majority of rights of way are in the category known as 'claimed' in which the basic requirements for establishment of a right of way appear to have been met, but no formal process has taken place. In the middle, are rights which have been 'asserted', where the local authority is interested in protecting them, or where the landowner affected has accepted the use of the route by the public.

SRWAS deals with hundreds of enquiries every year about problems with particular rights of way and other access matters, and can be asked to provide details of any rights of way or other routes affecting the property being purchased. For more information, go to their website at www. scotways.com. The offer should provide that:

> 'there are no servitudes, rights of way, wayleaves or similar rights affecting the Property other than those disclosed in the titles. Written evidence of the position regarding rights of way will be exhibited prior to settlement, both by way of the titles and by way of letters from the Scottish Rights of Way and Access Society and the Local Authority Access/Rights of Way Department.'

(ii) Access rights (the right to roam)

The general public have enjoyed rights of access of one sort or another over our beautiful countryside for a variety of recreational purposes, and for passage, for many years and these have been expanded over the years by local government and town and country planning legislation, and by the Countryside (Scotland) Act 1967 and the Countryside (Scotland) Act 1981. However public rights of access were transformed significantly by Part 1 of the Land Reform (Scotland) Act 2003, which extended statutory access rights to 'everyone' to encompass: (i) the right to be on land (which includes inland waters, canals and the foreshore) for (a) recreational purposes, (b) carrying on a relevant educational activity or (c) carrying on a commercial activity, provided it is an activity that is capable of being carried on uncommercially; and (ii) the right to cross land.

These access rights are exercisable above, below and on all land, other than land over which rights cannot be exercised defined in s 6 of the LR(S)A 2003 and including land with buildings or other structures on it or forms the curtilage of a building or land used for the purposes of a school, etc. There is power to exclude or restrict land from the exercise of access rights for the purposes of defence or national security. Included within the exemption is 'sufficient adjacent land' next to a house so that the occupants of the house can have a reasonable amount of privacy. This will normally mean the garden around the house.

There have been several quite high profile cases in the courts since the introduction of access rights, the first of which was *Gloag v Perth & Kinross Council* [2007] SCLR 530 a well publicised case due to the celebrity of the applicant, business woman Ann Gloag. Mrs Gloag successfully applied for a declaration that certain land adjacent to her house at Kinfauns Castle was not land in respect of which access rights were exercisable, arguing that an area of approximately 11 acres fell within the 'privacy exemption' in s 6 of the LR(S)A 2003, which allows an owner 'sufficient adjacent land to enable persons living there to have reasonable measures of privacy in that house…and to ensure that their enjoyment of that house…is not unreasonably disturbed'. This was an unpopular decision not only with the Ramblers' Association, but also in the Scottish Parliament where Sarah Boyack, a Labour MSP, obtained a parliamentary debate on a motion which was strongly critical of the decision, stating that it was contrary to the intention of the Act and 'undermined the clear will of Parliament, which legislated for the widest possible access to the countryside'. See also *Snowie v Stirling Council* [2008] SLT (Sh Ct) 61.

Access rights must be exercised responsibly, and for the most part they are. Landowners must use and manage their land and otherwise conduct their ownership of it in a responsible way, and for the most part they do. As directed by s 10 of the LR(S)A 2003, Scottish Natural Heritage produced the Scottish Outdoor Access Code (see www.outdooraccess-scotland.com) which gives detailed guidance to both access takers and land managers about enjoying and facilitating the access rights.

Local authorities have the duty to provide a plan for a system of core paths for giving access rights to the public throughout their area. Part of the idea here is that, if there are designated paths for ramblers and other access takers to use, they will use those paths, rather than randomly wandering across land. For this purpose, local authorities can enter into core path agreements with landowners. Such agreements do not need to be recorded in the Sasine Register or registered in the Land Register, (although their predecessors under the Countryside (Scotland) Act 1967 did). If a core path agreement cannot be obtained, the local authority has compulsory powers to delineate paths in land by way of core path order. Such an order is an overriding interest.

Arguably, the wording concerning rights of way or similar rights suggested in para 6.17(e)(i) would cover rights exercisable over core paths and subject to a core path agreement or core path order, and it would be expected that any such arrangements would be disclosed in any letter obtained from Local Authority Access/Rights of Way Department. Additional wording to cover the matter specifically could be included:

> 'If the property is affected by the exercise of rights of access exercisable by the public in terms of Part 1 of the Land Reform (Scotland) Act 2003, whether routinely or infrequently, then full details of the routes of such access and the quantity and frequency of such exercise will be provided with your acceptance of this offer, along with copies of any path agreements or path orders affecting the Property.'

(f) Community right to buy

Part 2 of the LR(S)A 2003 created a new concept of the Community Right to Buy, by which communities are allowed to register their interest in land within their neighbourhood, and have a right of first refusal to buy the land if it comes on the market for sale. Accordingly it is a pre-emptive right, ie it is only triggered by the proposed sale of land over which an interest has been registered. If the landowner never puts the land on the market or takes steps to transfer it, the right to buy will never by triggered. A registered interest will lapse after 5 years, but the community body can apply to re-register it for another 5 years. The community's interest (through a community body which must be set up specifically for the purpose) must be registered in the Register of Community Interests in Land (see para 7.09), and Scottish Ministers must have given written confirmation that they are satisfied that the main purpose of the community body is consistent with furthering the achievement of sustainable development.

The type of land over which the Community Right to Buy may be exercised is predominantly rural. Land over which the right to buy cannot be exercised is defined as 'excluded land', details of which are contained in the Community Right to Buy (Definition of Excluded Land) Order 2009. The order specifies 'settlements' which are excluded from the right to buy, because of their population size, and includes cities and major towns in Scotland. Plans showing the extent of these excluded areas are accessible on the Scottish Government website at www.scotland.gov.uk/ Topics/farmingrural/Rural/rural-land/right-to-buy/MappingTool. Once a community interest has been registered against land, and for five years from the date of its registration (or longer if renewed), the owner of that land (or heritable creditor with a right to sell the land) is prohibited from transferring the land, or taking any action with a view to transferring the land, except in certain exempt cases (for example if missives have already been concluded for the sale of the land) (see s 40 of LR(S)A 2003) and any transfer in breach of this prohibition will be of no effect.

Since the existence of a Community Right to Buy will effectively prevent a sale of the land affected (unless of course the community decides to decline to purchase) then any offer for land that is not excluded land should contain the following clause:

> 'Where the Subjects or any part of them are registrable land for the purposes of Part 2 of the Land Reform (Scotland) Act 2003, the Seller warrants that there is no interest of a community body either registered against the Property or any part of it, or any larger area of which the Property form part, nor is an application for registration of such an interest pending, and the Seller knows of no proposals either

for formation of a community body or for making an application for registration of an interest. If the Search in the Register of Community Interests in Land referred to in Clause [see below] of this offer contains a registered interest or application the Purchaser will be entitled to rescind the Missives without any penalty'

and the following additional section should be added to the searches clause in the offer:

'Where the Property or any part of it is registrable land for the purposes of Part 2 of the Land Reform (Scotland) Act 2003, the Seller will deliver prior to the date of settlement a Search in the Register of Community Interests in Land, from the date of commencement of the Register, or (if later) from the date occurring 5 years prior to the date of conclusion of the Missives, which Search will disclose no entry in the Register as at the date of conclusion of the Missives which would prohibit the Seller from transferring the Property to the Purchaser'

For wording that should be incorporated into a Disposition in case of a registered interest in land see para 9.10(1).

By contrast a Crofting Community Right to Buy under Part 3 of the LR(S)A 2003 does not depend upon the landowner putting the land up for sale, and can be exercised by eligible crofters at any time.

(g) Grants, Schemes, Agreements and Zoning

Many rural areas are affected by a variety of grants, schemes, or agreements, or may be zoned or specially designated in some way. It is as much a matter of finding out what sorts of arrangements affect the property, some of which will of course be beneficial, but in some cases, there might be a repayment or apportionment required, or certain conditions applied to the land which must be complied with, eg as to use of the land. Note that the names of and availability of various schemes and grants change over the years and it is prudent to check which types of schemes and other arrangements are likely to affect the type of property being purchased when drafting the offer. However some grant and other schemes which have been discontinued may continue to apply to properties already subject to them:

'No part of the Property is affected by (i) any Access Agreement, Countryside Stewardship Scheme, Designed Landscape designation, Environmentally Sensitive Area Scheme, Farm Business Development Scheme, Farm Woodland Premium Scheme, Forestry Dedication Agreement, Forestry or Woodland Grant Scheme, Grazing Agreement, Habitats Scheme, Mineral Agreement, Nitrate Vulnerable Zone designation, Rural Development Contract, Rural Stewardship Scheme, Section 75 Agreement, Set Aside Order or Scheme, actual or proposed Special Areas of Conservation, Tree Preservation Order or actual or proposed Special Areas of Conservation, or any other schemes, designations or restrictions or (ii) any sites of Special Scientific, Historic or Archaeological Interest. The Property is not situated in a National Scenic Area or Environmentally Sensitive Area.'

(h) Woodland and timber

If the Property contains any woodland areas, particularly if these are being worked or have economic value, then in addition to checking for schemes, grants and other arrangements in terms of para (g) above, provision should be made for protection of and preservation of the resources that exist as at the date of the offer, and the offer should specify that all forestry records are delivered at settlement:

(i)   There are no timber harvesting contracts which remain uncompleted and no timber on the Property will be cut or removed between the date of this offer and the date of entry;

(ii)   Until the date of entry the seller will maintain and manage the Property and, in particular, the whole timber on the Property in accordance with the rules of good husbandry and prevailing principles of silvicultural practice, and will not do anything to obstruct or limit the harvesting potential of the existing timber planted on the Property;

(iii)   the Seller will maintain adequate insurance cover in respect of all timber against damage by fire, storm, windblown trees and public liability and such other risks as the Purchaser, acting reasonably, may require.

If the Property is subject to an existing Forestry Dedication Agreement (in terms of s 5 of the Forestry Act 1967) then further information will be required and specific provision made in the missives depending on circumstances. Forestry Dedication Agreements can be recorded in the Sasine Register or registered in the Land Register. While the use of Forestry Dedication Agreements discontinued some years ago, there may still be exiting agreements in effect, and when they exist, they provide that the land must not be used for any use other that the growing of timber or other forestry products. It is possible to apply for a release from a Forestry Dedication Agreement at any time, and if that is required, then provision should be made to ensure that any obligations due by the seller to the Forestry Commission are fulfilled and nothing is outstanding at the date of entry.

SALES BY INSOLVENT PARTIES

6.18 Missives for the purchase of property from a trustee in sequestration, administrator, receiver or liquidator (known generally as Insolvency Practitioners or IPs) are likely to be much shorter than the usual form of offer, due to the limited knowledge of the IP, both in respect of the insolvent owner, and the property itself. The IP is unlikely to have anything other than the most basic knowledge of the property, and in corporate insolvencies in particular, he may have incomplete or even chaotic records from the company. Accordingly he is usually unable to provide much information or assurance on matters affecting the property. The requirement to exclude any personal liability on the part of the IP also means that there are few if any warranties or confirmations given, and the purchaser will have to satisfy himself on most aspects of the purchase from his own investigations, observations and reports, and accept the property and any moveables in their current condition.

The IP may not be able to ascertain the VAT status of the property from the company's records, and so it may be some time before it can be established for example whether the sale of the property will qualify as a TOGC. Even if that status can be established, the IP may not be in a position to produce other VAT documentation or make any warranty as to the tax status of the company

Often IPs will arrange for their own solicitor to produce an offer to sell, which will contain the various protections that IPs seek, as well as omitting much of the seller's warranties that traditional offers contain. In addition, the offer will contain (i) a clause that deals with the exclusion of any personal liability on the part of the IP (and this will be repeated in the Disposition (see para 9.05 (h)), and (ii) a clause that extracts acknowledgements from the purchaser that it is not relying on any representations or warranties from the IP or the insolvent seller. These clauses are belt and braces affairs and now follow a fairly standardised format. A typical example appears below (para 6.18(b)).

In sales of commercial premises by insolvent owners, there are often issues relating to moveable items that may be left in the property. If they do not belong to the insolvent owner, for example office equipment like printers and photocopiers, or vending machines, refrigerated cabinets and the like, that are the subject of hire purchase or leasing arrangements, they are frequently affected by a 'retention of title' clause in the hire agreement, which means that the supplier of the item has a prior claim to the item in preference to any of the creditors. Where such clauses validly (apply) to any of the moveables, the items will need to be restored to the supplier, and so the purchaser should be careful to identify any items which might fall into this category and at the very least not take their value into account when purchasing, as it will be very difficult to recover any costs from the IP, or argue that the price should be reduced accordingly.

(a) **Limitation of conveyancing procedures**

In an insolvency sale, generally the IP will not grant any warrandice and the usual procedure is also now that no warrandice will be granted by or on behalf of the insolvent seller (see para 9.10(o)). This is normally specified in the missives, so the purchaser is in no doubt.

Invariably no letter of obligation will be granted by the solicitors acting for the IP and again this will be stated in the offer. Although there is no duty on a solicitor to provide a letter of obligation in any sale, such is the strength of traditional practice, that the fact that none will be granted should be specified to avoid arguments that silence denoted that the normal conveyancing procedures would be followed.

Usually the missives will provide that the purchaser must satisfy himself as to matters of title, statutory compliance, searches and that no representations or warranties as to condition or fitness for purpose of the property will be made or implied. Accordingly the purchaser will have to carry out his own surveys, which would in any event be usual, satisfy himself as to title which again, his solicitors would expect to do, and also obtain his own PECs, searches and any other reports required, and which are usually provided by the seller but which often the IP will not provide.

(b) Exclusion of personal liability

This is arguably the most important clause in insolvency missives (from the viewpoint of the seller, at any rate) as it is essential to the IP that they have no personal liability in respect of either the property or the transaction. It states the exclusion from any liability and underlines that the purchaser will have no claim against the IP in respect of any aspect of the transaction. For good measure it excludes any personal liability that might be imposed on the IP by the provisions of the Insolvency Act 1986 as well:

(i)   The [IP] contracts solely as agent of the seller and will incur no personal liability of any nature (whether directly or indirectly, express or implied) and howsoever arising including without prejudice to the foregoing generality, personal liability in respect of any action or actions in pursuance of the seller's rights and/or obligations under the missives and whether formulated in contract and/or delict, or by reference to any other remedy or right, and regardless of the jurisdiction or forum in which it is raised;

(ii)   No claim which may be or become competent to the Purchaser arising directly or indirectly from the missives or any deed or document executed in connection with the missives or under any arrangement collateral to the missives will lie against the [IP] personally and the [IP] will be entitled at any time to have any such deeds or documents amended to include an exclusion of personal liability in terms of this clause; and

(iii)   Any personal liability of the [IP] which would arise in terms of the Insolvency Act 1986, but for the provisions of this clause, is expressly excluded.

(c) Exclusion of Representations and Warranties

The purpose of this clause is to ensure that the purchaser is relying entirely on its own investigations and advice received from its own advisers, and that nothing that may have been said or implied by the seller or the IP or any information or paperwork provided in the course of the marketing of the property or the transaction should be relied on. The following example clause sets out the main exclusions normally provided, but some offers on behalf of IPs will contain additional specific provisions along similar lines. Note also that if there are any moveable items included in the sale the exclusions should apply to them as well:

(i) The Purchaser agrees that in effecting the purchase of the property it is not relying on any information, warranty, statement, undertaking, representation or silence on the part of the seller or the [IP] or any of their solicitors, advisers, valuers, employees, agents, or representatives, or anyone acting for them or on their behalf, or all or any of them, whether or not made within any document prepared by or on behalf of the [IP] (whether acting as agents of the seller or otherwise) and that the Purchaser is not relying on any other written or oral representation made to it or to its representatives or agents by the [IP] or their representatives or agents.

(ii) All representations, warranties and conditions, express or implied, arising under statute, at common law or otherwise (including representations, warranties and conditions as to the right, title or interest of the seller or the [IP] to the property are expressly excluded.

(iii) It is agreed by the Purchaser that the provisions of the missives are fair and reasonable in the circumstances of the insolvency of the Seller, and are in accordance with normal practice, particularly in the light of the fact that:

(a) the Purchaser is aware of the need to rely on its own inspections and investigations of the property, by reason of the absence of representations, warranties and conditions, and has had every opportunity to do so;

(b) the Seller is insolvent and consequently faces the constraints on selling necessarily imposed on it in that circumstance;

(c) the knowledge of the property available to the [IP] and their partners, staff and advisers, including but not limited to solicitors and valuers, is necessarily limited;

(iv) Nothing in the missives or any deed or document executed in terms of the missives will oblige the seller and/or the [IP] to discharge in whole or in part any liability or obligation of the seller, regardless of how it arises, outstanding at the time of the [IP's] appointment.

In addition there will usually be some form of specific statement about the purchaser being totally satisfied as to the quality, state and condition of the property (and any moveables included in the sale if applicable):

(v) The Purchaser is deemed to have satisfied itself entirely from its own inspections and enquiries, and/or from its own opinion and/or professional advice as to the nature, condition, quality, state, description, fitness for purpose, use, operation, compliance or any other aspect of

    (a) the property;

    (b) any movable items in the property and

    (c) all systems, any mechanical or electrical apparatus and all service media in or serving the property and agrees that as neither the seller nor the [IP] have given any warranty, guarantee or other assurance they will have no responsibility or liability arising from any such aspect of the property, and or moveable items, systems, apparatus and/or service media in the property.

SALES BY HERITABLE CREDITORS IN POSSESSION

6.19 Purchasing property from a Heritable Creditor in possession is also likely to mean that the seller has very little actual knowledge about the property, and that can affect the due diligence process. However, the missives do not usually limit the searches and reports available to the purchaser in the same way as they do in insolvency sales, although the purchaser will be expected to satisfy itself as to title, and the heritable creditor is unlikely to be interested in engaging in arrangements that might reduce the amount of the funds that it receives as sale proceeds.

The heritable creditor exercising its power of sale must obtain the best price that could reasonably be obtained (see para 8.18(c)). Even though a heritable creditor's principal concern is to recover the amount that it lent to the borrower, the duty to obtain the best price means that if the borrower considers that the price obtained is not the best price that could have been obtained, which might for example mean the difference between the borrower receiving some of the sale proceeds, and not, then they can challenge the sale.

THE *DE PLANO* ACCEPTANCE

6.20 If the seller is able to accept all the condition in the offer without qualification then his solicitors can issue a letter concluding the missives in the following terms:

Dear Sirs

Seller

Purchaser

Property address

On behalf of our clients, [   ], we hereby accept your offer on behalf of your clients [   ] dated [   ] confirm that we are holding the Missives concluded on the basis of:

1. Your offer of [   ];and

2. This letter.

Yours faithfully

[solicitors]

(Signed by a partner and witnessed)

Quite often the original offer will contain a time limit for acceptance – see clause (Second) of the standard offer in para 6.09. If the seller's solicitor fails to comply with the time limit, then the usual practice is to issue a qualified acceptance with one qualification, namely the deletion of the time limit, which then needs to be accepted in writing by the purchaser's solicitors. Note however that the terms of clause (Second) state that if not accepted within the time limits specified, the offer is deemed to be withdrawn. Strictly speaking therefore, if the seller's solicitors fail to issue the acceptance in time, there is no offer to accept, it having been withdrawn. The five working day period referred to in the clause is considered sufficient time within which even the most disorganised seller (or solicitor) ought to be able to respond. A time limit will of course not be relevant if the parties are both treating the offer as a draft.

CONCLUDED MISSIVES

6.21 Once missives are concluded, remember that unless the risk is shifted back to the sellers in missives, the risk passes to the purchasers on completion of the missives. It is however, usual and normal for the sellers to accept the insurance risk until entry, but if for any reason this has not been agreed, then it will be necessary for the purchaser to arrange insurance cover immediately on completing missives. In this connection, remember that most general insurance contracts are regulated insurance contracts, which are regulated by the Financial Services Authority, and that solicitors may not arrange insurance for their clients without authorisation from the FSA, or licensed to conduct incidental financial business by the Law Society of Scotland.

The insurance cover, whether in name of the seller or the purchaser should be for full reinstatement value, and not for market value. In a modern property there may not be much difference between the two values but in an older building, built of traditional materials, the cost of repairing it to the same standard may well be considerably in excess of what the house cost to buy. Most commercial clients will expect to make their own insurance arrangements and would not expect their solicitor to be involved in this process.

Don't forget to inform your client that missives have been concluded and particularly for purchasers of residential property to remind them that they have entered into a formal binding contract. They should, of course, have been kept informed at all stages of formation of the contract.

FURTHER READING

Law of Contract in Scotland 3rd Edn (William McBryde, W Green)

RICS: Service Charges in Commercial Property – Code of Practice 2nd edition
www.rics.org/servicechargecode

Chapter 7

Searches and Enquiries

'Care and diligence bring luck' — *Thomas Fuller*

Part of the 'due diligence' process, the purchaser's searches and enquiries are of paramount importance in a system of *caveat emptor* (let the buyer beware). If there is any defect with the property, in the period before the purchaser settles, she should know about it and be able to decide how - or whether - to proceed.

If there are any mistakes in, or omissions from, this vital process, then the purchaser could end up buying a property that may be difficult to sell on for the right price, or at all, because of the failure in due diligence. Due diligence falls into one of two categories: 'private' due diligence, where enquiries are made of the seller as to the position of any matter; and 'public due diligence, where public registers are interrogated to disclose the position of any relevant matter. This Chapter will consider the latter, whilst the following chapter on examining title will consider the private due diligence aspects.

Precisely what public due diligence enquiries will be made will be dictated by the missives, as we have seen in the previous Chapter.

The good news is that although the due diligence must be thorough, it need not be exhaustive. There are standard searches and enquiries that solicitors should make, and any expert searches or determinations should be carved out of the scope of services in the initial letter of engagement.

THE SELLER'S KNOWLEDGE

7.01 We have already seen in Chapter 5 that the seller's knowledge of the property can be a considerable resource for the purchaser, whether contained in the Property Questionnaire of the Home Report or the Disclosed Documents section of the PSG Offer. The analysis of that knowledge can inform the nature and extent of the public due diligence package. The generally available public searches are as follows:

PROPERTY ENQUIRY CERTIFICATES (PECS)

7.02 Also variably called 'Property Clearance Letters' or 'Property Clearance Certificates' in some areas of Scotland, PECs can be obtained from the local council or from specialist searching agencies, on payment of a fee. The PEC should be obtained as early as possible by the seller, in case it presents any difficulty, preferably before missives are concluded, but it should be borne in mind that the information contained is out of date, and that some solicitors require a PEC to be dated after conclusion of missives (see para 8.10(s)). To be satisfactory to a client bank, the PEC must comply with the current edition of the Council of Mortgage Lenders' (CML) Handbook (or the bank's loan instructions). The standard position in the Combined Standard Clauses is that the PEC must be dated not more than three months prior to the date of entry, which is consistent with the CML Handbook. Check, however, that your client bank accepts PECs from private firms. Most do, but it is always better to check. The seller's solicitor should ask the purchaser's solicitor for an updated PEC (or parts of it) before settlement if no warranty from the seller can be obtained.

There is no standard form of PEC. Each of the 32 Councils and each private searching firm take a similar but different approach. Broadly speaking, the PEC encompasses searches of the following statutory registers:

Planning

This search will disclose any planning applications and consents (or refusals). Any planning information will of course just be in abstract form: you will need to ask the purchaser's solicitor for any blueprints or drawings that you need to see. Make sure that the versions you see are certified copies or originals, with the planning authority's approval stamped on its face.

As with building warrants etc, the purchaser's solicitor should match up known alterations to the approved documentation and refer to the surveyor or architect in cases of any doubt (see example in Appendix 1). Whether the property is a listed building, whether it is in a conservation area, whether it is affected by an Article 4 Direction (where some developments might have had deemed consent in general law, this Article disapplies the deemed consent), or whether it is subject to any enforcement action.

The listing of a building may make an enormous difference to the purchaser as to the desirability of a property. Some purchasers may be antiquarians, art historians or the like and actively welcome a listing. For most purchasers it means that there will be significant restrictions as to what they can do with the property (or the site, since demolition is seldom an option).

There are three grades of legal protection for listed buildings: A, B and C, with A being the greatest protection for national treasures. Any alterations to listed buildings will need listed building consent, which will involve the consultation and approval of Historic Scotland. Alterations to listed buildings will therefore require patience and deep pockets. See www.historic-scotland.gov.uk/listing for more details. For guidance on conservation areas and Article 4 directions, see the Scottish Government's guide at www.scotland.gov.uk/publications/2005/03/29141519/15200.

Building Control

This will disclose if there is are any building warrants that have been applied for in respect of alterations to the property. Crucially, it will also show whether the corresponding completion certificate confirmation has been issued by the Council, approving the works. The importance of this information will be considered in more detail in the following Chapter. The purchaser's solicitor should analyse the information that the Council holds about the Building Warrants and Completion Certificates to ensure that all works have been properly documented and that the necessary documentation in is in place. Almost as important, is to consider the information in the register in light of what the single survey (and perhaps even the Schedule of Sales Particulars) to ensure that any work revealed to have been carried out has been properly authorised. If not, then the solicitor should insist on a letter of comfort (or property inspection report) to ensure that the Council will not take any enforcement action in relation to the breach. See Appendix 1 for an example.

Roads

The Council is the Roads Authority. Roads authorities have the power (and duty) to adopt roads as public roads, to be maintained at public expense. Your client will need to know whether the road is adopted *ex adverso* (to the boundary) of the property. If the road is so adopted, then you need not make further enquiry, since you can assume that the roads authority has confirmed that a public right of passage exists over the road, which provides rights for any type of traffic to use the road at any time, subject only to the Road's Authority's regulations and road traffic law generally. The purchaser's solicitor will require to ensure that the property enjoys adequate rights to and from the adopted road. If the road is not adopted, then further investigation of the ownership and maintenance of the private road will be required and you should look at para 8.19 for further information. This section will also disclose whether the property is affected by any transportation proposals, such as a proposal for a bypass or road widening scheme.

Statutory Notices

This will disclose whether the Council has served any statutory notices under the Civic Government (Scotland) Act 1982, requiring the owners to deal with defects or disrepair. If a statutory repairs notice has been served on a building, the responsibility for this will usually remain with the seller. The purchaser's solicitor would normally retain an adequate amount from the purchase price delivered at settlement to cover the liability, which would arise after settlement.

Other Statutory Notices

This search will disclose whether the Council has served any notices under housing, environmental protection, and health & safety legislation. Environmental health, health and safety notices etc will be very important to a purchaser who is buying a business, not least in the catering industry.

The following are optional, but usually included:

Water and sewerage

For a separate charge, Scottish Water will produce a report stating whether the property is connected to the water and sewerage mains, and usually produce a helpful OS plan with the route of the mains. Most urban properties will be connected and, if this is the case, there should be no need for further enquiry. That said, as with roads, the purchaser's solicitor should ensure that the property enjoys adequate rights for the pipes to and from the main. Do not assume that Scottish Water has statutory powers to compel owners of other properties to allow your client to connect to the main – Scottish Water's powers are limited to the route of the main itself. In the same way as access can be 'ransomed' by a ransom strip, so can services for a property.

If the water supply and sewerage outflow is not connected to the main, then the purchaser's solicitor will need to consider the adequacy of any private arrangements. See para 6.17(c).

Contaminated land

Most Councils will disclose only whether the property is actually contaminated, by virtue of being on the contaminated land register kept under the Part IIA of the Environmental Protection Act 1990, which is the extent of their statutory duty. There are few properties on the register. Councils would rather money was spent on remediating properties through giving grant assistance and imposing planning conditions rather than effectively 'blighting' land by declaring it to be actually contaminated. One Council stands out, however. Since 2003, the Moray Council has included information on *potential* contamination as a standard component of its PEC from its own map-based database. The solicitors in Moray have made the provision of the envirosearch a standard part of their conveyancing process, whether it is provided by the Council through the PEC or from a third party provider. This addition of a contaminated land search in the conveyancing process might not always make the conveyancing transaction smooth, but this policy has had an appreciable effect on tackling the problem.

COAL MINING REPORT

7.03 As a rapidly industrialising country in the 19th and 20th centuries, Scotland needed masses of coal to power the great manufacturing industries. Coal was mined across Scotland. However, in the post-war period demand slumped due to clean air initiatives and cheaper imports of coal and coke. The majority of coal mines have been closed down.

However, in place of heavy industry, property development flourished. The result is that some houses may have been unwittingly built over old, disused coal mines and they may now be liable to movement or worse, subsidence or collapse.

Therefore, it is important to ensure that a search is requested from the Coal Authority, which holds records of where mines were constructed. There are some areas where there has never been any history of coal mining and therefore the Law Society allow solicitors to dispense with the requirement in these areas. You can check lists of the Coal Authority website www.coal.decc.gov.uk to find out whether the property your client is selling (or buying) is in an area where a coal mining search either is or is not required.

COMPANIES SEARCH

7.04 If the seller is a company, the purchaser's solicitor requires to be satisfied as to the continued good standing of the company. A company is a 'legal person' which has the legal personality to transact property in its own name, but as a legal person, it can be killed off more easily than a natural person. Therefore, a specialist company searcher is engaged to search the records held by Companies House (the companies registrar, named after the building). All being well, the companies search will disclose that there are no proposals to strike off or wind up the company.

In addition the purchaser's solicitors will require to check if there are any outstanding charges granted by the company as these need to be dealt with or discharges prior to completion. Accordingly the searchers should be asked to provide a search in the company's Register of Charges as well, and you should also ask to see a search disclosing the details of the current directors and the secretary so that you can check these details against the signatories to the disposition or other deeds.

PROPERTY REGISTER SEARCH

7.05 One of the main concerns of the purchaser is to obtain a good and marketable title to the property. As we will see in the next chapter, the purchaser's solicitor will satisfy himself or herself on the sufficiency of the title by examining the title deeds that have either been recorded in the General Register of Sasines or registered in the Land Register. Those titles clearly show an historical position. The purchaser's solicitor must therefore ensure that he or she has seen recent evidence of the continuing good and marketable title position.

If the title to property is already recorded in the Register of Sasines and the transaction does not involve a valuable consideration, then the new title will be recorded in the Sasines, too. The solicitor will already have examined the Report on Search from the last transaction. He must now ask the seller's solicitor to produce an Interim Report on Search, which will disclose whether there have been any other deeds recorded since the last Report on Search. The Interim Report on Search is 'brought down' before settlement, so that the seller's solicitor has a final Report on Search added to the composite document and then sends this to the purchaser's solicitor. Sasine transactions are becoming increasingly rare in practice.

If the title to property is recorded in the Sasines and the transaction does involve a valuable consideration, then the transaction will involve a First Registration in the Land Register. The seller's solicitor should send the Form 10 request to the Keeper or a searcher as early as possible. This will be a search in the Register of Sasines, in the same way as an Interim Report on Search. The reply is called a Form 10A Report. The application for the update of the Form 10A Report, just before settlement, is called a Form 11 and the response is a Form 11A Report. If these reports show any entries, then they clearly have to be dealt with before the transaction can proceed.

Alternatively, the title to the property will already be registered in the Land Register. That being so a Form 12 request is submitted and a Form 12A Report is generated. The update of this Report is a Form 13A Report. The Form 12A and 13A Reports are the result of searches in the Land Register.

PERSONAL SEARCHES

7.06 As part of the procedure for a Property Search, there is a personal search included at no extra cost. In this case, the seller's solicitor enters the full name and address details of each party to the transaction that will grant a deed. In the request to bring down the search just before settlement, the names and addresses of all the parties are added. The search is in the Register of Inhibitions (the personal register) and it will look for any impediment against the parties. It's not like a credit search or a County Court Judgement search. The most usual impediment that would be disclosed would be an inhibition, which is an interim or final court order preventing a party from selling the property. The case of *Park, Petitioners* (see paras 2.08 and 6.05) is an excellent example of how an inhibition can prevent the sale of property.

ENVIRONMENTAL SEARCH

7.07 We touched on contaminated land in chapter 3 in relation to letters of engagement and in section 7.02 above. We also look at this issue in the context of new houses in para 5.11. The position is that an environmental search is not a standard requirement as part of the Scottish conveyancing process (other than in Moray) and they are routinely excluded by solicitors because the Law Society and the CML do not require solicitors to obtain these (although note that some lenders may have requirements in this connection, so you should always check the relevant Part 2 of the CML Handbook (see para 10.05(b)). There is perhaps a danger that once the client has become aware of the potential contamination but does nothing about it, they can become a 'knowing permitter' in terms of the Environmental Protection Act 1990 - see *Circular Facilities (London) Ltd v Sevenoaks District Council* [2005] Env LR 35; [2005] JPL 1624. The current advice from the Law Society, informed by contaminated land specialists, is as follows:

> The Professional Practice and Conveyancing Committees of the Law of Society of Scotland have reconsidered that guidance in the light of the complexity of this area and the availability of specialist advice from Scottish Solicitors accredited in environmental law. The Committee's view is that if a Scottish Solicitor does not feel qualified to comment regarding environmental matters whether in general and/or in particular in regard to contaminated land matters, then, whatever the nature of the property in the transaction (including for the avoidance of doubt both residential and commercial property) that Solicitor is entitled to seek to exclude liability for environmental law matters and/or contaminated land matters provided that exclusion of indemnity is made clear in the initial terms of business issued to the client with respect to the transaction in question.

In reality, few solicitors will feel qualified to comment on environmental matters other than in the abstract and will therefore exclude liability automatically in the letter of engagement. However, an environmental search contains potentially interesting pieces of information that a residential purchaser (or commercial one for that matter) might really care about — and that may sway their purchasing decision. It seems illogical that there is so much information provided upfront in the Home Report, without any environmental or contamination information being made available. The reports generally include information about the site history, standard environmental enquiries, past uses that are potentially contaminative, and mining and stability history. Almost as importantly, in these days, is the flood risk information where flooding data is matched to the property's location.

A typical residential environmental report is comparatively easy to interpret. It has two outcomes, summarised as PASSED or REFERRED. If a report is referred, then a specialist will consider the nature of the potential contamination and whether any further investigation will be required. The reports are based on historical uses, mainly based on old OS maps. Such maps are not always helpful. So, if a property is within 500m of a railway line, it may deemed to be potentially contaminated. The purchaser has to take a view - should further investigation be considered necessary, it will invariably take the shape of drilling for soil samples that are then analysed by scientists for evidence of contamination. This is expensive for the seller (usually a few thousand pounds) and hugely disruptive to the conveyancing process. If remediation is required, then the seller may have a horrible liability to face up to.

It is, however, interesting to reflect that contaminated land is one area where the seller of land cannot ordinarily walk away from liability, despite the *caveat emptor* principle. The liability will remain, whether the seller is aware of it or not. In terms of the EPA 1990, the principle of the legislation is that the 'polluter pays'. To effect that principle, the Act creates a chain of liability all the way up the ownership chain to the original polluter. The seller can, however, end his or her liability by 'selling with information'. This means that the purchaser is provided with environmental reports and has enough information to make a decision.

It is interesting to note that the banks do not routinely require to see environmental reports. According to the CML this is because:

- They are not detailed enough to inform on current or future risk;
- There are no details of actual contamination or risks from contamination, what remediation would be required, or any effect on valuation; and
- There are a small number of properties affected by actual contamination, possibly less than 5%.

The practical position is that the jury is out on these reports. It is not common practice in Scotland to obtain these reports routinely for residential purchases. As a seller, there may be little advantage in offering an environmental report, as it would seem to opens a Pandora's Box. On the other hand, some clients may want to be reassured that there will be no continuing liability. For a purchaser, 5% (one in every twenty) can sound like a high risk of the nightmare of discovering that their new property is built on contaminated land or prone to flood for the sake of £150 (approximately) report. At some point they will have to sell on when the sentiment may be different. Although we reiterate the advice from the Law Society's Committees that this is not a requirement for a solicitor in terms of exercising a duty of care, you will be doing a good job in protecting their interest by insisting on a report from the seller with an option to resile if anything materially prejudicial is discovered. Even if that is resisted, a report is relatively modestly priced, so many clients might not object to paying for this. Either way, it's best to discuss the options with clients and keep a file note of the discussion.

The position with commercial clients is different in that, generally speaking, sophisticated property developers are well aware of the position and the risks and will have their own procedures for dealing with the risk. Equally, the financial risk may be higher, so again it is prudent to flag the issue with clients. However you should not give advice unless you have appropriate expertise, so refer the matter to someone who does.

P16 REPORT

7.08 Prior to registering a title in the Land Register for the first time a P16 Report should be obtained from the Registers of Scotland. Private searchers also provide this service, described for example as a 'Property Definition Report'. This compares the legal extent of the title with the occupational extent, by reference to the current Ordnance Survey sheet. It will confirm whether the description of the property in the title deeds coincides with the actual extent of the property on the ground.

The Keeper will reply to a Form P16 in one of the following ways:

(1)   *'The subjects are not identifiable on the Ordnance map.'* This may be a sign of a serious problem, and steps need to be taken to resolve this before matters progress further. If there is a defect in title the Keeper may restrict his indemnity. For this reason the form P16 report should be ordered as soon as possible, particularly if you are not familiar with the title. In practice this reply may not necessarily be difficult to overcome—the property may be a 'floating shape', ie it is not related in any way to adjoining geographical features, and the land could be situated anywhere. This can be easily corrected by the insertion of necessary details, such as streets or geographical features.

(2)   *'The boundaries of the subjects coincide with those on the Ordnance map.'* This is the answer you hope for, and if you get it, you can proceed without worry.

(3)   *'The boundaries do not coincide with those on the Ordnance map. Please see print herewith.'* This indicates a minor, but material, discrepancy, which will have to be cleared up. It does not, however, go to the root of the sale as does answer 1.

However, failing this discrepancy in the boundaries being clarified, the Keeper would have to give a qualified indemnity, because of the uncertainty of the boundaries. This is contrary to the obligation in the missives. This matter is clarified in an article by the then Deputy Keeper from 1995 JLSS 15, which states:

> If the comparison confirms that the Ordnance map is correct and there is a discrepancy between the legal extent and the occupied extent, what will require to be done will depend on which extent is the greater. If the legal extent is greater than the occupied extent and the latter is contained wholly within the former then, if the purchaser is prepared to accept a title to the occupied extent, the Keeper should be informed of this when the application is made and he will process the application accordingly. The second additional question provides an opportunity to do so. Where, however, the occupied extent exceeds the boundaries of

the legal extent, remedial conveyancing will be necessary and should be completed before application for registration is made.'

A form P16 report will only be available for properties that are capable of being shown on the Ordnance Survey map and are not therefore available for a flat in a tenement.

REGISTER OF COMMUNITY INTERESTS IN LAND (RCIL)

7.09 The RCIL was set up following on the introduction of the Community Right to Buy in Part 2 of the Land Reform (Scotland) Act 2003. Before a community body can exercise the Community Right to Buy, it must register its interest in the RCIL, which is maintained by the Registers of Scotland.

It is accessible online at http://rcil.ros.gov.uk and contains information relating to each community interest registered in it, including the name and address of the registered office of the company which constitutes the community body which has registered the interest; and a description of the land, including maps, plans or other drawings. Particulars of agricultural tenants' interests are also available at this Register.

Instructions to search in the RCIL should be included when instructing searches against land that could potentially be affected, although the seller should know whether such an interest has been registered against land that they own, as notification has to be given to landowners affected. The online facility is kept up to date, so it is easy to run an informal check. When offering to purchase land that could potentially be affected by a registered interest, confirmation should be sought from the seller that the land is not, and will not at the date of conclusion of missives be, affected by any registered interest by a community body. See also para 5.17(f).

OTHER SEARCHES

7.10 Other searches that may be carried out will vary according to the nature of the property. In some cases, there may be a heightened risk from radon gas. Radon is a colourless, odourless radioactive gas. It is formed by the radioactive decay of the small amounts of uranium that occur naturally in all rocks and soils. Breathing in high levels of radon can damage the lungs and cause lung cancer. The UK Health Protection Agency can provide a radon risk report for under £5.

For rural properties, it will be of interest to know whether the Forestry Commission has any schemes or dedication agreements over the land. The Forestry Commission provide a useful, interactive map at the link below. The Registers of Scotland operate a Register of Sites of Special Scientific Interest, which it is also prudent to check in rural or semi rural areas, particularly if development is proposed.

FURTHER READING

SEPA's contaminated land information can be found at:

http://www.sepa.org.uk/land/contaminated_land.aspx

Guidance

The Law Society of Scotland has issued the following guidance to solicitors:

Advice from Law Society of Scotland leaflet on what enquiries solicitors should make on contaminated land (Journal, April 2003).

A reminder that contaminated land is an issue that will not go away in property transactions (Journal, August 2007).

Recent advice from the Conveyancing and Professional Practice Committees

Contaminated Land – the story continues (Journal, March 2011).

Commentary on Two recent English cases highlighting the significance of the contaminated land regime, and the need for the greatest care over the history of land in any transaction (Journal, September 2007).

Radon Risk Report

http://www.ukradon.org/search.php

Forestry Commission

http://maps.forestry.gov.uk/imf/imf.jsp?site=fcscotland_ext&

Chapter 8

Examination of and Reporting on Title

INTRODUCTION

8.01 When land registration was introduced to Scotland in 1979, many experienced practitioners at the time forecast the demise of the art of the conveyancer: title would be reduced to a few lines on a title sheet, and no skill would be required to decipher the provisions that applied to the property. Reflecting on that view more than 30 years later, the reality has been quite different, and with the additional layers, more recently added, of feudal abolition and the revised regimes of title conditions and tenement law encapsulated in statute, the practicalities of title examination can seem increasingly complicated.

The similarities between various aspects of the conveyancing process for residential and commercial properties are most apparent when examining title. Precisely the same legal fundamentals come into consideration, although the implications of what the title examination discloses may be quite different. A use restriction limiting the use of the property for residential purposes matters not at all when purchasing a dwellinghouse for residential occupation, but could represent a major obstacle if the purpose of the purchase is to build a retail park.

WHY IS IT NECESSARY TO EXAMINE TITLE?

8.02 An essential element of the conveyancing process is to ensure that the purchaser obtains a good and marketable title to the property. In their book *Conveyancing* (3rd edn, 2004, W Green, page 111) Professors Reid and Gretton define a marketable title as one:

(a) which makes the buyer the owner of the property; and

(b) after acquiring ownership, will not be subject to any third party rights, other than title conditions of an ordinary nature and with the possible exception of title leases.

To this might be added that a marketable title is one that can be sent to the Keeper immediately after purchase, and on the basis of which the Keeper will, without making further enquiries or requisitions (or none that cannot be resolved in 60 days), issue a land certificate without any exclusion of indemnity (see para 2.05).

Examination of title is a process: a voyage of discovery with an identified destination in mind. We embark on it to discover:

(a)   who is the current owner of the property (it should be the seller)

(b)   what is the extent of the property and its boundary features

(c)   what rights and pertinents benefit the property

(d)   whether there are any restrictions on the use of the property

(e)   what obligations fall on the owner of the property

(f)   whether any third parties have rights in relation to the property

(g)   whether the title is valid and marketable

It is for the seller to show that they have a valid marketable title, and for the purchaser to be satisfied that this is so. It will usually be the preference of the seller that missives are concluded before the titles are passed to the purchaser's solicitors for examination. Using the appropriate version of the Residential Standard Clauses (see para 6.08) will invariably result in a swift conclusion of missives, and solicitors who use the PSG Offers to Sell (see para 6.13) often find that an agreed contract can be achieved more quickly than when starting from the polarised position of a purchaser- or seller- orientated first offer.

In both residential and commercial circumstances it is preferable to achieve conclusion of missives before sending the titles to the purchaser's solicitor for examination. Experience shows that once the purchaser's solicitor has received the titles he starts looking at them, and starts incorporating requirements that arise as a result of title examination into the missives. Guidance for the Standard Residential Missives advises not to send the titles until missives are concluded. It is not always as easy to achieve this in commercial transactions, and there might be compelling reasons to submit the titles (or some parts of them) to the purchaser's solicitors to establish some point, which will help to facilitate the progress of the transaction, so sensible judgement should be exercised in those cases where refusing to show the titles might well be considered obstructive.

In the disposition, the sellers will (usually) grant absolute warrandice (see para 9.10(o)), that is to say, they undertake to indemnify the purchasers against any title defect. When a title is registered in the Land Register, the Keeper will (usually) issue a land certificate with a guarantee of indemnity. Why then should the purchaser's solicitor have to examine the title in such detail? Can they not just assume, or expect that previous solicitors will have checked, that the title is in order and rely on that?

The short answer is no. Title is examined for a number of reasons, and has to be checked on each transfer to ensure that it is in order and that no new dealings affect the property. The purchaser is owed no duty of care by solicitors who have previously investigated the title, and generally there will be a degree of *caveat emptor*. The precise terms of the title may be unacceptable to your client depending upon what he plans to do with the property, if it is a commercial property, and your title examination will be needed to establish that there are no impediments to what is proposed.

As many experienced conveyancers know, errors and mistakes can exist in titles that have been passed along several times, and it is therefore the role of the purchasers solicitors to conduct a proper investigation of title as part of what is known as the 'due diligence' process of examining all elements that affect the property being purchased. It may be the case that the solicitor is required certify the title to the purchaser's lender. In some cases (usually commercial transactions) the seller's solicitor can be asked to certify title to the purchaser, and those parties will be entitled to rely on the certificate as though the solicitor giving the certificate were acting for them (although note that often in such cases, the party being certified to will have their own solicitors who will often be expected to advise their client on the terms of the certificate being given) (see para 8.38). Warrandice is not a particularly effective remedy, in practice, as it depends on 'eviction' having taken place, and the victim has to go through the process of losing his property before he can claim warrandice (see *Welsh v Russell* (1894) 21 R 769) 'Eviction' in this case means any interference with the property right, rather than being put out of the property. Even if there is a valid remedy under warrandice, it might prove impossible to trace the granters of warrandice, or if appropriate, their predecessors in title.

THE STUFF OF CONVEYANCING

8.03 Title examination is truly the stuff of traditional conveyancing.

It is a usual stipulation of missives that the title will contain 'no unduly onerous conditions or restrictions'. The meaning of this expression can be quite subjective, and depends very much on the circumstances of each case. This is an unsatisfactory state of affairs. If the sellers give this assurance in the missives, purchasers can claim at a later date that there is, in their opinion, an onerous condition or restriction in the title, and the matter will have to be argued and compromised, although, at worst, the purchasers may withdraw. Often a stipulation of this type in a purchaser's offer will have been qualified by the seller to the effect that the purchaser must satisfy himself as to the adequacy of the title, and will have imposed a time limit within which he will be deemed to have done so.

Lord Young commented on the phrase in *Whyte v Lee* ((1879) 6 R 699 at 701) as follows:

'If a man simply buys a house he must be taken to buy it as the seller has it, on a good title of course, but subject to such restrictions as may exist if of an ordinary character, and such as the buyer may reasonably be supposed to have contemplated as at least not improbable.'

The leading case is *Armia Ltd v Daejan Developments Ltd* (1979 SC (HL) 56), where a property in Kirkcaldy High Street, which had been bought for redevelopment, was found to be subject to a servitude right of access, along a 10-feet wide passage through the property from front to rear, coupled with a prohibition on building on the passage. The width of the passage was just slightly over a sixth of the length of the entire frontage of the property which would effectively sterilise the development. It was held that this was a sufficiently unusual condition to allow the purchaser to resile.

In the case of *Morris v Ritchie* (1992 GWD 33–1950) a piece of ground being sold turned out to be burdened by a servitude right of access, which would have reduced the number of car parking spaces by 7 out of 18, and would therefore have a bad effect on turnover and consequently, the market value of the property. This only became known to the pursuer after missives had been concluded, and a deposit had been paid. The pursuer was allowed to withdraw from the purchase because of the diminution in value of the ground. On a practical note, sellers who know of restrictions of this nature would do well to disclose them to the purchasers before missives are concluded.

In *Snowie v Museum Hall LLP* [2010] CSOH 107, 2010 SLT 971, in which six sets of missives were concluded to buy six flats in the same development, all subject to a requirement that the title to the development should 'contain no unduly onerous or unusual conditions', the purchasers sought to resile, in reliance on this provision, when they learned that the Deed of Conditions affecting the development contained a prohibition of use of a residential apartment for any trade, business or profession, even in an ancillary capacity. This is a very typical burden in residential deeds of conditions, and indeed, features in a style Deed of Conditions to be found in Greens Practice Styles. Lord Glennie was clear that restrictions of this type were not unusual, and the fact that they were not uncommon showed that neither were they unduly onerous.

TITLE EXAMINATION

8.04 Examination of title needs to be methodical and thorough. While principally it involves checking the provisions of the title deeds, it will also involve looking at the terms of other documentation that affects the property, which depending on the type of property, will or may include Property Enquiry Certificates, Planning and Building Warrant documents, Leases and other leasehold documents, construction documents and contracts, VAT and other taxation matters, Coal Authority Reports, Searches in the Property, Personal and Companies registers, energy performance certificates and so on (see Chapter 7: Searches and Enquiries).

A comprehensive list of items that you might need to examine in the course of your investigations is contained in the 'Due Diligence Questionnaire' available on the PSG website. The purpose of the Due Diligence Questionnaire is to provide the seller and the seller's solicitors and advisers with a comprehensive list of the purchaser's and the purchaser's solicitors' due diligence requirements at an early stage of the transaction. The Questionnaire is an information gathering exercise and is not a substitute for the normal conveyancing procedures. Often practitioners will use the Questionnaire as an *aide-memoire* of items they might need to examine during the course of a transaction. Bear in mind of course that not all items in the Questionnaire will be relevant for every transaction. See also paras 4.07(i) and 5.10.

GETTING STARTED

8.05 You will need to make a record of what you find during your examination of the titles and other ancillary papers, and the best way to do this is to write down 'Notes on Title' with all the salient details from the titles and other papers. While senior conveyancers might find that they are able to dictate their Notes, experience shows that it is much more effective to hand write these notes, particularly for the more junior practitioner. Your notes should be sufficiently comprehensive so that if need be you, (or a colleague) would be able to check an aspect of the title from them, without having to ask to get the title deeds back from the seller's solicitor. For some titles, particularly where the text is dense (and this can include some sections of Land Certificates) it can help to use coloured highlighters on the photocopies you have taken, to emphasise particular parts of the title, perhaps adding handwritten annotations in the margin, but this should be supplementary to your main notes.

While you may find it helpful to take photocopies of certain title deeds or sections of the Land Certificate, you should resist the temptation to substitute copying for making notes. There is no doubt that, particularly with old archaic titles, it is very easy to miss or misinterpret provisions if you do not subject the documents to careful and thorough scrutiny. You may need copies of certain writs for the purposes of reporting on the title to your client or, in some cases, certifying the title, and you will definitely need to take photocopies of any plans included in the title.

There will be issues that arise out of the titles as you progress through them, that you may need further information on, or that may give cause for concern or require some clarification. Ideally you should make a note of these as they occur, rather than once you have finished your examination, so that you can be sure that none are missed. Make a separate list, or dictate a running note of these, by all means. You will find that some of your queries or observations are answered when you look at other parts of the titles, but there are inevitably going to be matters that you will need to raise with the seller's solicitors (see para 8.34).

EXAMINING A SASINE TITLE

8.06 In theory the requirement to examine a title that is in the Sasine Register should diminish over time, as more properties move from the Sasine Register to the Land Register on sale. In practice however, it is still the case (at the time of writing) that title to the majority of Scotland by land mass is still recorded in the Sasine Register, so that the skills and knowledge required to examine a Sasine title will continue to be essential to the conveyancer for some time to come. Changes are however afoot that are intended to accelerate the move of titles from the Sasine Register to the Land Register, in the Scottish Law Commission's Report on Land Registration in a process called 'completing the Register'. See para 2.09 for a summary of the SLC proposals. In most cases your examination of a Sasine title will be in the course of a transaction which will induce a first registration in the Land Register, but there are still occasions when first registration will not be triggered, for example if examining the title for the purposes of taking a security over property that is already owned by a borrower, and the approach to title examination is no different, although the follow-on processes may be.

8.07 In a first registration, or in a Sasine transaction, the first thing that you must do is to check the title deeds against the Inventory of Writs, that (if the seller or his solicitors have been properly organised, should accompany the titles (whether these consist of a bundle or a couple of boxes)). This is your first opportunity to get a feel for what is involved in the title and possibly also identify if there are titles missing. It is usual and courteous to acknowledge receipt of the titles and some solicitors ask you to mark a copy of the Inventory and return it to the seller's solicitors. If there is a 'Search for Incumbrances' with the titles this will help you put the title deeds into order and check against the Search or Form 10 A Report and make sure that all the deeds mentioned in the search or form 10A have been sent to you. This helps you to start to form a rough history of the property in your mind, and in particular spot any split-offs or acquisitions and the writs referred to for burdens. Some fairly basic organisational techniques will help you at this stage. Sort the titles into categories: the prescriptive or foundation writ (see para 8.09) and writs within the prescriptive progress; the descriptive writ; writs referred to for burdens; undischarged securities and so on. Identifying writs with a visible Post-it note is a good way of seeing at a glance what role that writ plays in the overall title picture.

8.08 Some of the deeds that have been sent to you may not need to concern you. Conveyancers never seem to throw anything out and even when a Land Certificate has been issued, the prior underlying titles may still accompany the Land Certificate. In fact, this can be quite helpful, as we shall see. But some deeds can be ignored, such as some writs that are well outwith the prescriptive period, and old discharged securities. It can be quite satisfying to make a bundle of these at the start, and then concentrate on what you need to look at.

SECTION 1 OF THE PRESCRIPTION AND LIMITATION (SCOTLAND) ACT 1973 (POSITIVE PRESCRIPTION)

8.09 Where a person has possessed land openly, peaceably and without interruption for ten years, on the basis of a sufficient recorded or registered title, then after ten years the title will not be challengeable. This process is known as positive prescription. Prescription does not operate however, where the title was not valid *ex facie* (on its face), or if it turns out to have been forged.

It is not thought that many pieces of land are acquired in this way, yet this is, for another reason, a vital provision for the conveyancer. It has often been said that good titles have no need of prescription (see for example *Duke of Buccleuch v Cunynghame* (1826) 5S 53). Prescription is only required to cure bad titles. What it means, however, from the point of view of title examination, is that prior titles that fall outside the prescriptive period need not be checked, since the effect of prescription is to give an absolute presumption that the title deed is good. So, if you take the first recorded transfer of the land that you are buying, which is more than ten years old, (**the prescriptive or foundation writ**) and find that it is free from an intrinsic objection (that is an objection showing on the face of the title, and not requiring proof from outside sources) then that is a valid foundation for a prescriptive title, and you need look back no further. Therefore you may set aside all older transfers of the land, unless these contain valid land obligations to which you must refer. You must, however, check this foundation writ for any intrinsic objection, and check everything after it to make sure that it correctly flows down to the present seller (see para 8.13).

An intrinsic objection is one which can be observed from the terms of the deed itself. An example of this is given in *Cooper Scott v Gill Scott* (1924 SC 309), where a destination detailed in the narrative clause did not correspond with a further narration of the same destination in the dispositive clause. A majority of the seven judges, however, held that this deed was not intrinsically null and was therefore a good foundation for prescription (see also *Simpson v Marshall* (1900) 2 F 447).

An extrinsic objection, that is to say an objection which can only be proved from outside evidence, or an intrinsic objection that can be proved only by extrinsic evidence, does not affect the use of the disposition as a foundation of title.

A NON DOMINO DISPOSITIONS

8.10 As a demonstration of the power of prescription, consider the disposition *a non domino* (a disposition granted by someone who is not the owner). If a piece of land lies vacant, and the owner cannot be traced, it is possible for someone who does not own that land to obtain a disposition, granted by anyone in favour of a grantee. Note however that a disposition granted by the granter in favour of himself is ex facie invalid and will not be a foundation writ for prescription. This reflects the principle that a man cannot contract with himself. As Lord Clyde said in *Kildrummy (Jersey) Ltd v Inland Revenue commissioners* [1990] STC 657; [1992] SLT 787: '…where the same person is both debtor and creditor in the same matter there can be no obligation created. It is in my view ineffective to enter into a contract with continuing mutual rights and obligations with oneself, and it is whimsical to grant a lease of one's own property to oneself'. The principle is clearly settled for a non domino dispositions in *The Board of Management of Aberdeen College v Stewart Watt Youngerson and Anor* [2005] CSOH 31.

Only simple warrandice is given, for the granter has no claim to the land at all. The disposition is then recorded to make it public and the disponee occupies the land 'openly and peaceably', as if it was owned, so that anyone who has a better title may see the occupation and object. If no objection is made by anyone having a better title, within ten years, the disponee then becomes the owner of the land. If prescription can perfect a title in such circumstances, it will be seen that it can also cure much more minor defects in a deed.

It should not be thought however that the *a non domino* disposition is an easy way to acquire odd bits of land. The policy of the Registers of Scotland is quite strict on allowing *a non domino* deeds to be registered and applications for registration of such deeds will be carefully scrutinised and may be rejected. See the Registers Update 15 at http://www.ros.gov.uk/pdfs/update15.pdf.

SECTIONS 6, 7 AND 8 OF THE PRESCRIPTION AND LIMITATION (SCOTLAND) ACT 1973 (NEGATIVE PRESCRIPTION)

8.11 Together these sections provide that where an obligation has subsisted unacknowledged, or a right has not been enforced or exercised, for the continuous period specified, then that obligation or right will be extinguished. This is known as negative prescription. Sections 7 and 8 relate to the long negative prescriptive period of 20 years. These provisions can be of benefit to the conveyancer where, for example, the titles include an old bond or a security that is over 20 years old, but in respect of which no payments have been made in that time, and it has not been enforced by the creditor, it can be said to have prescribed. Servitudes which have not been exercised for a period of twenty years can be extinguished by prescription as well. The snag of course can be getting sufficient evidence of absence of payment or non use.

Section 6 provides for a five-year period of prescription for obligations to pay sums of money and obligations to pay compensation that fall within certain categories. These categories are set out in Sch 1 of the PL(S)A 1973 and include obligations to pay rent and interest.

The well equipped conveyancer should be thoroughly familiar with the rules relating to prescription. An excellent commentary on the PL(S)A

1973 is contained in an annotated edition of the PL(S)A 1973 by David M Walker *Law of prescription and limitation of actions in Scotland* 6th edn W Green 2002).

GOOD FAITH

8.12 Some conveyancing defects can be cured by *bona fides* or good faith. Section 17 of the Succession (Scotland) Act 1964 provides that where a person for good faith and for value acquires title to land from an executor, or from somebody who has derived title directly from an executor, the title will not be challengeable on the ground that the Confirmation of the executor was reducible, or had in fact been reduced, or even that the title should not have been transferred by the executor to the person who is offering the title.

For example, say you are buying from sellers David and Nicholas who do not have recorded or registered title to the property in question. Instead they produce (a) a Confirmation in the estate of their Uncle Vincent, which appoints George as executor and (b) a docket of nomination in terms of s 15 of the Succession (Scotland) Act 1964, signed by George, transferring that property to David and Nicholas, describing them as the persons entitled to take the property under Vincent's will. Provided your client is buying in good faith and for value, it need not concern you (i) if someone produces a later dated will appointing Edward as executor and nominating Harriet as the legatee entitled to the property, or (ii) someone alleges that the will is a forgery. You need look no further than the Confirmation itself.

There is an analogous provision in s 2 of the Trusts (Scotland) Act 1961 which provides that titles acquired from trustees or executors are also protected from being challenged on the ground that the transaction was at variance with the terms or purpose of the trust.

When checking discharges of previous standard securities, s 41 of the Conveyancing and Feudal Reform (Scotland) Act 1970 provides that where a discharge of a security bears to be granted by a person entitled to do so (eg the creditor), subsequent acquirers of land *bona fide* and for value, will not have their title to the land challenged after the expiry of a five-year period from the recording or registration of the discharge, merely by reason of the discharge being reduced. This means that, if a discharge is more than five years old, and appears to have been granted by the creditor of the security that is discharged, you need not examine the origins of that discharge any further.

Statutory protection also exists for parties dealing in good faith with companies. Section 40 of the Companies Act 2006 (which restates the provisions of ss 35A and 35B of the 1985 Companies Act) safeguards such parties, by providing that the power of the directors to bind the company, or authorise others to do so, is deemed not to be limited by the company's constitution. Accordingly, a third party dealing with a company in good faith does not need to concern himself about whether a company is acting within its constitution. Note also that although Section 40 does not apply to companies that are charities, nevertheless third parties acquiring property for full consideration from a charity, even if not permitted by its constitution, or its directors exceeded any limitation on their powers, does not affect the title of the third party if they do not know that the company is a charity or that the act is not permitted by the company's constitution or, that it is beyond the powers of the directors (s 42 of the Companies Act 2006 and s 112 of the Companies Act 1989).

There is also a protection afforded to a third party who acquires to any right or interest in good faith and for value from or through the recipient from a bankrupt in a gratuitous alienation (s 34 (4) Bankruptcy (Scotland) Act 1985). In practice given the importance of enquiry concerning gratuitous alientations and unfair preferences (see para 8.18(e)) good faith is likely to be difficult to demonstrate.

Further the Bankruptcy and Diligence (Scotland) Act 2007 s 17 provides some protection for a good faith purchaser from a post-sequestration dealing by the debtor, being an exception to the rule that such a dealing is void, unless consented to by the trustee. If a person who has been sequestrated grants a disposition (or other deed) to a good faith grantee, who has paid (or is willing to pay) adequate consideration for the property to which the deed relates, the sequestration does not invalidate that deed, provided that it is delivered not later than seven days after the sequestration has been registered in the Register of Inhibitions.

THE PRESCRIPTIVE PROGRESS

8.13 Start your title examination by looking first at the disposition (or dispositions) in favour of the seller, and noting down its terms. This will tell you what it is the seller owns and has to sell, and will either be all that the purchaser is acquiring, or may be a larger property of which your client is purchasing only a part. Compare the description of the title and any plan on this deed with whatever information you have – eg a survey report or Heads of Terms about what your client is purchasing. This disposition will also contain references to other rights and pertinents of title from which the seller benefits, such as servitudes. These may be expressly mentioned or reference made to other parts of the titles for more details. This disposition will also contain details of, or references to, burdens and title conditions that burden the property. Such burdens may be set out in full in much older titles, which will need to be examined in detail (see para 8.25).

Now you should identify the foundation writ, (see para 8.09) and examine it for intrinsic defects.

Next you have to examine all the writs that follow the foundation writ, until you get to the seller's title, ensuring that each one links with and follows on from every other one correctly.

LINKS IN TITLE

8.14 If the grantee (disponee) of one deed is not the granter (disponer) of the next deed, then you need to identify what the 'link in title', or midcouple, is between the two. Only certain deeds, according to s 3 of C(S)A 1924 (dispositions of land, or assignations, discharges or restrictions of heritable security), may be granted by uninfeft proprietors. Strictly speaking, following the abolition of the feudal system, the words 'infeft' and 'uninfeft' no longer have current meaning, but in the absence of a post feudal equivalent, they remain a convenient expression for many to distinguish between being a proprietor of property with a recorded/registered title (infeft), and being a proprietor of property without a recorded or registered title (uninfeft). Formerly, heritable securities could not be granted by persons without a recorded title, but standard securities and their transmissions may now be granted by uninfeft proprietors in terms of s 12 of CFR(S)A 1970.

A link in title can be a variety of things, and in some cases there may be more than one unrecorded link. Confirmation in favour of an executor and a docket of nomination (see para 8.12) is one example. Often, residential properties will be held in the joint names of a husband

and wife, and there may be a survivorship destination in the disposition in their favour, that means that the title will transfer automatically to the survivor on the death of the first of the owners, so the death certificate of that person would be the link. Generally any statute, conveyance, deed, instrument, decree or other writing, by which a right to land or to any real right in land is vested in or transmitted to any person, is competent, and includes a minute of a meeting at which any person is appointed to any place or office, if such appointment involves such rights to land.

The relevant links must be narrated in the disposition, by incorporating a clause of deduction of title (although note that once the property is registered in the Land Register no deduction of title clause is required (s 15(3) of LR(S)A 1979). A style of deduction of title clause is provided in C(S)A 1924, Sch A, form 1:

> 'Which lands and others (or subjects) were last vested [or are part of the lands and others (or subjects) last vested] in A.B. (designation of person last infeft), whose title thereto is recorded in (specify Register of Sasines and date of recording, or if the last infeftment has already been mentioned say in the said A.B. as aforesaid), and from whom I acquired right by (here specify shortly the writ or series of writs by which right was so acquired).'

It is important to note that this statutory style requires a designation of the person last infeft (usually their address and if the last vested person is deceased it is usual to say 'who resided latterly at…'), and is ineffective otherwise.

Note however that if the difference between the last grantee and the next granter is merely a change of name, then no deduction of title clause is necessary, but the fact of the change of name should be narrated in the narrative clause. For people this is simply a question of stating their current name and previous name eg Mrs Joan McMillan (design), formerly Miss Joan Spencer (design). For changes of Company name, the narrative should narrate the current and previous name or names and refer to the Certificates of Incorporation on Change of Name by which the name changes were formalised.

It will be necessary to check the links themselves to ensure that they exist and are valid and correctly referred to in the deduction of title.

Obviously the links must be sufficient to connect the previous title with the subsequent one.

THE DESCRIPTIVE WRIT

8.15 The first time a property or piece of land is fully described may be many years earlier than the foundation writ. When a property or piece of land is conveyed for the first time it needs to be sufficiently identified. This may be by way of a particular or bounding description in which the piece of land is identified by reference to its boundary features. This can range from a broad reference: 'bounded on the south by the road leading from Kinlochalmond to Kelvinforth' to a more detailed description: 'bounded on the north by the centre line of a stone wall separating the subjects from land now or formerly belonging to Richard Byron Childs and forming part of the lands and estate of Kinlochalmond and Dunvorlich, along which it extends 306 feet or thereby'. In older titles however, the description of the property, particularly of land, might be expressed in a more generalised way, where the physical boundaries of the lands are not specified, but instead the land may be described in general terms such as 'ALL and WHOLE the lands and estate of Marchmain in the County of Sutherland'. The extent of these lands is generally established over time through prescriptive possession, but this means of course that it can be difficult if not impossible to be certain of the exact extent of the land in question. Often it is necessary to decide whether or not the description is habile to include the property or area concerned (in other words that the general description is sufficient to competently include the area concerned, and with nothing to indicate to the contrary). The plan annexed to an 1837 Feu contract which delineated the high water mark meant that the description in the deed was not habile to include the foreshore (*Luss Estates Co v BP Oil Grangemouth Refinery Ltd* [1987] SLT 201).

This first description frequently arises when an area of land is split off from a larger area. It is customary to refer in the description to this larger area of which the property forms a part. Known as the 'part and portion' clause, this will refer to the larger area, usually by referring to the descriptive writ of that larger area, although it might also refer to a more general description of the larger land.

Check carefully the first description of the land, either with your own observations or with a survey plan of the property. This first full description does not however need to be repeated each time the property is conveyed. The property can be referred to in subsequent conveyances with a description by reference to that earlier descriptive writ, in accordance with the provisions of s 61 of the Conveyancing (Scotland) Act 1874 and s 8 and Sch D of the C(S)A 1924. Make sure that the first full description has been validly referred to throughout the progress of titles in conformity with these provisions.

You should also take note of all additions to the land, and disposals of any part of the land, where this is relevant, to ensure that no part of the property you are acquiring has already been conveyed by the seller to another party. This is particularly relevant in titles of large estates, where parcels of land have been conveyed off over a long period of time. There might be photocopies of dispositions and other conveyances of these parcels with the titles deeds that have been sent to you, but it might be that these split-offs are only apparent from a Search, or are disclosed by the Form 10A report, and you will need to ask for copies of the actual conveyances or title sheets to check their terms.

It can sometimes be difficult to identify the areas conveyed in previous split off writs, however, particularly if the conveyances contain no plan. Again this is more common in older titles as more modern conveyances tend where at all possible to include a plan of some sort for easier identification.

BOUNDARIES

8.16 Where a particular description is used, there are a number of rules that determine what is the precise nature of a physical boundary, depending on the words used in the deed to describe it, although the position may not be capable of determination without recourse to other evidence. Generally, if land is described as being bounded 'by' something, such as a lane, then that thing will be excluded.

Land described as being bounded by a road will usually exclude that road. However if it is a public road, or a private road situated between two estates or feus, then the mid-line (or *medium filum*) of the road will be presumed to be the boundary.

As a general rule, fences, walls and gables that lie between the properties of two persons are owned to the centre line by each proprietor, with each proprietor having an interest in the other half. It is possible, however, that the wall is owned jointly, in which case the boundary of each property is the nearest outside face of the wall, and the wall is jointly owned and maintained. Obviously this must be closely checked from the deeds to establish the exact nature of the ownership of the fences or walls.

When there is no adjoining proprietor, the wall, fence or gable is usually owned and maintained solely by the landowner. Some titles provide, however, that at a future date when someone builds on the adjoining property and uses that fence, wall or gable then that person should refund one-half of the cost of building to the person who paid for it, and become partly responsible for its maintenance. You should check that there are no outstanding charges for formation or maintenance of mutual fences, walls or gables.

Where a property is bounded by a non-tidal river, and there is no specification of the boundary, this is taken to be the middle line of the river. This includes the fishing rights, but not salmon fishing, which must be specifically transferred to the purchasers (see *McKendrick v Wilson* 1970 SLT (Sh Ct) 39). The same applies to non-tidal lochs. Care should be taken when purchasing a riparian property (ie one situated on a river bank or lochside) that the landowner has not retained a narrow strip of land between the property purchased and the loch or river. If this is the case, the purchaser is not a riparian proprietor and has no rights in the loch or river. This last point is something that would be well to be addressed in the missives as a condition of purchase, if the purchaser expects to have rights in the river or loch.

Using Google Earth and Google Streetview to view the actual physical features of the boundaries can be a useful way of clarifying the terms of a title description.

VALIDITY OF EACH DEED

8.17 Check that all parties granting deeds had the capacity to do so. For capacity generally see para 8.18.

Check also that the parties have been correctly named. This is particularly important in relation to limited companies, where even a minor error in the name of the company can be fatal to the deed. This is because the legal personality of the company resides in the company of that name only. Check the name of the company against a copy of the certificate of incorporation or an online search at Companies House. It is also good (and these days, invariable) practice when designing a company to refer to its company number, as this is a unique identifier for UK registered companies.

Opinions have been expressed that even the omission of an apostrophe, or brackets in the company name is a sufficient flaw. See *The Conveyancing Opinions of J. M. Halliday* (W Green 1992 page 265). Ensure that the form of all deeds is correct, that they are properly executed and witnessed and that the testing clause is correctly completed, that all deletions, interlineations, additions and erasures have been properly acknowledged and referred to in the testing clause.

When the deed has been granted by a limited company, the requirements for valid execution by companies since 1995 are contained in Sch 2 of the Requirements of Writing (Scotland) Act 1995. If you are checking a deed granted by a company dated prior to 1 August 1995 then different execution provisions apply. For example, deeds executed by companies prior to 31 July 1990 usually required to have the common seal impressed on them, accompanied by the signature of two directors or a director and the company secretary. In 1990, several methods of company execution applied, depending on the month in which the document was signed. This happened because new provisions that were introduced into the companies legislation that year were quickly discovered to be defective and had to be amended by further legislation. Gretton and Reid provide a chart, beloved of conveyancers, in *Conveyancing* (3rd edn, 2004, W Green para 14.07) which provides the relevant dates and method of execution competent for companies since time immemorial until the coming into force of the Requirements of Writing (Scotland) Act 1995.

Check that each deed, if completed prior to 1 December 2003, has been correctly stamped with an impressed stamp reflecting the amount of stamp duty paid on the deed. A list of historical rates of stamp duty from 1 March 1958 is available on the HMRC website currently at http://www.hmrc.gov.uk/stats/stamp_duty/00ap_a9.htm. Finally, check that each deed has actually been recorded in the appropriate Division of the General Register of Sasines. This is denoted by an ink stamp impressed on the first page of the deed in one of the margins. In very old deeds it is handwritten. It will give the County in which the deed is recorded, the Book and Folio number (latterly the Fiche and Frame numbers once the Registers started storing copies of deed on microfiche) and the date of recording.

CAPACITY OF THE PARTIES

8.18 Where a sale is made by a person or persons on behalf of someone else, or in default of someone else, care must be taken to ensure that the power of sale is competent, and that it was properly exercised.

(a) Trustees

Trustees have wide powers to sell, lease and grant securities over heritage under the Trusts (Scotland) Act 1921, s 4. The term 'trustee' includes (s 2) trustee *ex officiis* (namely trustees who are appointed by virtue of an office they hold, say a president and secretary of a golf club, and who cease to be trustees when they demit office, giving way to the next incumbents automatically), executors-nominate and judicial factors. Executors-dative also have this power of sale by virtue of s 20 of the Succession (Scotland) Act 1964.

(b) Executors

An executor on the estate of a deceased person can either be nominated in the will (executor nominate) or under the rules of intestacy, if there is no will or the nomination fails (executor dative). Although it is possible for an executor to deduce title through the will, this is not regarded as entirely safe, due to the fact that the good faith purchaser protection available under s 17 of the Succession (Scotland) Act 1964 (see para 8.14 above) is not available. In practice the executor obtains Confirmation in the estate of the deceased, which will include heritable property, and the executor can sell the property by virtue of the Confirmation in his favour. A beneficiary or legatee under the will of the deceased can have the property transferred to him by way of a docket of nomination (s 15 of S(S)A 1964) which is endorsed onto a certificate of Confirmation that gives details of the property. The docket is signed by the executor, and that effectively passes the property out of the executor's control. Actual title is not transferred but the docket endorsed on the certificate of Confirmation is an effective link in title for that person either to convey the property to a third party, or to complete their own title.

(c) Creditors selling under a standard security

The power of sale may be exercised among other remedies when the debtor is in default. Following on the Supreme Court decision in *Royal Bank of Scotland v Wilson* [2010] UKSC 50, heritable creditors must serve a calling up notice as an essential part of the repossession of the subjects.

The Home Owner and Debtor Protection (Scotland) Act 2010 made changes to procedures for enforcement of standard securities over residential properties, and provided for new forms of calling up notice and notice of default for both residential and commercial properties. For residential repossessions, unless the debtor voluntarily surrenders the property, calling up notices must be followed by an action for possession under s 24 of the CFR(S)A 1970. The HODP(S)A 2010 also imposed new obligations on heritable creditors in respect of securities over residential properties to go through certain pre-action procedures with a debtor before they can raise an action.

In addition, s 11 of the Homelessness etc (Scotland) Act 2003 requires notice of any calling up, or the fact that proceedings for re-possession have been commenced in respect of a dwelling house or 'land used to any extent for residential purposes' to be given to the relevant local authority in the form required in terms of Regulations issued under the H(S)A 2003. This provision affects residential landlords (but not local authorities) who seek to recover possession of property which they have let, and heritable creditors who take steps to call up any security where all or part of the security subjects is used for residential purposes.

The CFR(S)A 1970, s 25 entitles a selling creditor to sell the property either by private bargain (ie a sale normally concluded as outlined in previous chapters) or by exposure to sale (by which is meant sale by public auction), and imposes a duty on the selling creditor to advertise the sale and to take all reasonable steps to ensure that the price at which the property is sold is the best that can reasonably be obtained. There are now no defined rules for advertising, but the approach that was set out previously for advertising of a sale under a bond in the Conveyancing (Scotland) Act 1924 is generally still used as a rule of thumb.

Those rules provided that advertisements had to be placed:

(i)   if the property is in Midlothian in a daily paper published in Edinburgh;

(ii)   if the property is in Lanarkshire in a daily paper published in Glasgow; and

(iii)   if the property is elsewhere in Scotland in a daily newspaper published in Scotland circulating in the district where the property is situated and in one newspaper (ie a local paper that may be weekly or twice weekly) circulating in the district and published in the county where the property is situated (or in an adjacent county).

The frequency of advertisement required was: where the sale is by public roup, one advertisement a week for three consecutive weeks and where the sale is by private bargain, one advertisement a week for two consecutive weeks.

If your client is purchasing a residential property from a heritable creditor in possession (and note that this applies to commercial properties where a part is residential), then, in addition to the certified copy calling up notice, (ie a copy of it, on which the creditor's solicitors have written a certification that it is a true copy of the original) you will also need to see the s 24 decree as well (or, if the property has been voluntarily surrendered, copies of the relevant statements and any supporting evidence necessary to give the purchaser comfort this has been properly documented). For commercial properties, calling up on its own is sufficient to entitle the creditor to take possession and sell the property.

When acting for a purchaser from a heritable creditor in possession acting under the power of sale, you should ask to see copies of the advertisements certified as to date of publication by the newspaper publisher. Advertisement in the property lists of the ESPC or the GSPC for example is generally regarded a sufficient to comply with the advertisement requirement. The relevant SPC will be asked to certify that the property was so advertised.

Sale by a heritable creditor in this way, provided the requisite procedures have been followed will, on registration of the disposition in favour of the purchaser, result in the property conveyed being disburdened of the standard security and of all other heritable securities and diligences ranking *pari passu* (equally) with, or postponed to that security. Where the property is affected by a prior security, the registration of a disposition will not affect the rights of the creditor in that security, but the creditor who has effected the sale will have the same right as the debtor to redeem that prior security. In practice a postponed ranking creditor is unlikely to bother with calling up his security and selling the property unless there is a prospect of some repayment of the debt owed to him, which will mean having to satisfy the sums due to the prior ranking security holder first. In that event the creditor will be entitled to a discharge from the prior security holder to clear the title. Section 27 of CFR(S)A 1970 sets out the priority in which the proceeds are to be applied (see para 4.09).

(d) Sellers under a bond and disposition in security

It would now be extremely rare for an old style bond and disposition in security to be the current document securing a property to a heritable creditor, since no new bonds of this type will have been capable of being created after 29 November 1970. Prior to CFR(S)A 1970 the rules of sale under a bond and disposition in security were strict, in that the sale had to be by public auction, and certain rules of advertisement had to be implicitly followed. Section 69 of the Abolition of Feudal Tenure etc (Scotland) Act 2000 now applies the rules relating to assignation, variation, discharge and calling up of standard securities contained in ss 14 to 30 of CFR(S)A 1970 to any heritable security granted before 29 November 1970 (except securities constituted by way of *ex facie* absolute disposition).

(e) Trustees in sequestration (bankruptcy)

Sequestrations of individuals are governed by a statutory code set out principally in the Bankruptcy (Scotland) Act 1985 (B(S)A 1995) as amended by various enactments, and in particular Part 1 of the Bankruptcy and Diligence etc (Scotland) Act 2007 (BAD Act 2007). Different arrangements apply depending on whether the bankruptcy commenced before or after 1 April 2008. Detailed Notes for Guidance by the Accountant in Bankruptcy are available at http://www.aib.gov.uk/guidance/notes-guidance and should be closely read by anyone practising in this field.

The procedure, in summary, is that a trustee in sequestration will be appointed by the sheriff, on application by a creditor or a trustee acting under a trust deed, or by the Accountant in Bankruptcy on application by the debtor. Prior to 1 April 2008, an interim trustee would be appointed and that appointment would be followed by the appointment of a permanent trustee. Since invariably, the interim and permanent trustee was the same person, and that person was usually the Accountant in Bankruptcy, the two-tier appointment has been dispensed with under the BAD Act 2007. An interim trustee may still be appointed before the sequestration is awarded by the sheriff, to protect the assets of the debtor, provided either the debtor agrees or the petitioner can show cause why an interim trustee should be appointed. A trustee must be a qualified insolvency practitioner and must have given a written undertaking that they will act as interim trustee in the sequestration.

The date of sequestration is either (i) the date on which sequestration is awarded, where the application for sequestration has been made by the debtor or (ii) where sequestration is being sought by a creditor or a trustee acting under a trust deed, the date (or if more than one, the first date) on which the Sheriff grants warrant to cite the debtor.

The Sheriff Clerk must send a copy of the court order making the award of sequestration to the Register of Inhibitions 'forthwith' (B(S)A 1985, s 14), so that this will be disclosed in any search in the Personal Register. Where the Accountant in Bankruptcy awards the sequestration, she must send a copy of that determination for registration in the Register of Inhibitions.

Accordingly, the trustee's appointment (known as the act and warrant) consists of the court order or the determination of the Accountant in Bankruptcy. By virtue of the appointment, the whole of the debtor's property vests in the trustee on behalf of the creditors, as at the date of sequestration. You should ask to see a copy of the appointment. The name of the trustee in the Disposition in favour of the purchaser must be the same as the name of the trustee in the order.

However, there is a 28 day moratorium, starting with the date on which the order or the determination is registered in the Register of Inhibitions, during which neither the trustee, nor any one deriving title from him or her can complete title to any of the debtor's heritable property. This takes much of the haste out of the 'race to the register' that might have ensued if the debtor had sold the property just before sequestration, but the purchaser had not managed to register his title until after the trustee's appointment. Formerly the trustee could, immediately upon appointment, register his title to the property, by submitting the act and warrant to the Keeper if the property is registered in the Land Register, or by way of notice of title in the Sasine Register, as happened in the celebrated case of *Burnett's Trustee v Grainger* [2004]UKHL 8.

The appointment of the trustee will be confirmed at a statutory meeting of creditors, at which creditors also have the opportunity to select an alternative trustee. If there is no statutory meeting or no creditors attend, the original trustee will be the trustee.

The trustee cannot sell the property without the consent of the heritable creditors unless there are sufficient funds realised to pay off the heritable creditors. Further, the trustee cannot sell the property if a heritable creditor has already intimated an intention to sell (B(S)A 1985, s 39). Similarly if the trustee intimates to the creditor his intention to sell the property first, the creditor is precluded from taking steps to enforce his security over that property. In the case of a sale of a 'family home' (as defined in s 40(4) of B(S)A 1985), the consent of the bankrupt's spouse or civil partner, or of the debtor if he has no spouse or civil partner, is required. If consent is not given, the authority of the court will be required (B(S)A 1985, s 40). The court may, having regard to the factors set out in s 40(2) of BSA 1985, grant or refuse consent or postpone granting consent for up to 12 months subject to conditions being met. 'Family home' in this context means any property in which, at the relevant date, the debtor had a right or interest (either on his or her own or in common with another person), and it was property which was occupied at that date as a residence by the debtor and his/her spouse or civil partner, or just by the debtor's current or former spouse or civil partner (and with or without a child of the family) or by the debtor with a child of the family.

Note that, on the expiry of 3 years from the date of sequestration the debtor's right or interest in the debtor's family home will cease to form part of the debtor's sequestrated estate and be reinvested in the debtor (without disposition, conveyance, assignation or other transfer) (B(S)A 1985 s 39A). This period may be extended by the court on application by the trustee (B(S)A 1985 s 39A(7)). Post April 2008, the debtor is discharged from his sequestration after one year (the period was previously three years). Discharge from sequestration may, however, be deferred by the court on cause shown. Multiple deferrals are competent (s 54 B(S) A 1985). Inhibitions against the bankrupt need not be discharged (B(S) A 1985, s 31(2)). There is no requirement for any further sequestration orders to be lodged in the Personal Register. If discharge is deferred, the Sheriff Clerk will send a copy of the order deferring it to the Registers (s 54(7) B(S)A 1985) so that a search will disclose that the debtor has not been discharged.

Title is deduced through the trustee's act and warrant.

(f) A trustee under a trust deed

A trust deed is a document signed by the bankrupt, under a voluntary arrangement with his creditors, without the necessity of a court order. The trust deed is in effect a conveyance by the debtor of all of the debtor's property to the trustee, for the benefit of the creditors. Trust deeds executed after 1 April 1986 are subject to Sch 5 of B(S)A 1985. A 'protected trust deed' is one which has been given protected status under Sch 5 of B(S) A 1985 ie it binds both acceding creditors (those that accede to the trust deed) and non-acceding creditors.

The trustee grants the disposition, deducing title through the trust deed, which will usually have been registered in the Books of Council and Session.

(g) Liquidators of limited companies

The powers of a liquidator are detailed in the Insolvency Act 1986 Sch 4 and include the power to sell or otherwise dispose of property by public sale or private bargain. When a company is in liquidation, any disposition of heritable property will normally be granted in the name of the company (in liquidation) and the liquidator, who will sign on behalf of the company. However, since 28 November 2004, a liquidator can deduce title to land belonging to the company under the provisions of s 3 of the Conveyancing (Scotland) Act 1924, or complete title by way of notice of title in terms of s 4 of C(S)A 1924, entitling the liquidator to grant the disposition in his own name. Notice of title would be required if the liquidator wished for example to grant a lease of property.

It is not usual for a liquidator to complete title to the property himself, and so it will be necessary to see and refer to the liquidator's appointment, by which he is empowered to intromit with the property of the company, which remain vest in the company, unless the liquidator specifically asks for a court order for the company's assets to vest in him (although such a procedure is only exceptionally used). Title is deduced through the interlocutor ordering the winding up, if the liquidation is compulsory, and through the special resolution of the company, if it is voluntary. The interlocutor should have been registered in the Companies Register, and notified to the Accountant in Bankruptcy, as should the appointment of the liquidator.

As an aside it is worth noting here that at the time of writing (June 2011) the Scotland Bill was proceeding through the UK Parliament, with provisions for responsibility for some insolvency matters that had previously been dealt with by the Accountant in Bankruptcy to return to central UK control. On that basis some of the practical detail in this section may change, depending on the final outcome of the provisions of the Scotland Bill

In practice, the liquidation of a company is a matter of public knowledge, and is intimated in the *Edinburgh Gazette* and in the public notice sections of newspapers, although in all cases of dealing with a limited company the searchers should be asked if there has been any liquidator, receiver or administrator appointed, or if the company has been struck off for failure to lodge documents (see para 7.04)

(h) Receivers

A receiver (or administrative receiver) is an insolvency practitioner appointed by virtue of a floating charge, and his appointment will mean that the charge ceases to 'float' and becomes fixed on the assets of the company at the time of the appointment. Receiverships have become rare since they were effectively prohibited, except in a few quite specific circumstances by s 250 of the Enterprise Act 2002 which introduced ss 72A to 72H of the Insolvency Act 1986. Receivers can only now be appointed under floating charges which were created before 15 September 2003, unless they fall into one of the restricted categories set out in ss 72B-72H of IA 1986. Where a receiver has been appointed, the floating charge should be carefully inspected to see that it has been properly executed and registered in the Companies Register within 21 days of the date of its execution. The floating charge and the appointment of the receiver, which should be registered in the Companies Register, and which should also be checked, are the receiver's authority to convey the property. Floating charges do not need to be registered in the Land Register or Sasine Register. The deed by the receiver runs in the name of the company (in receivership) and the receiver, but is signed by the receiver only.

(i) Administrators

Holders of qualifying floating charges that were created after 15 September 2003 may appoint an administrator, but an administrator may also be appointed by a court order, or the directors of a company may pass a resolution to appoint an administrator. Anecdotally, it appears that administration is becoming the most popular method of corporate insolvency in cases of corporate distress. Whereas liquidation is a terminal process for a company, and receivership may or may not result in the survival of the company depending on what assets it has left, after the floating charge holder has satisfied its crystallised claim, administration is more generally perceived as and can, indeed, often be used as a corporate rescue process. In reality, administrations are used in a wide variety of circumstances, from cases where rescue is possible through to cases in which the company is to be effectively wound up.

As with receivership, the heritable property of the company does not vest in the administrator, and a disposition by an administrator runs in the name of the company (in administration) and the administrator, and is signed by the administrator. Title is linked through either the court interlocutor granting the administration order, the floating charge and the appointment by the charge holder of the administrator, or formal notice of appointment by the directors of the company, which has been lodged in court. In each case the relevant link needs to be registered with the Registrar of Companies and the Register of Inhibitions and Adjudications. The administrator also needs to advertise his appointment in the Edinburgh Gazette and a relevant local newspaper.

Finally it should be noted that a liquidator or administrator or receiver acts as an agent of the company.

(j) Limited companies

Most limited liability companies are reputable, especially public limited companies which have to submit to very rigorous scrutiny, although they can quite suddenly get into serious financial difficulties. Unfortunately, however, not all limited companies are sound, and it should never be forgotten that the forming of a limited company is a way to escape unlimited personal liability in the event of liquidation, although in terms of the Insolvency Act 1986, s 214, personal liability for a company's debts may be placed upon directors of a limited company where, before the commencement of the winding up of that company, they knew or ought to have concluded that there was no reasonable prospect that the company would avoid going into insolvent liquidation.

A limited company is a legal person, separate from its owners, directors and shareholders, and therefore some specific checks are required when dealing with companies, unless you are dealing with a company of unimpeachable credentials. The events of the recession have taught us however that no commercial organisation can be regarded as immune from financial difficulties, and there are no prizes for getting it wrong. Much of the information you will need to know about the company will be available in the searches in the companies registers (see para 7.04)

There are a number of aspects that you will need to check when purchasing, or taking security, from a limited company:

(i) Has the company been properly incorporated and constituted? You do not want to buy property from a company that does not yet exist. This information will be evident from the search in the Companies Register. And as already stated, it is imperative to check that you have the exact name of the company absolutely correct.

(ii) Is the company incorporated in the UK, which means it will be subject to the Companies Act 2006, and other company legislation and safeguards? Companies incorporated elsewhere are classified as foreign or overseas companies and this includes companies that are incorporated in the Isle of Man and the Channel Islands, as well as the more obvious places such as the British Virgin Islands, the Cayman Islands and Gibraltar, for example.

When a foreign company is involved in a transaction, there is not necessarily the same type of protection available in relation to issues such as the capacity of the company to enter into the transaction. Normally, any judgement obtained against a foreign company will have to be enforced by action taken in the country of its domicile. If it transpires that the contract or transaction in question did not bind the company in the first place, remedies against the company might not be available.

To ensure that a foreign company has the relevant powers and capacity to transact, the usual procedure is to obtain an opinion letter from a lawyer qualified in the relevant jurisdiction. The content of such an opinion will vary, but the usual requirements are that it should confirm that the contract in question, when executed, will be legally valid and binding as an obligation on the company. Transactions where such an opinion letter would normally be sought are purchases/sales, security transactions, lease transactions (including assignations etc) and the grant of guarantees. Failure by solicitors to take steps to establish whether a document granted by a foreign company has been duly authorised within that country may amount to negligence. See for example *Roker House Investments Ltd v Saunders & Another* (1997) EGCS137.

Obtaining an opinion letter may take some time and there is usually a fee involved, so it is important to identify this requirement in good time and let the seller's solicitors know that you will require an opinion letter dated to coincide with conclusion of the transaction. The PSG has produced a style Foreign Opinion letter which is available on its website www. psglegal.co.uk, accompanied by Guidance Notes explaining when it is required and what it should contain. Most firms of foreign lawyers who routinely provide foreign company opinions will probably have their own preferred style of letter, in which case the PSG style can be used as a basis for checking that the basic component assurances are available.

(iii) Is the company properly registered, and is it still registered, and not dissolved by the Register of Companies, without formal liquidation, in terms of Companies Act 2006 s 1000 (formerly CA 1985, ss 652 and 653). If you buy property from a dissolved company the disposition is invalid, and your only remedy would be to petition the court for a restoration of the company to the Register. That is not always possible or straightforward, and where a company has been dissolved any property or rights vested in it prior to its dissolution falls to the Crown as *bona vacantia*. The Companies Search (see para 7.04) will identify that the company has been continuously registered, and that it is still in existence.

(iv)   It used to be necessary to check the memorandum and articles of association of the company, to examine what the objects and powers of the company were, to ensure that the transaction was *intra vires* (within the powers) of the company. Parties dealing with a company were presumed to be aware, or required to make themselves aware of the purpose for which the company was set up. If a transaction was outside the company's objects (ie *ultra vires*), then the transaction was null and void. This issue has however eroded through successive legislation. The now repealed CA 1985, s 35 provided that where a person dealt with a company in good faith, a transaction entered into by the directors would be deemed to be within the capacity of the company. The Companies Act 2006 now permits companies to have unrestricted objects. Companies incorporated before 1 October 2009 can now amend their articles of association to remove the objects clause, which would have the effect that nothing the company does will be *ultra vires*.

(v)   If the company has granted a floating charge, this will show up in a search in the Charges Register. For so long as it 'floats' over the property and undertaking of the company it will not concern a party transacting with that company, but if it 'attaches' to the companies property then it is in effect converted into a fixed charge over such property as is then owned by the company (see para 10.06(e)). This happens when the holder of a floating charge appoints a receiver, but note that as a consequence of the Enterprise Act 2002, s 250, the holder of a floating charge created on or after 15 September 2003 may not appoint or apply to the court for the appointment of an administrative receiver of property of the company. This provision has meant that the use of receivership has diminished over time. Receivers may still be appointed in floating charges created prior to that date. In practice where a floating charge exists, you should seek a Letter of Non Crystallisation (see paras 10.06(e) and 11.05(i)). The seller's solicitor should obtain a letter from the holder of the floating charge confirming that it has taken no steps and does not intend to take steps to crystallise the charge. Ideally the letter should also incorporate a specific consent to the sale of the property in question.

(vi)   There exists the possibility that a deed has been recorded adversely, affecting the company's property, or that the company is no longer solvent, and that these events have occurred so recently that they have not been included in the search or advertised (see *Gibson v Hunter Home Designs Ltd* 1976 SC 23). It is a practical problem, and one solution that used to be popular was requesting a personal warranty by the company's directors. In reality such a warranty is rarely given and the practice of seeking such a warranty has died out somewhat over recent years. It is questionable what the value of such an undertaking would have been in any event if the directors themselves were of limited means or became insolvent. A style of the form of warranty appears in Handbook of Conveyancing Practice in Scotland 5th Edition para 8.32. No particular alternative practice has replaced the directors warranty but given the comparatively rare use of such warranties we have decided not to reproduce the style in this edition. In extreme cases the parties might agree to consign the price until the title is registered without any adverse entries and then release the funds to the seller when a clear company search is available, but this is by no means done routinely. Companies searches should be as up to date as possible at settlement /completion and deeds should be presented for registration immediately.

(k) Partnerships

A partnership can be a separate legal entity in Scotland, as distinct from the partners of the firm, and while this has always been the position, (s 4(2)

Partnership Act 1890), until 28 November 2004, it was not thought that a partnership could own land on its own account. Section 70 of AFT(S)A 2000 provided that a firm may own land, if it has separate legal personality. How much this option will be used in practice is unknown, as the legal and practical effect of this provision is uncertain. Normally, the partners of the firm will hold title to the property as trustees for the firm. Under s 5 of PA 1890, every partner is an agent of the firm and the other partners for the purposes of the business of the partnership, and as such may bind the firm and the partners, unless he has no authority to do so, although actings of a partner is excess of his authority can be later ratified by the other partners, and s 6 of the PA 1890 provides that the firm and all the partners are bound by an act or instrument relating to the business of the firm and done or executed in the firm name or in any other manner showing an intention to bind the firm, by any authorised person. If a partner acts when he has no authority to do so, the firm and the other partners may still be bound, unless the third party dealing with the partner knew either that he had no authority for the act, or neither knew nor believed the partner to be a partner.

Note that there is no public register of firms, which will normally be constituted by a private partnership agreement, (although there is no requirement that there has to be a written agreement), and it would not be usual to be allowed to inspect the partnership agreement, which will invariably contain confidential information about the constitution of the firm. The law of partnership in both Scotland and England is the subject of a comprehensive joint review by the Law Commission and the Scottish Law Commission: *Report on Partnership Law (Scot Law Com 192)*. As with most publications by the Scottish Law Commission, this Report is a rich source of information on the current law.

(l) Limited Partnerships

A limited partnership is a particular type of legal entity constituted under the Limited Partnerships Act 1907, and not to be confused with Limited Liability Partnerships (see para (l) below). Although governed by the LPA 1907, limited partnerships are also subject to the provisions of the PA 1890 so far as not inconsistent. Limited partnerships are (or were) quite often used in farming or agricultural tenancies. A limited partnership will have one or more 'general' partners and one or more 'limited' partners. Conceptually the idea behind a limited partnership was to allow investment in an entity without necessarily being subject to all the liabilities of that entity. So the general partner (or general partners) will have liability for all of the obligations including the debts of the partnership, while limited partners will not have liability beyond their initial stake. So for example in an agricultural tenancy, the general partner will be the farmer running the day to day operation and usually living on the farm, while the limited partner will be the owner of the land, but otherwise not involved in the farm business.

All limited partnerships have to be registered with the Registrar of Companies, and are issued with a certificate of registration which provides evidence of the existence of, and date of registration of, the limited partnership.

(m) Limited Liability Partnerships

More akin to companies than partnerships, but benefiting from elements of both, limited liability partnerships, established under the Limited Liability Partnerships Act 2000 are bodies corporate, and as such have separate legal personality. On incorporation, particulars of the LLP must be registered with the Registrar of Companies, who will again issue a certificate of incorporation of the LLP confirming its name and allocating a registered number and containing the date of incorporation of the LLP. The name of the LLP must end with the words 'limited liability partnership' or 'LLP'. Many legal and other firms of professionals have taken advantage of the benefits of the limited liability of these entities and incorporated as LLPs since introduction of the LLPA 2000.

(n) Power of attorney

A power of attorney is a mandate granted by a person who for any reason (be it illness or absence abroad, or in the case of companies and commercial organisations such as banks, for convenience), is unable, or chooses not to deal with their affairs either temporarily or permanently, in favour of another person or persons known as 'the attorney'. The power of attorney must contain an exact specification of the act or acts that the attorney is permitted to carry out. Unlike a will, no powers are vested in the attorney by law. Accordingly, if the power of attorney does not give the attorney power to sign a disposition of heritable property, for example, then no such power exists, and the power is valueless for that purpose. Consequently, where a deed is granted by an attorney, the conveyancer should ensure that the power of attorney authorises it.

A power of attorney may be either in general terms, empowering the attorney to do literally anything, or it may be in particular terms, empowering the attorney to do only one thing, such as to sell a property. An example of such a power is as follows:

'I, (name and designation), CONSIDERING that I am about to be absent from the United Kingdom and temporarily absent abroad and to facilitate the management and sale of subjects at (specify property to be sold), owned by me (the 'Property') it is convenient that I should grant a Power of Attorney and having full trust and confidence in the integrity and competence of (name and design Attorney) THEREFORE I appoint the said (name) as my Attorney with full power to enter into any agreement for the sale of the Property and to sign all conveyances and other documents relating to the sale on my behalf, and from the proceeds of sale to discharge any standard security or other form of security in connection with the Property and to sign any documents related to the Property; Thereafter from the net free proceeds of sale, to settle all expenses legally incurred in connection with the sale and generally to do whatever in his discretion my Attorney may think expedient for enforcing, carrying out and settling the said transaction; And I further grant to my said Attorney power to employ the firm of (name and design) to attend to the legal matters arising from the sale of the Property; And I further authorise my Attorney to institute on my behalf, pursue to finality, defend, compromise, all and any suits or actions, disputes or differences arising from the execution of these presents or otherwise affecting me or my property; And I do hereby ratify and confirm and hereby promise to ratify, allow and confirm all and whatever my Attorney lawfully does or causes to be done in the premises in virtue of this Power of Attorney without prejudice always to my right to demand just count and reckoning with me for the whole intromissions of my Attorney in terms of this Power of Attorney; And I declare that this Power of Attorney will subsist until it is recalled in writing; And I consent to registration it for preservation: IN WITNESS WHEREOF.'

The Law Reform Miscellaneous Provisions (Scotland) Act 1990, s 71 provided that powers of attorney granted on or after 1 January 1991 could continue, despite the supervening incapacity of the grantor. This provided a tremendous administrative advantage, as it no longer meant that a curator bonis would have to be appointed in those circumstances. However, the Adults with Incapacity (Scotland) Act 2000 s 15 repealed that provision, and now provides that a continuing power of attorney executed after 2 April 2001, will be valid only if it contains a statement which clearly expresses the granter's intention that the power be a continuing power.

The Adults with Incapacity (Scotland) Act 2000 places all continuing powers of attorney under the supervision of the Public Guardian at Callander Park in Falkirk. Regulations have been made to ensure that these continuing powers are signed and used properly.

When a deed is signed under a power of attorney, it is signed by the attorney. The narrative of that deed may either (a) run in the name of the attorney narrating the power, and state in the testing clause that it is signed by the named attorney or (b) run in the name of the constituent without mentioning the power, and then state in the testing clause that it is signed by the attorney on behalf of the constituent, by virtue of the power, which is then specified. Either method may be used, but in both cases the power of attorney must be produced with the deed to authorise the signature of the attorney.

ROADS AND ACCESS

8.19 It is essential to ensure that the property possesses suitable rights of access. This can be particularly relevant for rural property. Without proper rights of access ownership of land is useless. On 4 August 2002, it was reported in the press that a couple had bought a farmhouse (for £130,000) from a bank who had repossessed it. Unfortunately, however, the original owner still owned a small strip of land controlling access, and was not prepared to sell it. This is usually termed a ransom strip, and the owner of such a strip may be able to command a premium price for a comparatively small area of land. In 2004, an area of land in West Lothian extending to nine square metres was sold for over £1 million as it was required by a developer to obtain access into its site. The retention of this strip was a deliberate 'clawback' strategy by the owner to share in the profits of the subsequent planning permission for a multi-million pound development on the site, unlocked by the strip.

Depending on circumstances, the common law may imply a servitude right through necessity, or by implication, such as rights that are implied on severance of a property from adjoining property over which rights are necessary for the proper enjoyment of the property, but such rights can be extremely difficult to ascertain, and it is risky to rely on this as a satisfactory alternative to adequate and effective rights of access.

The problem is not so acute in the city and towns where, generally, but not universally, the streets have been adopted for maintenance by the local authority. In that case anyone can use the road not only to exercise a public right of passage over it, but also to access private property that abuts it.

As part of your due diligence examination you should ask to see a property enquiry certificate confirming the status of the roads *ex adverso* the property (see para 7.02) and if the road is not adopted for public maintenance, you will need to check that the titles contain the necessary rights of access. In certain circumstances it may be relevant to ask for a roads adoption plan, which can be provided by the local authority or the PEC providers, on which is marked the precise extent of the adoption. This can be relevant to ensure there are no ransom strip issues, or gaps where part of the access route is not actually adopted. For residential property in urban areas, this is probably unnecessary, but you may need to exercise your judgement in circumstances where it may be appropriate to request a plan.

Where the road is a public road, the roads authority (either the local authority or Transport Scotland) maintains the road, and is responsible for any accident that occurs through lack of maintenance (see Roads (Scotland Act 1984 ss 1 and 2). Where the road remains private, and this can be found even in towns and cities, there may be no-one with a specific obligation to maintain the road. Even though there is still a public right of passage, all that this imposes on the owner or owners is a requirement not to obstruct that right of passage. In *Johnstone v Sweeney* 1985 SLT (Sh Ct) 2, two individuals were injured on a towpath over which there was a public right of way, by falling into a gap on the towpath that had been covered over by a metal plate. In an action against the owner of the towpath, in which it was contended that the owner had a duty of care to pedestrians to ensure that the towpath was safe, the action was dismissed on the basis that the only duty to users of the public right of way was to take such care as in all the circumstances was reasonable, but there was no duty to make the public right of way (a close cousin of the public right of passage) safe for pedestrians.

In new developments, if a road is built to a standard that is sufficient for adoption by the local roads authority for maintenance, the builders can, and invariably will, ask the local authority to take over the maintenance of the road. Owners of existing private roads seldom do this, usually because the cost of making the road up to an adoptable standard would be prohibitive.

When buying rural property, it is more likely that some part of the access route to the property will be private road. The purchasers' solicitors must ensure that the purchasers will enjoy an unrestricted right to all necessary rights of access, and are not expected to pay a disproportionate amount of maintenance. Often the road will be owned by someone else, such as the owner of a larger estate or the owner of surrounding agricultural land. In such cases it is usual to obtain a servitude right of access over the road. This may be created by an express grant from the owner of the road, or might have been acquired by prescription – exercise of access over the road openly peaceably and without judicial interruption for a period of twenty years (Prescription and Limitation (Scotland) Act 1973 s 3). It is sometimes overlooked by purchasing solicitors that this is still a perfectly valid way in which to acquire a right of access, and is as valid a right of access as one given by express grant. However, it should be remembered that a servitude acquired in this way might be limited in its extent.

The Journal of the Law Society of Scotland used to run a regular column entitled 'Caveat' (a monthly article of legal cautionary tales). In Caveat (1993 JLSS 490), the story of a couple who bought a house in the country with an adjoining disused water mill as a holiday development, is highlighted. The access to the mill was over a farmer's land. There was nothing in the titles about this right, which had arisen from use, and positive prescription. The farmer objected to the proposed use of the road to the mill, which was intended for use as a holiday cottage. It was held by the court that the access had been created for use of the building as a mill, and not as a cottage. The solicitor who had acted for the pursuers was liable for the costs of forming an alternative access, and loss of income.

In addition, the owners of the benefited property (or dominant tenement in the traditional language of servitudes) cannot increase the burden on the burdened property (the servient tenement), and cannot therefore increase the use. If the prescriptive use has been for access to a single dwellinghouse, then it is unlikely that the servitude will be good for using it to access a new industrial estate to be built at the end of the road, and new rights would need to be obtained or a different route found. Professor Halliday (*Conveyancing Law and Practice in Scotland* (2nd edn, W Green, 1996) vol II, 20.11), suggests that when an express servitude of access is created, words such as the following should be used: 'The servitude has been granted with reference to the present state of the property and shall not be extended to apply to any substantially different condition thereof.' Such words would make it clear that the parties intended to restrict the use. Alternatively, when acquiring land for development, the purchaser might want any servitude rights granted to acknowledge that the type and volume of use might increase over time.

Grants of servitudes should be drawn very carefully, and in the case of any ambiguity will be construed *contra proferentem* (ie against the party who seeks to rely on it). When examining the terms of a servitude, you should ensure that it is sufficient to provide the access your client requires to the property. A lesser right will not include the greater right, but the greater will usually include the lesser. In other words a servitude right of access for pedestrian purposes will not permit the exercise of vehicular access, but conversely the right to access using vehicles will normally permit access on foot as well.

Servitudes are subject to servitude conditions which are for the benefit of the burdened property (as to which generally see DJ Cusine and RRM Paisley *Servitudes and Rights of Way Chapters 13 and 14* (W Green, 1998)). One of the principal legally implied servitude conditions is that a servitude should be exercised *civiliter* (ie so as to cause the least disturbance or inconvenience). Unless the provisions of the grant of servitude provide otherwise, the owner of the burdened property is not under any obligation to maintain the burdened property, he merely has to permit the servitude to be exercised, and he should not obstruct the way. In the absence of express provision the benefited owner is not obliged to maintain the burdened property or remedy defects which might affect the exercise of the servitude but do not damage or put the property at risk. In practice there will often be express provision about responsibility for the maintenance of a road, often, where the use of the road is shared, stated to be apportioned according to the extent of the respective uses. Maintenance 'according to user' is a common if unhelpful expression, as it would be rare for actual volume or frequency of use by several parties to be monitored in any detailed way (see *Cusine and Paisley Servitudes and Rights of Way* para 14.68).

ROADS IN NEW DEVELOPMENTS

8.20 The position with newly or recently constructed properties is rather different. Construction of the roads within a development, whether residential or commercial, takes place during the construction of the whole development. While access roads are formed early on in the development to allow access, some roads may not be finalised until later on in the development as, during the course of construction, heavy construction traffic may also be using these roads, and the finishing touches will usually only be added near the end, when the surface is not going to be damaged by heavy plant. This means that the purchaser of a new house or a commercial unit that is being constructed within a development could be buying property before the roads are completed, and certainly in that case, before the roads are maintained by the roads authority. In some commercial developments, although roads and other infrastructure is constructed by the developer, the decision is taken to keep the roads private and not apply for public maintenance, but this is the exception rather than the rule, and the invariable practice in residential developments is for the builder to form the road to the appropriate local authority standard and to apply to the local authority to take over liability for future maintenance.

To be able to construct roads within a development, the developer must obtain a roads construction consent from the local authority (Roads (Scotland) Act 1984 s 21). When acting for the purchaser of a newly or recently constructed property you must ask to see the Roads Construction consent to check that it (a) exists and is current (b) applies to the property your client is purchasing and (c) does not contain any conditions that would impact directly on the property your client is purchasing. This will usually mean that you also need to see the plan relating to the consent (which may be large unwieldy item) as this will show the roads to which the consent relates.

Many years ago it was common in cases where the road was incomplete at the time of purchase of a dwellinghouse in a development, for the purchaser to make a retention from the purchase price, to meet a proportion of the liability for completion of the roads, in case the developer failed to do so. This was particularly relevant since the cost of the house usually includes a provision for making up the roads to the necessary standard by the developer. The Roads (Scotland) Act 1984 s 17 requires a road bond to be provided by the developer to guarantee the cost of completion of the roads within a development of dwellinghouses. This can either be the deposit with the roads authority of the requisite sum of money or a bond lodged with them. The amount of the deposit or the bond must be sufficient to meet the cost of constructing or completing the road to such satisfactory standard. Again you should ask to see a copy of the road bond at the same time as requesting a copy of the construction consent, if these are not already with the title package that has been exhibited to you.

SERVICES

8.21 Just as a property needs to be adequately served by access rights, so too, if there are buildings on it, does it require connection to services including supply of water, gas, electricity etc and drainage, and the existence of these services, particularly water and drainage, should be checked as part of your investigations. In most cases of urban property, confirmation of connection to mains water and mains drainage will be disclosed in the property enquiry certificate (see para 7.02). In a rural or even semi-rural area, the position might not be so straightforward and the titles may need to be consulted to ascertain the position.

(a) Water

Scottish Water is the entity responsible for ensuring supplies of water and provision for sewerage through the public water supply system and the public sewerage system respectively. Not all properties are directly connected to the public water supply, and particularly in more remote rural areas, you might find that a property obtains its water supply from a private source such as a stream, reservoir or well, and that stream, reservoir or well will often be located on land belonging to someone else, and transmitted to the property by private pipes. In these cases the title needs to be checked to ensure that adequate servitude rights exist, both in relation to the water supply and the pipes (which potentially might run through several lands in different ownership). Typically what you might see is a split off title from a much larger estate in which rights over the lands retained are granted in favour of the property being conveyed. Where pipelines cross the land of another, make sure that there are clear servitude rights for running the pipe, and a right to gain access to the pipe if it requires maintenance.

Private water supplies are by their nature subject to the vicissitudes of the weather and quantity may not be guaranteed. Enquiries should be made of the sellers as to availability of supply, and you should check that the terms of the grant include that the supply may not be interfered with. It is advisable to check on water quality. Private water supplies are subject to environmental legislation, and public health considerations, and for supplies for property that is to be used for human consumption or use, you will want to ensure that the water supply is wholesome and potable, which may involve having water quality tests conducted.

(b) Gas, electricity and telephone

The relevant utilities companies should take care of the servitude rights (or wayleaves) for cables and pipes needed for transmission of these supplies, under statutory powers, and these will not therefore normally be of concern in most urban transactions of existing properties, although you should note details of wayleaves for cables and pipes leading to other properties, which must not be disturbed by digging, or obstructed in any way, eg by building over the wayleave area. So, for example, if there is a mains water pipe, or a gas pipe-line, leading through the property, the route of this should be identified.

(c) Drainage

In many rural areas drainage is not to a mains, but to a private septic tank. It would be a matter of survey to ensure that this tank is in order, and capable of treating the volume of waste generated by the property it serves. The main issue is to ascertain the exact location of the septic tank. If it is located in other property than the subjects being purchased, then servitude rights are required, and you should check that rights have been granted, both in relation to locating the septic tank and for all pipes and connections that lead from the tank through adjoining property to the subjects being purchased. There is, according to Professors Gretton and Reid (*Conveyancing* (3rd edn, 2004, W Green para 13.04), a servitude of 'sinks' which covers this, although this is not one of the classic servitudes (perhaps it should be). The responsibility for emptying septic tanks rests with Scottish Water to whom request can be made.

The discharge of effluent is controlled by the Scottish Environmental Protection Agency (SEPA). The Water Environment (Controlled Activities) (Scotland) Regulations 2011 (CAR) (which replace 2005 Regulations of the same name) require all 'controlled activities' to be authorised either by general binding rule, registration or licence. Septic tanks with discharges to land via full soakaway are controlled activities and therefore require registration. General provision regarding private drainage arrangements should have been covered by the missives (see para 6.17(c)), and accordingly if consent is required to be obtained retrospectively this should have been identified at an early stage. If the septic tank discharges were authorised prior to 1 April 2006 by a Control of Pollution Act 1974 (CoPA) consent, that consent will have been transferred automatically into CAR and will be deemed as registered. However many more septic tanks, that did not require registration under CoPA, require registration under CAR. Either way you probably need to see a piece of paper.

The CAR regime is more likely to affect residential purchases, but there may also be implications for developers if their activities will result in abstraction or impoundment of water bodies or if, for example, they carry out works and need to re-divert or culvert a burn.

DISCHARGE OF SECURITIES

8.22 Bearing in mind the valuable protection afforded by CFR(S)A 1970, s 41(1), it is important to check discharges which have been recorded within a five-year period. You should therefore check: (1) the details of the discharge—does it fully discharge the obligation that was created? (2)

the form of the discharge; (3) the execution of the discharge; and (4) the recording of the discharge.

As to the form of the discharge, the required forms are:

(a) Discharge of Standard security

The form is provided in the CFR(S)A 1970, Sch 4 Form F. This is a simple form. Many lenders have their own 'style' of discharge, although most are a variation on the theme of this statutory style. Note also that with mergers, takeovers, changes of name, dissolutions and acquisitions of many former high street lenders, many discharges will probably need to incorporate some form of deduction of title from the original creditor in whose favour the discharge was granted to the current entity. See the example in the Purchase file in Appendix 1. When the Keeper becomes aware of such a change, the documentation relating to it will have to be requisitioned and examined before the application can be processed. The Registers of Scotland maintains an index of these changes of name or status, in the Common Links Index, which is maintained by the Land Register intake section. Once the details are in the Common Links Index, it is not necessary to submit copies with future documents relying on the same information.

Although s 15(3) of the Land Registration (Scotland) Act 1979 dispenses with the need to deduce title in the case of a disposition or standard security granted by an uninfeft proprietor of a property that is registered in the Land Register, that section does not apply to discharges or deeds of restriction, so it is still necessary to deduce title in terms of note 1 to sch 4 of CFR(S)A 1970. However, according to the Registration of Title Practice Book: 'as a practical matter, the Keeper will not reject an application for registration merely because the assignation, deed of restriction or discharge, as the case may be, does not contain a deduction of title provided sufficient links are produced to (him) in support of that application for registration'.

(b) Bond and disposition in security

The requirement to discharge an old bond and disposition in security can still arise occasionally. Section 69 of the Abolition of Feudal Tenure etc (Scotland) Act 2000 now applies the rules relating to assignation, variation, discharge and calling up of standard securities contained in ss 14 to 30 of CFR(S)A 1970 to any heritable security (but not a security granted by way of *ex facie* absolute disposition) granted before 29 November 1970.

(c) *Ex facie* absolute disposition in security

Again, over time, the requirement to 'discharge' this type of security will diminish. This covert security may be discharged in one of two ways:

(i) traditional method—a disposition back to the owner of the subjects, which takes the form of an ordinary disposition but which sets out in the narrative that the original disposition to the lenders was truly in security of a loan of £X which has now been repaid, and it is now 'right and proper' that the subjects be reconveyed. The lenders grant warrandice only from their own facts and deeds;

(ii) shorter statutory method—CFR(S)A 1970, s 40 and Sch 9, provides for a short form of discharge, analogous to discharges (a) and (b). This has the effect (on being recorded) of disburdening the land and vesting the land in the person entitled to it.

Generally, it makes little difference which method is used. One school prefers to discharge securities in the manner in which they were created (*unumquodque eodem modo dissolvitur quo colligatur*); the other school prefers the shorter modern method.

A security may also be partially discharged on part payment, or restricted to any part of the land, freeing the remainder for sale. This is done by way of a Deed of Disburdenment or Deed of Restriction. For the appropriate forms see CFR(S)A 1970, Sch 4, forms C and D.

EXAMINING A REGISTERED TITLE

8.23 Once the title to a property has been registered in the Land Register, a considerable amount of the foregoing steps become redundant. Although the procedure of examining title is very much the same (ie you are looking to identify owner, extent, rights and obligations etc), the recording of title deeds in the Sasine Register is replaced by registration of interests in the property on the Title Sheet for the property held in the Land Register.

The contents of the Title Sheet, which is permanently based at the Land Register, will be reproduced in a Land Certificate which the Keeper issues following on completion of the first registration of the property, and thereafter updates it on subsequent dealings that require the production of an updated Land Certificate. It is therefore the most recent version of the Land Certificate that you will be required to examine to identify what is in the title. It is important to note however that any Land Certificate is only a snapshot of what was in the Title Sheet at the time the Land Certificate was produced. To an extent therefore, as soon as a Land Certificate is issued, it immediately starts becoming out of date, and any dealings which are subsequently added to the Title Sheet (and that do not generate a new Land Certificate) will not appear. It is important therefore to ensure that the Form 12 Report you are given is dated from the date of the Land Certificate and there is no gap.

The Title Sheet and its corresponding Land Certificate contains all the essential parts of the title, in four sections: a property section, a proprietorship section, a charges section and a burdens section. In theory, the fact that all inessential details from the prior Sasine titles are stripped out, and the remainder is clearly printed, should make examining a registered title a much easier business, but the reality often is that for any title that is less than straightforward, it can be unclear what the true position is. This is particularly so with tenement titles where the 'steading' method of registration (ie where the property is identified as 'lying within' an area shown outlined in red on a plan) can leave the title examiner in some doubt about what exactly is included in the title. In *North Atlantic Salmon Conservation Organisation v Au Bar Pub Ltd* [2009] GWD 14-222, a small area lying to the rear of the Au Bar pub in Edinburgh was used for alfresco dining and drinking. The right to do so was disputed by adjoining owners, but the title to the Au Bar pub was described as being within the land edged red on the title plan – which red outline included the disputed area. 'Within' does not mean 'comprises' of course, and in this case in fact there was no unequivocal evidence that either property was the clear owner, but the adjoining proprietor's entitlement was held to be more consistent with the original feuing plan.

Much of the checking as to validity required with Sasine titles is unnecessary with a registered title. Titles that are registered in the Land Register benefit from the 'curtain principle' which means that it should not be necessary, or in fact possible to look behind the Title Sheet to the underlying Sasine title where the title has been registered with full indemnity. Accordingly a purchaser is entitled to rely on the accuracy of the title sheet, even when it is, in fact, inaccurate.

It should be recognised however that it is possible that, during the process of transferring material from the previous Sasine title onto the Title Sheet that errors or omissions can occur. While it ought not to be necessary to revert to the Sasine title for clarification, experience shows that sometimes this is the only way to ascertain the true position.

Subject to getting updated searches, the Land Certificate contains all information relevant to the title to the property and it should therefore be a much simpler task to note the title. Where the Land Certificate is reasonably short, it is perfectly sensible to take a copy and highlight portions of it and add notes in the margins. With lengthier Land Certificates, given that the details of writs are presented in a continuous block of text, it can be quite easy to misread the provisions, and so care should be taken to read through the details carefully and note the terms separately in the same way as you would for a set of Sasine titles (see *Willimse v French* [2011] CSOH 51 and para 8.05 et seq.).

Office Copies and Registers Direct: It is becoming more common for elements of the title examination of registered property to be conducted through using Registers Direct.

Registers Direct is an internet based service from Registers of Scotland which provides access to information from the Land Register, Sasine Register, Personal and other registers direct to your desktop. It is primarily for use by business such as solicitors and other professionals, local authorities and HMRC, the police and fraud prevention authorities etc. Users have to register with the Registers of Scotland to be given secure login details to access the records.

Solicitors frequently use Registers Direct for research and information gathering during examination of title, or to find out who owns a property or piece of land, or what title conditions affect a client's property etc. Access to information in the Land Register allows you to view any one of the four Title Sheet sections, (property, proprietor, burdens and charges), as well as being able to look at the Title Plan for any particular registered property.

It is also possible to check records of title to properties in the Register of Sasines: the Search Sheet shows transactions affecting a property in chronological order as well as the parties to the deeds, a description of the property, the price paid and the date of recording. The Presentment Book, which shows details of any pending deeds awaiting recording can also be viewed.

Using Registers Direct™ has the advantage of ready access and speed, as, if your firm is signed up to use Registers Direct, you can search the records in real time and see details of what is currently on the title sheet of any registered property. However it is important to bear in mind that the information obtained from Registers Direct is not guaranteed by the Keeper. When you obtain information from Registers Direct it will state: 'This is a Quick Copy which reflects the date the Title Sheet was last updated. It does not have the evidential status of an Office Copy'. To be able to rely on the information from the Title Sheet, you must examine either the original Land Certificate or an Office Copy Land Certificate that can be obtained direct from the Registers. It will be formally stamped by the Registers and certified: 'This Office Copy has been issued in terms of s 6(5) of the Land Registration (Scotland) Act 1979, which provides that it shall be accepted for all purposes as sufficient evidence of the original'. Clearly therefore, although obtaining information from Registers Direct can be useful and convenient, it should not be relied upon for examining title and if no Land Certificate is available for inspection, you should ask the seller's solicitors to obtain an Office Copy for your examination. It is also good practice to print and retain a copy of what you have viewed on Registers Direct™, in case of any discrepancy between what you have examined on Registers Direct™ and what is disclosed by the Land Certificate or an Office Copy.

Not all dealings with a registered property will generate a new Land Certificate. The Land Registration (Scotland) Rules 2006 which came into effect in January 2007 proved that a Land Certificate would be issued on a transfer of all or part of the property and on the registration of a standard security over a registered property, but not for variations and discharges of standard securities. When Land Registration was first introduced the date to which the Land Certificate was last brought down was shown on the inside of the front cover. This is no longer the case and now a note in the Property Section will tell you when the Land Certificate was last updated.

The Keeper's Indemnity: A key element of the system of land registration in Scotland is that a person who suffers loss is entitled to indemnity in four circumstances:

(i)   where the register is rectified under s 9 of the Act;

(ii)   where the Keeper refuses or omits to make a rectification;

(iii)   where the loss is as a consequence of the loss or destruction of a document while lodged with the Keeper; and

(iv)   in a case where the loss is as a result of an error or omission in any land or charge certificate or in any information given by the Keeper in writing (or some other prescribed form).

See also para 2.05.

One aspect of title examination of a registered interest, that does not apply to Sasine titles of course, is the possibility of qualifications to or exclusion of the Keeper's indemnity, when some defect is apparent from the documents submitted for registration. An obvious example is a disposition *a non domino*, which, if the Keeper accepts it for registration, will be excluded from indemnity, the defect being that the granter has no title. There are few instances where such qualifications or exclusion should be ignored, and even if you think you know why it has been done, it should be raised with the seller's solicitors, and where appropriate their proposals for having it removed or dealt with in some other way should be sought. This is also a matter that needs to be reported to your client and in some circumstances will be a reason to withdraw from the purchase.

If the Land Certificate discloses any registered charges then there will also be a separate Charge Certificate which you should also obtain and examine. Often the original Standard Security will be attached to the Charge Certificate so that you will be able to check its terms, if appropriate.

OVERRIDING INTERESTS

8.24 An overriding interest is, in general terms, an interest in land which while not registered in the Land Register or recorded in the Sasine Register can nonetheless be a real right. It includes: a right or interest over land of a lessee under a lease which is not a long lease who has acquired a real right by virtue of possession; a crofter or cottar; the proprietor of the dominant tenement in a servitude; the Crown or other authority under an enactment which does not require the recording of a deed in the register to complete the right; the holder of a floating charge, whether crystallised or not; a member of the public in respect of a public right of way; *regalia* *majora* (property in right of the Crown); or any person having a right which has been made real other than by registration.

The full definition of overriding interests is contained in s 28(1) of the Land Registration (Scotland) Act 1979 (as amended) and consists of the right or interest over any interest in land of:

(a)   the lessee under a lease which is not a long lease (ie less than 20 years);

(b)   the lessee under a long lease who, prior to the commencement of the LR(S)A 1979, had acquired a real right to the subjects of the lease by virtue of possession of them;

(c)   a crofter or cottar within the meaning of s 3 or 28(4) respectively of the Crofters (Scotland) Act 1955, or a landholder or statutory small tenant within the meaning of s 2(2) or 32(1) respectively of the Small Landholders (Scotland) Act 1911;

(d)   the proprietor of the dominant tenement in any servitude which was not created by registration in accordance with s 75(1) of the Title Conditions (Scotland) Act 2003;

(e)   the Crown or any Government or other public department, or any public or local authority, under any enactment or rule of law, other than an enactment or rule of law authorising or requiring the recording of a deed in the Register of Sasines or registration in order to complete the right or interest;

(ee)   the operator having a right conferred in accordance with para 2, 3 or 5 of Sch 2 to the Telecommunications Act 1984 (agreements for execution of works, obstruction of access, etc);

(ef)   a licence holder within the meaning of Part I of the Electricity Act 1989 having such a wayleave as is mentioned in para 6 of Sch 4 to that Act (wayleaves for electric lines), whether granted under that paragraph or by agreement between the parties;

(eg)   a licence holder within the meaning of Part I of the Electricity Act 1989 who is authorised by virtue of para 1 of Sch 5 to that Act to abstract, divert and use water for a generating station wholly or mainly driven by water.

(eh)   insofar as it is an interest vesting by virtue of s 7(3) of the Coal Industry Act 1994, the Coal Authority;

(f)   the holder of a floating charge whether or not the charge has attached to the interest;

(g)   a member of the public in respect of any public right of way or in respect of any right held inalienably by the Crown in trust for the public or in respect of the exercise of access rights within the meaning of the Land Reform (Scotland) Act 2003 by way of a path delineated in a path order made under s 22 of that Act;

(gg)   the non-entitled spouse within the meaning of s 6 of the Matrimonial Homes (Family Protection) (Scotland) Act 1981;

(gh)   the non entitled civil partner within the meaning of s 106 of the Civil Partnership Act 2004;

(h)   any person, being a right which has been made real, otherwise than by the recording of a deed in the Register of Sasines or by registration; or

(i)   any other person under any rule of law relating to common interest or joint or common property, not being a right or interest constituting a real right, burden or condition entered in the title sheet of the interest in land under s 6(1)(e) of the LR(S)A 1979 or having effect by virtue of a deed recorded in the Register of Sasines, but does not include any subsisting burden or condition enforceable against the interest in land and entered in its title sheet under s 6(1) of LR(S)A 1979.

While each of these interests will be of relevance in your examination of the title, the ones most usually encountered are leasehold interests, rights of floating charge holders, and non-entitled spouses or civil partners.

It would be unusual but not impossible for a house to be purchased subject to a lease. Most houses are bought with vacant possession, but occasionally a house may be sold subject to a tenancy (colloquially 'with a sitting tenant'). Private residential tenancies are heavily regulated and the terms of any lease should be carefully examined to ensure that the purchaser as landlord can terminate the tenancy at the end of the let. Most residential tenancies are structured on a short assured tenancy basis for this purpose. More common in commercial properties, the terms of a lease which is not a long lease (ie for less than 20 years) will normally be known about, and in fact be one of the principal reasons for purchasing the property. Investment purchases are common in commercial property where the buyer is purchasing the property, not for its own occupation, but subject to a lease or leases which form an income stream for that purchaser. The trend these days is for commercial leases of less than 20 years, and so it is more common for these leases not to be registered but to be noted as overriding interests on the title sheet.

Where you are acting for an investment purchaser, of course, it is the terms of the leases that are of the most interest as in effect they are the 'investment' element of the property. A detailed examination of the terms of the leases and other leasehold documentation also requires to be undertaken, and a report on the terms of the leases provided to the purchaser. An investment purchaser will usually be looking for leases that are in their terms full repairing and insuring (known as an FRI lease), which means that the tenant pays for all repairs and maintenance to the property and the costs of insuring it, in addition to paying the rent.

REAL BURDENS

8.25 The title to an individual property may contain a number of conditions that operate to limit or restrict what can be done on the property, regulate the liability for maintenance of parts of the property, facilitate the use of, access to, or servicing of the property, or entitle others to use the property or parts of it for access or servicing. These real burdens and servitudes need to be checked carefully, and their terms where appropriate, reported to your client.

The subject of real burdens affecting property in Scotland has undergone a revolution in recent years. The abolition of the feudal system under the Abolition of Feudal Tenure etc (Scotland) Act 2000 and the introduction of a new statutory regime of creation, enforcement, variation and discharge of real burdens under the Title Conditions (Scotland) Act 2003, coupled with the transformation of the law of the tenement by the replacement of the old common law rules with a new statutory regime under the Tenements (Scotland) Act 2004, has left even the most experienced practitioner struggling to come to terms with all of the implications and effect of the new legislative structure.

While you might expect that replacing the old complicated common law rules with a new statutory regime ought to simplify the position, the opposite appears to be most practitioners' experience. At the time of writing (June 2011, some six and a half years into the post feudal world, there is still precious little case law on interpretation of this legislation. The Lands Tribunal, its powers significantly increased by s 90 of the TC(S)A 2003 have used the greater flexibility afforded to them by s 100 of TC(S)A 2003 to apply the terms of some of the legislation in the course of applications for variation or discharge of title conditions, but in a significant number of cases, this is largely a matter of balancing the different factors which they are entitled to take into account in terms of s 100, with reference to the particular facts and circumstances of the application before them.

The feudal system was abolished on 28 November 2004 which is the same day on which the majority of the provisions of the TC(S)A 2003 and the T(S)A 2004 came into force, and this date is often referred to as the 'appointed day'. There was a perception in some quarters in the days immediately following feudal abolition, that all burdens had been effectively wiped out, and the realisation that this was far from the truth came as a bitter disappointment to many practitioners. In fact, the realisation that not only were many burdens, and feudal ones at that, still in force, but also that there appeared to be some new enforcement rights that we hadn't had to consider before, left many practitioners yearning for the good old feudal days.

There are a number of ways in which feudal title conditions may have survived abolition, and therefore, when examining title, whether Sasine or land registered, it is necessary to consider each of the burdens in the title to identify whether or not they are still 'live', although surviving feudal abolition does not necessarily mean that the burden is valid and enforceable. Many burdens contained in titles are unenforceable for reasons other than feudal abolition, as we shall see. Not all burdens in titles will have been created in feudal deeds, of course, and those created in non-feudal deeds are unaffected by feudal abolition. So, there are a number of considerations to bear in mind when examining the burdens in the title, and in determining whether they are acceptable to the purchaser, or have the potential to have an adverse effect on what the purchaser plans to do with the property.

Not all burdens will fall to be treated in the same way and so there might be a different outcome for each burden in your title. In considering each burden it is very much a process of elimination that you must work though to determine whether the burden remains in force and who has rights to enforce it. You should also check of course that the provision is a real burden and not some other condition such as a servitude or a servitude condition.

The key thing to remember about a burden imposed on a property is that it is only of concern if someone has the right to enforce it. In other words for every burdened property there has to be a benefited property (unless the burden falls into one of the narrow post feudal categories of 'personal real burdens' (see para 8.25(d) below)). In addition to the owner of the benefited property having title to enforce a burden however, other interested persons also have such title, including a tenant or liferenter in the benefited property or a non-entitled spouse of an owner of the benefited property with occupancy rights in that property.

Rights of enforcement consist of two elements: title to enforce and interest to enforce. Both elements must exist for enforcement to be possible. The following paragraphs provide you with a guide to how to find out whether there are parties with title to enforce a burden, because they own (or have some other relevant right to) a benefited property. See para 8.25(f) for how interest to enforce affects the position, because, even if title to enforce can be determined, interest to enforce may be more difficult to establish.

(a) Is the burden a feudal burden?

The first elimination criterion is whether the burden has in fact been extinguished by feudal abolition. Clearly the first check is to ascertain if the burden was created in a feudal writ (eg a Feu Disposition, Feu Contract or Feu Charter). If it was not, then there are other tests to apply, but extinction as a consequence of feudal abolition is not one of them. However, if the burden was created in a feudal writ, then there are some specific points to check to determine if the burden has survived or been abolished. An example of a feudal writ to set out in the purchase file documents in Appendix 1.

(b) Feudal burdens that have already been extinguished

It was not uncommon, prior to abolition, for a party wishing to remove a feudal burden from his title, to approach the feudal superior for a discharge or waiver of the burden or burdens in question. Accordingly, if before the appointed day, the superior had granted a waiver of the burdens, and the superior was the only person entitled to enforce the burdens, then they will already be extinguished. The waiver will be disclosed in the titles or by a search. Unfortunately what was often overlooked in these cases was that sometimes other parties –usually co-feuars – also had rights of enforcement. It was rarely the case that these co-feuars were also approached to waive the burdens and, as feudal abolition only extinguished the superior's right to enforce, if the third parties had **express** rights to enforce the burdens before the appointed day, these rights would survive feudal abolition. Such rights might have been expressed as a *ius quaesitum tertio* (third party right) in favour of other feuars in the estate or development, or merely referred to rights to enforce burdens against the other feuars. All **implied** rights of enforcement were extinguished by TC(S)A 2003 s 49, and although new implied enforcement rights are created for co-feuars and co-disponees by ss 52 to 56 of TC(S)A 2003, nothing in those sections will revive a right of enforcement waived or otherwise lost prior to the appointed day.

(c) Feudal burdens that automatically survive abolition

There are several categories of burden, which even if feudal, were not extinguished and as part of your title examination you will need to consider the provisions of the burden and identify if it falls into any of these categories:

(i) *Facility or service burdens:* If a feudal burden is a 'facility burden' or a 'service burden' then it was automatically preserved on the appointed day (TC(S)A 2003 s 56). A 'facility burden' is a real burden which regulates the maintenance, management, re-instatement or use of heritable property which constitutes a facility of benefit to other land. Examples of this are: a common part of a tenement, a common area for recreation, a private road, private sewerage and a boundary wall (TC(S)A 2003 s 122(1) and (3)). A 'service burden' is a burden imposed on one property relating to the provision of services, water or electricity perhaps, to other land (TC(S) A 2003 s 122(1)). The party with rights to enforce these types of burdens will be the owner (or owners) of the land or properties that benefit from the facility, or that is provided with the services.

(ii) *Rights relating to minerals reservations:* It should be remembered that the minerals in or under land, if reserved, constitute a separate tenement of ownership and consequently, any reservations of minerals in a feudal deed are not affected by feudal abolition. The former superior (or any person to whom the former superior may have conveyed the minerals) is the owner of the minerals, and any conditions which relate to the reservation which generally relate to the manner in which the reservation may be exercised, remain in force. A typical feudal minerals reservation clause would be:

> 'There is reserved to (a) the British Coal Corporation (now the Coal Authority, of course) the whole coal, mines of coal and other minerals, if any, in or under the Feu and interests therein now vested in the said British Coal Corporation and (b) the Superiors the whole minerals, metals and substances other than those vested in the said British Coal Corporation in so far as the Superiors have right thereto (all hereinafter referred to as 'the said other minerals') as also reserving to the Superiors full power to work, win and carry away the said other minerals but without entering on the surface of the Feu, on payment to the Feuars for all damage to the surface of the Feu or the buildings and other erections erected or to be erected thereon that may be occasioned by the Superiors' working, winning and carrying away of the said other minerals as such damage shall, failing agreement, be ascertained by two arbiters, one of whom to be named by the Superiors and the other by the Feuars or by an oversman to be named by the said arbiters in case of their differing in opinion'

A distinction however needs to be made between these typical minerals reservation conditions, and any burdens imposed on the property title, which may be said to be for the benefit of the minerals title (usually restricting the use of property title to the surface of the land in some way, such as preventing building within a certain distance of actual mine workings). Burdens of this type in a feudal writ would have to have been preserved prior to the appointed day in the same way as other feudal burdens as described in para (c) below (AFT(S)A 2000 s 18(7)(c)(i)) by way of a notice registered against the title to the surface of the land. (for a detailed commentary on this point see Robert Rennie: *Minerals and the law in Scotland* EMIS Professional Publishing 2001 para 1,10).

(iii) *Rights relating to salmon fishings:* Title to salmon fishings can also be held as a separate tenement, in a manner similar to title to minerals, and conditions integral to such title, and burdens on other land for the benefit of such title, fall to be dealt with in a similar manner where the fishings have been reserved in a feudal title. So while conditions that are an essential part to the right of salmon fishing such as rights to use the shore will be unaffected, burdens imposed on the other land which are intended to benefit the fishings title would have to have been preserved by registered notice (AFT(S)A 2000 s 18(7)(c)(ii)).

(iv) *Sporting rights:* The definition of real burden in AFT(S)A 2000 specifically excludes sporting rights, and thus excluded such rights from the immediate effects of feudal abolition. However, these rights, which include freshwater fishing and shooting of game (but exclude salmon fishings which are a separate tenement in land) had to be preserved before the appointed day in a different way. Instead of being preserved as a real burden, the former superior had to preserve the rights as a separate tenement in land by registering the appropriate form against the title to the land to preserve the sporting rights as a separate tenement (AFT(S)A 2000 s 65A). Accordingly if this was done the right will be disclosed on the property title or in a search against it.

(v) *Manager burdens:* A 'manager burden' is a condition in the title that permits a person to be, or appoint (and dismiss) a manager of related properties. Although such burdens existed before feudal abolition they are specifically defined in s 63 of TC(S)A 2003. They often appear in some form or another in Deeds of Conditions relating to developments, and typically provide that the developer controls who is to be the manager in charge of coordinating maintenance and repairs. This type of burden – essentially personal in nature, could not be preserved by the preservation notice procedure described in para 8.25(c) below. Instead s 63 of TC(S) A 2003 provides that this power will survive feudal abolition, but this only for a limited period, which for the majority of property types is 5 years from the date of registration of the deed in which the burden was constituted (or 3 years in the case of manager burdens relating to sheltered or retirement housing developments). That means that the majority of feudal manager burdens will have now expired. The only exception in the case where the manager burden has been imposed in terms of s 61 of the Housing (Scotland) Act 1987, on the purchase by a council house tenant exercising his right to buy, where the power will endure for 30 years.

New manager burdens created after the appointed day are not feudal of course but are subject to the same time limits. In these cases, it should be noted that the burden is essentially a time limited monopoly to be or to appoint the manager, but is not the actual appointment of the manager.

(vi) *Maritime burdens*: these are burdens in favour of the Crown, which relate to the seabed and foreshore, and where created in a feudal deed, were automatically preserved to continue to be enforceable by the Crown following feudal abolition (s 60 AFT(S)A 2000).

(d) Feudal burdens that have been preserved

If the burden does not fall into one of the categories of automatic preservation referred to in para 8.25(c), the next step is to ascertain if the feudal burden has been preserved. AFT(S)A 2000 (as amended) set out a series of preservation notices that a superior could complete and register, prior to the appointed day, against the title of the burdened property, and through which the superior could (usually) nominate other land which he owned to be the benefited property entitled to the benefit of enforcing the burden, in lieu of the superiority enforcement right. Over 3,000 such notices were registered, the vast majority of which were registered in terms of s 18 of AFT(S)A 2000, which provided for a number of qualifying criteria for preservation, the most common of which was that the superior could nominate as the benefited property, other land on which there was a permanent building used wholly or mainly for human habitation or resort, and located at some point within 100 metres of the burdened property.

In addition to the ability to nominate a new benefited property, certain categories of feudal burden could be preserved as 'personal real burdens' which would nominate a person or body to be the person entitled to enforce the burden after the appointed day. These include conservation burdens, enforceable by conservation bodies or Scottish Ministers, economic development burdens, enforceable by Scottish Ministers or a local authority, and healthcare burdens, enforceable by an NHS Trust (until repealed) or Scottish Ministers. Feudal rights of pre-emption and redemption could be preserved either by nomination of a new benefited property or as a personal pre-emption or personal redemption burden, as the case may be. Maritime burdens, which were automatically preserved, (see para 8.25(c) above) are also a form of personal real burden in favour of the Crown.

To be preserved the notice had to be registered against the burdened property before the appointed day and so will be disclosed in the title or in a Form 10/12 Report. However, even though a preservation notice was registered prior to the appointed day and appears on the Register, this does not mean necessarily that the notice has been validly made. The Keeper was specifically excused from having to verify that the notices were correct or that the requisite procedure (eg as to service of the notice) had been followed, or that there was a building on the re-allotted property within 100 metres of the burdened property and so on. There might be an error in the description of the property, or in identification of the burden, or even in the way the notice is executed, which might render the notice invalid, and capable of challenge. How likely or prevalent errors or inaccuracies in the notices may be is impossible to quantify, and some errors may be such that they are not fatal to the validity of the notice. It might be possible however to challenge a notice and refer the matter to the Land Tribunal who will look into the facts and circumstances surrounding the procedure and/or terms of the notice, and consequently it will be important in some cases where a burden has been preserved by notice, to check the terms of the notice itself, in case there is an opportunity for challenging the preservation of a burden that your client would prefer did not apply to the title.

(e) Feudal burdens that are enforceable in terms of new implied enforcement rights

Establishing whether or not a party had a right to enforce a burden arising by implication was often a complicated business under the feudal system, and clarity at least was provided by s 49(1) of TC(S)A 2003 which provided that all previously arising implied enforcement rights were abolished. However, due to the requirement to protect the property rights of individuals, or provide for compensation to be made where such rights are affected (under Article 1 of the First Protocol to the European Convention on Human Rights) it was necessary to replace the abolished rights with new statutory equivalents, and therefore new statutory implied rights of enforcement were created by ss 49, 50, 52, 53, 54 and 56 of TC(S)A 2003.

Feudal burdens which do not fall into any of the categories described in paras 8.25(b) to (d) might still be enforceable under one of the implied enforcement right rules. The provisions also apply to non-feudal burdens created prior to 28 November 2004, where the benefited property or properties have not been expressly identified. All burdens created after that date, unless they are personal real burdens, require not only to identify the benefited property, but also, the terms of the burden must be registered against the title to that benefited property as well, or in the case of burdens that apply to a number of units in a community, the extent of that community has to be identified (s 4 TC(S)A 2003). See para 9.10(f) regarding creation of community burdens.

In addition to the enforcement rights that arise by implication in cases of facility and service burdens, (see para 8.25(c) above) these provisions of TC(S)A 2003 apply to three other principal categories of burden, where the benefited property or properties have not been expressly identified: (i) 'neighbour' burdens, where burdens have been imposed when part of a property is split off from a larger area (ii) common schemes, where two or more properties are affected by the same or similar burdens, and (iii) sheltered or retirement housing developments.

(i) Implied Enforcement rights arising on subdivision

Where a real burden is imposed on a property before 28 November 2004 by the person conveying that property, which forms part of land they own, but the benefited property is not expressly identified in the deed creating the real burden, the implication is that the retained property will be the benefited property. This is the rule expressed in *J A Mactaggart & Co v Harrower* (1906) 8 F 1101, 14 SLT 277 and applies to properties conveyed by disposition only, not in a feudal deed. A typical example of this is where a person sells off part of their large garden, for the purpose of building another house on it. In the disposition, a burden is imposed on the garden prohibiting the erection of more than one house, and specifying that the house to be built must not exceed a particular height! Such provisions are clearly designed to preserve the outlook and amenity of the rest of the seller's property, but often that is not expressly mentioned in the deed. These implied rights are abolished by s 49 of TC(S)A, but where the right to enforce has been created by subdivision of a property in this way, that right will endure for a period of ten years from 28 November 2004, during which period the benefited proprietor has the opportunity to preserve the right by registering an appropriate notice (TC(S)A 2003 Sch 7), failing which the enforcement right will be lost. After 28 November 2014, therefore it will be possible to discount a number of burdens that fall into this category, if there is no Sch 7 notice registered against the title.

(ii) Implied Enforcement rights arising in Common Schemes

In situations where two or more properties are affected by the same or similar real burdens, created prior to 28 November 2004, enforcement rights may have arisen due to the existence of a 'common scheme'. Burdens that affect common schemes in this way are now known as 'community burdens' (see para 9.10(f)) which has the effect that each burdened unit in the common scheme is also a benefited property, so that obligations and enforcement rights are reciprocal. However note that the rules relating to implied enforcement rights under common schemes do not arise in relation to rights of pre-emption, redemption or reversion.

There is no definition of 'common scheme' in TC(S)A 2003, but the Explanatory Notes to the Act indicate that the new implied rights of enforcement are based on the previous common law rules and also specify that 'Common schemes exist where there are several burdened properties all subject to the same or similar burdens (Explanatory Note 234)'. Given that the requirement for community burdens is satisfied where there are two or more properties affected (see para 9.10(f)), it seems likely that 'several' in this case will mean 'two or more'. The burdens imposed on each of the properties in the common scheme must be either identical, largely similar (*Botanic Gardens Picture House Ltd v Adamson* [1924] SC 549) or at least in some way equivalent (*Lees v North East Fife District Council* [1987] SLT 769).

Another indicator of the existence of a common scheme would be where the burdens come from a common source, for example: they have been granted by the same person, although this is not essential, and there is nothing specifically to this effect in TC(S)A 2003. Indeed, the Explanatory Notes to the Act specifically state that 'it will no longer be necessary for title to have been obtained from a common granter' and to that extent it diverges from the rules in *Hislop v MacRitchie's Trustees* [1881] 8 R (HL) 95 (see below). In reality however, it is more likely to be the case that the burdens in a common scheme will have been granted by a common author or its successors. So for example, Lightyear Development Company Limited may sell off the first twenty plots in a development all with the same burdens, and then sell the remainder of the land to Dunvorlich Homes Limited who continue to convey plots using the same style documentation with the same burdens.

There are two categories of implied enforcement rights in common schemes and these are set out in s 52 and s 53 of TC(S)A 2003. Sections 52 and 53 have proved to be problematic to the conveyancer, as it is not always easy to recognise or be sure of when a common scheme exists, or the extent to which enforcement rights arise.

The main distinction between these two sections is that in section 53 common schemes, the properties must be 'related properties', whereas for section 52 to apply there need be no such relationship. Section 53 is new law and the definition of what constitutes related properties, although some examples are given in the Act, is not altogether clear. The Act itself says that whether or not properties are related properties is to be inferred from all the circumstances and so, to that extent, there is still a lot of guesswork involved in working out whether or not section 52 or section 53 will apply.

The definition of 'related properties' does provide some examples, but the list is illustrative and not exhaustive, and there has not yet been any significant judicial determination of this provision (although it has been cited in several Sheriff Court and Lands Tribunal cases). Properties might be considered to be 'related' where (i) it is convenient to manage the properties together because they share some common feature, or an obligation for common maintenance of some facility; or (ii) there is shared ownership of common property; or (iii) they are subject to the common scheme in terms of the same deed of conditions; or (iv) they are flats in the same tenement. However, even if a case does not fall within the illustrative examples in the definition, it may still be possible for third party enforcement rights to exist.

Section 52 resembles a recognisable law, in that it is more or less a restatement of the old common law rules concerning third party rights of enforcement (or *ius quaesitum tertio*), formulated in *Hislop v MacRitchie's Trustees*. For common scheme enforcement rights to exist under Section 52 there must be:

- notice, express or implied, in the title that there is a common scheme of burdens and also
- nothing in the title that negates the creation or existence of the third party enforcement rights, such as the reservation to the superior to vary the conditions.

So at least with Section 52 we know what we are looking for, even although sometimes it is still tricky to recognise. Notice of a common scheme may appear in different ways – it may be apparent by virtue of the fact that a Deed of Conditions imposes the burdens on a number of units, for example a block of flats. Alternatively, there might be a deed in the title that imposes burdens, but it transpires that those burdens were imposed on a larger area of which the property that you are considering forms a part. The other parts of that larger area, which may also have been conveyed off in parts, are similarly burdened since they stem from the same original title of the larger area. Or the landowner might have individually sold off a series of plots of land or units, using Feu Dispositions to impose the burdens on a plot by plot basis, so while there is no common document containing those burdens, each of the individual conveyances contains similar title conditions. This technique was commonly used by local authorities when selling off housing stock, and is also common in sales of parcels of land in large estates.

By way of illustration, consider the provisions in the Feu Charter for 29 Sardinia Terrace, Kelvinforth, set out in Appendix 1. The terms of the Feu Charter are typical of the way in which parts of estates were feued and given the similarity of adjoining properties, it may be a safe assumption that they are similarly burdened. There is no indication that this and adjoining properties are 'related properties' and so there is a possibility that s 52 might apply. However, note the provisions of clause (Seventh) in the burdens section, by which the feudal superior reserves the right to alter the feuing plan and vary title conditions. This effectively eliminates third party rights of enforcement.

Section 53, on the other hand is far more wide ranging than section 52. On the face of it, it ought to be more straightforward – the properties have to be related properties, and that relationship clearly has to be factual. So, for example, the properties may all share a common access road or be subject to the same common scheme because they are all subject to the same Deed of Conditions. Those, however, are the simple section 53 situations, because section 53 differs from section 52 in that there is no requirement for the title to contain notice of the existence of a common scheme for section 53 to apply. So even if there is nothing apparent from the title, a common scheme may still be in place. Neither does the requirement that there be nothing negating the existence of a common scheme apply. The only qualifying condition for section 53 is the 'related properties' requirement. This makes section 53 extremely flexible and gives rise to the possibility that enforcement rights which did not exist before the appointed day, arise after that date.

It is worth bearing in mind that sections 52 and 53 are not complementary – they stand separately, so that even if section 52 enforcement is out of the question because of some negatory wording in the title, section 53 may apply, since such wording will have no effect on those enforcement rights. One other key distinction between section 52 and section 53 is that, for section 52 to apply, the deed by which the burdens are imposed must have been registered before the appointed day. In section 53 common schemes, at least one of the deeds imposing the burdens in a common scheme must have been registered before the appointed day, but it will also apply to burdens imposed on properties within the common scheme, by deeds registered after the appointed day, and that even if the deed imposing the burden registered after the appointed day does not make any express nomination of the benefited properties. This exception to the requirement to identify the benefited property in any burden created after the appointed day is allowed by s 57(2) of TC(S)A 2003.

(iii) Examining and reporting on title affected by common scheme implied enforcement rights

Where the conditions in sections 52 or 53 are satisfied, the other properties in the 'common scheme' will have third party enforcement rights in respect of the burdens. Conversely, of course, the property your client is purchasing will have enforcement rights in relation to the burdens against the other properties. But how do you identify what those other properties are? The short answer in some cases is that you may never be able to say with absolute certainty precisely what other properties are involved. Often the only way to identify whether other properties have enforcement rights under a common scheme is to examine the title to those other properties, because unless there is a common deed in which the burdens were imposed, such as a Deed of Conditions, it is only by looking at the title of surrounding properties that you will be able to discover whether they contain the same or similar burdens.

But it is not always possible to be totally certain, even if you do conduct an examination of the titles of neighbouring properties, that you have identified **all** of the neighbouring properties that are similarly affected and therefore form part of the common scheme. In cases where the area affected by the burdens is a larger area identified in an earlier deed, when the title is in the Land Register, it will often not be possible to ascertain from the title sheet what area is affected, and you would need to obtain a copy, with a plan of the original deed itself, to be able to identify where the other properties are. If the copy plan is poor or unclear, the position may remain unascertainable.

Trying to identify all of the other properties in a common scheme can sometimes be a rather hit and miss affair. Clearly the consequences for your client in terms of the time it takes to conduct investigation of other titles, and the cost involved could be quite unacceptable. If you are working to a fixed fee for the transaction, it could be simply impractical to conduct these investigations, while on the other hand a purchaser will be unwilling to pay for additional researches only for the outcome to be inconclusive.

It is just as likely that the individual plots could have been sold off without the benefit of all burdens being located in a single Deed of Conditions; each deed may have contained its own burdens and therefore, again, there may be many other titles which are similarly burdened, but it can be harder to spot given that there is no requirement for notice in the title. For example there might be no common deed, but simply reference to maintaining areas along with others having right to them. That could mean different properties have enforcement rights against each other depending on the nature of the relationship. For example only some of the units might use a particular road, while another different combination of units might use a car parking area. The enforcement rights in those circumstances will be different.

Where the position is unclear it can help to consider the burdens in the context of the whole facts and circumstances surrounding the title and the property, including its location and physical features. Ideally, a site visit to the property should be conducted. Realistically, however, particularly if you are on a fixed fee, or the property is located in a remote area, the practicalities of conducting a site visit may be difficult. Do try to visit the site if you can though. If you can't, it is a good idea to see if you can locate the property on Google Earth and Google Street view, which can give you a good idea of what the actual physical features on the ground look like. A restriction on building more than four storeys in height may not be considered too problematic if, when you view the property, it is clear that all the buildings round about it that are likely to be subject to the same title restriction are all ten storeys high.

It will be necessary therefore to find an appropriate balance for how far your investigations need to go. This will depend on (a) the importance of the burden to your client and whether it might potentially prevent or inhibit them from doing what they want to do on the property eg a prohibition in the title against using the land for residential purposes, when your client is purchasing it with a view to converting the buildings into houses, would be a major consideration and (b) the relevance of the burden: for example old burdens that are concerned with the construction of roads that are no longer applicable can be ignored, and obligations relating to maintenance of roads and drains etc that are now the responsibility of the local authority or Scottish Water are also no longer relevant.

It is often the case that the final position cannot be stated with complete accuracy, and reporting on title conditions may often have to be caveated to the extent that it is impossible to say with certainty who has rights to enforce and what measure of success they may have in securing those enforcement rights in the case of a breach.

For possible options to resolve these issues see para 8.35.

(f) Compensation for Development Value Burdens

AFT(S)A 2000 Act did not allow superiors to preserve feudal development value burdens, (essentially a clawback arrangement payable where land sold by the superior for a nil or nominal amount was subsequently developed in contravention of a burden restricting such development) but did permit them to register a notice entitling the former superior to claim compensation in the event of a breach of the relevant title conditions (s 33 of AFT(S)A 2000). However one of the conditions for entitlement to such compensation is that there is or was a breach of the title condition either during the period of five years immediately before the appointed day, or during the period of

20 years after the appointed day. If the breach occurred before the appointed day, the claim for compensation had to have been made not more than 3 years after the appointed day (ie by 27 November 2007), and if the breach occurred after the appointed day, the claim for compensation must be made not more than 3 years after the date of the breach. Only about fifty of these notices were registered prior to feudal abolition.

(g) Interest to enforce

A key consideration in the enforceability of burdens however, even if you have established that they are still in existence, and who has title to enforce them, is whether or not those parties also have **interest to enforce**. The right to enforce consists of two elements: title to enforce and interest to enforce, and both must be present if enforcement of the burden is to be possible. This can often be the final stumbling block for enforceability of a burden, and should always be an element in your deliberations when looking at title conditions.

Interest to enforce is not a new concept – it existed prior to the appointed day but was often overlooked, largely because, prior to feudal abolition, the interest of a feudal superior to enforce a burden was implied, and it tended to be forgotten that others might have interest to enforce too. The concept of interest to enforce has now been enshrined in statute in s 8(3) of TC(S)A 2003, which sets out two independent criteria for interest to enforce: a 'material detriment' test, and entitlement to payment in respect of some cost.

A person will have interest to enforce the burden if in the circumstances of any case, failure to comply with the real burden is resulting in, or will result in, material detriment to the value or enjoyment of the person's ownership of, or right in, the benefited property.

Interest to enforce also exists in the specific case of burdens that relate to payment of some cost: where the real burden is an affirmative burden (ie an obligation to do something) that consists of an obligation to defray, or contribute towards, some cost, a person will have interest to enforce it, if that person seeks (and has grounds to seek) payment of, or in regard to, that cost.

So after considering the terms of the burden and surrounding circumstances, you should apply the interest to enforce test. Would the persons who have, or who might have title to enforce have interest to enforce? Even if you can be fairly sure that there is title to enforce, the nature of the burden and other circumstances can often mean that those parties who have title to enforce would find it very difficult to show that they have interest to enforce.

The threshold for 'material detriment' is high, as determined in the case of *Barker v Lewis* [2008] SLT (Sh Ct) 17, in which the owners of houses in a small development were unsuccessful in enforcing a burden that the properties for were to be used for no purpose other than as 'a domestic dwellinghouse with relative offices for use by one family only' against one of the owners who was running a bed and breakfast business. Quite how high is a matter of debate, although while the Sheriff in *Barker v Lewis* decided that it meant 'substantial', on appeal, the Sheriff Principal indicated that was too strong a word, so that although the Sheriff had reached the correct result on the facts of the case, 'it is impossible to give a real meaning to the word ('material') except by considering the context in which it is used'. However qualification of the word 'detriment' by the word 'material' imported a question of degree.

Some commentators have remarked that, as a consequence of that decision, precious few burdens would actually be enforceable at all. In developments where there may be many properties all affected by the same burdens either as a consequence of a Deed of Conditions, or because of the application of s 52 or s 53, and thus all having title to enforce, the reality is more likely to be that only a few of those properties could actually be able to demonstrate interest to enforce. Although it is not included as a factor in the legislation, distance between the properties may be a consideration ie the further away the benefited property is from the burdened property, the less likely it would be to be able to demonstrate detriment to enjoyment of the benefited property from a breach of the condition, or detriment to value.

Earlier this year, however, the Sheriff at Paisley held that the pursuers in the case of *Kettlewell and Others v Turning Point Scotland* (Paisley Sheriff Court 8 March 2011) had established interest to enforce a burden requiring dwelling houses in a small development of 20 houses to be used only as private dwelling houses for occupation by one family only not to be subdivided and not occupied by more than one family. The defenders planned to convert one of the houses into a residential care home for up to 6 unrelated individuals suffering from learning disabilities, mental health problems, homelessness or drug or alcohol abuse. The pursuers were able to demonstrate an adverse effect on values of nearby properties in other areas where the defenders ran similar homes and were also able to demonstrate an adverse effect on their enjoyment of their properties due to the potential for unacceptable noise levels of increased traffic, and physical attacks on residents.

Accordingly, the cautious conveyancer examining title and reporting to his client, should start from the point of view that the burden may be enforceable and then try to establish through various tests and checks whether or not it actually is enforceable.

(h) Construction of the feudal terms

Although many burdens were extinguished by feudal abolition, as we have seen, many feudal burdens survived. That poses another difficulty in interpreting what feudal terms and phrases in these burdens now mean. Section 73 of AFT(S)A 2000 provides for substitution of certain feudal terms with their post-feudal equivalent, in other primary or secondary legislation passed before feudal abolition, in any document executed before the appointed day and in the Land Register issued before that day. So, for example, vassal becomes owner, *dominium utile* means the land or ownership of the land, references to feuing will be construed as disponing, and so on. References to a superior are replaced with references to the party who is now the owner of the benefited property, where the burden has been re-allotted onto land that is to be the new benefited property by way of preservation notice, and becomes a 'neighbour' burden (by virtue of ss 18, 18A, 18B, 18C, 19, 20, 28, 28A or 60 of AFT(S)A 2000) (see para 8.25(d)) or, in the case of facility burdens and service burdens, by the owner of the land which benefits from that facility (by virtue of s 56 of TC(S) Act 2003).

Not all references to superiors can be replaced in this way, however, and in the case of enforcement of community burdens, including those which arise under s 52 and 53 the expression 'superior' will not convert to all of the owners in the community, and those acquiring enforcement rights under those sections are specifically excluded from the provision replacing references to superior.

In addition, there are circumstances where a reference to 'superior' in a community burden can actually be ignored. Any provision in a deed, the effect of which is that anyone other than the person entitled to enforce the burden may waive compliance with, or vary the burden, is to be disregarded (for example, a community burden that provides that additions to buildings may not be constructed without the consent of 'us and our successors as superiors') (s 73(2A) of AFT(S)A 2000) That requirement for consent does not extend to all of the other parties in the community, and instead the wording is, in effect removed altogether because the superior no longer exists. The effect of this will often be to convert the burden into an outright prohibition, which would require a formal discharge rather than an informal consent. This provision does not only affect feudal superiors. In *Strathclyde Business Park (Management) Ltd v BAE Systems Pension Funds Trustees Ltd* 2010 GWD 39-791, Sh Ct, a deed of conditions contained a prohibition against putting up signs without the prior written consent of the 'Promoter' who was a management company: Strathclyde Business Park (Management) Ltd. This company did not own any part of the Park, and had no title to enforce on its own account as it wasn't an owner or tenant, nor was its mandate as manager clear, meaning that it was not a 'person entitled to enforce the burden' in terms of s 73(2A).

(i) Contractual rights in real burdens

Not only could superiors enforce real burdens against the vassal for the time being, but feudal real burdens could also be enforced as a personal contractual provision as between the superior and the original vassal. There was some doubt as to whether it could also be enforced in this way against successive disponees, however.

While feudal abolition extinguishes real burdens, it does not extinguish these contractual rights, and therefore if the original vassal is still the owner of the land, then the conditions in the original feudal grant will remain enforceable as a matter of contract. This needs to be borne in mind when reporting on the survival of feudal burdens. Section 75 of AFT(S)A 2000 confirms this but excludes rights to feuduty, and also confirms that contractual enforcement rights do not extend to successive disponees. Community burdens are also excluded from this contractual effect.

While these contractual enforcement rights are assignable, meaning a successor of the superior would be able to enforce against the original former vassal, the contractual liability ends when the original vassal ceases to own the land.

Contrast this with the effect on real burdens created after feudal abolition: the terms of s 61 of TC(S)A 2003 mean that a real burden is enforceable either as a real burden or as a contractual provision between the original parties, but not both. If it is successfully created as a real burden, then on registration any contractual entitlement ceases. However, if it fails in some way as a real burden, it may still be enforceable contractually.

(j) Use and building restrictions

Real burdens that contain use and/or building restrictions can be the most troubling for a prospective purchaser, if they limit or prevent what the purchaser wishes to do with the property. Many dwellinghouses are affected by conditions that prohibit certain uses: usually any trade or business or profession (although see *Snowie v Museum Hall LLP* para 8.03). An unreasonable restriction in the title might entitle your client to withdraw from the contract, but if the restriction is usual for the type of property then it should be expected and would not permit a purchaser to resile from the missives because of an unusual or unduly onerous burden (see *Snowie v Museum Hall LLP* again). It is important to identify at the outset what your client's plans are, so that appropriate provision has been made in the contract, and so that you will know what title conditions are likely to be problematic or unacceptable. Whatever the terms of any restriction, this should be noted and reported to your client, who may have other plans they haven't told you about.

Bear in mind that even the most 'usual' conditions can be unacceptable to a particular purchaser. The standard prohibition against keeping pets, for example, that appears in many modern deeds of conditions can be a source of much distress for your animal loving client, so it is important that your client is aware of the conditions that apply to the property they are buying.

The most common applications to the Lands Tribunal for variation or discharge of title conditions relate to building or use restrictions. If the use restriction is unacceptable to your client who still wants to proceed with the purchase, then an application to the Lands Tribunal for a discharge of the condition is one option open to him. It would then be a matter of the seller making the application, as the owner of the burdened property at the time. Although it is a matter of negotiation in the circumstances of the transaction, ideally your client would want the issue to be resolved before the purchase takes place, rather than taking the risk of waiting until after he has acquired the property, to apply for a discharge.

(k) Minerals

Minerals can be held as a separate tenement in land, and this happens when the minerals are reserved in a conveyance, whether feudal or non feudal. If no reservation has ever been made, the minerals are included in the title to land, based on the principle of ownership *a coelo usque ad centrum* (from the sky to the centre of the earth). More often than not however the minerals will have been reserved. Indeed sometimes the title may contain several successive reservations of minerals, sometimes caveated with the words 'so far as we have right thereto' However it is not always possible to be certain that there has not been a reservation of the minerals, because this may have been effected long ago, but the deed in which the reservation was made is no longer available. For these reasons, the treatment of ownership of minerals in the Land Register is subject to special provision. If there is no mention of the minerals in the title sheet there is a statutory exclusion of indemnity in case of any loss arising in respect of an interest in mines and minerals, and the title sheet of the interest, which includes the surface, does not expressly provide that the interest in mines and minerals, is included. So there may be ownership of the minerals, but that ownership does not benefit from the Keeper's guarantee. The proposals for reform of the system of land registration (see para 2.09) propose to continue this practice given the difficulties in establishing a good title to minerals.

Much of the time it will not matter to a purchaser whether the minerals are included in the title or not, although the position regarding minerals should always be reported to the client, particularly if they are reserved. Minerals reservations clauses have been known to cause problems unless adequate arrangements for compensation for any damage to the surface or buildings are expressed. Without this, the title is unmarketable, and particularly so if the reservation permits entering the surface and allows sinking bores and pits. In some parts of Scotland however, such as Lanarkshire, (where historically there was a significant amount of mining) there are many titles that contain clauses of reservations of minerals that contain these onerous provisions. It is customary for the missives to contain provisions for any reservation of minerals to be in satisfactory terms and also a requirement to obtain a Coal Authority Report (see paras 6.10(t), 6.13(k) and para 7.03).

You should bear in mind of course that all coal is vest in the Coal Authority, and that there are statutory provisions providing for payment of compensation for subsidence caused by the working of coal, covering damage to land or buildings, structures or works in or over land caused by the withdrawal of support in relation to lawful coal mining operations. Reservations of titles to minerals will exclude coal and sometimes (unnecessarily) state so. It is therefore the existence of, and working of minerals other than coal that will be of concern, if the minerals reservation clause is onerous, and it is possible to conduct investigations, firstly by inspecting the terms of the Coal Authority report, and if further more detailed information is required, by requisitioning a report on the existence of minerals in the area from the British Geological Survey (www.bgs.ac.uk). If ownership of the minerals can be identified, another possibility is to negotiate a purchase of them, which would effectively remove the problem of the reservation. However this is not always a simple task given the difficulty with minerals titles referred to above, and in any event might be a disproportionate remedy. Clearly of course if there are viable minerals in the land suitable for working then the cost of acquiring them would probably be out of proportion to the value of the land – indeed the real value in the land may be the minerals themselves.

(l) Pre-emption rights

This is a particular class of burden which gives a person who has sold land or buildings an opportunity to repurchase them the first time they are resold. The right is usually expressed as an obligation on the owner of the land, if he decides to sell the property, to offer it back to the pre-emption holder at the amount of the highest offer received from other parties, and on the same terms and conditions. A classic style of a typical clause of pre-emption can be found in Halliday: *Conveyancing Law and Practice* para

32.80 (W Green 1997 2nd Edition, Volume 2). For all pre-emptions created after 1 September 1974 the pre-emption holder has only one opportunity to exercise the right and if he declines the offer, then the pre-emption right is extinguished. It is important to note however that non feudal pre-emption rights created before 1 September 1974 can be exercised more than once, so if an offer is refused the first time the property is sold, the right remains live and can be exercised on subsequent sales.

Former feudal rights of pre-emption could be preserved by the former superior by registration of a preservation notice (see para 8.25(d)) prior to 28 November 2004, either by nominating land to be the benefited property, or as a personal real burden. Note also that even if the feudal superior has not preserved the right, and despite the elaborate scheme for preservation of feudal pre-emptions set out in AFT(S)A 2000, it seems clear in many cases that, even although the pre-emption has not been preserved under one of the preservation notices, it may still enforceable as a matter of contract by the original former superior where the original vassal is still in place. However, rights to enforce pre-emption rights do not arise by virtue of the common scheme provisions in ss 52 and 53 of TC(S)A 2003.

The existence of a right of pre-emption should be disclosed to purchasers at the missives stage, if not before. The contract should be made conditional on the pre-emption holder declining the offer. Otherwise, if missives are concluded and a pre-emption clause has been overlooked, the sellers cannot give a valid title without offering the property back to the person entitled to benefit from the pre-emption. If that person then accepts the offer, the sellers will not be able to fulfil the missives to the purchaser and will be in breach of contract. Where a right of pre-emption has not been observed, the pre-emption holder is entitled to seek a court order to reduce the disposition granted in contravention of the pre-emption, and all other deeds flowing from it, but not to a right to purchase the property as well (see *Roebuck v Edmunds* 1992 SLT 1055). Note however that the negative prescription provisions in s 18 of TC(S)A 2003 will apply after 5 years, so that if the pre-emption holder does not make any claim within that period then the pre-emption will be extinguished (although it seems that pre-1 September 1974 non-feudal pre-emptions will not extinguish completely).

From the seller's point of view, a valid clause of pre-emption is particularly irksome, as they may not know whether the pre-emption holder will exercise the right but still have to go through the process of a *bona fide* sale to establish the market value. The prospective purchasers are put to the trouble of obtaining a survey and submitting an offer. The dilemma is that if the seller warns prospective purchasers of the true position, they might not get as high an offer for the pre-emption holder to match. The practice therefore developed of approaching the pre-emption holder in advance of a sale to ascertain if they would be minded to exercise the right. If not then often a letter would be provided by the pre-emption holder confirming that they did not wish to exercise the pre-emption, and the sale to a third party would proceed unencumbered. The difficulty with this approach is that strictly speaking the pre-emption has not been validly declined since it was never formally offered on the same terms as a third party offer.

Section 83 of TC(S)A 2003 provides a solution to the problem, by providing for a statutory pre-sale undertaking that can be obtained from the pre-emption holder (the form of the undertaking is set out in Sch 10 of TC(S)A 2003) that, subject to any conditions specified by the holder of the pre-emption right, they will not exercise the pre-emption right during the period specified in the undertaking. The sale to a third party of the land can proceed without triggering the pre-emption, provided any conditions specified in the undertaking are met, and on registration of the conveyance to the third party, the pre-emption right will be extinguished. However, if a sale does not take place within the specified period, then the pre-emption right will revive at the end of that period.

The existing method of dealing with a pre-emption right can also be used ie offering the property to the pre-emption holder on the same terms and conditions as offered by a third party and the pre-emption holder has 21 days to accept (42 days in the case of a rural housing burden). Section 84 of TC(S)A 2003 re-states the previous law, and also provides that the terms on which the property is offered to the pre-emption holder are either as set out in the pre-emption clause, or if no terms are stated, then it can be on such terms as are reasonable in the circumstances.

(m) Right of redemption

A right of redemption is a right of re-purchase granted to the holder of that right. It is similar in effect to the clause of pre-emption, but in this case the original owners may call for the land to be resold to them at any time they choose, and not just when a resale takes place. When that right can be exercised depends on what the deed creating it says: it may be at any time at the instance of the holder of the right, on the occurrence of a trigger event, or after the expiry of a pre-determined period of time.

It has not been possible to create new rights of redemption as real burdens since 28 November 2004 s 3(5)(a) of TC(S)A 2003 (although they can still be created as personal contractual rights). Rights of redemption created before then still exist if non feudal, but any granted after 1 September 1974 are only exercisable for a period of 20 years from the date of creation (LTR(S)A 1974, s 12). (The reason for this provision was to prevent owners circumventing the restriction on creation of residential leases for more than 20 years, by selling property subject to a redemption clause, and then redeeming it some time after a period of 20 years had expired). Such clauses granted before September 1974 (many such clauses are contained in very old deeds) do not suffer from this 20 year restriction, so will need to be considered carefully. Potentially, it would have a damaging effect on marketability, so ideally you would want to require that it is discharged, or if it is sufficiently old, terminated.

Feudal rights of redemption were abolished on 28 November 2004 unless they were preserved by the former superior, either by nominating land to be the benefited property, or as a personal real burden (see para 8.25(d)).

If there is a sale in breach of a right of redemption, the redemption right will be extinguished 5 years after the sale by virtue of negative prescription, provided there is no claim.

(n) Reversions

Similar provisions apply to rights of reversion, which are very similar to rights of redemption, and it can sometimes be difficult to decide which type the burden is. So, any reversion created after 1 September 1974 must be exercised within twenty years of its creation, and while reversions created prior to that date are still valid, feudal reversions will have been extinguished on feudal abolition unless preserved (see para 8.25(d)). Nor is it competent to create rights of reversion after 28 November 2004 (s 3(5)(a) of TC(S)A 2003).

Statutory reversions can be subject to special provisions however. Section 86 of TC(S)A 2003 provides for extinction of rights of reversion in respect of land originally conveyed for schools, playgrounds and schoolhouses, under the School Sites Act 1841, but provides compensation may be payable by the local education authority. The Registers of Scotland produced *Update 7: School Sites Act 1841* at http://www.ros.gov.uk/pdfs/update7.pdf in 2003, which deals with the approach the Keeper will take to reversions under this Act.

(o) Burdens that are or may be unenforceable

(i) Restraint of trade

Simply because a burden appears in a deed or in the burdens section of a Title Sheet does not of course always mean that the burden is valid and enforceable. Non-feudal burdens may be unenforceable for a number of reasons, such as, for example, burdens that are intended to restrict a particular type of trade for competitive reasons, to confer commercial benefit (see *Aberdeen Varieties Ltd v James F Donald (Aberdeen Cinemas) Ltd* 1940 SC (HL)). In commercial property titles, burdens that in essence constitute a restraint of trade are quite common. The seller may plan to set up a similar business half a mile down the road and does not want his buyer to operate in direct competition to him, so places a prohibition in the title of the property being sold against using the property for that particular type of business. While there may be some contractual nexus between the original parties to the deed, such provisions have no validity as real burdens.

(ii) Reference to external documents

Another common obstacle to validity is the fact that the burden has to be set out in 'the four corners' of the deed, so that references to external documents, or material like an Act of Parliament for the purposes of establishing the precise content of the burden was not and still, except in some limited circumstances (s 5(2) of the TC(S)A 2003), is not a valid burden. A typical example of this is where a burden imposing a use restriction refers to the schedule to the Town and Country Planning (Use Classes) (Scotland) Order 1997 to define the use permitted. Section 5(2) of the TC(S)A 2003 permits a real burden that relates to an obligation to pay, or contribute towards some cost, to refer to some other, public document (which includes an enactment, public register or some record or roll to which the public readily has access) for specifying the way in which the cost or the proportion or share of the cost can be arrived at. A typical example of this would be a reference to the valuation roll for determining the respective shares of the costs of repairing common parts to be borne by the flats in a building.

(iii) Burdens for payment of money

We can distinguish here between pecuniary real burdens which are now definitely abolished (s 117 of TC(S)A 2003), so that any attempt to secure payment of sums of money, such as for example clawback payments, by way of imposing a real burden in the title, are definitely out of the question. However it is perfectly legitimate to create burdens that are about paying or contributing towards the cost of something (s 2(1)(a) of TC(S)A 2003) – often maintenance of something like a fence, or common areas of a development or common parts of a tenement.

(iv) Lack of Praediality

To be valid a burden must be praedial, in other words it must relate to the land: both the burdened property and the benefited property. A burden should burden the burdened property for the benefit of the benefited property. This is something that is often missing from older burdens, particularly 'neighbour' burdens. The lack of praediality can manifest itself in a number of ways. It may be because the benefited property is simply too far away from the burdened property for there to be any genuine praedial connection, although it might also be simply because the burden is conveying a personal benefit to the owner of the benefited property, and not a praedial one.

(v) Burdens imposed on retained property

Another common blow to validity is where, prior to 28 November 2004, the burden is set up in a disposition of part of a property, but burdens the part of the property being retained. This is not effective, because prior to the coming into force of TC(S)A 2003, it was a requirement that for a burden to be created it had to be done in a conveyance of the burdened property (or in a deed of conditions) whereas of course, there is no transfer of the restrained property. It is now possible to create real burdens in any kind of deed provided the deed is registered against both the benefited and the burdened properties (see paras 9.10(d), (e), (f) and (g)).

(vi) Lack of a benefited (or burdened) property

Where burdens are created in a disposition which conveys the whole of the property owned by the granter (so that there is no implied right of enforcement arising as a result of the rule in *Mactaggart* (see para 8.25(e)) or where the burdened property has not been sufficiently clearly identified, no effective burden is created.

Real burdens created post appointed day, ought in theory, and for the most part in practice, to be more likely to be valid, because of the requirements of dual registration and because we have, in TC(S)A 2003, a statutory code that tells us what we can and cannot do with burdens. It is still possible, however, that burdens which have been created since 28 November 2004 may fail some validity test, so don't assume that just because the burden has been created in the current climate of greater awareness, it automatically means that it is valid.

(p) Cleansing and updating of the Registers

(i) Feudal abolition

The Keeper is not required to remove a real burden extinguished by feudal abolition from a title sheet, unless she is requested to do so in an application for registration or rectification, or in terms of an order for rectification of the register by the court or the Lands Tribunal. However such a request or order will not be competent until after a period of 10 years from the appointed day. During that period therefore, a real burden, despite being so extinguished, may at the discretion of the Keeper, for the purposes of entering enforceable real rights in title sheet, be taken to subsist. Where burdens have been removed in this way, the following certificate will appear on the title sheet:

'Where the Keeper considers that any real burdens which affected the subjects in this title were extinguished by virtue of s 17 of the Abolition of Feudal Tenure Etc (Scotland) Act 2000, these have been removed or omitted from the title sheet.'

(ii) Implied enforcement rights

In the period of 10 years from the appointed day, the Keeper may, and after the expiry of that 10 year period must, where she is satisfied that a real burden subsists by virtue of any of ss 52 to 56 of TC(S)A 2003 or s 60 of AFT(S)A 2000 (preserved right of Crown to maritime burdens), enter a statement on the title sheet of the burdened property that the real burden subsists by virtue of the section in question. Where there is sufficient information to enable the Keeper to describe the benefited property, a description of that property will be included. In these cases she will also put the statement on the title sheet of the benefited property too, along with a description of the burdened property in the following terms:

'Note: In terms of s 58 of the Title Conditions (Scotland) Act 2003, the Keeper is satisfied that real burdens in the foregoing entry subsist by virtue of having been imposed as [eg facility burdens in terms of s 56,] of that Act.'

(q) Preserving neighbour burdens that arise by implication, and negative servitudes

The right to enforce neighbour burdens that arise by implication under s 49 and 50 of TC(S)A 2003, which are those which generally arise where a part of land is sold off subject to burdens which are enforceable by the land that is retained, may be preserved in perpetuity at any time during the period of 10 years from the appointed day, by registration of the appropriate notice against the title to the benefited property. Note that this provision does not apply to implied enforcement rights that arise in common scheme situations where there are reciprocal rights of enforcement.

All negative servitudes ceased to exist on the appointed day and were converted automatically to real burdens (s 80 TC(S)A 2003). These burdens, now known as 'converted servitudes', will, unless they are already registered against the burdened property prior to the appointed day, extinguish after 10 years, unless preserved by a notice registered against both benefited and burdened properties within the 10 year period.

Accordingly unless there is a preservation notice registered in respect of these types of burdens and servitudes by 27 November 2014, they will extinguish and you can ignore them.

FEUDAL LEFTOVERS

8.26 As a consequence of feudal abolition, in addition to the effect this had on feudal real burdens, there are a number of other consequences that the conveyancer should bear in mind when examining title, particularly Sasine titles. Most of these are in the category of no longer having to trouble us.

(i)   Feu duties, whether cumulo, allocated or unallocated, ground annuals, and other payments that are like feuduty, such as teinds, skat, and standard charge, are all abolished and the period within which a former superior could claim compensation (2 years after feudal abolition) has now long passed. These charges have to be extinguished if the recipient took the necessary steps to request repayment, but arrears no longer attach themselves to the property. Note however that while we do not have to be concerned with payment re feuduty, the amount of feuduty was often used as a basis on which to calculate the proportion or share of contribution towards common repair costs in tenements and this information may therefore still be relevant for that purpose.

(ii)   Thirlage, which is the duty of the vassal to have corn ground at the local mill. This had long fallen into disuse, but had never been formally abolished.

(iii)   Title relating to the superiority, including searches, minutes of consolidation, conveyances and the like can all be ignored following feudal abolition. You may come across a disposition of the superiority in pre-registration titles, and while it can be ignored, the trick is distinguishing between it and a normal disposition. The only guaranteed way is by looking at the warrandice clause—if it grants warrandice but excludes from the warrandice all feu rights in the land that have been granted, then it is a superiority disposition.

(iv) The superior's remedy of irritancy was abolished by the AFT(S) A 2000 with effect from 9 June 2000 so irritancy, or 'irritant and resolutive' clauses in feudal deeds can safely be ignored, and could not be preserved.

TENEMENTS

8.27 Historically, the common law of the tenement in Scotland was either unclear or unsatisfactory in many respects, and the Tenements (Scotland) Act 2004, which also came into force on 28 November 2004, has codified the previous common law in respect of boundaries and pertinents, regulated the rights and duties of owners of properties in a tenement, and also filled in some gaps in the law and clarified some areas of doubt.

(a) Ownership and Maintenance

Although it has its complications, the introduction of the T(S)A 2004 has simplified title examination of tenement properties in a number of respects, and rendered marketable some titles that would in the past have been considered unmarketable. For example, a top floor flat in a tenement where the titles were silent as to liability for maintenance of the common parts, would be liable for the whole burden of maintenance of the roof of the tenement, and a failure to grant a right in common to the *solum* of the tenement also would have an adverse effect on the marketability of upper floors. The T(S)A 2004 effectively restates the common law rules of ownership and applies both to existing tenements and new tenements. A top floor flat will include the roof over the flat, and a ground floor flat will include the *solum* beneath the flat.

The Act restates the common law in relation to the boundaries of the flats, which make default provisions in the event that the titles do not provide otherwise. In particular:

- each flat will own up to mid-point of the walls;
- a structure serving one flat only will belong to that flat (eg a bin store);
- the bottom flat will own the solum and the top flat will own the roof. A close (passage, stairs and landings) includes the solum and roof;

- the airspace above the tenement is owned by the owner(s) of the *solum*. In the titles this is very often expressed as common property, whereas in the statutory scheme it will belong to the owner of the ground floor flat; and

- where there is a pitched roof, the triangle of airspace between the extent of the actual slope of the roof and the imaginary horizontal and vertical lines from the highest and widest points of the building will belong to the owner of the top floor flat. This allows owners of top floor flats to install dormer windows, without encroaching on airspace owned by someone else.

In the same way, the T(S)A 2003 makes default provisions for common property or pertinents of the tenement. A close or a lift will be owned only by the owners who make use of them for access. Any land (other than the solum, a path, outside stair or other access) will belong to the ground floor flat nearest to it. Any other pertinents (which includes such things as a path, outside stair, fire escape, rhone, pipe, flue, conduit, cable, tank or chimney stack) will be owned by the flat they serve or, if serving more than one, equally among them. The only exception to the latter rule is a chimney stack, where ownership in common will be determined according to the ratio which the number of flues in the stack serving a flat bears to the total number of flues in the stack. In other words, if one flat uses five flues, but five other flats only use one flue each, the first flat will own a one-half pro-indiviso share of the chimney stack whereas the other flats will each own one-tenth.

(i) Scheme property

Where the Act changes the previous law, however, is in relation to maintenance. Ownership and maintenance no longer co-incide. The T(S) A 2004 provides a default Tenement Management Scheme (TMS) in Sch 1, which will apply to all tenements, except to the extent that the titles provide otherwise. It provides principally for certain parts of a tenement, such as the roof, foundations, *solum* and external walls always to be common parts for the purposes of maintenance and repair, regardless of ownership of these parts. These parts are referred to as 'scheme property' (see Rule 1.2 of the TMS for the full definition). It may have the effect, in some instances, of imposing obligations on owners that they did not have in the past. But this provison removes the adverse effect on marketability that ownership of the roof previously had, where the title did not provide for shared maintenance.

(ii) Application to all tenements

The key aspect of the T(S)A 2004 that the conveyancer should understand is that the T(S)A 2004 applies to all tenements to the extent that the title deeds do not. So even if the title deeds do contain provisions relating to maintenance of common parts, in other areas such as decision making, where the titles are silent, the TMS will apply. The practical significance of this is that now **all** existing tenement titles have to be read against the background of the TMS and the T(S)A 2004, and so, when dealing with tenement properties, whether residential, commercial or a mixture of both, it is necessary to have a good grasp of the provisions of T(S)A 2004.

(b) Tenement Management Scheme

The TMS is a common scheme of management for tenement properties, which applies to both existing and new tenement buildings, except to the extent that the burdens in the title deeds already make provision. However, one of the problems often encountered, particularly with elderly tenement properties, is that the provisions in the titles of each flat are inconsistent with each other. The TMS will rectify gaps and inconsistencies in such titles.

(i) Proportion of costs

Rule 4 of the TMS provides for how the costs of maintenance etc of scheme property ('scheme costs') are shared. Where the costs relate to scheme property which is owned in common by two or more of the owners in the tenement, in terms of the title, then the costs are shared among the owners in the proportions in which they share ownership of that common property. For the other types of scheme property Rule 4 states that the costs will be shared equally, except, where the floor area of the larger (or largest) flat or unit, is more than 1½ times that of the smaller (or smallest) unit, then each owner is liable to contribute in the proportion which the floor area of each owner's flat bears to the total floor area of both (or all) flats.

(ii) Inconsistencies in the Title

The provisions of Rule 4 of the TMS will apply in relation to scheme costs, unless there is a burden in the title which provides that the entire liability for those scheme costs is to be met by one or more of the owners (to the extent that that amount is not met by someone else).

What this means in practice is that Rule 4 will apply in cases where the titles of all flats or units in the tenement, taken together, do not contain provisions which provide for the full amount of scheme costs to be paid (s 4(6) of T(S)A 2004). There are titles where the shares of maintenance costs do not add up, and 100% of the total liability is not fully accounted for. Often this can arise where, for example, the titles to seven out of the eight flats in a tenement contain provisions for liability for maintenance of common parts and the remaining title is silent. In these cases Rule 4 will apply.

From the examination of title point of view, the requirement to examine the titles to all of the other flats in the tenement building becomes less imperative. It used to be necessary to see the titles of the other flats to check that they were all appropriately burdened, as otherwise there could be a gap in liability which the other properties in the tenement might have to absorb. Now, if the titles of all the flats in the tenement do not provide for 100% liability it does not matter as s 4(6) resolves the discrepancy.

(c) Reporting on tenement titles

Much of the terms of T(S)A 2004 provide for equitable arrangements in relation to ownership of a flat or floor in a tenement property, but because much of this is now contained in a statutory codified form, it will not be apparent to your client from the title. It will be necessary therefore to report to your client on some of the 'default ' provisions in the T(S)A 2004 that apply to their ownership.

(i) Scheme decisions

Rule 2 of the TMS deals with what are referred to as 'scheme decisions' relating to maintenance, appointment of manager, common insurance and other such matters. If the titles already provide for a method of making decisions these will apply. Otherwise Rule 2 will apply. Decisions on the repair of scheme property can be made by a majority of owners.

(ii) Access and installation of services

The owner of any flat in a tenement must give access to that flat to any other owner in the tenement, on reasonable notice being given, for the purposes of carrying out maintenance work or for inspection and for measuring the floor area where that is relevant for determining liability for costs.

An owner will be entitled to lead certain service pipes, cables or other equipment over other parts of the tenement but not so as to lead anything through, or fix anything to any part of the tenement which is wholly within some other flat. Scottish Ministers have still to specify both the types of services to which this part of T(S)A 2004 will apply and the procedure that must be adopted when exercising this right, so that although the relevant provision (s 19 of T(S)A 2004) is in force, until regulations are made, the scope of this right is undermined.

(iii) Insurance

Each owner has an obligation to insure his flat and any part of the tenement attached to that flat as a pertinent against certain prescribed risks (s 18 of T(S)A 2004). The duty to insure may be satisfied by way of a common insurance policy for the whole tenement.

The current prescribed risks (as set out in the Tenements (Scotland) Act 2004 (Prescribed Risks) Order 2007) are: (a) fire, smoke, lightning, explosion, earthquake; (b) storm or flood; (c) theft or attempted theft; (d) riot, civil commotion, labour or political disturbance; (e) malicious persons or vandals; (f) subsidence, heave or landslip; (g) escape of water from water tanks, pipes, apparatus and domestic appliances; (h) collision with the building caused by any moving object originating outside the building; (i) leakage of oil from fixed heating installations; and (j) accidental damage to underground services. It is likely that most reputable insurance companies will cover these risks.

(iv) Demolition and Abandonment

Demolition of a tenement building will not affect ownership rights. Where flats have been owned exclusively, each former owner will own the slice of air space which that flat formerly occupied. However, it is extremely difficult to measure air space of a flat or of a building which no longer exists and the T(S)A 2003 provides some solutions. Unless the title provides otherwise, the cost of demolition is to be shared equally except, as before, where the largest flat is more than one and half times that of the smallest, in which case liability is based on floor area. The liability arises from the date the owners agree to demolish, or in any other case from the date on which demolition is instructed. Partial demolition is also included.

No owner may build on or otherwise develop the site unless all agree, or there is a rebuilding requirement in the title. If all of the owners do not agree, any one owner is entitled to require the entire site to be sold, by applying to the courts, and the net sale proceeds would be divided equally or in accordance with floor area. Similar provisions apply for tenements that have been abandoned due to their poor condition.

The Scottish Government published a useful guide entitled Management and Maintenance of Common Property, available at: http://www.scotland.gov.uk/Resource/Doc/76169/0019425.pdf, intended to help professional staff who are involved in advising owners of flats in tenements, including housing officers, solicitors, surveyors, architects and staff in advice bureaux. It is a useful practical guide to the effects of T(S)A 2004.

EXAMINING AND REPORTING ON DEEDS OF CONDITIONS

8.28 Many multi occupancy sites, both residential and commercial, as well as mixed use sites, are subject to burdens that are contained in a Deed of Conditions. These deeds generally conform to a particular structure and also raise their own particular issues during the title examination process.

Many people regard Deeds of Conditions as something a bit scary and complicated. That perception is not helped by the often extremely dense drafting that can sometimes be used, particularly in Deeds of Conditions that relate to commercial developments, together with pages of Defined Terms, complicated Service Charge structures, convoluted meeting and voting structures, not to mention the slight anxiety that arises from concerns about ensuring that the document complies with all the legislative requirements of the TC(S)A 2003.

(a) Amenity and maintenance

Deeds of Conditions are generally used in developments or estates where there are several units or blocks or buildings of a similar kind, and where each of the owners or occupiers of these units will be expected to adhere to certain rules as to use, management, and maintenance of the units for the general benefit of the development as a whole.

The sorts of conditions that are imposed are concerned primarily with the preservation of the amenity of the whole development, so you can expect to see conditions that relate to the use to which units can be put, or prohibitions against particular types of uses. In a residential development for example, you will often see restrictions against trade or prohibitions against certain activities, like carrying out car repairs, as well as prohibitions against erecting additional buildings or adding extensions.

Usually there will be external areas in the development to deal with as well, and Deeds of Conditions will concern the use and maintenance of these areas which will include roads and pavements, landscaped and recreational areas such as play parks, grassed areas and areas of planting, possibly parking as well as more exotic things like ponds and fountains, street lighting, directional signs and so on. These provisions are about keeping the estate, office development, retail park or whatever it happens to be, nice and attractive for the people living, working or shopping there.

(b) Community burdens

The expression 'community burdens' was first used in TC(S)A 2003 Part 2, but the general idea is not new, and often the burdens set out in pre-abolition Deeds of Conditions will have been imposed on every unit in the development for the benefit of that community and may have provided for express rights of enforcement by each proprietor against the others. However, this element of reciprocity did not always exist in respect of units in a development, although there might be implied rights of enforcement created in terms of s 53 of TC(S)A 2003 (see para 8.25(e)(ii)).

Community burdens created in terms of the TC(S)A 2003 now mean something specific. By calling such burdens 'community burdens', they will automatically be enforceable by every unit in the community against any other unit in the community. Every burdened property is also a benefited property (s 27 of TC(S)A 2003). Some burdens created in Deeds of Conditions may be neighbour burdens – ie imposed on one or more properties for the benefit of other different properties - and strictly speaking, the Deed should make clear that they are not community burdens. The usual way would be to identify those Conditions in the Deed which are community burdens, the others being identified merely as 'real burdens'.

(c) Interest to enforce

As outlined in para 8.25(g), interest to enforce can be difficult to establish. The leading case of *Barker v Lewis* related to a community burden imposed in a Deed of Conditions and found that interest to enforce in respect of a breach had not been proved. The more recent decision in *Kettlewell and Others v Turning Point Scotland* (see para 8.25(g)) provides guidance about the type of evidence that is required to establish the material detriment test for interest to enforce. It should be borne in mind that interest to enforce applies to community burdens as for other burdens and that depending on the nature of the burden, not all proprietors in the development will have any interest to enforce even though it is clear that they will have title to enforce.

(d) Ownership of Common parts

In any development on land, there will be parts of the development that are to be used in common by the owners of units in the development, whether they be roads, car parks, recreation or play areas and so on. There are several ways of dealing with title to these common areas, which will also need to be looked after, maintained and sometimes repaired and renewed.

The first option is for the developer to retain ownership of these areas. This may be acceptable but invariably, once the developer has finished the development, he doesn't want any lingering involvement in it, particularly now that developers no longer have any continuing interest as feudal superior. Sometimes, in fact, the developer or owner of the land being developed may be a special purpose company set up for the duration of the development, and which it is intended to wind up once the development is complete, so continuing ownership simply isn't an option.

An alternative is for the common areas to be conveyed at the end of the development to an owners association, or to some third party, often a management company, which will look after the common parts and recover the cost of doing so from the owners of units. There have over the years been well publicised problems with some of these arrangements, with bitter complaints from owners in developments about the standard of service, lack of service and heavy handed tactics – allegedly – in recovering outstanding sums.

In the past, having common areas conveyed to owners associations, which generally do not have any legal personality has been somewhat problematic. Where they have been set up, they usually operate in favour of trustees *ex officio* – eg the chairman, secretary and treasurer for the time being of the owners' association. It is however now possible to have an Owners' Association, set up by using the Development Management Scheme arrangements under Part 6 of TC(S)A 2003 (see para 9.10(g)) which has a separate legal personality and can hold title to parts of the development, as well as contract in its own name.

The third main option, and one which was formerly extremely common, is to convey *pro-indiviso* shares – usually equal shares – of ownership in the common areas to each owner along with the conveyance of their unit. There are a couple of ways in which this has been done in the past: (i) by reference to a detailed plan of the development, identifying all the areas that are to be communal and conveying shares in those areas in the Disposition with the plan attached, or by reference to the Deed of Conditions in which those parts are identified, and to which there is a plan attached or (ii) by describing those common areas in the Deed of Conditions on an exclusion basis – in other words by referring to every part of the development that is not to be conveyed individually to plot owners.

This second alternative, which was the more popular of the two options, was seen to give developers the flexibility that they often needed to make alterations to the precise location of the common parts, perhaps slightly alter the route of roads, or amend the configuration, if adjustments to the way in which the development was being built out were made. This approach was however resoundingly discredited in the Lands Tribunal decision in *PMP Plus Ltd v The Keeper of the Registers of Scotland* LTS/LR/2007/02.

The original developer had purported over time to convey *pro-indiviso* shares in the external common parts in the development to each of the plot owners, in the Dispositions in their favour. These common areas were identified described by reference to whatever was going to be left at the end of the development once all the plots had been conveyed. However at some point before the end of the development, the developer sold off a chunk of the same external common areas to PMP Plus for the purposes of building a health centre. Initially, because of the prior conveyances of *pro-indivsio* shares, the Keeper indicated that indemnity would be excluded in PMP Plus's title, but on appeal of this decision to the Lands Tribunal, it was decided that the conveyances of these prior *pro-indiviso* shares were invalid, due to the fact that the area of ground – the common areas – was not capable of being identified or mapped and consequently it was not possible validly to convey an uncertain area or a share in an uncertain area. This is due to the specificity principle – which requires that land being conveyed must be specific, not uncertain – 'that which cannot be identified cannot be conveyed'.

Because it was such a common and popular method, it was a device employed in many developments, both residential and commercial, no doubt reinforced by the fact that the Keeper was happy to accept such deeds and produce land certificates reflecting the purported conveyances. Following on the decision in *PMP Plus*, of course the Keeper has changed her policy, but only in relation to developments where the first conveyance of a unit takes place after August 2009. (see Registers of Scotland Update 27 'Creation, Identification and Transfer of Rights in Common Areas of Developments at http://www.ros.gov.uk/pdfs/update27.pdf). For consistency, she will continue to accept conveyances of such *pro-indiviso* shares in developments where such conveyances had already been accepted by her prior to August 2009. That policy doesn't necessarily make such conveyances any more valid, but it does represent equal treatment.

In its draft Land Registration (Scotland) Bill, (attached to the SLC Report 222 on Land Registration at http://www.scotlawcom.gov.uk/publications/reports/2010-present/) (see para 2.09 for a summary of the proposals for reform of the Land Registration system), the Scottish Law Commission put forward proposals for dealing with the issue of *pro indiviso* shares of common parts in ss 29 to 31 of its draft Bill. The idea is that if a developer wants to structure and convey his development in that way, but still retain some flexibility about what the common parts are finally going to look like, he can apply to the Keeper to set up a separate title sheet for what will be known as a 'provisional shared plot', and as and when the *pro-indiviso* shares are 'conveyed' to plot owners, the title number for the main unit will be added to the provisional shared plot title sheet. Once the extent of the common parts are known the developer will submit an ascertainment plan attached to a deed which will act as a proper disposition to all of the individual *pro-indiviso* shares, and the Keeper will perfect the title to those shares at that stage in respect of all the title numbers that have been added to the provisional shared plot. So, rights of property wouldn't pass until the areas are clearly defined, but they sit in a visible pending tray until that stage.

It is not necessarily an ideal solution, and there are those who do not favour such an approach, so it remains to be seen whether these proposals, or something like them, will ever make it to the statute book. Clearly however, some imaginative commercially aware thinking is required to adequately resolve this issue. In the meantime, it seems that a reasonably pragmatic approach might be possible where this issue arises: while individual circumstances always have to be taken into account, the practical effect of a lack of title to a share of the common parts may be negligible, if, as is usually the case, there are rights to use the common parts anyway (subject usually to a corresponding obligation to contribute to maintenance). Neither is there any evidence of an adverse effect on value of the units. However, at the time of writing, there is no settled approach to the issue.

(e) Examining and reporting

As the Deed of Conditions, if there is one, is likely to be the main document containing burdens and servitudes affecting the property, it is important that you read it, so that you can report on its terms to your client. For residential developments particularly it can be tempting to assume that it will contain the 'usual conditions' and that taking a photocopy to send to the purchaser is all that need be done. However, while the usual conditions may be familiar to the conveyancer, the chances are that this is the first (and possibly only) time that the purchaser will see one, and it can be a daunting prospect to read through and understand the significance of all its terms without some guidance. At the very least you should be pointing out provisions such as restriction on trade and the no pets rule, if there is one, as these things may be of great importance to your client. In fact there is a strong argument, since you know the sort of conditions that that these deeds are likely to contain that you should be highlighting the prospect of such conditions at the initial stages of purchase, so that the purchaser does not find herself contractually bound to a purchase of a property that contains conditions that, while an 'industry norm', may be unpalatable to her lifestyle.

Commercial Deeds of Conditions tend to be far more bespoke affairs. However given the nature of the commercial purchaser you will be expected to read and report in some detail on the terms of the Deed, and flag up any conditions of which a commercial buyer should be aware and that might affect your client's business. There are likely to be a lot of definitions at the start of the Deed, or possibly in a Schedule and while reading the document from the start is always a good idea, it can be counter productive to read all the definitions first until you know how the structure of the Deed itself operates. The meaning or effect of some definitions sometimes only becomes clear when you read it in the context of the operative clauses of the Deed.

(f) Importing pre-abolition Deeds of Conditions

Some Deeds of Conditions registered before 28 November 2004 dis-applied s 17 of the Land Registration (Scotland) Act 1979. Dis-application of s 17 meant that the burdens and servitudes contained in the pre-2004 Deed of Conditions would not be registered against the land affected at the time the Deed of Conditions was recorded or registered, but only when it, or parts of it, were conveyed in a deed, and the terms of the Deed of Conditions were stated in that conveyance to apply to the land conveyed. Section 17 was repealed by the TC(S)A 2003. However in some cases these pre-November 2004 Deeds of Conditions will still apply to plots or units in the development that are conveyed after 28 November 2004. In that case, s 6 of the TC(S)A 2003 provides for transitional provision to allow such Deeds of Conditions to cross the bridge between the old and new law. This is done by using words which will import the old deed of conditions into the title of the units being conveyed (see para 9.10(k)). If this wording has not been used in the relevant circumstances then the burdens in the Deed of Conditions will not be validly imposed on the unit concerned.

SITE ASSEMBLY ISSUES

8.29 When examining a title you should always have in mind the type of property it is, and where appropriate, the type of property your client intends it to be after purchase, where that is different. So if you are examining title for shop premises which your client plans to buy, you must check for prohibitions against the sale of alcohol, which could cause problems if your client intends to have an off-sales section in the shop. In rural locations, you need to be extra particular about access and drainage rights (amongst many other issues) and when your client is buying land or property for development, there are some specific issues that it is important to bear in mind, particularly when, as can often be the case, the site is being put together from several parcels of land or sites. By way of illustration of some of these issues, consider the following case study:

(a) A typical site

Your client is Lightyear Development Company Ltd (LDCL), a company with considerable experience in putting together sites for development and onward sale or letting, which has been engaged in property development on a small scale for several years. Over the years, LDCL has acquired small to medium pieces of ground, sites and bits of property on a speculative basis, and land-banked these for future development potential when the circumstances are right. Having owned properties in the middle of Sardinia Terrace, in the market town of Kelvinforth, for several years, LDCL now has the opportunity to buy from the owner, Kelvinforth Investments Ltd (KIL), the block at the corner of Sardinia Terrace and Lombardy Street (see plan A on page 352), which is close to the main residential parts of town. LDCL has been in talks with the estates director of Prontomart plc, a national supermarket chain, with a view to building a supermarket on the cleared site (see plan B on page 352) which LCDL would then let to Prontomart on a long lease.

Agents for a major pension fund have indicated to LCDL that their client is looking to expand their portfolio and would be interested in acquiring the developed and tenanted site as an investment, along with five other sites in Scotland currently being developed for Prontomart.

PLAN A

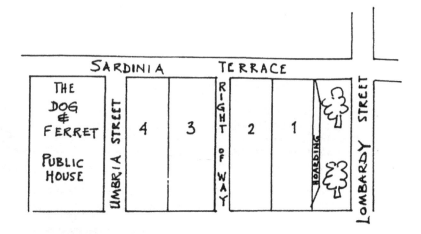

PLAN B

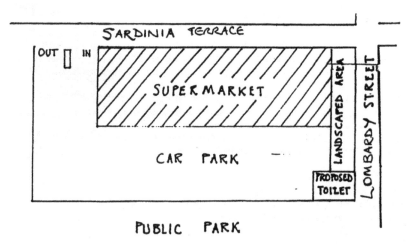

(b) Title considerations

While it is often preferable to wait until conclusion of missives before looking at the title, given the importance of title boundaries and conditions when assembling a development site, it is often more prudent to look at the title as early as possible, perhaps while the contract is being negotiated, because it is important for the developer to establish sooner rather than later whether the site is going to be suitable for development. Developing a site is a major investment in time and money for a developer, particularly as the acquisition will normally be subject to obtaining the necessary planning consent, which can take some time, so the developer wants to know that his expenditure in that regard, which can be considerable, is not going to be wasted due to an insurmountable obstacle with the title to the land. This usually will mean that the missives that are negotiated will address some issues that the title examination throws up, and which the developer might be expected to take a view on, but the contract will in all probability be conditional, or suspensive, on a number of conditions and other factors.

At an early stage you should identify the precise extent of the land required. This is usually assisted by obtaining a draft plan of the proposed development from the client or the surveyors. You need to ensure that there are no gaps in the title, and also that all the land you need is available and not owned by someone else, or unavailable in some other way, such as being the subject of an option in favour of some other party. Checking the title early on will identify whether the seller has title to all of the land required and if there are any 'ransom strips' or rights in favour of others such as servitudes or rights of way.

In the Sardina Terrace site, it is clear from the Plan B proposals, produced by Prontmart's surveyor, that there are several issues: (i) Plan A shows a right of way which runs between Numbers 2 and 3 Sardinia Terrace, leading to the public park, and is regularly used by children from the nearby school. Note that rights of way and other third party rights are often not apparent from the titles or plans and may only be apparent from a site visit; (ii) Umbria Street, between the pub and Number 4 Sardinia Terrace is a public road; (iii) a plot of ground with two large trees sits at the corner of Sardinia Terrace and Lombardy Street. These trees are the subject of a tree preservation order under the Town and Country Planning (Scotland) Act 1997, s 160, although they have become large and unwieldy and overhang Lombardy Street, and the tree roots are intruding under No 1 Sardinia Terrace causing difficulties in the foundations; (iv) KIL does not have title to the land on which the Dog And Ferret Public house on Umbria Street is situated, although an associated company, Kelvinforth

Leisure Pursuits Ltd (KLPL) is the tenant of the pub. KLPL's employee, Desmond Moore, runs the pub and lives in the flat above, and (v) there is an advertising hoarding on the east gable of number 1 Sardinia Terrace, which is in regular use. It may be the subject of a lease or licence.

(c) Boundaries

Clearly defined boundaries are of considerable importance and the site visit is of huge assistance here, once a preliminary title check has been made, to identify whether there are any problems. It is essential to have good quality plans based on the Ordnance Survey map, to identify what is being acquired, and whether the boundary features themselves could pose any difficulties, for example where the site is bounded by a river or a road, or perhaps a wall that is listed, or a gable of an adjoining building with windows overlooking the development. A boundary feature may turn out to be onerous with significant maintenance obligations – a canal bank for example or some other infrastructure, and this needs to be taken into account. Proximity to a river may give rise to considerations regarding flooding which could have significant impact on the construction costs.

A visual inspection at this point can be extremely revealing, as what looks like one thing on a two dimensional plan can take on a completely different complexion once it is seen in reality, such as when a boundary over which some oversailing rights (for the boom of construction cranes to use adjoining airspace) are required turns out to be a vertical cliff. It is important to ascertain at an early stage in the process what if any oversailing rights will be needed, so that the relevant parties can be approached for consent. You should also make enquiries of the sellers about any existing disputes with adjacent proprietors, whether in relation to boundaries or otherwise. Access and possibly oversailing rights will be needed over the public park next to the Sardinia Terrace site, since the site itself is quite tight and there are buildings on the other sides of the surrounding streets.

(d) Site Visit

A site visit with your client and development team could be useful, when involved in a development. It enables physical issues that might not be clear from the title to be easily checked, and it also gives you an opportunity, along with the development team, to look at issues of access to and from the site during construction and for the final development, and consider servicing arrangements, which might be affected by the topography of the land: a steep incline on the site will affect the route and locations for laying of drainage and water pipes, and might mean that different servitude rights are needed. It is also an ideal opportunity to get to know and benefit from the knowledge and perspective of the development team. A visual inspection of the Sardinia Terrace site discloses that locals are using the ground to the rear of the Dog and Ferret for car parking and as a site for car boot sales. How long the parking area has been used may need to be investigated. You also note that there is a small grocer's shop at the corner of Sardinia Terrace and Lombardy Street. These issues may well elicit objections to the planning proposals.

(e) Access

A crucial part of any development is ensuring that there are adequate access rights, which can mean not just owning the land where points of access are taken, but also checking existing servitude rights and the sufficiency of them to allow the site to be accessed for all necessary purposes, both during the construction phase and for the final built out development. Even when a site abuts a public highway, it is still important to consider access carefully. The best position for forming a new entry point off the highway and into the site, may clash with the position on the site where the developer proposes to put new buildings, and so new rights might be needed or development proposals might have to be re-visited. For sites that are being acquired for residential development there are considerations of density of population and consequent traffic management issues, as well as increasing the burden on existing servitude rights, depending on how they are expressed. It is also important to check whether the site or any part of it is used as access by third parties, whose rights may need to be accommodated or re-negotiated. And remember that not all access rights will necessarily be set out in the title.

Access points to consider:

(i)   What are the current access arrangements: adopted public road or private access route?

(ii)   What is the exact extent of adopted highway, pavement or verge? While a Property Enquiry Certificate may confirm that the road serving the property is adopted and maintained by the Local Authority, it will not (usually) show the extent of the adoption. It can often be the case that little strips of land between the road and the title to the site exist in a no-mans land and are not included in the adopted extent. A plan should be obtained from the local authority showing the exact extent of adoption.

(iii) Can the current access be used for the development or will new roads need to be constructed for which a Road Construction Consent will be required?

(iv) If the site is for residential development, and roads are to be constructed, a road bond will be required (s 17 Roads (Scotland) Act 1984).

(v) Are the current entry points from the public road suitable for the development?

(vi) Where new access points off a public road are needed, does the site include sufficient ground for bell-mouth openings, visibility splays or deceleration lanes? If not, can land be acquired or servitudes obtained? Even in rural areas this can be an issue if lorries which require large turning circles are transporting large loads, such as turbines for wind farms need to swing over adjoining land as they turn off the main road.

(vii) Check that there are no other proposals – for example local authority plans for road widening or closure that might adversely impact on access to, or development proposals for, the site.

(viii) If new access rights are required, who are the land owners that will need to be approached either for renegotiating existing servitudes or obtaining new ones. There could be significant cost consequences which might have an impact on the viability of the development. It is important to ensure that any new grants of access will be forthcoming and at what cost.

(ix) Are existing servitudes adequate for the proposed use of the development eg if the servitude is for agricultural purposes, then it is unlikely to be sufficient for use as access to a retail park.

(x) What if any third party access rights are there across the site? These might be constituted be express grant but there are, of course classes of servitude that can exist but which are not evident from the title, as well as rights of way.

(xi)   Is there sufficient access for service vehicles and delivery lorries? In a small site where there are already built up areas, this can be an important consideration. If the Prontomart supermarket is build on the Sardinia Terrace site, the architect will need to make sure that the access into the site and provision within the site is sufficient to accommodate the large articulated transporters that the supermarket chain uses to deliver supplies from its centralised distributions centres.

(f) Ransom Strips

As described in the context of roads at para 8.19, so-called 'ransom strips' can occur in any title, but clearly when assembling a title for development which is made up of various component parts of different titles and properties, there is greater scope for areas of ground, small or large, that are not within the seller's title, to be found necessary to complete the 'jigsaw' of the development site.

Some parties may seek to exploit ransom strips by holding back small areas of land when selling off sites, or may adventitiously find themselves in a position where they hold land that suddenly becomes important for a development proposal to come to fruition. The good news is usually that the owner of the ransom strip does want to sell, however the downside is likely to be the cost, since such a piece of land will command a much higher value than the actual value of the land itself.

It seems likely that the site of the Dog and Ferret pub could be a ransom strip (or plot) for the Sardinia Terrace project. The pub is somewhat run down and although it has a small hard core of loyal regulars, it is not a particularly profitable enterprise, and the lease to KLPL is due to expire in 2 years' time.

(g) Services

Checking the arrangements for services to the site; water, drainage, electricity, gas telecoms etc is as important as checking the physical access arrangements.

Services points to consider:

(i)   Check with the development team where services routes are intended and what additional rights they consider will be required.

(ii)   Are the existing services and associated servitude rights sufficient for the purposes of construction and eventual use of the development?

(iii)   Do any existing services require to be relocated or enlarged, and if so are the existing rights sufficient and is there adequate land available to do so? More modern servitudes for services will often incorporate 'lift and shift' provisions for relocating pipes and cables, but older servitude rights often don't specify these.

(iv)   Will third parties such as adjoining land owners need to be approached for servicing arrangements? Do you need to inspect titles to adjoining land in connection with services arrangements?

(v)   Does any service media serving adjoining property run through or over the site? A gas mains that needs an unbuilt on strip of land 20 metres wide across its route could effectively sterilise land for development purposes. Moving or diverting existing pipe and cable routes could be time-consuming and potentially prohibitively expensive.

(h) Surveys and Reports

Any development will involve a number of professionals and specialists who will produce surveys and reports on various aspects of the site and the proposals for development. While you are not expected to be expert in all the terminology or implications of these reports (unless of course that is your particular specialism), it is important that you obtain and read these reports, particularly the main surveyors report and any environmental and conditional reports. Note of course that environmental issues in particular are an extremely specialised area, and if there are environmental or contamination issues, then advice should be sought from persons specialised and experienced in these matters. On larger sites, and with most developers, Environmental Consultants will be instructed, retained or even employed in-house, and will cover these issues, but you should always check that these issues are being picked up.

However there might be aspects that emerge from your title examination that should be reported in this context. Previous uses of the site your client is buying may contain clues that point to possible contamination. If the site was a former gas works or used for some industrial process for example, then this fact should spark a recommendation for an environmental survey if none has been carried out. Once the title is registered in the Land Register of course, access to these older titles is less common and they might no longer be available. A wealth of ancillary information is lost in this way. However it is also good practice, where appropriate, to obtain old maps of the area concerned which will often show up features of old uses, and can also be invaluable in piecing together parcels of land that suffer from vague or archaic or historical descriptions.

Standard reports such as PECs, Coal Authority reports, British Geological Survey reports and utilities searches will all disclose information that may be relevant, and should be passed on to your client and/or his surveyor and advisers.

(i) Existing buildings and features

Where the site includes existing buildings or other features that will need to be demolished or removed to allow the development to take place, this will also need to be catered for. Older buildings that are to be demolished may contain asbestos, which needs to be removed and disposed of in a carefully controlled and regulated manner. Consents for demolition will need to be obtained. If any of the buildings on the site are listed then any alterations to them will require listed building consent in addition to other consents. The design of the site may need to accommodate protected structures that it is not possible to remove, and trees that are subject to tree preservation orders can also pose an obstacle to development.

(j) Planning and other consents

It may be that the site your client is buying already benefits from planning or other consents for its development. Invariably planning consents will relate to a number of physical features of a site and make provision for access, services, servicing, traffic management, parking, density, use and so on. The terms of the consents may require for example that the access to the site is to be widened to improve visibility or that additional entry points need to be created and these can impact on how much land the developer needs to acquire, as well as the other terms and conditions of the title. If additional land or rights are needed to comply with the terms of the planning permission, then this needs to be addressed early on. Indeed, you may need to make it a condition of the purchase of the site that any necessary additional land or rights are obtained. As well as inspecting the reports and surveys of your client's other advisers, they also need to see a copy of your Title Report, and elements of it should be composed with this in mind.

If the consents and other documentation produced are complex, then it will be necessary to consult planning and construction lawyers, if you do not have this expertise yourself. Otherwise you should make it clear in your letter of engagement that these aspects will not be covered by you, or your firm.

Clearly the earlier that you can establish whether additional land/areas will be required the better. Therefore ensure your title report is something that the architects/planning consultants (and indeed planning lawyers) have seen and are aware of in the context of their discussions with the planning officers as they prepare the planning application. You do not want to end up with a consent that cannot be implemented because additional land/access is required, or where payment will be required to a third party (who will by then be aware of the planning consent) to secure the land/access.

SERVITUDES

8.30 Servitudes such as rights of access, rights to lay pipes etc are unaffected by feudal abolition and although it is now no longer possible to create a negative servitude (ie servitudes prohibiting certain action), negative servitudes were not extinguished on the appointed day, instead they were converted into 'negative real burdens' for a transitional period of 10 years. Servitudes are often couched with conditions that apply specifically to the exercise of the servitude, and while they may look like real burdens, they are in fact 'servitude conditions' which survive with the servitude itself. Remember that servitudes can be validly created by the running of prescription for 20 years and can be extinguished in this way too. See also paras 8.19 and 8.21 for servitudes rights that should be checked for, when examining title.

ADJUDICATION TITLES

8.31 An adjudication may be granted against a person who either (a) does not pay a debt or (b) contracts to sell property under missives and then refuses or delays to transfer the property. Adjudication titles are not very common.

In case (a): adjudication for debt - the title given to the creditor is a security title only, and the debtor may redeem within 'the legal', which is a ten-year period from the date of decree. The decree obtained is registered in the Register of Sasines or Land Register. Such a title should not be accepted by a purchaser until the legal has lapsed. Any title registered prior to expiry of the legal will exclude indemnity, and the charges section of the title sheet will disclose the security aspect of the decree, for the purposes of ranking in relation to other securities. To remove the exclusion of indemnity on expiry of the legal, the adjudger has to obtain and register a decree of declarator of expiry of the legal.

In case (b): adjudication in implement - the title is absolute and may be accepted by a purchaser or a lender in security. A decree of adjudication in implement is equivalent to a conveyance of lands, and the creditor (or 'adjudger') completes title by recording the decree in the Register of Sasines or registering it in the Land Register.

Section 79 of the Bankruptcy and Diligence etc (Scotland) Act 2007 will, once commenced, abolish adjudication for debt and replace it with a diligence called land attachment.

GRATUITOUS ALIENATION AND UNFAIR PREFERENCE

8.32 During the course of your examination of title, you have to be alert to the possibility that a transfer of the property may have taken place at a price under its true value, or in favour of one creditor in preference to the general body of the transferor's creditors. While a person is free to convey their property at less than market value, as a gift, or to anyone they choose, the status of such transfers alters significantly if the person was insolvent at the time, or the transfer in question renders that person insolvent. This is a complex area of the law, and the following description is, of necessity, no more than a general summary of the main provisions.

(a) Gratuitous alienation

A gratuitous alienation is a transfer for no, or inadequate, consideration by an insolvent granter (s 34 Bankruptcy (Scotland) Act 1985 (individuals) and s 242 Insolvency Act 1986 (companies)). If a transfer of this type takes place and the transferor is subsequently sequestrated or grants a trust deed for the benefit of his creditors, or, if a company, it is wound up or an administrator is appointed, then the insolvency practitioner (IP) or any creditor may challenge the transfer. A receiver may not challenge a gratuitous alienation but the holder of the relevant floating charge would be entitled to challenge. Gratuitous alienation provisions can also apply where the debtor is deceased, and within twelve months, his estate is sequestrated or a judicial factor appointed.

Where the recipient is an associate of the debtor the alienation must have taken place within the period of five years immediately preceding the date of sequestration, and in the case of any other type of recipient from the debtor within two years prior to that date.

The term 'associate' has a wide meaning (see s 74 of B(S)A 1985). It includes the debtor's husband, wife or civil partner or a relative (brother, sister, aunt, uncle, nephew, niece etc) or the spouse or civil partner of a relative of the debtor or the debtor's spouse, or any person with whom the debtor is in partnership, and includes an employee and an employer. A director or other officer of a company is treated as being an employee of that company for these purposes, and a company can be an associate of another company in certain circumstances (s 74(5A) to (5C) and (6) of B(S)A 1985).

Note that, in addition to the statutory challenge, there remain certain rights of challenge at common law. The onus of proof on the pursuer is higher, since fraud must be shown, therefore these are rarely used. However, the common law challenge is available for up to 20 years. See McBryde on Bankruptcy 2nd Edition paras 12.11 to 12.57.

(b) Challenge

A challenge to a gratuitous alienation may be made by action of reduction in the Court of Session or seeking other redress in the sheriff court. A challenge will not be successful if it can be shown that the debtor was solvent immediately after (or at any time after) the alienation was granted (ie that the debtor's assets were greater than his liabilities) or that the alienation was for 'adequate consideration' or that it was a birthday or Christmas or other conventional present or a charitable gift which it was reasonable for the debtor to make. Note that the challenge is against the recipient, not the debtor.

If the challenge is successful, the remedy is a decree of reduction of the alienation, or such restoration of property to the debtor's estate as is appropriate, or 'other redress'. The courts will seek to reduce the alienation or restore the property in preference to other routes – see *Short's Trustee v Chung* 1991 SLT 473 at 476 per Lord Sutherland.

(c) Unfair preference

An unfair preference is a transaction entered into by a debtor, which has the effect of creating a preference in favour of one creditor or creditors to the prejudice of the general body of creditors (s 36 B(S)A 1985 (individuals) and s 243 Insolvency Act 1986 (companies)). To qualify as an unfair preference under statute, the preference must have been created not earlier than 6 months before the date of insolvency. Some types of transaction, such as transactions in the ordinary course of business, are exempt from challenge (s 36(2) B(S)A 1985 and s 243(2) IA 1986) and may be plead as a defence by the recipient. An unfair preference can be challenged by creditors and insolvency practitioners (but not receivers).

As with gratuitous alienations, preferences may also be challenged at common law. Again, the transaction must be shown to be fraudulent in nature and is therefore rarely used, despite the long prescriptive period.

A challenge to an unfair preference is either by way of action of reduction in the Court of Session or seeking other redress in the Sheriff Court.

(d) The position of a third party acquirer

A third party who has acquired a property from or through a recipient of a gratuitous alienation or unfair preference, for value and in good faith is protected (s 34(4) and s 36(5) of B(S)A 1985 and ss 242(4) and 243(5) of IA 1986).

While it may be difficult to tell from the face of a title that it was given by way of unfair preference, it might be easier to spot a gratuitous alienation, as this may refer to a nil or nominal consideration, or consideration that appears to be clearly inadequate for the size or likely value of the property concerned. References to 'certain good (and onerous) causes and considerations' should be carefully considered in their context. If faced with a transfer of this nature in the title being offered, can a third party purchaser be said to be 'in good faith' if they proceed with their purchase without further enquiry?

(i) Is the transferor solvent?

Much of this is about identifying whether there is any risk to your client. If the transaction effecting the transfer took place more than 5 years ago and the granted has not been sequestrated or wound up etc, then it is outwith the statutory challenge period. If not then you should raise a query with the seller's solicitors as to the solvency of the transferor. The search in the Personal registers will disclose whether any insolvency proceedings have been applied against that party.

(ii) Certificate or declaration of solvency

It is debatable whether there is anything that can be obtained that would provide complete protection from challenge, however, if you are acting for a transferee from an individual and the consideration is nil or clearly significantly less than full value, in order to ensure that in the future the transfer cannot be perceived as a gratuitous alienation, it might be possible to obtain either a declaration or affidavit from the granter, or (possibly) a certificate from their accountant confirming that as at any date after the transfer, the granter was absolutely solvent (a formal expression meaning that the assets of the granter were greater than their liabilities).

How willing accountants may be to give such a certificate is a moot point, but in family transactions there might be a greater chance that something of the sort would be forthcoming. It should not be assumed that there is a problem with solvency just because the accountant is unwilling to produce the certificate. The accountant can only comment on the basis of the information that has been given to him, so if it transpires that information has been withheld from him, the value of the certificate would be questionable, although having made enquiry and having received some form of assurance can help to demonstrate good faith. Also useful would be a statement of the reasons why the transfer is being made. So for example a father who decides for reasons of tax efficiency, or for 'love, favour and affection' to transfer property to his daughter, could confirm that this was the reason why the transfer was being made.

It is much harder to obtain a declaration or certificate of this type retrospectively, but where you are acting for a purchaser from the transferee, enquiry should be made as to the circumstances of the transfer, and ask for confirmation that the granter was solvent when, and immediately (or at any time) after the property was transferred. It is a matter of judgement how far it will be necessary to pursue this issue. You can also consider audited accounts for business transferors as these show the financial position at a particular point in time. Although these are based on assumptions, they have at least been subject to audit. Also qualified statement in the accounts would be a sign of something to look into ie where auditors state they are unable to certify.

(iii) The insolvent transferor

If the search discloses that the transferor is in some form of insolvency, a sensible course of action is to ask the seller's solicitors to find out from the IP if he intends to challenge the transfer. On appointment any IP will look into transfers effected in the past 5 years with a view to indentifying any gratuitous alienation or unfair preference, and will have investigated the circumstances.

OCCUPANCY RIGHTS

8.33 The occupancy rights of spouses in the matrimonial home have been recognised as an overriding interest on the title to any property that qualifies as a matrimonial home, since 1982, when the Matrimonial Homes (Family Protection) (Scotland) Act 1981 came into force. As the name suggests, the policy reason behind the Act was to protect spouses (predominantly wives) from domestic abuse and provide that even if they did not own the marital home, they had rights to stay there that did not depend on the consent of their spouse, and in extreme circumstances could apply to the courts to exclude that spouse from the home. The Civil

Partnership (Scotland) 2004 extended similar rights to civil partners. These occupancy rights of the non-entitled spouse or civil partner are such that they would have priority over the rights of a purchaser or a heritable creditor, and so it is necessary when purchasing from a single individual to ascertain his or her marital status and ensure that the rights of any spouse or civil partner are addressed.

This will normally involve either (i) incorporating the consent of the spouse or civil partner into the documentation, either within the disposition or standard security, or as a stand-alone form, or (ii) a renunciation of the occupancy rights by that spouse or civil partner. Where the seller is unmarried, the position is covered by obtaining (iii) a declaration from the seller to the effect that the property is not a matrimonial home in relation to which a spouse or civil partner of the seller has occupancy rights. For further details, see para 4.08(d). Occupancy rights of a non entitled spouse or civil partner will extinguish after of period of two years of non-cohabitation and non-occupancy (s 5 and Sch 1 para 3 of the Family Law (Scotland) Act 2006).

RAISING OBSERVATIONS ON TITLE

8.34 It would be a rare title indeed that did not throw up some question or requirement for clarification. During the course of your title examination, or once you have finished looking at the titles provided to you by the seller's solicitor, you may need some further information or require to see further documents, and these are generally known as 'observations on title' or 'title requisitions'. They may include standard requests such as the request for search reports or updates of these, asking for information about something that is in the knowledge of the seller, such as when the last common repairs were carried out, and confirmation that there are no outstanding repairs bills; details of the identity of any managing agent or factor and so on. You might find the PSG Due Diligence Questionnaire of some assistance here as well, and use it as a checklist of issues that might be relevant to your particular title, as well as an indication of what to ask for if they are.

This is also the time to be requesting clarification about any matters arising during the course of your title examination and which you were jotting down as you went along. It is good practice to raise all of these observations at the same time, where you can, as this will let the seller's solicitors know the general extent of your requirements. However since there may be other matters you wish to raise that you haven't at that stage identified, or you might have supplementary observations to make when you see the seller's solicitors responses, it is sensible to make it clear that your list of queries is not exhaustive, by saying for example that these are preliminary queries and that you will let the seller's solicitor know if you have any others.

There will come a point however, and this will depend on how the missives are worded, that the seller's solicitor may ask you to declare that you are satisfied as to title. Caution should be exercised before making such a declaration, or you may need to caveat it by saying that it is subject to seeing updated clear searches, for example.

REMEDIES FOR AN UNMARKETABLE TITLE

8.35 The purchasers are of course entitled to resile if presented with an unmarketable title, but we can presume that the purchasers and sellers both want to complete the purchase if they can. Often a problem with a title can be remedied, and the seller should be given the chance to try to do so.

There are many ways of reaching a satisfactory position, enabling the transaction to proceed, and the following suggest some of the ways in which a problem can be rectified or resolved. Not all of these will be suitable solutions if the property is already registered in the Land Register rather than still in the Sasine Register and *vice versa*.

(a) Disposition *per incuriam*

If a disposition has a bad mistake in it, for example it conveys the top floor flat right instead of the top floor flat left, the error can be rectified by getting the original granter to grant this form of disposition. It simply narrates that *per incuriam* the earlier disposition conveyed the wrong flat, and then goes on to dispone the correct one. The use of the Latin tag hides the fact that it was done (literally) 'by mistake'. A disposition of this type cannot however be used to correct the error, once the title has been registered in the Land Register, although remedial conveyancing is still possible if the parties agree.

(b) By use of the *Requirements of Writing (Scotland) Act 1995, ss 4, 5*

Section 4 of RoW(S)A 1995 sets up a presumption as to the granter's subscription or date or place of subscription by application to the court, where the deed has not been witnessed. This is likely only to be useful where the granter is unavailable whether through incapacity or death, or untraceable or unwilling to assist, since it will usually be far more straightforward to simply have the granter acknowledge his signature to a witness. Section 5 of RoW(S)A 1995 sets out provisions for dealing with alterations to deeds, both prior to and after execution. Careful use of the provisions of these sections may assist in resolving a number of defects of execution and mistakes in the deed.

(c) By use of the *Law Reform (Miscellaneous Provisions) (Scotland) Act 1985, s 8(1)(a)*

This useful provision of law allows a disposition (or other defectively expressed deed) to be rectified by the court, if it does not reflect the common intention of the parties to the deed. This applies both to deeds in the Sasine Register and interests in the Land Register.

(d) Rectification of the register

Inaccuracies and errors in the Land Register can be rectified by the Keeper in accordance with the provisions of s 9 of the Land Registration (Scotland) Act 1979. This can be done either by the Keeper herself, or at the request of an interested party, and must be done if the court or the Lands Tribunal so orders, but the power is severely curtailed if rectification would prejudice a proprietor in possession. See also para 2.06.

(e) Positive and negative prescription

The running of prescription can cure a number of defects, including absence of title itself (see para 8.10). The right to enforce a real burden in the event of a breach now prescribes after 5 years, regardless of any knowledge on the part of the benefited proprietor, although only to the extent of the breach and provided there has been no 'relevant claim' or 'relevant acknowledgement' (as these expressions are defined in s 9 and 10 of the Prescription and Limitation (Scotland) Act 1973) made which would interrupt prescription.

(f) The Keeper's 'discretion'

In terms of the Land Registration (Scotland) Act 1979, the Keeper has a discretion as to what documents and other evidence she requires to register a title in the Land Register (s 4(1) of LR(S)A 1979). It may also be said to be in the discretion of the Keeper whether to exclude indemnity, or to refuse to register an application at all, although there are circumstances in both these cases where there is a clear path set out for the Keeper to follow. However there may be said to be discretion in a more informal sense, in relation to decisions taken on a wide variety of aspects of an application for registration, and this manifests itself in the generally pragmatic approach that the Keeper takes to registration. There is however no hard and fast rule and it is not the role of the Keeper to paper over cracks in a dubious title. Nor is it the role of the Keeper to correct carelessness in conveyancing.

Pre-registration enquiries will, for a fee, consider any requests for clarification of the approach that the Keeper will take to an issue you may have in the title. It is prudent, if the view of the Keeper is required in your transaction to raise a pre-registration requisition at the earliest opportunity, and this can be done by either seller or purchaser. For a general indication of how the Keeper will approach a number of issues, access to information on the Keeper's registration policy practice and procedure is available at http://www.ros.gov.uk/foi/regpolicypracticeprocedure.htm.

(g) Indemnity insurance

An indemnity policy can be taken out to cover a defect in title, which recompenses the purchaser if a claim arises from a third party. Title indemnity policies are available for all manner of risks including: absence of matrimonial affidavit, giving rise to a claim by a non-entitled spouse; *a non domino* disposition, where there is a claim by the true owner within the prescriptive period; failure to establish a link in title; lack of access rights; burdens imposed on the property and a possible claim by the benefited proprietor when they have been contravened without having been discharged; discrepancies in the description of land and incorrect detailing of plans. A purchaser is not, however, obliged to accept an indemnity, as it does not render a title marketable. It is only an indemnity until prescription corrects the defect. Indemnity policies are usually taken out for a period that coincides with the relevant prescriptive period applicable. If considering this option, remember that arranging insurance is a regulated activity and you must comply with Financial Services Authority (FSA) requirements. As a general rule, most practitioners will not be individually authorised and you should check what authorisation status, if any, your firm has, and what internal compliance procedures you have to observe.

(h) The *actio quanti minoris*

This remedy, which applies automatically in terms of the Contract (Scotland) Act 1997, unless specifically excluded by contract, involves a reduction of the price where there is something wrong in the title of the property.

(i) *De minimis non curat lex*

('The law does not care about little things'.) If the defect is minor or trivial, then it may be possible to ignore it.

(j) Variation or discharge of burdens and title conditions

It is not necessary to tolerate unacceptable burdens in the title. There are a number of ways that these can be varied or discharged, and one of these options may prove appropriate in the circumstances. Note that in the case of a purchase it will be usual for the purchaser to require the seller to obtain the variation or discharge, particularly if this involves an application to the Lands Tribunal, when the burdened owner must make the application.

(i) Applications for variation or discharge under s 90 of TC(S)A 2003. This section contains the main powers of the Lands Tribunal and is the one under which most applications to the Tribunal for variation of discharge of title conditions tend to be made. An owner of burdened property or any

other person against whom a title condition is enforceable can apply to the Tribunal for a discharge or variation of the condition. Notice must be served on the parties entitled to enforce the condition who will have 21 days to make representations to the Lands Tribunal in respect of the application.

When applications for variation or discharge of a real burden are made under s 90 or 91 of TC(S)A 2003, affected parties are entitled to make representation to the Tribunal during the notice period. This includes, not just the owner of the benefited property, but any person who has title to enforce the title condition, and any person against whom the title condition is enforceable. This may include tenants, non entitled spouses, liferenters and heritable creditors in possession, as well as, in appropriate circumstances, the owners association and the owner of any unit in a development where a Development Management Scheme applies.

The Lands Tribunal also has the power to determine the validity, applicability or enforceability of any real burden or rule under a Development Management Scheme, or how a burden or rule may be interpreted. Generally Lands Tribunal orders come into effect on registration, but this does not apply to orders stating that a burden is invalid or unenforceable or as to interpretation. This is because contractual enforceability (as opposed to enforceability as a real burden that runs with the land) is unaffected by any order of the Lands Tribunal (s 104(4). In practice however, it seems that any application for determination is usually accompanied by an application for discharge.

(ii) Applications for variation or discharge of community burdens: There are three procedures for varying or discharging community burdens. The first under s 91 of TC(S)A 2003 provides that owners of 25% of the units in a community may apply to the Lands Tribunal for a variation or discharge of a community burden. Again, 21 days are to be given for representations to be made to the Lands Tribunal in respect of the application.

Section 33 of TC(S)A 2003 provides for variation or discharge by a majority of owners (or such other percentage as may be expressly stated in the constitutive deed). Intimation requires to be made to other owners in the community who have a period of eight weeks to apply to the Lands Tribunal to have the burden preserved unvaried in respect of the minority dissenting owners.

Section 35 of TC(S)A 2003 provides for variation and discharge by owners of affected units or by the owners of all adjacent units (within four metres of the affected unit). Intimation has to be sent to other owners in the community either by notice, or by lampposting or by local advertisement, with an eight week period allowed for other owners to make application for preservation, unvaried, of the burden

(iii) Factors to which the Lands Tribunal are to have regard in determining applications: Whereas, prior to 28 November 2004, the criteria which the Land Tribunal could consider under CFR(S)A 1970 were somewhat limited, now, the Tribunal's powers have been expanded significantly by TC(S)A 2003. Section 100 sets out a list of factors for the Tribunal to take into account to a greater or lesser extent, and in whatever combination, as they see fit. The factors are:

(a)   any change in circumstances since the title condition was created (including, without prejudice to that generality, any change in the character of the benefited property, of the burdened property or of the neighbourhood of the properties);

(b)   the extent to which the condition (i) confers benefit on the benefited property; or (ii) where there is no benefited property, confers benefit on the public;

(c)   the extent to which the condition impedes enjoyment of the burdened property;

(d)   if the condition is an obligation to do something, how (i) practicable; or (ii) costly, it is to comply with the condition;

(e)   the length of time which has elapsed since the condition was created;

(f)   the purpose of the title condition;

(g)   whether in relation to the burdened property there is the consent, or deemed consent, of a planning authority, or the consent of some other regulatory authority, for a use which the condition prevents;

(h)   whether the owner of the burdened property is willing to pay compensation;

(i)   if the application is under s 90(1)(b)(ii) of TC(S)A 2003, the purpose for which the land is being acquired by the person proposing to register the conveyance; and

(j)   any other factor which the Lands Tribunal considers to be material.

Very usefully, in an early Lands Tribunal case of *Ord v Mashford* [2006] SLT (Lands Tr) 15 and LTS/LO/2004/16 the Lands Tribunal made a point of setting out the approach that they expected to take to each of the factors contained in s 100. In general terms, it seems that the main factors that the Tribunal look at are the balance between factor (b) namely the extent to which the condition confers a benefit on the benefited property (or the public) and factor (c), the extent to which the condition impedes the enjoyment of the burdened property. In addition, factor (a): any change in circumstances since the title condition was created, is also major consideration. Factors (a), (b) and (c) are very similar to the original grounds to be considered by the Lands Tribunal under s 1(3) of CFR(S)A 1970, which is repealed. The Lands Tribunal has an overriding duty to act reasonably in considering any application. In respect of applications for variation of community burdens under s 33 or 35, where a representation is made for preservation of the burden unvaried, the Lands Tribunal has to consider whether the variation or discharge in question is in the best interests of the owners of all the units in the community, or is unfairly prejudicial to one or more of those owners.

(iv) Termination of burdens over 100 years old (the 'sunset rule'): Old burdens of over 100 years old (counting from the date of registration of the constitutive deed) may be extinguished by application to the Lands Tribunal for termination. This is designed to help to remove outdated amenity burdens, and does not apply to facility or service burdens, nor rights to work minerals, nor conservation or maritime burdens. The termination procedure also involves an intimation and notification procedure which is set out in ss 20 to 24 of TC(S)A 2003.

(v) Discharge by agreement: Traditional routes to extinction of real burdens continue to apply, so that parties may agree between themselves to extinguish burdens, whether neighbour burdens or community burdens, although in the latter case, unless the community is small, reaching agreement of all parties can be problematic. A Discharge of real burdens is often described as a 'Minute of Waiver'.

(k) Acquiescence

Under s 16 of TC(S)A 2003, where a real burden has been breached in a way that involves the incurring of material expenditure, and any benefit from the expenditure would be lost if the burden were to be enforced, acquiescence will apply, if the person entitled to enforce the breach consents to the breach, or is aware or (because of its nature) ought to be aware of the breach. They will be personally barred from objecting. If the party entitled to enforce the breach has not objected to the breach by the end of a reasonable period, not exceeding 12 weeks, from the date on which the activity constituting the breach is substantially completed, then the burden is extinguished to the extent of the breach. An important point to note concerning this provision, however, is that everyone who has an interest to enforce must not object to the breach for acquiescence to apply. If, for example, a tenant or a non-entitled spouse of a benefited owner objected, even if the owner did not, this would prevent the operation of this statutory acquiescence.

REPORTING ON TITLE

(a) **Reporting on residential property**

8.36 If you are acting for a residential client purchasing a house, the chances are they do not expect to get, and probably would not welcome, a detailed Title Report in the form in which you would report to a commercial client. However it is just as important that you ensure your client is made aware of the things about their property that they should, or need to, know and that you have ascertained from your title examination and inspection of searches and reports. The terms of the title to their house are just as important to a residential purchaser as the terms of a commercial purchase are to a commercial client. More so in some respects, particularly in relation to restrictions on use, access arrangements, boundary and other maintenance obligations. Depending on deadlines or timescales in the Missives, you may be sending them information, or having conversations or email exchanges with them from an early point in the transaction, to ensure that the extent of the property is correct for example. Letting your client see a plan of the property is essential, and it may also be prudent to let the surveyor see the plan as well.

While purchasers of residential property do not need a formal title report for their record purposes, it is a good idea to send them copies of key items such as a Deed of Conditions for houses in an estate, provided of course that you provide them with a bit of an explanation. A single letter or email summarising the important parts of their title that they will need to know for future reference, along with a plan, is a helpful reminder, both for your client and you.

(b) Reporting on commercial property

The Report on Title is a fairly essential element of the purchase of commercial property, although again it is likely that, if there are issues arising during your examination of the title, you will have communicated with your client about them as you go along. Producing an interim draft Report at a key point in the transaction can be a useful way of drawing together the current state of play and summarising all of the issues that have been advised and discussed in phone calls and correspondence. If there are matters in the title or other aspects of your due diligence where remedial action or corrective steps are required, this draft report will flag these. It can also identify reports or documents that you have still to examine, such as final searches or updated reports, and that might alter the terms of your final report.

(c) Content and style of reporting

In any report on title, the essential thing to remember is that it should not look anything like your notes on title. The object of reporting on title is to give your client the key facts about the property, in a clear and readable format. They do not need to see details of the deeds in which some of the information is contained. For example, they need the report to tell them that there is a use restriction preventing the property being used for industrial purposes, not that the use restriction is contained in a deed that was 'recorded in the Division of the General Register of Sasines for the County of Perth and registered in the Books of Council and Session on.....'

Consider whether you need to report to your client on *de minimis* issues or spent burdens. A lot of old title conditions were about regulating the use of properties in Victorian times and earlier, when there was little or no planning control. The fact that there is a prohibition against using the common yard as a dunghill, or that there is a prohibition against using the property as a candlemakers or a tannery, is probably irrelevant in modern times.

Use plans to identify both the extent of the property, and issues that affect parts of the property or burdens that affect only specific areas of it. If you are reporting on a site assembly, try to produce a composite plan showing how the title is made up and what conditions affect it. Attaching copies of old and mutually inconsistent plans that make up the overall site are less helpful (although might be necessary for some elements of your report) as it can be difficult for the client to piece together the different component parts from this motley collection, and this is one area where misunderstandings or lack of clarity can arise.

Finally, once you have put together your Report it is a good idea to insert an 'Executive Summary' at the start, highlighting the critical points that your client either needs to make a decision about, or at least that you need him to be consciously aware of. This is a particularly useful and helpful aspect of reporting for a client if the Report itself is lengthy and complicated, or if you are reporting on a number of properties.

EXAMINING TITLE ON BEHALF OF COMMERCIAL LENDERS

8.37 In commercial transactions involving funding, the lenders will instruct their own solicitors to act on their behalf and this will involve examination of the title, unless arrangements have been made for the purchaser's solicitors to produce a Certificate of Title to the lender (see para 8.38). There are no real differences between examining title on behalf of a purchaser, and your examination of a title when acting for a lender in the taking of a standard security. A good rule of thumb is to bear in mind that if the borrower should default in the future and your client the lender finds itself in the position of having to sell the property, it will want to be able to sell the security subjects without any difficulties arising out of the title. This means you must be scrupulously thorough (as you would always be) in your examination of title and in raising observations on title and ensuring that any title problems are rectified. While purchasers may, or may be expected to 'take a view' on certain title matters and accept them as they stand, lenders are less inclined to do this, and may simply be unprepared to compromise. However it is also the role of the lender's solicitors to advise his client, and where possible a pragmatic approach should be taken. Remember however that when acting for a lender, you have a contractual obligation to them to adhere to their general 'standing instructions to solicitors' in the majority of cases. If a client lender decides to depart from the position as indicated by those instructions – for example if it agrees to lend, despite there being some flaw with the title to the property, you must record the lender's instructions to that effect on your file, and to confirm these instructions in writing to them, or request written confirmation from them for record purposes. For the most part though, a lender is unlikely to accept something that might give it a problem with marketability in the future, as a future purchaser might not take a similar view, making the property difficult to sell, or resulting in a reduction in the price.

CERTIFYING TITLE

(a) Residential property

8.38 It is usual for the solicitor for a purchaser of residential property to also act for the lender to the purchaser, and to draw up the security documentation as well as the conveyance. The lender will expect that the purchaser's solicitor will certify to them that there is a good and marketable title to the property that is being given in security for the mortgage, and this will normally be done on the lender's form of certificate that comes with the loan instructions. You should ensure that you comply with any standards terms and conditions that the lender expects of the solicitor in this case. These may be contained in documents that accompany loan instructions, and in particular you must note and comply with any specific conditions that are applied to the particular borrower or the particular property, such as ensuring that building warrants and certification of completion are available for alterations to the property. Conditions with which you are expected to comply will also be included in the CML handbook which contains not just general conditions but also specific requirements of particular lender which may diverge from the standard position.

(b) Commercial property

In anything other than *de minimis* situations, the commercial property lawyer will not act for the borrower and the lender in the same transaction.

Lenders will often instruct their own solicitors to examine the title that you have just examined for the purchaser. However it is quite common for the purchaser's solicitor to be asked to produce a Certificate of that title for the benefit of the lender, base on the examination that they have already carried out for the purchaser.

Although some lenders (banks) have their own preferred style of certificate that they require solicitors to use, the industry standard style is the City of London Law Society Land Law Committee (CLLS) long form certificate of title. The Scottish equivalent produced in liaison with the CLLS is the PSG Certificate of Title, which adopts the same approach and format and is therefore particularly useful in cross border transactions, where English solicitors will work from the CLLS Certificate and will expect the Scottish solicitors to work from a Scottish version of that document. It can of course be used on a stand alone basis for Scottish transactions. Although principally for use in lending situations, it can be adapted for other purposes. The assumption is that the certificate will be granted by the solicitors acting for the purchaser/borrower, and it would require to be adapted if it were to be granted by the seller's solicitors in any given transaction.

The PSG Certificate is available on the website of the PSG at www. psglegal.co.uk along with Guidance Notes and a Client questionnaire for use in conjunction with the Certificate. The current version at the time of writing is the 6th edition. However, work is in hand by CLLS to produce a 7th edition and the PSG will produce a Scottish 7th edition to reflect the changes.

(i) Basic Structure of the Certificate

The certificate takes the form of a front end certificate, with a Schedule of 5 Parts attached, each Part serving a specific purpose: some provide further statements forming part of the certification or details or descriptions of the Property, and some detail documents and searches or disclosures against the statements in the earlier part of the certificate. There are therefore essentially two distinct elements to the certificate – the *Certification*, contained in the front end and in parts 1-4 of the Schedule, and the *Disclosures*, contained in Part 5 of the Schedule.

The Certification sections provide a template setting out the ideal position that the recipient wants to have certified: that the title is good and marketable; that there are no onerous conditions; that the property enjoys all rights required etc. The Disclosure section is then used to provide further information on details of title, leases etc and most importantly, to make any qualifications necessary in relation to matters where there is any departure from the ideal position stated in the Certification, in effect, proceeding by way of exception reporting. There will usually be a number of disclosures and it is usually the role of the lender's solicitor to decipher these and advise the lender of the acceptability or otherwise of the resultant title position.

The Certification sections should therefore be preserved unamended (subject to necessary drafting to tailor defined terms etc to the particular circumstances) unless there are specific transactional requirements (on which both parties agree) to make amendments to the text. The Certificate states that no changes have been made to the certificate and would need to be disclosed against if amendments were agreed. Any qualifications or disclosures should be incorporated in the Disclosure sections. For example, if there is a title issue, the Certification sections of the certificate should still state that the title is valid and marketable, but the appropriate Disclosure section should contain details of the defect or flaw or other issue affecting the title, in effect qualifying the statement made in the Certification. It is essential that this principle is followed if the certificate is to be used properly.

One of the principal changes that the 7th Edition will make is to this format. It is intended that, instead of having a separate disclosure section, any disclosures against statements in the Certificate will be inserted immediately beneath the statement, in effect, integrating disclosures throughout the document.

(ii) Content of the Certificate

As a general rule, the certificate should summarise the effect of the title and other documents, instead of simply attaching copies of the relevant writs. This is because the certificate is intended to replace an investigation of title by the recipient's solicitors. If they have to read, not only the certificate, but also a bundle of documents attached to it, the point of the certificate is to some extent lost. Having said that, there are occasionally circumstances when a document, or a part of a document, is so important and so complex that it cannot be summarised accurately. While such circumstances may be rare, where they do exist, it would be appropriate for the document, or an extract from it, to be annexed to the certificate.

In practice each statement of certification in the front end Certification part of the Certificate needs to be checked to decide whether the statement can be given without qualification. If it cannot, then the disclosure in the Disclosure section should identify which statement or paragraph it is intended to qualify, rather than making a general statement. This way it is quite clear what the granter of the Certificate is certifying, and it is also clear to the recipient of the certificate the extent of the certification that can be relied on. This process should become clearer once the new format of the 7th Edition is introduced.

(iii) Addressees of the Certificate

It is an important consideration to whom the certificate is to be addressed, as the solicitor giving the certificate will have a duty to that addressee, as though it was his own client. Multiple addressees should be resisted, as should the ability for the addressee to assign the benefit of the Certificate to other parties. Usually the granter of the Certificate will have in mind the nature of the addressee when he is drafting the Certificate. He does not want to suddenly find that he owes a duty to an assignee who may have a completely different set of requirements.

(iv) Cap on liability for those giving the Certificate

The solicitors giving the Certificate may seek a limitation or 'cap' on liability where the same Certificate is addressed to more than one person, in order to prevent a double claim against the solicitors and to ensure that the solicitors' liability to all ultimate addressees does not exceed the liability to the original addressee of the Certificate. Any such limitation or cap must be a matter to be agreed by the solicitors and the addressees on a case by case basis.

FURTHER READING

Other helpful reading on this topic includes:

Ransom strips: 'Bower of Bliss?' by Prof Roddy Paisley Edinburgh Law Review, Vol 6, pp 101–108

Minerals: Minerals and the Law of Scotland Robert Rennie

Real Burdens

The excellent and comprehensive 'The Abolition of Feudal Tenure in Scotland' (Kenneth Reid, LexisNexis Butterworths 2003);

The detailed commentary in 'Land Tenure in Scotland' (Robert Rennie, W. Green 2004)

Professor McDonald's Conveyancing Manual 7th edition Chapter 17 (David A Brand, Andrew JM Steven and Scott Wortley LexisNexis UK 2004), and

A two part essay, published in JLSS by Andrew Steven and Scott Wortley of Edinburgh University entitled 'Is that Burden Dead Yet?'

(Part 1: http://www.journalonline.co.uk/Magazine/51-6/1003142.aspx and

Part 2: http://www.journalonline.co.uk/Magazine/51-7/1003234.aspx)

Bankruptcy – McBryde

Tenements

Management and Maintenance of Common Property (Scottish Government) www.scotland.gov.uk/Resource/Doc/76169/0019425.pdf

Chapter 9

Conveying the Property: The Disposition and Other Deeds

INTRODUCTION

9.1 Having completed examination of title (or having examined enough of the title to know what is to be conveyed to the purchaser) it is time for the purchasers' solicitors to draft the conveyance. This is done by way of Disposition these days, since with the demise of the feudal system, the complications of feu contracts, feu dispositions, charters of novodamus and dispositions *ad perpetuam remanentiam* are a thing of the past.

Once drafted, the disposition is sent to the seller's solicitor for revisal or approval. The seller's solicitor revises or approves the disposition and returns it to the purchaser's solicitor, who in turn has this document engrossed and then sends the typed principal deed known as the 'engrossment', back to the seller's solicitor for signature by their clients. The draft disposition is also returned for comparison purposes. It is just as likely these days that this process will be done electronically, with the final version being sent to be printed out by the seller's solicitor, and the previous draft is compared using revision indicator tools.

A disposition needs to contain the following clauses:

(a) narrative clause: granter, grantee, any consents, and the consideration;

(b) dispositive clause: words of transference, destination of grantee, description (which can include postal address) of subjects, reference to burdens or title number;

(c) ancillary clauses: date of entry, and warrandice;

(d) testing clause (see para 11.03(c)).

Drafting a disposition can be a very straightforward matter if your client is buying a property that is registered in the Land Register and no new rights or burdens are being created.

If the title to the property is still in the Sasine Register then a few more clauses are required, but the structure of a disposition follows a tried and tested format.

Things start to get a little more complicated when it is also necessary to impose new burdens and/or servitudes to implement the transaction, but help is at hand with a series of style dispositions that cater for these situations, available from the PSG website at www.psglegal.co.uk (and see paras 9.10 (d), (e) and (f)).

There are specific considerations when the nature of the property means that the owner is selling it off in several parcels. This is what happens when a developer or builder buys land to build a number of houses or retail units or office buildings, and plans to sell each unit to individual purchasers. Very often a standard form of disposition will be prepared by the seller's solicitor for use by the purchaser's solicitor, departing from the normal procedure, in which the disposition is drafted by the purchaser's solicitor. The imposition of new burdens and servitudes is handled differently, by using a deed that will be common to all of the units – a Deed of Conditions. Since the introduction of the Title Conditions (Scotland) Act 2003, a number of new drafting options are also open to the conveyancer.

There are also a variety of circumstances when an additional clause or two may need to be incorporated into your disposition: trust clauses; special destinations; Lands Tribunal application time limits; or supersession clauses for example. These are all considered in detail in this Chapter.

DISPOSITION OF REGISTERED PROPERTY WITH NO NEW CONDITIONS

9.02 The title is already registered in the Land Register, your client is purchasing everything in the title, and no new rights or obligations need to be imposed. Provided you refer to the correct title number, the property along with all its rights, pertinents and burdens will be effectively referred to and, upon registration, conveyed in a very simple form of disposition. Such a disposition might look something like this:

> I, JAMES BROWN, residing at as Forty Three Piemonte Place, Kelvinforth, Perthshire IN CONSIDERATION of the price of THREE

HUNDRED AND FIFTY THOUSAND POUNDS (£350,000) Sterling paid to me by MICHAEL MONK, residing at 27 Lombardy Street, Kelvinforth, Perthshire HAVE SOLD and DO HEREBY DISPONE to and in favour of the said Michael Monk and his executors and assignees whomsoever heritably and irredeemably ALL and WHOLE the subjects known as Forty Three Piemonte Place, Kelvinforth registered in the Land Register of Scotland under Title Number PTH12345; WITH ENTRY as at 30 November 2011; and I grant warrandice: IN WITNESS WHEREOF

DISPOSITION OF PROPERTY ON FIRST REGISTRATION IN THE LAND REGISTER

9.03 A sale of any property or land for valuable consideration will induce a first registration in the Land Register. The form that the disposition takes is exactly the same as for previous dispositions in the Sasine Register, so you need to ensure that the description of the property adequately describes the property, for example by incorporating a description by reference to a previous descriptive writ; that all rights and pertinents are clearly identified and that the writs that are referred to for burdens affecting the property are clearly listed. Usually the approach is to take the terms of the disposition in favour of the seller and replicate its terms, substituting the seller's name and address for that of the previous disponer and inserting the purchaser's details as the disponee. The disposition could look something like this:

I, JAMES BROWN, residing at as Forty Three Piemonte Place, Kelvinforth, Perthshire IN CONSIDERATION of the price of THREE HUNDRED AND FIFTY THOUSAND POUNDS (£350,000) Sterling paid to me by MICHAEL MONK, residing at 27 Lombardy Street, Kelvinforth, Perthshire HAVE SOLD and DO HEREBY DISPONE to and in favour of the said Michael Monk and his executors and assignees whomsoever heritably and irredeemably ALL and WHOLE the subjects known as Forty Three Piemonte Place, Kelvinforth in the County of Perth more particularly described in, disponed by and shown outlined in red and coloured pink on the plan annexed to Disposition by Lightyear Estates Limited in my favour recorded in the Division of the General Register of Sasines for the County of Perth on Eleventh May Nineteen

Hundred and Ninety Six; Together with all rights of common property, the parts, privileges and pertinents thereof, including all servitude and other rights, all fittings and fixtures therein and thereon, and my whole right, title and interest present and future in the said subjects; BUT THE SUBJECTS HEREBY DISPONED are so disponed always with and under, in so far as still valid, subsisting and applicable thereto the burdens, servitudes and other conditions contained in: (One) Feu Disposition by Walter John McFarlane in favour of Caroline Rowan recorded in the said Division of the General Register of Sasines on Twenty Fifth September Nineteen Hundred and seventy eight; and (Two) Feu Disposition by Rowan Homes Limited (in liquidation) in favour of Lightyear Estates Limited recorded in the said Division of the General Register of Sasines on Eleventh May, Nineteen hundred and ninety four; WITH ENTRY and actual occupation [or vacant possession] as at 30 November 2011; And I grant warrandice: IN WITNESS WHEREOF

DISPOSITION WITH CONSENT OF SPOUSE AND TO JOINT DISPONEES

9.04 The examples in paras 9.02 and 9.03 give the two basic forms of disposition for use when conveying a property, but there are many additional clauses that may be incorporated or sub-forms used depending on the circumstances. In the two examples already given, which relate to the transfer of a residential property, the marital position of the disponer James Brown, should have been checked. He may be single and have given a declaration to that effect (see para 4.07(d)) or if married or in a civil partnership, his spouse or civil partner may have already signed a form of consent or a renunciation. It is usually more convenient however to incorporate the consent of a spouse or civil partner in the disposition.

Where a husband and wife or both civil partners are purchasing a property jointly, both parties should be included in the disposition as disponees. There also needs to be a discussion with them as to how they want the title to be taken. For spouses and civil partners the implications of the options open to them need to be discussed carefully, particularly within the wider context of their testamentary intentions, so that the appropriate destination is used in the deed. For spouses who plan to leave their whole estate to the other, then the use of a survivorship destination

386

in the disposition can be attractive, because it provides that automatically on the death of the first spouse, the whole title in the property will be vest in the survivor. No further action would be necessary to transfer the whole title to that surviving spouse. This can be extremely convenient.

However, it is essential that both parties are quite clear about this and agree, since it will override any provisions in the will of either party even if made subsequently. A survivorship destination has to be effectively discharged, or evacuated, by the parties who have put it in place, by another deed. Even that is not without its difficulties (see *Board of Management of Aberdeen College v Youngson* [2005] CSOH 31 and commentary on that case in Gretton and Reid Conveyancing 2005 pages 77 to 78). Gretton and Reid's suggestion is to incorporate a renunciation within a disposition in which the destination is evacuated – a belt and braces approach that must surely work. A style clause is provided at page 78 of that text, although you might want to replace 'hitherto' with 'until now'.

Such destinations also used to cause considerable problems, if the spouses split up. To address this particular problem, s 19 and Sch 1 para 11 of the FL(S)A 2006 provide that unless the provision of the survivorship destination expressly provides otherwise, then on divorce or annulment of the marriage, or dissolution or annulment of the civil partnership, the survivorship destination will no longer apply, so that on the death of either party their share will instead form part of their estate. There may be many reasons why the couple prefer to deal with the property in a different way, and own half (or some other proportion) shares *pro indiviso* in the property. It is important never to assume that your client will take title in a particular way, and you must always take instructions on this point. In the following example, Mrs Brown joins in the disposition as consenter for the purposes of the MF(FP)(S)A 1981, and two alternative options are shown for the way in which Mr and Mrs Monk will hold title:

I, JAMES BROWN, residing at 43 Piemonte Place, Kelvinforth, Perthshire IN CONSIDERATION of the price of THREE HUNDRED AND FIFTY THOUSAND POUNDS (£350,000) Sterling paid to me by MICHAEL MONK and MRS JESSICA LAPIN or MONK, spouses, both residing at 27 Lombardy Street, Kelvinforth, Perthshire HAVE SOLD and DO HEREBY with the consent and concurrence of MRS ELEANOR JARVIE BROWN, residing with me at 43 Piemonte Place, aforesaid, the spouse of me the said James Brown for the purposes of the Matrimonial Homes

(Family Protection) (Scotland) Act 1981 (as amended) DISPONE to and in favour of the said Michael Monk and Mrs Jessica Lapin or Monk equally between them [*option 1 survivorship*: and to the survivor of them and to their respective assignees and disponees and to the executors of the survivor] [*option 2 equal shares*: and to their respective executors and assignees] whomsoever heritably and irredeemably ALL and WHOLE the subjects known as Forty Three Piemonte Place, Kelvinforth in the County of Perth more particularly described in, disponed by and shown outlined in red and coloured pink on the plan annexed to Disposition by Lightyear Estates Limited in my favour recorded in the Division of the General Register of Sasines for the County of Perth on Eleventh May Nineteen Hundred and Ninety Six; Together with all servitude and other rights of servitude to the subjects, all rights of common property, the parts, privileges and pertinents thereof, all fittings and fixtures therein and thereon, and my whole right, title and interest present and future in the said subjects; BUT THE SUBJECTS HEREBY DISPONED are so disponed always with and under, in so far as still valid, subsisting and applicable thereto the burdens, servitudes and conditions contained in: (One) Feu Disposition by Walter John McFarlane in favour of Caroline Rowan recorded in the said Division of the General Register of Sasines on Twenty Fifth September Nineteen Hundred and seventy eight; and (Two) Feu Disposition by Rowan Homes Limited (in liquidation) in favour of Lightyear Estates Limited recorded in the said Division of the General Register of Sasines on Eleventh May, Nineteen hundred and ninety four; WITH ENTRY and actual vacant possession as at 30 November 2011; And I grant warrandice: IN WITNESS WHEREOF

DESIGNING THE PARTIES TO THE DISPOSITION

9.05 The parties to the disposition: the granter (disponer) and the recipient of the title (disponee) need to be sufficiently identified, and in the case of the disponee, provision should be made regarding their successors in title as well (see eg para 9.04 regarding survivorship destinations).

(a) Natural persons

It is usual to identify people by their full name, and their current address. There are proposals in the Scottish Law Commission's Report on Land

Registration (see para 2.09) for individuals to also be identified by reference to their date of birth. When a natural person is the disponee, it is usual to provide that the title is granted to the disponee 'and his/her executors and assignees whomsoever'.

Where title is taken in joint names, the destination will depend on the shares in which the title is to be held and whether or not a special destination is required (see survivorship clause in para 9.04).

Sometimes titles can be held in specific shares. These share are usually referred to as *pro indiviso* shares which mans that each *pro indiviso* share holder owns a share of the whole property, indivisible from the others. They can transfer their *pro indiviso* share independently of the others if they want, although in practice this can be difficult, if for example the *pro indiviso* shares are of the title to a house occupied by the parties. However this is a typical way of dealing with shares in common parts of developments (but see para 8.28) but is also typical in family titles, such as where the title to a farm is held by the father and his three sons who operate the farming business. The actual amount of the share is usually expressed (having fully designed the parties in the narrative clause) as eg:

> 'to and in favour of (One) the said Eric Sweet and his executors and assignees to the extent of a one-half *pro indiviso* share; (Two) the said David Alexander Sweet and his executors and assignees to the extent of a one-sixth *pro indiviso* share; (Three) the said Preston Maxwell Monk Sweet and his executors and assignees to the extent of a one sixth *pro indiviso* share and (Four) the said Christopher Gavin Sweet and his executors and assignees to the extent of the remaining one sixth *pro indiviso* share'

(b) Companies

A limited company incorporated under the Companies Acts should be designed by referring to their registered office and their unique company number, and if it has changed its name since the date on which it acquired title then the changes should be narrated eg

> We, LIGHTYEAR DEVELOPMENT COMPANY LTD, (formerly known as Lightyear Estates Ltd, our name having changed conform

to Certificate of Incorporation on Change of Name dated 12 August Two thousand and four) incorporated under the Companies Acts (Registered Number 809908) and having our registered office at 65 Registration Row, Perth

Where the change of name takes place following on re-registration of a plc the reference is to 'Certificate of Incorporation on Re-Registration of a Public Company as a Private Company'.

When a company is the disponee it is usual to convey the title to the company 'and its successors and assignees whomsoever'.

(c) Partnerships

A partnership can take title in its own name, but it is far more common that title will be held by the partners in trust for the firm. A partnership granting a disposition may be designed as:

We, CAROLINE ROWAN, residing at Piemonte House, Kelvinforth, Perthshire and ERIC SWEET, residing at The Old Railway House, Florence Park, Kelvinforth, Perthshire, Partners of and (as such partners) Trustees for the firm of Rowan Retirement Homes of Piemonte House, Kelvinforth

The partnership as disponee will be designed in the same way in the narrative clause and the destination will run as:

the said Caroline Rowan and Eric Sweet, the Partners of the firm of Rowan Retirement Homes as trustees for the said firm, and their successors in office as such trustees and the survivor of them as trustees and their or his/her assignees whomsoever

(d) Executors

An executor can either be nominated in the Will of the deceased (executor nominate) or if there is no will or none of the executors nominate survived the deceased, then a family member identified through the rules applicable on intestacy (executor dative). There may be more than one executor. The executor's entitlement to the estate of the deceased including heritable property is confirmed by the Confirmation of the deceased's estate, which is obtained by submitting an inventory of all of the property in the deceased's estate to the Commissary department of the relevant Sheriff Court for the area, which will then (subject of course to payment of any inheritance tax and confirmation dues) issue the formal Confirmation. When transferring title belonging to the deceased, the executor will narrate the terms of the Confirmation:

> I, ERIC SWEET, residing at The Old Railway House, Florence Park, Kelvinforth, Perthshire, Executor nominate of the late MRS NORMA McNAUGHT MONK or SWEET who resided sometime at Lionheart Farm, Kinlochalmond, by Kelvinforth, and latterly at Rowan Retirement Home, Calabria Crescent, Kelvinforth conform to Confirmation issued by the Commissariot of Glasgow and Strathkelvin at Glasgow in my favour on 10 March 2006 and as such Executor nominate now in right of the subjects hereby disponed IN CONSIDERATION of the price of [   ] paid to me, as Executor foresaid…

(e) Trustees

In dispositions granted by trustees, the trustees are named and the deed of trust or other document under which they are appointed is narrated:

> WE, the RIGHT HONOURABLE RICHARD BYRON CHILDS, Earl of Kinlochalmond and Dunvorlich, of Lochalmond House, Kinlochalmond by Kelvinforth Perthshire, THE RIGHT HONOURABLE ANN CHILDS, Countess of Kinlochalmond and Dunvorlich, of Lochalmond House aforesaid, and HENRY ROSE PINK of 65 Registration Row Perth the Trustees now acting under Deed of Trust by The Right Honourable Richard Glenalmond Childs, 4th Earl of Kinlochalmond and Dunvorlich dated 18 September 1982 and registered in the Books of Council and Session on 28 March 1988 (the 'Seller') heritable proprietors of the property hereinafter disponed

When trustees acquire title, the dispositive clause may run along the following lines:

> to and in favour of the said Richard Byron Childs, Ann Childs and Henry Rose Pink as trustees foresaid and their successors in office and the survivors and survivor of them as trustees and trustee foresaid

(f) Limited Partnerships

The limited partner does not get involved in the day to day business of the limited partnership. Title is held in name of the General partner:

> We, LIONHEART GENERAL PARTNER LIMITED, incorporated under the Companies Acts (Registered Number SC090909) and having our Registered Office at Lionheart Farm by Kinlochalmond Perthshire, as General Partner and Trustee of The Lionheart Limited Partnership, registered as a Limited Partnership under the Limited Partnership Act 1907 (Registration Number LP9999) and having its principal place of business at [   ]

When the limited partnership is taking title, the dispositive clause will generally say:

> to and in favour of the said Lionheart General Partner Limited as the General Partner of and as such, Trustee for Lionheart Limited Partnership and its successors and assignees whomsoever

(g) Limited Liability Partnerships

Limited Liability Partnerships refer to their incorporation under the Limited Liability Partnerships Act 2000 and provide their registered number:

> DUNVORLICH RENEWABLES LLP, incorporated in Scotland as a limited liability partnership under the Limited Liability Partnerships Act 2000, with Registered Number SO909090, and having its Registered Office at 204 St Kentigern Street Glasgow G2

(h) Insolvency practitioners

For dispositions granted by insolvency practitioners on behalf of insolvent companies the usual format is for the company to grant the disposition acting by the administrator, receiver or liquidator. Generally the disposition would not be granted by the administrator, receiver or liquidator itself as there is no vesting in the administrator, receiver or liquidator, who instead takes control of the Company. In a sequestration of an individual however the trustee becomes vest in the property of the bankrupt by virtue of the act and warrant.

In all cases of a disposition by an insolvency practitioner, they will want to exclude any personal liability on their part. The disposition should therefore contain words like:

acting solely as agent(s) of the company and without any personal liability whatsoever and regardless of how it arises (whether directly or indirectly, express or implied)

In some dispositions you may see a more detailed narrative of the facts and circumstances of the appointment of the insolvency practitioner.

(i) Administrator

We, [   ] LIMITED, (in administration) incorporated under the Companies Acts (Registered Number [   ]) and having our Registered Office at [   ] (the 'Company'), acting through its joint administrators [   ], of [   ] and [   ], of [   ], appointed [joint] administrator[s] of the Company to manage the affairs, business and property of the Company pursuant to an appointment by the directors of the Company on [   ], acting solely as agents of the Company and without any personal liability whatsoever or howsoever arising (whether directly or indirectly, express or implied)

(ii) Receiver

WE, [   ] LIMITED (IN RECEIVERSHIP), incorporated in the British Virgin Islands (Company Number 121212) and having our Registered Office sometime at [   ] Tortola, British Virgin Islands and previously registered at Companies House as an overseas company (Company Number FC212121) (the 'Company'), acting through our Joint Receivers, [   ] and [   ], Chartered Accountants both of [   ], (hereinafter referred to as the 'Joint Receivers') appointed by Instrument of Appointment by Scotland Bank plc in favour of the Joint Receivers dated [   ] pursuant to Bond and Floating Charge in favour of the Bank granted by the Company dated [   ]

(iii) Liquidator

We, [   ] LIMITED (IN LIQUIDATION), incorporated under the Companies Acts (Registered Number [   ]) and having our registered office [previously] at [   ] [and now at [   ]] (the 'Company') heritable proprietor of the subjects hereinafter disponed, acting through its Liquidator [   ] of [   ], appointed by virtue of Interlocutor granted by the Court of Session at Edinburgh on [   ], thereafter being appointed Interim Liquidator on [   ] and thereafter being appointed Permanent Liquidator on [   ], acting solely as agent of the Company and without any personal liability whatsoever or howsoever arising (whether directly or indirectly, express or implied) (the said liquidator acting as aforesaid, being hereinafter referred to as the 'Liquidator')

(iv) Trustee in sequestration

I, [   ], of [   ], the Permanent Trustee on the Sequestrated Estate of [   ] residing at [   ] duly confirmed conform to Act and Warrant by the Sheriff of the Sheriffdom of [   ] at [   ] dated [   ], IN CONSIDERATION of the price of [   ] POUNDS (£[   ]) STERLING paid to me as Trustee aforesaid by [   ], residing at [   ] of which sum I hereby acknowledge the receipt and discharge him HAVE SOLD and DO HEREBY DISPONE

As the trustee in sequestration is vest in the property by virtue of the act and warrant, a deduction of title clause is required (unless the property is already registered in the Land Register):

Which subjects were last vested in the said [   ] and from whom I acquired right as Trustee foresaid by the said Act and Warrant in my favour, dated as aforesaid;

(i) Heritable creditor in possession

The heritable creditor must comply with various statutory requirements before it can convey the property, and then it then does so by virtue of the power of sale imported into the original standard security in its favour by Standard Condition 10 (CFR(S)A 1970 Sch 3). It is customary to narrate the process in the disposition:

WE, SCOTLAND BANK plc incorporated under the Companies Acts and having our Registered Office at Alba House, Corries Road, Edinburgh WHEREAS in virtue of a power of sale contained in Standard Security [for £X] by Y residing formerly at [   ] and now at

[   ] in our favour registered in the Land Register of Scotland under Title Number [   ], we advertised the subjects hereby disponed for sale and sold the said subjects by private contract to [   ] residing at [   ] at the price of [£   ] being the best price that could reasonably be obtained and considering that the said [   ] has paid to us the said price of [£   ] therefore we HAVE SOLD and DO HEREBY DISPONE to the said…..

(j) Charities

The Charities and Trustee Investment (Scotland) Act 2005 requires that any body wishing to refer to itself as a charity, and that has a significant presence in Scotland, must be registered in the Scottish Charity Register. To be eligible to be entered in the Scottish Charity Register a body must meet the charity test set out in the CTI(S)A 2005: its purposes must consist only of one or more of the 'charitable purposes' specified in s 7(2) of the CTI(S)A 2005 and the body must provide public benefit in Scotland or elsewhere.

Under the Charities References in Documents (Scotland) Regulations 2007, any body entered in the Scottish Charity Register must state legibly on all documents listed in the regulations (which includes all conveyances which provide for the creation, transfer, variation or extinction of an interest in land), and which are issued or signed on behalf of the charity after 31 March 2008:

(i)   its name as entered in the Scottish Charity Register;

(ii)   any other name by which it is commonly known;

(iii)   its registered number and,

(iv)   where the name of the body does not include the word 'charity' or 'charitable', that it is a charity by using one of the terms referred to in the CTI(S)A 2005: ie charity; charitable body; registered charity; charity registered in Scotland; Scottish charity; or registered Scottish charity. The last two terms may only be used if the body is established under Scots law or is managed or controlled wholly or mainly in Scotland.

There does not appear to be a standardised form of words for designation of charities, but the wording will be competent provided it complies with the provisions of the CRD(S) Regulations 2007. Examples of designations are:

THE UNIVERSITY COURT OF THE UNIVERSITY OF EDINBURGH, a charitable body registered in Scotland with registered number SC005336 and established under the Universit Real Burdens

ies (Scotland) Acts and having our principal offices at Old College, South Bridge, Edinburgh, EH8 9YL

KELVINFORTH LEISURE PURSUITS LIMITED incorporated under the Companies Acts (Registered number SC876543) and a registered Scottish charity (Scottish Charity Number SC444444) and having its registered office at 999 Lally Street Glasgow G2 4XX

SCOTTISH SOCIETY FOR THE PREVENTION OF CRUELTY TO ANIMALS, a Company limited by Guarantee, Company Number SC201401, a registered Scottish Charity Number 006467 and having its registered office at Kingseat Road, Halbeath, Dunfermline, Fife, KY11 8RY

DEDUCTION OF TITLE

9.06 Where the granter of the disposition does not have a recorded title, it is necessary to deduce title through the documents that link the granter and his entitlement to dispone the property, with the person having the last recorded title (see para 8.14). The C(S)A 1924, Sch A, form 1 provides a statutory style of deduction of title clause that should be used:

'Which lands and others (or subjects) were last vested [or are part of the lands and others (or subjects) last vested] in A.B. (designation of person last infeft), whose title thereto is recorded in (specify Register of Sasines and date of recording, or if the last infeftment has already been mentioned say in the said A.B. as aforesaid), and from whom I acquired right by (here specify shortly the writ or series of writs by which right was so acquired).'

An example of a deduction of title clause in a Disposition by an Executor would accordingly look like this:

Which subjects and others were last vested in the said Mrs Norma McNaught Monk or Sweet whose title thereto is recorded in the said Division of the Register of Sasines on Twenty ninth November Nineteen hundred and ninety and from whom I, as Executor foresaid, acquired right by the said Confirmation in my favour dated as aforesaid

And for Trustees might run along these lines:

Which subjects were last vested in the said Richard Glenalmond Childs and me the said Henry Rose Pink as the then Trustees acting under the said Deed of Trust whose title thereto is recorded in the said Division of the General Register of Sasines on 2nd September 1989 and from whom we acquired right as Trustees foresaid by virtue of (One) Minute of Resignation by the said Richard Glenalmond Childs dated 11th and 27th both November and registered in the Books of Council and Session on 31st December all 1993; (Two) Deed of Assumption and Conveyance by me the said Henry Rose Pink in favour of myself and the said Richard Byron Childs and Ann Childs dated 14th, 24th and 29th all August and registered in the Books of Council and Session on 14th September all 1994.

CONSIDERATION

9.07 It is most common for the consideration for the conveyance of property to be a full monetary consideration. To ensure that there is no doubt, in case of a typographical error for example, it is usual to set out the price in both words and figures.

(a) References to VAT

The sale, grant, assignation or surrender of a major interest in land for consideration is a supply of goods for the purposes of VAT. However sales of a dwellings or a residential purpose building converted from a non-residential building or part of a building are zero-rated and therefore no VAT is payable on sale. However commercial buildings which are more than three years old are treated differently. Such buildings are exempt from VAT, which means that no VAT will be payable on sale, unless the owner of the building opts to tax the building. It is therefore necessary when purchasing commercial property to ascertain at the outset its VAT status (see 6.13(d)). Since SDLT is payable on the grossed up consideration it is necessary to narrate in the Disposition of commercial property either that VAT is payable (in which case the consideration stated will be the total of the Price plus VAT at the current rate) or that none is payable (for whatever reason):

> IN CONSIDERATION of the price of [   ] POUNDS (£[ ]) STERLING [on which sum no Value Added Tax is payable][exclusive of Value Added Tax which will be payable in addition]

(b) Non monetary consideration

The 'payment' made for property may not be in cash. There may be an exchange of property for shares in a company or the adoption of a debt. The usual way to narrate this is to say 'for certain good and onerous causes and considerations'

(c) Gifts

Property may change hands with no payment being made at all: a transfer from one family member to another for example. In such cases the deed can refer to 'certain good causes and considerations' omitting the word 'onerous', or the consideration can be stated as 'Love favour and affection' as in:

> I, ALEXANDER RUPERT SWEET residing at Lionheart Farm, Kinlochalmond, by Kelvinforth IN CONSIDERATION of the love favour and affection which I bear towards my wife MRS NORMA McNAUGHT MONK or SWEET residing with me at Lionheart Farm, aforesaid DO HEREBY DISPONE to the said Mrs Norma McNaught Monk or Sweet and her executors and assignees.....

DESCRIBING THE PROPERTY

9.08 A key element in successfully conveying property is to ensure that it is clearly identified. How this is best achieved will depend on the type of property that it is, and how its title is currently constituted.

(a) Registered title

Describing the property could not be simpler. Referring to the correct Title Number will ensure that the property and its pertinents are correctly and sufficiently identified.

(b) Description by reference

We have already considered descriptions by reference in the context of examination of title (see para 8.15). When conveying a property that has already been fully identified in a deed recorded in the Sasine Register, it can be competently described in the next transfer of the property (which includes a disposition that will induce first registration) by reference to that earlier descriptive writ, in accordance with the provisions of s 61 of the Conveyancing (Scotland) Act 1874 and s 8 of the C(S)A 1924. These sections permit a particular description of property contained in a recorded deed to be inserted in subsequent writs by reference to that recorded deed. A statutory form of words is provided in Sch D of the C(S)A 1924, although it is fine provided the reference is in this form or 'as nearly as may be'. The form of words given in Sch D is:

> All and whole the lands and others (or subjects) in the country of (or in the burgh of and county of as the case may) described in (refer to the conveyance, deed, or instrument in such terms as shall be sufficient to identify it, and specify the Register of Sasines in which it is recorded and date of recording, or where the conveyance, deed, or instrument referred to is recorded on the same date as the conveyance, deed, or instrument containing the reference substitute for the date of recording the words of even date with the recording of these presents)

Terms sufficient to identify the writ are: the names of the granter and grantee, or of the parties to the deed (no designations necessary) and if there are several granters or grantees or several parties acting in the same category, then it is enough to give the first named person followed by 'and others', eg

> being the subjects more particularly described in, disponed by and delineated in red and partly coloured green and partly coloured pink on the plan annexed and subscribed as relative to Feu Disposition by

Richard Glenalmond Childs, 4th Earl of Kinlochalmond and Dunvorlich in favour of Alexander Rupert Sweet and others dated Fourth April and recorded in the Division of the General Register of Sasines for the County of Perth on Fourth July both Nineteen hundred and sixty four;

If any of the parties act in a fiduciary capacity (eg trustees), it is unnecessary to list all the names and instead, reference can be made to that role eg 'in favour of the Trustees of A.B.' This format for description by reference can be used when describing a larger area of which the property being conveyed forms a part - in other words you have particular description of the part, and then identify it further by reference to a recorded disposition in which the larger area was described (see para 9.08(d) below). Or if the property being conveyed forms part of only part of the lands described in the earlier deed, reference need only be made to that part eg 'being the subjects more particularly described (In the First Place) in, and disponed by Disposition by....' Note that while this obviously helps identification purposes, from a technical point of view it does not matter if this distinction is made or not (ie it is just as valid to refer to the whole subjects described in the deed referred to for particular description, missing out '(In the First Place)').

(c) Bounding Description

The first time a plot of land is conveyed as a separate entity, it needs to be clearly identified. While a taxative plan, such as one based on the Ordnance Survey map, will often be sufficient to identify the location and extent of an area, a verbal description is often also required, particularly to establish the actual physical features of the boundary, eg, the inner face of a wall, which a red line on a plan will not necessarily communicate.

The format of a full bounding description therefore will involve all, or a sufficient combination of (i) a plan, (ii) an area measurement (iii) boundaries identified by reference to (1) orientation (eg the points of the compass) (2) physical attributes (3) length and (4) direction. Areas and lengths should be expressed in metric measurements. It is recognised that there are limitations in scaling on maps. On a plan that uses a scale of 1:1250, one millimetre on the plan represents 1.25 metres on the ground, so the accuracy of the boundaries plotted on such plans is limited. Some leeway is afforded to take account of the limitations of scaling in maps, and the possibility of minor discrepancies in measurements or orientation, by use of the expressions 'on or towards' and 'or thereby'.

An example bounding description would be:

> ALL and WHOLE that area of land extending to 1.12 hectares or thereby situated in Kinlochalmond in the County of Perth and bounded as follows: on or towards the northeast by the outer edge of the grass verge of the road leading from Kelvinforth to Kinlochalmond along which it extends in a southeasterly direction 51 metres or thereby; on or towards the southeast, again on or towards the northeast and again on or towards the southeast by the centre line of a stone wall separating the property hereby disponed from other property belonging to us known as Dunvorlich Cottage along which it extends 64.2 metres or thereby, 18 metres or thereby and 20.5 metres or thereby respectively; on or towards the southwest and on or towards the northwest by parts of the lands and estate of Kinlochalmond and Dunvorlich, following the outer face of a fence or wall to be erected by our said disponee as provided for in Part 2 of the Schedule annexed to this Disposition along which it extends 69 metres or thereby, and 84.7 metres or thereby respectively, all as the said area of land is shown delineated in red and coloured pink on the plan annexed and subscribed by us as relative to this Disposition;

(d) Part and portion/Conveyance of part

When the property being conveyed in the disposition is being described for the first time, this is dealt with by reference to the deed describing the larger area of which it formed a part. This might be a whole estate, or it might just be the title of the larger house and garden, a part of which is being sold off for a new house to be built, or a development which is being sold off in individual plots or units. Either way the approach is the same. Following the description of the part conveyed a reference is made to it being part and portion of the larger title. So the bounding description above (para (c)) would continue:

> which area of land hereby disponed forms part and portion of ALL and WHOLE that area or piece of land lying in the said County extending to 151.61 acres or thereby described (In the Second Place) in, disponed by and delineated in red and coloured pink on the plan annexed and subscribed as relative to Feu Disposition by Richard Glenalmond

Childs, 4th Earl of Kinlochalmond and Dunvorlich in favour of Alexander Rupert Sweet and others dated Fourth April and recorded in the Division of the General Register of Sasines for the County of Perth on Fourth July both Nineteen hundred and sixty four

Note that the reference to an imperial area measurement (acres) is permissible, because it is (i) the measurement specified in the deed referred to, which is historical and (ii) is not part of the particular bounding description of the actual area being conveyed.

A conveyance of part of property registered in the Land Register is a much simpler affair:

I, ERIC SWEET, residing at The Old Railway House, Florence Park, Kelvinforth, Perthshire in consideration of the price of £100,000 paid to me by SAMANTHA MIRREN DARLING, residing at 19 Lionheart Farm Cottages, Kinlochalmond HAVE SOLD and DO HEREBY DISPONE to the said Samantha Mirren Darling and her executors and assignees whomsoever ALL and WHOLE that plot of ground at Lionheart Farm, Kinlochalmond in the County of Perth extending to 2.8 hectares or thereby Metric measure and shown delineated in red on the plan annexed and signed as relative to this Disposition; being part of the subjects registered In the Land Register of Scotland under Title Number PTH41192 (insert any new title conditions; date of entry; warrandice)

(e) Tenement flat

There has always been a bit of a problem in providing an accurate description of a flat in a tenement building, whether residential or commercial. While in modern multi-occupancy buildings it is possible to produce drawings showing floor layouts, it is still necessary to revert to verbal descriptions if the seller wants clearly to identify the limits of the title – such as by way of reference to the point between the floors at which one floor starts and another floor ends. This method of identification is more typical when describing floors or parts of floors in buildings that are the subject of a lease, rather than sale, although recourse can be had to these methods for describing parts of a tenement building being sold where the internal configuration of the property is complex.

Traditionally, descriptions of floors in tenements have been quite short: 'the westmost first floor flat entering by the common passage and stair at

12 Sardinia Terrace, Kelvinforth' is sufficient to identify the location of the flat in question, and the common law dealt with horizontal separation and ownership of other parts of the tenement. This form of description of a tenement flat is still acceptable.

Tenement boundaries are now defined in the Tenements (Scotland) Act 2004 s 2 to the extent that the title to the tenement does not make any provision. The definition is quite technical, stating that the boundary between any two contiguous sectors (flats that are next to each other) is the median (mid point) of the structure that separates them (eg a floor or a wall). A sector (flat) extends in any direction to such a boundary. If the flat is not next to another flat at any of its boundaries, then it extends to and includes the solum or any other part of the tenement which is an outer surface of the tenement building; or it extends to the boundary that separates the flat from an adjoining, but separate building.

If part of the boundary between two flats is some feature, for example a door or a window which wholly or mainly serves only one of the flats, then the entire thickness of that feature is part of that flat.

So far as ownership of 'common' parts of the tenement is concerned (as distinct from liability for maintenance) then, again in the absence of specific provision in the titles, the T(S)A 2004 provides that a top flat will include the roof of the tenement over that flat, and where the roof of the tenement building slopes, will also include the airspace above the slope of the relevant part of the roof up to the level of the highest point of the roof. A ground floor (or basement where there is one) flat will include the solum under that flat, and will also include the airspace above the tenement building that is directly over the relevant part of the solum (except the portion of airspace that goes with the top flat where the roof is sloped). A close (or common stair) extends to and includes the roof over, and the solum under, the close.

For most normal purposes therefore there should not be any need to describe the boundaries of a tenement property, provided the parties do not, for some reason, need or want to depart from the provisions of the T(S)A 2004, which would be rare.

(f) General name

An early form of description by reference, describing property by a 'general name' is provided by s 13 of the Titles to Land Consolidation

(Scotland) Act 1868. When several lands are brought together in one conveyance in favour of the same person, the conveyance could incorporate a clause declaring that the whole lands were to be known in future by a general name that is specified in the conveyance. Wording is provided in Sch G to the TLC(S)A 1868. Although still competent, this format is rarely (if ever) used in modern conveyancing, having been overtaken by the description by reference, and of course any transfer for value of such land will induce a first registration in the Land Register after which any description or conveyance will identify the lands by reference to a title number.

(g) Plans

The system of registration of title in the Land Register is plan based, therefore it is important to have a good quality (as to clarity and accuracy) plan annexed to the title deeds. When the sale of the property is a transaction that induces a first registration, it is particularly important to ensure that the property is sufficiently identified for the purposes of registration. The Sasine title may contain maps, plans or descriptions that adequately identify the property, and a P16 report will establish if these are adequate for registration purposes, or whether it would be advisable to commission a plan of the property for annexation to the disposition.

The Registration of Title Practice Book (which is available online from the Registers of Scotland website at http://www.ros.gov.uk/rotbook/index. html provides guidance on the Keeper's requirements in the preparation of deed plans. This guidance is reproduced below under Crown copyright arrangements:

Recommended criteria for preparation of plans attached to deeds for conveyancing

- A scale and the orientation of north must be shown. A drawn or bar scale is to be preferred, because it allows distortion from any subsequent photocopying to be identified.
- The Keeper produces title plans using 1:1250, 1:2500, and 1:10,000 base scale ordnance survey mapping for properties falling in

urban, rural, and mountain and moorland areas respectively. Deed plans drawn for properties in these areas should be adequate for the corresponding scale - but see below.

- If the scale of the most suitable map is insufficient to reflect the necessary detail, an inset plan at a larger scale may be used. Situations will invariably arise when even the 1:1250 scale map cannot provide enough detail, in which case plans at 1:500 are the preferred option.

- Scales based on the imperial system (eg 1 inch to 8 feet) are no longer acceptable.

- The plan must not be stated to be 'demonstrative only and not taxative'.

- The plan must contain sufficient surrounding established detail (eg fences, houses, road junctions etc) to enable its position to be fixed with accuracy on the ordnance map.

- Where it is necessary for any measurement to be shown on the plan, metric units must be used to two decimal places.

- Where measurements are deemed necessary, then the dimensions shown on the plan ought to agree, as far as possible, with the scaled measurements.

- A plan employing dimensions which are simply a perimeter measure are incapable of being accurately plotted or proven. Dimensioned plans must therefore include proof measurements which may consist of:
  - cross/diagonals;
  - angles at each change of boundary direction; or
  - local or national grid co-ordinates of boundary changes supported by tape checks along each boundary; or
  - any other form of independent check which is capable of proofing the survey.

- The property forming the transaction must be clearly indicated by means of suitable graphic references (eg edging, tinting, hatching).

- Exclusive and shared areas must be properly differentiated and referenced as above and consistent with the text of the deed.

- Undefined boundaries (ie where no physical boundary exists) must be accurately fixed to existing detail by metric measurements shown on the plan.

- Where buildings, pathways, etc, require to be referenced on the plan to reflect shared or common interests they must be shown in the correct position relative to other surrounding detail.

- Boundaries should be identified by description (eg centre line of wall, outer face or inner face of hedge, etc).

- Details of how, by whom, and when the survey was completed. Information as to the currency of the survey detail and whether or not it relates to the as-built positions or merely the proposed layout should also be noted.

- Extracts from proposed development plans must not be employed if the property involved physically exists.

Once a property is registered in the Land Register, no plan is required for conveyances or other dealings of the whole of the subjects in the Title Number. However, if the dealing relates to only a part of the registered interest, then as well as identifying the larger area by reference to the title number, a description or plan of the part, which is sufficient to enable the Keeper to identify the part on the existing title plan, is required. This applies to any dealing of part, not just transfers, for example if an owner is granting a standard security over only part of the property in the Title Number.

If preparing a new plan for this purpose then the guidelines set out above should be followed, and it should be clear from the new plan how the area relates to the larger subjects in the title, by showing sufficient detail of the adjoining property. However, it is acceptable in these cases to use a copy of the Title plan with the relevant part carefully delineated, (if that can be done clearly) and with the addition of boundary measurements marked on the plan, in case of any distortion in the copying process. Note that if this option is used, copyright issues need to be addressed. If your firm has an Ordnance Survey licence this will cover such copying. A plan may not be necessary if the relevant portion subject to the dealing is sufficiently separately identified, such as already being tinted a different colour from the rest of the subjects in the Title number.

Any plan used must be taxative, that is to say it can be founded on. It was common in older deeds to refer to the plan being 'demonstrative only and not taxative', but a demonstrative plan will not be accepted by the Keeper, and this form of words can no longer be used.

(h) Airspace

In some circumstances, the property being conveyed may consist of a portion of airspace that is going to be occupied in the future by some structure, but, at the time of the conveyance that structure has not yet been erected. Say a purchaser is acquiring several upper floors in a new building about to be constructed, or the building being acquired requires to be described on a separate title from a sub-terranean car park or storage facility beneath it. In such circumstances it is possible to describe the 'box of airspace' that will comprise the title, and this is typically done by reference to datum levels (Ordnance Datum). A datum level is a horizontal surface, for example sea level, which is taken as a reference point for identifying altitudes for maps, and is used in this context to determine the precise position of elevations, heights, or depths of the property or portion of airspace to be occupied by the property.

Mean sea level (MSL) is generally used. The level used by the Ordnance Survey is Ordnance Datum Newlyn which is based on the MSL at Newlyn in Cornwall between the years 1915 and 1921. With increasingly sophisticated technology, other measurement techniques may also start to be used. The datum level figures will be produced by the professional team involved in the construction project.

For example in the description of a building which will exclude a self contained storage facility area being constructed beneath the building, and which will support the building structure, references to datum levels can be incorporated like this:

> ALL and WHOLE that area of ground and the building erected on it known as Unit 5A Lochalmond, Perth comprising five storeys including the ground floor storey, which area of ground is shown delineated in red on the Plan annexed and signed as relative hereto, the subjects hereby disponed commencing at Ordnance Datum level 24.500 MSL in respect of that area shown hatched black, and coloured pink on the Plan; at Ordnance Datum level 27.500 MSL in respect of

that area shown cross hatched black and coloured green on the Plan
and at Ordnance Datum level 29.100 MSL in respect of that area shown
hatched black and coloured yellow on the Plan; but always excluding
the Storage Facility Area beneath the area of ground

This technique is not without risk, as locations and levels may change
during the construction process.

(i) Pertinents

References to pertinents, or 'parts, privileges and pertinents' were often
used as a bit of a conveyancing 'catch-all' and often without particular care
or precision. The reference is generally understood to mean rights such as
servitudes or common rights such as rights to common parts, for example
the common passage and stair of tenements. There may be circumstances
however where a general reference to parts and / or pertinents will
be sufficient to transfer rights or parts that have been omitted from the
description, but it will be a question of the particular circumstances of
each case whether such rights or parts are effectively transferred. Where
a servitude has been properly constituted in favour of a property, strictly
speaking there is no need to refer to it specifically, but this is often done
for clarity and certainty.

The relevance of a pertinents clause is less significant these days. It is
normal conveyancing practice when conveying property to refer to rights
such as servitudes specifically, and other pertinents that apply, and this is
good practice when describing the property in a first registration, or when
describing a split off from another title for the first time.

However the effect of registration is such that, once title to property
is registered in the Land Register, no reference to pertinents is required
in future transfers, since the effect of registration is to vest in the person
registered as entitled to the registered interest in land a real right in the
interest and in any right, pertinent or servitude, express or implied, forming
part of the interest (s 3(1)(a) of the Land Registration (Scotland) Act 1979).

Various common rights as pertinents were a feature of descriptions
of tenement properties, and when examining old tenement titles you will
often see lists of parts referred to. Section 3 of the Tenements (Scotland)
Act 2004 now sets out what the pertinents in a tenement property are, and
provides that these will attach to each flat as a right of common property.

These are equal rights except where the pertinent is a chimney stack, when the proportion will be according to the number of flues pertaining to a flat.

The parts are a close, and a lift which provides access to more than one of the flats. If any flat is not accessed from such close or lift then it will not be a pertinent of that flat. Land, that pertains to a tenement, other than the solum on which the tenement is built, will be a pertinent of the bottom flat closest to the land, but does not apply a path, outside stair or other way that also provides access to other flats.

Other parts that may attach as a pertinent to one or more flats may include a path, outside stair, fire escape, rhone, pipe, flue, conduit, cable, tank or chimney stack that wholly serves one flat or two or more flats. If serving more than one flat it will attach to each of the flats served, as a pertinent, a right of common property in (and in the whole of) the part.

(j) Common property

As can be seen from para (i) above, pertinents in tenement flats are often held as common property by the owners of the flats in the tenement. But other land and property can also be held in common by specific reference in the title. Common property can be held by two or more owners, who will own the property in equal shares, unless some other configuration of shares in the property is specified. These shares are referred to as *pro indiviso* (undivided) shares, and the effect is that each of the owners owns an indivisible share of the whole of the property. This means that each co-owner has a say in what happens to the whole of the property, and if one owner wants to realise the property (eg by sale), but another does not, the matter can be forced, through an action for division and sale.

For style wording for *pro indiviso* shares, see para 9.05(a). When describing common property, reference should be made to a 'right of common property' and not merely a 'right in common' which, while it will probably be taken to mean a property right, is imprecise.

Common property should be distinguished from joint property, which is generally the way in which trustees and unincorporated associations hold title to property. In joint property there are no individual shares. Instead the trustees all hold title jointly to the whole property, and the removal, resignation or death of a trustee does not affect the title of the remaining trustees, which continues without the departed trustee, and without any conveyance being required, joint ownership being an incidence of the office of trustee.

EXISTING BURDENS AND SERVITUDES

(a) First registration

9.09 As previously indicated, when conveying property in a sale or other transaction that induces a first registration, you should describe the property and the burdens that apply to it in the same way as though it was a transfer in the Sasine Register. So you must refer to all the relevant writs referred to for burdens, and of course if new burdens are also being created, these should be set out in full (see para 9.10). For a style disposition see para 9.03.

(b) Registered property

Reference to the Title Number of a registered property transfers all rights, pertinents and burdens.

(c) Servitudes in conveyance of part

If the title to the larger area is still in the Sasine Register, then you should specify the servitude and other rights that are to pass with the part being conveyed in clear terms. It should be noted, however, that unless a servitude has been created by express grant, the Keeper will not include servitude rights that may have been created by other methods eg prescription. Formerly the Keeper would accept affidavit evidence of the exercise of a servitude, but this posed problems when many instances of contrary evidence were subsequently produced in relation to the exercise of such rights. In the face of a dispute, the Keeper has no powers to adjudicate the issue. Consequently the Keeper stopped accepting affidavit evidence of the exercise of servitudes. There is only one exception to this and that is in relation to servitudes that may be granted *a non domino* in a conveyance where despite all attempts to trace the owner of the servient tenement he cannot be found. Such a servitude will be subject to exclusion of indemnity for a twenty year period. However servitudes validly constituted other than by express grant are perfectly legitimate and, as already stated, the effect of registration includes vesting in the owner a real right in any servitude whether express or implied.

Once property is registered in the Land Register, any servitudes form part of the title. Theoretically therefore it should not be necessary to refer to rights and pertinents when transferring part of a registered title, but in practice it may not be entirely clear which rights should pass with the part being conveyed and whether some should not. Accordingly it is good practice, and a requirement of the Keeper, to specify in the conveyance of the part of the registered property the rights and servitudes that are to apply to that conveyed part.

In cases where the rights are narrated in a deed of conditions which is entered in the title sheet of the whole subjects a reference in the dispositive clause of the conveyance to the deed of conditions, such as 'together with the rights specified in the deed of conditions...', will suffice.

> I, MICHAEL RUPERT MONK residing at [   ], in consideration of the price of Forty two Thousand Pounds Sterling paid to me by CHRISTOPHER GAVIN SWEET, residing at Lionheart Farm, Kinlochlmond, by Kelvinforth HAVE SOLD and DO HEREBY DISPONE to the said Christopher Gavin Sweet and his executors and assignees whomsoever ALL and WHOLE (describe the part conveyed in sufficient detail, preferably by reference to a plan, to enable the Keeper to identify it on the ordnance map) being part of the subjects registered in the Land Register of Scotland under title number(s) (   ) [All and Whole the subjects (First) registered under title number (   ) or All and Whole the subjects marked (   ) on the plan of title number (   )] [but always with and under the following reservations, burdens and conditions viz.:- (insert additional burdens or conditions where appropriate)] [but declaring that the following rights (burdens, conditions) set out in title number(s) (   ) are not to apply to the subjects hereby conveyed]; with entry on (date of entry); and I grant warrandice: IN WITNESS WHEREOF

(d) Division of burdened properties

Depending on the terms of the burden, on a division of a property that is a burdened property, each part of the property as divided will continue to be a burdened property, unless the burden cannot relate to a part or parts of the property once it is divided. So a use restriction affecting a property would continue to apply to each of the split o other than the solum on which the tenement is built, ff parts, but a facility burden relating to a wall located in one part of the property, but not the part conveyed, will no longer apply to the conveyed property (s 13 of TC(S)A 2003).

(e) Division of benefited properties

Before 28 November 2004, if a benefited property was divided, each part became an independent benefited property. The rules are now changed for divisions of property made by a deed registered on or after that date. Section 14 of TC(S)A 2003 provides, as a default rule, that the part conveyed will cease to become a benefited property – unless the break-off conveyance provides otherwise. The break-off conveyance can provide for both properties, or just the part being sold, to be benefited properties instead. It will also be possible to allocate different burdens from the larger title to the separate parts of the divided titles.

The rules regarding division of benefited properties apply in a different way to pre-emptions and other options, where only one property can be benefited. If the rule that the retained land is to be the benefited property is disapplied, the only alternative is that the conveyed property is to be the benefited property.

CREATING NEW BURDENS AND SERVITUDES

9.10 The rules relating to the creation of new real burdens are now set out in the Title Conditions (Scotland) Act 2003. Many of the rules reflect the law that applied before the commencement of the TC(S)A 2003, but several new rules were created and some of the previous rules were changed. It is important therefore, to be familiar with the provisions of TC(S)A 2003 when drafting new real burdens. The rules relating to servitudes were not innovated on to anything like the same extent by the TC(S)A 2003, but a few changes and clarifications were set out in Part 7 of TC(S)A 2003.

(a) Rules for creation of real burdens

The system set up by the TC(S)A 2003 for creating real burdens provides the following rules:

(i) Affirmative, negative and ancillary burdens

Section 2 of the TC(S)A 2003 divides burdens into three categories: affirmative, negative and ancillary burdens. Affirmative burdens are obligations to do something and can include a requirement to meet or contribute towards the cost of something, for example maintenance costs. Negative burdens consist of obligations to refrain from doing something. A prohibition against carrying out alterations or a use restriction prohibiting a particular use would fall into this category.

There had previously been some doubt about whether ancillary burdens, such as a right to enter a property in order to carry out repairs, ran with the land. The TC(S)A 2003 permits ancillary burdens which, in addition to a right to enter or make use of a property, can also include provision for management or administration, provided these burdens are for a purpose ancillary to an affirmative or negative burden that is imposed. An obligation to maintain common areas would support an ancillary burden that set out arrangements for management of the common areas, instructing repairs and recovering costs.

(ii) Burdens must 'run with the land'

The mantra is that: a burden must burden a burdened property for the benefit of the benefited property. Only personal real burdens are excluded from this requirement. This was the law before 28 November 2004, but is now enshrined in s 3(1), (2) and (3) of TC(S)A 2003. This is known as the 'praedial rule', which always applied to real burdens but which often was (and sometimes still is) overlooked, particularly in connection with the type of real burden which relates to commercial activity, for example a restriction on a type of trading. Often, there is no benefit to the benefited property in such a burden – the benefit is to the owner. Section 3 TC(S)A 2003 provides that a real burden must relate in some way to the burdened property and that relationship may be direct or indirect, but must not merely be that the obligated person is the owner of the burdened property – so, unless it is a community burden, a real burden has to be for the benefit of the benefited property where there is one. A community burden may either be for the benefit of the whole of the community to which it relates or just some part of that community.

(iii)   Content of real burdens

There are various rules peppered through the TC(S)A 2003 that relate to what a real burden may contain. A lot of prior case law in this respect continues to be relevant.

A real burden may not be contrary to public policy eg as an unreasonable restraint on trade, (s 3(6)). This restates the pre-existing law. This is not to say that any burden which restricts trade is not permitted. Prohibition against use for business purposes may be considered quite reasonable in a residential development (although the case of *Snowie v Museum Hall* (see para 8.03) in 2010 appears to cast that contention in some doubt). Typical examples of an unreasonable restraint on trade are burdens which may be seen as being anti-competitive. Generally these types of burdens are imposed for commercial reasons eg to prevent a business being set up in competition to an existing similar business nearby. Understandable perhaps, but not enforceable as a real burden.

A burden may not be repugnant with ownership. Repugnancy with ownership would apply to burdens which attempt to impose unreasonable restrictions on freedom to use the property, such as prohibitions against selling or leasing.

A burden cannot be created to secure payment of money, such as the 'clawback' type of burden previously popular, particularly in cases of land being sold for speculative development. Section 117 of TC(S)A 2003 prohibits the creation of 'pecuniary real burdens', although, in fact, since 29 November 1970 the only competent method of taking a fixed security over heritable property in Scotland is by way of standard security (see para 10.02). In contrast, however, it is permissible to provide in a burden for someone to pay for or contribute towards the cost of something, like maintenance of the property or common parts (s 2(1)(a)).

A burden must not have the effect of creating a monopoly (s 3(7)). Examples given are the provision that a certain person is to be the manager of a property or supplier of services to the property. This can be contrasted with the short term monopoly that can apply when using a manager burden under s 63 of TC(S)A 2003 which gives a period of exclusive right to appoint or be the manager of properties for up to five years.

Pre-emption rights are still allowed, but it is no longer competent to create rights of redemption or reversion, or other options to acquire the burdened property, as real burdens (s 3(5)).

A burden which provides that someone other than the holder of a burden can waive compliance with it, or vary it is not competent. This again should be contrasted with the ability in community burdens to appoint a manager to do these things.

Personal real burdens, which are in favour, not of another property, but of a person, such as Scottish Ministers or a local authority, are introduced by Part 3 of the TC(S)A 2003, and there are various statutory instruments that nominate relevant bodies that are entitled to the benefit of such burdens. These burdens are each quite limited in their application and must be framed to relate to a particular purpose. Personal real burdens are created by statute and, as a concept, are not freely available for the ordinary benefited owner. Instead they are of named types and the parties in whose favour such burdens can be created is also set out in statute. A **conservation burden**, (s 38 of TC(S)A 2003) for example, which can be created in favour of a conservation body or Scottish Ministers, must be for preservation or protection for the benefit of the public, of architectural or historical or other special characteristics of the land. **Economic development burdens** (s 45 of TC(S)A 2003), for the benefit of a local authority or Scottish Ministers, have to promote economic development, and **healthcare burdens** (s 46 of TC(S)A 2003) in favour of an NHS Trust, or Scottish Ministers, have to relate to the provision of healthcare. **Maritime burdens** (s 44 of TC(S)A 2003) relate to the sea bed or foreshore and benefit the Crown. A **rural housing burden** (s 43 of TC(S)A 2003) is a type of pre-emption in favour of a rural housing body. **Manager burdens** (s 63 of TC(S)A 2003) are also a type of personal real burden although not in the same category as those just described, and they also have a limited life span (see para 9.11(f) below). Other types of personal real burdens can be created, for example the Climate Change (Scotland) Act 2009 s 68 provides for a **climate change burden** which can be created in favour of a public body or trust, (essentially the same bodies that are conservation bodies) or Scottish Ministers for the purpose of reducing greenhouse gas emissions, by requiring that a property meets specified mitigation and adaptation standards in the event of development.

The terms of the burden must be set out in full in the constitutive deed (s 4(2)(a) of TC(S)A 2003). The expression used is that it must appear in 'the four corners of the deed' (Lord Guthrie in *Anderson v Dickie* 1914 SC

706), because an owner or a buyer of property must be able to ascertain from the face of the title what limitations or restrictions are placed upon his use of that property. This is another restatement of the position as it has always been in law. Burdens which refer to extrinsic information or documentation such as a reference to statute eg 'only to be used for Class 1 Use under the Town and Country Planning Use Classes Order' are ineffective. The only exception is in relation to payment of or contribution towards costs, where the amount is not specified in the deed, reference to some other document for the purposes of calculating the cost will be permitted, provided that the other documents referred to as the basis of calculation must be public documents or records (s 5 of TC(S)A 2003). Referring to the valuation roll for example as a way of working out the proportion of liability for common repairs would be permissible on this basis.

(iv) Referring to 'real burden' or other named burdens

When drafting a real burden, you must use either the expression 'real burden' (s 4(2)(a) of TC(S)A 2003) or, if creating a type of burden which is 'a nameable type of real burden' then you can use that expression instead (s 4(3) of TC(S)A 2003). The nameable types of real burden in TC(S)A 2003 are: affirmative burden, negative burden, ancillary burden, community burden, facility burden and service burden and also all the types of personal real burdens. There might be a danger however in naming the burden as a particular type of burden incorrectly (other than the personal real burdens) and so it is probably safest to stick with 'real burden' except in the case of community burdens, when using that expression had additional significance (see para (vii) below). The commonly coined expression 'neighbour burden' is **not** one of the nameable types of burden, so should not be used in drafting.

(v) The burden must be created by the owner of the burdened property

There is no change from the previous law (s 4(2)(b) of TC(S)A 2003), and s 123 of TC(S)A 2003 clarifies that 'owner', for the purposes of creating real burdens, means a person who has right to the property whether or not that person has completed title.

(vi) The constitutive deed

The TC(S)A 2003 provided a major change in the way in which real burdens can be created. Previously only competent in a conveyance of the burdened property or in a Deed of Conditions, now any deed may be used, provided of course it complies with the other rules relating to creation of real burdens. The main benefit of this in practice is that burdens can be created in stand-alone deeds – which have come to be known as Deeds of Real Burdens – without the need for a property to be conveyed. This can be useful for regulating or regularising title conditions between or among adjoining properties, and it has become not uncommon to use Deeds of Real Burdens, even when there is property being conveyed, to impose burdens that are not community burdens, on the properties being conveyed and the property being retained, where these arrangements are complex. It is also competent now to impose burdens in a split-off disposition that affect the land that is retained. Formerly it was not possible to impose real burdens in this way (despite frequent attempts to do so).

For styles of Deeds of Real Burden, and Dispositions imposing real burdens and servitudes, see the PSG website, and further details on their use in paras 9.10(d) and (e).

(vii) Identify the burdened and the benefited properties

In non feudal deeds imposing burdens before the appointed day, there was no legal requirement to identify the benefited property. Identification of the benefited property or any benefited party was therefore often omitted, making it difficult to work out who had a right to enforce the burden. Now a proper description of both the burdened and the benefited property is necessary (s 4(2)(c) of TC(S)A 2003), sufficient for the Keeper to identify both properties affected. For real burdens created since 28 November 2004, therefore, all enforcement rights must be express, and implied enforcement rights will not arise.

(vii) Dual registration

Following on from the requirement to identify both the burdened and the benefited properties, the burdens must be registered in the title to both those properties (or recorded, if the title to one or both of the properties is in the Sasine Register). In pre 28 November 2004 titles, invariably burdens do not appear on the title of the benefited property, and in many cases benefited proprietors may have no idea that they are entitled to enforce certain conditions. This requirement for dual registration has meant that we must now identify both the benefited and burdened property and the owners of these properties to effect registration against both titles. In the case of community burdens, which are often set up in a Deed of Conditions, the very fact of calling them 'community burdens' means that each property that is affected by the burdens is (or will be) both a benefited and a burdened property (s 27 of TC(S)A 2003), and so registration of the Deed once is all that is required.

(viii) Effect of registration

Formerly, parties could rely on the fact, where the benefited proprietor and the burdened proprietor were the original contracting parties, that even if there was no longer enforceability of the burden, such as where there is no interest to enforce, it might have been possible to enforce as a matter of contract. Section 61 of TC(S)A 2003 disapplied that rule, so that now any such contractual link is extinguished on registration, and the burdens will only be enforceable as real burdens. Conversely, however, if the burden fails as a real burden, it may be enforceable as a matter of contract between the original parties.

It is possible to postpone the coming into effect of the burden by making appropriate provision in the deed, either for a future date when the conditions will come into effect, or by specifying some future event when the conditions will come into force such as, for example, the date of registration of a conveyance of particular units (ss 4(1)(a) and 4(1)(b) of TC(S)A 2003). Careful thought should be given to the effect of postponement if this option is chosen.

(b) Changes to Servitudes

A number of changes were made to the law of servitudes by the TC(S)A 2003, but the underlying law of the servitude has not otherwise changed. While TC(S)A 2003 uses the expressions 'benefited property' and 'burdened property', the more traditional expressions 'dominant tenement' and 'servient tenement' are still applicable, although are less used nowadays.

(i) New categories of servitude

Historically, a servitude had to be of a known and recognised type, many of the classes derived from Roman law, and it was very rare for new categories of servitude to be added to the list. Section 76 of TC(S) A 2003, permits, within reason, new types of servitude to be created provided they are created in writing, dual registered and not repugnant with ownership. Creating a servitude right of parking by express grant, it seems, is now possible (and in any event see *Moncrieff v Jamieson* [2007] UKHL 42; [2008] SC (HL) 1). Servitudes created by other means, such as by prescription, are not affected, but will still need to fit into one of the categories of recognised servitudes.

(ii) Registration for written servitudes

A servitude that is contained in a written deed now needs to be registered to be effective. This does not affect unregistered deeds creating servitudes prior to 28 November 2004, however, and it will still be possible to obtain a right by prescription following on an unrecorded deed after 20 years. In addition, and reflecting the arrangements for real burdens, servitudes need to be dual registered against the benefited property and the burdened property (s 75(1) of TC(S)A 2003), with the exception of 'pipeline servitudes' (see para (iv) below)

(iii) Same person can own the benefited and the burdened properties

Section 75(2) of TC(S)A 2003 disapplied the rule that the benefited and burdened properties must be in separate ownership at the time of registration of the servitude. If properties are in the same ownership at the time of registration of the servitude, it will remain inactive until the date when the two properties come into separate ownership. Thus, 'community' servitudes affecting a development can be effectively created in advance of conveying off plots or units – and will come into effect on registration of the conveyances of the plots or units.

(iv) Pipeline servitudes

The competence of a servitude to lead a pipe, cable or wire over or under land for any purpose is confirmed by s 77 of TC(S)A 2003, and is deemed always to have been the case, so that previously created servitudes of this type are valid. Servitudes of this type do not need to be dual registered to be effectively created (s 75(3)(b) of TC(S)A 2003).

However, this does not alter the position that to be a valid servitude, there must be both a burdened and benefited property. The difficulty with pipeline servitudes has always been in identifying a benefited property that will benefit from the pipe or cable that is subject to the servitude. Some ways of addressing this include: identifying a substation to which electricity cables will run, or, a waterworks or sewage works served by pipelines may be considered to be the benefited property. It may be that there is not an easily identifiable property in the ownership of the utility provider that can obviously be identified as benefiting from the servitude, and the longer the cable or pipe route, the more difficult it can be to identify the benefited property. While it is preferable to attempt to identify the benefited property, for example the originating source of the water ie the waterworks or reservoir or the substation or power station, it seems, however, that a full conveyancing description of the benefited property is not necessary, and that something general will suffice. Careful consideration may need to be given to this issue and it may be necessary to get pre-registration clearance from the Keeper in some circumstances.

(v) Discharge of positive servitude

A positive servitude which has been registered, if discharged by deed, can only be discharged by deed registered against the title (s 78 of TC(S) A 2003). The position regarding extinction through non use for the prescriptive period, or by other legitimate methods, is not changed.

(vi) Negative servitudes

It is no longer competent to create negative servitudes (eg servitudes *non aedificandi* (no building or not to build above a certain height) or *altius non tollendi* and *luminibus non officiendi* (not to obstruct prospect or light)). These type of provisions must now be created as negative burdens and dual registered.

Negative servitudes in existence on 28 November 2004 were automatically converted into negative burdens, ie obligations to refrain from doing something (s 80 of TC(S)A 2003). These are known as converted servitudes and will be extinguished 10 years after the appointed date, ie on 28 November 2014 unless they are preserved (as real burdens) by notice procedure and registered against the burdened property and the benefited property before expiry of the 10 year period.

(vii) Conversion of certain burdens to positive servitudes

Any real burden that consists of a right to enter or use a property (unless it could be classified as an ancillary burden) ceased to exist on 28 November 2004 and became a positive servitude (s 81 of TC(S)A 2003). This happened automatically and no notice procedure is required. Note that this does not affect burdens that were extinguished by feudal abolition.

(c) The need for real burdens

The first thing to decide before you even get into the drafting issues is whether or not you need a real burden at all. Many real burdens of a certain vintage are all about control, either personal – in the form of the superior, or social or public in the form of regulating the style and appearance of buildings. Much of what used to be covered by real burdens is now a matter of planning regulations. Indeed there is a potential risk, if your drafting is over-prescriptive in these matters, of having conflicting provisions. In developments for example, some developers still impose burdens about what the proprietors can and cannot do, according to what they want to happen in the development, in the same way they used to do when they were feudal superiors and had a continuing role in enforcement after completion.

A more realistic approach is to concentrate on what is necessary to ensure the smooth operation of the development. If everyone is required to maintain a uniform colour scheme for example and all front doors must be blue – is there really going to be a material detriment to the value or enjoyment of everyone else's property if I paint my door yellow?

The same considerations apply when drafting 'neighbour' burdens. Ensure that your client has a clear idea of what it is possible to achieve with a burden, particularly in the light of having to establish not only title to enforce, but also interest to enforce. Some clients will still want the burden to be imposed, even if there is a possibility or likelihood that it will be difficult to enforce. In that case it is important that you have made it clear to your client what the realistic prospects of enforcement, in the event of a breach, are likely to be.

(d) Creating real burdens and servitudes in a Disposition

While it no longer matters what form of deed you use as the vehicle for your real burdens (see para 9.10(a)(vi) above), it is often still the case that the constitutive deed will be a disposition when the parties want to impose burdens on the property being sold for the benefit of property being retained by the seller. Sometimes it is appropriate to impose burdens on the property being retained too. The PSG has two styles of disposition for use in these circumstances: a Disposition that imposes new Burdens and servitudes on the property being conveyed; and a Disposition that imposes new real burdens and servitudes on both the property being conveyed and the property being retained (Reciprocal). To access these styles, go to the 'Title Conditions' section of the website at www.psglegal.co.uk. These styles can be freely used and can of course easily be adjusted to suit other circumstances.

The format of each disposition provides for the details of the new burdens and servitudes to be set out in a schedule at the end of the Disposition. The Keeper has confirmed that this approach will assist her in entering details of the burdens and servitudes on the title sheets and land certificates for the benefited and burdened properties (see comment from the Registers of Scotland in the article 'Easing the burdens' JLSS 18 April, 2011. (http://www.journalonline.co.uk/Magazine/56-4/1009611.aspx)).

There are detailed guidance notes that accompany the PSG deeds, however the following drafting suggestions are offered:

(i)   Using schedules: If you are only creating one or two new burdens or servitudes, a separate schedule may not be necessary. Experience has shown however that it is easy to get provisions confused in a format that uses continuous block of text, so do not feel that you cannot use the Schedule approach with only a few provisions. This also makes the deed easier to revise during the transaction, and review when examining title in the future.

(ii)   Using definitions: Traditionally, conveyancers did not use defined terms in dispositions, (preferring references to 'the said' or 'as aforesaid') but as a drafting technique it often simplifies drafting and clarifies provisions, so it is now quite common to see defined terms in conveyances, either in the body of the deed, or in a schedule (or both as in the PSG style). It is particularly useful to use defined terms for the property being conveyed and the property being retained. In the PSG style, the definitions 'Conveyed Property' and 'Retained Property' are used, but alternative, more descriptive terminology can be substituted. It is recommended however that you do not use the expressions 'benefited property' and burdened property' as your definitions in a grant of reciprocal burdens and servitudes, as your drafting will quickly become tangled and confused.

(iii)   Keep in mind the rules for creation: Even if the wording of the burden is 'standard' wording that has been used many times in the past, be critical about any style wording you find. It is an easy trap to fall into, since a lot of the time we are drafting new burdens that are the same burdens we always used to draft, that we fail to notice, because we are so used to them, that the burdens may not comply with the rules for creation. One of the commonest failings is failure to adhere to the praedial rule - that the burden must burden the burdened property for the benefit of the benefited property. Both elements need to be in place. Too often, burdens burden the burdened property for the benefit of the *owners* of the benefited property, and it can sometimes be tricky to distinguish between the two. Distance between the two properties can be relevant too – although not an exact science, the further away the benefited property is from the burdened property, the weaker the praedial interest is likely to be, and the nature of the burden itself can often determine the extent to which interest to enforce will be able to be sustained.

(iv)   Use clear and precise language: Remember that the burden or servitude you are drafting will (or probably will) be perpetual, and it is important therefore that you compose it in language that is as unambiguous and unequivocal as possible, so that future generations will be able to ascertain with ease the meaning and effect. It is crucial that, under no circumstances, should you take the wording about the nature of the burden, that your client has thrown into an email to you, and transfer it straight into your drafting. Please. It is the responsibility of the conveyancer, armed with knowledge of what is required to create a clear and enforceable burden, to use their skill to fashion wording that will do the job it is supposed to do. Also remember the rule of interpretation that burdens and servitudes will be interpreted *contra proferentum* (in other words in case of doubt or ambiguity the wording will be construed against the party in whose favour it was cast).

(v) Check that your drafting does what it is supposed to do: Once you have drafted the burden or servitude, review it critically and in the context of what it is intended to achieve. It is particularly important to stress test provisions that involve some kind of calculation, in this way. Run a couple of examples to ensure that the right outcome will be achieved. It might even be appropriate to include a worked example for illustrative purposes only to make it clear what the effect of the provision is supposed to look like.

Example wording for a burden involving a calculation:

In each year, the total cost of carrying out landscaping maintenance will be arrived at by applying the formula:

$(10 \times OA) \times B$

Where OA (overall area) equals 52.83 and
B equals the Unit Multiplier

By way of example, only, if the Unit Multiplier is £150 then the total cost of landscaping maintenance would be

$(10 \times 52.83) \times 150 = £790.245$

A definition of Unit Multiplier would be needed in this example.

(e) Creating real burdens and servitudes in a stand-alone deed

It has always been possible to create servitudes in a freestanding deed, and the TC(S)A 2003 does not change this. This is particularly useful when no property is being conveyed but burdens are required, and a deed of conditions would be too cumbersome or inappropriate to create the burdens required.

(i) Deeds of Real Burdens

Two styles of Deed of Real Burdens have been produced by the PSG to allow the creation of real burdens in this way. The Deed of Real Burdens (Unilateral) can be used where burdens are being imposed on one property in favour of the other, and the Deed of Real Burdens (Reciprocal) may be used where each property will have burdens imposed upon it in favour of the other property.

In each case it is assumed that there will be only two properties involved, but deeds of real burdens can be used in transactions where there are multiple properties, and of course combined Deeds of Real burdens and Servitudes can be created where required.

Creating real burdens in this way is otherwise no different from their creation in a Disposition. The same rules of creation apply and dual registration is necessary.

(ii) Deed of Personal Real Burden

From time to time you may be required to draft a deed that imposes a personal real burden on land or property in favour of the relevant body entitled to the benefit of the personal real burden in question (see para 9.10(a)(iii) above)

Again there is a PSG style for this purpose, suitable for creating the five types of personal real burden introduced by Part 3 of the 2003 Act, ie conservation burdens, rural housing burdens, maritime burdens, economic development burdens and health care burdens. It is not suitable for the creation of manager burdens, which are also a type of personal real burden, to the extent that they operate in favour of persons, not property, but which are subject to their own set of requirements, and which are more properly created in Deeds of Conditions. The Deed of

Personal Real Burden could also be used for drafting other types of personal real burdens created in other legislation, such as climate change burdens.

When framing the terms of the Deed of Personal Real Burden, the relevant section of the TC(S)A 2003, and the relevant statutory instrument under which the entitled body is appointed, should be specified.

For the relevant sections of the TC(S)A 2003 see para 9.10(a)(iii).

At the time of writing there are eleven Scottish SIs by which conservation bodies and rural housing bodies are entitled to the benefit of a personal real burden in their favour, and you will need to check for the correct SI (the one that refers to the body in whose favour the burden is being granted) to incorporate into the Deed. The main SI is The Title Conditions (Scotland) Act 2003 (Conservation Bodies) Order 2003 (SSI 2003/453).

Note that all personal real burdens, except for maritime burdens, require the consent of the relevant body in whose favour the burden is created to be obtained before the Deed of Personal Real Burden is registered. While the TC(S)A 2003 does not require the consent to be incorporated into the deed creating the personal real burden, it is a simple and conclusive way of evidencing such consent to do so, and the style contains a suggested clause for this purpose.

The correct terminology (ie conservation, rural housing, maritime etc) must be used otherwise the personal real burden will be ineffective. When drafting the terms of the personal real burden, it should be considered whether what it is intended to create as a personal real burden is permitted by the terms of the relevant section of the TC(S)A 2003 or other relevant statute (eg Climate Change (Scotland) Act 2009 for climate change burdens).

(iii) Deed of Servitude

Creating a servitude in a stand-alone deed has always been competent and nothing in the TC(S)A 2003 changes that, except that of course deeds creating servitudes must be dual registered unless they relate to pipeline servitudes, and only positive servitudes may now be created. To complete the suite of documents creating real burdens and servitudes, the PSG styles also include a style Deed of Servitude drafted to incorporate the requirements of the TC(S)A 2003 and in a format that reminds the drafter to identify both the burdened and the benefited properties.

Invariably when drafting a servitude right, there will be corresponding servitude conditions that will also apply. It is important to distinguish between a condition that applies to the burdened property, and one that applies to the benefited property. Properly, servitude conditions regulate the use and terms of the servitude rights, and are for the benefit of the burdened property. If the conditions that are to be applied are for the benefit of the benefited property, such as an obligation on the owner of the burdened property to form a road or build a wall, then these should be created as real burdens burdening the burdened property for the benefit of the benefited property. The importance of remembering this, when you are drafting a Deed of Servitude is that when creating real burdens the expression 'real burden' or one of the equivalents must be used. Since this expression will not otherwise appear in a Deed of Servitude (which is designed to create only servitudes, for which no special expression is required) the absence of these words would render the real burdens in the deed ineffective (see para 9.10(a)(iv)).

Where possible, the agreed basis for the way in which costs, such as maintenance and repair are to be shared in the particular circumstances should be specified as clearly as possible, to avoid any potential dispute in the future as to the proportion of costs due.

(f) Creating real burdens and servitudes in a Deed of Conditions

Probably the most recognisable document for creating real burdens and servitudes, the Deed of Conditions, is both familiar and daunting. Before the TC(S)A 2003, it was all we had if we wanted to create real burdens where there was no conveyance of the property concerned (although it was not without its issues). If parties wished to impose burdens on one property in favour of another, then a Deed of Conditions – something of a conveyancing sledgehammer in such cases – was the only alternative.

With the introduction of the concept of 'community burdens' in TC(S) A 2003, the Deed of Conditions comes into its own. Often used already for estates of houses or retail or office parks, the format lends itself to the situation where a number of properties are to be subject to the same conditions, and each proprietor is concerned to ensure that his neighbours also comply. Many examples of Deeds of Conditions have their origins in the feudal system, where the developer would be the feudal superior and would retain a high degree of control and enforcement rights, after the units – usually houses, in fact – were built, sold and occupied.

(i) Problems with drafting

It is in that context of familiarity that some of the problems with modern day Deeds of Conditions can occur. In many cases, experienced developers still expect to apply the same kinds of title conditions as they did before feudal abolition. For the lawyer drafting the Deed, it is all too easy to use the same drafting that was used the last time – and that drafting probably dates back many years. If you compare a variety of residential deeds of conditions, drafted over a period of time, you are bound to find many similarities in the content. This is unsurprising – developments of houses usually need the same kind of regulation – preservation of amenity: no ball games; no trade or business; no breeding of dogs; no parking on the roads and so on.

Many of these conditions are perfectly fine, however some of the conditions are concerned with 'control', such as not to change the appearance or colour scheme of the front elevation without consent. In feudal deeds the consent required would be that of the superior, but this does not translate itself well into a large community, where in reality only a handful of neighbouring owners have any real interest – in the actual sense as well as probably in the legal sense of interest to enforce.

It is important in drafting terms therefore to move away from the feudal mentality and to help clients who might still have a lingering 'feudal hangover' to consider the purpose, effect and desirability of imposing real burdens, and not simply to replicate the same kinds of burdens and conditions that we were accustomed to drafting into pre-feudal abolition Deeds of Conditions. Developers are far less likely to have any continuing interest in the development once it is completed, compared with the ongoing involvement of superiors in the past. While some of that wording and those clauses are still perfectly fine for modern developments, it is important for the drafter and the client to be realistic about what it is possible to create as enforceable real burdens. By all means continue to draft for extensions and alterations and the like, but these should be framed in a way that recognises who should have enforcement rights.

There are a number of elements in a Deed of Conditions that are affected by the provisions of TC(S)A 2003. The PSG style Deed of Conditions, which can be used for any kind of development such as a retail park, housing development or industrial estate, provides a structure that addresses the principal issues that need to be taken into account to ensure that the Deed complies with the provisions of the TC(S)A 2003, including the need to identify real burdens and servitudes separately, identifying relevant burdens as community burdens, providing for variation and discharge, and a suitable manager burden.

(ii) Amenity

One of the principal purposes of burdens in a community is the preservation of the amenity of the community. The Deed should provide for reciprocal burdens that the owners of the units in the community are prepared to adhere to, and want to see imposed on their neighbours. These burdens will relate to such things as maintenance and use.

(iii) Management

Inevitably, because of the numbers of units involved, issues of management need to be addressed in some form or another in Deeds of Conditions. Usually this involves the appointment of a manager or factor to be responsible for the organisation, and carrying out of repairs and maintenance of common parts, and for collecting shares of the costs from each of the owners. A majority of the owners in a development can appoint a manager and dismiss him, and set out what they want the manager to do (s 28 of TC(S)A 2003).

A 'manager burden' created in accordance with s 63 of the TC(S) A 2003 has precedence over the power of the majority, for a maximum period of 5 years from the date of registration of the Deed of Conditions. A manager burden allows the developer to be, or to appoint, a manager to act as the manager of related properties, such as the units in the development and, where it applies, gives a period of exclusivity of appointment for up to 5 years. (Note however that in the case of sheltered housing, the period of exclusivity of appointment is 3 years and in the case of manager burdens relating to right to buy housing, the period is 30 years). This means that the manager may not be dismissed by the owners until the expiry of the 5 year period, although if the developer ceases to own one of the related properties before expiry of that period, (ie because he has sold all of the units in the development) the manager burden will cease to have effect. The meaning of 'related properties' for this purpose is outlined in s 66 of the TC(S)A 2003, and is different from the way in which this expression is used in the context of implied enforcement rights. However, while that exclusivity of the power to appoint applies only for a period of up to 5 years, the same manager may well be approved to continue to act beyond the 5 year period, by the owners, but of course is at risk of dismissal by them after that date. A manager burden can be used by the developer to exercise or retain some control over how the common parts of the development are run, in the early years of the development.

Complex management and administrative arrangements may also be needed, particularly in relation to service charge estimates, billing and accounting. Some form of decision making structure is also required, with arrangements for meetings, quorums, proxy voting and so on. Much of these arrangements have been provided for in the Development Management Scheme, a statutory model scheme of management provided by Part 6 of TC(S)A 2003, and it is worth considering incorporating some or all of these rules either as they are drafted or amended to suit the particular circumstances of the development, into your Deed of Conditions or on a stand-alone basis (see para 9.10(g) below).

(iv) Commencement

You need to think quite carefully about whether you want to postpone the effect of the terms a Deed of Conditions. If nothing is said in the Deed, then on registration in the Property Register, the whole land affected by the Deed of Conditions will be burdened with the provisions in the deed. It is possible to postpone the creation of the burdens by making express provision in the deed for creation to take place on some other date, either a fixed date or the date of registration of some other deed, like the Dispositions of each individual plot (s 4(1) of TC(S)A 2003).

In the past this was seen as a useful mechanism if the developer wanted to retain the flexibility to make changes to the layout of the development in the future. It is difficult to see, nowadays, how such changes could be made, given the requirement for a deed constituting community burdens (which these are going to be) to specify the community that is affected, and with greater certainty of the extent of the development being required at an early stage in the process, it seems that there is little to be gained from postponement of the effect of community burdens. If you do decide to postpone the date of effect of the burdens however, then clearly it is important to remember to trigger their creation in the Disposition of each plot. Recommended wording to incorporate into each disposition is:

> but always with and under the real burdens contained in the Deed of Conditions by [   ] dated [   ] and registered in the Land Register for Scotland under Title Number [   ]

If there is no wording in the Dispositions applying the conditions in the Deed of Conditions, then the plots will not be burdened by the conditions, and there is a risk that not all maintenance and other costs can be recovered.

(v) Identify the community

For burdens to qualify as community burdens, the 'community' must be identified (s 4(4) of the TC(S)A 2003). More often than not, this will be the whole development, and using the words 'community burden' has the effect of making the units which are subject to those burdens both benefited and burdened, setting up the reciprocal arrangement typical of communities. This is further support of the notion that communities should get on with it themselves without external interference, once they are set up, by providing that each owner has (subject to establishing interest to enforce) enforcement rights against the others.

When identifying the property to which the community burdens will apply, care must be taken to ensure that no parts of the development, which may be held in separate ownership, but which do not form part of one of the units, are inadvertently included as a burdened or a benefited property.

For example the development may consist of a number of units which are conveyed to individuals, and extensive common parts which are retained in the ownership of the developer or held by a management company. It would not be the intention for the owner of the common parts either to have burdens that affect the units imposed on them, or to be entitled to enforce those burdens against the units. In such a case, the community burdens should be imposed on the units in the development rather than the whole development. Separate burdens, for example restricting the use of the common parts to open space, should be imposed on the common parts for the benefit of the units.

(vi) Common parts – identification

We have already considered the effect of the case of *PMP Plus v the Keeper of the Registers of Scotland* an identification of common parts of a development, in relation to examination of title (see para 8.28(d)). Instances where developers sell off large parts of the common amenity areas to other commercial interests will be rare. And the view has been expressed (Gretton and Reid Conveyancing 2008 pages 145-146 that while the conveyance from the developer may be void, future transfers by plot or unit owners to a purchaser may operate as an a non domino title which will be perfected through prescription. It seems that the sensible approach is to be aware of the issue and flag it to purchasers and their lenders, but not to over-react.

However, in drafting new Deeds of Conditions, we have to be mindful of the PMP Plus decision and define elements of the development, such as common parts, in a better way. Using a plan to devote them is one option, but it is not without risk, particularly for larger developments, where, for perfectly good reasons, the developer might need to depart, even slightly from the original layout, meaning the initial delineation is no longer correct.

Another possibility is to identify certain community rights, such as access over roads and liability for external boundaries, in an over-arching Deed, followed by later Deeds over smaller areas, confining liability for common areas for example to those in the immediate vicinity. Again this option is not entirely satisfactory particularly if a park or play area in one section is intended to be used by everyone. The individual circumstances of each development need to be considered with care, and an appropriate structure devised.

(vii) Common parts – Ownership

Much of the concern expressed about the *PMP Plus* case stems from the fact that ownership of the common parts needed to be transferred to the individual owners. But, of course, that is not the only alternative. There does not appear to be any objection to the alternative approach of having the common parts owned by the developer, or some third party, provided the burdened properties have some interest in the common parts. Section 3 of the TC(S)A 2003 says that a real burden must relate in some way to the burdened property and that that relationship may be direct or indirect so, provided that the owners of the units have freedom to use the common parts for leisure and recreation for example, and use the roads for access and egress, then it seems quite clear that there is a sufficient connection and praedial interest for the burden to be validly constituted without the necessity for the common parts to be owned by the individuals responsible. This view would appear to be supported by comments in the Lands Tribunal case of *Greenbelt Property Ltd v Riggens* 2010 GWD 28-586.

The Development Management Scheme (see para 9.10(g)) has the potential to be of considerable assistance in the setting up of provisions to regulate developments.

(viii) Servitude rights

As well as real burdens, a Deed of Conditions will typically contain a number of servitudes. The sensible use of servitudes in a Deed of Conditions can help to resolve some of the difficulties that we might encounter with real burdens affecting common parts. For example, it is of course perfectly valid and acceptable to grant servitude rights of access over access roads to be constructed within the development, meaning there would then be no requirement to convey the property. It is also perfectly valid for such servitudes to have, as a servitude condition, an obligation to contribute towards the cost of maintenance.

As well as access, a typical Deed of Conditions will contain servitude rights over other units for the purposes of maintenance, repair, cleaning and similar purposes. There may need to be construction servitudes for access for construction traffic or for oversailing, and also rights reserved and granted for laying, maintaining and renewing service media. Style wording for these types of servitude is contained in the PSG Deed of Conditions. For further exploration of the use of servitude in development titles see the article 'Servitudes, developers and flexible rights' by Professor Roddy Paisley JLSS, February 2011 (http://www.journalonline. co.uk/Magazine/56-2/1009301.aspx)

(ix) Plans and site visits

Before starting on the drafting of a Deed of Conditions, it is essential to have a reasonably detailed plan showing what the developer proposes for the site. This will identify issues relating to access, emergency access, what is to happen in communal external areas, areas that are to be exclusive or shared among only some of the owners, parking and access to parking spaces, boundaries, service strips, amenities such as play areas, recreational areas. Although not always possible, it can help to conduct a site visit – not necessarily when the development is a muddy field (although if you act for an active developer, it can be a good idea to keep a pair of wellies in the boot of your car just in case) – but once some of the infrastructure is in and foundations have been laid. Actually visiting the site may flag up issues on the ground that are not obvious from a two dimensional plan – in just the same way as a site visit can be of immense value when examining title – access issues, land contours that may require height restrictions to be imposed, or issues that may affect privacy or amenity can be identified.

(g) Creating real burdens and servitudes using the Development Management Scheme

Although there is not yet much anecdotal evidence of the use of the Development Management Scheme, it has a number of extremely attractive elements that can help to provide a structure for the maintenance of a development. Practitioners who advise developers on a regular (or even infrequent) basis would benefit from becoming closely acquainted with the rules of the scheme, and the way in which it can operate and be adapted for use in any development.

(i) A statutory scheme for management

The Development Management Scheme (DMS) provided for in Part 6 of the TC(S)A 2003, and the full details of which are contained in the Title Conditions (Scotland) Act 2003 (Development Management Scheme) Order 2009 (SI 2009/729)S.2)) consists of a set of rules, similar to real burdens, that can be applied to land, which it is intended to develop with a number of units that will be subject to the same provisions ie as you would do in a Deed of Conditions. However, in contrast to the rules for management of tenements in the Tenement Management Scheme attached to the Tenements (Scotland) Act 2004, which automatically apply to tenements in default, the DMS is an optional scheme that you can choose to apply to your development or not, and with the ability to vary or omit some of the rules.

The rules provide a structure for management of shared facilities, and set out arrangements for a number of administrative matters, such as appointment of, and duties of a manager; convening meetings, and procedures at such meetings, eg constituting a quorum and voting arrangements; instructing emergency work; and financial matters including fixing a budget and applying service charge.

These rules function like real burdens and, in particular, community burdens, and specific provisions of the TC(S)A 2003 apply to these rules as they do to real burdens. With the exception of the rules that relate to having, and naming an Owners' Association, the rules in the DMS can be varied as you wish, added to or omitted, so that it is possible to tailor the DMS to the requirements of any development.

(ii) Form of deed of application of DMS

The DMS can be applied to the title by a deed of application. However, there is no fixed form required for such a deed and the DMS rules could either be used on their own, with some words of application attached, or, as is envisaged in the PSG Deed of Conditions, incorporated as a schedule into the Deed, with a clause of application of the DMS in the body of the Deed. Any variations to the DMS can be drafted in the Deed of Conditions or by amendment to the Schedule. Alternatively the DMS rules themselves could be incorporated in the body of the Deed, with the addition of amenity burdens dealing with use and maintenance.

(iii) Owners' Association

Application of the DMS to a development will set up an Owners' Association for the land, which will be a body corporate, and thus able to own land in its own name, enter into contracts and conduct other juristic acts of an entity with legal personality, which previous owners' associations were not able to do without incorporating or setting up some form of trust arrangement. All owners of units in the development will automatically be members of the Owners' Association, and the Owners' Association must have a manager to deal with the day to day management of the shared facilities.

With separate legal personality meaning that that the Owners' Association can take title to land, it is clearly an ideal vehicle for taking title to common parts of the development, either during the course of the development or at the end, and there is no reason why the common parts could not be conveyed to the owners' association in several parcels so there would appear to be no impediment to different sections of eg common parts being conveyed at different times. This raises interesting possibilities.

(iv) Enforcement of DMS rules

Under the rules of the DMS, the manager manages the development for the benefit of the members and has the power (so far as it is reasonable to do so) to enforce the provisions of the DMS and of any regulations which have taken effect, and any obligation owed by any person to the association (Rule 8). Accordingly the members (owners) themselves do not have enforcement rights in respect of the rules, although provision can easily be made for this if wanted (Article 10 of the TC(S) 2003 (DMS) Order 2009). One advantage of enforcement through the manager is that he does not need to show interest to enforce. This is another aspect of the DMS that may make it more attractive than the traditional Deed of Conditions route, given the uncertainty that surrounds interest to enforce.

(h) Trust clauses

Trust clauses go in and out of popularity according to the vicissitudes of the decisions of the courts. The purpose of the trust clause is to offer some protection to the purchaser from the seller's insolvency occurring in the period between settlement or completion (when the price has been paid and the disposition delivered), and perfecting a real right to the property by registering that disposition in the Land Register. A real right of ownership only passes when the purchaser effects such registration. Until then, the real right remains with the seller. The purchaser is exposed to the risk of the seller's sequestration or liquidation between settlement and registration. And because the real right in the property remains with the seller, it continues to form part of the seller's estate in the sequestration/ liquidation, and will be available to the seller's creditors. Floating charges are an exception as per the earlier House of Lords decision in *Sharp v Thomson* [1997] SC (HL) 66 the purchaser is safe even if the company goes into receivership on crystallisation of a floating charge in the 'gap' period.

Since the decision of the House of Lords in *Burnett's Trustee v Grainger* (2004 SC (HL) 19) (see KGC Reid and GL Gretton *Conveyancing 2004* pp 79-85) which confirmed that in cases of insolvency of any legal person (other than in the floating charge exception referred to above), there is still a race to the register, trust clauses have reappeared, although opinion is divided on their use and effectiveness, and even whether it is appropriate for the seller to be holding the property in trust for the purchaser at all. Some firms have taken the view neither to ask for a trust clause in dispositions in favour of their clients, nor to give trust clauses in dispositions by their clients. Academic opinion appears to be firmly against them, the consensus being that 'they have never really worked', and there is no clear trust purpose. It is also felt that recent changes to bankruptcy legislation render the clause unnecessary (s 17 BAD Act 2007 and see para 8.18(e)) (although note there is no such 28 day moratorium in corporate insolvency) and that the use of such clauses should be discontinued.

It is always incumbent on the purchaser's solicitor to submit the purchaser's disposition for registration as soon as possible after settlement/ completion. However if you **do** decide to seek a trust clause the following style may be of assistance:

The Seller declares that he/she/it/they hold[s] the Property in trust for the Purchaser absolutely until the earlier of 14 days from the date of entry, and the date of registration in the Land Register of Scotland of the Purchaser's interest in the Property, but for the sole purpose of holding title to the Property. From the Date of Entry the Seller qua trustee under the trust will not be under any duty to maintain or preserve the Property nor to insure the Property against fire or other insurable risks.

Some seller's solicitors will also include provision that the purchaser will indemnify the seller in respect of anything that imposes any liability on them in the period as a result of the trust.

(i) Supersession

The former rule that delivery of the disposition superseded the missives was considered to be a 'Bad Rule' and generated elaborate provisions in missives that were never entirely satisfactory in their effect. The SLC 'Report on Three Bad Rules in Contract Law' (Scot Law Com No 152) resulted in the Contract (Scotland) Act 1997 which flipped the rule over, so that as a result of s 2 of the C(S)A 1997, on delivery of a deed in implement of a contract, any unimplemented terms of the contract will not be superseded.

The practical effect of this is that, instead of having to provide in missives and in dispositions for the contract to survive delivery of the disposition for a period of time, it is now necessary to provide for expiry of the missives after a period – usually two years – from the date of delivery of the disposition, but according to circumstances if there are particular elements of the contract that require to remain in force for a longer time.

This is normally now dealt with in the missives and, strictly speaking, there is no longer any need to make provision in the disposition – since delivery of it no longer supersedes the contract which was really the point of 'non-supersession' clauses. The contract will normally provide for the provisions of the missives to cease to be enforceable after the specified period except in so far as they are founded on in any court proceedings which have commenced within the period stated (see paras 6.10(v) and 6.13(cc)). If, however, the missives are silent but the parties want to put a cap on the period then there is no reason why this could not be put into the disposition (s 2(2) of the C(S)A 1997) along similar lines:

And the Missives [either a defined term or (constituted by letters between [   ] and [   ] dated [   ] and [   ]) will cease to be enforceable after a period of [two] years from the Date of Entry except insofar as they are founded on in court proceedings which have commenced within the said period;

(j) Division of benefited properties

No form of words is necessary if it is intended that on the sale of part of a property which is already a benefited property in an existing burden, the part conveyed will cease to be a benefited property (see para 9.09(e)). If both the part conveyed and the part retained are separately to constitute benefited properties, or if the part retained is to cease to be a benefited property, then specific provision to this effect must be made in the disposition, for example:

> And we nominate the Conveyed Property to be a benefited property in respect of burden (Two) contained in Feu Disposition by Rowan Homes Ltd (in liquidation) in favour of Lightyear Development Company Ltd recorded in the Division of the General Register of Sasines for the county of Perth on Eleventh May, Two thousand;

(k) Importing Deeds of Conditions

The now repealed s 17 of the Land Registration (Scotland) Act 1979 provided that burdens set out in a deed of conditions would become real obligations burdening the land on recording or registration of that deed. It was possible to disapply s 17, so that the burdens would only have effect on a conveyance of plots of (or other units in) that land and reference was made in the disposition to application of the terms of the deed of conditions. A number of pre 28 November 2004 deeds of conditions disapplied s 17.

Accordingly the TC(S)A 2003, in repealing s 17 had to make provision to allow such deeds of conditions which applied to units or plots conveyed after 28 November 2004 to be capable of being imported into the title of the unit or plot, essentially to correct the old and new law. Section 6 of TC(S)A 2003 makes provision for importing the old deed of conditions into the title of the units being conveyed. Wording is given in Sch 1 of the TC(S)A 2003:

> There are imported the terms of the title conditions specified in Deed
> of Conditions by [ ] dated [   ] and [recorded in the Division of the
> General Register of Sasines for the County of [   ] on [   ]] [registered
> in the Land Register of Scotland under Title Number [   ] on [   ]];

There is no need to use this import wording in pre-2004 Deeds of
Conditions where s 17 had **not** been dis-applied, nor of course is it required
in relation to titles where Deeds of Conditions have been registered after
the appointed day.

(l) Community interest in land declaration

If the property is subject to an entry in the RCIL (see para 7.09) by which
a community body has registered an interest, the property cannot be sold
other than to that community. Section 40 of the Land Reform (Scotland)
Act 2003 sets out certain circumstances in which a property can be sold
regardless of an entry in the RCIL, including the situation where the sale
is in implement of missives that were concluded on a date before the entry
appeared on the RCIL.

Where one of the s 40 exemptions applies, the disposition must contain
a declaration to that effect. The PSG wording for this declaration is:

> [The Seller declares that the transfer effected by this disposition is
> excluded from the operation of s 40(1) of the Land Reform (Scotland)
> Act 2003 by virtue of para [insert appropriate para number] of s
> 40(4) of that Act][*If, but only if, the exempting paragraph is (a),
> (e) or (h) insert the following*: The Seller further declares that the
> transfer effected by this disposition does not form part of a scheme
> or arrangement and is not one of a series of transfers mentioned in s
> 43(1) of the said Act];

Part of the difficulty here is one of timing. There may be no entry in
the RCIL when you draft the disposition, but if one appears just before
completion, a declaration is required. Obviously if the property is in an
area which is excluded land for the purposes of the community right to
buy provisions in Part 2 of the LR(S)A 2003, no wording will ever be
necessary, since it is not possible to acquire excluded land by way of the
community right to buy. Excluded land is defined in The Community
Right to Buy (Definition of Excluded Land) Order 2009 (SSI2009/207),

and plans are available online, which delineate the excluded areas so it is easy to check.

However, if there is a possibility that an entry could appear in the RCIL at the last minute (and of course the owner of the land should be well aware of this possibility since the preparations of a community body leading up to registration will be well known), then it would be worth inserting the necessary declaration into the disposition anyway, to avoid the deed being rejected by the Keeper. A declaration that turns out to be unnecessary will not invalidate a disposition.

If you have incorporated a declaration on a 'just in case' basis but it turns out not to be necessary, because no interest is registered in the RCIL, you should point this out in your application for registration, to avoid unnecessary requisitions having to be made by the staff at the Registers. The PSG suggests the following wording for a covering letter to the Keeper:

> The Property disponed in favour of the Applicant does not lie within 'excluded' land as defined in regulations made under Part 2 of the Land Reform (Scotland) Act 2003. Accordingly we have included in the disposition a declaration, under s 40/43 of the Land Reform (Scotland) Act 2003, to allow registration of the disposition in the event of an entry, affecting the Property, being made in the Register of Community of Community Interests in Land ('RCIL') in the period between conclusion of missives for the sale of the Property, and registration of the Applicant's title.
>
> We understand that a declaration of this type will neither invalidate a deed, nor an application for registration, in the event that the declaration is not ultimately required. No such entry in the RCIL has been made as at today's date. If this remains the case [(and we have no reason to believe otherwise)] as at the date of registration of the Applicant's title, please disregard the declaration.

(m) Application to the Lands Tribunal

There is in theory no reason why a burdened owner could not now apply to the Lands Tribunal for discharge of a burden as soon as it has been created (although it is not known how the Lands Tribunal would regard such an application). Section 92 of the TC(S)A 2003 allows the parties to impose a moratorium on applications to the Lands Tribunal to vary the terms of the burdens or servitudes, for up to a maximum period of five years, and if the parties agree, the following clause preventing applications to the Lands Tribunal can be included. It is now fairly common to insert this clause as a matter of course in deeds that create new burdens and servitudes:

> No application may be made to the Lands Tribunal for Scotland under s 90(1)(a)(i) of the Title Conditions (Scotland) Act 2003 in respect of the [real burdens set out in [Part [ ] of the Schedule] [and] [the servitudes set out in Part [ ] of the Schedule] for a period of [five years] after the registration of this disposition in the Land Register of Scotland;

(n) Entry

Generally expressed either as 'entry and actual occupation' or 'entry and vacant possession'. It is customary to insert the date on which the purchaser is entitled to take entry to the property into the disposition. The clause may also refer to 'vacant possession', although this is not appropriate if the property is leased and is being bought for investment purposes. Traditional wording also distinguished the date of entry from the date of execution of the deed, but this wording is often now omitted:

> WITH ENTRY and actual occupation as at 14 March 2012 [notwithstanding the date hereof];

(o) Warrandice

Warrandice in the context of transfer of heritable property is a guarantee from the granter that the title is good. A disposition of heritable property will usually contain a clause of absolute warrandice. If the deed omits a clause of warrandice, then warrandice is implied, and the type of warrandice implied will depend on the nature of the transaction. Accordingly if the granter intends to grant no warrandice, then the deed must say 'And I grant no warrandice'.

If the granter of the title knows that there is a problem with an aspect of the title, then that aspect can be excluded from the warrandice.

(i) Absolute warrandice protects the purchaser from the past and future acts and deeds of the disponer, and from the acts of third parties and is a

guarantee from the granter that the title is good, and not subject to unusual conditions of title that are unknown to the disponee. It is expressed by the words 'And I/we grant warrandice'.

(ii) Fact and deed warrandice is a guarantee against both the future acts or deeds and the past acts or deeds of the granter. In effect it is an undertaking by the disponer that he has not done anything in the past, and will do nothing in the future to prejudice the title granted in the disposition. This type of warrandice is usually given by granters acting in some representative capacity, such as executors or trustees, in which case generally they will also bind the trust or the executry estate in absolute warrandice. It is expressed by the words 'And I grant warrandice from my own facts and deeds only'.

(iii) Simple warrandice is usual where the property is being transferred for no consideration eg a gift, and indeed is implied in such deeds unless other provision is made. It offers protection from the future voluntary acts or deeds of the granter but not past ones, or third party acts. It is expressed by the words 'And I grant simple warrandice'.

Some examples of warrandice clauses used in particular cases are:

> And I grant warrandice, but declaring that warrandice is excluded to the extent that the Keeper has excluded indemnity in respect of that strip of ground shown shaded in pink on the attached plan.

> And we the said [   ] and [   ] grant warrandice from our own facts and deeds only and bind the Trust Estate under our charge in absolute warrandice:

> And I the said [   ] as Trustee foresaid grant no warrandice but in so far as I have power to do so bind the Sequestrated Estate under my charge in absolute warrandice

> And we grant warrandice, but excepting from warrandice the Lease between [   ] and [   ] dated [   ] and registered in the Land Register of Scotland under Title Number [   ]

(iv) Warrandice in insolvency transactions. It used to be reasonably usual market practice for the insolvent company to grant some form of warrandice. These days however, Insolvency Practitioners are far more cautious about incorporating such warrandice into any conveyance of property. The records of the company may be unclear or in disarray and

the IP may not be able to ascertain that the company did not in the past grant any deeds that might conflict with what is being granted in the transaction.

There might in any event be little value in a grant of warrandice by an insolvent company, whose assets may already be fully secured to or distributed among its creditors. Although it is possible that the company might one day recommence trading, it is equally possible that it will be wound up. An IP is also going to be very wary about committing the company to the possibility of a future claim on warrandice, the value of which is entirely unknown, and which potentially could impact on the position of the other creditors, not to mention the IP's own expenses.

Also and in particular, if the disposition is following on an asset sale or other transfer arrangement, it may be the case that it has already been agreed that no warrandice or title guarantee will be given. If that is the case then a purchaser would not be entitled to insist on any warrandice in the disposition, and so this should be checked.

There is considerable debate among the profession about whether or not to include fact and deed warrandice by the IP. On one view, this limited degree of warrandice is probably not of great value to the purchaser, although solicitors acting for purchasers do like to see something.

However, it is now the invariable practice of IPs to insist that nothing in the contract or in the conveyance in any way implies or expresses personal liability upon them. Indeed most also now insist, not only on no grant of warrandice, but also that the exclusion of personal liability is also incorporated into the disposition. In some drafting you may see both fact and deed warrandice and an exclusion of personal liability, and there is clearly an inconsistency between the two statements.

When acting for a purchaser from an insolvent company therefore, you should expect that neither the IP nor the insolvent company will grant any warrandice, and personal liability of the IP will also be excluded.

If the purchaser insists on having a grant of warrandice from the IP, then this might have to be explored in individual circumstances. Fact and deed warrandice does impose personal liability on the IP, however minor that may be. Solicitors acting for IPs in these circumstances **must** get specific instructions from the IP before agreeing to such a proposal.

For commentary on the issues surrounding warrandice and insolvency practitioners, see the article in JLSS by Kenneth Ross and Colin Gilchrist: 'To grant or not to grant?' 19 April 2010. (http://www.journalonline.co.uk/Magazine/55-4/1007936.aspx)

The absence of warrandice from either the company or the IP should not pose any problems with the Keeper's indemnity when it comes to registering the title, provided the title is good. The Keeper will exclude indemnity where there is a defect in the title, but the absence of warrandice is not a defect (although there are circumstances where a seller does exclude warrandice because of a defect). When faced with an absence of warrandice, the Keeper will enquire into the circumstances, and the Keeper recognises that a sale by an IP will invariably omit or qualify warrandice for reasons that are nothing to do with the title.

CONTRACTS OF EXCAMBION

9.11 Circumstances may arise where the parties wish to exchange areas of land and, while this can be done by way of separate dispositions, there is also a form of deed – the Contract of Excambion, whereby the whole exchange can be narrated in one deed. In the days before stamp duty land tax (SDLT) there used to be a benefit to using an excambion, if the values of the properties were the same, there was only a nominal payment of stamp duty. However under SDLT rules, the tax (if any is due) is calculated on each of the transfers, and as a result, the popularity of the Contract of Excambion has waned. They were never particularly easy documents to draft, incorporating, as they do, all the elements of two dispositions, with all the descriptive, part and portion and burdens clauses having to be incorporated, there was huge scope for a very confusing document to result. Drafting when both properties are registered in the Land Register would be significantly simpler, of course.

FURTHER READING

Conveyancing by GL Gretton and KGC Reid 4th Edition (W Green: Publication due Autumn 2011)

Servitudes and Rights of Way be DJ Cusine and R Paisley (W Green 1998)

There are a number of detailed commentaries on the PMP Plus case, the best of which is probably Gretton & Reid Conveyancing 2008 (pages 136 to 149) and Conveyancing 2009 (pages 122 to 127).

Chapter 10

Security

SECURED LENDING

10.01 Most purchasers of heritable property will need to borrow funds to finance the purchase. This applies equally to residential and commercial property. When a bank, building society or other lending institution makes money available for the purchase or financing of heritable property, it will require, amongst other things, to be granted a fixed charge over the title to the property. That fixed charge will be registered against the borrower's title to the property and gives the creditor a certain amount of control over the voluntary sale of the property, effectively preventing the borrower from selling the property and making off with the sale proceeds without repaying the loan. It also provides the lender with powers and remedies in the event the borrower defaults on the loan. While the lending criteria may be different depending on the type of property, the document by which such lending is protected is the same – the 'Standard Security'.

THE LEGISLATIVE BASIS FOR STANDARD SECURITIES

10.02 Since November 1970, the Standard Security is the only form of document by which a fixed charge over heritable property in Scotland may be created. You may, in the course of examination of title, come across earlier forms of heritable security such as the bond and disposition in security, or the *ex facie* absolute disposition, but none of these documents can now be used for creating a fixed charge over property.

Standard securities were introduced by the Conveyancing and Feudal Reform (Scotland) Act 1970 which also covered other aspects of property law reform, including the procedure for variation and discharge of land obligations by the constitution of a Lands Tribunal for Scotland – the precursor to the provisions in Part 9 of the TC(S)A 2003, and the reduction of the period of prescriptive possession from 20 years to 10 years.

The CFR(S)A 1970 contains a number of forms and styles of the documents and procedures which it introduces, including the Standard Security and forms for Assignation of a standard security, a Deed of Restriction, a Discharge, and a Deed of Variation of a standard security.

CFR(S)A 1970 also introduced a codified set of conditions which automatically apply to the provisions of any standard security, without the need to mention it in the document. These Standard Conditions, contained in Sch 3 of the CFR(S)A 1970, relate to practical matters aimed at preserving the value of the property, such as maintenance and repair, alterations and letting of properties, as well as enforcement such as calling-up and notices of default. Most, but not all of them can be varied to suit the lender's specific requirements.

The enforcement rights of heritable creditors in the event of default by the borrower are also set out in the CFR(S)A 1970.

THE STANDARD SECURITY AND OTHER FORMS

(a) Standard Security

10.03 The CFR(S)A 1970 provides that a Standard Security may be in one of two forms. Styles of Form A and Form B are given in Sch 2 of the CFR(S)A 1970. These statutory forms give some uniformity to securities, while providing flexibility to cater for the many different lending criteria.

Form A is used where both the personal obligation of the debtor as well as the details of the mortgage and the grant of security over the property are all contained in the one document. This form is the one that is most widely used by lenders in residential mortgages.

Form B just contains the grant security over the property, and the personal obligation and sometimes also the details of the mortgage do not appear on the face of the security, but are contained in a separate unregistered document. This method is mostly used in commercial loans where the lending arrangements are often complex and lengthy (see para 10.03(b)).

A simple form of Form A security using the style in Sch 2 of CFR(S) A 1970:

> WE, FREDERICK ROWAN, residing at Piemonte House, Kelvinforth Perthshire and MISS FLEUR LAPIN MONK residing at 27 Lombardy Street, Kelvinforth, Perthshire (the 'Borrower') hereby undertake to

pay [*this is the personal obligation part*] to SCOTLAND BANK PLC incorporated under the Companies Acts and having its registered office at Alba House, Corries Road, Edinburgh and its successors and assignees (the 'Bank') on demand the sum of TWO HUNDRED THOUSAND Pounds Sterling (£200,000) with interest from [date to be inserted] at 3.95 per centum per annum payable monthly on the First day of each month commencing on [date to be inserted] and all sums of principal, interest and charges now due and that may become due to the Bank in any manner of way by us whether solely or jointly with any other person or persons, corporation, firm or other body and whether as principal or surety; And any account or certificate signed by the Treasurer and General Manager, or other person so authorised by the Bank shall ascertain, specify and constitute the sums or balances of principal, interest and charges due and that may become due as aforesaid; For which sums we the said Frederick Rowan and Miss Fleur Lapin Monk GRANT a Standard Security in favour of the Bank [*this is the standard security part*] over ALL and WHOLE the subjects known as Flat 12 Florence Park, Kelvinforth, registered in the Land Register of Scotland under Title Number PTH2803; The Standard Conditions [*see para 10.04 below*] specified in Sch 3 to the Conveyancing and Feudal Reform (Scotland) Act 1970, as amended, and any lawful variation thereof operative for the time being shall apply and we agree that Standard Condition 5(a) shall be varied to the effect that the sum for which the security subjects shall be insured in terms of said Condition 5(a) shall be reinstatement value and not market value [*this variation is always made in practice*]; And we grant warrandice; And we consent to registration of these presents and of the said account or certificate aforementioned for execution; IN WITNESS WHEREOF

Note that it is sufficient to describe the security subjects so as to identify them so that a postal address or other common law description would be sufficient (AFT(S)A 2000 Sch 12, para 30(23)). For property registered in the Land Register the Title Number should also be included and, for safety, a Sasine description eg by reference to a descriptive writ should ideally be used.

A Form B security is made up as above, but omitting the personal obligation, the amount of the loan, the rate of interest and repayment details, and the consent to registration for execution, which are contained in a separate unregistered minute of agreement. In commercial loans this document may also carry heavy variations of the standard conditions and trading conditions.

The majority of lenders - banks, building societies and funding institutions will have their preferred style or format of standard security, and this will be provided to the lender's solicitors as part of their instructions. Most of these documents are now produced electronically and a number of lenders provide their solicitors with electronic versions of their branded documents in their preferred style and format.

Usually, lenders try to resist revisals to their house style. It is rare for any amendments to be made to residential standard securities, which are usually pretty straightforward affairs. For commercial securities, permitted revisals will depend upon individual circumstances.

If any collateral security is given to the lender, such as a life assurance policy, an assignation of that additional security must be drawn up, signed by the borrower and intimated to the life assurance company. Forms of assignation and intimation will also be provided by the lender with their instructions.

After a standard security has been granted and registered, it is possible to assign it to another creditor (s 14 of the CFR(S)A 1970); to make amendments to the extent of the property it secures, or the amount of the debt to which it relates (s 15 of the CFR(S)A 1970); vary its terms as between debtor and creditor (s 16 of the CFR(S)A 1970), or to discharge it completely when the loan has been repaid, or the obligations it secures have been satisfied (s 17 of the CFR(S)A 1970). See paras 10.03 (c) to (f) below.

(b) Personal obligation – personal bond

As we have seen the security must contain two components – the obligation to pay or perform, and the grant of the security over the property. When a Form B style of security is used, the personal obligation is contained in a separate document, the simplest form of which is the personal bond. Instead of the undertaking to pay, the Form B standard security will say:

> 'We..........hereby IN SECURITY of all sums due and that may become due to Scotland Bank plc.....and its successors and assignees (the 'Bank') in terms of Personal Bond granted by us the said...in favour of the Bank dated......'

The Personal Bond will contain more or less the first section of the wording in the style Form A security, with reference to rates and payment, or may relate to all sums that may be due at any time or from time to time and so can be used in a flexible way. The personal obligation of the debtor can relate to any obligation due, or to become due at a point in the future, to repay money or pay money, or to do something or perform some act, (an *ad factum praestandum* security). This type of security obligation is sometimes used to secure performance of development obligations. Where the personal obligation is located in a separate deed in this way, it can be referred to in several standard securities, which need not be granted at the same time as the personal bond.

Most commercial lenders will usually look for an 'all sums' security. This provides that the Borrower will pay all sums which are due to the lender in any manner of way, including interest, charges, costs etc, and thus can relate to several different loans. Some 'all sums' obligations may relate to a specific loan or facility arrangement between the borrower and the lender – for a particular project or development.

There is also a distinction that can be made between 'direct' and 'indirect' securities, and they appear in both residential and commercial loans. A direct security is one which is granted by the borrower over property that he owns, in security of his own debts and obligations. An indirect security is one where the borrower grants the personal obligation to pay or perform in respect of the debt or obligation, but someone else grants the security over property owned by that third party. Situations where this might arise are where an individual is prepared to give security over his house in security of borrowings by his business which he runs through a company, or a close relative may provide a property in security of the indebtedness of a family member. Clearly the circumstances in which such securities are taken must be considered with care, since the third party granting the security is placing their property at the risk of performance of the obligation to pay or perform of another party, and they may have little or no control over how that person manages their affairs.

Before an indirect security is granted, it is important to ensure that the third party has received independent legal advice. There are many cases of indirect security arrangements over matrimonial homes where the lender's security was reduced because the parties to the security were not given proper advice as to the effect of the document they were signing (see para 10.05(c)).

(c) Assignation

A standard security can be assigned by the lender (s 14 of CFR(S)A 1970) and there are two styles of assignation. These are contained in Sch 4 of CFR(S)A 1970 and may be in Form A (a separate document) or Form B (endorsed on the standard security). Unless provided for in ancillary documentation, the borrower's consent is not required to an assignation, nor does it require to be intimated, although it must be registered in the Register of Sasines or Land Register to be effective. This procedure can be used by lenders to raise finance, by selling their portfolio of loans to another lender.

Assigning a standard security is not without its pitfalls, however. Special care needs to be taken when assigning a Form B type standard security, where the personal obligation is contained in a separate deed, as the obligation in respect of the debt also has to be assigned. Otherwise the new lender would have security over the property, but no obligation from the debtor to make any payment to it. A document known as a bond of corroboration of the obligations of the debtor may be required in addition to the assignation in these circumstances. This will, in effect, confirm or corroborate the personal obligations of the borrower in favour of the new lender. It is always open to the lender to discharge the existing security, and for a new one to be constituted in favour of the new lender, but one of the advantages of assigning the existing security is that the priority or ranking of the original security is preserved. If there are other securities over the property that are registered after the original security, they would gain a prior ranking status if the original security is discharged (see para 10.06(f)).

It would be unusual, but not impossible, for a standard security to be assigned by the borrower to a new borrower, but it is not an attractive option, given that the assignation does not discharge the original borrower.

(d) Variation

Variation may be appropriate where any alteration of the standard security is required which is not a change of lender, when assignation might be suitable, or a change to the amount or area, when a deed of restriction would be appropriate. Variation of the security in the style of Form E in Sch 4 of CFR(S)A 1970 would deal for example with changing the debtor (eg transferring title to the property and the corresponding security from joint names to just one of the parties), or to correct an error in the original standard security, or to alter some of the original lending criteria.

(e) **Deed of Restriction**

The Deed of Restriction (also sometimes called a Deed of Disburdenment) operates to restrict the terms of the standard security by removing part of the security subjects from its ambit and can also operate as a partial discharge of the standard security. Again there are statutory forms in Sch 4 of CFR(S)A 1970 - either Form C which disburdens the property described in it from the security, or Form D, which incorporates a partial discharge as well. A full description of the subjects being disburdened, ideally (and usually) with a plan, should be incorporated in the deed of restriction. Such deeds are typical in transactions that deal with the sale of plots in a development, where the developer granted a standard security over the whole site. On the occasion of each plot sale, in addition to granting a disposition of the plot, the same description and plan are used to for the deed of restriction, which is signed by the creditor and delivered to the purchaser at settlement, to be registered along with title to the plot in favour of the purchaser.

(f) **Discharge**

Form F of Sch 4 of CFR(S)A 1970 contains the style to use for a document that discharges the standard security in its entirety.

All deeds assigning, varying, restricting or discharging a standard security must be recorded or registered in the appropriate Property Register. If the title to the property is still in the Sasine Register and all that it happening is that the security is being discharged, the discharge will not induce a first registration, so the discharge should be recorded in the Sasine Register too. The grant of a standard security on its own does not induce a first registration in the Land Register either (although it may be noted that under the proposals of the Scottish Law Commission (see para

2.09) there is a prospect that, in future, and to accelerate the completion of the Register, the grant of a standard security may induce first registration). There is an example discharge of standard security in Appendix 1.

THE STANDARD CONDITIONS

10.04 There are a number of typical conditions that all or most lenders would want to apply to the basis on which they are lending money on a property, and that the borrower should be obliged to do – maintain and insure the property for example, or comply with any statutory notices that are served on the property. Section 11 of the CFR(S)A 1970 provides that a number of conditions and obligations that are 'standard' in any lending situation should be incorporated automatically into every grant of a standard security. These conditions, known as the 'Standard Conditions' are listed in Sch 3 of CFR(S)A 1970 and are intended to make sure that the borrowers do not imperil the security of the lenders by allowing the value to deteriorate, and if they do, the lenders are entitled to several remedies.

(a) The Standard Conditions

The standard conditions are either variable (V), non-variable (NV), or partially non-variable (PNV). Variable conditions may be, and in practice often are, varied by the lenders either within the standard security itself or by a longer, separate deed of variations, which will usually be registered in the Books of Council and Session. Most large lenders tend to favour the latter method, and print the variations and give a print to the borrowers. The standard conditions are summarised as follows, and their appropriate status is marked:

(1) *Maintenance and repair:* The borrower is to keep the property in good and sufficient repair throughout the loan period, in order that the lender's security is not endangered. He must allow the lender to enter the property and inspect the state of repair on 7 days notice being given (V).

(2) *Completion of buildings and prohibition of alterations*: The borrower is to complete buildings but make alterations, extensions, or demolish the property only with the lenders' authority, in

accordance with any statutory consents or licences and exhibit evidence of these. Obviously, carrying out alterations, or failing adequately to maintain the property could have an adverse effect upon the value of the security subjects. (V)

(3) *Observance of conditions in title and general compliance with law*: The borrower is to observe any condition or perform any obligation that applies to the property, including paying rates (or Council Tax) and taxes, and comply with any requirements of law imposed by statute. This would include complying with any statutory repair notices. (V)

(4) *Planning notices etc*: The borrower is to deal with planning and other notices, and provide the lender with copies of any received, and if appropriate and the lender wishes to object to a planning notice, the borrower is to object or join with the lender in objecting to the notice: eg proposals for an unsuitable use of neighbouring property that might damage the value or amenity of the security subjects (V).

(5) *Insurance*: The borrower is to insure (or permit the lender to insure) the property for 'market value', and the proceeds of any claim are to be dealt with as directed by the creditor. 'Market value' is almost universally replaced in standard conditions by 'reinstatement value' (see eg the style in para 10.03(a)), especially in older buildings built with traditional materials and craftsmanship, where the cost of replacing on a like for like basis will be in excess of the market value. The borrower must pay the insurance premiums, and also let the lender know in the event of any claim. For commercial properties that are let to occupational tenants, the leases will usually provide that the landlord must insure on specific terms and the tenants will make payment of the premium. It may be necessary to vary this Standard Condition to ensure that it is compatible with the insurance provisions in the leases (V).

(6) *Restriction on letting*: The borrower is not to let the property without the lender's consent. In practice for residential property, this means that the lenders must approve the terms of the letting, and ensure that the requisite notices are served to prevent the

tenant obtaining security of tenure, which would affect the lender's security. For commercial properties which are, or are going to be, the subject of occupational leases, a suitable variation of this standard condition is required (V).

(7)　*General power of creditor to perform on failure of debtor*: If the borrower does not fulfil any of the duties imposed by the standard conditions, the lender may do so itself, at the borrower's expense, and is entitled, on giving notice, to enter the property for this purpose. (V).

(8)　*Calling up*: A lender is entitled to enforce the security by the calling up procedure set out in s 19 of CFR(S)A 1970, if the lender wishes to require repayment of the loan, where the borrower is in arrears and unable to pay, for example. See para 10.08. The lender may exercise the remedies provided in standard condition 10. (V)

(9)　*Default:* A borrower will be in default (a) where a calling-up notice in respect of the security has been served and has not been complied with; (b) where there has been a failure to comply with any other requirement arising out of the security; or (c) where the proprietor of the security subjects has become insolvent (V).

(10)　*Rights of creditor on default:* This Standard Condition sets out the remedies given to the lender if the borrower is in default:

　[(10)(1)　The lender will be entitled to exercise any other remedies arising from the contract to which the standard security relates, and also exercise the remedies given in the following paragraphs in accordance with the operative provisions of CFR(S)A 1970, in particular ss 19 to 25 and any other relevant enactment (V).

　(10)(2)　Sell the property (see para 8.18 (c)) (NV).

　(10)(3)　Enter into possession of the property and receive or recover rents (V).

　(10)(4)　Let the property (V).

　(10)(5)　Grant leases of the property, and manage and maintain it (V).

　(10)(6)　Repair, reconstruct, alter and improve the property (V).

(10)(7)   Foreclosure. This is a remedy carried forward from the C(S)A 1924, which enables the lender, after an unsuccessful attempt to sell the property, to petition the court to convert a security title into an absolute one. It is probably rarely appropriate, as the CFR(S) A 1970 gives lenders ample powers anyway, and is in reality rarely used. The Standard Condition relating to sale and foreclosure (Standard Condition 10) may not be varied either directly or indirectly. Any other variation of the Standard Conditions which may have the effect of varying this non-variable Condition will not be effective. (NV)]

(11)   *Exercise of right of Redemption:* The borrower is entitled redeem the loan on giving notice of intention to the lender. This provision was intended to prevent borrowers from being locked into loans on a long term basis. This does not affect any contractual provisions that may have been applied to a mortgage requiring payment of an early redemption penalty. This provision is non-variable (in other words, the debtor must always be entitled to a right to redeem the loan), but the lender may dispense with a formal notice, or choose to vary or dispense with any period of notice to which he is entitled (NV).

(12)   *Debtor liable for expenses:* The borrower is liable for the expenses of the preparation and execution of the standard security, any discharge or partial discharge or restriction of the security, registration dues, and any costs incurred by the creditor in enforcing the security. The borrower is, however, not liable for the expenses of the assignation of the standard security to a third party (V).

(b) Variation of Standard Conditions

Any changes can be made to the variable Standard Conditions, and are often done so according to circumstances and the type of loan facility being made available. If the property consists of a development in the course of construction, a borrower may wish to have the provisions relating to completion of buildings and the prohibition against alterations (Standard

Condition 2) tailored to suit the actual circumstances. For investment properties, which are subject to occupational leases, the borrower may want the standard conditions relating to letting and the insurance of the subjects varied. A Standard Condition can also be excluded in its entirety, provided it is not Non Variable.

(c) Additional Conditions

Entirely new conditions can also be imported into a standard security over and above the Standard Conditions. A number of lenders incorporate considerable additional conditions in their house style standard securities, either in the body of the deed itself, or, by way of a separate 'Deed of Variation of Standard Conditions' which is then referred to within each standard security. Conditions relating to specialist types of property, such as industrial or agricultural property or licensed premises can also be built in.

ACTING FOR THE RESIDENTIAL LENDER

(a) Acting for both purchaser and lender

10.05 Most loans for the purchase of residential property are made by banks or building societies, or former building societies that have become banks. Other bodies may be lenders, such as local authorities, particularly in the purchase of public sector housing. Broadly speaking, however, the procedure is the same whoever the lender may be. Lenders are now represented by a central body known as the Council of Mortgage Lenders (CML), the mortgage lenders' representative body, which produces a Handbook detailing the practices of various lenders, and issuing standard forms (see para 10.05 (b)).

Generally, lenders will permit solicitors acting for the borrower in the purchase of a house, to act on the lender's behalf as well, provided the solicitors are on their approved list or panel, if they have one. This practice, which is permitted under the Solicitors (Scotland) (Standards of Conduct) Practice Rules 2008 (which incorporates the conflict of interest provisions in the Solicitors (Scotland) Practice Rules 1986 preventing solicitors acting for two or more parties, with conflicting interests), means a substantial saving on duplication of work, and thus a saving of costs payable by the borrowers.

Law Society guidelines permit the solicitor to act for both borrower and lender, despite the apparent conflict of interest. In terms of Rule 5 (1) (f) of the S(S)P Rules 1986 the terms of the loan must have been agreed between the parties before the solicitor has been instructed by the lender and the granting of the security must only be to give effect to such agreement. It should always be borne in mind however, that if a genuine conflict of interest does emerge, the solicitors must immediately stop acting for both parties. You must always remember that the lender is also a client. Solicitors must not reveal information to one client and not the other, eg information as to prices paid for the property. This was clearly established in *Mortgage Express v Bowerman & Partners* ([1996] 2 All ER 808). If solicitors find themselves in possession of information that is clearly detrimental to one of the parties, they are under a duty to reveal it to the other party, for whom they also act. If they feel unable to do so, they should then withdraw from acting.

In residential lending, the borrower will receive an offer of loan which will set out the basic terms and conditions on which the loan will be made and there are usually also extensive standard terms and conditions which the borrower is required to acknowledge (see the example Offer of Loan in Appendix 1). The borrower's solicitor will receive a copy of the offer of loan, and should take time to explain the meaning and implications of the loan to his clients and encourage them to read the material and raise any questions they might have. There can be a bewildering amount of paper work generated at this time and the solicitor should make sure that his client understands the key elements of the mortgage he is taking, and particularly the details of any lock-in arrangements or early redemption penalties, and whether or not a fixed or capped rate mortgage is 'portable' (ie if the property is sold during the period of the fixed rate, but the borrower takes out a new mortgage with the same lender over his new property, that the fixed rate can be transferred to the new mortgage with no redemption penalties).

The following conveyancing steps should be taken by the solicitor acting for both purchaser and lender:

- Receive and carefully peruse the lender's instructions, noting any specific conditions that have to be complied with;

- Check provisions of CML handbook for particular lender (see para 10.05(b));

- After examining title (see Chapter 8), they draft a standard security and any other papers required by the lenders.

- Have the standard security and other papers signed by the borrowers.

- If title is taken in the name of one spouse or civil partner only, obtain consent by the non-entitled spouse/civil partner (Note that this can be incorporated in to the standard security or in a separate deed. See para 4.07 (d) for Matrimonial Homes and Civil Partnership documentation generally. In the same way that a seller's solicitor must obtain the necessary document for satisfying the purchaser's solicitors, so too must the borrower's solicitor ensure that the lender's position is protected against the occupancy rights of a non entitled spouse or civil partner.

- For single borrowers, obtain Matrimonial Homes or Civil Partnership declarations as appropriate relative to the granting of the standard security.

- Send the report on title to the lenders, with the firm's opinion that the title is in order, and request the loan funds. This should be done in good time for settlement, allowing sufficient time for funds to be organised and remitted to the solicitor's bank account. Loan instructions will often specify the amount of notice that the lender requires for draw down of funds. It can be as much as 10 working days.

- The standard security with a completed and signed form 2 should accompany the disposition to the Land Register.

- Intimate any assignation of a life assurance policy to the assurance company in duplicate to validate the transfer, and on return one receipted copy is put with the assignation document

- Check any insurance requirements. The lenders may insure the property against fire and other damage but may require that the borrower arranges this. If the latter make sure that the borrower has arranged for insurance cover from the date of entry, if not before.

(b) CML Handbook

The Council of Mortgage Lenders is the trade association for the mortgage lending industry, whose members, which includes banks, building societies and other mortgage lenders, are responsible for around 94% of residential mortgage lending in the UK. The CML provides support, and acts as a representative voice for its members and residential lending, as well as providing research, statistics, training and information.

One of the key resources produced by the CML is the Lenders' Handbook. This provides detailed instructions for solicitors acting on behalf of lenders in residential transactions, and has separate handbooks for Scotland, England and Wales, Northern Ireland and the Isle of Man. Your instructions from an individual lender will indicate if you are being instructed in accordance with the CML Handbook. If you are, the general provisions in part 1 and any lender specific requirements in part 2 must be followed. In addition you may receive further instructions applicable to the individual loan.

Part 1 is the main set of instructions that apply to all mortgages by CML lenders. Part 2 contains specific requirements of each lender who is a member, overlaid onto the provisions of Part 1. Many lenders requirements will be the same as the Part 1 provisions, in which case no changes will be made, but where they have different or additional requirements these will be specified.

Accordingly the CML handbook should be your first port of call whenever you receive instructions from a lender in a residential transaction. It may even be a good idea to check for a lender's specific requirements as soon as you know who will be providing finance to your client, in case of any specific variations which might affect your clients purchase or which might have to be incorporated into the missives. Your duty to the lender when acting on its behalf will include compliance with its CML handbook requirements.

The CML Handbook is available online at www.cml.org.uk/cml/handbook. First select the appropriate region/country from the dropdown menu, and then select the appropriate lender from the further dropdown selection. You can choose to see Part 1 only (the main conditions) Parts 1 and 2 (the main provisions overlaid with the particular lender's requirements) or Part 2 only (specific requirements only)

The handbook contains general instructions as to the standard of care expected of the conveyancer, and requirements to comply with Accounts Rules, Money laundering regulations and professional guidance and codes as well as the basis on which communications between the solicitor and lender should be conducted. It also provides instructions regarding the valuation of the property, and in the case of new properties whether a re-inspection is required before drawdown of funds. All of the due diligence elements are covered, such as title examination, reports and enquiries, title conditions and servitudes, adoption of roads and sewers, insurance, MH(FP)(S)A 1981 or CPA 2004 rights and planning and building regulations issues. Also covered are home warranty schemes for new build homes, or, in their absence, the requirement for a Professional Consultants' Certificate (see para 6.11(c)(xi)).

The Handbook also reminds you to explain the terms of the standard security and any other documentation to the borrower, and that your fees and outlays are payable by the borrower too.

Types of mortgages: A short word about residential mortgages. The 5th edition of this book provided details of some typical types of residential mortgages available and the different repayment methods. It was about that time that problems with terminal payments on endowment policies linked to mortgages was becoming a common theme, and given the borrowing difficulties encountered by purchasers during the recession, the mortgage market, never an uncomplicated place, has become increasingly elaborate. Residential purchasers seeking mortgage advice should consult specialist mortgage advisers with access to detailed product information, to ensure that they obtain the best mortgage product most suitable to their requirements.

(c) Acting for spouses

When conveyancers are asked to act for a married couple in a conveyancing transaction, they may do so, since acting for related parties is exempted from the general rule of conflict of interest, laid down by the Solicitors (Scotland) Practice Rules 1986. There is a temptation to treat a married couple as one unit, but it should be remembered that husband and wife have separate interests, and the solicitor must ensure that both partners signing the standard security understand its terms and effect.

Difficulties can, and frequently do arise in situations where a wife is asked to sign a standard security over the marital home, in support of the husband's business, (or vice versa, of course). These are referred to by George Gretton as 'cautionary wives'. It is essential to ensure that the spouse receives independent legal advice as to the nature and effect of the obligation, as the various cases over the years have illustrated (see *Barclays Bank v O'Brien* [1994] 1 AC 180; *Bank of Scotland v Smith* [1997] SC (HL) 111, *The Royal Bank of Scotland v Etridge (No 2)* [2001] 3 WLR 1021, and *Clydesdale Bank plc v Black* [2002] SC 555).

The House of Lords decision in *The Royal Bank of Scotland plc v Etridge (No 2)* set an extremely high threshold for the 'core minimum requirements' necessary for solicitors acting in cases where one party in the relationship, usually the wife, acts as guarantor of the other party's business debts. Given that it was a House of Lords decision, for a short period it seemed as though its requirements would apply in Scotland, but two Court of Session cases (*Clydesdale Bank plc v Black* decided in the Inner House in 2002 and the Outer House decision in *Thomson v The Royal Bank of Scotland plc* 28 October 2003 (unreported)) made it clear that the 'core minimum requirements' set out in the *Etridge (No 2)* case do not apply to the substantive law of Scotland, where the position is governed by the principles that were applied to Scots law by the House of Lords in *Smith v Bank of Scotland*.

Accordingly the approach required in Scotland may be summarised as follows:

- Lenders looking to take security from a third party for the indebtedness of a borrower must take 'reasonable steps' to advise the third party about the risks of the transaction, and should act in good faith throughout the proposed transaction.

- Good faith will be shown by warning the third party of the consequences of entering into the obligation, and by advising them to take independent legal advice.

- The duty applies whenever the third party is in a 'non-business relationship' with the person with the principal obligation to repay the debt (eg a marriage).

- If the lender does not take reasonable steps, the courts could set aside the obligations undertaken by the third party, but this is always subject to the proviso that the third party can demonstrate that they entered into the arrangement as a consequence of undue influence, misrepresentation or other coercion from the debtor.

- The lender has to have been put on notice that the third party may have entered into the transaction because of the undue influence of the borrower.

Undue influence may be identified by reference to the four elements in the definition in *Gray v Binny* 7R 332 at p 347, namely:

- The existence of a relationship between the parties which creates a dominant or ascendant influence;
- The fact that confidence and trust arose from that relationship;
- The fact that a material and gratuitous benefit was given, to the prejudice of the granter (ie the third party); and
- That the granter had entered into the transaction without the benefit of independent advice or assistance.

If all four elements exist then the lender should be put on notice, although whether there was in fact undue influence will depend on the individual facts and circumstances.

Although the decision in *Etridge* does not apply to Scotland, many lenders operating both north and south of the border, for consistency, will apply the core minimum requirements set out in Etridge.

The Law Society of England and Wales provided a style letter for its members to send when acting for the wife in an inter-spouse guarantee transaction, and a similar style was also adopted by the Law Society of Scotland. The style letter does not appear to be held currently on the Law Society website, but a copy of it is replicated in GL Gretton and K Reid Conveyancing 2003 at pages 80 to 82 and in Appendix 4 of this book.

On the question of conflict of interest, the Law Society guidelines are quite unequivocal

'...where the jointly owned home is to be put up as security for a business loan to only one of the owners, there is a clear conflict of interest between the owners and you should not act for both of them. Not only must you make it clear that you are not acting for the owner who is not getting the benefit of the loan, when sending the standard security for signature by that person you must accompany it with a letter in terms of Rule 7 of the 1986 Rules…..'

Rule 7 states that a solicitor acting on behalf of a party or prospective party to a transaction of any kind where it is permitted for the solicitor to act for both parties, must not issue any deed, writ, missive or other document requiring the signature of another party or prospective party to him without informing that party in writing that such signature may have certain legal consequences, and that he should seek independent legal advice before signature.

Acting for both spouses in this situation therefore would be a *prima facie* breach of the conflict rules. Even if there is no apparent sign of undue influence, and the wife may be fully aware of and have accepted the implications of signing the security and may even be involved in the business herself, the interests of husband and wife are to be treated as being in conflict in every situation where the wife is providing her guarantee for her husband's business borrowing in this way. It is also the Law Society Professional Practice Committee's view that the exceptions to the absolute prohibition under rule 3 specified in Practice rule 5 do not apply despite the parties being obviously related by marriage and the fact that both may be established clients of the same firm of solicitors.

The checklist at the end of this Chapter is taken from Alistair Sim's JLLS article dated 1 March 1999: 'Conflict of interest between borrower and spouse'.

(d) Acting for both seller and seller's lender

When property is sold and there is an existing security created by the seller, the seller's solicitors usually act for the lenders in attending to its discharge. There is rarely any conflict in doing so, and this is common in residential transactions and often adopted in commercial transactions. In conveyancing terms, the following steps should be taken:

- Inform the seller's lenders of the proposed sale and obtain the titles, if held by the lender.
- Draft a form of discharge and send the draft to the purchaser's solicitors for revisal.
- Request details of the sum required to repay the loan as at the date of entry (the redemption figure).

- On return of the draft discharge, have the principal discharge prepared and send to the seller's lender for execution.
- The seller's lender will return the signed discharge to the seller's solicitors to be held as 'undelivered' pending repayment of the loan. In some circumstances, the purchaser's solicitors or the purchaser's lender's solicitors need to be able to hold the discharge as undelivered before the purchaser's lender will release funds for the purchaser. As far as possible this should be facilitated.
- At settlement of the sale, the seller's solicitors deliver the discharge together with a signed form 2 and forms 4 in duplicate. These are sent to the Land Register by the purchaser's solicitors, and once the Keeper is satisfied with the discharge, the old standard security will simply be removed from the title sheet, and the new disposition and standard security will be registered.

ACTING FOR THE COMMERCIAL LENDER

(a) Separate representation

10.06 It has been standard practice for many years now for borrowers and lenders in commercial transactions to be separately represented by different solicitors, due to the increased risk in acting for both, and the potential for conflict of interest to arise at various stages throughout the transaction. The Law Society originally issued its guidance on this subject in 1994. It is accepted that there will be occasions where the lender may wish to instruct the same solicitors to act for both parties where the amount of the loan is regarded as '*de minimis*'. That is currently accepted as meaning less than £250,000. Funds required to redeem the standard security being discharged must be remitted to lenders after completion.

In commercial lending circumstances, most lenders will have a panel of solicitors that they have approved to act on their behalf, and will also produce standing instructions to panel solicitors, to which the solicitors acting for them will be expected to adhere whenever an instruction is given. In addition there may be transaction specific instructions that will be issued to the solicitor at the time. There is no commercial equivalent to the CML handbook, although it may a useful resource to check for a particular lender's policy on certain standard conveyancing procedures, such as when a PEC would be regarded as out of date.

(b) Conflict of interest in commercial security transactions

Any one acting for a commercial lender in Scotland should also be familiar with the Law Society guidance on this area, which is available on the Law Society website and is summarised below. The Professional Practice Team at the Law Society are always willing to provide advice or guidance in this type of transaction, as well as in other cases of doubt or uncertainty on professional matters.

The Law Society provides a definition of 'commercial security transaction':

> 'A commercial security transaction relates to the secured lending to a customer of a bank or other lending institution where the purpose of the loan is clearly for the customer's business purposes'.

While the key element is clearly a loan for business purposes, it is incumbent on the solicitor, when receiving instructions to act for a lender and a borrower in any type of transaction, (but particularly a commercial security transaction), to exercise the necessary judgment in the context of the Conflict of Interest Rules about acting for both parties. Some thought is required in this connection, and it is necessary to anticipate as far as possible, given the circumstances of the instruction, what type of conflict situation might arise. The Law Society provides some examples:

Disclosure of all relevant circumstances

Either the solicitor may know more of the borrower's position than has been communicated to the lender or vice versa; or there may have been a reluctance by the borrower or lender fully to disclose their respective positions because of dual representation. This clearly affects the extent to which impartial 'best advice' can be given.

Ongoing negotiations

Negotiations between the borrower and lender may only be at a preliminary stage, requiring further detailed consideration or negotiation of covenants/

undertakings/events of default. In such negotiations the borrower and lender may have different negotiating strengths and thus there may be competing pressures on the solicitor as to whose interests are to be promoted.

Defects in title

While a borrower may be prepared to 'live with' a minor defect in title or some lack of planning or building consent (ie he is prepared to 'take a view') the lender may take an entirely different stance.

Security by companies

Apart from the complexities and time restraints for registration of security, companies may well be subject to negative or restrictive covenants or powers affecting the security on which the borrower but not necessarily the lender, may be prepared to take a commercial view. This may merit separate consideration and advice.

Competing creditors' ranking agreements

The circumstances as to the inter-relationship/enforcement of security between lenders may merit separate consideration and advice. Banks may not have 'standard forms' of ranking agreements and this clearly may involve a solicitor in preparing a document and negotiating its terms on points which have a bearing on the borrower's position.

Security over commercial property

The permitted use, associated licences/quotas and specific standard conditions may merit separate consideration and advice, as they may not be covered by pre-printed 'standard' bank forms. Particular risks arise on the transfer of a licence where the lender's interests will sometimes conflict with the borrower's commercial ambitions.

Leased property as security

The circumstances in which a lender requires protection in the event of irritancy may merit separate consideration and advice. Invariably the borrower is trying to strike the best deal while he is in occupancy while the lender needs protection in the event of the borrower's failure through insolvency or otherwise.

Enforcement of security

The solicitor acting for both borrower and lender may be placed in difficulty in the event of subsequent enforcement of a security. For whom does the solicitor act in such circumstances? Do both clients know and understand their respective positions?

Powerful clients

A major business client may bring subtle or even open pressure on a solicitor to follow a particular course, or to turn a blind eye to a matter which could prejudice a lender's position, eg discrepancies between a valuation and purchase price.

'All sums due' securities

Solicitors should be mindful to advise fully joint obligants (eg husbands and wives) of the nature of an 'all sums due' security. In particular it should be drawn to their attention that additional loans for example in respect of one obligant's business, may give rise to further secured borrowings without the other obligant requiring to sign the documentation. In such circumstances there is also a conflict of interest between the joint obligants.

(c) Facility documentation

We have seen that in residential lending, the borrower will receive an offer of loan with basic terms and conditions of the loan and this is also sent to the borrower's solicitor. The terms and conditions of a commercial loan can be far more intricate, and often negotiating the terms of the loan facility takes some considerable time and may require specialist legal input before being finalised.

The facility documentation will contain a number of conditions, some of which, known as 'conditions precedent' have to be implemented by the borrower before any funds can be drawn down. These can include obtaining planning permission, a satisfactory examination of title, signing the standard security, obtaining a parent company guarantee and so on. There will be other 'conditions subsequent' which the borrower will have to implement at some later stage, after some or all of the funds have been drawn, for example in funding for a development there will be key milestones to be met for building out the development. Other consents or licences may be needed for the property. Failure to comply with facility conditions may be made an 'event of default' in terms of the facility agreement, entitling the lender to apply some penalty or call up the loan. The underlying forms and structure of commercial lending is beyond the scope of this book, but there are some key aspects of commercial secured lending that need to be borne in mind, which the following paragraphs introduce.

(d) Registration of Charges

If you take nothing else from this chapter, please remember the importance, when a standard security is granted by a company, of registering the details of that security, or 'charge', in the Company's Register of Charges, within the 21 day period allowed by statute. This **must** be done for a security to be effective, and for the rights of the creditor under the security to be exercisable against the borrower. The consequences of failing timeously to register a charge are too dreadful to contemplate. Without registration in the Register of Charges, the lender's rights to enforce the standard security are not protected. Failure to register would render the charge void as against a liquidator and any competing creditors. While registration after the 21 day period may be technically possible, the charge remains void against a liquidator or administrator appointed under proceedings which were started between the date of execution of the charge and the date of registration, and anyone who acquired an interest in the charged property in that period.

Invariably, it is the responsibility of the lender's solicitor to register the charge, and steps should be followed to ensure that this is done expeditiously (see para (iii) below). If the Company is registered in Scotland the relevant Register is in Edinburgh. If the Company is registered in England or Wales, the Registrar is based in Cardiff. The 21 day period begins on the day after the date of creation of the charge.

(i) Date of Creation

The date of creation of the charge for the purposes of registration in the Register of Charges depends upon the nature of the charge. Note that this need not necessarily be tied to the date of completion and action may be required before the transaction settles, for certain types of charge:

- Standard Security: date of creation of a Standard Security is the date of recording in the Sasine Register or registration in the Land Register
- Floating Charge: date of creation is the date of execution
- Ranking Agreement, incorporating an alteration of a Floating Charge: date of creation of the charge is the last date of execution, regardless of the date of subsequent recording or registration in the Property Register.

(ii) Forms

There is a selection of 'Companies House' standard forms that must be used when notifying the charge to the Registrar of Companies, and these vary according to the country in which the company is registered. These forms can be accessed and downloaded from the Companies House website. Some firms of solicitors subscribe to specialist software applications that provide forms of many types, including company forms, that can be completed on-screen and saved to a matter file, then printed for signing and submission to the Registrar of Companies

For registering a charge created by a company registered in Scotland, the appropriate form is MG01s, and it should be accompanied by a certified copy of the charge and submitted to the Edinburgh office. For companies registered in England, a certified copy of the charge requires to be submitted with forms MG01 and MG09, which are submitted to Cardiff.

There is a charge of £13 (at the time of writing) for registering each charge which must be prepaid to the Registrar ie accompany the forms and copy charge.

The restriction or discharge of a standard security may also need to be registered in the Company's Register. Deeds of Restriction and Discharges can be registered by way of Memorandum of partial or full satisfaction of the charge. The Company forms for this are MG02 and MG04 for English companies and MG02s and MG03s for Scottish Companies. There is not the same urgency for registering the discharge of the charge created by a standard security in the Companies Register, since the relevant property register will disclose the discharge, and sometimes this is overlooked or not done, without any adverse effect from the conveyancing point of view.

(iii) Procedure and Reminder System

There are, as they say, no prizes for getting it wrong, and never more so in the registration of a charge. It is essential to set up a system of reminders and diary entries to ensure that any charge for which you are responsible is registered on time, and so that the all important Certificate of Registration of a Charge is issued. In some firms, a particular partner may take responsibility for signing the forms and checking the timings.

- Remember to take a photocopy of the executed standard security as this is required to accompany the MG01s or MG01/MG09 forms (Company Form).

- Prepare the form. The information you need to complete includes the Company name in full and company number, a description of the charge, the amount secured (or 'all sums due'), short particulars of the property charged (usually put in the ALL and WHOLE description from the standard security), and in the case of a floating charge, details of any restrictions or ranking arrangements that it contains. The other key piece of information (which you have to wait for if the charge is a standard security) is the date of creation.

- Ask the Keeper to confirm the date of registration of the standard security. Although not legally obliged to do so, this is a service that the Keeper provides. The date of registration (or recording if in the Sasine Register) is the date of creation of the charge, when it is a standard security, and the 21 day period starts to run from that date.

- The usual format is to write in big block capitals on the top of the Form 2 (or SAF) submitting the standard security the words 'PLEASE CONFIRM DATE OF REGISTRATION'.

- Diarise to check for the Keeper's confirmation of registration in two or three days. Phone. If it is not yet available diarise again until you get it.

- If the charge you are registering is a floating charge or ranking agreement the 21 days start to run from the date of execution, and so that date is inserted in the Company Form, which is then signed and submitted to the Registrar along with a certified copy of the charge and a cheque for the filing fee.

- For a standard security, as soon as you have the date of registration, complete the Company Form, have it signed and submitted to the Register along with a certified copy of the charge and a cheque for the filing fee.

- Certifying a copy involves writing onto the copy document the words 'Certified a true copy of [description of the document]' with the date of certification and the signature of the solicitors. Some firms have an embossed stamp for this purpose.

- Once the Company Form and copy charge has been sent, diarise to check with the Registrar that they have received it – your 21 day clock is still ticking. If there is some major flaw with the submission, the Registrar may have to return the form for correction and this might mean that you run out of time (see 'Informal Corrections' below).

- Once you are satisfied that the charge will be registered in time, you can relax until the next time.

- When the Certificate of Registration of the Charge is received from the Registrar, send a copy of it to the Keeper so that there is no exclusion of indemnity issue. Retain the principal Certificate carefully. Breathe.

(iv) Informal corrections

The Registrar of Companies has the power under s 1075 of the Companies Act 2006 to informally correct a document delivered to the Registrar which appears to be incomplete or internally inconsistent, before registering it. The power only applies to documents for the registration of mortgages and charges, and the power is designed to help companies (and their advisers) meet the statutory time limit for the delivery of particulars of charges for registration. Informal Correction Guidance published by the Registrar contains a full list of the documents to which the power applies and exceptions to the exercise of the power are contained in that Guidance.

Anyone who wishes to take advantage of the power must first agree to be contacted and to give the Registrar whatever instructions are needed to correct the document. The registrar must be satisfied that the person giving instructions is authorised to do so. For solicitors, this means identifying a senior solicitor, and submitting their details to the Registrar, and obtaining an authorisation code.

Then, if any registration of charge forms submitted by anyone in the firm require to be corrected and can benefit from the informal correction arrangements, the Registrar can contact the authorised person, who can instruct the Registrar to make the correction. Once the Registrar has corrected the document, it will be treated as having been delivered when the correction was made, so any correction procedure must still be finalised within the 21 day period.

(e) Floating charges

A standard security is often characterised as a 'fixed charge'. It applies to the heritable property to which it relates on registration, and unless specifically varied, continues to do so until discharged. So the property over which the creditor would be able to enforce rights is fixed and known from the start.

By contrast, a 'floating charge' does not identify specific property to which it attaches, instead it 'floats' over the assets of the company named in the charge, usually in general terms eg 'the whole of the property, assets and rights (including uncalled capital) which are or may from time to time be comprised in the property and undertaking of the company'. A key aspect of the floating charge is that for as long as it continues to 'float' and does not 'crystallise', the company can intromit with, trade and sell the assets concerned (subject to any other fixed charge that may exist) without any discharge from or consent of the holder of the floating charge, unless restricted from doing so by the wording of the floating charge.

Scottish floating charges differ from their English counterparts, in that they derive their legal basis entirely from statute, however, the document can be in any form, so long as it is clear that it is 'for the purpose of securing any debt or other obligation (including a cautionary obligation) incurred or to be incurred by, or binding upon, the company or any other person, to create in favour of the creditor in the debt or obligation a (floating charge) over all or any part of the property (including uncalled capital) which may from time to time be comprised in its property and undertaking' (s 462 of the Companies Act 1985).

Floating charges must also be registered in the Companies Register. Unlike standard securities, they are not registered in any other register, and consequently registration in the Companies Register is required to make their existence public to those having dealings with the company, such as creditors and prospective creditors.

A floating charge continues to float over whatever property and assets it encompasses that are owned by the company from time to time, until it is caused to attach to those assets – known as 'crystallisation'. That will happen if the company goes into liquidation, or if a receiver (if it is a floating charge created prior to 15 September 2003) or an administrator (for floating charges after 15 September 2003) is appointed (see para 8.18 (h) and (i). It is then crystallised as a fixed charge over the assets and property of the company at the time of crystallisation. Where a company that has granted a floating charge sells property, the purchaser's solicitors should ask to see a letter of non-crystallisation from the floating charge holder (see paras 8.18(j)(v) and 11.05(i)).

The statutory basis of floating charges in Scotland is prospectively changed by the provisions of the Part 2 of the Bankruptcy and Diligence etc (Scotland) Act 2007. While not yet in force, and with no date for coming into force yet appointed, ss 37 to 49 of the BAD(S)A 2007 set out a structure for floating charges in Scotland for the future. As well as changing the law relating to floating charges in Scotland it will consolidate the existing law and prospectively repeals the relevant sections of CA 1985

(i) The prospective Register of Floating Charges. Part 2 of the BAD(S) A 2007 proposes the setting up of a new Register of Floating Charges, to be kept by the Keeper of the Registers of Scotland - not by the Registrar of Companies - and once the relevant provisions are in force, a floating charge will be created by registration in this new Register. As company law currently stands, security rights granted by companies have to be registered in the Companies Register. This includes fixed charges, which means that a standard security has to be registered twice: first in the Land or

Sasine Register and then in the Companies Register. This has often struck practitioners as unnecessary duplication. Since publication to a company's creditors and those planning to have dealing with the company is the object of the exercise in registration, it would be administratively burdensome if the introduction of the Register of Floating Charges were to mean that double registration would be required for floating charges as well.

However, s 893 of the Companies Act 2006 allows orders to be made dispensing with double registration. An order can be made which will provide that a charge granted by a company which is registered in a 'special register' will not have to be separately registered in the Companies Register. Whoever keeps that special register will send details of the charge to the Registrar of Companies direct, who will put the information in the Companies Register. 'Special registers' include the Land Register, the Sasine Register, the Patents Register, the Shipping Register and so on.

The prospective Register of Floating Charges will be a special register as well, and once it is activated (by s 893 order), a floating charge will only have to be registered once, in the new Register of Floating Charges. It is anticipated that there will also be a s 893 order made, at some point in the future, in relation to the Land and Sasine Registers, so that standard securities granted by companies will no longer have to be double registered either.

(f) Ranking Agreements and Arrangements

It is possible to have more than one standard security over the same property. But not everyone can be first in the queue for repayment in the event of a sale of the property. Instead, multiple securities will rank in relation to each other, in accordance with the rules of priority, which will determine the order in which they are entitled to payment in the event of enforcement of these securities.

A security can rank **prior** to another. In other words the creditor under the prior security will have first call on the sale proceeds of the property.

A security can rank **postponed** to another. In other words the entitlement of the creditor under the postponed security, to the sale proceeds of the property, will be subject to the rights of the prior security holder.

Securities can rank *pari passu*. In other words the securities rank equally.

The ranking implied by law without the need for a separate document is first past the post ie the order in which the securities were recorded or registered in the relevant Property Register. If they are received on the same day by the Keeper, they will rank equally. Note that a fixed security has priority over a floating charge, regardless of their respective dates (see para 10.06(e)(ii)) unless there is wording in the Floating Charge to the contrary.

(i) Section 13 Intimation

There is a statutory cut-off point for prior ranking however. Section 13 of the CFR(S)A 1970 provides that where the creditor under a standard security receives notice of the creation of a subsequent security over the same property, then the preference in ranking of that prior creditor is restricted at that point to security for its present advances, and any future advances which it is already contractually obliged to make, and interest and expenses on those advances. In other words, the security of a secured lender who receives an s 13 notice will only have priority ranking for any further advances it makes, if it is already committed to make them.

(ii) Ranking of Floating Charges

A Ranking Agreement, which is a document entered into among all of the creditors and the borrower, setting out the priority arrangements among them, will usually be needed where there is also a floating charge granted by the company, because a fixed charge has priority over a floating charge, regardless of the respective dates of registration of the securities (s 464 of the CA 1985 (prospectively repealed by s 46 of the BAD(S)A 2007, not yet in force)). However, floating charges will invariably contain what is called a 'negative pledge' by which the borrower is prohibited from creating any subsequent fixed security. Most creditors of fixed securities will want to rank prior to the floating charge or to restrict the entitlement of the floating charge holder, and therefore the respective ranking of fixed and floating charges where there is more than one creditor will need to be agreed between the creditors and the borrower, and the agreement set out in a Ranking Agreement.

A Ranking Agreement can be recorded in the Sasine Register or registered in the Land Register. If it alters the provisions of a floating charge, it requires to be registered in the Register of Charges at the Companies Office within 21 days of the last date of execution of the Ranking Agreement (see para 10.06(d)).

Once the provisions of Part 2 of the BAD(S)A 2007 come into force ranking of floating charges and fixed securities will change and they will then rank according to date of creation.

(g) Overseas Companies

As we have seen, (para 8.18 (j)) when transacting with an overseas company, it is necessary to obtain an opinion from a firm of solicitors in the jurisdiction in which the company is incorporated, to confirm that the company has the powers and capacity to enter into the transaction, and this applies equally when the borrower is an overseas company, to ensure that it can validly grant a valid and enforceable security. Such an opinion should confirm a number of things, including that the company is validly incorporated, validly exists and is in good standing, and has the necessary powers both to purchase or acquire property and to grant the security. It should also cover such matters as execution and any procedural formalities which require to be followed, as well as confirming the directors and secretary of the company.

(i) Registration Requirements

In addition to any UK registration requirements, the firm providing the opinion should also be asked to confirm whether there are any local registration requirements which require to be followed for the security to be valid.

Currently, overseas companies may register with the Registrar of Companies in the UK.

Since 1 October 2009, the position relating to registration of changes created by overseas companies has been governed by the Overseas Companies (Execution of Documents and Registration of Charges) Regulations 2009, which provided that the requirement to register a charge created by an overseas company (including standard securities and floating charges) only arises if that company has actually registered with the Registrar of Companies. In terms of the Overseas Companies Regulations 2009 an overseas company must, within one month of having opened a UK establishment, submit registration details to the Registrar, and it must do so each time it opens a UK establishment.

For the purposes of the OC(EDRC) Regulations 2009, the overseas company is not treated as registered unless and until its particulars are on the Register and accordingly available for public inspection.

However, in a consultation paper entitled 'Revised Scheme for Registration of Changes created by Companies and LLPs' published in August 2011 by the Department for Business Innovation and Skills, it was announced that overseas companies will cease to be subject to the scheme for registration of company changes from 1 October 2011.

ENFORCEMENT AND REPOSSESSION

10.07 The rights of heritable creditors to enforce their security in the event of default by the borrower, and the safety measures to protect debtors, that have been introduced over the years, since the establishment of the current regime by the CFR(S)A 1970, mean that the law in this area is becoming increasingly elaborate, and a whole book would be required to do justice to the topic (in which respect see DJ Cusine and R Rennie *Standard Securities*). Baldly put, if the debtor is in default and the lender requires to enforce its security, it is arguably not a job for a conveyancer, but is a matter that the conveyancer's litigation colleagues will attend to. Having said that, the conveyancer should have a high level knowledge, at the very least, of the remedies that are available to the lender, not least because, when acting for a client purchasing from a heritable creditor in possession, they need to know that the relevant statutory formalities have been complied with. The decision of the Supreme Court, in 2010, in the case of *Royal Bank of Scotland plc v Wilson* [2010] SLT 1227 rather upset most conventional wisdom regarding routes to sale for the heritable creditor. Also the restrictions placed on heritable creditors' remedies by the Mortgage Rights (Scotland) Act 2001 and Home Owner and Debtor Protection (Scotland) Act 2010, amongst others, mean that this is increasingly becoming an area of law where the uninitiated should not tread, and instead is becoming a legislative and judicially-determined labyrinth that demands a careful and informed approach.

Given the excoriating financial circumstances that the world has passed through recently, any text written at this time is a momentary snapshot of current practice, so, for this Edition, a high level commentary only is offered.

(a) CFR(S)A 1970 remedies

The provisions relating to enforcement of standard securities are contained in ss 19 to 29 of the CFR(S)A 1970 with Schs 6 and 7 providing statutory styles of notices. These sections have been amended by the MR(S)A 2001.

Scots Law on enforcement previously had a reputation for being relatively creditor-friendly. The CFR(S)A 1970 set out enforcement procedures which were challengeable only in fairly limited circumstances.

The CFR(S)A 1970 provided three methods of enforcement (or so we thought):

- Service of Calling-up Notices
- Service of Notices of Default
- Immediate court action – s 24 Action

Royal Bank of Scotland plc v Wilson tells us that the position is not so simple, and that for a heritable creditor to be in a position to sell the security subjects, the calling up procedure must always be followed.

(b) Calling-up Notice

A calling-up notice requires the owner of the property to pay to the creditor the whole sum secured by the standard security within 2 months of the date on which the calling-up notice is served on him. This period of notice may be dispensed with or shortened in certain circumstances. Generally, calling-up notices are served in circumstances where the creditor wants the debt secured by its standard security to be discharged in full. It is always competent for the creditor to serve a calling-up notice unless either:

- the creditor has agreed to restrict its ability to serve calling-up notices under a particular standard security (which in practice is very unlikely to happen); or
- where the creditor has received notice from the debtor's trustee in sequestration that the trustee intends to sell the security subjects (s 39(4)(b) of the Bankruptcy (Scotland) Act 1985).

Calling-up notices must be in the form set out in the CFR(S)A 1970, Sch 6 Form A, and must be served in accordance with s 19 of the CFR(S) A 1970 ie on the person with the last recorded or registered title to the property. Generally there is an obligation on the creditor to serve a copy of the calling-up notice on any other person against whom it wishes to preserve a right of recourse in respect of the debt, which will cover service on guarantors and joint and several debtors.

After service of the calling-up notice, the borrower has 2 months in which to pay the sums demanded. If the owner of the property does not comply with the calling-up notice, the creditor may exercise any of the remedies available to it in terms of Standard Condition 10, subject now to the provisions of the HODP(S)A 2010 in respect of residential properties (see para 10.07(g)).

(c) Notice of Default

A notice of default can be served in circumstances where there has been a breach of the terms of the standard security and the breach is remediable. The notice of default requires the debtor or the owner (as appropriate) to remedy the default specified in the notice within one month of the date on which the Notice is served. This period of notice may be dispensed with in certain circumstances.

Notices of default are typically used where a debtor has fallen into arrears or has failed to maintain the security subjects and the creditor simply wants to have the default remedied. Notices of default must be in the form set out in the CFR(S)A 1970 Sch 6 Form A and must be served in accordance with s 21 of the CFR(S)A 1970. The decision in *Royal Bank of Scotland plc v Wilson* now means that it cannot be used as an alternative to the calling up procedure, where the creditor wished to have the whole debt repaid.

(d) Section 24 Court Action

Prior to the decision in *Royal Bank of Scotland plc v Wilson* a practice had evolved of heritable creditors going straight for a section 24 court application and decree, to entitle them to enter into possession, bolstered by the Inner House decision in 1999 in the case of *Bank of Scotland v Millward* [1999] SLT 901 that the calling up notice was, in effect, optional. The practice has been despite wording in the CFR(S)A 1907 stating that where a creditor in a standard security intends to exercise its power of sale, that creditor '**shall** serve a notice calling up the security'. That wording had generally been regarded as a permissive and not a mandatory provision. The Supreme Court decision, which clearly overrules *Millward*, is that this interpretation of the legislation is wrong.

Section 24 procedure is therefore only now to be used after calling up or default procedure, and **must** be used after calling up procedure for residential properties as a consequence of the provisions of the HODP(S) A 2010 (see para 10.07(g)).

(e) Effect of the Mortgage Rights (Scotland) Act 2001

The MR(S)A 2001 allows the debtor (and certain other persons) to apply to the court for an order suspending the enforcement process, once enforcement steps have been initiated, (and before they have been completed) and provides that the court will have the power to make orders suspending the lender's rights 'for such periods' and 'subject to such conditions' as the court thinks appropriate. The provisions of the MR(S) A 2001 do not significantly change the initial enforcement procedures, other than amending the form of the notices, and making it necessary to serve notices on the occupier of the property (who may or may not be the debtor), but can impact considerably on the process after that.

Mortgage rights applications to the court can be made by the borrower, or the granter of the standard security if the security subjects (in whole or in part) are that person's sole or main residence; by the non-entitled spouse or civil partner of the debtor or proprietor where the security subjects (in whole or in part) are a matrimonial home or family home and the sole or main residence of the non-entitled spouse or civil partner, or by a co-habitee (for longer than 6 months) of the debtor or proprietor, where the security subjects (in whole or in part) are the sole or main residence of that co-habitee, and it is also the sole or main residence of a child of the co-habitee and the debtor or proprietor.

(f) Requirement for notices under Section 11 of the Homelessness (Scotland) Act 2003

Since 1 April 2009, heritable creditors who take steps to call up any security where all or part of the security subjects is used for residential purposes must give notice of the service of the calling-up notice to the relevant local authority in the form required in terms of The Notice to Local Authorities (Scotland) Regulations 2008 issued under the H(S)A 2003. This provision also affects residential landlords who seek to recover possession of property which they have let.

Note that some courts insist that the Notice must be in precisely the terms of the statutory style: in other words presented as a notice, and not converted to letter form. Whether that is a correct interpretation of the regulations or not, it would be prudent to conform exactly to the statutory style.

(g) Home Owner and Debtor Protection (Scotland) Act 2010

The Home Owner and Debtor Protection (Scotland) Act 2010 makes changes to procedures for enforcement of standard securities over residential properties, and provided new forms of Calling up notice and Notice of Default for both residential and commercial properties. For residential repossessions, unless the debtor voluntarily surrenders the property, Calling up Notices must now be followed by an action for possession under s 24 of the CFR(S)A 1970. The Act also imposes new obligations on creditors in securities over residential properties to go through certain pre-action procedures with a debtor before they can raise an action. This involves providing the debtor with prescribed information, including the terms of the standard security and the amount due under it including arrears and any additional charges, as soon as the debtor is in default. Lenders must now take reasonable efforts to agree proposals for future payments with the debtor, and must provide him with information including contact details on sources of advice and help with managing debt, and contact details for the local authority housing department.

Finally, it should be pointed out that, prior to conclusion of a contract to sell the security subjects, following on enforcement action having been taken, the debtor has the right to redeem the standard security without purging the default specified in the Notice of Default. A debtor, or proprietor as the case may be, in a standard security can redeem the security on giving two months' notice of his intention to do so. The procedure and forms to be used to exercise this entitlement are set down in Standard Condition 11 and Sch 5 of the CFR(S)A 1970.

The provisions of the MR(S)A 2001 and HOPD(S)A 2010 only apply to property used for residential purposes so it could be said that Scots Law remains relatively creditor–friendly in relation to enforcement of standard securities over commercial premises.

CERTIFICATES OF TITLE

10.08 We have already touched on Certificates of Title in the context of acting for the purchaser of the commercial property, and being asked to certify the title to the lender (see para 8.38(b)). In these circumstances, even though the lender's solicitors are excused from examining the title and other due diligence items, and reporting on their terms to the lender, there is still usually a requirement on the lender's solicitors to review and consider the provisions of the Certificate and advise the lender as to the acceptability of it, for the purposes of agreeing to lend.

The current version of the CLLS and PSG Certificates is the 6th Edition, and as indicated, at the time of writing, a new 7th Edition is being drafted. Solicitors acting for commercial lenders should make themselves familiar with the appropriate version of the Certificate in common use. Inevitably, in the period during changeover from the 6th Edition to the 7th Edition (when it is published) there will be some transactions where the 'old style' Certificate is used, although there will be a point at which the new edition becomes adopted and, importantly, PI insurers will expect that the most up to date version of the Certificate is being given.

Guidance on how to use the 6th Edition Certificate of Title is provided on the PSG website, and this is summarised at para 8.38(b)). The lender's solicitor is looking for the Certificate to be as clear as possible, and limited to matters which are material to the interests of the lender in the context of the loan and the value of the property. The disclosures in the Certificate should enable the lender to assess the extent of risk attached to the property being offered as security, and it should be clear to the lender's solicitors in reviewing the Certificate what those risks might be. Accordingly the lender's solicitor is entitled to expect that the Certificate will contain a fair summary of the effect of the title and other documents, but that copies of titles should not be attached, as this would defeat the object of the exercise. Only if the title contains documents that are so complex that their terms cannot be accurately summarised would it be acceptable for the document, or an excerpt from it, to be attached to the Certificate. Even complex documents, if they are in terms usual and acceptable for the type of property, may not need to be attached, unless there is reason why the lender must know the detail of them, and the purchaser's certification could be expressed along the lines of 'containing no unusual or unduly onerous conditions' or 'in terms usual for documents of this type relating to properties of the nature of the security subjects' or similar wording.

There is a balance to be achieved between the purchaser's solicitor and the lender's solicitor in these situations: the purchaser's solicitors must accept that they need to make sensible disclosures, based on commercial considerations that might have a bearing on the value or viability of the property from the lender's point of view, but should resist the temptation to produce pages and pages of disclosures on every point arising out of the title, some of which may relate to minor matters. Professional skill and judgement is required in deciding on what must appear in the Certificate, and what can be left out or modified.

On the other hand, the solicitors for the lender ought to accept that there will be limits to what the purchaser's solicitor is able to certify, and this will usually not include an assessment of the risks that might arise from any problems or issues that the Certificate discloses. The function of the Certificate is to provide specific information about the property, to allow the lender, with the help of its own professional advisers, to decide whether the property is one which can be accepted for the transaction in question.

That is not to say that the lender or its solicitors or other advisers are not entitled to ask for further information or clarification, to enable a proper assessment to be made of any risks disclosed by the Certificate.

Full detailed guidance on using the Certificate of Title and what its provisions are intended to achieve is on the PSG website at www.psglegal. co.uk

FURTHER READING

Professor Halliday's book on 'The Conveyancing and Feudal Reform (Scotland) Act 1970' which is a very good practical handbook full of practice points and styles as well as commentary. (2nd Edition: W. Green 1977)

Stair Encyclopaedia volume 20

Douglas Cusine Robert Rennie 'Standard Securities' (2nd edition LexisNexis 2002)

JLSS article by Conveyancing Committee 'Interspouse guarantees – an update 1 October 2003

JLSS article by Alistair Sim of Marsh 'Conflict of interest between borrower and spouse' 1 March 1999

Register of Companies: www.companieshousegov.uk

Informal Correction Guidance published by the Registrar of Companies at http://www.companieshousegov.uk/about/informalCorrection.shtml

CHECKLIST OF RELEVANT ISSUES TO CONSIDER WHEN ACTING FOR LENDER (by Alistair Sim of Marsh)

- There are many issues that need to be considered routinely when instructions from a lender involve arranging signature of security deeds, including the following points:
- Are you quite clear which party/parties is/are your client(s)? Lender, borrower, borrower's spouse? Are your instructions such that you could have a duty of care to more than one of these parties?
- Should you act for/advise more than one party?
- Is there an actual conflict of interest? If so, have you made it clear to the other parties that they should seek separate legal advice?
- Has the borrower's spouse been advised to take independent legal advice and, if so, has such advice been given?

If you are acting for the spouse

- Have you ensured that the spouse knows and understands who has instructed you and the basis on which advice has been given?
- Are you satisfied that the spouse was not subject to undue influence on the part of the borrower or the lender?

- Have you considered the implications of Rule 7 of the Conflict of Interest Rules (issuing deeds, etc, for signature by a party who has chosen not to instruct a solicitor)?

- Have you ascertained whether the spouse will receive direct financial benefit from the loan to which the security relates?

- Have you ascertained whether the spouse is involved in any way in the business to which the loan relates?

- Have you made other enquiries with a view to establishing whether the spouse might be advised not to sign the security deed? (Note: it may be only by examining the finances/accounts of the borrower's business that meaningful advice could be given in this regard)

- Has the spouse been advised of the implications of securing business borrowings over the matrimonial house/other matrimonial property?

- Has the spouse been advised that the security is an all sums security/a security for a fixed amount?

- Have you ensured that there are letters/attendance notes recording advice given?

When acting for the lender

- Have you considered whether it may be appropriate to qualify your report on title (to note, for instance, concerns in respect of potential conflict of interest)?

- If your instructions require you to warrant that the security deeds are properly executed, how have you satisfied yourself before reporting to the lender that the signatures are genuine? If you cannot warrant that signatures are genuine (eg by seeing the spouse sign and seeing evidence of identity), do not do so.

- Remember, if a claim a rises and the cause of the claim is or is attributable to breach of the Conflict of Interest Practice Rules, the self-insured amount will be double the standard amount.

Chapter 11

Settlement and the Final Steps

HEADING FOR COMPLETION

11.1 Commercial lawyers refer to 'completion', while residential conveyancers speak of 'settlement'. We mean the same thing, and much of the procedure is the same too, although commercial property lawyers probably see fewer keys.

Once title has been examined and any unsatisfactory points resolved, all reports and searches have been examined and are clear, the disposition, the standard security and any other documents required have been drafted, revised and approved, there are two essential things to set up to achieve settlement: signing and money. All of the conveyancing documents need to be properly executed, and arrangements made for the transfer of funds from the purchaser to the seller, either via their solicitors, or sometimes (in commercial purchases) directly between the parties or their respective banks.

The actual logistics of settlement of the transaction can become complicated, particularly in commercial deals. Usually residential settlements involve two or three documents (discharge, disposition, standard security) and the same solicitor organises requisitioning the loan monies and pays the price, although they can become more complex. Because of separate representation of the parties, however, sometimes even 'simple' commercial property completions can become rather tortuous. There are usually several parties involved, all of whom are separately represented: the purchaser, the seller, the purchaser's lender, the previous lender, perhaps the proposed occupier, and sometimes other parties such as the local authority can be involved in the conveyancing process too.

It is good practice to clearly establish the completion requirements of each party as early as possible, and work out how these are going to be achieved. Issues normally revolve around payment of funds and release of the key documents, and the tension that exists because of the respective requirements of the parties. The purchaser needs to have the disposition to register his real right, but must release the purchase price, while the seller will not deliver the disposition without payment; the lender will only release the loan funds if they are assured that they can perfect their security, which means having possession or control of both the disposition in favour of the borrower and the signed standard security. The previous lender may only be willing to release the discharge in exchange for repayment of the outstanding loan, funds for which are coming from payment of the purchase price.

The time-honoured way to resolve the apparent stalemate that these entrenched requirements creates, is for the respective solicitors to agree and undertake to hold documentation and sometimes also funds as 'undelivered'. The end recipient of the deeds (and funds) receives the deeds and/or funds but must not intromit with them in any way – so for example, the purchaser must not submit the disposition to the Land Register until the seller has received the funds. Usually when there are loan funds required to finance the purchase of commercial property, the lender's solicitors will require to be in possession of all of the documents, holding them as undelivered, so that, as soon as the funds arrive with the seller, the documents immediately become 'delivered' and the lender has immediate possession and can proceed to have them registered. The alternative would be for all of the solicitors to assemble in the same place for a completion meeting and wait for the funds to be transferred from one bank to another before handing over the documents. For those solicitors still using cheques, frequently the cheque will be sent to the seller's solicitor and simultaneously the seller's solicitor will send the settlement items to the purchaser's solicitor, in both cases to be held as undelivered until each confirms to the other that the items have been received. This is common and convenient in residential completions. Settlement cheques are virtually unheard of in commercial completions, particularly when there are often back to back telegraphic transfers of funds required on the same day, because, although a solicitor's cheque is guaranteed funds, it is not cleared funds. The sums of money involved are greater, therefore interest per day is much greater. It is also a more secure method of transfer of funds.

One of the key documents in any conveyancing transaction is the Discharge of the security granted by the seller. Here, however there is a bifurcation in conveyancing practice. Residential conveyancers are happy to accept an undertaking from the seller's solicitors to deliver the executed discharge after settlement. Such an undertaking is 'classic' for the purposes of the Master policy insurance (see para 11.04(a)). However, invariably in a commercial transaction, completion cannot take place without the executed discharge being available, to be held as undelivered and then treated as delivered at completion. Some lenders have been known to refuse to release the executed discharge, even to their own solicitors, until the loan is repaid, but thankfully these rather self-defeating instances are rare.

It should also be established who is going to attend to the post-settlement formalities of settling any stamp duty land tax payable by the purchaser and presenting for registration. In residential transactions where the solicitor almost always acts for both borrower and lender, this is not usually an issue. In commercial transactions, again it is often the lender's solicitors who will deal with these arrangements, to ensure that the standard security in favour of their client is put on the register as swiftly as possible. These days, with online submission of SDLT a comparatively straightforward matter, this is something that can often be achieved simultaneously at settlement, but arrangements need to be considered if there is going to be a slight time lag (see para 11.06).

A checklist of completion items and requirements is a vital tool in anything other than the most straightforward completion. This can be circulated around the other solicitors to make sure that everyone's requirements have been covered, and that everyone knows the settlement items for which they are responsible. The PSG Completion checklist (see the end of this Chapter for the checklist) is a reasonably comprehensive starting point for most transactions, and is available to download from the PSG website.

EXECUTION

11.02 For the present, we must leave the issue of electronic execution to one side. The advent of digital signature for contracts of heritable property is on the horizon for the conveyancer (and is of course currently possible within the ARTL system (see para 13.09), and is certain to become more prevalent in the future, but for now we are still dealing with 'wet' signatures of contracts and documents to give them effect.

The Requirements of Writing (Scotland) Act 1995 is the key piece of legislation when it comes to the formalities required for execution of documents in Scotland. Not always an easy Act to read, it is nonetheless vital for the conveyancer to be familiar with its provisions and effect. Note that RoW(S)A 1995 is subject to any statutory provision to the contrary. For the purposes of the conveyancer, it starts as relatively straightforward: writing is required - both for the constitution of a contract or unilateral obligation for the creation, transfer, variation or extinction of a real right in interest in land (eg missives), and for the creation, transfer, variation or extinction of a real right in land, (otherwise than by operation of a court decree, enactment or rule of law) (eg a disposition etc) (s 1(2)(a) and (b) of RoW(S)A 1995.

Rules for execution of these (and other) documents are also set out in RoW(S)A 1995, and there are two parts to this: validity and probativity. For formal **validity** all that is required is the subscription of the granter (s 2 of RoW(S)A 1995). So far, so good. But a document that has merely been signed, while valid, is not self-proving (ie probative or self-evidencing), and this is where witnessing comes in. If the granter's signature is witnessed – only a single witness is necessary – this bestows an evidential presumption that the document was signed by the granter (s 3 of RoW(S)A 1995). To be recorded in the Sasine Register or registered in the Land Register, a document needs to be self-proving (s 6 of RoW(S)A 1995) ie witnessed, although it should be mentioned that s 4 of RoW(S)A 1995 provides an alternative route to probativity for a document that has been merely signed, but not witnessed, by making application to the court. This may be appropriate in cases where the granter's signature cannot now be witnessed, such as where he is now deceased or incapax, so that it is likely to be of use in proving wills for example, rather than a realistic alternative for conveyancing transactions. A granter can always acknowledge his signature, in the presence of a witness, some time after he has signed, and execution by the witness at that stage will confer the self-proving presumption. Any collateral agreements need to be self-proving to be registered in the Books of Council and Session.

SUBSCRIPTION AND SIGNING: SPECIAL CASES

11.03 Sch 2 of RoW(S)A 1995 sets out the methods by which certain classes of person may sign, with, in some cases, adjustment to the witnessing arrangements. These, and some other common execution arrangement are itemised below.

(a) Subscription

A granter should subscribe at the end of the last page of the deed. If there is more than one granter, it is sufficient that at least one of them signs on the last page of the deed and the others can sign on an additional page (ie a blank sheet of paper). There must always be part of the deed on the signing page – even if it is one word.

If there are any annexations to the deed – such as schedules or plans, then (for deeds relating to land) each of those annexations must also be signed (but do not need any witnesses' signatures). For this reason, it is usual in Scottish deeds for any Schedule to be a single annexation of Parts, so that only one signature on the last page of the whole Schedule is required. Compare this with the practice in England where deeds can contain many individual Schedules, as there is not the same execution requirement. Note however that each plan, drawing or other representation that is attached to a deed must be individually signed (s 8 of RoW(S)A 1995).

An annexation should be referred to in the document (eg 'the real burdens set out in the Schedule annexed and signed as relative to this disposition') and identified on its face as being that annexation. There is no prescribed way of doing this set out in the RoW(S)A 1995, but in practice, (and it is good practice that should be followed) identification of any annexation is done by putting wording at the top of the first page of the annexation (eg 'This is the Schedule referred to in the foregoing Deed of Real Burdens between Lightyear Development Company Ltd and Kelvinforth Leisure Pursuits Ltd [dated [   ]]'). The interpretation of the 'face' of the document means that the Keeper will reject any plan where a label has been stuck onto the annexation and the signature is put on the label.

For plans and other representations that need to be signed on each page, the wording is endorsed onto it in some convenient place. If for example an A1 size plan is attached to a deed, it will often be folded in such a way that the bottom right hand corner of the plan is uppermost, and for convenience the wording (eg 'This is the Plan 1 referred to in the foregoing Disposition by Eric Sweet in favour of David Alexander Sweet and Preston Maxwell Monk Sweet') can be written on this uppermost section.

(b) Witnesses

A witness has to see the granter sign the document, and sign after him, or be present when the granter acknowledges his signature, and the witness must then sign. Signature and witnessing must be one continuous process. A witness has to be over the age of sixteen and not be mentally incapax, blind, or unable to write. The witness must know the granter whose signature he is witnessing. It is sufficient that at the time of witnessing he has 'credible information' as to the granter's identity. The witness should not be a granter of or other party to the deed.

(c) Testing clauses

The details of the execution of the deed are added after signature. There are broadly two ways of doing this: the first, and more popular with conveyancers is the testing clause, which is a narration of the date and place of signing, and the authority of the signatory if necessary, plus details of the witness typed into the document after signature. To ensure that there is enough room for a testing clause to be typed on to the deed afterwards, a space on the engrossment is 'ruled off', usually by drawing a diagonal pencil line after the words 'IN WITNESS WHEREOF' and adding the words 'please leave blank' in pencil. Underneath the diagonal pencil line, further pencil lines are marked with the initials of the party or the words 'witness' next to it and the signatories are instructed to sign along these pencil lines.

Any alteration to the deed before signature must be declared in the testing clause to be effective.

The alternative method is for a signing block or docquet to be typed onto the deed before execution, and the details of place and time can be written in at the time of signing. Signing blocks are becoming more prevalent and often appear on pre-printed security documentation already. See the example that follows. Testing clauses are still used a lot by conveyancers, though, and so some examples are also given below. Section 10 of RoW(S)

A 1995 tantalisingly offered the possibility of a prescribed form of testing clause, through regulations, but these have never materialised. Appendix B to the Scottish Law Commission's Report on Requirements of Writing (Scot Law Com 112) contains some model forms of testing clauses, which are a hybrid form of signing block, but these have never really been adopted for general use. A signing block looks like this:

IN WITNESS WHEREOF these presents consisting of this [and the [   ]] preceding pages are [together with] [the Schedule] [and the plan(s)] annexed] executed as follows:

SUBSCRIBED for and on behalf of LIGHTYEAR DEVELOPMENT

COMPANY LIMITED at [   ] on the [   ] day of [   ] 2010

by

_____ Authorised Signatory

_____ (Full   Name)   signing by virtue of Power of Attorney by Lightyear Development Company Limited in his favour dated [   ] 2010

before this witness

_____ Witness

_____ Full Name

_____ Address

(d) Individuals

Individual natural persons who are granters, or who are signing as, or on behalf of, a granter, sign in accordance with the principal provisions of RoW(S)A 1995 ie they subscribe the deed, and their signature should be witnessed at the same time as signing, by a single witness who also signs the deed. This applies for all individuals, so will include persons signing as executor, administrator, trustee etc. Where more than one granter signs at the same time, then only one witness to all of their signatures is necessary. Where a person grants a document in more than one capacity (eg as an individual and as an executor) that person only needs to sign the deed once. An example testing clause:

495

IN WITNESS WHEREOF these presents typewritten on this and the three preceding pages are executed by me the said Eric Sweet, as an individual and as Executor nominate of the said Mrs Norma McNaught Monk or Sweet, at Kelvinforth on Tenth April Two thousand and ten, in the presence of Wendy Robertson, Trainee Solicitor of 42 Piemonte Place, Kelvinforth.

(e) Partnerships

Para 2 of Sch 2 of RoW(S)A 1995 provides that where the granter of a document is a partnership, it is signed on its behalf by one of the partners, or by a person authorised to sign the document on behalf of the partnership. The signatory can either use their own name or the firm name. This deals with validity. For probativity, a witness will also be required. An important point to note, however, is that, invariably, title to heritable property is held, not in the firm name (although this is competent) but in the names of the individual partners as trustees for the firm. Accordingly where the document relates to heritable property, execution should be in accordance with trust law, ie all of the trustees, or a quorum, should sign the deed. There is a view that a quorum, or majority of trustees is sufficient, but the law is uncertain on this point. (See Gretton & Reid: Conveyancing 3rd Edn para 22–18). An example testing clause (incorporating how to refer to the firm name if signed):

IN WITNESS WHEREOF these presents consisting of this and the preceding two pages are, together with the Plan annexed, signed by the said and the Eric Sweet as partners of and trustees for the said firm of Rowan Retirement Homes, the firm name being adhibited by the said Caroline Rowan, one of its partners, all at Kelvinforth on First November Two thousand and four, in the presence of Samantha Mirren Darling of 7 Lionheart Farm Cottages, Kinlochalmond, Perthshire.

(f) Limited Partnerships

There is no specific reference in RoW(S)A 1995 to execution by a Limited partnership. Usual practice is for documents to be executed by the general partner, although the partnership agreement for the Limited Partnership may make specific provision regarding execution of documents, so this should always be checked. A limited partner has no power to bind the partnership and should not sign the deed. A witness is required for the deed to be self-proving.

(g) Limited Liability Partnerships

For self-proving execution by an LLP either the signature of one member with a witness, or the signatures of two members without a witness is required (para 3A of Sch 2 of RoW(S)A 1995). An example testing clause:

> IN WITNESS WHEREOF these presents consisting of this and the preceding page are subscribed for and on behalf of the said Dunvorlich Renewables LLP, acting by Stuart James, a Member for and on behalf of the said Dunvorlich Renewables LLP, at Glasgow on Twenty Ninth October Two Thousand and nine, in the presence of Alan John Gaunt of 204 St Kentigern Street, Glasgow.

(h) Companies

Section 78 of the Companies Act 2006 provides that Scottish companies executing a deed in accordance with RoW(S)A 1995 will have effect as if executed by a company affixing its common seal. Companies signing deeds have a variety of signing options under the provisions of para 3 of Sch 2 of RoW(S)A 1995. For self-proving status, a deed requires subscription by either:

- one director and one witness;
- the secretary and one witness;
- one authorised signatory and a witness;
- two directors;
- a director and the secretary; or
- two authorised signatories.

As a matter of practice, the Companies Search obtained for a seller should include details of the current directors and secretary. If however the company execution is by authorised signatory(ies) then confirmation of the basis of authority should be exhibited to the purchaser's solicitors. Example testing clauses:

Signatory and witness:

> IN WITNESS WHEREOF these presents consisting of this and the seven preceding pages are signed for and on behalf of the said Lightyear Development Company Limited by Richard Byron Childs, one of its Directors, at Perth on the Fifth day of April Two Thousand and Four in the presence of Celia Bloomsbury of 65 Registration Row, Perth PH12 5TJ.

Director and Secretary:

> IN WITNESS WHEREOF these presents consisting of this and the seven preceding pages are signed for and on behalf of the said Lightyear Development Company Limited by Richard Byron Childs, a Director of the said Lightyear Development Company Limited and Rory Redknapp, Secretary of the said Lightyear Development Company Limited at Perth on the Fifth day of April Two Thousand and Four.

As a matter of style, you can use defined terms such as 'the Company' or 'Lightyear'.

Where the company is the borrower, the lenders will often require to see a Board Minute or Officer's Certificate from the company, containing details of the resolution by the Board of directors that authorises the taking of the loan, the granting of the security, and naming or nominating the directors or other authorised signatories of the company who will sign the standard security. Many Banks will produce their preferred style of Board Minute, which the Company (or its solicitor) types and completes with the details of the relevant meeting of the directors of the company. This does not need to be a formally constituted occasion, and a normal meeting of the directors or a sufficient quorum of them will be adequate.

'BOARD MINUTE

of

Lightyear Development Company Limited

(Registered in Scotland, Registered Number 809908)

MINUTES of MEETING of the BOARD of DIRECTORS of

LIGHTYEAR DEVELOPMENT COMPANY LTD (the 'Company')

held at 65 Registration Row, Perth

on 16 July 2010 at 11am.

PRESENT: Richard Byron Childs (Chairman)

Rhuaridh John Darling (Director)

Rory Redknapp, Secretary

1. Quorum

The chairman confirmed that notice of the meeting had been given to the Directors and the Secretary, and noted that a quorum was present and accordingly it was competent to proceed to the business of the meeting.

2. Standard Security

There was then produced to the meeting a draft of the proposed Standard Security to be granted by the Company in favour of Scotland Bank plc relative to the proposed development at Sardinia Terrace, Kelvinforth.

After careful consideration, the Directors resolved that it was in the best interests of the company to grant the Standard Security

The terms of the Standard Security were approved and it was resolved that Richard Byron Childs be and was duly authorised to execute the Standard Security on behalf of the Company.

3. Further business

There being no further business, the meeting was closed.'

(i) Local authorities

For valid execution by a local authority, para 4 of Sch 2 of RoW(S)A 1995 provides that, unless an enactment expressly provides otherwise, signature on its behalf by the proper officer of the local authority is required. The local authority will have a scheme of delegation or a scheme of appointments of proper officers, and lenders will often ask to see a certified copy of the scheme.

To be probative, then either the document must also be signed by a witness, or in addition to the signature of the proper officer, the document is sealed with the common seal of the authority.

(j) Other bodies corporate

Para 5 of Sch 2 of RoW(S)A 1995 applies to any body corporate other than a company incorporated under the Companies Acts, or a local authority, which includes industrial and provident societies, universities, building societies, and companies incorporated by Royal Charter. Again, unless there is other provision in another enactment where a granter of a document is a body corporate the document is validly signed by the body if it is signed on its behalf by either:

- a member of the governing board of the body or (if there is no governing body) a member of the body;
- the secretary of the body by whatever name he is called; or
- an authorised signatory of the body.

For the document to be self-proving, the signature must either be witnessed, or the common seal of the body must also be applied, in addition to signature.

(k) Overseas companies

The rules relating to 'Other bodies corporate' apply to execution of documents by overseas companies. Regulation 5 of the Overseas Companies (Execution of Documents and Registration of Charges) Regulations 2009 modifies s 48 of the Companies Act 2006 so that it provides: 'For the purposes of any enactment (a) providing for a document to be executed by a company by affixing its common seal, or (b) referring (in whatever terms) to a document so executed, a document signed or subscribed by or on behalf of an overseas company in accordance with the provisions of the Requirements of Writing (Scotland) Act 1995 has effect as if so executed.' Note that English companies are not overseas companies.

(l) Ministers of the Crown and other office holders

Where a granter of a document is a Minister or an office holder, then, unless another enactment provides otherwise, the document is subscribed by the Minister or office holder if it is signed:

- by him personally; or
- where an enactment or rule of law permits a document by a Minister to be signed by an officer of his, or by another Minister, by that officer or other Minister, or
- where an enactment or rule of law permits a document by an office holder to be signed by an officer of his, by that officer; or
- by any other person authorised to sign the document on his behalf.

A witness is required to achieve self proving status. In terms of the Ministers of the Crown Act 1975, it is presumed that such a signature is in fact authorised. In practice, each UK ministry sets out its signing procedure in the incorporating statutory instrument. For example, Article 3(2) of the Secretary for State for Business, Innovations and Skills Order 2009/2748 provides that a document will be executed by adhibiting the corporate seal or by being signed by an authorised person.

(m) Scottish Ministers

In terms of s 59(4) of the Scotland Act 1998, deeds executed on or after 1 July 1999 by the Scottish Ministers are validly executed if signed by any member of the Scottish Executive (now known as 'the Scottish Government') or under the Ministers' delegated authority.

LETTERS OF OBLIGATION

11.04 Solicitors in other jurisdictions are amazed that Scottish solicitors provide a firm's undertaking that the searches and records in relation to their client will be clear, but the letter of obligation, given by the seller's solicitors at settlement, is a key part of the conveyancing process in Scotland, and covers the gap period between the last date to which the 10A/11A or 12A/13A Report is brought down, and the date of registration of the purchaser's title. There is a time lag between the date to which the Searchers can certify the records in the Property Registers, and in that period, the purchaser is vulnerable, because a competing title may be registered or the granter may become insolvent, or a standard security over the property could be granted without the purchaser's knowledge. The seller's solicitors' undertaking is covered by the Professional Indemnity

Insurance for solicitors - the Master Policy. If the letter of obligation is 'classic' which means not only that the letter must be in a particular form, but also that certain steps and checks have been carried out by the seller's solicitor before giving it, then in the event of any claim arising out of the firm having to honour the undertaking, this will be met by the Master Policy (subject to limits of cover etc), and there will be no adverse impact on the level of that firm's Master Policy premium.

(a) Classic undertakings

Letters of Obligation granted in a variety of situations will qualify as 'classic' when given in appropriate circumstances, which is defined in the Master Policy as any situation involving 'the disposal for onerous consideration of any interest in property of any description or the granting of security over any such property by a client of that solicitor'. This will include undertakings given in lender/borrower transactions as well as sale/purchase transactions. It also includes transactions involving leases.

Typical undertakings include clear property and personal searches, and executed/recorded discharges. The PSG produced a suite of letters of obligation relating to sale, loan and lease transactions, in situations where title to the property is in the Sasine Register, or induces a first registration in the Land Register, and where the title is already registered. These are free to download from the PSG website, along with detailed Guidance Notes, which provide a full explanation of each provision in the style letters. These letters are generally now regarded as the industry norm. For a style letter of obligation see Appendix 1 (purchase transaction), which you will note additionally potentially undertakes to deliver the executed discharge if it is not available at settlement. In commercial property transactions this undertaking would not normally be given - see para 11.01

To qualify as 'classic' certain risk management controls must be observed:

- a search must have been carried out 'immediately prior to settlement' (which in practice will mean dated not more than 3 days prior to settlement, although the CML Handbook specifies 3 **working** days). In Sasine cases, this should include a search in the Computerised Presentment Book, and the search must be clear (Note: Insurers will require to see the clear searches in the event of a claim);

- the granter of the letter of obligation must have control of sufficient funds to pay the loan (and must know the identity and whereabouts of the party entitled to the redemption money) before giving an undertaking to deliver a discharge of a standard security;

- the granter of the letter of obligation must have made proper enquiry of the client regarding any outstanding security or other matter which might adversely affect the search (Note: in the event of a claim, Insurers will require evidence of such enquiry having been made and it is therefore prudent for the position to be documented in writing); and

- the granter of the letter of obligation must be unaware of any other security or matter which might adversely affect the search.

These are the minimum, essential risk management controls which must be complied with so that the undertaking should be 'classic'. Other additional risk management controls which, although not requirements of the Master Policy, may further reduce the risk of a claim arising. This might include making enquiry of the client regarding any impending insolvency or threat of inhibition, as well as ensuring that no part of the property has already been sold. Such enquiries must of course be judged appropriately, and if relevant broached with sensitivity. Any additional enquires which it is appropriate to make will depend upon the individual circumstances of the transaction and the client.

The period that the letter of obligation covers is not indefinite, for obvious reasons. The 'gap' that the letter of obligation will cover for clear records must be no more than 14 days from settlement. This is the maximum period that will be covered by the Master policy.

(b) Other undertakings

Any obligation by the Seller's solicitor, other than delivery of searches, and, where there are sufficient funds available, delivery of a recorded discharge, would be non-classic. All non-standard obligations ought therefore to be given on behalf of the client.

Delivery or exhibition of a Charges Search is a perfect example. A firm's undertaking to deliver a clear search in the Register of Charges should never be given, as this is something over which the firm has no control. That tends to be the rule of thumb for obligations: if the firm has absolute control over the thing that is being undertaken then it may be possible to give a firm's undertaking. These should not be given lightly however, and anything other than the standard classic undertakings need to be approved by a partner in the firm, whose policy excess and PI premium is on the line.

The thirty-six day continuation period provided in the undertaking to produce Charges Searches is to allow for a combination of the period of 14 days after settlement, by the end of which the disposition has to be recorded, plus the period of 22 days after the date of completion/settlement, during which a charge created by the seller immediately prior to the date of completion/settlement would normally appear in the Charges Register.

(c) Back-to-back undertakings

In loan transactions where the borrower is also purchasing the Property, the seller's solicitors will be granting a letter of obligation in favour of the borrower's solicitors, which they should ensure is also in classic terms, to enable them to grant a letter of obligation to the lender's solicitors in classic terms.

Where the seller and the purchaser/borrower are companies, the lender's solicitors will also require an undertaking to exhibit or deliver a clear Charges Search against the seller, as well as one against the borrower. Such undertakings are given on behalf of the client only, but the borrower's solicitor should ensure that they have a similar obligation from the seller's solicitor to produce the Charges Search to enable them to give a similar undertaking to the lender's solicitors.

(d) Insolvency sales

It is becoming more common for no letter of obligation to be given in a sale by an insolvency practitioner, although the question of whether any letter of obligation is to be granted is a matter for negotiation in each case, but it is becoming increasingly rare. Any letter of obligation which the seller's solicitors agree to grant would be (a) on behalf of the Company in receivership only and (b) in terms which expressly exclude any liability on the part of the receiver.

(e) The future for letters of obligation

Solicitors would rather not be exposed to the risks of granting letters of obligation, but they are regarded as a necessary evil. The Master Policy insurers would rather not be exposed to the risks of solicitors granting letters of obligation and there are strict rules that apply to the circumstances in which these are classic. It is clear however that there is a distinct impression that such undertakings will become harder to insure against. Proposals by the Scottish Law Commission in the Land Registration Bill will assist. One aspect of the English system of title registration of which we have long been envious is the 'priority period'.

In Scotland, when searches in the Property and Personal Registers are carried out there is an obvious gap from the date of that search until the date of completion. There is a similar 'gap' in England, but the purchaser is able to benefit from the protection afforded to him by the priority period that is available following an application for an official search. This gives the purchaser a period of grace within which to register their title, and serves as a form of protection against other applications for registration against the property. The SLC proposals include a recommendation that a similar arrangement of 'advance notice' should apply in the Land Register. This has come from considerable pressure within the profession, and is likely to be one element of the Land Registration proposals that may be fast tracked through the parliamentary process. If we have an advance notice procedure in Scotland, then Letters of Obligation could become a thing of the past. Imagine.

11.05 FUNDS AND SETTLEMENT

(a) Funds

The purchaser's solicitor must ensure that the necessary financial arrangements are in place in good time for completion. If there are any payments that are made in respect of the property that require to be apportioned between the seller and the purchaser as at the date of entry, then the seller's solicitors prepare a State for Settlement, or Completion Statement which will show the purchase price and the plus or minus effect on it of any apportionments. A State for Settlement is usual in commercial investment properties where the rents received from the tenants are apportioned. Usually, since the seller will have received the current quarter's rent already, the proportion of these to which the purchaser is entitled will be reflected as a deduction from the price. The draft completion statement is sent to the purchaser's solicitors to approve:

'[STATE FOR SETTLEMENT][COMPLETION STATEMENT]

in connection with the Sale of 104 to 110 Lombardy Street, Kelvinforth

Sellers:	Dunvorlich Investments Ltd Per Gaunt Mitchell LLP, Solicitors, Glasgow
Purchasers:	Lightyear Investments Ltd Per O'Neill Middleton, Solicitors, Perth
Date of Entry:	9 January 2011

Purchase Price	£1,950,000
Less	
Portions of rents due to Purchasers as per Schedule:	51,523
	£1,898,477

SCHEDULE OF APPORTIONMENTS

104 Lombardy Street, Kelvinforth

Rent £120,000 pa from 9 Jan 2011 to 27 Feb 2011 (50 days) (£328.76 per day)	£16,438.00

106 Lombardy Street, Kelvinforth

Rent £89,750 pa from 9 Jan 2011 to 27 February 2011 (50 days) (£245.89 per day)	£12,294.50

108 Lombardy Street, Kelvinforth

Rent £64,930 pa from 9 Jan 2011 to 27 February 2011 (50 days) (£177.89 per day)	£8,894.50

110 Lombardy Street, Kelvinforth

Rent £101,440 pa from 9 Jan 2011 to 27 Feb 2011
(50 days) (£277.92 per day)   £13,896.00'

Where funding for the purchase is coming from a bank or building society, the purchaser's solicitor must ensure that sufficient notice is given so that funds are in the solicitor's clients account in time for settlement. When also acting for the lender in residential transactions, the loan instructions should be checked at the start to note any period of notice that the lender requires for draw down of funds. When separate solicitors are acting for the lender, bank account details for where funds are to be sent should be given to them in good time.

Where funds are coming from the client, any cheque must be given to the solicitors in plenty of time for it to be cleared through the banking system. This is crucial. A solicitor's cheque from their clients' account is treated as guaranteed funds. If, therefore, a solicitor issues a cheque, it is incumbent on them to ensure that they have funds to meet it, as the solicitors may not stop the cheque once issued, other than in the most exceptional circumstances. So, if the solicitor issued a cheque and then the cheque from his client was not honoured, the risk rests with the solicitors, and any attempt to shift the problem to the sellers may amount to professional misconduct. The following statement by the Law Society (1981 JLSS 357) makes the position clear:

'A solicitor acting for a purchaser in a conveyancing transaction has a duty to ensure either that he has cleared funds in his clients' account for the settlement of such a conveyancing transaction or that any cheque which he has received for his client will be met by the paying bank. There is a principle that a cheque drawn by the solicitor acting for a purchaser on his client bank account and handed over in settlement in a conveyancing transaction to the solicitor acting for the seller should not be stopped except in exceptional circumstances.

Such exceptional circumstances would arise in the event of circumstances amounting to breach of contract on the part of the seller, as for example when the purchasers are unable to receive vacant possession or if the subjects have been destroyed (and these circumstances are contrary to the terms of the missives) or in the event of a postal settlement where the disposition which is delivered contains a defect in execution.'

In this unfortunate event the purchasers' solicitors would be well advised to inform the Law Society before they stop their cheque.

(b) Council tax and rates

Apportionment of council tax, for residential properties and non domestic rates, for commercial properties are dealt with by the relevant local authority. A notification of the change of ownership is prepared by the seller's solicitors, approved by the purchaser's solicitors and sent to the local authority at settlement. (For an example notice see Appendix 1 (purchase transaction).

(c) Notice of Change of Landlord

In investment purchases of commercial property, the occupational tenants may be oblivious to the fact that the identity of their landlord is about to change. There is no need or requirement to involve the tenants in the sale, but once ownership changes hands, there is an administrative and management requirement to ensure that future rents and other payments are made to the new owner, or its managing agents, and for future interactions between landlord and tenants, the tenants should know who to contact or send intimations to for the future.

Accordingly, the seller's solicitor and the purchaser's solicitor will adjust draft notifications of the change of landlords to be sent to the tenants at completion. Either the seller's solicitor or the purchaser's solicitor can deal with this. Each party has an interest in ensuring that the new arrangements are put in place. The following style notification (which forms a Part of the Schedule to the PSG Offer to Sell Investment Property) is suitable for this purpose:

'To: [Insert name of Tenants]

Dear Sirs

[ ] (the 'Property')

On behalf of our clients, [   ], [incorporated under the Companies Acts (Registered Number [   ]) and having their registered office at [   ] we intimate to you (the **'Tenants'**) that, as from [   ] 20[   ], our clients have sold their interest as your landlords in the Property to [   ], [incorporated under the Companies Acts (Registered Number [   ]) and having their registered office at [   ]] (the **'Purchaser'**).

Future rent demands will be issued to you by or on behalf of the Purchaser and future communications concerning any matter arising from the letting should be addressed to the Purchaser or their managing agents, namely [   ].

[We also intimate that we have received a retrocession from [   ], [as agent and trustee], of their right, title and interest to the rent and other sums receivable in terms of the assignation of rents granted by [   ] in their favour dated [   ] and created on [   ] (a copy of which accompanies this letter).]

This letter is enclosed in duplicate. Kindly post the duplicate, with the docquet on it duly signed, [using the accompanying pre-paid addressed envelope] to [   ], the solicitors acting for the Purchaser.

Yours faithfully'

These notices are usually sent in duplicate, with a receipt docquet endorsed on the duplicate for the tenant to sign in acknowledgement and return.

(d) Common charges

Where a flat in a tenement building is sold, any property manager or factor (if there is one) should be asked by the seller's agents to apportion the common charges for maintenance of the building between the parties. This can be done when the property manager or factor is informed of the change of ownership by the sellers' solicitors. In modern practice it is usual for the property manager or factor to ask an incoming owner for a deposit to meet future charges. This deposit is set against these charges. Purchasers' solicitors should ask to see the latest common charges receipt.

Practice seems to vary geographically in relation to factors. It is common in Glasgow, for example, for residential tenement buildings to have a factor appointed to deal with common repairs and routine matters. Such arrangements are more the exception rather than the rule in Edinburgh tenements however. It is more typical for commercial properties in multiple ownership or occupation to have a property manager, who will deal with matters or repair and maintenance and collect the costs from the owners or occupiers through a service charge arrangement.

Over the years the activities of some factors have received a poor press, with complaints of poor service and high costs. This has resulted in the Property Factors (Scotland) Act 2011, which, at the time of writing, is due to come into force on 1 October 2012.

The PF(S)A 2011 is designed to protect homeowners who contract with property factors by establishing a public register of property factors in Scotland and making it a criminal offence for a property factor to operate without being registered. A mandatory code of conduct is to be introduced, setting out minimum standards of practice required of registered property factors. A Homeowner Housing Panel will be established to deal with disputes between homeowners and property factors.

(e) Interest

When settlement takes place properly on the agreed date of entry, the question of interest does not arise—that is to say when the full purchase price is paid by the purchaser and the property is made available with the disposition, the titles and the keys. Where, however, one party or the other cannot meet their obligation, the question of interest arises and this will generally be regulated by the provisions of the missives - see paras 6.10(m) and 6.13(c). If there is any delay that results in an interest payment being required then the parties will need to agree the amount of the additional payment due at settlement/completion. It will usually fall to the seller's solicitor to do the calculation, and agree this with the purchaser's solicitor. It is sensible to work out the daily amount, so that it is clear what sum will be due on any particular day. See para 12.04(d) for further detail.

(f) Bridging loans

If the date of entry arrives and the purchaser's funds are not yet available, it may be possible for the purchasers to ask their bank for a bridging loan to avoid being in default on the date of entry. However, if the purchasers have not yet sold their house or do not have an approved offer of mortgage, the bank may not be willing to provide 'open-ended bridging' (see para 12.04(c)). For this reason it is essential to ensure that availability of funds is certain.

(g) Settlement/Completion

If funds are available in good time, and settlement is being dealt with by way of cheque, then settlement can usually be effected by post – ie the purchaser's solicitor send the cheque by post or DX/Legal Post the night before the date of entry. The settlement documents are similarly sent to the purchaser's solicitors overnight. On the day of settlement a phone call should confirm receipt by each solicitor of the respective items, and the seller's solicitor then authorises release of the keys. Alternatively, settlement in person can be arranged, in which case the tradition is that the purchaser's solicitor goes to the seller's solicitor. More often than not however, settlements nowadays are carried out by post overnight, or by courier on the day.

To get round the difficulty of the cheque or the disposition reaching the other solicitor before the other part is received, and being misused, the sender of the cheque or disposition will usually present it on the basis that it is held as undelivered until the corresponding settlement items are received. The Law Society guidelines on settlement cheques being held as undelivered, from 1998, is still current guidance. The text is set out below:

> 'Settlement cheques sent to be held as undelivered (1998)
>
> As part of their Review of Practice Guidelines, the Professional Practice Committee have considered Guidelines which were issued in 1992 and 1994, and have agreed that there should be no change to the most recent Guideline, which was published in 1994. The Committee reaffirmed that such matters should be agreed in advance if at all possible, and that it is improper professional practice to impose unilaterally a condition that a cheque in settlement of a transaction be

held as undelivered pending confirmation that the sender is in funds. The Committee accepted, however, that while as a matter of law the seller's solicitor may be entitled to encash the cheque and ignore the condition, such action would not be good professional practice as it would destroy the professional trust between agents. The text of the Guideline is as follows:

In the 1992 Journal at page 323 a note was published after a purchaser's agent, without prior agreement or discussion, sent the selling agent a cheque for the purchase price to be held as undelivered until the purchaser's agent telephoned to say it could be cashed. The chief accountant's advice as contained in the note was that the selling agent should have ignored the unilaterally imposed condition relating to delivery of the cheque and should have cashed it.

Exception was taken to this view and the matter was extensively debated within the Society's Conveyancing Committee, the Professional Practice Committee and the Council. The considered view of the majority, approved by Council, contradicted important elements in the chief accountant's note.

It is not competent unilaterally to impose a condition, whether made verbally or in writing, in a contract such as for the sale of heritable property. In the absence of subsequent agreement, the missives prevail. It is professionally wrong for an agent to impose a unilateral condition, the first intimation of which to the other side is in a letter on the morning of settlement. Prior discussion and agreement is necessary. Professors Cusine and Rennie touch on this at para. 6.15 of their recent book, Missives, where they state: It is not open to the purchasing solicitor, at the time of dispatch of the cheque, to require the cheque to be held as undelivered where the seller's obligations under the contract are unimplemented, unless of course that has been agreed with the seller's solicitor.

It is acknowledged that a practice that has developed of sending cheques to be held as undelivered with both sides being agreeable to this. This practice avoids alternative courses of action such as bridging or effecting settlement in person, all of which can be viewed as adding expense, though agents should be aware of the benefits of electronic transfer of funds. Assuming trust between practitioners, arrangements which rely on mutual acceptance of an undertaking not to cash the cheque can be made. It is analogous to the customary sending of the settlement cheque to be held as undelivered pending dispatch of a duly executed disposition, etc

It is also important to bear in mind that the question of conditional delivery of a cheque is dealt with in s.21 of the Bills of Exchange Act 1882.

The Society's view is that it was wrong and improper professional practice for the purchasing agent to impose the unilateral condition which he did. However, that did not entitle the selling agent to cash the cheque, given that it was sent subject to the words to be held as undelivered. The Professional Practice Committee and the Council have confirmed that where money or deeds are sent to be held as undelivered pending purification of a condition, they should be so held if the condition is not purified. Settlement will not take place until they can be treated as delivered, with consequent penalty interest if provided in the missives. The matter is one of practice between agents rather than of law.'

Current practice is such that invariably the solicitors will have agreed by phone or email that items and funds are to be held as undelivered in this reciprocal way.

It is increasingly common for bank to bank transfers of funds, and probably the norm in commercial transactions. A CHAPS (Clearing House Automated Payment System, or telegraphic transfer) payment is arranged from the purchaser's solicitors account to the seller's solicitors' account. Again, this obviously necessitates the purchaser's solicitors having cleared funds in their clients' account, since the removal of funds from one account to the other takes place that day – no period of clearing is required. Bank to bank transfers do not happen instantaneously however, and waiting for funds to arrive can be a stressful part of the completion day for all concerned, as the process sometimes takes several hours. Careful planning is required and the instruction should be given to the bank as early as possible.

Holding funds that have arrived in the seller's solicitors' bank account as undelivered can be slightly more complicated. Again the Law Society has produced Guidelines (in 2008) which are reproduced below:

'Guideline on settlement by cheque, loan redemption and remit of the free proceeds of sale effective 1 November 2008

The Professional Practice Committee has seen an increasing number of requests for information or guidance on the question of whether settlement of house purchase and sale transactions should take place by cheque or electronic (CHAPS) transfer. This is also getting to be a frequently asked question by clients, and the issues are not well understood.

Almost all transactions now settle by post. A solicitor can send a cheque subject to conditions but cannot attach conditions when sending a CHAPS transfer. It is perfectly proper to reach agreement with the other Solicitor in advance of sending funds by CHAPS transfer that those funds will be held as undelivered pending fulfilment of certain conditions, but if that is not agreed in advance, it is too late to impose the condition at the time the funds are sent by CHAPS transfer.

If such pre-arranged conditions are not fulfilled, the Solicitor receiving the funds would risk a finding of Professional Misconduct if the funds are treated as delivered and paid out to clients or third parties.

An electronic transfer cannot be stopped, but if the buyer's Solicitor does not receive the titles, Letter of Obligation, keys etc in return for a client's account cheque which has been sent to be held as undelivered he can either demand the return of a cheque or stop the cheque (in extreme circumstances). Settlement by cheque therefore protects the buyer by giving the buyer's solicitor control over the money even after the cheque has been sent. A seller's solicitor can also protect the seller by attaching conditions to deeds etc sent by post, including a condition about interest on the price if settlement has been delayed (a not infrequent problem these days).

Traditionally, when a selling Solicitor received and banked another Solicitor's client account cheque, he could write his own client account cheques to redeem his client's loan or settle his client's purchase on the same day. Problems are encountered very occasionally if the Solicitor receiving the cheque banks at the same branch of the same bank as the Solicitor sending the cheque although that is rare.

Since the introduction of the cheque clearing process known as 2-4-6 there is a risk that the cheque sent out will be presented for payment at the sender's bank before the cheque paid in has cleared. The Professional Practice department at the Society has received a number of telephone calls from Solicitors affected in this way.

These problems may be surmounted by either

(1) clients arranging short term bridging loans or

(2) solicitors arranging a temporary facility with their own bank that would allow the bank to transfer sufficient funds into the client bank account to meet the presentation of an outgoing cheque where the incoming cheque has still to clear. Any interest payable could be charged to the client although that would have to be specified in the relevant Terms of Business.

If neither of these options is adopted, a third option namely

(3) settlement by CHAPS transfer is suggested to avoid the possibility of a shortfall in the client account that may in turn lead to a failure to comply with Rule 4(1)(a) of the Solicitors (Scotland) Accounts etc Rules 2001.

If a selling Solicitor is also purchasing for his client on the same day and wishes the sale to be settled by CHAPS transfer the selling solicitor should put a clause in the missives requiring the sale to be settled electronically. That will be subject to agreement by the buyer, but it must be in the missives or it cannot be insisted upon.

Subject to these considerations the Professional Practice Committee remains of the view that settlement by cheque between solicitors is in both clients' interests as the cheque can be sent in advance to be held as undelivered pending delivery of relevant items and/or confirmation that the sender is in funds, and the disposition can be sent in advance subject to the seller's conditions.

Lenders and clients

The Committee agreed however that so far as settlement with the client and the lender are concerned the seller's agent should ascertain in advance whether the seller would prefer to meet the cost of a CHAPS transfer of funds or opt for the issue of a cheque in relation to (a) redemption of the loan (if the method is not prescribed by the lender) and (b) remit of the free proceeds of sale to the seller. Such instructions will of course be subject to the solicitor ensuring that there are sufficient cleared funds to meet whatever method of payment is adopted.

England and Wales

If a client is purchasing a property in England or Wales out of the proceeds of sale of a property in Scotland, it is important to ascertain the requirements for settling the purchase at the earliest possible stage. Purchase and sale transactions routinely settle by CHAPS transfer in England and Wales and the clients English or Welsh Solicitor will assume that he will receive funds by CHAPS transfer. If there will not be sufficient time for a cheque to clear before funds are required in England or Wales, the selling Solicitor should explain that to the client and conclude the bargain for the sale on the basis that settlement will be by CHAPS transfer or advise the client that he will need to arrange temporary bridging facilities to await cleared funds. Failure to address these issues at an early stage is likely to lead to a dissatisfied client and a possible complaint to the Scottish Legal Complaints Commission.'

When the settlement items change hands, this amounts to delivery of the disposition, in its technical sense. Before the disposition is registered, the fact of delivery can be an important issue for the purchaser, particularly if insolvency of the seller intervenes.

(h) VAT

The rules on whether VAT is payable on the purchase of commercial property are complex but the basic rule is that no VAT is payable unless:

- The property is less than three years old;
- The type of commercial property falls within one of a number of special categories (a common example being where the property comprises parking facilities); or
- The seller of the property has opted to tax the property for VAT.

In any of these situations, VAT will be payable on the price of the property at the standard rate which is currently 20%. However if the sale of the property constitutes a Transfer of a Going Concern (TOGC), the purchase will fall outwith the scope of VAT as the transfer of a business (namely, the letting of the property), resulting in no liability to VAT on the price (see para 6.13(d)). If VAT is payable on the price, (only in commercial transactions as VAT is not payable on residential purchases) then the seller should produce a VAT receipt for the purchaser, to allow it to offset the

VAT in its VAT return. The seller's solicitor should ask his client for this in good time for completion.

(i) Letter of Non-crystallisation

When purchasing from a company that has granted a floating charge, the seller's solicitors should deliver a letter of non-crystallisation from the floating charge holder dated not more than one or two days prior to the date of settlement/completion. See paras 8.18(j)(v) and 10.06(e).

STAMP DUTY LAND TAX (SDLT)

11.06 Since December 2003, purchases of property above a certain price level have attracted a tax known as Stamp Duty Land Tax. The Finance Act 2003 abolished its precursor, stamp duty, except on instruments relating to stock or marketable securities, and replaced it with SDLT. Although amended frequently by regulations and successive Finance Acts, Part 4 and various Schs to the FA 2003 contains the basic provisions by which the SDLT regime was set up. The main elements of the basis of charge are

- SDLT is payable on a land transaction which is not exempt from charge;
- the charge is based on a percentage of the chargeable consideration;
- the liability to pay the charge falls on the purchaser (which definition includes tenants, assignees etc)
- a Land Transaction Return (which is made on an SDLT1 Form – see para 11.6(f)) – must be made within thirty days of the effective date and must be accompanied by the relevant tax (unless online submission is made).

This is the technical stuff:

(a) Land Transaction

A land transaction is any acquisition of a chargeable interest ie:

- any estate, interest, right or power in or over land in the UK or
- the benefit of an obligation, restriction or condition affecting the value of any such estate, interest, right or power,

other than an exempt interest, which is: any security interest (a standard security); a licence to use or occupy land (as distinct from a lease); and any other interest provided by the Treasury through regulations. This means that the purchase of land or the taking of a lease of land will be a land transaction.

(b) Chargeable Consideration

Chargeable consideration amounts to any consideration given in money or money's worth and includes any VAT actually paid. In other words: the price, or a premium paid by a tenant or assignee. A just and reasonable apportionment must be made of any consideration that does not relate only to the land transaction (eg apportionment to fittings). If non-monetary consideration is paid, it is valued at market value on the effective date of the transaction.

The charge is based on the 'slab system', ie once the threshold is reached, all of the consideration is chargeable at the higher rate. For current rates of SDLT see the Stamp taxes section of the HMRC website: http://www.hmrc.gov.uk/so/index.htm.

(c) Definition of Purchaser

The purchaser is the person who acquires the subject matter of the transaction and the vendor is the person who disposes of the subject matter of the transaction. The subject matter of the transaction is the chargeable interest acquired or disposed of. These expressions apply even if no consideration is given. The expressions translate into lease transactions so that the 'purchaser' will also be the tenant under a new lease; the assignee of a lease; and the landlord in a renunciation.

(d) Effective Date

Where a contract is entered into which will be completed by a conveyance of the property, the contract itself is not the land transaction which is taxable. The effective date is determined by the following rules:

If a transaction is completed without having been previously substantially performed, then the contract and the completion are treated as a single transaction and the effective date of the transaction is the date of completion. However, if the contract is substantially performed without being completed, (for example if the purchaser were allowed to take entry to the property, before the disposition is delivered), the contract is treated as if it were the transaction provided for in the contract. The effective date of the transaction is when the contract is substantially performed.

A contract is substantially performed if:

- the purchaser or a person connected with the purchaser takes possession of the whole, or substantially the whole, of the subject matter of the contract; or

- a substantial amount of the consideration is paid or provided.

Although the legislation does not define what constitutes a substantial amount of the consideration, it seems HMRC regards this as meaning 90% or more of the consideration (see HMRC Stamp Taxes Manual page SDLT07950).

(e) Practical effects

It is important to be familiar with the concepts of SLDT – especially 'effective date' and 'substantial performance' as these will trigger not just liability on the part of your client but also the requirement for action on your part. Actually, the subtleties of 'substantial performance' tend to come into play more in lease transactions, but might from time to time be an issue in sale/purchase transactions. The usual situation however will be that settlement or completion will trigger the requirement to make an SDLT return and pay any tax that is due.

As the liability to pay any SDLT that is due falls on the purchaser, it is up to the purchaser's solicitor to ensure that they have sufficient funds at settlement to meet the tax, since it is not possible to register the disposition in favour of the purchaser, without producing evidence to the Keeper, of submission of an SLDT return to HMRC.

(f) SDLT submission

The SDLT1 application form and cheque for SDLT must be submitted to HMRC not later than 30 days after the effective date of the transaction.

The due date is known as the 'filing date' and there are penalties for late filing. The SDLT forms you may need to use are:

SDLT 1	Main form required for all transactions that are notifiable to HMRC.
SDLT 2	Supplementary form to SDLT 1 where there are more than two vendors and/or purchasers.
SDLT 3	Supplementary form to SDLT1 where need to provide additional details re land that can't fit on the limited space provided on SDLT1.
SDLT 4	Supplementary form to SDLT1 called 'Additional details re Transactions, including Leases'. This is required to be submitted with SDLT1 where the purchaser or tenant is a company.

Submission can be made on paper forms, or on electronic forms generated by specialist software which many firms of solicitors use. If you are able to use the ARTL system for your transaction, then the SDLT return will be completed as part of that process. Alternatively you can register to make SDLT submissions online via the HMRC website.

The SDLT return is a tax return that is the responsibility of the purchaser to make. Accordingly, and even if submission is being made online, there is a point at which a hard copy needs to be printed and sent to the purchaser himself for signing. There are two options here – either the purchaser signs the principle certificate that is submitted by post, or an agent's copy is produced (which usually contains all the information except the effective date). This can be given to the purchaser to sign as authority for you as his solicitor to sign and send the final submission – either in paper form, or online. In the latter case of course no signature is possible, instead there is a declaration that you have the purchaser's authority to submit.

When the SDLT1 form has been submitted to HMRC – either by post, by personal presentment at the Stamp Office HMRC in Edinburgh (see below), through ARTL, or online, along with payment of the tax due (although if submission is made through the online facility, the purchaser has 30 days to pay the tax. In practice the solicitors must ensure that they have funds to meet the tax before pressing the 'submit' button in the online application, and should send a cheque to HMRC that day).

You will receive an SDLT5 certificate back from HMRC once they have processed the application. It is this certificate that should accompany your application to the Registers of Scotland with your deed.

Always keep copies on file of any SDLT forms that relate to the transaction.

(g) Personal Presentment

It is possible for the purchaser's solicitor to personally present SDLT forms (and cheque) at the Edinburgh Stamp Office at Sighthill in certain circumstances. Part of the problem with the paper submission procedure is that the completed form and the cheque in payment of the tax requires to be sent by post to HMRC in Netherton (HM Revenue & Customs, Stamp Taxes/SDLT, Comben House, Farriers Way, Netherton, Merseyside L30 4RN (or by DX to: Rapid Data Capture Centre DX725593 Bootle 9)

However, in many commercial transactions in particular, this is too slow. The lender's solicitors require to be in a position to present their standard security for registration immediately. To do that they require the disposition as well to present for registration, because without it, the borrower would not yet have a registered title over which the security is granted, so the two deeds must go together. If SDLT is due on the purchase, they must also have the SDLT5 to present to the Keeper. Online submission solves this problem, because it generates an SDLT5 immediately, but an alternative is the arrangement for personal presentation in Scotland to which the HMRC agreed several years ago. They produced a style letter for solicitors to sign, which should accompany personal presentation. The letter is reproduced below.

This service can only be used in one of the three circumstances identified in the letter: ie

(i)   The seller is a company and its solicitors will not give a firm's undertaking in relation to the charges search – which solicitors will never do of course;

(ii)   No letter of obligation is being given – eg in insolvency sales; or

(iii)   The loan funds cannot be used unless the purchaser's title is registered. In practice this means the ability to be able to register the title straight away – so that the draw down of funds, completion and registration are simultaneous.

This form of presentation is only available within two days of the effective date.

'Dear Sirs

Unique reference number of SDLT1:

Address of Property:

We confirm that the land transaction return with the above unique reference falls within the Special Arrangements criteria agreed between the Inland Revenue and the Law Society of Scotland as detailed below and that **[immediate registration] [registration within two working days]** is required.

Please tick
box to indicate
which applies

	The Seller is a corporate entity and the Seller's solicitor has not given a solicitor's personal letter of obligation in respect of the Charges register and the Company file, or
	The Seller's solicitor has been requested to give a solicitor's personal letter of obligation but has refused to do so, or
	The Purchaser needs to register ownership on or before obtaining access to the transaction funding.

Yours faithfully'

(h) 16th Day Procedure for late SDLT5 certificates

HMRC and the Law Society have agreed a procedure, which only applies in Scotland, for being able to obtain a handwritten SDLT5 from the Edinburgh Stamp Office, if there is no sign of the SDLT5 certificate from submission by post to HMRC in Netherton.

Where the SDLT5 certificate has not been received within 16 calendar days after the effective date, an emergency telephone enquiry service to be operated by the Edinburgh Stamp Office has been set up, to be used strictly in these circumstances only.

If a cheque was sent with the return, obtain the cheque number and amount of the cheque, and establish whether the cheque has been cashed (and if it has, the date on which it was cashed). Do not stop an uncashed cheque. Make sure you have to hand a copy of the SDLT return(s) as submitted to HMRC and any SDLT8s (letters about incorrectly completing SDLT returns) or other communications received from or sent to HMRC.

Contact the Edinburgh Stamp Office and ask for this service. They may ask you to fax the SDLT return to them or to provide additional information. Provided that there are no errors in the returns, they will arrange for a handwritten SDLT5 certificate to be provided to you, and it may be possible for you to arrange for the SDLT5 certificate to be collected from the Edinburgh Stamp Office.

It is important to note that the availability of this procedure is subject to early submission of the SDLT Return (preferably on the effective date), if you are to expect receipt of your SDLT5 Certificate within 16 calendar days of the effective date of the transaction.

(i) Lending Transactions

Where the lender's solicitors insist on presenting both the purchaser's disposition and the standard security in favour of the lender for registration together, they may also take the signed SDLT submission forms and a cheque in payment of the tax and attend to all these formalities. The respective solicitors may be perfectly happy to let this happen, but there may be a concerns that since payment of SDLT is the purchasers' legal duty, which if they fail to do can result in penalties, then some audit trail of responsibility may be necessary. The PSG has produced a series of simple undertakings which can be used in these circumstances which are shown below. These cover the following situations:

- Where the Borrower's solicitor is to submit the SDLT application
- Where the Lender's solicitor is to submit the SDLT application
- Where submission is being made Online/Electronically by the Borrower's Solicitor

As with any undertaking which is being granted by the firm, the borrower's or the lender's solicitor should ensure that implementation of the undertakings (other than those on behalf of the client) is entirely within its control (eg it has funds to pay the SDLT, or is in possession of a signed SDLT1 form etc). The style Letters of Undertaking caters for either personal presentation or online submission. Detailed Guidance notes for these undertakings are available on the PSG website.

Online submission via the HMRC website is of course subject to the availability of the online facility, and it is important to check, before giving the undertaking, that there is no planned downtime on the website that conflicts with the timings of the obligations in the letter of undertaking. Where the online facility is unavailable, personal presentation is still possible, and would be the preferred alternative, to ensure that the purchaser's interest, and consequently that of the lender, is registered as quickly as possible.

There is no requirement to produce one of these undertakings in the circumstances described, and many solicitors may be content to trust the other solicitors to carry out the SDLT formalities without seeking a formal undertaking. It is a matter of judgement or practice whether to seek an undertaking in these, or similar, circumstances, although the issue of late submission penalties for SDLT should be borne in mind.

Undertaking 1 – Borrower to Lender

'(To be given by the Borrower's solicitors to the Lender's Solicitors)

Dear Sirs

[   ] ('Borrower')

[   ] ('Lender')

[   ] ('Property')

With reference to the completion of this transaction [today] [on [   ] ('effective date')], we hereby:

(i)   undertake to submit the SDLT1 to HM Revenue & Customs either: (a) within two working days of [today's date][the effective date] [by way of Special Presentation at Edinburgh] together with cheque or other payment for the SDLT due or (b) by electronic submission within one working day of [today's date][the effective date]

(ii) undertake to deliver the SDLT5 to you [as soon as it is received by us] [within one working day of receipt if specially presented at Edinburgh, or within one working day of electronic submission if submitted online].

(iii) undertake to advise you of any rejection by HM Revenue & Customs of the Borrower's SDLT application, prior to the issue of an [SDLT5 Certificate] [electronic receipt], and provide you with a copy of any such rejection and other relevant correspondence

(iv) in the event of any rejection by HM Revenue & Customs, undertake on behalf of the Borrower, to correct the application and resubmit it and a remittance for the correct amount of SDLT to HM Revenue & Customs without delay [and]

(v)   where alternative (i)(b) applies, undertake to make payment of the correct amount of SDLT to HM Revenue & Customs within 30 days of the effective date.

Yours faithfully'

Undertaking 2 - Lender to Borrower

'(To be given by the Lender's solicitors to the Borrower's Solicitors)

Dear Sirs

[   ] ('Borrower')

[   ] ('Lender')

[   ] ('Property')

With reference to the completion of this transaction [today][on [   ] ('effective date')], we hereby:-

(i)   undertake to submit the SDLT1 and cheque or other payment for the SDLT due within two working days of [today's date][the effective date] to HM Revenue & Customs [by way of Special Presentation at Edinburgh],

(ii) undertake to present the Disposition in favour of the Borrower for registration in the Land Register as soon as reasonably practicable after, and in any event no later than [two] working days after, receipt by us of the SDLT5 Certificate,

(iii) undertake without delay, (i) to advise you of any rejection by HM Revenue & Customs of the Borrower's SDLT application, prior to the issue of an SDLT5 Certificate, and (ii) provide you with a copy of any such rejection and other relevant correspondence.

Yours faithfully'

Undertaking 3 – Borrower to Lender

'(To be given by the Borrower's solicitors to the Lender's Solicitors)

Dear Sirs

[   ] ('Borrower')

[   ] ('Lender')

[   ] ('Property')

With reference to the completion of this transaction [today][on [ ] ('effective date')], we hereby:

(i) undertake to deliver to you the SDLT5 within 1 working day if it is received by us,

(ii) undertake without delay, (i) to advise you of any rejection by HM Revenue & Customs of the Borrower's SDLT application received by us, prior to the issue of an SDLT5 Certificate, and (ii) provide you with a copy of any such rejection and other relevant correspondence received by us, and

(iii) in the event of any rejection by HM Revenue & Customs, undertake on behalf of the Borrower, to correct the application and resubmit it and a remittance for the correct amount of SDLT to HM Revenue & Customs without delay.

Yours faithfully'

FURTHER READING

Stair Encyclopaedia: Re-issue 5 Conveyancing Part 8

The Importance of Being Classic' by Alistair Sim JLSS April 2001

Law Society of Scotland Letter of Obligation FAQs: http://www.lawscot. org.uk/members/member-services/a-to-z-rules--guidance/g---m/letters-of-obligations---faqs

SDLT Manual and other information on SDLT on the HMRC website at: http://www.hmrc.gov.uk/so/index.htm

CHECKLIST

- The PSG Completion Checklist is reproduced here with kind permission of the PSG. It has been compiled for use with any property transaction and you will need to tailor the checklist for your transaction.
- The missives will contain details of all the documents to be delivered at settlement. Ensure that all documents that the seller has undertaken to deliver are included in the list.
- The responsibility for producing most of the documents will fall on the seller although the purchaser's solicitors will be responsible for producing the SAF or Forms 2 & 4 for registering the disposition and any new standard security and for the SDLT forms.
- While the Checklist attempts to cover most eventualities, it does not purport to be appropriate or sufficient for any particular transaction, which will need to be carefully considered on a case by case basis.

COMPLETION CHECKLIST for: [Name of Property]		
PROPERTY DOCUMENTS	*RESPONSIBILITY*	*COMMENTS*
Disposition/Assignation (with landlord's consent)/ Lease (the 'Deed')		
SAF/Forms 1, 2 or 3 & 4 for registering Deed and SAF or Form 2 if necessary for registration of any new burdens/ servitudes against benefited property, cheques for recording/ registration dues (including fee for dual registration if necessary)		
SDLT Return and payment of any SDLT due		
Particulars of signing for Deed [and evidence of authorised signatories power to sign document or any other authority needed eg Power of Attorney ('signing authority')]		
Title deeds/Land Certificate		
[Discharge/Deed of Restriction of existing standard security, particulars of signing and any signing authority required]		
[SAF/Forms 2 & 4 for Discharge/ Deed of Restriction and payment for recording/registration dues]		
Letter of Obligation		
Charges search & company file search showing where relevant directors and/or company secretary who have signed Deed are duly appointed		

COMPLETION CHECKLIST for: [Name of Property]		
PROPERTY DOCUMENTS	*RESPONSIBILITY*	*COMMENTS*
Form 11/13 or Interim property and personal searches [including searches in community interests and agricultural tenant's interests sections of the RCIL if appropriate]		
[Any other searches due in terms of missives eg P16 Report, Property Enquiry Certificates, coal mining search, search in the register of insolvencies]		
Original planning and building control documents		
CDM Health & Safety File		
[Maintenance agreements/ operating manuals]		
Energy Performance Certificate		
[Collateral warranties, particulars of signing and any signing authority required]		
Letters of non-crystallisation of any floating charges		
Notice of change of ownership to the rating authority		
Signatories certificate		
Capital Allowances Election (s.198 Capital Allowances Act 2001) for fixed plant and machinery.		
LEASE DOCUMENTS (delete if no occupational leases)		
Principal or extract leases and lease documents (including any subleases and sublease documents)		

COMPLETION CHECKLIST *for: [Name of Property]*		
PROPERTY DOCUMENTS	*RESPONSIBILITY*	*COMMENTS*
Notifications of change of ownership to tenants		
[Back letters due to be granted by purchasers to existing tenants]		
[Assignation of any guarantees, signing particulars and any signing authority required]		
[Assignation of any rent deposits, signing particulars and any signing authority required]		
[Assignation of any service contracts, signing particulars and any signing authority required]		
FINANCE DOCUMENTS		
State for Settlement		
[VAT invoice]		
[Insert details of any TOGC documents which remain outstanding]		
Account details where purchase monies to be sent		
SECURITY DOCUMENTS (delete if no security being granted)		
New standard security, particulars of signing and any signing authority required and SAF/Form 2		
[Assignation of rent, signing particulars and any signing authority required]		
[Intimations of assignation of rent]		
[Board minute authorising granting of standard security]		

COMPLETION CHECKLIST *for: [Name of Property]*			
	PROPERTY DOCUMENTS	*RESPONSIBILITY*	*COMMENTS*
	[Ranking Agreement, particulars of signing and any signing authority required]		
	SDLT undertaking(s) to submit SDLT Return and any SDLT payable, deliver Inland Revenue Certificate (if appropriate) and deal with any Inland Revenue requisitions prior to Certificate being issued		
	OTHER		
	[Insert here any other documents or things to be handed over at settlement in terms of the missives]		
	Keys		

Chapter 12

The Collapsing Contract

'Contract: an agreement that is binding on the weaker party' —
Frederick Sawyer

THE THREE 'RS'

12.01 Contracts are, in effect, private legislative acts. As we have already seen in Chapter 5 on Contract, once a contract is agreed, the law requires it to be observed by the parties. The courts are traditionally very reluctant to depart from this principle unless there are very exceptional and compelling reasons to do otherwise.

You need to understand the legal position of the other party's failure in order to understand the remedies available, so let's be clear about the 'three Rs' in contract law:

(a) **Repudiation** - means to indicate clearly, by words or acts, that the repudiator will not perform the obligation, but having no right to withhold or refuse performance. A repudiation is a wrongful rejection or renunciation of the contract. It does not end the contract but gives the other party an option to accept the repudiation, rescind and claim damages for the breach;

(b) **Recission** (verb: to rescind) - means the 'un-making' of a contract, bringing it to an end, at least so far as concerns the future performance of primary obligations, in response to a repudiation or material breach by the other party. Recission puts the parties back to the position that they were in before the contract was made; and

(c) **Resile** - means to withdraw from a contract lawfully, in the exercise of a right to do so, but not in response to a repudiation or breach. For example a party may be unable to purify a suspensive condition, entitling the other to resile. The parties effectively 'call it quits'.

There is a lot of confusion between resiling and rescinding and sometimes they are incorrectly used interchangeably. However, this difference is this: if you look at Condition 2.4 of the PSG Offer to Sell, you will see that the seller is entitled to *rescind* the contract if the purchaser has effectively repudiated the contract by not paying on time. A damages claim would normally follow recission. In Condition 6.3, however, the purchaser is entitled to *resile* from the contract, should the seller's title disclose any aspect that is materially prejudicial to the purchaser. There is no obligation in the contract or at common law to make good any losses of the seller.

Should you find yourself in a collapsing contract situation, there are remedies available to your client but which one to use will be largely dictated by the circumstances.

WHAT IS THE CONTRACTUAL POSITION?

12.02 First, review the missives. The Combined Standard Clauses, the PSG Offers to Sell and almost all other standard and bespoke missives will contain a detailed clause, setting out what is to happen if settlement does not proceed as planned.

It is important to note that both the Combined Standard Clauses and the PSG Offers to Sell contain an 'entire agreement' clause and in the case of the Combined Standard Clauses also a 'non-reliance' clause. This is important to interpretation of the contract, as it will generally speaking exclude any extraneous evidence as to the parties' intention in reaching the agreement. The courts will only intervene in cases of misrepresentation or if the contract is unclear as to what is meant. Thus in *Houldsworth v Gordon Cumming* 1910 SC (HL) 49, a plan used by the parties during negotiations was admitted by the House of Lords to define what the missives meant by 'the estate of Dallas', when this description did not feature in the title deeds.

It is usual, and it is the position in Clause 16 of the Combined Standard Clauses, that the parties agree that the obligation to settle will be that the price has to be paid in exchange for a signed disposition in favour of the purchaser, good and marketable title, vacant possession and the other items agreed to be deliverable on the Date of Settlement. Time is not expressed to be of the essence, but Clause 13 has already set out what is to happen in the event of a breach by either party.

If the seller is unable to settle on the date of entry, there is no obligation upon the purchaser either to take entry or pay interest (see *Bowie v Semple's*

Executors 1978 SLT (Sh Ct) 9). If, however, the purchaser wishes to take entry, they have the option to consign the price on deposit with a bank (see *Prestwick Cinema Co v Gardiner* (1951 SC 98)) (although it would not be possible to consign the price if it was being funded by a lender, as the lender will usually only release funds on condition that its standard security is being presented for registration immediately). When the money is on deposit neither party has control over it without the consent of the other.

WHEN ARE YOU DUE TO PERFORM?

12.03 There are three dates that you need to be aware of:

The **Date of Entry** is defined in the covering offer to the Combined Standard Clauses as being a specific date '…or such other date as may be mutually agreed in writing';

The **due date** is defined as the later of:

- the Date of Entry; or
- The date on which payment of the price was due having regard to the circumstances of the case, including any entitlement to withhold payment owing to the non-performance by the seller; and
- Settlement or **Date of Settlement** means the date on which settlement is actually effected whether that is the Date of Entry or not.

These could all be the same day, but sometimes they are not. So the date of entry is when settlement should take place, the due date is when the liability to pay interest or damages arises and the date of settlement is the end point, when the price plus any interest or damages is paid.

REMEDIES

(a) Non-performance by the seller

12.04 Before you take any action, you should ascertain whether there has been any non-performance by the seller that would entitle non-payment by the purchaser. This would mean that the due date for payment is, in fact, after the date of entry.

In practice, non-performance by the seller is likely to manifest itself long before settlement: in standard missives, the seller is obliged to produce a number of items on which the purchaser has to satisfy itself within the agreed timescale, failing which the purchaser can resile. Once the seller has produced these satisfactorily, there should be no reason why the seller should not be in a position to settle.

It would not be unknown for the seller's solicitor, for whatever reason, to exhibit the disclosed documents too close to the agreed date of entry for the purchaser's solicitor to satisfy themselves within the timescale set out in standard missives. In that case the purchaser's solicitor would be entitled to claim that there was non-performance on the date of entry, and that consequently the due date would be once the appropriate period (eg 10 working days) has elapsed. Communication between solicitors is the key here and often a mutually acceptable position can be agreed.

(b) Renegotiate the missives

You may have noted from the definition of the Date of Entry, the door is not closed on re-arranging the date, provided the other party agrees. The next option, if a default looks likely is, therefore, to explain to the other party's solicitor the reason for the anticipated delay and seek to amend the date of entry in the missives. The solicitor would need to take clients' instructions. Some parties will take a generous view and try to accommodate your client's request as a matter of goodwill and not wishing to stray into the default minefield, others may insist on sticking to the letter of the contract, as they are entitled to do, often because they have to co-ordinate with an onward transaction.

Remember that when acting in a conveyancing transaction, you are dealing with real people in what, for some, can be a very stressful situation. A house move has to be meticulously planned well in advance and your purchasing client will care little for the legal niceties when they are sitting in the street in front of their new home, surrounded by all their furniture and belongings. Similarly, a commercial client may need immediate entry to start or continue trading. Most sellers are also purchasers and vice versa. Problems at settlement may also have knock-on impacts on other transactions or arrangements with removals, or fitting out for example.

Neither party will want long-drawn out litigation, but will look to you to provide a practical remedy. Delays are possibly slightly less stressful for the commercial purchaser, unless the property is being acquired for owner occupation and they have to be out of their existing premises by a deadline. But although it may be more expensive than they planned, putting office furniture into store or leaving it in a removal van overnight does not have the same personal impact on a business and their employees who still have homes to go to.

(c) Bridging finance

The next practical solution, should a rescheduling not be available, is for the purchaser to ask his bank for a 'bridging loan', that is to say, a short-term loan, usually given on the basis of the probability of the borrower receiving funds on a certain future date. The purchaser can say to his bank: 'My bank loan is coming through next week and I'll repay you then'. It should be emphasised that bridging loans are expensive and should only be taken on a short-term basis; further the bank may ask for a hefty 'arrangement fee' for arranging the loan which may make these loans unattractive, except in an emergency.

Banks are not, however, so keen on lending against a payment on an uncertain future date; for example, if the purchaser is still selling his own house and has not found a buyer yet, his bank may not be willing to provide open ended bridging finance. Banks like their loans to be short term and repayment to be certain, unless they make a specified arrangement as in a 'personal loan'. This provides for regular payments to account, and the banks charge more handsomely for a personal loan.

At the time of writing, interest base rates have been at an historically low level of 0.5% for three years. Banks are risk averse and an arrangement fee could be as high as £1,000 for bridging finance. Your client might consider other options, maybe an inter-family loan or an inter-group loan. We would never advocate that a party breaches a contract intentionally, but it might be the case that default interest would be cheaper than bridging, especially for less than two weeks delay. Some sellers may be prepared to delay and collect default interest. This sort of situation needs to be managed carefully, and tempers can become a bit frayed in these circumstances. Again, we cannot over-emphasise that communication between the solicitors is crucial.

(d) Default (NOT penalty) interest

If none of these practical remedies can be agreed, and the payment price is still not forthcoming, the purchaser will be in default on the date of entry. Both the Combined Standard Clauses and the PSG Offer to Sell make provision for what is to happen in the event of default by the purchaser. See commentary in respect of these clauses at paras 6.10(m) and 6.13(c). Provisions of this type in contracts have to be carefully drafted to ensure that they are not perceived as a penalty clause, which would be unenforceable, as opposed to a liquidated damages clause which usually would not.

Liquidated damages clauses: Parties can agree in the contract the basis on which damages will be calculated in the event of a breach, and often, to avoid disputes in quantifying the amount of the actual loss, such a clause sets out in advance what the defaulting party must pay. These are known as liquidated damages clauses, and are generally regarded as enforceable. Such clauses assume that the aggrieved party will suffer loss because of the breach, and this type of provision provides a basis for calculating what the parties agree will be paid as damages for that loss. If however, the purpose of the provision is to punish the defaulting party for his failure to perform, or frighten him into performing, then it is likely it will be seen by the court to be a penalty provision in the strict sense and will be unenforceable.

Whether a clause is enforceable as a liquidated damages clause or unenforceable as a penalty clause will depend on the facts and circumstances, at the time of entering into the contract, not when the breach occurred, and also on what was intended by the parties. What the clause is called in the contract is not necessarily a material factor, since if the effect of a provision is to penalise, then the fact that the contract describes it as a liquidated damages provision will be irrelevant.

The case of *Dunlop Pneumatic Tyre Co Ltd v New Garage and Motor Co Ltd* [1915] AC 79 sets out various tests that earlier case law had formulated to assist in the correct construction of such a provision in the contract:

- If the amount of the sum specified is 'extravagant and unconscionable' compared with the largest amount of loss that could conceivably be proved to have followed from the breach, then it will be held to be a penalty.

- If the breach is simply not paying a sum of money, and the amount specified in the provision is greater than the amount which was due to be paid, then it will be a penalty.

- There is a presumption that it is a penalty when there is provision for a single sum to be payable as compensation on the occurrence of different events, some of which may be serious but others trivial.

- The sum specified must be a genuine pre-estimate of damage, even where the consequences of the breach would have made accurate pre-estimation impossible.

As we have seen at para 6.10(m), the settled figure for liquidated damages is 4% over the base rate of a UK clearing bank. The Bank of England base rate (and that of many other UK clearing banks) has been pegged at 0.5% for three years and looks set to stay low. Given that most ordinary bank lending rates are considerably in excess of 4.5%, consider carefully whether liquidated damages might leave your client out-of-pocket.

(e) Enforcing the missives

The position of a seller in default is the common law position that the purchaser will either seek a decree of implement, requiring the seller to deliver a disposition in their favour in exchange for the price, or alternatively, if that is not possible, treat the seller as being in material breach of contract, rescind the missives and seek damages to make good their losses.

The heads of claim for wasted expenditure are covered in some detail in both the Combined Standard Clauses and the PSG Offer. There is a danger from the seller's perspective that, unless these heads are comprehensively set out, the courts at common law may not allow a claim under a particular head to succeed. In *Tiffney v Bachurzewski* 1984 SC 108 it was held that the equitable principles governing restitution of the seller will be narrower than the usual contractual provision and unforeseen expenses not within the contemplation of the parties (in this case, bridging finance) will be disallowed.

If the purchaser has repudiated the contract, there are two options open to the seller:

- Accept the repudiation, rescind and claim damages for losses sustained under the heads of damages; or

- Keep the missives alive and raise an action for specific implement (an order to implement the contract by paying the price against delivery of the disposition). See the Sheriff Principal's judgment in *AMA (New Town) Ltd v McKenna* [2001] ScotSC 11 for analysis on the current law relating to implement.

It should be remembered that, if settlement or completion finally takes place after a delay, searches will need to be updated by the seller's solicitor, and other checks re-made, to allow the seller's solicitor to grant a letter of obligation in classic form (see para 11.04).

INSOLVENCY OF THE SELLER

12.05 Only a few words now need be said about the risk to a purchaser, having paid the money in settlement to a seller who **subsequently** becomes insolvent. The disposition in favour of the purchaser will have been delivered before any appointment, or registration of a competing title in favour of the insolvency practitioner, and therefore (because it is incumbent on the purchaser's solicitor to ensure that the dispositon in favour of the purchaser is presented for registration as swiftly as possible after settlement) will have reached the Land Register first. There were some horror stories in the cases of *Sharp v Thomson* 1997 SC (HL) 66 and *Burnett's Trustee v Grainger* 2004 SC (HL) 19.

AVOIDING CONTRACT DISPUTES

12.06 Without wishing to sound trite, when you reflect upon this chapter, consider that the risks of a contract dispute can sometimes be minimised or avoided by the simple expedients of:

(a) inserting a suitable contractual clause in missives to cover delays;

(b) ensuring that the purchaser has made satisfactory financial arrangements;

(c)   choosing a sensible and realistic date of entry; and

(d)   keeping the transaction running on schedule until settlement.

FURTHER READING

Scottish Law Commission – discussion paper on Interest on Debt and Damages [2005] SLC 127(2)

Conveyancing 2006 pp 85–97 (K G C Reid and G L Gretton)

Chapter 13

Tidying Up and Feeing

'Do not plan for ventures before finishing what's at hand.' — *Euripides*

So the transaction has settled satisfactorily and the clients are happy. You can give yourself a well-earned pat on the back, but not yet plan for ventures. There is still work to do.

FEES AND BILLING

13.01 Both sets of solicitors should attend to their fee. Your firm is a business and has been laying out expense for weeks, sometimes months, on behalf of the client. Now is the time to recover.

The purchaser's solicitor should have sent the purchaser a settlement/completion statement before the date of completion, showing the funds required and including his own fee and any outlays. The fee note should be ready in anticipation of the funds coming in for settlement. If this is not done, experience dictates that it sometimes becomes harder to recover from a client who has moved on to other interests (and is himself planning for ventures!). Having to instigate debt recovery procedure against what was once a happy client is never a pleasant task, far less being desirable for business development.

The seller's solicitor has to attend to the distribution of the sale proceeds. Usually there is a bank loan to be redeemed and a cheque or bank transfer for the amount stated in the redemption statement should be sent immediately. If there is any doubt about extra day's interest, then it may be sensible to hold some money back which you can repay to the clients later, if not needed. It is always better to be sending an unexpected reimbursement than an unexpected demand!

Estate agents and surveyors often have an understanding with the seller that they will be paid by the seller's solicitor from the proceeds of sale. In fact this will often be stated in the estate agent's terms of engagement. So you must ensure you have received their a final account in advance and pay this immediately too.

An organised solicitor will have arranged to deduct their fee from the proceeds of sale. The ideal position is that the fee note is ready before settlement, and to achieve this, there must be a high degree of administrative organisation. All final outlays should be noted on the ledger. Check back to the letter of engagement as to what was proposed for the fee, even if you think you remember. All time entries must be up-to-date across the firm, so that the fee is reflective of the work carried out (unless it is a fixed fee with no additional work).

The vital job of the seller's solicitor is to transmit the net free proceeds of sale to the client as soon as they have cleared, unless they are required for purchasing another property in a back-to-back transaction. However good the conveyancing has been and however clearly it was set out in the initial letter of engagement all those weeks ago, experience has shown the seller will not understand why there is a delay in remitting the money to them unless it has been recently and explicitly explained to them.

FILE CLOSING

13.02 Once everyone has been paid, and all documentation received (see paras 13.03 and 13.04), it is time to close the file. Check with the cashroom whether there are any balances held on the ledger, particularly if, as suggested above, you retained a small positive balance to cover any unforeseen expenses. Now that all accounts have been settled, you should send any remaining balance.

All filing should be up-to-date, including all emails, letters, scribbled notes and sorted into chronological order. Many draft documents can be securely disposed of. Once principal contract documents have been agreed, drafts are of no help in interpreting the contract. That said, it can sometimes be useful to see how certain elements of a document evolved during a transaction, in case of ambiguity or uncertainty later, even if (at the moment at any rate) they do not have any evidential status. The file should then be closed by being sealed and archived if a paper file, or electronically archived onto a cryoserver if an electronic file, with original signed documents being retained in a sealed and archived 'papers' file.

The Law Society requires that client files are held for at least ten years, so it is useful to date stamp the file with the date of review in ten year's time.

TITLES, LAND CERTIFICATE AND DEMATERIALISATION

13.03 The purchaser's solicitor has to attend to the registration of the title. That means gathering up all the original documents from settlement and sending them to the Keeper with the requisite forms and cheques (unless paying by direct debit). All relevant titles are sent to the Keeper with the application. The Keeper will acknowledge the application and assign a Title Number (if a first registration) and an application number to the application with a priority date. ARTL will provide an electronic acknowledgement of applications on submission. See Chapter 14 for registration procedures.

Some titles will remain and are no longer of much use. Some titles contain historical information that may be of interest to the client. These can be returned to client, securely disposed of, or retained as part of a title package held on behalf of the client. Documentation such as planning permissions, building control documents etc are usually held with the titles rather than in the file, so that they are not destroyed unwittingly.

There is a possibility that the Keeper will requisition certain documents as part of the registration process. These requests must be complied with within 60 days or the Keeper will abandon the application, and return all the papers to the submitting solicitor, resulting in a loss of priority for titles and securities. There must be a system in the office to ensure that these requisitions are promptly dealt with.

Assuming that all has gone well with the registration process, then a Land Certificate (and Charge Certificate containing the security, if there is one) will eventually be produced in certain types of transactions. The Keeper now has a policy of dematerialisation, which is to say that the official title is kept on the Land Register itself as a database, rather than a printed piece of paper, and applicants can opt whether to have an electronic or paper version of the Land Certificate in due course. In terms of the amended Land Registration (Scotland) Act 1979, a Land Certificate will only be issued on the creation of a new title sheet and following the registration of a disposition or the assignation of a lease, and on subsequent transfers.

IMPLEMENTING THE LETTER OF OBLIGATION

13.04 Once the Land Certificate is received from the Keeper, it is necessary to re-open the file, if you have already closed it. Often due to lack of space in modern offices, it can make sense for the file to be temporarily closed and stored, pending the receipt of these final documents, which may take months (or sometimes years) to arrive.

The first thing that the purchaser's solicitor should arrange to be done is a comparison between the disposition (and other titles) that was submitted to the Keeper, with the terms of the resulting Land Certificate. There can occasionally be omissions in the Land Certificate and in that case, the Land Certificate should be returned for correction immediately. For an example of a Land Certificate that wasn't checked - and the consequences that followed - see *Willemse v French* [2001] CSOH 51.

If the Land Certificate is in accordance with your submissions and you are now satisfied that your client has received a good and marketable title, the final thing the purchaser's solicitor should do is to retrieve the seller's solicitor's Letter of Obligation from the file, score through it and mark it as 'implemented' — the seller's solicitors are now released from their obligation and the Letter of Obligation, duly marked as implemented, should be returned to them.

Now you can plan for ventures.

Chapter 14

Registration of Title

COMPLETING THE CONVEYANCING PROCESS

14.01 As soon as settlement/completion has taken place, the purchaser's title needs to be registered, and if there is a lender, that lender's standard security must also be registered. On taking delivery of the deeds, any testing clause is added, or the signing docquet checked and any missing information as to date and place of signing, or witness details added in. It is perfectly permissible to do this after the event, (just as, of course, it is correct to add the testing clause later). If SDLT is due, then the SDLT return must be made and the duty paid (unless online submission is used) (see para 13.06) and the SDLT5 must accompany the application for registration.

The relevant application forms for recording (SAF, which is an abbreviation of 'Sasine Application Form') or registration (either a Form 1, Form 2, or Form 3, and in each case a Form 4) are completed, signed and submitted to the appropriate register along with the deeds themselves (see Appendix 1 for examples of completed forms). Recording/registration dues must be pre-paid, so either a cheque for the correct amount of dues should accompany the application, or alternatively, solicitors can set up a dedicated account through which payment of registration dues can be made. A Variable Direct Debit account will be drawn from by the Registers whenever that firm of solicitors makes an application for registration. Careful checks and protocols must be in place at the solicitor's firm to ensure that funds from the clients account are put into the direct debit account to meet the liability for registration dues as they arise. The solicitors should not send the application for registration without checking that they have sufficient funds to meet the registration dues. Every firm of solicitors is given a FAS number by the Registers. This number (eg FAS4040) must appear on every application form for registration or recording of a deed. It identifies the firm for billing purposes. Firms with variable direct debit accounts are given an additional FAS number for that account, which must be put in the form when payment is to be debited from that account.

Before the application is submitted, the deeds and forms should be carefully checked to avoid the application being rejected by the Keeper. Make sure that all boxes in the Form 1, 2 or 3 are completed and that the Form is signed at the bottom of the first page (usually by a partner of the firm, or by someone authorised to sign the Form by the firm). A copy of the Registration Application Checklist from the Registers of Scotland is reproduced at the end of this chapter under Crown Copyright rules. The following paragraphs provide some more detail to help ensure that the registration process is as trouble-free for you as possible. There are numerous Guidance Sheets and an information section on the Registers of Scotland website that you can also consult.

WHY REGISTER TITLE?

14.02 The missives and the disposition give the purchaser personal, contractual rights in relation to the property, but it is the effect of registering that disposition that creates a real right in the property. Personal rights are rights against persons, such as the obligations contained in a contract, whereas real rights consist of rights in things, and ownership of property is one of the principal real rights. Obtaining a real right in something means that it is protected from challenge 'against all mortals' as the saying goes. Registration of a person's title to property is the essential last stage of the conveyancing process and may be characterised as the method by which the personal right – in the disposition – is converted into the real right – the registered title.

Security over property is another of the real rights in property and this is relevant in relation to the rights of a heritable creditor under the standard security.

The recording of a deed in the Register of Sasines confers a real right to the property, although this does not in itself guarantee valid title to a property. In the Land Register, the act of registration gives a real right of ownership on the person entered on the Title Sheet as proprietor, and the Keeper's indemnity (see para 2.05) provides a form of state guarantee of title.

RECORDING IN THE SASINE REGISTER

14.03 Usually, if the title to a property is still in the Sasine Register, a transaction dealing with that property will result in the title moving out of that Register and into the Land Register. Not all types of transaction will induce a first registration in the Land Register, however, and where the title to the property is still recorded in the Sasine Register, the documents in implement of a transaction that does not trigger first registration (see below) will be recorded in that Register. While we talk of interests (or, inaccurately, but inevitably, deeds) being 'registered' in the Land Register, deeds are 'recorded' in the Sasine Register. The following types of transactions will not induce first registration:

- a gratuitous transfer, such as a conveyance for 'love, favour and affection' rather than for a consideration;
- a heritable security or discharge of a heritable security over an unregistered interest;
- the grant of a liferent;
- a grant or transfer of an incorporeal heritable right (other than salmon fishing) even if for valuable consideration (eg a Deed of Servitude) and
- a renunciation of a long lease if the landlord's interest is not registered;

In general, gratuitous transfers, and transactions not involving a transfer will not induce a first registration. Proposals by the Scottish Law Commission for the reform of the land registration system propose that all transfers of property, including gifts and other gratuitous transactions, and the grant of a heritable security should induce a first registration, as part of the process of speeding up the completion of the Land Register (see para 2.09)

The Sasine Register is a register of deeds, and so all that is required when submitting a deed for recording in the Sasine Register is:

- the deed itself
- a completed and signed SAF form
- cheque for the correct amount of the recording dues, or where the firm has a VariableDirect Debit account, the special FAS number for that account should be put on the SAF form.

Once the recording process has been completed, the actual deed is returned to your with a recording stamp on the first page of the deed giving the recording County, the folio and fiche number (which denotes where a facsimile of the deed has been stored in the records of the Registers) and the date of recording.

PRE-REGISTRATION ENQUIRIES

14.04 During the course of a transaction, there may be issues that arise, where it is unclear to the solicitor how the Keeper might react to, and deal with those matters. To assist, the Land Register staff will take 'Pre-registration Enquiries' from the solicitor, by which the solicitor can submit a query in writing to the Keeper and ask for a statement from them of how they will deal with the matter when the application for registration is submitted. The response from Pre-Registration Enquiries may suggest a course of action that must be followed for the application to be acceptable to the Keeper.

The Pre-Registration Enquiries team will provide guidance on current transactions that are soon to be submitted for registration, where, for example defects or anomalies have been discovered during examination of the title. You should check the FAQ section of the website before you commit to asking them to advise on the Keeper's position. Experience has also shown that the Keeper's staff will refer extensively to the Keeper's policy in the 'Legal Manual' which is available at www.ros. gov.uk/foi/legal/Frame%7EHome.htm. They will only deal with specific questions and will not look at the whole title, although they do provide a separate Title Investigation Service (at a cost). One of the key aspects of a pre-registration query is to ascertain whether the Keeper will exclude indemnity in relation to any matter, although they will usually not commit to confirming that there will be none until the application has been received, and they have had an opportunity to fully check the title. It is suggested that your date of entry is marked clearly on any enquiry, so that they are able to prioritise requests, if the date is imminent.

Advice is confined to registration issues and they will not advise on legal matters, or on 'hypothetical issues'. Queries in respect of possible *a non domino* dispositions should be raised with the Pre Registration team, who will be able to assess the evidence you have gathered to support an *a non domino* approach, and might also be able to suggest any additional evidence that might be required, although they will be unlikely to confirm what will be sufficient to satisfy the Keeper in advance of the submission of the application, but this correspondence can be very helpful in identifying a suitable course of action for dealing with a problem in the title.

Once an application has actually been submitted, any enquiries should be directed to the relevant team at the Registers.

Requests to Pre Registration Enquiries have to be made in writing and a fee of £50 plus VAT (at the time of writing) will be charged for each written enquiry. Letters should be sent to Pre Registration Enquiries, Registers of Scotland, Meadowbank House, 153 London Road, Edinburgh EH8 7AU (DX 550907 LP55 Edinburgh 5). Email enquiries to pre-reg@ros.gov.uk or fax to 0131 479 3675

Any correspondence with Pre-Registration Enquiries should be submitted along with the actual application for registration when it is made in due course.

FIRST REGISTRATION

14.05 Any transfer of unregistered property for valuable consideration (ie money or money's worth) will induce first registration in the Land Register. Transactions which induce first registration are set out in s 2(1) (a) of the LR(S)A 1979, summarised as follows:

- a conveyance on sale or for any valuable consideration;
- the interest of the tenant under the grant of a long lease, ie a lease for more than 20 years and regardless of whether it is for valuable consideration or not (a lease with a duration of less than 20 years will induce first registration if it contains a provision allowing the landlord to extend its term to exceed 20 years);
- a conveyance in consideration of marriage (marriage being considered 'valuable consideration') (but not simply when a title is transferred on the occasion of the parties getting married);
- any transfer of a long lease, or an interest held on udal tenure (a form of land tenure applicable in Orkney and Shetland and essentially allodial (ie outright ownership, as our system also now is, following feudal abolition); and

- a transfer of an interest by which it is absorbed into a registered interest; and

- a voluntary registration (see the following paragraph).

In some circumstances, the Keeper may accept an application for a voluntary registration in the Land Register, of property which does not strictly qualify to be registered under s 2 (1)(a) of LR(S)A 1979. This may be appropriate in developments where the title to the land is still in the Sasine Register, but it is now being developed and sold off in individual plots. In this situation, an application may be made to register the entire estate voluntarily. Once an interest in land has been registered voluntarily, the entire registration provisions under the 1979 Act will apply, and therefore no further writs relating to that interest may be registered in the Sasine Register. One of the proposals in the Scottish Law Commission's recommendations for completion of the register is that all voluntary registration applications will be accepted by the Keeper. At present she has a discretion to decline to register, if there is no evident benefit from doing so (see para 2.09).

On the first occasion when the registration of title to the property moves from the Sasine Register to the Land Register, the staff at the Registers will have to examine the title, so your application for registration of the disposition should be accompanied by all the relevant title deeds:

- the prescriptive progress
- the descriptive writ and any deed outside the prescriptive progress which contains a plan that identifies the property
- any break off writs that are relevant
- all writs referred to for burdens
- any links in title
- the P16 report, and
- any other deeds relevant to the application, such as the discharge of the seller's standard security. Standard securities granted by the purchaser will also be submitted at this time.

All the relevant information from the title deeds is extracted and put into a new Title Sheet that is created by the Registers for that property, divided into four sections: the property (A) section; the proprietorship (B) section, the charges (ie standard securities) (C) section and the burdens (D) section. The property is also given a unique Title Number, and its extent, (unless it is a tenement flat or other property which it is more appropriate for the Keeper to identify by the 'steading method' (see paras 8.27 and 9.08(e)) is delineated on an Ordnance Survey Map, and this Title Plan also forms part of the Title Sheet.

The Title Sheets for all properties that are registered in the Land Register stay at the Register, but the information from the Title Sheet is put into a document called a Land Certificate, which is issued to the agents who presented the application for registration on behalf of the owner. This Land Certificate effectively replaces the bundle of title deeds of titles in the Sasine Register. The Land Certificate is a record of the information registered in the Title Sheet for the property as at the date the Land Certificate is issued, so it should be borne in mind that it simply represents a snapshot in time of what the Title Sheet contained. The Land Certificate will only be updated by the Keeper when the property or part of it is transferred.

Remember that the Title Sheet and corresponding Land Certificate will not show up overriding interests, but any exclusion of the Keeper's indemnity will appear as a prominent note on both.

For commercial property that is subject to leases, the Keeper can be asked to note short particulars of these in the Property section too. These are usually put into a schedule or table under the property description.

Application for registration of the Disposition that induces the first registration is made using a Form 1, and an inventory of all of the other titles and documents submitted is produced on the Form 4. If the same solicitor is submitting more than one deed eg both disposition and standard security for a residential property, then they can both appear on the same Form 4. If different solicitors are submitting the applications, then each submission requires to be accompanied by a separate Form 4 listing all the deeds relating to the property being submitted by that solicitor. The Keeper sends a letter acknowledging receipt of the application, which should be retained for record purposes. It will provide the Title Number that has been allocated, and an application number that you will need to quote when making any enquiries to the Registers about the progress of the application.

Application for registration of an accompanying Standard Security is made on a Form 2, as it follows the registration of the disposition, and is therefore a dealing with a registered interest, as the disposition has triggered registration of the whole title. As well as appearing in the Charges section of the Land Certificate, every standard security gets its own separate Charge Certificate, and usually the actual security document itself is attached to the Charge Certificate.

REGISTERED TITLE

14.06 Once the title to a property is registered in the Land Register a lot of the conveyancing procedures become a lot simpler. The disposition is shorter and the speed at which the Registers can update the title sheet and produce a Land Certificate showing the purchaser as registered proprietor and updating the Charges section with the new lender's details, is much quicker.

Land Certificates will only be issued in the case of an application for first registration, a transfer of a registered title and a transfer of part of a registered title. No Land Certificate is issued for any other type of application for registration in the Land Register. Charge Certificates are issued following the registration of a standard security, but while any other deed affecting the standard security will be registered on the Tile Sheet, the Charge Certificate does not get updated.

Application for registration of the Disposition is made using a Form 2, as the title is already registered, and an inventory of any other accompanying documents is produced on the Form 4. This is a much shorter list than for a first registration, obviously, and again can include all deeds relevant to the application being submitted by that solicitor. You should not submit the prior Land Certificate of Charge Certificate with any applications for registration in a registered interest. The Keeper neither wants nor needs these, and will destroy them if they are submitted.

DUAL REGISTRATION

14.07 If new burdens or servitudes are being created in the documents being presented for recording, then they require to be dual registered ie registered against both the benefited property and the burdened property. This will mean an additional set of application forms from the seller or granter of the deed, to register the burdens or servitudes against his property as well.

COMPLETING THE REGISTRATION FORMS

14.08 The Registers of Scotland website contains Guidance for completion of the Land registration application Forms 1. 2, 3 and 4 and should be consulted when completing applications for registration.

In addition, guidance is given for completion of Form 5: Application for noting or entering on the register; Form 9: Application for rectification of the register; also for completing the Report Forms 10, 11, 12 and 13. There is also guidance for Form 14: Application for a report to ascertain whether or not subjects have been registered; Form 15: Application for an office copy; the Form P16 and the lesser used Form P17, which is an application to compare boundaries on the title plan with the OS map

All forms, whether they are generated electronically using forms software or the e-forms service provided by the Registers, or handwritten or manually typed, must contain a Unique Identifier inserted in the UID number field at the bottom of every page of the Form and any additional information sheets used. In the case of electronic forms, the UID number will be generated automatically. When using paper forms, you must manually insert a number. This can be based on your file reference for example. It is important to ensure that the same UID is inserted on every page of a Form, but each separate Form requires a different number or identifier.

Because the information from each application form is machine scanned in the Land Register, the forms should be filled out using black ink or type and capital letters, and keeping within the white response areas in the form. The Keeper requires use of following fonts: OCR-B font (9pt) - (available for download from website adobe. com); or Courier 12pt or Arial 10pt.

Most of the questions in the forms are self-explanatory and must be answered correctly and truthfully. During the conveyancing process the purchaser's solicitor will pass a draft of the application form to the seller's solicitor for confirmation that the answers to the Questions on their form are correct. The letter of obligation that the seller's solicitor gives in land registration transactions confirms the accuracy of these responses. The applicant's solicitor signs a declaration on the form that the information supplied in the application is correct to the best of their knowledge and belief. The Keeper will also rely in the answers to certain questions and her indemnity is given in the context of reliance on these answers.

(a) Basic information

Basic information about the property and the applicants is provided:

- the price or other consideration;

- if already registered, the Title Number or Numbers affected by the deed;

- a short description only of the property to which the deed being registered relates; that is an identifiable postal address, for example, rather than a full conveyancing description;

- the name and address of the applicant (eg purchaser or lender) who is applying for registration. If they are acting in some capacity eg as executor, then that is stated;

- the full name of the person granting the deed (i e the seller) or the last recorded title holder if it is not the granter. For example if Alexander Sweet owned the property, but has died, and his executors are granting the deed, the purchaser's solicitors would insert the late Alexander Sweet's name here, as the last proprietor;

The forms are also an information gathering and certification exercise for the Keeper's benefit. Some of the questions require confirmation to be given so that the Keeper can proceed with the registration without further enquiry into these matters. If a 'No' response cannot be given, then full information must be provided. Some of the questions require some further explanation:

(b) First registration – plan of the property

As the Land Register is a map-based system, the Keeper must be able to identify the property by reference to the OS map. The title must therefore include a full description of the property that is sufficient to identify it, or better still, a plan. The P16 comparison that will have been carried out at the early stages of the transaction will have identified whether the title description and the OS map coincide (see para 7.08). If the description of the property is such that it cannot be identified on the OS map through the P16 comparison, then the solution is to produce a new plan, which will be attached to the Disposition. The plan must be taxative and otherwise comply with the Keeper's requirements for plans

– see para 9.08(g). This means either that a surveyor or other professional should prepare an appropriate plan, or an OS plan may require to be obtained and used for this purpose, and any copyright considerations complied with.

Questions 1 and 2 in the Form 1 are designed to confirm if the property is properly identified in the title, and if it is not, the Keeper will require a plan. Naturally this should have been established and dealt with during the conveyancing process in anticipation of the Keeper's requirements.

(c) **Companies**

Form 1 Question 6 or Form 2 (and Form 3) Question 2. As currently drafted, this question asks for confirmation on a number of points:

(i)   Is any party to the deed inducing registration a company registered under the Companies Acts? A yes or no response is all that is required.

(ii)   If yes has a receiver, or administrator or liquidator been appointed? If yes, then details must be provided, including the date of the appointment.

(iii)   Has any resolution been passed or court order made for the winding up of the company or petition presented for its liquidation? Again if the answer is yes, details including dates of the resolution or court order should be inserted.

(iv)   (a) Is it a charity as defined in *s 112 of the Companies Act 1989* and (b) Is the transaction to which the deed gives effect one to which *s 322A of the Companies Act 1985* applies. These questions refer to the ultra vires doctrine which used to be applied strictly, but is no longer relevant except for (a) where the company selling property is a charity and (b) where the company is transferring property to a director of the company, or its holding company or a person connected with a director. In both cases the power to transfer property in these circumstances must be seen to exist. Note that in fact s 322A of CA 1985 has been repealed and replaced by s 41 of CA 2006, although the registration forms still refer to s 322A.

(d) Matrimonial and Family Homes

The Keeper does not now require any matrimonial home or civil partnership documentation to be sent with applications. For documents like this, her policy is 'Tell Me, Don't Show Me'. So, instead, the submitting solicitor must answer a series of questions (Form 1 Question 8 and Form 2 (and Form 3) Question 4).

The principal question is: Is the application for registration a dealing within the meaning of the Matrimonial Homes (Family Protection) (Scotland) Act 1981 or the Civil Partnership Act 2004? And then a series of related questions have to be answered according to the circumstances, including certifying whether all necessary consents, declarations or renunciations exist. From the responses provided, the Keeper can decide whether or not to enter a statement on the Title Sheet that she is satisfied there are no subsisting occupancy rights, or a qualified statement when she is not satisfied in respect of the occupancy rights of spouses or civil partners of certain named persons.

The statement or a qualified statement would appear in the form:

'The Keeper is satisfied that there are in respect of the subjects in this title no occupancy rights in terms of the Matrimonial Homes (Family Protection) (Scotland) Act 1981, or the Civil Partnership Act 2004 of spouses or civil partners of persons who were formerly entitled to the said subjects, [except AB.....who ceased to be entitled on ...]'

(e) Adverse entries in the Register of Inhibitions

The purpose of Form 1 Question 9 and Form 2 (and Form 3) Question 5 is to identify that a personal Search against all relevant parties has been carried out in respect of transactions where the deed changes the status of the interest in the title. The first part of the question is *'Does the deed inducing registration grant, transfer, create, vary or discharge an interest in land?'* Guidance on this question indicates that if the deed being submitted for registration is not a voluntary act of the registered proprietor eg Compulsory Purchase or a Notice of payment of a Repair Grant, then the answer to this question is No. Otherwise a series of further questions and information have to be completed in relation to the obtaining of a report on the Register of inhibitions and dates and details of any entries that it disclosed. If no Personal Search had been obtained the appropriate response should be given and all this means is that the staff at the Land Register will check the Register of Inhibitions themselves.

(f) Heritable creditor's power of sale

The Keeper's 'Tell Me, Don't Show Me' policy also applies to sales by heritable creditors under their power of sale. Form 1 Question 10 and Form 2 (and Form 3) Question 6 asks *'Is the deed inducing registration in implement of the exercise of a power of sale under a heritable security?'* Where the answer is yes, the supplementary question is *'Have the statutory procedures necessary for the proper exercise of such power been complied with?'*

In the course of the due diligence process the purchaser's solicitors will have checked that the necessary forms and procedures for calling up the security, marketing and advertising etc have been complied with so that they are able to certify this question (see paras 4.09, 8.18(c), and 10.07).

An issue arises, since the Supreme Court decision in *RBS v Wilson* (see para 10.07(d)), although it is hoped that it is a short term issue. In cases where the enforcement of the creditor's standard security had proceeded by way of s 24 application alone, with decree being obtained following on which the creditor entered into possession and proceeded with a sale, it will not be possible for the purchaser's solicitor to confirm that the statutory procedures have been complied with. Answering 'no' to this question will result in an exclusion of the Keeper's indemnity.

One option would be for the creditor to start at the beginning again, go through the calling up procedure (plus a s 24 application if the property is residential as required under the Home Owner and Debtor Protection (Scotland) Act 2010 (see para 10.07(g)). This is problematic if the property has already been marketed and missives entered into with the successful purchaser. The conveyancing sticking plaster that has been adopted is for the heritable creditor to finance the cost of, or obtain a Title Indemnity Policy, covering the possibility of a challenge to the purchaser's title as a consequence of this lack of compliance. The Keeper will still exclude indemnity, and for this reason, the heritable creditor may qualify the warrandice it gives in the Disposition with the words 'and I grant warrandice, but excepting from warrandice any exclusion of indemnity arising from the requirement to give a negative answer to question 6 of Form 2'

ARTL

14.09 The System of Automated Registration of Title to Land at the Land Register has been operating since August 2007 (see para 2.07). Although the system has been used for sales of property where the title is already registered, the vast majority of transactions in ARTL are remortgages and discharges of standard securities. While it might seem incongruous for a text book to provide a commentary on such an electronically based system as ARTL, some comment on a few of the 'high level' elements of the system is appropriate. In any event there is a comprehensive text available dealing with ARTL and wider Scottish conveyancing technology issues by Robert Rennie and Stewart Brymer: *Conveyancing in the Electronic Age* (2008 W Green), which we would commend to the budding ARTL practitioner. Robert Rennie is also the author of Opinions on the use of mandates in the ARTL system that the Law Society commissioned for the profession. These opinions are on the Law Society's website

When your firm registers for a licence to use the system, the ARTL team from the Registers will help you through the process, come and visit your offices to set up the system, and provide training for all users of the system. There are also online training demonstration modules in the ARTL section of the Registers of Scotland website. Further details and copy forms of mandate that must be obtained from clients are located on the Law Society website.

There are a number of procedures, including appointments, registration, obtaining of digital signatures, obtaining of smartcards to be able to submit forms and smartcard readers to connect to PCs, required for a firm to be able to use ARTL.

(a) Local Registration Authority and Practice Administrator

Each firm needs to appoint an individual to be the 'local registration authority' (LRA), responsible for administering ARTL within the firm. The Law Society recommend this should be a solicitor.

A practice administrator (who can be the same person as the LRA) should also be appointed. The practice administrator is responsible for compliance with the terms and conditions imposed by the Keeper in connection with ARTL. The practice administrator is responsible for the actions of all members of staff who are given access to the system. Both the practice administrator and the LRA have to ensure compliance with internal procedures and are responsible for preserving usernames, passwords, PIN numbers and the like in connection with digital execution of documents.

The Law Society recommend that the firm should apply the same criteria allowing people access to digital signatures to complete application forms for registration as they do in allowing individuals to sign Forms 1 and 2 etc. Digital signatures of actual documents will be or may be a different matter.

(b) Digital Signatures and Mandates

To be able to digitally execute any document on behalf of a client, it will be necessary to obtain a mandate from the client authorising an individual in the solicitor's firm to do so. The mandates have to be submitted electronically to the Keeper along with ARTL application.

Standard wording for the style of mandates appear in pdf format on the website of the Law Society. There are two forms – mandate A is for use in general cases, and Mandate B is for use in unrepresented borrower cases (eg in remortgages). Firms using the ARTL system should create their own styles of these mandates to have available and obtain the client's signature at a reasonably early point in the transaction.

Protocols will need to be put in place within the firm as to who may have authority to execute a digital signature in implement of a mandate. This is likely to be partners or very senior solicitors.

(c) Digital Signatures and Execution of Application Forms

A digital signature will be required to execute the Form 1, Form 2, Form 3 etc application forms with which an application for registration through ARTL is made. This does not require the authority of the client, and it is likely that more individuals within a firm will be enabled to digitally sign applications forms, than are authorised to digitally execute deeds.

(d) Digital Signatures – Smartcards and Smartcard Readers

The Registers of Scotland will provide ARTL users with digital smartcards which contain encrypted signatures for users. These are free of charge. Smartcard readers will be required, to permit verification of the digital signature card. These are small gadgets which plug into the individual's PC. The Law Society has identified a preferred supplier of these readers which are modestly priced. Ideally and ultimately everyone who uses the ARTL system should have a smartcard reader and smartcard with encrypted signature.

(e) IT Matters

The Registers of Scotland will require to obtain information about a firm's IT compatibility with ARTL. This is done as part of the initial application by the firm for an ARTL licence. A firm's IT staff will require to be involved throughout the registration and implementation period and for ongoing IT support.

(f) SDLT

One benefit of using the ARTL system is that it will integrate submission and payment of SDLT and provide for instantaneous production of a virtual SDLT5. There will be no delay in obtaining the necessary SDLT authorisation to be able to submit deeds to the Land Register as this will all be done seamlessly within the ARTL process. This alone means that, if it is possible to use the system in more commercial high value transactions, it will be a significant procedural improvement.

(g) Letters of Engagement

There is a saving in registration dues if transactions are submitted through ARTL. Accordingly if a firm of solicitors is ARTL-enabled and able to deal with a transaction through that system, then it is recommended that reference of this is incorporated within the firm's terms and conditions of engagement. It may be appropriate to quote two sets of registration dues depending upon whether or not ARTL can be used. It needs to be borne in mind that even if the solicitors are ARTL-enabled, the solicitor on the other side of the transaction also has to be ARTL-enabled for the system to be used. So it may not be possible for a solicitor to offer this procedure, and the concomitant reduction in recording dues to his client, if the solicitor on the other side of the transaction is unable to transact in this way.

(h) Risk Management

Each firm of solicitors that signs up for ARTL will also need to carefully consider the risk management issues for their organisation, and ensure that the necessary procedures and protocols are put in place and incorporated within the firm's guidelines, particularly in relation to the implementation of mandates, the submission of digitally executed documents, and confirmation of completion of an ARTL transaction which will trigger the requirement to pay registration dues and any SDLT. Both payments will be debited from the Variable Direct Debit account that the firm must set up to be able to use ARTL, as the electronic nature of the system will not operate on a cheque based method of payment.

THE LAND CERTIFICATE

14.10 On completion of the registration process, the Land Certificate is duly sent to the applicant's solicitors. In first registrations, depending on the complexity of the title, this can take many months and sometimes several years. The deeds sent with the original application are also returned.

The purchaser's solicitors should check that there is no exclusion of indemnity contained in the Land Certificate, and that it contains no mistakes. If any mistakes are found, the Land Certificate should be returned to the Keeper for correction.

Once they are satisfied, the purchaser's solicitors can discharge the letter of obligation (usually by writing the word 'implemented' on it and dating and initialling it) and return it to the sellers' solicitors.

The Land Certificate, when sent in hard copy, has a bright yellow cover (making it easy to find in even the untidiest of workspaces) and contains:

(a)   **The Title Number** and a short description of the property (eg the postal address)

(b)   **Statement of indemnity:** 'Subject to any specific qualification ... a person who suffers loss as a result of any of the events specified in s 12(1) of the [1979] Act shall be entitled to be indemnified in respect of that loss by the Keeper of the Registers of Scotland in terms of that Act.'

(c) **Section A—the property section.** A description of the property and a coloured plan based on the Ordnance Survey scale 1:1,250 for densely populated urban areas; 1:2,500 for less densely populated urban areas and farms; or 1:10,000 for hill farms, mountains and moorland.

(d) **Section B—the proprietorship section.** The name and designation of the proprietor, the date of registration (ie when the real right was created), the price and the date of entry.

(e) **Section C—the charges section.** Details of charges affecting the property whether previously existing or created by the proprietor. A separate charge certificate (form 7) is also issued.

(f) **Section D—the burdens section.** A verbatim note of all land obligations affecting the property, in so far as still relevant and existing. The Keeper discards what she considers all irrelevant information: such as narrative and ancillary clauses; descriptions etc

The Land Certificate completely takes the place of the title deeds. If it is lost, an office copy can be obtained from the Keeper who prepares this from the Title Sheet, but the Keeper no longer issues substitute Land Certificates if the original is lost or destroyed. You can, in theory at least, tear up all the title deeds—but before you do so remember: (1) it is better to keep them until at least the first sale, just in case there has been a mistake that has been overlooked; (2) they belong to the owner of the property who might want to keep them; and (3) the deeds may have historical interest and may be worth preserving for that purpose. The writer remembers examining the title to a property in Edinburgh's Ann Street some years ago. The original Feu Charter, granted by Sir Henry Raeburn (after whose wife Ann, the Street is named) would probably be worth quite a tidy sum these days, and definitely not one to throw into the shredder.

Equally importantly, the original titles can often help to clarify unclear or obscure aspects of the title as it has been reproduced in the Title Sheet, such as the extent of application of burdens.

In the drive towards dematerialisation, the Keeper will offer an electronic version of the Land Certificate, rather than a hard copy and there is a box to tick on the applications form to choose which you want. However, the electronic option is not yet technically possible.

If the purchaser sells the property in the course of registration, there can be a difficulty, as the titles are all in the Keeper's possession for the purposes of the first registration application. The Keeper can be requested to return the title deeds, but this only delays the registration. Alternatively, the Keeper can be asked to supply photocopies of the title deeds, but this is an expensive and time-consuming procedure. The Keeper suggests that, if there is any likelihood of the property being sold before registration is complete, the applicants' solicitors should take photocopies of the deeds presented before sending them. This is not totally satisfactory either particularly as the purchaser's solicitors are entitled to expect to examine the principal titles. It is the practice of some solicitors to keep copies of all writs presented anyway.

SOME OTHER REGISTRATION PROCEDURES

14.11 Although by far and away the most common applications in the Land Register are applications for first registration and dealings with the whole of the registered property, there are a number of other procedures that are designed to assist in property transactions involving registration in the Land Register. Further guidance for completion of land registration forms is available on the Registers of Scotland website - see 'Notes for LR'.

(a) Form 3

Application for registration of a transfer of part of registered holding. This procedure is similar to that for a registered title (see para 14.06), except that the disposition needs to contain a description of the part of the registered title being transferred. A Form 3 should be used when applying to register a dealing in part only of a registered title. This is perhaps most commonly seen in house plot sales, where the developers title to the development is registered in the Land Register and allocated a Title Number. Each time a house or other unit is sold off, the 'parent title' reduces. Equally if a title is being split into two, for example where the garden of a large house is being sold to build another separate home, the same procedure applies.

The disposition should contain a proper conveyancing description for the plot of land being split off the larger, registered, property (see para 9.08(d)).

(b) Form 5

Application for noting an over-riding interest or the removal or discharge of an over-riding interest, or for noting additional information. An over-riding interest is defined in s 28(1) of LR(S)A 1979 (see para 8.24). Such over-riding interests can be notified on a Form 1, 2 or 3 at the time of registration and are then shown on the title sheet. Any interest or discharge of an interest not notified in this way, should be notified on Form 5.

(c) Form 9: Application for rectification of the Register

Where it appears to any party that there is a mistake or inaccuracy in the Register, the Keeper may be requested to rectify this mistake, using a Form 9. A mistake or inaccuracy will include any incorrect or erroneous entry in, or omission from the Register. All relevant supporting deeds and documents in connection with a Form 9 application should be listed on a Form 4, and submitted with the application.

(d) Form 14: Application to ascertain whether or not the subjects have been registered

This form may be used in the course of a normal transaction, but it is more usual to obtain this information from the relevant part of the Form 10.

(e) Form 15: Application for an office copy of a land certificate or charge certificate or any part of one of these

An office copy of the title sheet kept by the Keeper may be requested if a Land Certificate is in constant use or is misplaced. The office copy may be of the whole title sheet or any part of it, or of any document referred to in it.

RECTIFICATION OF BOUNDARIES

14.12 When there is a discrepancy in a common boundary between two properties as shown in their respective titles, an agreement in terms of s 19 of LR(S)A 1979, may be signed by the parties concerned and registered. This is a short cut in conveyancing procedure when otherwise a contract of excambion (see para 9.11) or two dispositions would be required. This agreement should also contain a plan showing the agreed boundary. The agreement is registered in the Land Register, in the case of registered interests, or in the Register of Sasines, in the case of unregistered interests, and the respective titles will show the boundary line as the new agreed line:

> WE, (First) CAROLINE ROWAN, residing at Piemonte House, Kelvinforth, Perthshire ('Proprietor 1') proprietor of ALL and WHOLE [   ] (Property 1) and (second) ERIC SWEET, residing at The Old Railway House, Florence Park, Kelvinforth, Perthshire ('Proprietor 2') proprietor of ALL and WHOLE [   ] (Property 2) WHEREAS Property 1 is situated to the north of and immediately adjacent to Property 2, but the title deeds of Property 1 and Property 2 disclose a discrepancy in the line of the common boundary between Property 1 and Property 2; and whereas in terms of s 19 of the Land Registration (Scotland) Act 1979 we have agreed to regularise the common boundary between Property 1 and Property 2 and to that end have agreed the terms of a plan of that boundary, which plan is annexed and executed by Proprietor 1 and Proprietor 2 as relative to this agreement THEREFORE we agree that the common boundary between Property 1 and Property 2 is and will in all time coming be as shown by the red line on the said plan being the centre line of a mutual fence. IN WITNESS WHEREOF

LONG LEASES

14.13 The transfer of an interest which is held under a long lease is also a registerable event. A long lease is defined in the Land Tenure Reform (Scotland) Act 1974, as being a lease of over 20 years' duration. In practice, many commercial leases, particularly ground leases, were for a long period, (up to 175 years (s 67 of AFT(S)A 2000)). One reason for that is that only by registering a lease may a security over that lease be created. The LTR(S)A 1974, s 12, also prohibited the creation of leases of residential property for a period exceeding 20 years. This is therefore a matter principally for commercial leases, although a pre-1974 residential long lease may still be registered, if it hasn't been already. Similarly an assignation of a registered long lease, or a sublease, or a sub sublease, or a standard security over any part of the property contained in the registered lease, may be registered. In passing, it is worth noting that the trend over recent years has been for much shorter periods in commercial leases, so that fewer require to be registered.

If an unregistered long lease has less than 20 years to run, but its length was originally over 20 years, it may still be registered. Thus (writing in 2011) a lease for a 25-year period, granted say in 1992, may still be registered although it has only a life of a further six years. The registration of a long leasehold interest proceeds in similar fashion to the registration of a right of ownership.

FURTHER READING

Real rights – See generally Stair Institutions, Bell Principles, Erskine Institutes and Hume Lectures. For a modern explanation see KGC Reid: The Law of Property in Scotland, Chapter 13 (Butterworths 1996)

Robert Rennie and Stewart Brymer: *Conveyancing in the Electronic Age* 2008 W Green

Registration of Title Practice Book: www.ros.gov.uk/rotbook/index.html

Registers of Scotland Update 29: http://www.ros.gov.uk/pdfs/update29.pdf

Registers of Scotland Update 31: http://www.ros.gov.uk/pdfs/registers_update31.pdf

CHECKLIST

Registration Application Checklist (**reproduced from the Registers of Scotland under Crown copyright rules**):

Before submitting an application for registration, solicitors should check the following points:

Application Forms

- Use the correct application form.
    - if the transaction will induce registration in the Land Register for the first time use a Form 1;
    - if it is a transaction involving the whole of a property registered in the Land Register use a Form 2;
    - if it is a transaction of part of a property registered in the Land Register use a Form 3.
- Sign and date the application form.
- Answer all the questions on the application form and provide any necessary additional information.
- Include a unique identifier on each page of the application form. (This is so the Registers can be certain about the individual pages that go together to comprise an application form.)
- To meet the scanning requirements ensure that all information provided on the application form is within the marked boxes. (Information outwith the boxes may result in the application form not being compatible for scanning.)
- Where application forms 2 and 3 are being used ensure you include the title number of the already registered property.
- Check that the information on application forms matches that in the deed inducing registration (ie the parties and property are the same).
- Is it the correct form? – ie Form 1, 2 or 3

Form 4

- A single inventory form 4 should accompany the application for registration.

Registration Fee

- The application must be accompanied by a cheque for the correct amount or include the necessary direct debit reference

Deeds

- Check that the deed inducing registration accompanies the application form.

- Ensure the parties to the deed are correctly named and designed.
- For DW (dealing of whole) or TP (transfer of part) Applications - subjects must be described by reference to Title Number
- For applications for first registration and applications for transfer of part the description of the subjects must be sufficient to enable identification on the Ordnance Survey map.
    - include all deeds referred to for extent;
    - consider if a fresh plan is necessary.
- Include prescriptive progress deeds (including breakaway and any unrecorded links in title).
- Include deeds referred to for burdens unless you are aware the deeds contain common burdens and you know that the Keeper has previously examined the deeds.

Stamp duty land tax

- Include a SDLT5 certificate if the transaction requires one.

Competing title/*a non domino* titles

- If title problems exist, enclose evidence of any investigations undertaken to resolve these, with outcomes. Further enquiry may be required depending on circumstances of the individual case.

Appendix I

Transaction file: Purchase of 29 Sardinia Terrace, Kelvinforth

File note by Henry Pink, partner of Brown, Jarvie & Walker dated 06.02.06.

Attendance at meeting with Stuart and Parveen James. I met them through mutual friends recently, who had recommended the firm to them. Noting that Mr and Mrs James are selling their house Hope Cottage in Kinlochalmond and are keen on purchasing the house at 29 Sardinia Terrace, Kelvinforth, and wanted us to act on their behalf. Saying that we would be pleased to act on their behalf, and roughly explaining what we would charge for each transaction, and what other expenses there would be, with special reference to Stamp Duty Land Tax on the purchase, which if they bought at £450,000 would be £13,500. When they expressed surprise at the extent of this outlay, explaining that it was something we had no control over, it was simply another tax from which there was no escape. Similarly the Land Register charges and VAT are on a fixed scale, over which we have no control. Reviewing Home Report Mr and Mrs James brought with them. House valued at fixed price. No apparent problems, but noting there appears to be some alteration work that has been carried out. Explaining that I would make the offer conditional on alteration documentation being available. Instructed to proceed with offer at £450,000 and a date of entry as at 20 November 2011.

Explaining that I would have to see some evidence of their identity, such as passports or driving licences. Further explaining that although they were consulting the firm as a married couple, we would have to treat them as separate individuals with separate interests to protect which might lead to our having separate consultations with only one or the other being present. Saying that we would write a letter setting out the terms of our engagement and what would be likely to be the charges we would make.

Noting they will return later today with their ID.

Engaged 1/2 hour.

Abridged property schedule

Kelvinforth – 29 Sardinia Terrace

Fixed price £450,000

This is a delightful and spacious mid-terraced villa on a sought-after street, quietly situated in the market town of Kelvinforth. The villa has front garden and a delightful sunny back garden. Close to the railway station, with regular trains to Perth station, and to the motorway network, providing easy access to extensive shopping, cultural and sporting facilities. Nearby sporting facilities include Kelvinforth Leisure Centre and Swimming Pool and Tennis, Bowling and Golf Clubs. For enthusiastic dog walkers, nearby Almond Glen provides ample exercise areas. Good local shopping area with an excellent gastro-pub nearby. Close to Kinlochalmond Primary School and Inveralmond High School.

The accommodation comprises on the ground floor – vestibule, hall, lounge with bay window, large open-plan kitchen/dining room with Aga, playroom study, utility room and w.c.; and on the first floor – landing, master bedroom with bay window, double bedroom 2, double bedroom 3, bedroom 4 and bathroom. There is also a large storage basement.

The property retains many fine period features, in particular fireplaces, cornice work, sanded wooden floors and natural wood doors. The house is heated by gas central heating. All fitted carpets, blinds and light fittings are included in the sale price. The curtains may be for sale by separate negotiation. There is free parking on the street outside the property.

The home of Home Reports.

**29 Sardinia Terrace
Kelvinforth
Perthshire
PH36 5KF**

property questionnaire

Property Address	**29 Sardinia Terrace** **Kelvinforth** **Perthshire** **PH36 5KF**
Seller(s)	**Angus George McDuff** **and Susannah Marjorie McDuff**

Completion Date of Property Questionnaire

property questionnaire

Note for sellers

- Please complete this form carefully. It is important your answers are correct.

- The information in your answers will help ensure that the sale of your house goes smoothly. Please answer each question with as much detailed information as you can.

- If anything changes after you fill in this questionnaire but before the date of entry for the sale of your house, tell you solicitor or estate agent immediately.

Information to be given to prospective Buyer(s)

1.	Length of Ownership

How long have you owned the property?   5 years

2.	Council Tax

Which Council Tax band is your property in? Please tick one.

☐ A   ☐ B   ☐ C   ☐ D   ☐ E   ☐ F   ☒ G   ☐ H

3.	Parking

What are the arrangements for parking at your property?

(Please tick all that apply)

Garage	☐	On street	☒	Driveway	☐
Allocated parking space	☐	Resident Permit	☐	Metered parking	☐
Shared parking	☐				

Other (please specify):

4.	Conservation Area

Is your property in a designated conservation area (that is an area of special or architectural interest, the character or appearance of which it is desirable to preserve or enhance)?

Yes /No
/Don't Know
no

5.	Listed buildings

Is your property a Listed Building, or contained within one (that is a building recognised and approved as being of special architectural or historical interest)?

Yes /No
no

6.	Alterations/additions/extensions

property questionnaire

a.   i) During your time in the property, have you carried out any   Yes /No
structural alterations, additions or extensions (for example
provision of an extra bath/shower room, toilet or bedroom)?   yes

If you have answered yes , please describe below the changes

which you have made:

(ii) Did you obtain planning permission, building warrant,   Yes /No
completion certificate and other consents for this work?   yes

If you have answered yes , the relevant documents will be needed by

the purchaser and you should give them to your solicitor as soon as
possible for checking.

If you do not have the documents yourself, please note below who
has these documents and your solicitor or estate agent will
arrange to obtain them:

---

b.   Have you had replacement windows, doors, patio doors or double   Yes /No
glazing installed in your property?   no

If you have answered yes , please answer the three questions below:

(i) Were the replacements the same shape and type as the ones   Yes /No
you replaced?

(ii) Did this work involve any changes to the window or door   Yes /No
openings?

(iii) Please describe the changes made to the windows doors, or patio doors (with
approximate dates when the work was completed):

Please give any guarantees which you received for this work to your solicitor or
estate agent.

7.	Central heating

a.   Is there a central heating system in your property?   Yes /No /
Partial
(Note: a partial central heating system is one which does not heat all
the main rooms of the property - the main living room, the bedroom   yes
(s), the hall and the bathroom).

If you have answered yes or partial   - what kind of central heating is
there?

(Examples: gas-fired, solid fuel, electric storage heating, gas warm
air).

If you have answered yes , please answer the three questions below:

property questionnaire

i) When was your central heating system or partial central heating system installed?

1980s

(ii) Do you have a maintenance contract for the central heating system?	Yes /No
	no

If you have answered yes , please give details of the company with which you have a maintenance contract:

(iii) When was your maintenance agreement last renewed? (Please provide the month and year).

8.	Energy Performance Certificate	

Does your property have an Energy Performance Certificate which is less than 10 years old?	Yes /No
	no

9.	Issues that may have affected your property	

a.	Has there been any storm, flood, fire or other structural damage to your property while you have owned it?	Yes /No
		no
	If you have answered yes , is the damage the subject of any outstanding insurance claim?	Yes /No

b.	Are you aware of the existence of asbestos in your property?	Yes /No
		no

If you have answered yes , please give details:

10.	Services	

a. Please tick which services are connected to your property and give details of the supplier:

Services	Connected	Supplier
Gas or liquid petroleum gas	☒	e-on
Water mains or private water supply	☒	Scottish Water
Electricity	☒	e-on
Mains drainage	☒	Scottish Water
Telephone	☒	talktalk

property questionnaire

Cable TV or satellite	☐	
Broadband	☒	talktalk

b. Is there a septic tank system at your property? Yes /No

If you have answered yes, please answer the two questions below: no

(i) Do you have appropriate consents for the discharge from your septic tank? Yes /No / Don't Know

(ii) Do you have a maintenance contract for your septic tank? Yes /No

If you have answered yes, please give details of the company with which you have a maintenance contract:

11. Responsibilities for shared or common areas

a. Are you aware of any responsibility to contribute to the cost of anything used jointly, such as the repair of a shared drive, private road, boundary, or garden area? Yes /No / Don't know

no

If you have answered yes, please give details:

b. Is there a responsibility to contribute to repair and maintenance of the roof, common stairwell or other common areas? Yes /No / Not applicable

n/a

If you have answered yes, please give details:

c. Has there been any major repair or replacement of any part of the roof during the time you have owned the property? Yes /No

no

d. Do you have the right to walk over any of your neighbours' property - for example to put out your rubbish bin or to maintain your boundaries? Yes /No

no

If you have answered yes, please give details:

e. As far as you are aware, do any of your neighbours have the right to walk over your property, for example to put out their rubbish bin or to maintain their boundaries? Yes /No

no

If you have answered yes, please give details:

property questionnaire

| f. | As far as you are aware, is there a public right of way across any part of your property? (public right of way is a way over which the public has a right to pass, whether or not the land is privately-owned.) | Yes /No
no |

If you have answered yes , please give details:

---

12. Charges associated with your property

| a. | Is there a factor or property manager for your property? | Yes /No
no |

If you have answered yes , please provide the name and address, and give details of any deposit held and approximate charges:

| b. | Is there a common buildings insurance policy? | Yes /No /Don't know
no |

If you have answered yes , is the cost of the insurance included in your monthly/annual factor's charges?

| c. | Please give details of any other charges you have to pay on a regular basis for the upkeep of common areas or repair works, for example to a residents' association, or maintenance or stair fund. |

---

13. Specialist works

| a. | As far as you are aware, has treatment of dry rot, wet rot, damp or any other specialist work ever been carried out to your property? | Yes /No
no |

If you have answered yes , please say what the repairs were for, whether you carried out the repairs (and when) or if they were done before you bought the property.

| b. | As far as you are aware, has any preventative work for dry rot, wet rot, or damp ever been carried out to your property? | Yes /No
no |

If you have answered yes , please give details:

---

property questionnaire

c. If you have answered yes   to 13(a) or (b), do you have any   Yes /No
    guarantees relating to this work?

    If you have answered yes   these guarantees will be needed by
    the purchaser and should be given to your solicitor as soon as
    possible for checking. If you do not have them yourself
    please write below who has these documents   and your solicitor
    or estate agent will arrange for them to be obtained. You will also
    need to provide a description of the work carried out. This may
    be shown in the original estimate.

    Guarantees are held by:

14. Guarantees

a. Are there any guarantees or warranties for any of the following:

(i)	Electrical work	No / Yes / Don't know / With title deeds / Lost	don't know
(ii)	Roofing	No / Yes / Don't know / With title deeds / Lost	don't know
(iii)	Central heating	No / Yes / Don't know / With title deeds / Lost	don't know
(iv)	National House Building Council (NHBC)	No / Yes / Don't know / With title deeds / Lost	no
(v)	Damp course	No / Yes / Don't know / With title deeds / Lost	no
(vi)	Any other work or installations? (for example, cavity wall insulation, underpinning, indemnity policy)	No / Yes / Don't know / With title deeds / Lost	no

b. If you have answered yes   or 'with title deeds', please give details of the work or
    installations to which the guarantee(s) relate(s):

c. Are there any outstanding claims under any of the guarantees listed above?   Yes /No

    If you have answered yes , please give details:

15. Boundaries

So far as you are aware, has any boundary of your property been moved in   No
the last 10 years?

property questionnaire

If you have answered yes , please give details:

16.	Notices that affect your property	

In the past three years have you ever received a notice:

a.	advising that the owner of a neighbouring property has made a planning application?	Yes /No no
b.	that affects your property in some other way?	Yes /No no
c.	that requires you to do any maintenance, repairs or improvements to your property?	Yes /No no

If you have answered yes to any of a–c above , please give the notices to your solicitor or estate agent, including any notices which arrive at any time before the date of entry of the purchaser of your property.

Declaration by the seller(s)/or other authorised body or person(s)

I/We confirm that the information in this form is true and correct to the best of my/our knowledge and belief.

Signature(s): _____

_____

Date: _____

single survey

survey report on:

Property address	29 Sardinia Terrace Kelvinforth Perthshire PH36 5KF

Customer	Angus George McDuff and Susannah Marjorie McDuff

Customer address	29 Sardinia Terrace Kelvinforth Perthshire PH36 5KF

Prepared by	Mr Stephen Andrew MRICS, Archibald + Grant

single survey

1. Information and scope of inspection

This section tells you about the type, accommodation, neighbourhood, age and construction of the property. It also tells you about the extent of the inspection and highlights anything that the surveyor could not inspect.

All references to visual inspection refer to an inspection from within the property without moving any obstructions and externally from ground level within the site and adjoining public areas. Any references to left or right in a description of the exterior of the property refer to the view of someone standing facing that part of the property from the outside.

The inspection is carried out without causing damage to the building or its contents and without endangering the occupiers or the surveyor. Heavy furniture, stored items and insulation are not moved. Unless identified in the report the surveyor will assume that no harmful or hazardous materials or techniques have been used in the construction. The presence or possible consequences of any site contamination will not be researched.

Services such as TV/cable connection, internet connection, swimming pools and other leisure facilities etc. will not be inspected or reported on.

Description	Two storey terraced house

Accommodation	Ground Floor: Entrance Vestibule, Hall, Sitting Room, Open plan Kitchen/Dining Room with Playroom/Study off, Utility Room and WC. First Floor: Four Bedrooms, Bath/Shower Room, WC Basement: Storage

Gross internal floor area (m^2)	166

Neighbourhood and location	Established popular good class residential district. Usual local amenities reasonably convenient.

Age	Appoximately 100 years

Weather	Dull and overcast. The weather over the past few weeks has been mixed.

Chimney stacks	Brick harled. Visually inspected with binoculars.

single survey

Roofing including roof space	The roof is of pitched timber construction overlaid with timber sarkingboard, underfelt and slates to the front, with a timber platform overlaid with bituminous felt to the rear. The roof is principally flat. The structure at the roof appeared 'sound with no significant defects noted within the scope/limitations of the inspection. Externally routine maintenance is required to reinstate loose and slipped slates. Ongoing maintenance will be necessary. Feltwork to the main roof is starting to show signs of age and patching repair is likely to be required within the foreseeable future, although no significant defects were apparent at the time of inspection. Roofing felt has a limited life span and it is likely the flat roofs will require to be renewed within the next 10 years. You should budget accordingly.
Rainwater fittings	Traditional cast iron. No significant defects were noted within the scope/limitations of the inspection and report
Main walls	Principally solid stone drylined internally. Brick roughcast outshot to rear. No significant-defects requiring immediate attention noted within the scope/limitations of the inspection and report.
Windows, external doors and joinery	The majority of the windows are original comprising single glazed sash and casement units. Some modern double glazed windows have been installed within the Playroom\Study.
External decorations	External vent pipes should be capped to prevent water ingress.
Conservatories/porches	None.
Communal areas	None.
Garages and permanent outbuildings	None.
Outside areas and boundaries	Private, garden ground is provided to the front and rear of the property. This has been adequately maintained with boundaries well defined.
Ceilings	Principally lath and plaster (original).
Internal walls	Solid plastered on the hard, lath and plaster and plasterboard lined.
Floors including sub floors	These are of suspended timber construction boarded. A solid floor with tile finish is provided within the Entrance Vestibule.

single survey

Internal joinery and kitchen fittings	Solid plastered on the hard, lath and plaster and plasterboard lined. No significant defects noted to internal walls and partitions within the scope/limitations of the inspection and report. Some repairs are required to areas of damaged and cracked plasterwork noted to wall surfaces at the various points throughout.
Chimney breasts and fireplaces	The majority of the open fires have been retained as features.
Internal decorations	Softwood, original. Some maintenance repair required.
Cellars	Basement used for storage.
Electricity	Mains supply. The meter and fuse box are located within the Entrance Vestibule and are of a modern pattern. Although the system was not tested no evidence of any significant defects were noted within the scope/limitations of the inspection and report.
Gas	Mains supply. Gas supplies and installations were not tested.
Water, plumbing, bathroom fittings	Mains supply. Water supplies and installations etc were not tested and are assumed to function satisfactorily at present. Where visible the plumbing installation appeared to be of a modern pattern comprising of copper and plastic piping. The original lead cold water tank has been retained, but we believe is now obsolete.
Heating and hot water	Central heating is provided by means of a floor mounted gas fired boiler located within the cellar under the Playroom/Study. The boiler serves panel radiators located throughout the house. The heating system was not tested and was not in operation at the time of inspection.
Drainage	Drainage is assumed to be connected to the main sewer.
Fire, smoke and burglar alarms	Smoke alarm fitted to hall ceiling.
Any additional limits to inspection	Our valuation is made on the assumption any alterations which may have been carried out to the property satisfy all relevant legislation and have full certification where appropriate.

585

single survey

Sectional Diagram showing elements of a typical house

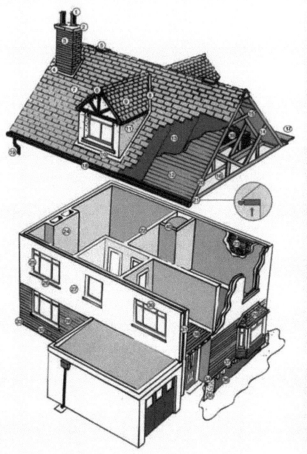

1. Chimney pots
2. Coping stone
3. Chimney head
4. Flashing
5. Ridge ventilation
6. Ridge board
7. Slates / tiles
8. Valley guttering
9. Dormer projection
10. Dormer flashing
11. Dormer cheeks
12. Sarking
13. Roof felt
14. Trusses
15. Collar
16. Insulation
17. Parapet gutter
18. Eaves guttering
19. Rainwater downpipe
20. Verge boards /skews
21. Soffit boards
22. Partition wall
23. Lath / plaster
24. Chimney breast
25. Window pointing
26. Window sills
27. Rendering
28. Brickwork / pointing
29. Bay window projection
30. Lintels
31. Cavity walls / wall ties
32. Subfloor ventilator
33. Damp proof course
34. Base course
35. Foundations
36. Solum
37. Floor joists
38. Floorboards
39. Water tank
40. Hot water tank

Reference may be made in this report to some or all of the above component parts of the property. This diagram may assist you in locating and understanding these items.

single survey

2. Condition

This section identifies problems and tells you about the urgency of any repairs by using one of the following three categories:

Category 3	Category 2	Category 1
Urgent repairs or replacement are needed now. Failure to deal with them may cause problems to other parts of the property or cause a safety hazard. Estimates for repairs or replacement are needed now.	Repairs or replacement requiring future attention, but estimates are still advised.	No immediate action or repair is needed.

Structural movement

Repair category	1
Notes	No significant defects apparent.

Dampness, rot and infestation

Repair category	2
Notes	No significant defects apparent.

Chimney stacks

Repair category	1
Notes	No significant defects apparent.

Roofing including roof space

Repair category	2
Notes	No significant defects apparent.

Rainwater fittings

Repair category	1
Notes	No significant defects apparent.

Main walls

Repair category	2
Notes	No significant defects apparent.

Windows, external doors and joinery

Repair category	1
Notes	No significant defects apparent.

External decorations

Repair category	1
Notes	No significant defects apparent.

single survey

Category 3	Category 2	Category 1
Urgent repairs or replacement are needed now. Failure to deal with them may cause problems to other parts of the property or cause a safety hazard. Estimates for repairs or replacement are needed now.	Repairs or replacement requiring future attention, but estimates are still advised.	No immediate action or repair is needed.

Conservatories/porches

Repair category	not applicable
Notes	

Communal areas

Repair category	not applicable
Notes	

Garages and permanent outbuildings

Repair category	not applicable
Notes	

Outside areas and boundaries

Repair category	2
Notes	No significant defects apparent.

Ceilings

Repair category	2
Notes	No significant defects apparent.

Internal walls

Repair category	2
Notes	No significant defects apparent.

Floors including sub-floors

Repair category	1
Notes	No significant defects apparent.

Internal joinery and kitchen fittings

Repair category	1
Notes	No significant defects apparent.

Chimney breasts and fireplaces

Repair category	not applicable
Notes	

Internal decorations

Repair category	3
Notes	No significant defects apparent.

single survey

Category 3	Category 2	Category 1
Urgent repairs or replacement are needed now. Failure to deal with them may cause problems to other parts of the property or cause a safety hazard. Estimates for repairs or replacement are needed now.	Repairs or replacement requiring future attention, but estimates are still advised.	No immediate action or repair is needed.

Cellars
Repair category	1
Notes	No significant defects apparent.

Electricity
Repair category	1
Notes	No significant defects apparent.

Gas
Repair category	1
Notes	No significant defects apparent.

Water, plumbing and bathroom fittings
Repair category	1
Notes	No significant defects apparent.

Heating and hot water
Repair category	1
Notes	No significant defects apparent.

Drainage
Repair category	1
Notes	No surface evidence of chokage or leakage.

single survey

Set out below is a summary of the condition of the property which is provided for reference only. You should refer to the previous comments for detailed information.

Structural movement	1
Dampness, rot and infestation	2
Chimney stacks	not applicable
Roofing including roof space	2
Rainwater fittings	1
Main walls	2
Windows, external doors and joinery	1
External decorations	1
Conservatories / porches	not applicable
Communal areas	not applicable
Garages and permanent outbuildings	not applicable
Outside areas and boundaries	2
Ceilings	2
Internal walls	2
Floors including sub-floors	1
Internal joinery and kitchen fittings	1
Chimney breasts and fireplaces	not applicable
Internal decorations	3
Cellars	not applicable
Electricity	1
Gas	1
Water, plumbing and bathroom fittings	2
Heating and hot water	1
Drainage	1

Category 3

Urgent repairs or replacement are needed now. Failure to deal with them may cause problems to other parts of the property or cause a safety hazard. Estimates for repairs or replacement are needed now.

Category 2

Repairs or replacement requiring future attention, but estimates are still advised.

Category 1

No immediate action or repair is needed.

Remember

The cost of repairs may influence the amount someone is prepared to pay for the property. We recommend that relevant estimates and reports are obtained in your own name.

Warning

If left unattended, even for a relatively short period, Category 2 repairs can rapidly develop into more serious Category 3 repairs. The existence of Category 2 or Category 3 repairs may have an adverse effect on marketability, value and the sale price ultimately achieved for the property. This is particularly true during slow market conditions where the effect can be considerable.

single survey

3. Accessibility information

Guidance notes on accessibility information

Three steps or fewer to a main entrance door of the property: In flatted developments the 'main entrance' would be the flat's own entrance door, not the external door to the communal stair. The 'three steps or fewer' are counted from external ground level to the flat's entrance door. Where a lift is present, the count is based on the number of steps climbed when using the lift.

Unrestricted parking within 25 metres: For this purpose, 'Unrestricted parking' includes parking available by means of a parking permit. Restricted parking includes parking that is subject to parking restrictions, as indicated by the presence of solid yellow, red or white lines at the edge of the road or by a parking control sign, parking meters or other coin-operated machines.

1. Which floor(s) is the living accommodation on?	Ground
2. Are there three steps or fewer to a main entrance door of the property?	Yes [X] No [ ]
3. Is there a lift to the main entrance door of the property?	Yes [ ] No [X]
4. Are all door openings greater than 750mm?	Yes [ ] No [X]
5. Is there a toilet on the same level as the living room and kitchen?	Yes [ ] No [X]
6. Is there a toilet on the same level as a bedroom?	Yes [X] No [ ]
7. Are all rooms on the same level with no internal steps or stairs?	Yes [ ] No [X]
8. Is there unrestricted parking within 25 metres of an entrance door to the building?	Yes [X] No [ ]

591

single survey

4. Valuation and conveyancer issues

This section highlights information that should be checked with a solicitor or licensed conveyancer. It also gives an opinion of market value and an estimated reinstatement cost for insurance purposes.

Matters for a solicitor or licensed conveyancer
Normal legal enquiries.

Estimated reinstatement cost for insurance purposes
£325,000

Valuation and market comments
£450,000

Report author	Mr Stephen Andrew MRICs, Archibald + Grant

Address	Archibald +Grant, Chartered Surveyors, 50 Lombardy Place, Kelvinforth, Perthshire PH36 7TH

Signed	Electronically prepared by The Valuation Exchange

Date of report	22nd June 2011

energy report

energy report on

Property address:	29 Sardinia Terrace Kelvinforth Perthshire PH36 5KF

Customer:	Angus George McDuff and Susannah Marjorie McDuff

Customer address:	29 Sardinia Terrace Kelvinforth Perthshire PH36 5KF

Prepared by:	Mr Stephen Andrew MRICs, Archibald + Grant

Energy Performance Certificate

Address of dwelling and other details

29 Sardinia Terrace
Kelvinforth
Perthshire
PH36 5KF

Dwelling type:	Semi-detached house
Name of approved organisation:	RICS Protocol for Scotland
Membership number:	RICS068511
Date of certificate:	22nd June 2011
Reference number:	2082-1008-3209-6870-5900
Total floor area:	50 m²
Main type of heating and fuel:	Boiler and radiators, mains gas

This dwelling's performance ratings

This dwelling has been assessed using the RdSAP 2005 methodology. Its performance is rated in terms of the energy use per square metre of floor area, energy efficiency based on fuel costs and environmental impact based on carbon dioxide (CO_2) emissions. CO_2 is a greenhouse gas that contributes to climate change.

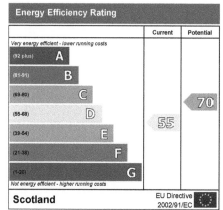

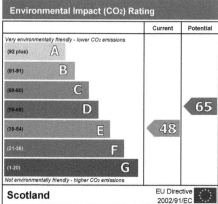

The energy efficiency rating is a measure of the overall efficiency of a home. The higher the rating the more energy efficient the home is and the lower the fuel bills are likely to be.

The environmental impact rating is a measure of a home's impact on the environment in terms of carbon dioxide (CO_2) emissions. The higher the rating the less impact it has on the environment.

Approximate current energy use per square metre of floor area: 447 kWh/m² per year

Approximate current CO_2 emissions: 75 kg/m² per year

Cost effective improvements

Below is a list of lower cost measures that will raise the energy performance of the dwelling to the potential indicated in the tables above. Higher cost measures could also be considered and these are recommended in the attached energy report.

1 Increase loft insulation to 270 mm	4 Low energy lighting for all fixed outlets
2 Cavity wall insulation	5 Hot water cylinder thermostat
3 Increase hot water cylinder insulation	6 Upgrade heating controls

A full energy report is appended to this certificate

Information from this EPC may be given to Energy Saving Trust to provide advice to householders on financial help available to improve home energy efficiency.

For advice on how to take action and to find out about offers available to make your home more energy efficient, call **0800 512 012** or visit **www.energysavingtrust.org.uk**

N.B. THIS CERTIFICATE MUST BE AFFIXED TO THE DWELLING AND NOT BE REMOVED UNLESS IT IS REPLACED WITH AN UPDATED VERSION

Energy Performance Certificate

RRN: 2082-1008-3209-6870-5900

Energy Report

The Energy Performance Certificate and Energy Report for this dwelling were produced following an energy assessment undertaken by a member of RICS Protocol for Scotland. This is an organisation which has been approved by the Scottish Ministers. The certificate has been produced under the Building (Scotland) Amendment Regulations 2006 and a copy of the certificate and this energy report have been lodged on a national register.

Assessor's name:	Mr. Stephen Andrew MRICS
Company name/trading name:	Archibald +Grant, 50 Lombardy Place, Kelvinforth
Address:	
Phone number:	01738 614900
Fax number:	01738 614909
E-mail address:	steve.andrew@archibald-grant.co.uk
Related party disclosure:	

Estimated energy use, carbon dioxide (CO₂) emissions and fuel costs of this home

	Current	Potential
Energy use	447 kWh/m² per year	293 kWh/m² per year
Carbon dioxide emissions	3.8 tonnes per year	2.5 tonnes per year
Lighting	£48 per year	£26 per year
Heating	£452 per year	£364 per year
Hot water	£237 per year	£128 per year

Based on standardised assumptions about occupancy, heating patterns and geographical location, the above table provides an indication of how much it will cost to provide lighting, heating and hot water to this home. The fuel costs only take into account the cost of fuel and not any associated service, maintenance or safety inspection. This certificate has been provided for comparative purposes only and enables one home to be compared with another. Always check the date the certificate was issued, because fuel prices can increase over time and energy saving recommendations will evolve.

About the building's performance ratings

The ratings on the certificate provide a measure of the building's overall energy efficiency and its environmental impact, calculated in accordance with a national methodology that takes into account factors such as insulation, heating and hot water systems, ventilation and fuels used.

Not all buildings are used in the same way, so energy ratings use 'standard occupancy' assumptions which may be different from the specific way you use your home.

Buildings that are more energy efficient use less energy, save money and help protect the environment. A building with a rating of 100 would cost almost nothing to heat and light and would cause almost no carbon emissions. The potential ratings in the certificate describe how close this building could get to 100 if all the cost effective recommended improvements were implemented.

About the impact of buildings on the environment

One of the biggest contributors to global warming is carbon dioxide. The way we use energy in buildings causes emissions of carbon. The energy we use for heating, lighting and power in homes produces over a quarter of the UK's carbon dioxide emissions and other buildings produce a further one-sixth.

The average household causes about 6 tonnes of carbon dioxide every year. Adopting the recommendations in this report can reduce emissions and protect the environment. You could reduce emissions even more by switching to renewable energy sources. In addition there are many simple everyday measures that will save money, improve comfort and reduce the impact on the environment. Some examples are given at the end of this report.

RRN: 2082-1008-3209-6870-5900

Summary of this home's energy performance related features

The following is an assessment of the key individual elements that have an impact on this home's performance rating. Each element is assessed against the following scale: Very poor / Poor / Average / Good / Very good.

Elements	Description	Current performance	
		Energy Efficiency	Environmental
Walls	Cavity wall, as built, partial insulation (assumed)	Average	Average
Roof	Pitched, 100 mm loft insulation	Average	Average
Floor	Suspended, no insulation (assumed)	-	-
Windows	Fully double glazed	Average	Average
Main heating	Boiler and radiators, mains gas	Average	Good
Main heating controls	Programmer, TRVs and bypass	Poor	Poor
Secondary heating	None	-	-
Hot water	From main system, no cylinderstat	Poor	Average
Lighting	Low energy lighting in 14% of fixed outlets	Poor	Poor

Current energy efficiency rating	D 55
Current environmental impact (CO2) rating	E 48

Low and zero carbon energy sources

These are sources of energy (producing or providing electricity or hot water) which emit little or no carbon dioxide into the atmosphere. There are none applicable to this home.

Recommendations

RRN: 2082-1008-3209-6870-5900

Recommended measures to improve this home's energy performance

The measures below are cost effective. The performance ratings after improvement listed below are cumulative, that is they assume the improvements have been installed in the order that they appear in the table. However you should check the conditions in any covenants, warranties or sale contracts, and whether any legal permissions are required such as a building warrant, planning consent or listed building restrictions.

Lower cost measures (up to £500)	Typical savings per year	Performance ratings after improvement	
		Energy efficiency	Environmental impact
1 Increase loft insulation to 270 mm	£15	D 56	E 49
2 Cavity wall insulation	£83	D 62	D 56
3 Increase hot water cylinder insulation	£43	D 65	D 59
4 Low energy lighting for all fixed outlets	£17	D 66	D 60
5 Hot water cylinder thermostat	£25	D 68	D 62
6 Upgrade heating controls	£35	C 70	D 65
Sub-total	£218		
Higher cost measures (over £500)			
7 Replace boiler with Band A condensing boiler	£99	C 77	C 74
Total	£317		
Potential energy efficiency rating		C 77	
Potential environmental impact (CO₂) rating			C 74

Further measures to achieve even higher standards

The further measures listed below should be considered in addition to those already specified if aiming for the highest possible standards for this home. Some of these measures may be cost-effective when other building work is being carried out such as an alteration, extension or repair. Also they may become cost-effective in the future depending on changes in technology costs and fuel prices. However you should check the conditions in any covenants, warranties or sale contracts, and whether any legal permissions are required such as a building warrant, planning consent or listed building restrictions.

8 Solar water heating	£21	C 79	C 76
9 Solar photovoltaic panels, 2.5 kWp	£172	A 93	B 90
10 Wind turbine	£12	A 94	B 90
Enhanced energy efficiency rating		A 94	
Enhanced environmental impact (CO₂) rating			B 90

Improvements to the energy efficiency and environmental impact ratings will usually be in step with each other. However, they can sometimes diverge because reduced energy costs are not always accompanied by a reduction in carbon dioxide (CO₂) emissions.

597

RRN: 2082-1008-3209-6870-5900

About the cost effective measures to improve this home's performance ratings

If you are a tenant, before undertaking any work you should check the terms of your lease and obtain approval from your landlord if the lease either requires it, or makes no express provision for such work.

Lower cost measures (typically up to £500 each)

These measures are relatively inexpensive to install and are worth tackling first. Some of them may be installed as DIY projects. DIY is not always straightforward, and sometimes there are health and safety risks, so take advice before carrying out DIY improvements.

1 Loft insulation

Loft insulation laid in the loft space or between roof rafters to a depth of at least 270 mm will significantly reduce heat loss through the roof; this will improve levels of comfort, reduce energy use and lower fuel bills. Insulation should not be placed below any cold water storage tank, any such tank should also be insulated on its sides and top, and there should be boarding on battens over the insulation to provide safe access between the loft hatch and the cold water tank. The insulation can be installed by professional contractors but also by a capable DIY enthusiast. Loose granules may be used instead of insulation quilt; this form of loft insulation can be blown into place and can be useful where access is difficult. The loft space must have adequate ventilation to prevent dampness; seek advice about this if unsure. Further information about loft insulation and details of local contractors can be obtained from the National Insulation Association (www.nationalinsulationassociation.org.uk). It should be noted that building standards may apply to this work.

2 Cavity wall insulation

Cavity wall insulation, to fill the gap between the inner and outer layers of external walls with an insulating material, reduces heat loss; this will improve levels of comfort, reduce energy use and lower fuel bills. The insulation material is pumped into the gap through small holes that are drilled into the outer walls, and the holes are made good afterwards. As specialist machinery is used to fill the cavity, a professional installation company should carry out this work, and they should carry out a thorough survey before commencing work to ensure that this type of insulation is suitable for this home and its exposure. They should also provide a guarantee for the work and handle any building standards issues. Further information about cavity wall insulation and details of local installers can be obtained from the National Insulation Association (www.nationalinsulationassociation.org.uk).

3 Hot water cylinder insulation

Increasing the thickness of existing insulation around the hot water cylinder will help to maintain the water at the required temperature; this will reduce the amount of energy used and lower fuel bills. An additional cylinder jacket or other suitable insulation layer can be used. The insulation should be fitted over any thermostat clamped to the cylinder. Hot water pipes from the hot water cylinder should also be insulated, using pre-formed pipe insulation of up to 50 mm thickness, or to suit the space available, for as far as they can be accessed to reduce losses in summer. All these materials can be purchased from DIY stores and installed by a competent DIY enthusiast.

4 Low energy lighting

Replacement of traditional light bulbs with energy saving recommended ones will reduce lighting costs over the lifetime of the bulb, and they last up to 12 times longer than ordinary light bulbs. Also consider selecting low energy light fittings when redecorating; contact the Lighting Association for your nearest stockist of Domestic Energy Efficient Lighting Scheme fittings.

5 Cylinder thermostat

A hot water cylinder thermostat enables the boiler to switch off when the water in the cylinder reaches the required temperature; this minimises the amount of energy that is used and lowers fuel bills. The thermostat is a temperature sensor that sends a signal to the boiler when the required temperature is reached. To be fully effective it needs to be sited in the correct position and hard wired in place, so it should be installed by a competent plumber or heating engineer. It should be noted that building standards may apply to this work.

6 Heating controls (room thermostat)

The heating system should have a room thermostat to enable the boiler to switch off when no heat is required. A competent heating engineer should be asked to do this work. Insist that the thermostat switches off the boiler as well as the pump and that the thermostatic radiator valve is removed from any radiator in the same room as the thermostat. Building regulations may apply to this work, so it is best to obtain advice from your local authority building standards department and from a qualified heating engineer.

Higher cost measures (typically over £500 each)

7 Band A condensing boiler

A condensing boiler is capable of much higher efficiencies than other types of boiler, meaning it will burn less fuel to heat this property. This improvement is most appropriate when the existing central heating boiler needs repair or replacement, but there may be exceptional circumstances making this impractical. Condensing boilers need a drain for the condensate which limits their location; remember this when considering remodelling the room containing the existing boiler even if the latter is to be retained for the time being (for example a kitchen makeover). Building regulations may apply to this work, so it is best to obtain advice from your local authority building standards department and from a qualified heating engineer.

RRN: 2082-1008-3209-6870-5900

About the further measures to achieve even higher standards

Further measures that could deliver even higher standards for this home. You should check the conditions in any covenants, planning conditions, warranties or sale contracts before undertaking any of these measures. If you are a tenant, before undertaking any work you should check the terms of your lease and obtain approval from your landlord if the lease either requires it, or makes no express provision for such work.

8 Solar water heating

A solar water heating panel, usually fixed to the roof, uses the sun to pre-heat the hot water supply. This will significantly reduce the demand on the heating system to provide hot water and hence save fuel and money. The Solar Trade Association has up-to-date information on local installers and any grant that may be available or call 0800 512 012 (Energy Saving Trust). Building regulations may apply to this work.

9 Solar photovoltaic (PV) panels

A solar PV system is one which converts light directly into electricity via panels placed on the roof with no waste and no emissions. This electricity is used throughout the home in the same way as the electricity purchased from an energy supplier. The British Photovoltaic Association has up-to-date information on local installers who are qualified electricians and on any grant that may be available, or call 0800 512 012 (Energy Saving Trust). Planning restrictions may apply in certain neighbourhoods and you should check this with the local authority. Building regulations may apply to this work, so it is best to obtain advice from your local authority building standards department and from a suitably qualified electrician.

10 Wind turbine

A wind turbine provides electricity from wind energy. This electricity is used throughout the home in the same way as the electricity purchased from an energy supplier. The British Wind Energy Association has up-to-date information on suppliers of small-scale wind systems and any grant that may be available, or call 0800 512 012 (Energy Saving Trust). Wind turbines are not suitable for all properties. The system's effectiveness depends on local wind speeds and the presence of nearby obstructions, and a site survey should be undertaken by an accredited installer. Planning restrictions and/or building regulations may apply and you should check this with the local authority.

What can I do today?

Actions that will save money and reduce the impact of your home on the environment include:

- Ensure that you understand the dwelling and how its energy systems are intended to work so as to obtain the maximum benefit in terms of reducing energy use and CO_2 emissions.
- If you have a conservatory or sunroom, avoid heating it in order to use it in cold weather and close doors between the conservatory and dwelling.
- Check that your heating system thermostat is not set too high (in a home, 21°C in the living room is suggested) and use the timer to ensure you only heat the building when necessary.
- Make sure your hot water is not too hot - a cylinder thermostat need not normally be higher than 60°C.
- Turn off lights when not needed and do not leave appliances on standby. Remember not to leave chargers (e.g. for mobile phones) turned on when you are not using them.
- If you're not filling up the washing machine, tumble dryer or dishwasher, use the half-load or economy programme. Minimise the use of tumble dryers and dry clothes outdoors where possible.
- Close your curtains at night to reduce heat escaping through the windows.

SPM Ref No

Mortgage Valuation Report

Instructing Source	Case Ref	Valuer Ref
Millar & Bryce Limited - SPM	424000	

1) Applicant Details

Applicants Name(s)   Angus George McDuff and Susannah Marjorie McDuff

Property address (inc. postcode)   29 Sardinia Terrace, Kelvinforth, Perthshire

Town

Postcode   PH36 5KF

2) Description of Property

Year built: 1900

Type of property	House	X	Detached		If Flat / Maisonette: Purpose Built	
	Bungalow		Semi detached			Converted	
	Chalet		Mid terrace	X	Floor number of subject property	
	Flat / Maisonette		End terrace		No. of floors in block	
	Other*		*Specify under General Comments		No. of flats in block	

Type of Construction: (*Specify under General Comments) *Traditional [X]   *Non Traditional [ ]

3) Accommodation - give number of:

Receptions	1	Bedrooms	4	Kitchens	1	Bathrooms	1	Inside W.C.s	2
Other	Basement and Playroom			No. of floors	2	Garage(s) /* Outbuilding	0	Garden	1

4) If Newly Built

Name of builder   Stage reached:

NHBC [ ]   Other* [ ]   (*Please specify)

Roadways and pathways adopted?   Yes [X]   No [ ]

5) Tenure   Ex-Feudal [ ]   Freehold [ ]   Leasehold [ ]   Other* [ ]   (*Please specify)

If Leasehold, years unexpired:

Any known or reported problems with onerous or unusual ground rent or service charges?

Owner occupied [X]   Tenanted [ ]   Vacant [ ]

If part tenanted, please give details:

6) Subsidence, Settlement and Landslip

Does the property show any signs of, or is the property located near any area subject to landslip, heave, settlement, subsidence, flooding, mining?   Yes [ ]   No [X]

If yes please clarify: Evidence of previous movement was noted in the property. We found no evidence to suggest that the movement appears serious or that there were obvious signs of recent movement having occurred.

7) Condition of Property

General standard of constructions	Good	X	Average		Poor	
Structural Repair	Good	X	Average		Poor	
Decorative Repair	Good	X	Average		Poor	

Are essential internal repairs required?   Yes [ ]   No [X]

Are essential external repairs required?   Yes [ ]   No [X]

Should the repairs be effected before the advance is made?   Yes [ ]   No [X]

Is a mortgage retention recommended?   Yes [ ]   No [X]

If the answer to any of the above questions is Yes, please provide further detail:

SPM Ref No [   ]

8)	**Services**	Mains water [X]	Mains Drainage [X]	Electricity [X]	Gas [X]
	Central Heating?	Full [X] Part [ ]	None [ ]		
		Gas [X] Electric [ ]	Oil [ ] Solid Fuel [ ]	Warm Air [ ]	Mixed [ ]

9) <u>Demand For Letting (Buy To Let)</u> (fill in this section only if applicable).

Monthly rental value from the property: **(on a furnished basis)**	£	
Monthly rental value from the property: **(on an unfurnished basis)**	£	

10) <u>Insurance Reinstatement Value</u>
Total area of all floors measured externally.   180   m²

Cost of rebuilding inc. demolition, site clearance, professional fees, local authority requirements,   £325,000
and main building (including all other structures within the site boundaries unless specifically excluded).

11) <u>Market Valuation for Mortgage Purposes (Assuming Vacant Possession)</u>

Do you recommend the property as suitable security for a mortgage?   Yes [X]   No [ ]

If No, please provide reasons.

If Yes, please provide your valuation.

Valuation in present condition: [   ]

Valuation on completion of any works required under Question 7:   [   ]

Valuation on completion of the property per Question 4:   £450,000

12) <u>General Comments</u>

Please advise of any special features of the property and/or the location, which affects the property.
The general condition of the property appears consistent with its age and type of construction.

IMPORTANT - THIS IS A CONFIDENTIAL REPORT PREPARED FOR MORTGAGE PURPOSES.

Certificate: I have personally inspected the property described herein and confirm adequate professional indemnity cover is held.

Signature   Mr Stephen Andrew   **Company / Firm Name**   Archibald + Grant, Chartered Surveyors

Address   50 Lombardy Place
              Kelvinforth
Qualification   MRICS [X] FRICS [ ]   Perthshire
                                                        PH 36 7TH
Date of Inspection   20/6/2011

Date of Report   22/6/2011   **Tel No**

601

Anti-Money Laundering Checklist:

VERIFICATION OF CLIENT IDENTITY CHECKLIST

FOR CLIENT

Name: Parveen James

A. Evidence not obtained – reasons:

1. Client previously identified in Month............... Year...............

2. Client identified personally by – Name_____

  Position_____

3. Other – state reason fully_____

  _____

B. Evidence obtained to verify name and address

Full National Passport   x

Full National Driving Licence   x

Pension Book

Armed Forces ID Card

Signed ID Card of employer known to you

Young person NI card (under 18 only)

Pensioner's travel pass

Building Society passbook

Credit Reference agency search

National ID Card

Copy Company Certificate of Incorporation

Gas, electricity, telephone bill

Mortgage statement

Council tax demand

Bank/Building Society/credit card statement

Young persons medical card (under 18 only)

Home visit to applicants address*

Check of telephone directory*

Check voters roll*

Suitable for proof of address only

C. Evidence for unquoted company or partnership

Certificate of Incorporation or equivalent

Certificate of Trade or equivalent

Latest report and audited accounts

Principal shareholder/partner

Principal director

I confirm that:

a) **I have seen the originals of the documents indicated above and have identified the above Customer(s), or**

b) **In accordance with the Regulations, evidence is not required for the reasons stated.**

Signed___*Wendy Robertson*_____ **Date**_____

(a)   Letter of engagement from Brown Jarvie & Walker to Mr and Mrs James

Brown Jarvie & Walker
Solicitors and Estate Agents
42 Piemonte Place
KELVINFORTH PH36 3RT

Mr and Mrs S G James
Hope Cottage
Kinlochalmond
Perthshire
PH36 7GH

14 August 2011

HP/VV/ Jame 232

Dear Mr and Mrs James

29 Sardinia Terrace, Kelvinforth

Terms of Engagement

I refer to your recent meeting today with Mr Pink of this firm.

I am pleased to confirm that Brown, Jarvie & Walker will be acting on your behalf in connection with the purchase of 29 Sardinia Terrace, Kelvinforth.

I will be assisted by Veronica Vanbrugh, paralegal, and Wendy Robertson, trainee solicitor. We all work very closely together on all transactions and keep each other appraised of progress on the transactions.

Fees and Outlays

I will have (if requested) provided you with details of our charges and the likely outlays under separate cover and will keep you advised of any change to these as we progress, based on our original quotation guidance notes. For the avoidance of doubt, even if your transaction is not completed, we reserve the right to charge a fee for all work carried out up to the point where the transaction ends. Please refer to the guidance notes attached to our quotation or ask us if you require any further information in this regard. By instructing us to proceed it is assumed that you have accepted the terms and conditions of our quotation and guidance notes etc. We would be happy to answer any queries in that regard if you so wish. If you do not accept this please advise us immediately.

It should be noted that it is a requirement of Brown, Jarvie & Walker that all fees and outlays are paid prior to completion of any transaction. If the transaction involves the sale of property or other transaction where we will be receiving funds for the client, and these funds are sufficient to pay fees and outlays, no up front payment of fees will be required. In all other cases we will require payment of fees and outlays prior to completion.

In the majority of cases we will be carrying out work in terms of a quotation (particularly for house purchases, sales, other conveyancing matters etc). However, on some occasions the work we do will not be covered by a quotation because we have to do extra work not included as part of the original quotation. Unless we specify otherwise to you in writing at any stage, we will charge a fee for work carried out by a solicitor at £190 plus VAT per hour.

If you wish to be kept appraised as to the cost to date in any transaction please contact us and we can provide you with a rough idea and, insofar as we are able to, we can appraise you as to what is likely to be the further additional cost for completing the transaction. Any figures given are and will only be given as a very rough guide. At the end of every transaction involving work that was not carried out under a quotation with a set fee, we will issue a fee note based on the amount of work conducted. If you are not in agreement with any fee then, in the first place, please feel free to discuss this with us further. If still not happy then there is a process where the file can be audited by the Auditor of the Court of Session so that a reasonable fee can be decided upon independently. We will pass on the cost of any outlays incurred during any transaction to the client. Again, if requested, we can advise you as to the possible outlays involved, although it may not be possible to determine these at the outset of any transaction if the exact nature of the work to be carried out is not known at that time.

Client Relations

Our aim is to provide a service which is satisfactory in every respect. However, if you, or either of you, have any concerns about the manner in which work is carried out on your behalf, please contact our client relations partner, Mr Brown, who will be happy to discuss your concerns.

Anti-Money Laundering Procedures

We have to ensure that we comply with the Money Laundering Regulations and accordingly we must obtain suitable identification and information from you. In that respect, unless I already hold recent copies of identification from you on a previous file, I would be obliged if you could provide me with two forms of identification as a matter of urgency. **In terms of the regulations we may not be able to carry out any work on your behalf until we have suitable ID.** It may also be necessary to request further information from you for Money Laundering Regulations at the outset. One item of photo ID such as a passport, driving licence or employee ID card with a photograph of you is required to confirm your identity and another item such as a recent household utility bill, recent bank statement, credit card bill or other recent official correspondence is required to confirm your present address. Please note that we require to have sight of the original items of ID, or copies certified by a solicitor or other professional who is regulated by International Money Laundering Regulations. If you have any difficulty in providing ID or information up front, please contact us to discuss immediately.

In addition and particularly where you will be providing funds over the value of about £8,000 towards any transaction, we will have to discuss with you the source of the funds and, also, the method by which we will require payment. Depending on the amount of funds being invested by you, we may need to obtain further evidence from you as regards the source of the funds. For the avoidance of all doubt, please note that under no circumstances can we accept cash of more than £500 from clients and we absolutely cannot accept any cash paid direct into our firm's bank account. Please contact me for details as to what is necessary given your individual circumstances. Any alteration in the source of your funding must be notified to us urgently and could result in a delay before we are able to proceed with the matter. It is very important that there is no last minute change in your financing. Please note that in conveyancing transactions it is normal for there to be a serious financial penalty for delay in completing. If you are unable to complete on the contractual date this could mean that you are in breach of contract.

If you are arranging for a telegraphic transfer of funds to our account, or are to provide us with a Bankers Draft, the bank which transfers these funds or issues the draft must also confirm to us the name and number of the account from which it was drawn and the bank branch details. Any failure to do this may result in a delay in completing your transaction. We reserve the right to withdraw from acting for you if you fail to provide us with the information requested above which is necessary to comply with the Money Laundering Procedures required by the Law Society of Scotland. In addition, where circumstances merit it, we may be legally bound to report individuals to SOCA (the Serious Organised Crime Agency) without warning, if any financial dealings may be considered suspicious.

The Money Laundering Regulations are now very strict and we trust that you will realise that we have a legal obligation to make necessary enquiries where thought appropriate. Perhaps you can call me at your earliest convenience to provide me with the ID and discuss your particular circumstances. If anyone else is providing you with money towards any particular transaction the same rules will apply to them as far as ID etc. is concerned. As a result we will only accept payment of any funds directly from the client (with the exception of funds received from your mortgage lender). If anyone is helping you finance any transaction funds should pass through your own bank account first of all as we cannot receive funds direct from third parties nor will we pay out any funds to third parties other than mortgage lenders and other parties where outlays are usually incurred in such transactions. Please advise us immediately if anyone else will be providing any funds towards the transaction so we can confirm what requirements there may be. It would also be helpful if you could confirm your National Insurance number as this is often required during transactions.

Funds

Clients should note that, for sale and purchase transactions, the purchase price is normally paid over by way of a cheque from the purchasing solicitors Client Account (and not by bank transfer). Therefore, cleared funds are not usually available for distribution on the date of entry and, consequently, if selling, some additional days interest will be charged by the selling client's lender. Please also refer to our Guidance Notes in our Quotation for further details in this respect.

For your information, we will hold any funds on your behalf in our client account which is held with the Southern Cross Bank plc. If sums need to be invested then we will invest these on your behalf in a Southern Cross Bank plc Professionals account. We cannot accept any liability for any losses in the very unlikely event of a bank going out of business.

Standard Conveyancing Clauses

There is now a standard form of contract for property purchases and sales, which is used by many firms of Solicitors. We will forward a copy of the Standard Clauses to you once an offer has been accepted. We will use the Standard Clauses in any purchase on your behalf. If you are selling your property it is possible that the purchaser may not use the Standard Clauses in which case we will send you a copy of the relevant contract letters and discuss the terms of these with you in detail. Now that the Standard Clauses have been adopted by many solicitors in the Central Belt, this has resulted in the speeding up and simplification of the contract process which is of benefit to all concerned. The Standard Clauses are hopefully self explanatory, but if you have any questions regarding the terms of the Standard Clauses we can discuss them with you in due course, or if you have any queries at this time, please do not hesitate to contact us. If you are purchasing a property please be aware that by instructing us to put in an offer for a property, you must be willing to be legally bound to purchase the property. It is possible that the seller's solicitor may issue a formal letter accepting the offer which would immediately result in a legally binding contract. You should therefore not instruct us to put an offer in for a property unless you are willing to be legally bound to the purchase.

Home Report

Since 1 December 2008, anyone who begins marketing their property for sale must produce a Home Report which is to be made available to prospective purchasers. We can of course provide further advice with regard to the requirements, but thought it best to provide some additional detail in that this will affect the services that we provide for you and it is important that you are aware as to the requirements and what this means when it comes to the services we provide to you. We therefore provide the following guidance:-

- It should be noted that there is a general life span on Home Reports of twelve weeks. For anyone purchasing, we would suggest that you do not rely upon Reports which are more than 12 weeks old. For those selling, it may be appropriate, depending on circumstances, to consider updating the Report if it is more than 12 weeks out of date. We can provide further advice about the general reliability of reports and the suitability of these as far as your proposed lender is concerned. It is possible that the surveyor's cost for updating a Report may be about a quarter of the amount for their initial survey.

- In terms of the legislation, solicitors are able to charge prospective purchasers a reasonable fee for providing the Home Report to them. We will not do so except in exceptional circumstances.

Environmental Searches

With reference to Conveyancing transactions there are various standard searches that are obtained and examined in most cases. However it is not standard practice to obtain environmental reports which may give details as regards the likes of contaminated land etc. However, such searches are unlikely to be obtained or examined as part of any Conveyancing process by us as we are not qualified to give advice in this connection and environmental matters do not form part of our remit.

This letter is purely designed to set out the position insofar as your transaction is concerned. The Law Society of Scotland has advised that such a letter should be sent to clients at the outset of every transaction. Please do not hesitate to contact me should you wish to discuss this letter or any other matter.

Yours sincerely

Henry R Pink

Partner

Note: Under the Solicitors (Scotland) (Client Communications) Rules 2005, it may be an inadequate professional service not to send a letter to cover these points.

Southern
Cross Bank

Southern Cross Bank PLC
Mortgage Centre
15 Brisbane Way
Edgbaston
Birmingham
BX4 7HG

Stuart James & Parveen James
Hope Cottage
Kinlochalmond
Perthshire
PH36 7GH

Dear Mr and Mrs James

Application Number: ZGG684-9404-45

We can confirm that your mortgage application has now been approved. The enclosed Offer of Advance provides full details of the terms and conditions of your mortgage, including our Standard Conditions for Borrowing. Your Legal Representative has been sent copies of these.

May we draw your attention to the Special Conditions enclosed. Please make sure that you understand the rules that apply to the mortgage product you have selected.

Please ensure that you have read the documentation carefully and note any conditions that require action on your part.

Please refer to the lending terms for your chosen scheme on our website www.scbmortgages.co.uk.

Please contact us if you have any queries.

Your home may be repossessed if you do not keep up repayments on your mortgage.

Yours sincerely

Additional Information

Southern Cross Bank PLC, is regulated by the FSA, and our register number is 2322. You can check the FSA register on FSA's website, www. fsa.gov.uk/register or by contacting the FSA on 0845 606 1234

1. No right of cancellation applies to your mortgage under the Financial Services (Distance Marketing) Regulations 2004. You may however repay your mortgage at any time in accordance with its terms and conditions.

2. The terms and conditions applicable to your mortgage are supplied in English, and all communications between us throughout the life of your mortgage will be conducted in English.

3. If the property over which you give us a mortgage is situated in England or Wales, English law and the jurisdiction of the English courts apply. If it is in Scotland, Scots law and the jurisdiction of the Scottish courts apply. If it is in Northern Ireland, Northern Irish law and the jurisdiction of the Northern Ireland courts apply.

4. Southern Cross Bank PLC is making this loan for its commercial purposes.

5. You must be over 18 years of age. You are responsible for notifying Southern Cross Bank PLC of any change in your circumstances that may affect the application or mortgage and you agree to pay any costs or expenses in connection with the application.

6. Southern Cross Bank PLC may inspect the file held by your Solicitor in relation to this application at any time and for whatever purpose.

7. By entering into this mortgage you confirm that you have received, read and understood our document entitled Important Customer Information and that you have made the statements set out in it.

Date produced: 11 August 2011	
This offer is valid until 10 December 2011	
Personalised offer for:	**Stuart James and Parveen James**
Property: 29 Sardinia Terrace, Kelvinforth PH36 7GH	
Tenure: Freehold	
If you do not take out this loan any fees already paid which are detailed in Section 8 as non-refundable, will not be refunded to you.	
Once you have signed the legal charge and the funds have been released you cannot withdraw from this loan, however, you can pay off this loan at any time (see Section 10 for the cost involved in this).	
Solicitor:	Brown Jarvie & Walker, 42 Piemonte Place, Kelvinforth PH36 3RT

1. About this offer document	
• You are not bound by the terms of this offer document until you have signed the legal charge and the funds are released.	
• You should compare this offer document with the illustration given to you before you applied for this mortgage, to see how the details may have changed.	
2. Which service were you provided with?	
X	Harvey & Jones recommended that you take out this mortgage. If you have any queries about this service, you should contact Harvey & Jones. Southern Cross Bank PLC is not responsible for the advice or information you received.
	did not recommend a particular mortgage for you. You must make your own choice whether to accept this mortgage offer. If you have any queries about this service, you should contact . Southern Cross Bank PLC is not responsible for the advice or information you received.

3. **Your mortgage requirements**		
Loan amount required:	£150,000.00	Plus £2,725 for fees that will be added to the loan. These and the additional fees that you need to pay are shown in Section 8.
Therefore,		
Gross Advance amount:	£152,725.00	
Net Advance amount:	£150,000.00	
Purchase price:	£450,000.00	
Value of the property:	£450,000 on 14 July 2011	
Term:	22 years 0 months	
Repayment method:	Interest-only	

4. Description of this mortgage

This mortgage is provided by Southern Cross Bank PLC, which is a division of BankOZ Group.

As this mortgage is made up of more than one part, these parts are summarised below:

Part	Loan Amount	Product description	Initial rate payable
1	£152,725.00	a variable rate which is 3.85% above the Bank of England base rate, currently 0.50%, for 12 months, to give a current rate payable of 4.35%. When the Bank of England base rate changes, the interest rate on your loan will change on the 1st of the following month.	4.35%
2	£	a fixed rate of 0% for the term of the loan.	0.00%
	£152,725.00		

The following table summarises these parts once any initial special rates detailed above end

Part	Product description
1	a variable rate which is 4.19% above the Bank of England base rate, currently 0.50%, for the remaining term of the loan, to give a current rate payable of 4.69%. When the Bank of England base rate changes, the interest rate on your loan will change on the 1st of the following month.

The following restrictions apply to the product for part 1 of the loan:

This product is not available for additional borrowing

You can only have another Non-Flexible product with this product

5. Overall cost of this mortgage

The overall cost takes into account the payments in Sections 6 and 8 below.

However, it excludes any payments that you may need to make into a separate savings plan, to build up a lump sum to repay the amount borrowed, but assumes that you pay off the amount borrowed as a lump sum at the end of the mortgage.

The total amount you must pay back, including the amount borrowed is	£297,813.75
This means you pay back	£1.95 for every £1 borrowed
The overall cost for comparison is	8.9% APR

The figures in this section will vary following interest rate changes and if you do not keep the mortgage for 22 years 0 months.

Only use the figures in this section to compare the cost with another interest-only mortgage.

6. What you will need to pay each month

These payments are based on a loan amount of £152,725 and include the fees that are shown in Section 8 as being added to your mortgage and assume that the mortgage will start on 20/11/2011

Part	Loan amount	Repayment method	Number of monthly payments	Initial interest rate payable	Monthly payments
1	£152,725	Interest-Only	240	Variable rate, currently 4.35%	£543.75
2	£0	Interest-Only	0	Fixed rate of 0%	£0.00
	£152,725				

The payments shown for part 1 of the mortgage will only repay the interest charged, and do not include any amount to repay the loan amount

You will still owe £152,750.00 at the end of the mortgage term. You will need to make separate arrangements to repay this. Southern Cross Bank PLC does not know, or need to know details of these arrangements.

It is important to check regularly that your repayment vehicle is on track to repay the mortgage at the end of the term.

6a. What you will need to pay in future

When change will occur	Reason for change	Total monthly payments
After 12 months	Special rate on part 1 ends	£543.75
After 119 months	Final payment	£543.75

These payments assume interest rates will not change.

Remember to add the cost of any savings plans to the monthly payments.

7. Are you comfortable with the risks?

What if interest rates go up?

The monthly payments shown in this offer document could be considerably different if interest rates change. For example, for one percentage point increase in the Bank of England base rate, your monthly payment will increase by around £75.77.

The interest rate on part 2 of your mortgage is fixed for the term of the loan so the payment on this part of the loan will not change.

RATES MAY INCREASE BY MUCH MORE THAN THIS SO MAKE SURE YOU CAN AFFORD THE MONTHLY PAYMENT

What if your income goes down?

You will still have to pay your mortgage if you lose your job or if illness prevents you from working. Think about whether you could do this.

MAKE SURE YOU CAN AFFORD YOUR MORTGAGE IF YOUR INCOME FALLS

8. What fees must you pay?

8. What fees must you pay?	Fee amount
Fees payable to [ ]	
The product fee is payable at the start of the loan. This fee is not refundable. You have selected to add this fee to your mortgage.	£1,500.00
The valuation fee is payable on application. This fee is not refundable. You have already paid this fee.	£150.00

The mortgage account fee is payable on completion and is not refundable. The fee will be added to the loan.	£150.00
The telegraphic transfer fee is payable at the start of the loan. This fee is not refundable. The figure quoted here is the current fee amount which may change.	£25.00
Other fees	
A non-refundable legal fee to your conveyancer before the loan starts. The figure quoted here is an estimate – the total cost of conveyancing may be higher.	£650.00
You may have to pay other taxes or costs in addition to any fees shown here.	

9. Insurance	Monthly payments
Insurance you must take out through Southern Cross Bank PLC or BankOZ Insurance Ltd	
You do not need to buy any insurance through Southern Cross Bank PLC or BankOZ Insurance Ltd	x
Insurance you must take out as a condition of this mortgage but that you do not have to take out through Cross Bank PLC or BankOZ Insurance Ltd	
As a condition of this mortgage you must take out buildings insurance on the property.	x

10. What happens if you do not want this mortgage any more?
Early repayment charges
Early repayment charges apply to part 1 of this mortgage for the first 12 months as follows:
The maximum charge you could pay is £1,500

What happens if you move house?

You can keep the product shown as part 1 in Section 4 if you move house and take out a new mortgage with Southern Cross Bank PLC, provided you meet our lending criteria and product terms and conditions, at the time. The new mortgage must be taken out within 6 months of repayment of this loan. If this occurs, on redemption of your existing loan any early repayment charges (detailed above) will be payable, these will be refunded on completion of your new loan. If redemption of your existing loan and completion of your new mortgage is simultaneous the early repayment charges will not be payable. If the new mortgage is taken out in different names we will not allow you to keep this product or refund these early repayment charges without the written consent of all original borrowers. If the new mortgage is for less than the balance on the product being transferred, any early repayment charges will be payable on the difference. If the new mortgage is for more than the balance on the product being transferred, the additional amount must be taken on a new product, from our product range available to you at the time.

You cannot keep the product shown as part 2 in Section 4 if you move house or do not want this mortgage anymore.

If either the type of mortgage scheme or our lending terms change, you may not be able to keep the product shown as part 1 in Section 4, and any early repayment charges (detailed above), will be payable.

11. What happens if you want to make overpayments?

You are free to make lump sum or regular overpayments to part 2 of this mortgage.

You are free to make lump sum or regular overpayments to part 1 of this mortgage, however the early repayment charges, for this part of the loan, detailed in Section 10, will apply if you make lump sum or regular overpayments within the period that these early repayment charges apply.

If you do make a lump sum payment or overpayment then the amount you owe, and the amount of interest you are charged, is reduced immediately. This means that you will get the benefit straightaway.

12. Additional features

There are no additional features for this mortgage.

Your home may be repossessed if you do not keep up repayments on your mortgage

BROWN JARVIE & WALKER
Solicitors and Estate Agents
42 Piemonte Place
KELVINFORTH PH36 3RT

O'Neill Middleton
Solicitors and Estate Agents
65 Registration Row
PERTH PH12 5TJ

BY COURIER

14 August 2011

HP/VV/ Jame 232

Dear Sirs

For the purposes of this offer and the Combined Standard Clauses (2011 Edition) aftermentioned.

The Purchaser means Stuart Alfredo James and Parveen James, spouses, residing together at Hope Cottage, Kinlochalmond, Perthshire PH36 7GH.

The Property means 29 Sardinia Terrace, Kelvinforth PH36 5KF.

Together with any garden, carport, garage, parking space and/or outbuildings pertaining thereto and all other parts and pertintents.

The Price means Four Hundred and Fifty Thousand Pounds Sterling (£450,000).

The Date of Entry shall be 20 November 2011 or such other date as may be mutually agreed in writing.

The Purchaser hereby offers to purchase from your client (hereinafter referred to as 'the Seller') the Property at the Price and upon the conditions contained in the Combined Standard Clauses (2011 Edition) specified in the Deed of Declaration by Ross Alexander MacKay and Others dated [ ] and registered in the Books of Council and Session for preservation on [ ], both 2011, and upon the following further conditions:

(One) The Price will include the following additional items:

The moveables specified in the Seller's sales particulars.

(**Two**) This offer, unless previously withdrawn, is open for verbal acceptance by midday on 15 August 2011 with a written acceptance reaching us no later than 5.00 pm on the fifth working day following the date of this offer, and if it is not so accepted will be deemed to be withdrawn.

(**Three**) With reference to Standard Clause number 7, it is understood that there have been alterations to form the open plan kitchen/dining room, to the additional shower in the bathroom and the new windows in the playroom. Suitable alteration documents will be provided in respect of these alterations as provided for in the Standard Clause.

Yours faithfully

(*signed*) Brown Jarvie & Walker

Witness Wendy Robertson
Legal Trainee

Covering letter

Dear Sirs

Stuart and Parveen James
29 Sardinia Terrace, Kelvinforth

We enclose an offer for the above property, at the fixed price.

We shall be pleased to have your acceptance, within the time limit imposed, if so instructed.

Yours faithfully

(*signed*) Brown Jarvie & Walker

Email to clients

To: Stuart and Parveen James <jamesfamily26@tiscali.co.uk>
Sent: 14 August 2011, 15:33
From: Veronica Vanbrugh on behalf of Henry Pink
<vvanbrugh@bjw.co.uk>

Subject: 29 Sardinia Terrace, Kelvinforth

Attachment: jame232offer.doc

We enclose a copy of an offer lodged by us today for 29 Sardinia Terrace.
We will be back in touch as soon as we hear further.

Kind regards

Henry Pink

Letter to clients 15.08.11

Dear Stuart and Parveen

Purchase of 29 Sardinia Terrace, Kelvinforth

I refer to the above transaction and I am pleased to confirm that your offer
for the above subjects has now been verbally accepted by the selling agents
and that at a price of £450,000, with a date of entry of 20/11/11. Accordingly,
I now enclose a copy of the offer for your information and retention. I would
expect to hear from the other side with their formal qualified acceptance
in the next day or so. I shall of course forward a copy of the acceptance as
soon as it is received and we can go over it together with a view to moving
towards conclusion of the bargain as swiftly as possible. I enclose the
Combined Standard Clauses referred to in the offer and a Client Guide to
Missives, which you may find helpful.

I also take this opportunity to confirm the expected costs involved in your
purchase, as noted below. Our firm has a practice of requiring settlement
of the total amount before settlement. I trust this will not cause any
inconvenience. Our firm also require cleared funds for any balance over and
above the mortgage at least one week prior to entry, to ensure that funds
are cleared in time. If your sale of Hope Cottage settles shortly prior to the

settlement date, some or all of these costs, together with any fees and outlays for your sale can be deducted from the proceeds of sale, if there are sufficient funds available after redemption of the mortgage.

Kind regards

Yours sincerely

H R PINK

Partner

Note referred to:

Fee	£690.00
VAT thereon at 20%	£178.00
Outlays on your behalf	
Land Registration fee for:	
Disposition	£720.00
Standard security	£60.00
Stamp Duty Land Tax @ 3%	£13,500.00
TOTAL	£15,148.00

The proposed fee is for a normal transaction involving the normal amount of work. In the event of the work required involving more than normal time or being of an unusually complex nature, the proposed fee may require to be increased. You will be advised of any such development in the course of the transaction. Outlays are estimated at current rates.

Note: It is as well to allow an increase if something horrible is found in the title, and the matter requires to be sorted after much work. The outlays are stated to be at current values. The Chancellor might, for instance, change SDLT in a Budget prior to settlement, in which case you need to alert your clients straight away with a revised estimate.

Response from O'Neill Middleton

15 August 2011

Dear Sirs

Mr Angus McDuff and Mrs Susannah McDuff

Mr Stuart James and Mrs Parveen James

29 Sardinia Terrace, Kelvinforth

We are pleased to enclose our Qualified Acceptance, together with the titles and our draft letter of obligation, Form 10, Discharge and Council Tax Notification of Change of Ownership, all for your revisal/approval. We also enclose a P16 Report for perusal and return.

Our clients are bridging in connection with their purchase and it would therefore be of assistance if the price could be paid by electronic transfer. We are advised by our clients that they have two telephone lines - one is a land line with BT and the other is a broadband line with Tiscali. It would be helpful if you would confirm whether your clients also would want to take on the broadband line.

We look forward to hearing from you in conclusion of the contract as soon as possible.

Yours faithfully

Acceptance of Offer by O'Neill Middleton dated 15.08.1.

Dear Sirs

Mr Angus McDuff and Mrs Susannah McDuff ('the Seller')

Mr Stuart James and Mrs Parveen James ('the Purchaser')

29 Sardinia Terrace, Kelvinforth ('the Property')

On behalf of our clients Mr Angus and Mrs Susannah McDuff, we hereby accept your offer dated 14 August 2011 on behalf of Mr Stuart and Mrs Parveen James, to purchase the property at 29 Sardinia Terrace, Kelvinforth, and that at the price of FOUR HUNDRED AND FIFTY THOUSAND

POUNDS (£450,000) and on the terms and conditions stated in the Combined Standard Clauses but subject to the following qualifications, namely:

Condition (two) of your said offer dated 14 August 2011 is delete.

With reference to Condition 1(b) of the Standard Clauses, the wooden corner shelf in Bedroom 3 is excluded from the sale.

With reference to Condition 1(d) of the Standard Clauses, the bird baths in the front and the rear gardens are excluded from the sale.

Schedule Condition 3 of the Standard Clauses is delete. The Seller does not have any specialist treatment paperwork and therefore none will be exhibited or delivered.

Condition 3 of your said offer dated 14 August 2011 and Schedule condition 7 of the Standard Clauses is delete. Enclosed with the titles is the following alteration paperwork:

(a) building warrant reference 98/1734 dated 22 May 1998;

(b) stamped building warrant plans reference 98/1734 dated 22 May 1998; and

(c) Certificate of completion dated 28 July 1998.

By your acceptance hereof, the Purchaser is deemed to be satisfied regarding the abovementioned alteration paperwork. For the avoidance of doubt, no further alteration paperwork will be exhibited or delivered.

With reference to Schedule Condition 16 of the Standard Clauses, payment of the purchase price will be made by electronic transfer at the option of the Seller.

Yours faithfully

Letter to clients 18.08.11:

Dear Stuart and Parveen

Purchase of 29 Sardinia Terrace, Kelvinforth

I refer to the above and I am now pleased to enclose a copy of the acceptance received from the Seller's solicitors. I would ask you to read this document carefully as it, along with offer, will form the basis of your contract of purchase. Please contact me to discuss the acceptance. Please note that I will be unable to make any further progress with this transaction until such time as I have your instructions.

I also enclose the copy of the covering letter from O'Neill Middleton for your information. The ability to pay by electronic transfer will very much depend on whether or not your sale in Kinlochalmond is to settle at roughly the same time and, by what means the settlement is due to be effected.

Unless I hear from you to the contrary, I assume that you would wish to take the title to the property in equal shares. It is possible to take the title to the property in unequal shares and if you would prefer this, please let me have details in early course. In some cases co-purchasers make a co-purchase agreement regulating the use of the property and what would happen if the couple separated and the property were to be sold or transferred to one of the parties. This is a specialist area and if you were interested in this, I would refer you to Harriet Roe, our Family Lawyer (unless there is a conflict of interest).

As a firm, we do not normally include a 'survivorship' clause, which would automatically provide for the transfer of the share of the property to the surviving spouse, should either of you die, without discussing this with you. Accordingly, should either of you die, that person's share will fall into the deceased's estate to be distributed according to their will. I am proceeding on this basis, but should you need clarification or wish to instruct otherwise, please contact me immediately on receipt of this letter and I will be happy to discuss your options.

I confirm that I will write to you under separate cover regarding the title to the property.

With kind regards

H R PINK

Partner

Extract from Feu Charter by the Kinlochalmond Real Estate Co Ltd in favour of Frederick John Gretton, recorded GRS (Perth) 16 May 1904

We, the Kinlochalmond Real Estate Company Limited, incorporated under 'the Companies Acts 1862 to 1890' and having our registered office in Edinburgh, heritable proprietors of the subjects hereby disponed (we and our successors and assignees being embraced where the term 'the superiors' is used in these presents) In Consideration of the sum of One thousand and fifty pounds sterling instantly paid to us by Frederick John Gretton, University Professor, of which we hereby acknowledge the receipt ... Sell and in feu farm dispone to and in favour of the said Frederick John Gretton and his heirs and assignees whomsoever (the said Fredrick John Gretton and his foresaids being embraced where the terms the 'said disponees' is used in these presents) ... heritably and irredeemably ALL and WHOLE that area or piece of ground extending to eighty decimal or one thousandth parts of an acre Imperial Measure or thereby part of the lands of Kinlochalmond aftermentioned and bounded as follows, videlicet: On the north west by north by the centre of a mutual front division fence, mutual gable and mutual back green separating the subjects hereby disponed from the adjoining property on the north feued to William James Burness along all which together it extends One hundred and thirty eight feet eleven inches or thereby; On the west or south west by the centre of a mutual wall dividing the subjects hereby disponed from ground still belonging to us along which it extends thirty feet six inches or thereby; On the south or south east by the centre of the mutual front division fence, mutual gable and mutual back drying green separating the subjects hereby disponed from the adjoining property on the south feued to John Shepherd Wedderburn along which altogether it extends One hundred and forty four feet two inches or thereby; and on the east or north east by the street of Sardinia Terrace along which it extends Twenty three feet nine inches or thereby, all as the said area or piece of ground hereby disponed is delineated and coloured red on the plan annexed and subscribed as relative hereto, together with the dwelling-house number Twenty-nine Sardinia Terrace erected on the said area or piece of ground (but reserving always to us and our assignees the unused half of the west boundary wall of the subjects hereby disponed) which area or piece of ground before disponed is part and portion of ALL and WHOLE that ground extending to five hundred and sixty three acres and four hundred and forty-four decimal one thousandth parts of an acre Imperial Measure, being the remaining portion of the lands and estate of Kinlochalmond belonging to the Testamentary Trustees of the late the Right Honourable Sir George Shelley Childs, Baronet, Earl of Kinlochalmond and Viscount Dunvorlich ...

...And also with and under the burdens, conditions, permissions, prohibitions and declarations after written videlicet: (First) the said disponees shall be bound and obliged in all time coming to maintain and when necessary to renew and rebuild upon the said area of ground above disponed as a self contained dwelling-house consisting of two stories of the value of at least one thousand pound sterling which dwelling-house shall always be of the same design, materials and dimensions and on the same site as the present dwelling-house, and no building of any description shall at any time be erected on said area of ground until the site and the plans and elevations thereof and materials therefor shall have approved of in writing by the superiors or their architect (Second) the said disponees shall be bound and obliged to keep and maintain in good order and repair in all time coming the division walls and fences surrounding the subjects hereby disponed, the gables, division walls and fences on the west north and south boundaries shall be mutual between and be maintained at the mutual expense of the feuars of the subjects adjoining respectively and the said disponees, but the said disponees shall have no claim against us or our foresaids under any circumstances for any part of the expense of maintaining such gables or division walls and fences, (Third) the said disponees shall be bound to keep constantly insured against loss by fire with some responsible insurance company to the extent of nine hundred pounds said dwelling-house erected upon the ground above disponed and to exhibit to the superiors the receipts for the premiums upon the insurance policies as the same fall due, declaring that any sums that may be recovered under such policies shall be expended by the said disponees in immediately rebuilding and restoring the said buildings, which, in the event of destruction, shall be rebuilt of the same value according to the same plans and elevations and upon the same sites as the original buildings, and the superiors shall be entitled to see the money recovered under any insurance policy applied in terms hereof; (Fourth) the ground in front of and behind the dwelling-house erected on the area of ground hereby disponed shall at no time be used or applied for the purpose of buildings of any description except in the event of the superiors authorising the erection of relative offices in connection with said dwelling-house, declaring that said ground in front of and behind said dwelling-house shall be kept and used in all time as ornamental pleasure ground only, the only exception being that the ground behind may be used as a drying green; (Fifth) the said disponees are hereby expressly prohibited from erecting upon the said area of ground hereby disponed any building other than those herein specifically provided for, and the said disponees are further expressly prohibited from converting any building on the said area of ground to any purpose other than that of a self -contained dwelling-house for the occupancy of one family only, and from using the said buildings on said area of ground for any other purpose than as a private family residence; (Sixth) in respect we or our authors have formed the macadamised carriage with surface water channel and kerb stone for footpath on both sides of the said road of Sardinia Terrace along the east boundary of the area of ground hereby disponed and have also formed in the said roadway a common drain for carrying off the sewage from the lands and buildings belonging to us and our feuars, including the subjects hereby disponed, the said disponees shall be bound along with the feuar on the opposite side of said road at mutual expense in all time coming or until the same shall be taken over by the County Authorities and kept up at the public expense, to maintain and uphold the same so far as ex adverso of the said area of ground hereby disponed. The said disponees shall also be bound to pay the proportion of the cost of putting said road and others in repair preparatory to their being taken over by the County Authorities and also to maintain and uphold in good repair in all time the concrete footpath along the whole length of the frontage of the area of ground hereby disponed and all drains within the area of ground hereby disponed, including the service drains which run from north to south through the ground for the use of said dwelling-house and the houses erected or to be erected to the north and west thereof; (Seventh) Notwithstanding that the lands belonging to us have been laid out according to a feuing plan, it shall be competent to us or our successors in said subjects to alter the said feuing plan and the streets and roads not yet formed in any way which we or our foresaids may hereafter consider desirable, and also to appropriate as we and our foresaids may see fit, the lands at any time remaining unfeued and to vary or depart entirely from the burdens, conditions, provisions and others under which the same may be held; (Eighth) In the event of the said disponees contravening or failing to implement any of the foregoing burdens, conditions, provisions, prohibitions and declarations herein written, this feu-right and all that may followed thereon shall, in the option of us or our foresaids become void and null, and the said disponees shall omit, lose and forfeit all right and interest in the said area of ground hereby disponed and buildings thereon, which shall thereupon revert to and become the property of us and our foresaids, freed and disburdened of these presents and all burdens whatsoever in the manner as if this feu right had never been granted and we and our foresaids shall have right to remove the said disponees and to levy the rents of said subjects in all time thereafter, but without prejudice to the legal rights and remedies of us and our foresaids against the said disponees for payment of bygone feu duties and performance of the obligations incumbent upon them under these presents prior to the date of their forfeiture (Ninth) Notwithstanding and without prejudice to anything herein contained, it is hereby provided and declared that should we or our foresaids either expressly or by silence allow any of the burdens, conditions, provisions, prohibitions and declarations herein written to be in any way relaxed or modified the doing thereof shall not entitle any other feuar or proprietor to act without the consent of us or our foresaids as if he had obtained or was entitled to obtain similar or other relaxations or modifications, nor shall it hinder us or our foresaids from preventing his so acting any law or custom to the contrary notwithstanding, and providing in like manner that should we or our foresaids either expressly or by silence modify or relax any of the burdens, conditions, provisions, prohibitions and declarations in the feu right of any other of the feuars of our lands at Kinlochalmond, the doing thereof shall not entitle the said disponees to act without the consent of us or our foresaids as if he or they had obtained or were entitled to obtain similar or other relaxations or modifications, nor shall it hinder us or our foresaids from preventing the said disponees from so acting all which burdens, conditions, provisions, prohibitions and declarations before written are hereby declared real burdens and conditions in favour of us and our foresaids ...

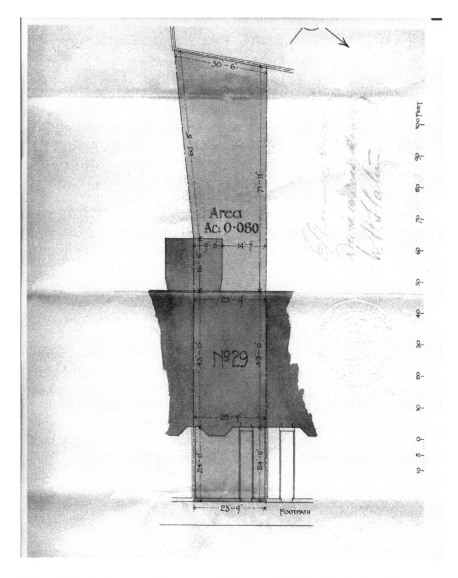

Disposition in favour of Angus and Susannah McDuff—the last Sasine title deed

I, ROBERT McROBERT, residing at Twenty-nine Sardinia Terrace, Kelvinforth IN CONSIDERATION of the sum of Fifty Thousand pounds (£50,000) paid to me by ANGUS GEORGE McDUFF and

MRS SUSANNAH MARJORIE MACDUFF residing at Forty Three Ariel Drive, Edinburgh DO HEREBY DISPONE to and in favour of the said Angus George McDuff and Susannah Marjorie McDuff and their executors and assignees heritably and irredeemably ALL and WHOLE that area or piece of ground extending to eighty decimal or one thousandth parts of an acre Imperial Measure or thereby part of the lands of Kinlochalmond, being the subjects more particularly described in, in feu farm disponed by and delineated and coloured red on the plan annexed and executed as relative to the Feu Charter by The Kinlochalmond Real Estate Company Limited in favour of Frederick John Gretton dated Third and recorded in the Division of the General Register of Sasines applicable to the County of Perth on sixteenth, both days of May in the year Nineteen hundred and four TOGETHER WITH (One) the whole rights common, mutual or sole effeiring thereto; (Two) the whole parts, privileges and pertinents thereof: (Three) the whole fittings and fixtures therein and thereon and (Four) my whole right, title and interest present and future in and to the said subjects; BUT ALWAYS WITH AND UNDER in so far as still valid, subsisting and applicable the burdens, conditions and others specified and contained in the said Feu Charter dated and recorded as aforesaid; WITH ENTRY as at the Tenth day of August Nineteen Hundred and Seventy Five; and I grant warrandice: IN WITNESS WHEREOF these presents are signed by the said Robert McRobert at Glasgow on the Fifth day of August Nineteen Hundred and Seventy Five in presence of these witnesses Charles Spence, Writer to the Signet, and Mary Griffiths, Typist, both of Thirty Three Cornwallis Street, Perth.

REGISTER on behalf of the within named Angus George McDuff and Susannah Marjorie McDuff in the Register for the County of Perth.

'Spence & Spence'

Writers, Perth, Agents

REGISTERS OF SCOTLAND
GENERAL REGISTER OF SASINES
COUNTY OF PERTH
FICHE 4477 FRAME 22
PRESENTED & RECORDED ON 12 AUGUST 1975

Draft disposition on first registration

WE, ANGUS GEORGE McDUFF and SUSANNAH MARJORIE MCDUFF, spouses, residing together at Twenty nine Sardinia Terrace, Kelvinforth, Perthshire, heritable proprietors of the subjects hereinafter disponed IN CONSIDERATION of the sum of FOUR HUNDRED AND FIFTY THOUSAND POUNDS (£450,000) paid to me by STUART ALFREDO JAMES and PARVEEN JAMES, both residing at Hope Cottage, Kinlochalmond, Perthshire HAVE SOLD and DO HEREBY DISPONE to the said Stuart Alfredo James and the said Parveen James and to their executors and assignees whomsoever heritably and irredeemably ALL and WHOLE that area or piece of ground extending to eighty decimal or one thousandth parts of an acre (0.080 acre) Imperial Measure or thereby part of the lands of Kinlochalmond, being the subjects more particularly described in, disponed by and delineated and coloured red on the plan annexed and executed as relative to the Feu Charter by The Kinlochalmond Real Estate Company Limited in favour of Frederick John Gretton dated Third and recorded in the Division of the General Register of Sasines applicable to the County of Perth on sixteenth, both days of May in the year Nineteen hundred and four; Together with all parts, privileges and pertinents thereof, all fittings and fixtures therein and thereon, and our whole right, title and interest in the said subjects; BUT ALWAYS WITH AND UNDER the burdens, conditions and other in the said Feu Charter; WITH ENTRY at the Twentieth day of November Two Thousand and Eleven; AND we grant warrandice: IN WITNESS WHEREOF

Southern Cross Bank

Standard Security

By STUART ALFREDO JAMES AND PARVEEN JAMES

in favour of

SOUTHERN CROSS BANK PLC

Date: 2011

Property: 29 SARDINIA TERRACE, KELVINFORTH PH36 5KF

Solicitors: BROWN WALKER & JARVIE

SOUTHERN CROSS BANK PUBLIC LIMITED COMPANY STANDARD SECURITY

In this deed the expressions set out below shall have the meaning and effect respectively set opposite to them:-

1. The Borrower means

Where the Borrower is more than one person the singular includes the plural and all obligations of the Borrower are undertaken jointly and severally.

Stuart Alfredo James and Parveen James, spouses, residing together at Hope Cottage, Kinlochalmond, Perthshire PH36 7GH

....

2. SOUTHERN CROSS BANK PLC means SOUTHERN CROSS BANK
PUBLIC LIMITED COMPANY registered in England, number 2434567, of
Canberra House, 10 Dover Street, London SE10 4FD which expression shall
include their successors and assignees whomsoever.

....

3. The Property means: The heritable subjects known as

`29 Sardinia Terrace, Kelvinforth PH36 5KF`........

being the subjects more fully described below.

The Borrower hereby binds and obliges himself and his executors and
representatives whomsoever to pay to Southern Cross Bank PLC on demand
all sums of money as are now or may from time to time become due by the
Borrower under the provisions of any loan agreement or otherwise and all
other monies in respect of which the Borrower either as principal or surety
is or may hereafter become indebted to Southern Cross Bank PLC on any
account whatsoever including (without prejudice to the foregoing generality)
legal costs and expenses relating to or incidental to the enforcement of this
Security and together with all other costs and expenses that may be incurred
by Southern Cross Bank PLC in respect of the property and all other monies
intended to be hereby secured for which the Borrower grants a Standard
Security in favour of Southern Cross Bank PLC over the Property being ALL
and WHOLE

```
that area or piece of ground extending to eighty
decimal or one thousandth parts of an acre (0.080
acre) Imperial Measure or thereby part of the lands of
Kinlochalmond, being the subjects more particularly
described in, disponed by and delineated and coloured
red on the plan annexed and executed as relative to the
Feu Charter by The Kinlochalmond Real Estate Company
Limited in favour of Frederick John Gretton dated
Third and recorded in the Division of the General
Register of Sasines applicable to the County of Perth
on sixteenth, both days of May in the year Nineteen
hundred and four
```

The Standard Conditions specified in Schedule 3 to the Conveyancing and Feudal Reform (Scotland) 1970 and any lawful variation thereof operative for the time being shall apply; And the Standard Conditions shall be varied to the effect that:-

(ONE) This Standard Security shall be a security to Southern Cross Bank PLC for all sums due by the Borrower to Southern Cross Bank PLC howsoever arising (including without prejudice to that generality all or any advances or re-advances made by Southern Cross Bank PLC to the Borrower in respect of the property and all interest and consequents due thereon).

(TWO) Interest at the rate of four per centum per annum above the base lending rate from time to time of Southern Cross Bank PLC will also be charged in respect of any expenditure incurred by Southern Cross Bank PLC in pursuance of the provisions hereof and on any monies becoming payable by the Borrower to Southern Cross Bank PLC in terms hereof on the date on which such expenditure is incurred or on the date on which such monies become payable as the case may be.

(THREE)

(a) Standard Condition 4 shall be varied to the effect that reference to any notice or order issued or made by virtue of the Town and Country Planning (Scotland) Act 1997 shall be construed as including all notices or orders howsoever signed, made, given or issued by any other party or person which may affect the value of the property in any way.

(FOUR)

(b) Standard Condition 5 (a) shall refer to full reinstatement value and not market value. The opinion of Southern Cross Bank PLC as to the full reinstatement value shall be conclusive and binding on the Borrower.

(c) Standard Condition 7 (3) shall be varied to the effect that the rate of interest chargeable by Southern Cross Bank PLC in the event therein specified shall be the rate specified in Clause (TWO) hereof.

(d) Standard Condition 9 shall be varied to the effect that references to 'proprietors' shall be construed as including references to the Borrower and in Standard Conditions 7 (3) and 12 references to 'expenses' shall be construed as including references to stamp duty land tax and registration dues.

The Borrower shall vacate the Property in so far as it is occupied by him or his dependants on the expiry of a period of seven days after the posting of a notice by recorded delivery given by or on behalf of Southern Cross Bank PLC and addressed to the Borrower at his last known address or at the address of the Property, at any time after Southern Cross Bank PLC shall have become entitled to enter into possession of the Property and the Borrower agrees that a Warrant of Summary Ejection may competently proceed against him at the instance of Southern Cross Bank PLC in the Sheriff Court of the County in which the property is situated. And in the event of Southern Cross Bank PLC entering into possession of the Property:-

(a) Southern Cross Bank PLC shall be entitled as Agent for the Borrower to remove, store, sell or otherwise deal with any furniture or goods which the Borrower shall fail or refuse to remove from the Property within seven days of being requested so to do by notice from Southern Cross Bank PLC;

(b) Southern Cross Bank PLC shall not be liable for any loss or damage occasioned to the Borrower and the Borrower shall be liable to indemnify Southern Cross Bank PLC against all expenses incurred by Southern Cross Bank PLC in relation to such furniture or goods.

(FIVE) A certificate given under the hand of a Director or Secretary for the time being of Southern Cross Bank PLC or any other duly authorised official of Southern Cross Bank PLC shall be conclusive and final and sufficient evidence (without the necessity of any other voucher) for instructing sums at any time due by the Borrower hereunder to Southern Cross Bank PLC and shall constitute the sum for which the Borrower may be charged and no suspension of a charge for the sum so ascertained shall pass except on consignation.

(SIX) The Standard Conditions contained in the said Schedule 3 to the Act shall except in so far as hereby varied apply to the said Standard Security.

IN WITNESS WHEREOF these presents consisting of this and the three preceding pages are executed by the said Stuart Alfredo James and by the said Parveen James at Kelvinforth on the nineteenth day of July Two thousand and eleven before the witness Henry Rose Pink, solicitor, of 42 Piemonte Place, Kelvinforth

Stuart James

Parveen James   Henry Pink

Draft discharge of standard security by Black County Bank PLC.

WE, BLACK COUNTY BANK PLC incorporated under the Companies Acts and having our Registered Office at Queer Street, Cheapside, London EC1 2LW in consideration of the sum of ONE HUNDRED AND THIRTY THOUSAND POUNDS (£130,000) paid by ANGUS GEORGE McDUFF and SUSANNAH MARJORIE McDUFF residing at Twenty nine Sardinia Terrace, Kelvinforth, Perthshire, being the whole amount secured by the Standard Security aftermentioned HEREBY DISCHARGE a Standard Security by the said Angus George McDuff and Susannah Marjorie McDuff in favour of BULL BANK PLC recorded in the Division of the General Register of Sasines applicable to the County of Perth on Twelfth August Nineteen hundred and Seventy Five; which Standard Security was last vested in the said Bull Bank PLC as aforesaid and from whom we acquired right on Fourth December Two Thousand by (one) the Black Bull Group Reorganisation Act 2002 and (two) resolution of Board of us, Black County Bank PLC, made on Twenty Eighth March Two thousand and three pursuant to the Act: IN WITNESS WHEREOF

Draft approved.

WR.

Draft letter of obligation by O'Neill Middleton

Messrs. Brown Jarvis & Walker.

(to be dated)

Dear Sirs

Angus George McDuff and Susannah Marjorie McDuff (the 'Seller')

Stuart Alfredo James and Parveen James (the 'Purchaser')

29 Sardinia Terrace, Kelvinforth (the 'Property')

With reference to the settlement of this transaction today, we hereby:

1. Undertake to clear the records of any deed, decree or diligence (other than such as may be created by or against your clients) which may be recorded in the Property or Personal Registers or to which effect may be given in the Land Register in the period from………….. to 14 days from today's date inclusive (or to the earlier date of registration of the Purchaser's interest in the Property) and which would cause the Keeper to make an entry on, or qualify his indemnity in, the Land Certificate to be issued in respect of that interest; and

2. Confirm that, to the best of our knowledge and belief, the answers to the questions numbered 1 to 14 in the draft form 1 adjusted with you (in so far as these answers relate to our client or to our clients' interest in the above subjects) are still correct. [and]

[3. Also undertake to deliver to you within 14 days of this date the duly executed Discharge of the existing Standard Security granted by our client with our forms 2 and 4,

and our cheque made payable to the Keeper for the registration dues]

Yours faithfully

Approved

WR.

Letter to clients 21.08.11:

Dear Stuart and Parveen

Purchase of 29 Sardinia Terrace, Kelvinforth

I enclose for your information and retention, a photocopy of the title deed which first divided the title of your property from that of the larger area of ground. It describes your property in detail and sets out various burdens, obligations and conditions relating to maintenance of the common parts of the terrace.

The property is described after the words 'ALL and WHOLE', where they appear about a third of the way down the first page. It is an area of ground extending to 0.080 acres. The boundaries are each narrated and there is a plan of the property at the back of the deed which also shows the measurements. You will note from the deed itself that the boundaries are as follows:

The boundary to the north west or north is the centre line of a mutual front division fence, mutual gable and mutual back green, extending to a total of 138 feet 11 inches approximately;

The boundary to the west or south west is along a mutual wall which extends 30 feet and 6 inches;

The boundary to the south or south east is the centre of a mutual front division fence, mutual gable and mutual back green division fence extending to a total of 144 feet 2 inches; and

The boundary to east or north east is street/pavement of Sardinia Terrace extending 23 feet 9 inches (meaning that any wall or fence at the front will be solely your property, as you would expect).

There are two previous deeds that lay down burdens and conditions that affect the property, most of which will be largely historic and therefore irrelevant. The most relevant burdens are in this deed itself and commence with paragraph (First) at the top of top of page Third. I would summarise these follows:

You are obliged to maintain, renew and if necessary rebuild a self-contained two storey house. The house will always be of the same design materials and dimensions and on the same site as the present house.

You are obliged to keep in order and maintain the division walls and fences. The division walls on west, north and south boundaries are mutual and to be maintained at joint expense with the corresponding neighbouring owner.

You must keep the house constantly insured for loss by fire with a 'responsible' Insurance Company and immediately rebuild to the same specifications as current in the event of destruction.

You must keep the front and back gardens as ornamental garden ground and not build on them, except for a drying green at the back.

You are expressly forbidden from erecting any other building on the ground and from converting any building for any other purpose than that of a self contained house for the occupancy of one family only and from using it for any other purpose than a private family residence.

None these burdens are enforceable by the original superiors, the Kinlochalmomnd Real Estate Company Limited, any longer but may well be enforceable by your neighbours. I would emphasise that the last burden in particular may be important if you were thinking about using the house for anything other than a family home. Recent case law seems to be clear that you could have a study and either of you could work from home, but running a business may be a breach of these conditions if it has an adverse effect on the amenity or value of adjoining properties. Your neighbours could take court action to try to stop any such business activity. If this is a concern, please let me know as soon as possible.

I confirm that I have received a clear Property Definition Report, confirming that the boundaries of the property match the current version of the Ordnance Survey plan.

If you have any queries, please do not hesitate to contact me.

Kind regards

Yours sincerely

H R PINK

Partner

Title deed referred to:-

[Copy of Feu Charter by the Kinlochalmond Real Estate Co Ltd in favour of Frederick Gretton, recorded GRS (Perth) 16 May 1904, enclosed]

E-mail from clients

> From: Stuart and Parveen James <jamesfamily26@tiscali.co.uk>
> Sent: 22 August 2011 08:32
> To: Henry Pink <hpink@bjw.co.uk>
>
> Subject: Re 29 Sardinia Terrace
>
> Hi Henry
>
> Thanks for your letters. We understand the position with the title conditions and we are not planning any sort of business to be run from the house. We may work from home sometimes, but that seems to be OK.
>
> Also confirmed that we would like title in joint names.
>
> Thanks
>
> Stuart & Parveen

Letter to O'Neill Middelton 21.08.11

> Dear Sirs
>
> **Mr Stuart James and Mrs Parveen James**
>
> **Mr Angus McDuff and Mrs Susannah McDuff**
>
> **29 Sardinia Terrace, Kelvinforth**
>
> We refer to the above and now return your title deeds together with your drafts, duly revised/approved. We also enclose our draft disposition and draft Forms 1 and 4 For your approval and return.
>
> We have the following observations on title:
>
> - We look forward to receiving the Form 10A Report;
> - We look forward to receiving the Property Enquiry Certificate;

- We have sent the alteration documents to the surveyor for his perusal and we will revert to you once these are returned to us;

Please advise as to whether or not there is any service history for the gas central heating /appliances and exhibit the evidence of this to us;

We understand that your clients have had regular repairs carried out to the property. It would be helpful if they could leave all associated paperwork for our clients;

We understand that the sittingroom fireplace is fully functional; can you please advise whether or not any servicing/sweeping of the chimney has taken place?

Please advise as to whether or not your clients have any knowledge as to when the property was last rewired.

We will take our clients' instructions on the terms of your qualified acceptance and will revert to you once we have heard from them and, in addition, the surveyor.

As to your request for payment by bank transfer, our clients will try to accommodate your request, but it will depend on whether or not our clients' sale will complete the same day. If it does, then it may well be difficult to settle this way. We will revert to you once the position is known, but we will have to delete your condition in the missives for the time being. If it is practicable, we take it that your clients agree that the cost of the bank transfer fee would be deducted from the sum sent.

Yours faithfully

Letter from O'Neill Middleton 23.08.11

We refer to your letter of 21 August and we now enclose the following, with apologies for our earlier omission:

Property Enquiry Certificate;

Property Definition Report; and

Form 10A Report.

Yours faithfully

Appendix I

Millar & Bryce Limited
5 Logie Mill, Beaverbank Office Park, Logie Green
Road, Edinburgh, EH7 4HH
Tel: 0131 556 1313
Fax: 0131 557 5960
DX: 550301 Edinburgh 24
Registered in Scotland No. 134475

Property Definition Report

O'Neill Middleton, DX 550099 Perth

DATE	23-Aug-2011
SEARCH REF. No.	PDR98765/RC/PDR
INSTRUCTIONS REC'D	22-Aug-2011
YOUR REFERENCE	Rory Redknapp

Subjects: 29 Sardinia Terrace, Kelvinforth

Client Name: Angus George McDuff and Susannah Marjorie McDuff

Dear Sirs,

We refer to your instructions dated 22-Aug-2011

The boundaries shown on the Ordnance Survey map coincide with those claimed in the deed provided by you.

We trust this meets with your requirements.

Yours faithfully

Millar & Bryce

As with the non-statutory P16 service offered by the Keeper, Millar & Bryce's Property Definition Service is not an examination or guarantee of title, nor is it possible to give an assurance that further examination during the process of registration will not lead to exclusion of indemnity.
Millar & Bryce Limited do not accept liability for any inaccuracy in the Ordnance Survey map on which their Property Definition Service is based.
All paper extract plans supplied as part of Millar & Bryce's Property Definition Service are subject to the full provisions of Crown copyright and are not to be reproduced without prior written permission of Ordnance Survey.

Email search@millar-bryce.com   Visit www.millar-bryce.com   © 2004 Millar & Bryce

Property Enquiry Certificate

O'Neill Middleton
DX: 550099 Perth

Date: 02/08/11
Search Ref: 0364530AAA
Your Ref: RR/MCD00021.1.0
Client Name: McDuff

Millar
&
Bryce

Subjects: 29 Sardinia Terrace, Kelvinforth
Council: Perth & Kinross

Planning Information

1. Local Planning
   The subjects are covered by the following Local Plan: Perth Area Adopted March 1996
   The subjects are covered by Policy 41, 41A and 42 zoned as Residential & Compatible Uses

	Yes	No
2. Do the subjects lie within a Conservation Area/Article 4 Area?	☐	☒
3. Are the subjects categorised as a Listed Building?	☐	☒
4. Do the subjects lie within a designated Smoke Control Area?	☐	☒

Planning Applications

5. Are there any planning applications in respect of the subjects?	☐	☒

Building Warrant Applications

6. Are there any Building Warrant applications in respect of the subjects?	☐	☒

Notices & Orders

7. Does a Notice/Order under the legislation searched affect the subjects?	☐	☒

Water Information

8. Is there a public water pipe ex adverso the subjects?	☒	☐

Sewer Information

9. Is there a public sewerage pipe ex adverso the subjects?	☒	☐

Road Schemes

10. Are there any Road Scheme proposals that affect the subjects?	☐	☒

Road Information

11. The status of the carriageways/footpaths/verges ex adverso the subjects is:
    Sardinia Terrace – Carriageway/Footway - Adopted

Legislation Searched

Acquisition of Land (Authorisation Procedure)(Scotland) Act 1947, Building (Scotland) Acts 1959/1970 [as amended by Building (Scotland) Act 2003], City of Edinburgh District Council Order Confirmation Act 1991 (where applicable), Civic Government (Scotland) Act 1982, Clean Air Act 1956/68 [as amended by Clean Air Act 1993], Environmental Protection Act Part IIA [Contaminated Land (Scotland) Regulations 2000 (SI 2000 No 178)], Housing (Scotland) Act 1987, Housing (Scotland) Act 2006, Planning (Listed Buildings and Conservation Areas) (Scotland) Act 1997, Roads (Scotland) Act 1984, Sewerage (Scotland) Act 1968, Town & Country Planning (Control of Advertisements) (Scotland) Amendment Regulations 1992, Town and Country Planning (General Development) (Scotland) Order 1992 [Amendment No.2 Order (SI 2001 No.266)}, Town & Country Planning (Scotland) Act 1997, Water (Scotland) Act

Certificate Notes

1. Information contained in this Property Enquiry Cerificate is based on searches of publicly available Private Rented Housing Panel (PRHP), Local Authority and Water Authority records, in accordance with the Local Government (Access to Information) Act 1985
2. Only Notices/Orders served on the subjects within the information period of search, identified in note 1, are disclosed.
3. Only Road Schemes that lie within 250m or less from the subjects are disclosed.
4. Only planning applications on the subjects validated within the past 5 years will disclosed.
5. Only building warrant applications validated in the past 5 years will be disclosed
6. Contaminated Land – Unless detials are confirmed in section 7 above, the answer to each question in para 5.2.6 of CML Handbook for Scotland 2nd edition is in the negative.
7. This Property Enquiry Certificate is covered by the Millar & Bryce Comprehensive Warranty, detials supplied on request.

Appendix I

0369304AAA
Millar & Bryce Limited
5 Logie Mill, Beaverbank Office Park, Logie Green Road, Edinburgh, EH7 4HH
DX: 550301 Edinburgh 24 – Legal Post No LP125 Edinburgh 2
Tel: 0131 556 1313 – Fax: 0131 557 5960
Registered in Scotland No. 134475

PRE-REGISTRATION REPORT
(FORM 10A)

O'Neill Middleton
DX: 550099 Perth

Date	23-Aug-2011
Search Ref. No.	0369304AAAx/AP
Instructions Rec'd	22-Aug-2011
Your Reference	PA
S/S No.	11111
County	Perth

SUBJECTS: 29 Sardinia Terrace, Kelvinforth

NOTE: There have been no alienations from the description

From the examination of the official Search Sheet, it would appear that the Keeper has not compiled a research area for the subjects in this report.

REGISTER OF SASINES (by the Search Sheets thereof)   As at: **23 Aug 2011**

Deed	Recording Date
1. Prescriptive progress of titles Disposition by Robert McRobert – In Favour of Angus George McDuff and Susannah Marjorie McDuff	GRS Perth 12 Aug. 1975 (4477.22)
2. Undischarged securities within the past 40 years Standard Security by Angus George McDuff and Susannah Marjorie McDuff - To Black County Bank PLC	GRS Perth 12 Aug. 1975 (4477.29)
3. Discharges (of securities) recorded within the past 5 years NIL	
4. Miscellaneous deeds recorded within the past 40 years NIL	

LAND REGISTER
The subjects have not been registered   As at: **23 Aug 2011**

SEARCHED FOR INHIBITIONS, ADJUDICATIONS AND INSOLVENCIES BY MILLAR & BRYCE'S COMPUTERISED PERSONALS SYSTEM

Searched against: Angus George McDuff; Susannah Marjorie McDuff – NO DEED

Searches of the Register of Insolvencies will not disclose;
Bankruptcy petitions, which are dismissed or which have not yet been awarded,
Bankruptcies, which have been recalled or discharged by the Trustee, more than 2 years back from the date of the Register and Protected Trust Deeds discharged by the Trustee more than 1 year back from the date of the Register

At the present time searches in the Register of Insolvencies do not include searches against Limited Companies. These can be obtained from our Company Search Department (cosearch@millar-bryce.com)

Further letter to clients 24.08.11:

Dear Mr and Mrs James

Purchase of 29 Sardinia Terrace, Kelvinforth

We have now seen a Property Enquiry Certificate relating to a search in the various statutory registers held at the Council. We would report the position as follows:

Alterations or extensions

The Sellers have already supplied us with a Building Warrant (reference 98/1734 dated 22 May 1998), accompanying stamped building warrant plans and a certificate of completion (dated 28 July 1998).

On inspection of the plans, this warrant and completion certificate relate to works undertaken on the ground floor. There is no warrant in respect of the (admittedly minor) works undertaken on the first floor. We are concerned that these works may not have been approved by the Council and may need retrospective permission. We have accordingly written to the surveyors to ascertain whether this is likely to be a problem. We will keep you advised of progress on this issue

There is nothing in the Property Enquiry Certificate to indicate that there are any other alterations or extensions in respect of which a building warrant has been issued but no certificate of completion has been issued.

Roads and Pavements

The roads and pavements are taken over and maintained by the local authority. There are no road proposals.

Water and sewerage

There is mains water and mains drainage outside the property and we presume that the property is connected to these.

Tree Preservation Orders

There are no tree preservation orders affecting the property. A tree preservation order prohibits the cutting down, topping, lopping, wilful destruction etc of trees situated on the property.

Listed building or conservation area

The property is not a listed building and is not in a conservation area. Where a property is a listed building or is in a conservation area, there may be restrictions on the way in which the property can be developed and it may be more difficult to obtain permission for any proposed building works, alterations, extensions or changes of use in respect of the property.

Contaminated Land

The property is not on the local authority's Register of Contaminated Land.

Yours faithfully

Letter from Archibald + Grant, Chartered Surveyors to BJW, 23.08.11

Dear Sirs

Mr Stuart and Mrs Parveen James

29 Sardinia Terrace, Kelvinforth

We refer to your letter of 18 August 2011, providing plans and documentation relating to alterations undertaken at the above subjects.

We confirm, within the limitations of our inspection, that the existing internal accommodation/layout appears broadly as shown in the warrant plan dated 22 May 1998. We would however point out that the layout of the appliances within the first floor of the bathroom is not as currently shown in the warrant plan. The position of the WC having been altered and an additional shower tray/unit installed. It is unclear whether or not any structural alterations have been carried out to accommodate the shower tray and this should be clarified with the vendors prior to conclusion of missives. If no structural alterations have been carried out, we are of the opinion that the incorporation of an additional shower tray/unit may not have required the obtaining of a building warrant.

We trust the above information is of assistance and return the plans and documents provided along with this letter.

Yours faithfully

Further Qualified Acceptance from BJW 24.08.11

Dear Sirs

Mr Stuart James and Mrs Parveen James

Mr Angus McDuff and Mrs Susannah McDuff

29 Sardinia Terrace, Kelvinforth

On behalf of and as instructed by our clients, Stuart Alfredo James and Parveen James, residing together at Hope Cottage, Kinlochalmond, Perthshire PH36 7GH, we hereby accept the qualifications contained in your formal letter on behalf of your clients, Angus Michael McDuff and Susannah Marjorie McDuff dated 17 August 2011, being a qualified acceptance of our formal offer on behalf of our said clients dated 14 August 2011 to purchase the subjects known as and forming 29 Sardinia Terrace, Kelvinforth, but subject to the following further qualifications, namely:

1. With reference to your qualification 2, the sellers will remain responsible for making good any damage to the decor caused by the removal of the wooden corner shelf.

2. With reference to your qualification 6, in addition to the documents which you have exhibited to date, we will require a clear Property Inspection Report as regards the alterations to the layout of the bathroom at the first floor level to incorporate an additional shower unit, including the position of the WC having been altered.

3. Your qualification 7 is delete. While the purchasers will endeavour to make payment by bank transfer, their ability to do so will depend on the situation with their sale. No guarantee is therefore given in this respect and the price will only be paid by bank transfer if this is suitable to our clients at the time, and on the understanding that your clients would pay any bank charge for the transfer and that they would agree to release the keys to our clients upon confirmation that the bank have been instructed to make any transfer in due course. If a bank transfer is not possible, payment will be made by way of a cheque from the Brown, Jarvie and Walker Solicitors Client Account.

Yours faithfully

Letter from O'Neill Middleton 24.08.11

Dear Sirs

Mr Angus McDuff and Mrs Susannah McDuff

Mr Stuart James and Mrs Parveen James

29 Sardinia Terrace, Kelvinforth

We thank you for your letters dated 21 and 24 August 2011. We are taking our clients' instructions regarding your further missive letter and will revert to you as soon as possible. As regards the observations contained in your letter of 21 August, we can advise as follows:

1&2 These will be forwarded to you once received.

3 Noted along with the qualification in your further Missive Letter.

4 Our clients have confirmed that the gas central heating has been regularly serviced. Our clients have also advised that there have been no problems with the appliances other than a new filter on the dishwasher.

5 Our clients have advised that there was minor work done to the top of the chimney but there is no paperwork in this connection.

6 Our clients have advised that the chimney has been swept on a regular basis.

7 We shall revert to you regarding this matter.

Yours faithfully

Letter to clients 24.08.11:

Dear Stuart and Parveen

Purchase of 29 Sardinia Terrace, Kelvinforth

I now enclose a copy of a further letter I have sent to the sellers' solicitors amending the terms of the previous missive letter. I hope to hear back from them shortly and I will contact you again as soon as I do. The missive letters form the basis of the contract but the contract is not complete until there is agreement on every point.

I also enclose Archibald + Grant's letter for your attention. The surveyor does not seem particularly concerned about this matter, but I prefer to err on the side of caution. The matter may well be raised again, should you sell the property in due course, so it is better to have the matter settled now. We will see whether the sellers agree to obtain a Property Inspection Report from the Council (at a cost of £125). If they could even provide evidence that this alteration would not require a building warrant then this would suffice.

If you have any queries, please do not hesitate to contact me.

H R PINK

Partner

Email from clients

From: Stuart and Parveen James <jamesfamily26@tiscali.co.uk>
Sent: 27 August 2011 08:32
To: Henry Pink <hpink@bjw.co.uk>

Subject: Re 29 Sardinia Terrace, Kelvinforth

Henry

Thanks for your letter. We agree with the stance you are taking on the alterations. We don't want to have any snags when we come to sell.

Stuart & Parveen

Letter from O'Neill Middleton 30.08.11

Dear Sirs

Mr Angus McDuff and Mrs Susannah McDuff

Mr Stuart James and Mrs Parveen James

29 Sardinia Terrace, Kelvinforth

We refer to your letter dated 24 August and now enclose our further Missive Letter. Our clients' architect considers that a Property Inspection Report is unnecessary as works to the bathroom were done at the one time and inspected and passed by Building Control with the Completion Certificate being issued. Our clients' architect is of the view that Building Control would have considered the minor repositioning of the WC and the addition of a shower to have been minor discrepancies which were not worthy of an amendment of warrant. We enclose a copy letter from ECHO architects dated 29 August 2011 which confirms this. In these circumstances we trust that your clients can accept the position and we look forward to hearing from you in conclusion of the contract.

Yours faithfully

Further Qualified Acceptance from O'Neill Middleton 30.08.11

Dear Sirs

Mr Angus McDuff and Mrs Susannah McDuff

Mr Stuart James and Mrs Parveen James

29 Sardinia Terrace, Kelvinforth

On behalf of and as instructed by our clients, Angus and Susannah McDuff, we hereby accept the terms of your formal qualified acceptance dated 24 August 2011 on behalf of and as instructed by your clients, Stuart and Parveen James in response to our qualified acceptance dated 17 August 2011 on behalf of our said clients of your said offer dated 14 August on behalf of your said clients, subject to the following qualification:

Qualification 2 of your said formal qualified acceptance dated 26 August 2011 is delete.

Yours faithfully

Letter from ECHO Architects to O'Neill Middleton 29.08.11

Dear Mr Redknapp

29 Sardinia Terrace

I understand the buyer's lawyers have queried the addition of a shower and bathroom and the minor repositioning of the WC in the main bathroom.

The works to install the shower and to move the WC were done at the same time as the other alterations covered by the building warrant. The building inspector would therefore have been aware of the minor discrepancies from the warrant drawings when he made his final inspection. I presume that he felt the changes were so minor that an amendment to warrant was therefore not required, and so he issued the completion certificate.

Yours sincerely

Letter to O'Neill Middleton 30.08.11

Dear Sirs

Mr Stuart James and Mrs Parveen James

Mr Angus McDuff and Mrs Susannah McDuff

29 Sardinia Terrace, Kelvinforth

We refer to your letter of 30 August 2011. We are no longer in possession of the Building Warrant Plans as these were returned to you on 24 August 2011.

We would have thought, however, that the Inspector would not have inspected first floor accommodation when the alterations were actually on the ground floor and the Warrant Plans would not even have shown the bathroom. We feel that your clients' Architect's letter is entirely unsatisfactory and even potentially misleading.

Unless you can provide us with a letter from the architect warranting that the alterations would not have required a building warrant along with a copy of his indemnity cover we feel it only appropriate to ask for a Property Inspection Report. Initial enquiries could perhaps be made with the Council to ascertain whether a Building Warrant would have been required for an additional shower being created, but given that this would have involved additional plumbing etc we would have thought that a Building Warrant would have been required.

We feel that our clients are paying more than a fair price for the property and do not think that they should be left in a difficult position when they come to sell due to the lack of alteration documentation relating to the period prior to their purchase.

We look forward to hearing from you.

Yours faithfully

Letter from O'Neill Middleton 01.09.11

Dear Sirs

Mr Angus McDuff and Mrs Susannah McDuff

Mr Stuart James and Mrs Parveen James

29 Sardinia Terrace, Kelvinforth

We refer to your faxed letter of 30 August 2001. We note your comments. Our clients' architect believes that he building control officer did look at the alterations to the first floor bathroom at the time of alterations being done on the ground floor but unfortunately has nothing on file to confirm this. We are therefore writing to the Building Control Department to ask whether a building warrant should have been obtained.

We enclose a further Formal Letter which we trust will allow you to conclude the bargain. We have provided that if Building Control advise that a building warrant is not required then no further documentation will require to be provided by our clients. However, if Building Control are of the view that a building warrant should have been obtained then our clients will obtain a clear Property Inspection Report prior to settlement.

We look forward to hearing from you.

Yours faithfully

Further Qualified Acceptance from O'Neill Middleton 01.09.11

Dear Sirs

Mr Angus McDuff and Mrs Susannah McDuff

Mr Stuart James and Mrs Parveen James

29 Sardinia Terrace, Kelvinforth

On behalf of and as instructed by our clients, Angus and Susannah McDuff, we hereby offer to amend our qualified acceptance dated 30 August 2011 on behalf of our said clients in response to your formal qualified acceptance dated 24 August 2011 on behalf of and as instructed by your clients, Stuart and Parveen James in response to our qualified acceptance dated 17 August 2011 on behalf of our said clients of your said offer dated 14 August on behalf of your said clients to the following extent:

In respect that we have written to the Building Control Department of Perth and Kinross Council to ascertain whether a building warrant should have been obtained for our clients' alterations to the first floor bathroom which included the relocation of the WC and the installation of shower unit (**'Alterations'**):

If the said Building Control Department advises that no building warrant is required in respect of the Alterations then your clients will be deemed to be satisfied regarding the alteration documentation already exhibited to you.

If, however, the said Building Control Department advises that a building warrant should have been obtained in respect of the Alterations then our said clients will exhibit a clear Property Inspection Report in respect of the Alterations prior to the date of entry.

Yours faithfully

Email to clients

From: Henry Pink <hpink@bjw.co.uk>
Sent: 1 September 2011 10:06
To: Stuart and Parveen James <jamesfamily26@tiscali.co.uk>
CC: Veronica Vanbrugh <vvanbrugh@bjw.co.uk>

Subject: 29 Sardinia Terrace, Kelvinforth

Attachments: jame232QA.pdf; jame232covlet.pdf

Please find attached a copy of a fax letter and further Qualified
Acceptance just in from O'Neill Middleton. I think that what they are
suggesting seems fair and I suggest that we conclude missives on that
basis. Please email or call to confirm that you are happy to do so. HP

Stuart and Parveen James reply.

From: Stuart and Parveen James <jamesfamily26@tiscali.co.uk>
Sent: 1 September 2011 11:57
To: Henry Pink <hpink@bjw.co.uk>

Subject: Re: 29 Sardinia Terrace, Kelvinforth

Hi Henry

That seems fair. Please proceed as you suggest.

Stuart and Parveen.

Letter concluding Missives 21.08.2011

Dear Sirs

Mr Stuart James and Mrs Parveen James

Mr Angus McDuff and Mrs Susannah McDuff

29 Sardinia Terrace, Kelvinforth

On behalf of and as instructed by our clients, Stuart Alfredo James and Parveen James, residing together at Hope Cottage, Kinlochalmond, Perthshire PH36 7GH, we hereby accept the qualifications contained in your formal letter on behalf of your clients, Angus Michael McDuff and Susannah Marjorie McDuff dated 30 August 2011 as amended by your formal letter on behalf of your said clients dated 1 September 2011 in response to our formal letter on behalf of our said clients dated 24 August 2011 in response to your qualified acceptance on behalf of your said clients dated 17 August 2011 in response to our formal offer on behalf of our said clients dated 14 August 2011 to purchase the subjects known as and forming 29 Sardinia Terrace, Kelvinforth and now hold the bargain to be concluded.

Your faithfully

Letter to clients 21.08.11:

Dear Stuart and Parveen

Purchase of 29 Sardinia Terrace, Kelvinforth

I refer to the above and enclose herewith copy formal letter in conclusion of the bargain for your information. Accordingly, you are now legally bound to purchase the property and pay over the purchase price on the date of entry (subject to the seller providing any outstanding documentation that remains to be exhibited) with the sellers bound to vacate the property at that time.

Kind regards

Yours sincerely

H R PINK

Partner

Letter to clients 11.09.11:

Dear Stuart and Parveen

Purchase of 29 Sardinia Terrace, Kelvinforth

I now enclose the Stamp Duty Land Tax return which you require to sign. This form is in effect a tax return, so it's important that it is accurate, as HM Revenue & Customs have powers to ensure that purchasers provide accurate information.

To assist you I have completed the return as far as possible. However you are responsible for checking over the parts we have completed to verify their accuracy.

You can access the HMRC guidance notes on the internet at http://www. hmrc.gov.uk/sdlt6/index.htm. If you have any difficulty, let me know and I will post or email a copy.

Yours sincerely

H R PINK

Partner

HM Revenue & Customs

Land Transaction Return

FOR CLIENT APPROVAL

For official use only

Your transaction return

How to fill in this return

The land transaction return guidance notes, SDLT6, available form the Orderline **0845 302 1472** will help in completion of this return.

- A unique reference number must be entered on the return, this is the number shown on the payslip in the 'Reference' box. Payslips, PS1/SDLT, are available from the Orderline.
- Show amounts in whole pounds only, rounded down to the nearest pound.

- Leave blank any boxes that do not apply.
- The completed return should be printed off and then signed.
- Staple the sheets in the top left-hand corner.
- Do not fold the return.

If you need help with any part of this return or with anything in the guidance notes, please phone the Stamp Taxes enquiry line on **0845 603 0135**, open 8:30am to 5:00pm Monday to Friday, except Bank Holidays. Calls are charged at local rates.

Starting your return

ABOUT THE TRANSACTION

1 Type of property

`01` Enter code from the guidance notes

2 Description of transaction

`F` Enter code from the guidance notes

3 Interest transferred or created

`FP` Enter code from the guidance notes

4 Effective date of transaction

5 Any restrictions, covenants or conditions affecting the value of the interest transferred or granted? Put 'X' in one box

☐ Yes   ☒ No

If 'yes' please provide details

6 Date of contract or conclusion of missives

| 4 | 6 | 2011 |

7 Is any land exchanged or part-exchanged?
Put 'X' in one box

☐ Yes   ☒ No

If 'yes' please complete address of location
Postcode

House or building number

Rest of address, including house name, building name or flat number

8 Is the transaction pursuant to a previous option agreement? Put 'X' in one box

☐ Yes   ☒ No

SDLT 1 (E)   Page 1

UTRN

657

FOR CLIENT APPROVAL

ABOUT THE TAX CALCULATION

9 Are you claiming relief? Put 'X' in one box

Yes ☐   **X** No

If 'yes' please show the reason

Enter code from the guidance notes

Enter the charity's registered number, if available, or the company's CIS number

For relief claimed on part of the property only, please enter the amount remaining chargeable

£ [   ] . 0 0

10 What is the total consideration in money or money's worth, including any VAT actually payable for the transaction notified?

£ [450,000] . 0 0

11 If the total consideration for the transaction includes VAT, please state the amount

£ [   ] . 0 0

12 What form does the consideration take?
Enter the relevant codes from the guidance notes

[30] [ ] [ ] [ ]

13 Is this transaction linked to any other(s)?
Put 'X' in one box

Yes ☐   **X** No

Total consideration or value in money or money's worth, including VAT paid for all of the linked transactions

£ [   ] . 0 0

14 Total amount of tax due for this transaction

£ [13,500] . 0 0

15 Total amount paid or enclosed with this notification

£ [13,500] . 0 0

Does the amount paid include payment of any penalties and any interest due? Put 'X' in one box

Yes ☐   **X** No

ABOUT NEW LEASES If this doesn't apply, go straight to box 26 on page 3.

16 Type of lease

Enter code from the guidance notes

17 Start date as specified in lease

18 End date as specified in lease

19 Rent-free period
Number of months

20 Annual starting rent inclusive of VAT (actually) payable

£ [   ] . 0 0

End date for starting rent

Later rent known? Put 'X' in one box

Yes ☐   No ☐

21 What is the amount of VAT, if any?

£ [   ] . 0 0

22 Total premium payable

£ [   ] . 0 0

23 Net present value upon which tax is calculated

£ [   ] . 0 0

24 Total amount of tax due – premium

£ [   ] . 0 0

25 Total amount of tax due – NPV

£ [   ] . 0 0

Check the guidance notes to see if you will need to complete supplementary return 'Additional details about the transaction, including leases', SDLT4.

SDLT 1 (E)   Page 2

UTRN [   ]

658

FOR CLIENT APPROVAL

ABOUT THE LAND including buildings

Where more than one piece of land is being sold or you cannot complete the address field in the space provided, please complete the supplementary return 'Additional details about the land', SDLT3.

26 Number of properties included

1

27 Where more than one property is involved, do you want a certificate for each property? Put 'X' in one box

☐ Yes ☐ No

28 Address or situation of land
Postcode

House or building number

29

Rest of address, including house name, building name or flat number

Sardinia Terrace

Kelvinforth

Is the rest of the address on the supplementary return 'Additional details about the land', SDLT3? Put 'X' in one box

☐ Yes ☒ No

29 Local authority number

9074

30 Title number, if any

31 NLPG UPRN

32 If agricultural or development land, what is the area (if known)? Put 'X' in one box

☐ Hectares ☐ Square metres
Area

33 Is a plan attached? Please note that the form reference number should be written/displayed on map. Put 'X' in one box

☐ Yes ☒ No

ABOUT THE VENDOR including transferor, lessor

34 Number of vendors included (Note: if more than one vendor, complete boxes 45 to 48)

2

35 Title Enter MR, MRS, MISS, MS or other title
Note: only complete for an individual

Mr

36 Vendor (1) surname or company name

McDuff

37 Vendor (1) first name(s) Note: only complete for an individual

Angus
George

38 Vendor (1) address
Postcode

House or building number

29

Rest of address, including house name, building name or flat number

Sardinia Terrace

Kelvinforth

SDLT 1 (E) — Page 3

UTRN

659

FOR CLIENT APPROVAL

ABOUT THE VENDOR CONTINUED

39 Agent's name

O'Neill Middleton

41 Agent's DX number

40 Agent's address
Postcode

PH12   5TJ

Building number

65

Rest of address, including building name

Registration Row

Perth

42 Agent's e-mail address

43 Agent's reference

MCD23.5

44 Agent's telephone number

01222 432109

ADDITIONAL VENDOR

Details of other people involved (including transferor, lessor), other than vendor (1). If more than one additional vendor please complete supplementary return 'Land Transaction Return – Additional vendor/purchaser details', SDLT2.

45 **Title** Enter MR, MRS, MISS, MS or other title
Note: only complete for an individual

Mrs

46 **Vendor (2) surname or company name**

McDuff

47 **Vendor (2) first name(s)**
Note: only complete for an individual

Susannah

Marjorie

48 Vendor (2) address

Put 'X' in this box if the same as box 38.

If not, please give address below
Postcode

House or building number

29

Rest of address, including house name, building name or flat number

Sardinia Terrace

Kelvinforth

UTRN

FOR CLIENT APPROVAL

ABOUT THE PURCHASER including transferee, lessee

49 | **Number of purchasers included** (Note: if more than one purchaser is involved, complete boxes 65 to 69)

`2`

50 | **National Insurance number (purchaser 1), if you have one.** Note: only complete for an individual

`YX    34    44    55    D`

51 | **Title** Enter MR, MRS, MISS, MS or other title
Note: only complete for an individual

`Mr`

52 | **Purchaser (1) surname or company name**

`James`

53 | **Purchaser (1) first name(s)**
Note: only complete for an individual

`Stuart`

54 | **Purchaser (1) address**

☐ Put 'X' in this box if the same address as box 28.
If not, please give address below
Postcode

House or building number

Rest of address, including house name, building name or flat number

`Hope Cottage`
`Kinlochalmond`

55 | **Is the purchaser acting as a trustee?** Put 'X' in one box

☐ Yes   ☒ No

56 | **Please give a daytime telephone number** – this will help us if we need to contact you about your return

`01413334000`

57 | **Are the purchaser and vendor connected?**
Put 'X' in one box

☐ Yes   ☒ No

58 | **To which address shall we send the certificate?**
Put 'X' in one box

☒ Property (box 28)   ☐ Purchaser's (box 54)

☐ Agent's (box 61)

59 | **I authorise my agent to handle correspondence on my behalf.** Put 'X' in one box

☒ Yes   ☐ No

60 | **Agent's name**

`Brown Jarvie & Walker`

61 | **Agent's address**
Postcode

`PH36        3RT`

Building number

`42`

Rest of address, including building name

`Registration Row`
`Kelvinforth`

62 | **Agent's DX number**

63 | **Agent's reference**

64 | **Agent's telephone number**

`01356 422223`

SDLT 1 (E)   Page 5

UTRN

661

FOR CLIENT APPROVAL

ADDITIONAL PURCHASER

Details of other people involved (including transferee, lessee), other than purchaser (1). If more than one additional purchaser, please complete supplementary return 'Land Transaction Return – Additional vendor/purchaser details', SDLT2.

65 **Title** Enter MR, MRS, MISS, MS or other title
Note: only complete for an individual

Mrs

66 **Purchaser (2) surname or company name**

James

67 **Purchaser (2) first name(s)**
Note: only complete for an individual

Parveen

68 **Purchaser (2) address**

Put 'X' in this box if the same as purchaser (1) (box 54).
If not, please give address below
Postcode

House or building number

Rest of address, including house name, building name or flat number

Hope Cottage

Kinlochalmond

69 **Is the purchaser acting as a trustee?** Put 'X' in one box

Yes   **X** No

ADDITIONAL SUPPLEMENTARY RETURNS

70 **How many supplementary returns have you enclosed with this return?** Write the number in each box. If none, please put '0'.

0   Additional vendor/purchaser details, SDLT2

0   Additional details about the land, SDLT3

0   Additional details about the transaction, including leases, SDLT4

DECLARATION

71 **The purchaser(s) must sign this return.** Read the guidance notes in booklet SDLT6, in particular the section headed 'Who should complete the Land Transaction Return?'.

If you give false information, you may face financial penalties and prosecution.
The information contained in this copy of the return is correct and complete to the best of my knowledge and belief. I authorise my agent to submit a return, containing this information, electronically on my behalf. If the information I have approved does not include the effective date, I also authorise my agent to enter the effective date in the return on my behalf.

Signature of purchaser 1   Signature of purchaser 2

Please keep a copy of this return and a note of the unique reference, which is in the 'Reference' box on the payslip.

Please don't fold this return – keep it flat. Staple the sheets in the top left-hand corner.

Fill out the payslip from which the unique reference was taken and pay in accordance with the 'How to pay' instructions.

Finally, please send your completed return to:
HMRC, Stamp Taxes/SDLT, Comben House, Farriers Way, NETHERTON, Merseyside, Great Britain, L30 4RN, or the DX address is: Rapid Data Capture Centre, DX725593, Bootle 9

SDLT 1 (E)   Page 6

UTRN

Letter from O'Neill Middleton 18.09.11

Dear Sirs

Mr Angus McDuff and Mrs Susannah McDuff

Mr Stuart James and Mrs Parveen James

29 Sardinia Terrace, Kelvinforth

We write to advise that the Building Control Officer, Ross Paisley, has confirmed that a Building Warrant should have been obtained for the alterations to the first floor bathroom. We are therefore applying for a Property Inspection Report and we enclose a copy of our application for your information.

Yours faithfully

Letter to clients 19.09.11:

Dear Stuart and Parveen

Purchase of 29 Sardinia Terrace, Kelvinforth

I enclose for your information a copy of a letter received from O'Neill Middleton. You will note that they are applying for a Property Inspection Report in connection with the alterations to the bathroom on the first floor.

Yours sincerely

H R PINK

Partner

Stuart and Parveen James reply

From: Stuart and Parveen James <jamesfamily26@tiscali.co.uk>
Sent: 20 September 2011 18:09
To: Henry Pink <hpink@bjw.co.uk>

Subject: Re: 29 Sardinia Terrace, Kelvinforth

Hi Henry

Thanks for your letter about the alterations saga. We are very pleased that you insisted on receiving the correct documentation from the seller's lawyer.

Stuart and Parveen

Letter to Clients 12.10.11

Dear Stuart and Parveen

29 Sardinia Terrace

I refer to the above. O'Neill Middleton have now sent me a copy of the Letter of Comfort obtained from the Council in respect of the alterations to the upstairs bathroom. This letter means that the Council are aware of the alterations but do not propose to take any enforcement action.

I take this opportunity to enclose a note of my fee and a Purchase Statement. You will see this shows a balance due by you of £24,380. As previously indicated, I will need to receive these funds from you at least one week before the settlement date.

Kind regards

Yours sincerely,

Fee Note:

Account No:	**JAME232**
VAT Reg No:	**474 8484 -848**
Tax Point:	**20 November 2011**
Invoice Number:	**00028844**

Stuart James and Parveen James
Hope Cottage
Kinlochalmond
Perthshire

In account with Brown, Walker & Jarvie

Purchase of 29 Sardinia Terrace, Kelvinforth

TO: Taking your instructions re the purchase of the above subjects; advising re offer and concluding a bargain on your behalf, examining title deeds; preparing disposition; preparing any necessary security deeds and obtaining funds from ledger; preparing SDLT form and remitting any SDLT due to HM Revenue & Customs where necessary; lodging deeds and registration dues with Registers of Scotland; including all meetings, telephone calls, correspondence, post and incidentals in respect thereto:

	£
Fee:	690.00
VAT @ 20%	<u>178.00</u>
TOTAL	<u>868.00</u>

Purchase statement:

Item	£	£
To Purchase price of subjects		451,000.00
Funded by:-		
By JAME232.03 – net free proceeds from sale of Hope Cottage	289,043.00	
By Southern Cross Bank plc – loan funds	152,725.00	
		441,768.00
Non VAT-able Outlays:		
To Registers of Scotland -		
disposition recording dues	720.00	
standard security recording dues	60.00	
To HM Revenue & Customs – SDLT	13,500.00	
		14,280.00
VAT-able fees and outlays:		
None		
Legal Fees:		
To fee for all work per fee note, attached	690.00	
To VAT thereon	178.00	
		868.00
Balance due from you:		24,380.00

Draft state of settlement

STATE FOR SETTLEMENT
Property: 29 Sardinia Terrace, Kelvinforth
Sellers Agents: O'Neill Middleton, Glasgow
Purchasers Agents; Brown Jarvie & Walker, Glasgow
Date of Settlement: 20 November 2011

Price agreed by Missives	£450,000
Price agreed for moveable property	£1,000
Total Price due	£451,000

Note: *Perth & Kinross Council have been requested to apportion the Council Tax and will issue separate accounts.*

Letter to clients dated 11.11.11

Dear Mr and Mrs James

This is to remind you that the settlement of your purchase is due on 20 November. It is therefore important that we have cleared funds in our account by that date. Please therefore send a cheque for the sum requested, or, better still, ask your Bank to send an electronic transfer of the funds to our Bank (details underneath). They will need to have cleared funds in their hands to be able to do this. Please therefore arrange this at the earliest opportunity.

The sum requested by us is as agreed in earlier letters.

Yours faithfully

Bank Details: Caledonian Commerce Bank, Perth Head Office.
Clearing Number: 08-15-06. Account Number: 00248833

Sum requested;	
Price of house	£450,000.00
Price of Moveable items	£1,000.00
Stamp Duty Land Tax @ 1%	£13,500.00
Our fee as agreed	£690.00
VAT thereon @ 17.5%	£178.00
Land Registration Fee	£780.00
	£466,148.00
Less	£441,768.00
TOTAL	£24,680.00

Note: *Remember the importance of having cleared funds in the bank. Cheques to you should be banked at least seven days before settlement, to ensure that they are met before you start signing cheques. Alternatively you may get an electronic transfer into your account, which guarantees that the funds are cleared. Please remember that an electronic transfer is not made instantly, and allow, say, a day for it to happen. Why electronic transfers cannot be made more quickly remains a mystery to all but the banks.*

Report on title to the Bank

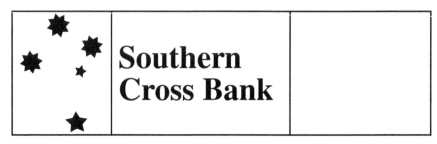

Certificate of Title (Scotland) CERTIFICATE OF TITLE

for Residential Mortgages Combined

with Further Advances MORTGAGE ACCOUNT NUMBER 8484-48484826	PROPOSED SETTLEMENT **DATE** **20 November 2011**
DATE OF CONCLUSION **OF MISSIVES** **21 August 2011**	**GROSS LOAN £152,725.00**
TO: **Southern Cross Bank PLC** Mortgage Centre 15 Brisbane Way Edgbaston Birmingham **BX4 7HG** **(DX577744 Birmingham 3)** ('the Bank' which expression shall include its successors in title and assignees and those deriving title through or under it and whether by way of an absolute transfer or other disposal or by way of security only and whether in relation to the whole or to part, and where the context so admits, its appointed agent or the appointed agent of any persons so deriving title or any trustee for such Bank or other persons)	**FROM:** **Brown, Walker & Jarvie......................** (Name of Solicitors/Qualified Conveyancers) **42 Piemonte Place................................** (Address) **Kelvinforth PH36 2RT.........................** **...** **TEL: .01738 658333....** **FAX:.01738 555666....** **REFERENCE..HRP/WRC/JAME232**

FULL NAME(S) OF BORROWER (PLEASE NOTE THAT TITLE TO THE PROPERTY MUST BE TAKEN IN THE NAME(S) OF THE BORROWER - WHERE THIS TERM INCLUDES ONE OR MORE BORROWERS, TITLE MUST BE TAKEN IN ALL NAMES). **Stuart Alfredo James and Parveen James, spouses, Hope Cottage, Kinlochalmond PH36 7GH**	

PROPERTY ADDRESS 29 Sardinia Terrace, Kelvinforth, Perthshire PH36 5KF ('the Property')	

PURCHASE PRICE £450,000.00 (as shown in the Disposition)	**IF A REMORTGAGE SHOW DATE OF PURCHASE**
IS TITLE SASINE (S) FIRST REGISTRATION TRANSFER OF WHOLE (FRW) **X** FIRST REGISTRATION TRANSFER OF PART (FRP) SUBSEQUENT REGISTRATION (SR)	**IF REGISTERED PLEASE STATE TITLE NUMBER** REGISTERED ON ARTL YES/NO NO
BUILDING INSURANCE	
Name of Insured: Stuart Alfredo James and Parveen James	**Sum Insured: £350,000.00**
Insurance Company: 2BIG2 Banking PLC	**Renewal Date: 21 August 2012**
Policy Number: ZG834856363	**Commencement Date: 20 August 2011**
INDEMNITY INSURANCE DETAILS	
Policy Number: HSJ-0084654	**Commencement Date: 1 November 2010**
Renewal Date: 31 October 2011	**Sum Insured: £10,000,000.00**
Name of Insured: Brown, Walker & Jarvie LLP	**Insurance Company: Lloyds & Company per Marsh**
THIS FORM MUST BE SENT TO US AT LEAST 7 WORKING DAYS PRIOR TO SETTLEMENT TO ENABLE US TO RELEASE THE FUNDS TO YOU THE DAY PRIOR TO SETTLEMENT. IMPORTANT NOTES! Have you dealt with the Buildings Insurance details? Remember the policy must be index-linked. Have you provided your Bank Account details on page 2?	

See Paragraph 4.2 of the Lenders' Handbook for Scotland issued by the Council of Mortgage Lenders and the letter of instruction for time-scales for re-inspection of the Property and submission of the Certificate of Title.

Please note that definitions used in the Standard Mortgage Conditions shall also apply to this Certificate of Title.

WE HEREBY CONFIRM TO THE BANK THAT:-

a) We have investigated title to the Property in accordance with the Bank's Instructions set out in parts 1 and 2 of the Lenders' Handbook issued by the Council of Mortgage Lenders' ('the Instructions') and any other requirements of the Bank and the Borrower has acquired or will acquire on Settlement a good and marketable title which is free of defect other than as is detailed on the reverse hereof but which will constitute good security to the Bank and may safely be accepted by the Bank for mortgage purposes.

b) All conditions of the Offer of Loan to the Borrower, other than those Conditions detailed in the Offer of Loan which do not require to be completed until after Settlement, have been or will be complied with before Settlement.

c) The Standard Security and all other documents relative to the Loan have been executed and will be in our possession before Settlement.

d) If the purpose of the Loan is to assist in the purchase of the Property the price is as stated in the Offer of Loan, the purchase monies including any deposit will pass through our Firm's Clients' Account and will be paid in full to the seller's solicitors.

All of the information in this Certificate of Title is correct and the Bank may rely on the accuracy of each and every statement.

* (i) We have explained to the Borrower (including any joint Borrower separately and independently where their interests might conflict) that the security covers all obligations of the Borrower(s) of whatever kind and whether incurred solely or jointly with any person, corporation, firm or other body and whether as principal or surety. We have also explained that it covers all such obligations which may arise in the future. Having received this advice we believe the Borrower(s) understand the nature and scope of the security they have granted.

* (ii) We have advised the solicitors acting on behalf of the Borrower(s) (including any solicitors acting for any joint Borrower being separately advised) of the fact that the Bank is providing or may in the future provide further facilities to the Borrower(s) and they have confirmed to us in writing that they have explained to the Borrower(s) (separately where appropriate) that the security covers all obligations of the Borrower(s) of any kind whatsoever and whether incurred solely or jointly with any person, corporation, firm or other body and whether as principal or surety.

* Delete as appropriate

WE HEREBY UNDERTAKE TO THE BANK:-

To hold the funds comprising the Loan strictly to the order of the Bank and to apply them only when the Borrower has provided us with sufficient cleared funds in order to complete the transaction and only then in order to secure a first ranking standard security over the Property in favour of the Bank.

If Settlement does not take place on the proposed date (as shown overleaf), except with the prior agreement of the Bank, to return the funds in full by close of business on the next working day to the Bank by CHAPS transfer (quoting the Sorting Code Number and Account Number detailed in the Bank's Part 2 instructions) and to advise the Bank's Mortgage Centre beforehand.

GUIDANCE NOTES:

1. Please retain a copy of the Certificate of Title for your file.

2. Please ensure that it is completed in full and signed by a Partner or authorised signatory on behalf of the firm.

3. By signing this document you are committing your firm to an undertaking.

4. If you have any difficulties regarding the contents of this Certificate of Title you must contact the Bank's Mortgage Centre **BEFORE** Settlement.

Letter from Brown Jarvie & Walker to O'Neill Middleton dated 12.11.11

Dear Sirs

We enclose the draft Disposition together with the engrossment for signature. We also enclose the draft form 11 and State for Settlement, both duly approved.

Yours faithfully

Letter from Mr and Mrs James dated 12.11.11

Dear Mr Pink

Thank you for your letter telling us how much we owe you. We enclose our cheque for £24,380 as the balance of the money. We would like to thank Messrs Brown Jarvie & Walker for their kind work on our behalf.

Yours sincerely

EMAIL

To: Veronica Vanbrugh <vvanbrugh@bjw.co.uk.;
Wendy Robertson<wrobertson@bjw.co.uk>
Sent: 13 November 2011 13:04
From: Henry Pink <hpink@bjw.co.uk>

Subject: JAME232 – 29 Sardinia Terrace

Please see accompanying letter from Mr and Mrs James. Well done! I have incidentally passed the cheque to the cashroom and asked them to bank it today! They will let you know when it has cleared. HP.

EMAIL

To: Wendy Robertson<wrobertson@bjw.co.uk>
Sent: 17 November 2011 10:53
From: Nisha Banerji <nbanergi@bjw.co.uk>

Subject: Mr & Mrs James JAME232

Please note that cheque from Mr and Mrs James cleared today. You may now write cheques on the client account.

Note: *The money is now safely in the client account, and accordingly cheques may be written for the price, the SDLT, the registration fees, and the firm's fee against a properly vouched fee note.*

Letter from O'Neill Middleton in settlement 19 November 2011

Dear Sirs

Angus McDuff and Susannah McDuff

Stuart James and Parveen James

29 Sardinia Terrace, Kelvinforth

We refer to the above and we enclose the following settlement items, to be held strictly as undelivered, pending our confirmation that the purchase price has been paid in full:

Disposition duly executed, together with the draft;

Title deeds;

Letter of Comfort from Perth & Kinross Council

Clear Form 11A Report;

Principal Property Enquiry Certificate;

Principal Property Definition Report;

Our Letter of Obligation with the approved draft;

Discharge of Standard Security and draft along with Form 2 and cheque

We understand that our respective clients are meeting at the property to hand over the keys etc.

We look forward to receiving the purchase price in exchange.

Yours faithfully.

0369304AAA
Millar & Bryce Limited
5 Logie Mill, Beaverbank Office Park, Logie Green Road, Edinburgh, EH7 4HH
DX: 550301 Edinburgh 24 – Legal Post No LP125 Edinburgh 2
Tel: 0131 556 1313 – Fax: 0131 557 5960
Registered in Scotland No. 134475

CONTINUATION OF A PRE-REGISTRATION REPORT
(FORM 11A)

O'Neill Middleton	Date	21-Nov-2011
DX: 550099 Perth	Search Ref. No.	0369304AAAxx/AP
	Instructions Rec'd	18-Nov-2011
	Your Reference	PA
	S/S No.	11111
	County	Perth

SUBJECTS: 29 Sardinia Terrace, Kelvinforth

NOTE: There have been no alienations from the description supplied

REGISTER OF SASINES (by the Search Sheets thereof)   As at: 21 Nov 2011

Deed	Recording Date
1. Deeds relating to Subjects of Search	
Nil	
2. Miscellaneous deeds	
Nil	
3. Discharges (of securities)	
Nil	

Searched the Register of Sasines from **12 June 2011** to **13 June 2011** and found as above.

LAND REGISTER
The subjects have not been registered   As at: **21 Nov 2011**

SEARCHED FOR INHIBITIONS, ADJUDICATIONS AND INSOLVENCIES BY MILLAR & BRYCE'S COMPUTERISED PERSONALS SYSTEM

Searched against:
Angus George McDuff
Susannah Marjorie McDuff
Stuart George James
Parveen James
NO DEED

Searches of the Register of Insolvencies will not disclose;
Bankruptcy petitions, which are dismissed or which have not yet been awarded,
Bankruptcies, which have been recalled or discharged by the Trustee, more than 2 years back from the date of the Register and
Protected Trust Deeds discharged by the Trustee more than 1 year back from the date of the Register

At the present time searches in the Register of Insolvencies do not include searches against Limited Companies. These can be obtained from
our Company Search Department (cosearch@millar-bryce.com)

Email search@millar-bryce.com   Visit www.millar-bryce.com   © 2001 Millar & Bryce

Letter from Brown, Walker and Jarvie in settlement 19 November 2011

Dear Sirs

Stuart James and Parveen James

Angus McDuff and Susannah McDuff

29 Sardinia Terrace, Kelvinforth

We refer to your faxed letter of today's date. We enclose our firm's cheque in the sum of £451,000, to be held as undelivered pending our confirmation that we have received all the items falling to be delivered in terms of the Missives.

Yours faithfully,

File Note by Wendy Robertson, 20 November 2011:

Att tel w. R Redknapp of ONM. Confirmed that all settlement items were in order and cheque can be encashed. Thereafter att tel clients confirming that they can collect keys from the McDuffs at the property. T/E 5 mins.

REGISTERS OF SCOTLAND

FORM **1**
APPLICATION FOR FIRST REGISTRATION
(Land Registration (Scotland) Rules 2006 Rule 9(1)(a))
Version 25/10/2007

1. From (see Note 1)
Brown, Jarvie & Walker
42 Piemonte Place
Kelvinforth
PH36 3RT

PART A - The notes referred to are contained in Notes and Directions for completion of applications for First Registration.

2. FAS No. (see Note 2)	**3. Agent's Reference**	**4. Agent's Tel No.** (see Note 3)
1058	HPR/WRC/JAME232	01738 854 6677

5. Agent's email Address
wrobertson@bjw.co.uk

6. Search Sheet Number (see Note 4)
77643

7. Name of Deed in respect of which registration is required
Disposition

8. County (see Note 5)
Perth

Mark X in box if more than one county

9. Monetary Consideration (see Note 6)
450,000

Non-monetary Consideration (see Note 7)

Value (see Note 8)

Fee (see Note 9)
720

Payment Method (see Note 10)
Direct debit

Date of Entry
20 11 2011

10. Subjects (see Note 11)

House No/Name: 29
Postcode: PH36 5KF

Street Name & Town/City: Sardinia Terrace, Kelvinforth

11. Name and Address of Applicant (see Note 12)

Mark X in box if more than two applicants

Applicant 1 Surname: James
Forename(s): Stuart James
House No/Name: Hope Cottage
Postcode: PH36 7GH
Street Name & Town/City: Kinlochalmond, Perthshire

Applicant 2 Surname: James
Forename(s): Parveen
House No/Name: Hope Cottage
Postcode: PH36 7GH
Street Name & Town/City: Kinlochalmond, Perthshire

And/or company/firm or council, etc

House No/Name:
Postcode:

Street Name & Town/City:

12. Granter/Last recorded title holder (see Note 13)

i. Surname: McDuff
Forename(s): Angus George
House No/Name: 29
Postcode: PH36 5KF
Street Name & Town/City: Sardinia Terrace, Kelvinforth

Page 1   UID Number:

REGISTERS OF SCOTLAND

FORM **1**

APPLICATION FOR FIRST REGISTRATION
(Land Registration (Scotland) Rules 2006 Rule 9(1)(a))
Version 25/10/2007

Mark an X in the appropriate box. If more space is required for any section of this form a separate sheet (s) may be added.

PART A Continued - The notes referred to are contained in Notes and Directions for completion of applications for First Registration.

II. Surname McDuff	**Forename(s)** Susannah Marjorie

House No/Name 29	**Postcode** PH36 5KF

Street Name & Town/City Sardinia Terrace, Kelvinforth

And/or company/firm or council, etc

Mark X in box if more than two granters

13. If a Form 10 Report has been issued by the Keeper in connection with this Application, please quote the Report No.

14. If a P16 Report has been issued by the Keeper in connection with this Application, please quote the Report No.

PART B

				YES	NO
1.	(a)	Do the deeds submitted in support of this application include a plan illustrating the extent of the subjects to be registered?		X	

If **YES**, please specify the deed and its Form 4 Inventory number :

1

	(b)	Have you submitted a deed containing a full bounding description with measurements?		X	

If **YES**, please specify the deed and its Form 4 Inventory number :

1

If the answer to both the above questions is NO:

• then you must submit a plan of the subjects that conforms to the Keeper's stated deed plan criteria policy;

• the plan should bear a docquet, signed by the Granter(s) and Grantee(s) of the deed accompanying the application, to the effect that it is a plan of the subjects to be registered.

NB: a plan will not normally be required where the property is part of a tenement or other flatted property, unless additional exclusive subjects are to be registered along with the flat.

		YES	NO	N/A
2.	Does the legal extent depicted in the plans or descriptions in the deeds submitted in support of the application coincide with the occupational extent?	X		

If **NO**, the Keeper will require further information to assist in the creation of the title sheet, therefore please advise:

	(a)	if the extent of the subjects as defined in the deeds is larger than the occupational extent, is the applicant prepared to accept the occupational extent?			
	(b)	if the extent of the subjects as defined in the deeds is smaller than the occupational extent, has any remedial action been taken?			

If **YES** to question 2 (b), please provide details of remedial action taken:

Page 2   UID Number:

REGISTERS OF SCOTLAND

FORM **1**
APPLICATION FOR FIRST REGISTRATION
(Land Registration (Scotland) Rules 2006 Rule 9(1)(a))
Version 25/10/2007

Mark an X in the appropriate box. If more space is required for any section of this form a separate sheet (s) may be added.

PART B CONTINUED

		YES	NO

3. Is there any person in possession or occupation of the subjects or any part of them adversely to the interest of the applicant?
If **YES**, please give details:

YES ☐ NO ☒

4. If the subjects were acquired by the applicant under any statutory provision, does the statutory provision restrict the applicant's power of disposal of the subjects?
If **YES**, please indicate the statute:

YES ☐ NO ☐ N/A ☒

5. (a) Are there any charges affecting the subjects or any part of them, except as stated in the Schedule of Heritable Securities etc. on page 6 of this application?
If **YES**, please give details:

YES ☐ NO ☒

(b) Apart from overriding interests are there any burdens affecting the subjects or any part of them, except as stated in the Schedule of Burdens on page 6 of this application?
If **YES**, please give details:

YES ☐ NO ☒

(c) Are there any overriding interests affecting the subjects or any part of them which you wish noted on the Title Sheet?
If **YES**, please give details:

YES ☐ NO ☒

(d) Are there any recurrent monetary payments (e.g. leasehold casualties) exigible from the subjects or any part of them?
If **YES**, please give details:

YES ☐ NO ☒

Page 3   UID Number: [   ]

678

REGISTERS OF SCOTLAND

FORM **1**
APPLICATION FOR FIRST REGISTRATION
(Land Registration (Scotland) Rules 2006 Rule 9(1)(a))
Version 25/10/2007

Mark an X in the appropriate box. If more space is required for any section of this form a separate sheet (s) may be added.

PART B CONTINUED

	YES	NO

6. Is any party to the deed inducing registration a company registered under the Companies Acts? — NO: X

If **YES**,

(a) has a receiver or administrator or liquidator been appointed?
If **YES**, please give details:

If **NO**, has any resolution been passed or court order made for the winding up of the company or petition presented for its liquidation?
If **YES**, please give details:

(b) (i) Is it a charity as defined in section 112 of the Companies Act 1989?

(ii) Is the transaction to which the deed gives effect one to which section 322A of the Companies Act 1985 applies?

Where the answer to either (b) (i) or (ii) is **YES**, please give details:

	YES	NO

7. Is any party to the deed inducing registration a corporate body other than a company registered under the Companies Acts? — NO: X

(a) If **YES**, is it acting *intra vires* ?
If **NO**, please give details:

(b) Has any arrangement been put in hand for the dissolution of any such corporate body?
If **YES**, please give details:

Page 4   UID Number:

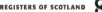

REGISTERS OF SCOTLAND

FORM **1**
APPLICATION FOR FIRST REGISTRATION
(Land Registration (Scotland) Rules 2006 Rule 9(1)(a))
Version 25/10/2007

Mark an X in the appropriate box. If more space is required for any section
of this form a separate sheet (s) may be added.

PART B CONTINUED

			YES	NO
8.		Is the application for registration of a dealing within the meaning of the Matrimonial Homes (Family Protection) (Scotland) Act 1981 or the Civil Partnership Act 2004?	X	
	(a)	If **YES**, could the subjects be a matrimonial home within the meaning of the 1981 Act or a family home within the meaning of the 2004 Act?		x
	(b)	If **YES**, do the necessary consents, renunciations, affidavits or written declarations exist confirming that the subjects will not be affected by any subsisting occupancy right of -		
	(i)	any spouse of the current registered proprietor and of any other party (excluding the applicant) who has subsequently been entitled to the interest in land, in terms of section 6 of the 1981 Act?		
	(ii)	any civil partner of the current registered proprietor and of any other party (excluding the applicant) who has subsequently been entitled to the interest in land, in terms of section 106 of the 2004 Act?		

			YES	NO
9.		Does the deed inducing registration grant, transfer, create, discharge or vary an interest in land?	X	
		If **YES**,		
	(a)	has a Land Register report been obtained which includes certification of a search in the Register of Inhibitions and Adjudications ('ROI') against 1. the granter of the deed and 2. any party whose right has vested in the granter by virtue of any unregistered mid-couple or link?	X	
	(i)	If **YES**, to what date was that search made? Date 20 11 2011		
	(ii)	If **NO**, has a search been carried out against the aforesaid granter/other party in the ROI?		
		If **YES**, to what date was that search made? Date		
	(b)	If you answered **YES** to any part of question **9(a)** does the Land Register Report or the search in the ROI disclose any subsisting entries in the ROI pertaining to the granter/other party aforesaid which are adverse to the interest in land?		x
		If **YES**, give details.		

		YES	NO
10.	Is the deed inducing registration in implement of the exercise of a power of sale under a heritable security?		x
	If **YES**, have the statutory procedures necessary for the proper exercise of such power been complied with?		

		YES	NO
11.	Is the deed inducing registration pursuant on a Compulsory Purchase Order?		x
	If **YES**, have the necessary statutory procedures been complied with?		

Page 5   UID Number:

REGISTERS OF SCOTLAND

FORM
APPLICATION FOR FIRST REGISTRATION
(Land Registration (Scotland) Rules 2006 Rule 9(1)(a))
Version 25/10/2007

1

Mark an X in the appropriate box. If more space is required for any section
of this form a separate sheet (s) may be added.

PART B CONTINUED

		YES	NO
12.	Is any party to the deed inducing registration subject to any legal incapacity or disability? If **YES**, please give details:		x

		YES	NO
13.	Are the deeds and documents detailed in the Inventory (Form 4) all the deeds and documents relevant to the title? If **NO**, please give details:	x	

		YES	NO
14.	Are there any facts and circumstances material to the right or title of the applicant which have not already been disclosed in this application or its accompanying documents? If **YES**, please give details:		x

SCHEDULE OF HERITABLE SECURITIES ETC. (N.B. New Charges granted by the applicant should not be included)

deed number 3 on Form 4

SCHEDULE OF BURDENS

Deed number 1 on Form 4

Mark X in the box to show if this property is Residential [x] Commercial [ ] Land Only [ ] Other [ ]

Do you wish to receive an electronic [ ] or paper [x] Certificate?

I/ We certify that the information supplied in this application is correct to the best of my/our knowledge and belief.

I/ We apply for registration in respect of Deed(s) No in the Inventory of Writs (Form 4). [2]

Signature	**Date of Signing**
Brown, Walker & Jarvis	20 11 2011

Page 6   UID Number: [ ]

681

REGISTERS OF SCOTLAND

FORM 4

INVENTORY OF WRITS RELEVANT TO APPLICATION FOR REGISTRATION (see Note 1)
(Land Registration (Scotland) Rules 2006 Rule 9(2))
Version 25/10/2007

1. From (see Note 2)

Brown, Jarvie & Walker
42 Piemonte Place
Kelvinforth
PH36 3RT

PART A - The notes referred to are contained in Notes and Directions for completion of Inventory of Writs

2. Agent's Reference

HRP/WRC/JAME232

3. Title No(s) (to be completed for a dealing with registered interests in land. see Note 3)   Mark X in box if more than 3 Title Numbers.

4. Subjects (see Note 4)

| House No/Name | 29 Sardinia Terrace | Postcode | PH36 5KF |

| Street Name & Town/City | Sardinia Terrace, Kelvinforth |

5. County (see Note 5)

Perth

PART B - The notes referred to are contained in Notes and Directions for completion of Inventory of Writs

Inventory - Particulars of Writs (Note 6), Continue overleaf if required

Item No.	Writ Submitted	Writ not Submitted	Writ	Grantee	Date of Recording		
1	S		Feu Contract	Frederick John Gretton	16	05	1904
2	S		Disposition	Angus George McDuff & spouse	12	08	1975
3	S		Standard Security	Black County Bank PLC	12	08	1975
4	S		Disposition	Stuart George James & spouse			
5	S		Standard Security	Southern Cross Bank PLC			
6	S		Property Definition Report				
7	S		SDLT 5				

Page 1   UID Number:

TO BE RETURNED TO:
Perth & Kinross Council
Executive Director (Housing & Community Care)
PO Box 7301
PERTH
PH1 5WL
Tel:(01738) 477430
Email: localtaxes@pkc.gov.uk
Fax: (01738) 475610
(Mon-Fri 8.45 to 5.00)

PERTH &
KINROSS
COUNCIL

NON DOMESTIC RATES
NOTIFICATION OF CHANGE OF OWNERSHIP /TENANCY

THIS FORM SHOULD BE COMPLETED TO NOTIFY THIS OFFICE OF ANY CHANGE IN OWNERSHIP OR TENANCY.

PLEASE COMPLETE SECTION A BELOW, TO ADVISE OF OWNERSHIP CHANGES.
SECTION B OVERLEAF, SHOULD BE COMPLETED TO ADVISE OF TENANCY CHANGES.

PLEASE RETURN THE COMPLETED FORM TO THE ADDRESS DETAILED ABOVE.

IF YOU REQUIRE ANY ASSISTANCE IN COMPLETING THIS FORM, PLEASE VISIT **THE RECEPTION AT PULLAR HOUSE, 35 KINNOULL STREET, PERTH. ALTERNATIVELY, YOU MAY TELEPHONE (01738) 477430.**

SECTION A: COMPLETE THIS SECTION TO NOTIFY OF A CHANGE IN OWNERSHIP.

Account Number (if known): PK 288495-958

Name of Seller: Angus George McDuff & Susannah Marjorie McDuff

Forwarding Address of Seller: 13 Chevening Row
Alnwick
Northamptonshire
NH15 8TR

Address of Property which has been Sold: 29 Sardinia Terrace
Kelvinforth
PH36 5KF

Date of Sale: 20 November 2011

Name and address of Solicitor acting for the Seller: O'Neill Middleton
65 Registration Row
PERTH PH36 3RT

Name and Address of Purchaser: Stuart Alfredo James & Parveen James

Date Property became Occupied: 20 Nov 2011

Please indicate form of Business (eg sole trader; Ltd Company; Partnership): N/A

Name and address of Solicitor acting for the Purchaser: Brown, Jarvie & Walker
42 Piemonte Place
Kelvinforth PH36 3RT

Please also complete overleaf.

683

SECTION B: COMPLETE THIS SECTION TO NOTIFY OF A CHANGE IN TENANCY.

Account Number (if known):

Name of Outgoing Tenant:

Forwarding Address of Outgoing Tenant:

Address of Property which has been Vacated:

Tenancy End Date:

Name and address of Landlord / Letting Agent:

Name and Address of Incoming Tenant:

Please indicate form of Business (eg sole trader; Ltd Company; Partnership) for incoming Tenant:

Tenancy Start Date for Incoming Tenant:

SECTION C: DECLARATION - MUST BE COMPLETED

I DECLARE THAT THE INFORMATION GIVEN ON THIS FORM IS, TO THE BEST OF MY KNOWLEDGE, ACCURATE AND COMPLETE.

Signature: .... **Date:**..

DATA PROTECTION

Any information you have provided will be used for the billing and collection of local taxes and the recovery of any unpaid debts due to the Council. Disclosures to third parties will only be made to agents employed by Perth & Kinross Council to recover unpaid debts and to those organisations with a legal right of access, e.g. Inland Revenue. This authority is under a duty to protect the public funds it administers, and to this end may use the information you have provided for the prevention and detection of fraud therefore it may also share this information with other bodies for these purposes.

In terms of the Data Protection Act 1998, you are entitled to know what information this Council holds about you, on payment of a fee of £10. Application should be made to the Executive Director (Housing & Community Care), Perth & Kinross Council, Pullar House, 35 Kinnoull Street, Perth, PH1 5GD.

(LAND REGISTRATION (SCOTLAND) RULES 1980, RULE 14)

LAND REGISTER OF SCOTLAND

LAND CERTIFICATE

VERSION 28/11/2010

Title Number: PTH87648

Subjects: 29 Sardinia Terrace
                  Kelvinforth PH36 5KF

THIS LAND CERTIFICATE, ISSUED PURSUANT TO SECTION 5(2)

OF THE LAND REGISTRATION (SCOTLAND) ACT 1979,

IS A COPY OF THE TITLE SHEET RELATING TO THE ABOVE
SUBJECTS

STATEMENT OF INDEMNITY

Subject to any specific qualifications entered in the Title Sheet of which
this Land Certificate is a copy, a person who suffers loss as a result of
the events specified in section 12(1) of the above Act shall be entitled to
be indemnified in respect of that loss by the Keeper of the Registers of
Scotland in terms of that Act.

ATTENTION IS DRAWN TO THE NOTICE AND GENERAL
INFORMATION OVERLEAF

LAND REGISTER OF SCOTLAND	Officer's ID / Date	TITLE NUMBER
	7347 12/12/2010	**PTH87648**
✦	ORDNANCE SURVEY NATIONAL GRID REFERENCE	Scale 1/1250
NW6347SE NW6347NE		

CROWN COPYRIGHT © - This copy has been purchased by the ROS Digital Mapping System on 12/12/2010 and was made with the authority of Ordnance Survey pursuant to Section 47 of the Copyright, Designs and Patents Act 1988. Unless that Act provides a relevant exception to copyright, the copy must not be copied without the prior permission of the copyright owner.

THE BOUNDARIES INDICATED HEREON ARE
MORE FULLY DEFINED IN THE TITLE SHEET

A1

TITLE NUMBER PTH87648

A. PROPERTY SECTION

DATE OF FIRST REGISTRATION
22 NOV 2011

DATE TITLE SHEET UPDATED TO
22 NOV 2011

DATE LAND CERTIFICATE
UPDATED TO
22 NOV 2011

INTEREST
PROPRIETOR

MAP REFERENCE
NW6347SE NW6347NE

DESCRIPTION

Subjects 29 SARDINIA TERRACE, KELVINFORTH PH36 5KF edged red on the Title Plan.

Note: the boundaries between the points indicated on the Title Plan are as follows:

A-B   North West boundary Centre line
B-C   South West boundary Centre line
C-D   South East boundary Centre line

See General Information, Note 2

B1

TITLE NUMBER PTH87648

B. PROPRIETORSHIP SECTION

ENTRY	PROPRIETOR CONSIDERATION	DATE OF REGISTRATION	

STUART ALFREDO JAMES and PARVEEN JAMES both Hope Cottage, Kinlochalmond   22 NOV 2011   £450,000

DATE OF ENTRY
20 NOV 2011

Note 1:   There are in respect of the subjects in this Title no subsisting occupancy rights, in terms of the Matrimonial Homes (Family Protection) (Scotland) Act 1981, of spouses or persons who were formerly entitled to the said subjects.

Note 2:   There are in respect of the subjects in this Title no subsisting occupancy rights, in terms of the Civil Partnership Act 2004, of partners of persons who were formerly entitled to the said subjects.

C1

TITLE NUMBER PTH87648

C. CHARGES SECTION

ENTRY	SPECIFICATION	DATE OF REGISTRATION
1.	Standard Security by the said STUART ALFREDO JAMES and PARVEEN JAMES to SOUTHERN CROSS BANK PLC	22 NOV 2011

TITLE NUMBER PTH87648

D. BURDENS SECTION

ENTRY SPECIFICATION

1   Feu Charter by the Kinlochalmond Real Estate Company (who and whose successors are hereinafter referred to as the superiors) to Frederick John Gretton and his heirs and assignees (who and whose successors are hereinafter referred to as the said disponees), recorded GRS (Perth) 16 May 1904, of the subjects in this Title, contains the following reservation and burdens:

Reserving always to us and our assignees the unused half of the west boundary wall of the subjects hereby disponed;

And also with and under (First) the said disponees shall be bound and obliged in all time coming to maintain and when necessary to renew and rebuild upon the said area of ground above disponed as a self contained dwelling-house consisting of two stories of the value of at least one thousand pound sterling which dwelling-house shall always be of the same design, materials and dimensions and on the same site as the present dwelling-house, and no building of any description shall at any time be erected on said area of ground until the site and the plans and elevations thereof and materials therefor shall have approved of in writing by the superiors or their architect;

(Second) the said disponees shall be bound and obliged to keep and maintain in good order and repair in all time coming the division walls and fences surrounding the subjects hereby disponed, the gables, division walls and fences on the west north and south boundaries shall be mutual between and be maintained at the mutual expense of the feuars of the subjects adjoining respectively and the said disponees, but the said disponees shall have no claim against us or our foresaids under any circumstances for any part of the expense of maintaining such gables or division walls and fences;

(Third) the said disponees shall be bound to keep constantly insured against loss by fire with some responsible insurance company to the extent of nine hundred pounds said dwelling-house erected upon the ground above disponed and to exhibit to the superiors the receipts for the premiums upon the insurance policies as the same fall due, declaring that any sums that may be recovered under such policies shall be expended by the said disponees in immediately rebuilding and restoring the said buildings, which, in the event of destruction, shall be rebuilt of the same value according to the same plans and elevations and upon the same sites as the original buildings, and the superiors shall be entitled to see the money recovered under any insurance policy applied in terms hereof;

(Fourth) the ground in front of and behind the dwelling-house erected on the area of ground hereby disponed shall at no time be used or applied for the purpose of buildings of any description except in the event of the superiors authorising the erection of relative offices in connection with said dwelling-house, declaring that said ground in front of and behind said dwelling-house shall be kept and used in all time as ornamental pleasure ground only, the only exception being that the ground behind may be used as a drying green;

(Fifth) the said disponees are hereby expressly prohibited from erecting upon the said area of ground hereby disponed any building other than those herein specifically provided for, and the said disponees are further expressly prohibited from converting any building on the said area of ground to any purpose other than that of a self -contained dwelling-house for the occupancy of one family only, and from using the said buildings on said area of ground for any other purpose than as a private family residence;

(Sixth) in respect we or our authors have formed the macadamised carriage with surface water channel and kerb stone for footpath on both sides of the said road of Sardinia Terrace along the east boundary of the area of ground hereby disponed and have also formed in the said roadway a common drain for carrying off the sewage from the lands and buildings belonging to us and our feuars, including the subjects hereby disponed, the said disponees shall be bound along with the feuar on the opposite side of said road at mutual expense in all time coming or until the same shall be taken over by the County Authorities and kept up at the public expense, to maintain and uphold the same so far as ex adverso of the said area of ground hereby disponed. The said disponees shall also be bound to pay the proportion of the cost of putting said road and others in repair preparatory to their being taken over by the County Authorities and also to maintain and uphold in good repair in all time the concrete footpath along the whole length of the frontage of the area of ground hereby disponed and all drains within the area of ground hereby disponed, including the service drains which run from north to south through the ground for the use of said dwelling-house and the houses erected or to be erected to the north and west thereof;

(Seventh) Notwithstanding that the lands belonging to us have been laid out according to a feuing plan, it shall be competent to us or our successors in said subjects to alter the said feuing plan and the streets and roads not yet formed in any way which we or our foresaids may hereafter consider desirable, and also to appropriate as we and our foresaids may see fit, the lands at any time remaining unfeued and to vary or depart entirely from the burdens, conditions, provisions and others under which the same may be held;

(Eighth) Notwithstanding and without prejudice to anything herein contained, it is hereby provided and declared that should we or our foresaids either expressly or by silence allow any of the burdens, conditions, provisions, prohibitions and declarations herein written to be in any way relaxed or modified the doing thereof shall not entitle any other feuar or proprietor to act without the consent of us or our foresaids as if he had obtained or was entitled to obtain similar or other relaxations or modifications, nor shall it hinder us or our foresaids from preventing his so acting any law or custom to the contrary notwithstanding, and providing in like manner that should we or our foresaids either expressly or by silence modify or relax any of the burdens, conditions, provisions, prohibitions and declarations in the feu right of any other of the feuars of our lands at Kinlochalmond, the doing thereof shall not entitle the said disponees to act without the consent of us or our foresaids as if he or they had obtained or were entitled to obtain similar or other relaxations or modifications, nor shall it hinder us or our foresaids from preventing the said disponees from so acting

Implemented letter of obligation

Messrs. Brown Jarvis & Walker.

20 November 2011

Dear Sirs   Implemented 16 July 2012

Angus George McDuff and Susannah Marjorie McDuff (the 'Seller')

Stuart Alfredo James and Parveen James (the 'Purchaser')

29 Sardinia Terrace, Kelvinforth (the 'Property')

With reference to the settlement of this transaction today, we hereby:

1. Undertake to clear the records of any deed, decree or diligence (other than such as may be created by or against your clients) which may be recorded in the Property or Personal Registers or to which effect may be given in the Land Register in the period from 19 November 2011 to 14 days from today's date inclusive (or to the earlier date of registration of the Purchaser's interest in the Property) and which would cause the Keeper to make an entry on, or qualify his indemnity in, the Land Certificate to be issued in respect of that interest; and

2. Confirm that, to the best of our knowledge and belief, the answers to the questions numbered 1 to 14 in the draft form 1 adjusted with you (in so far as these answers relate to our client or to our clients' interest in the above subjects) are still correct.

Yours faithfully

O'Neill Middleton

Note: That's it; transaction completed and happy clients. Check for any balances on the ledger and close the file.

Appendix II

Purchaser's solicitor's checklist

No	Item	Due	Done
1	Meet or talk to client(s). Discuss purchase in outline. Provide estimate of fees and outlays (it is useful to have a spreadsheet for this). Establish funding source. Consider whether any conflict of interest exists that would prevent you from acting.		
	Gather the facts surrounding the client's objective in purchasing the property. If it is to convert into a B&B, for example, this could be a material consideration when reporting on title and any planning constraints.		
	Ask about the shares in which the property will be held. Consider a co-habitation agreement for parties who are not married. Advise on the pros and cons of having a survivorship destination in the title. Seek mandate to act for both spouses. When acting for a company, establish authority of person giving you instructions.		
2	Carry out client due diligence and verification. Complete proforma checklist and keep copies of identification documents on file. Also send a copy to the MLRO for a central file, if that is the office practice.		
	Await clearance before carrying out any work or receiving any funds.		
3	Once the client has been approved, send letter of engagement and terms of business letter. Remember to carve out any areas where you are not qualified (e.g. taxation or environmental). Provide full estimate of fees and outlays. Check that the VAT rate is correct. Provide for a default hourly rate for complex work outside the scope of a fixed fee.		
4	Note the client's interest with seller's solicitors (unnecessary where property is fixed price).		

No	Item	Due	Done
5	Gather information about the property. Ask seller's solicitors for particulars and Home Report (if residential). Ask about other notes of interest to gauge interest.		
6	Take full instructions on the details of the offer, including parties, property (including any moveables), price, suspensive conditions, date of entry. If the date of entry depends on a trigger event, ensure that you advise on the need for a long-stop date allowing your client to resile for non-purification after a reasonable period.		
7	If the property is a home, consider the terms of the Home Report. Check that the lender will accept the valuation for mortgage purposes.		
	If a commercial property, arrange a survey on behalf of the purchaser (or the purchaser can arrange this themselves, if they prefer) or note that offer is to be 'subject to survey'.		
8	Consider whether to submit offer immediately or wait for closing date to be set. Remember that there is no requirement for the seller to set a closing date at all. If a closing date has been set, ensure that appropriate diary entries are made.		
9	Satisfy yourself that the client has access to funds, whether privately or from a bank loan.		
10	Draft offer, being careful to check all the details from your instructions. Ensure you are using the latest version, if using standard missives. Make sure the offer is checked and ready to go out and that a partner is available to sign the offer on behalf of the firm. If your firm's practice is to witness formal missives, ensure that a witness is on hand to witness the partner's signature.		
11	Submit offer and send a copy to the client. Make sure that the seller's solicitor has received the offer and record the acknowledgement in the file.		

No	Item	Due	Done
12	If the offer is acceptable in principle to the seller, both parties' solicitors adjust missives until conclusion. This is usually effected by adjustment of the formal offer, which is treated as a draft for these purposes. The purchaser's solicitor would then submit a fresh offer in the agreed terms for a *de plano* acceptance by the seller's solicitor.		
	During this period both parties' solicitors should appraise clients of the risk of "open missives", which is that neither party is legally bound until conclusion. Take instructions from clients on any new points arising. Send copies of all formal missive letters sent on behalf of the client to the client forthwith.		
	If the property is a commercial property and if the offer has been submitted as 'subject to survey', ensure that a survey is arranged as soon as possible so that the suspensive condition can be purified.		
13	Following adjustment of missives in consultation with your client. Send copies of all missive letters as soon as they are issued. Inform clients that missives have been completed and that they are now bound to purchase the property. Remind them of the penalties for not completing on time. If no loan instructions have yet been received, enquire into progress with the loan. Suggest an escalation to avoid late arrival of loan instructions causing last minute pressure.		
14	Advise client that, although risk passes at settlement, it is prudent for them to arrange buildings insurance. Double insurance is better than no insurance.		
15	Once loan instructions are received, peruse carefully for any unusual conditions. Refer to the online CML lenders' handbook relevant to the particular lender to ensure that the latest terms are understood where property is residential.		
16	Make diary entries for the date of entry, with appropriate reminders or file 'bring forward' entries. Ensure that double entries are made in another diary or at the very least that colleagues can access your diary.		

No	Item	Due	Done
17	Once title deeds are received, note that there is usually a tight timescale to satisfy your client on the title. If the property is on an estate with similar properties, check with colleagues to see if any of them have noted a similar title. Note title and raise any observations with the seller's solicitor. Consider that third parties may be entitled to enforce title conditions. Report any unusual or potentially restrictive conditions contained in the title to the client.		
	Check that you have examined all the titles disclosed by the Form 10A or Form 11A and ask to see quick copies of any deeds disclosed that have not been exhibited.		
18	Make sure that the seller has produced a suitable plan for annexing to the disposition for a first registration. Send a copy to the client to ensure that this plan accords with their expectations.		
19	If the transaction will trigger a first registration, ensure that a clear P16 Report has been exhibited. If there is an overlap or a gap, resulting in your client receiving more or less of the property, take your client's instructions on how they would like to proceed.		
20	Once Property Enquiry Certificate is received, note the position with planning and building control, roads, water and sewerage. If the road is adopted, check that there are no gaps from the verge of the adopted road to the entrance of the property. If water and sewerage are supplied from the main, ensure that there are sufficient rights to lead pipes from the mains to the property.		
	If water and sewerage services are not connected to the main, check that there are sufficient rights pertaining to the property, such as the right to use a septic tank or soakaway and a right of access or a right to lead pipes over others' land.		
	Check the position with planning and building control and that the requisite consents tie in with the surveyor's report in respect of the actual alterations that have been made to the property.		
	Report to the client on any issues relating to the Property Enquiry Certificate.		

No	Item	Due	Done
21	Approve or revise the seller's solicitors drafts, namely: – letter of obligation; – Form 11 or 13 (updated search); – discharge of any existing securities; – letter of non-crystallisation (if there is a floating charge);		
22	Draft the disposition in favour of your client. Remember to include any conditions that were expressly agreed to be inserted into the disposition in the missives.		
	If the property is a development site, ensure that there is a right to connect to any roads or services.		
	Draft the Form 1 or Form 2 (application for registration) and the Form 4 (inventory of deeds submitted).		
23	When acting for both purchaser and lender, draft the standard security in favour of the lender and a Form 2. Where acting for both parties, only one Form 4 is required. For a commercial purchaser, the lender will be separately represented. Revise the standard security and Forms 2 and 4 from the lender's solicitors		
	Draft a matrimonial home or family home declaration or consent to protect the lender's interest, if applicable.		
24	Consider making any further enquiries that the seller's solicitor has not undertaken in missives, but note that the opportunity to resile in the event of any item materially prejudicial to the purchaser must be included in the missives.		
25	Draft the Stamp Duty Land Tax (SDLT) Land Transaction Return (LTR) on behalf of the purchaser and send this to them for approval, signature and return. Make clear in any covering letter that the LTR is a tax return, that they should check the details thoroughly and that you cannot be responsible for any mistakes.		

No	Item	Due	Done
26	Agree any alterations to the disposition and Forms 1 or 2 and 4. Make corrections and engross (make a final version) the disposition. Make sure you have attached any plans and schedules and that these are the correct versions. Then send the engrossed disposition with draft for comparison purposes to the seller's solicitor for the seller to sign.		
27	Prepare final versions of the Forms 1 or 2 and 4.		
28	Meet clients to arrange for them to sign the standard security and any declaration or consent in good time for settlement.		
	If meeting clients is likely to be difficult, send the standard security and forms well in advance of settlement with clear instructions as to how and where they should be signed. It is advisable to enclose a stamped address envelope to ensure that the documents are returned as swiftly as possible.		
29	Send state for settlement to clients, outlining how much money you expect from them, and when. If funds are being sent by cheque ask to be placed in funds at least five working days in advance. It's a good practice to ensure that your fee is covered at this point, if you have provided for this in your letter of engagement.		
	If you have accepted the standard condition allowing client to report defects in central heating systems to the seller within five days, ensure that the client is aware of this requirement in plenty of time to arrange for an inspection immediately on entry.		
	Report on title to the lender and requisition funds. Funds are normally sent by telegraphic transfer the day that the funds are requested. These funds can arrive at any time up to 4pm, so it is advisable to requisition the funds for the day before the date of entry to ensure that these can in turn be transferred to the seller's solicitor before the cut-off point for transfer (usually around 2.30pm).		
	Explain to the purchaser why it is necessary for them to incur an extra day's interest.		
	Alert your cashroom that you await the funds, so that you will be informed as soon as the funds arrive.		

No	Item	Due	Done
30	Once your cashroom has confirmed that all the funds have arrived in the clients' account and have cleared, you are in a position to settle/complete.		
	Once you are satisfied that there are no points outstanding, requisition the firm's cheque. Again this will require to be signed by a partner, so ensure that a partner will be available to sign on behalf of the firm.		
	Similarly, authority for a telegraphic transfer of funds will require to be signed by a partner.		
	If posting a settlement cheque, ensure it is sent in good time to arrive at the seller's solicitor's office for settlement. If you are sending a cheque or transferring funds before you have the signed disposition in your possession, ensure that the seller's solicitor understands that these funds are to be held as undelivered and held to your order, pending settlement.		
31	Ensure the purchase funds have arrived.		
	Once the seller's settlement items have been delivered, check these over carefully and compare signed engrossments with the corresponding drafts. These should comprise: √ keys, or arrangements for their collection; √ signed disposition with draft; √ principal reports, certificates, guarantees, building control documentation etc; √ clear Form 11A Report; √ deliverable title deeds; √ signed letter of obligation with draft; √ letter of non-crystallisation (if applicable); √ charges search if seller is a company; √ any matrimonial home or family home declaration or consent (if applicable); √ receipted state for settlement and draft; √ discharge of any securities with draft and signed Form 2 with arrangements for paying the cost of registration; and		

No	Item	Due	Done
	√ signed Form 2 or Sasine Application Form (SAF) with arrangements for paying the cost of registration in respect of any burdens to be registered against the retained property. For a completion of commercial property, see the PSG checklist reproduced at the end of Chapter 11.		
	Check that all deeds have been signed and dated properly and that any plans and schedules are present and have been signed correctly. Ensure that deeds have been witnessed and that you have the witness' full details either on the deed or in separate schedule.		
	Once satisfied, contact the seller's solicitor to confirm that you are treating the transaction as settled and that the cheque or funds can be released.		
32	Submit LTR to HMRC and pay SDLT.		
33	Add the testing clause to the disposition, or complete details in the signing block.		
34	Collate and send application to the Land Register, including: ● Form 1 or 2; ● Form 4; ● cheque for registration costs (if not using direct debit); ● all items mentioned on the Form 4, which include: – relevant title deeds (marshalled in number order); – matrimonial home and family home affidavits (if -appropriate); – SDLT5 certificate; ● discharge of security and Form 2 and 4, with payment.		
35	Ensure that the client's building insurance arrangements have been put in place.		
36	Notify lenders of the completion of the transaction and the transfer of the funds.		

No	Item	Due	Done
37	Send the client a receipted fee note and a statement breaking down all the disbursements.		
38	Send notice of change of ownership to the Local Authority.		
39	Await any observations from the Keeper. These should be responded to within 60 days otherwise there is a danger that the application will be cancelled.		
40	Eventually the Land Certificate and Charge Certificate are received together the deeds.		
	Compare with the disposition and check for any exclusion of indemnity or other irregularity.		
	On being satisfied, the letter of obligation is marked as 'implemented' and is returned to the seller's solicitor.		
41	The Land Certificate, Charge Certificate and any other documents or certificates (e.g. NHBC, planning, treatment guarantees etc) are placed in the safe, sent to the lender, or returned to the client for safe-keeping.		

Appendix III

Seller's solicitor's checklist

No	Item	Due	Done
1	Meet or talk to client(s). Discuss sale in outline. Provide estimate of fees and outlays (it is useful to have a spreadsheet for this). Consider whether any conflict of interest exists that would prevent you from acting.		
	Gather the facts surrounding the ownership and the client's use of the property. Collate the various marketing materials in circulation. If you have an estate agency, try to cross-sell the marketing. Ask to see Home Report if the seller has commissioned one. If not, you could offer to arrange this. If the sale is a commercial property, ask if the client has already engaged a surveyor.		
	Ask about the ownership of the property and whether there are any legal formalities to be aware of, ie is the client acting as executor, or does a company director have authority to instruct you direct? Also ascertain the whereabouts of the title deeds, unless clients are already established and you hold these. Seek mandate to act for both spouses.		
2	Carry out client due diligence and verification. Complete proforma checklist and keep copies of identification documents on file. Also send a copy to the MLRO for a central file, if that is the office practice.		
	Await clearance before carrying out any work or receiving any funds.		
3	Once the client has been approved, send letter of engagement and terms of business letter. Remember to carve out any areas where you are not qualified (eg taxation or environmental). Provide full estimate of fees and outlays. Check that the VAT rate is correct. Provide for a default hourly rate for complex work outside the scope of a fixed fee.		

No	Item	Due	Done
4	Note the any interest that is registered with you from solicitors (unnecessary where property is fixed price). Ensure that client is kept appraised of developments on a regular basis.		
5	If multiple notes of interest are received, consider setting a closing date. Any offers before the closing date should be communicated to the client for consideration.		
6	Requisition title deeds or, to speed things up, download a quick copy Land Certificate from Registers Direct. Ask client to complete Property Questionnaire if they haven't already.		
7	Order P16 Report, Form 10 and a Property Enquiry Certificate for the property.		
	Check for any missing deeds or documents. Obtain quick copies of any missing deeds and apply for retrospective consent that may be required, eg a Letter of Comfort from the Council in respect of Building Control matters.		
8	If a plan is required, arrange for this to be drawn up. Check with client whether any land is being retained and whether any title conditions should be inserted into the title to the subjects.		
9	On receiving an offer, take full instructions. Report principal terms to the client, including parties, property (including any moveables), price, suspensive conditions, date of entry. Evaluate offers to assist client to differentiate. Send copy offers to the client. If the date of entry depends on a trigger event, check whether your client finds this acceptable and ensure that you advise on the need for a long-stop date allowing your client to resile for non-purification after a reasonable period.		
10	If the offer is acceptable, verbally confirm to purchaser's solicitor. Agree with purchaser's solicitor whether to use the offer as a draft or whether a formal Qualified Acceptance is required.		
11	Inform solicitors of unsuccessful offerors.		

No	Item	Due	Done
12	If the offer is acceptable in principle to the seller, both parties' solicitors adjust missives until conclusion. This is usually effected by adjustment of the formal offer, which is treated as a draft for these purposes. The purchaser's solicitor would then submit a fresh offer in the agreed terms for a *de plano* acceptance by the seller's solicitor.		
	During this period both parties' solicitors should appraise clients of the risk of "open missives", which is that neither party is legally bound until conclusion. Take instructions from clients on any new points arising. Send copies of all formal missive letters sent on behalf of the client to the client forthwith.		
	If the property is a commercial property and if the offer has been submitted as 'subject to survey', ensure that the purchaser's solicitor has arranged a survey as soon as possible so that the suspensive condition can be purified.		
13	Following adjustment of missives in consultation with your clients. Send copies of all missive letters as soon as they are issued. Inform clients that missives have been completed and that the purchasers are now bound to sell the property.		
14	Advise client that, because risk passes at settlement, they must not cancel their buildings insurance.		
15	Inform the lenders of the sale and the date of entry. Also ask them to state how much is to be repaid on redemption of the loan, with a daily interest figure, so the figure can be calculated in cases of delay.		
16	Make diary entries for the date of entry, with appropriate reminders or file "bring forward" entries. Ensure that double entries are made in another diary or at the very least that colleagues can access your diary.		

No	Item	Due	Done
17	Send titles, Form 10A Report, Property Enquiry Certificate and P16, draft Form 11, draft discharge of security and relative Forms 2 and 4, draft state for settlement, and any guarantees, certificates, consents or other paperwork that may be useful to purchaser's solicitor for examination.		
	Deal with any observations on title from the purchaser's solicitor.		
18	Contact the local Council and intimate forthcoming change of address details.		
19	Advise your client to contact their utility providers to arrange for final readings to close the accounts. Also notify if the purchaser is going to take over any of the services.		
20	Revise the draft disposition received from the purchaser's solicitor and the draft Forms 1 or 2 and 4. Remember to ensure any conditions that were expressly agreed to be inserted into the disposition in the missives are included. Ensure that your clients retained property is adequately described (or shown on plan) as the benefited property, if applicable.		
	Engross discharge of security and send to lender in plenty of time for settlement. Some banks charge a "sealing" fee of around £50. Although this will be added to loan, advise your client of this extra outgoing. Send redemption statement to the client so that there are no nasty surprises after settlement.		
	Expeditiously deal with all observations on title and requisitions from the purchaser's solicitor.		
21	Arrange to receive all sets of keys for delivery or agree alternative handover arrangement with purchaser's solicitor.		
22	Compare the engrossed disposition with the draft. Arrange for your clients to sign the disposition and any declaration or consent required.		
	Return draft disposition to the purchaser's solicitor.		
23	Ensure that the signed discharge of security is available, type on a testing clause (if there is no signing block) and engross the Forms 2 and 4.		

No	Item	Due	Done
24	Engross letter of obligation onto firm's notepaper and arrange for a partner to sign it on behalf of the firm. Ensure that checks have been carried out to make the letter of obligation 'classic'.		
25	Once everything is ready, arrange logistics of settlement with purchaser's solicitor. Most settlements will be carried out by an exchange of items in the mail.		
26	Arrange for a Form 11A to be sent just prior to settlement. A Form 11A more than two days old may need to refreshed for settlement.		
27	Send the following settlement items to the purchaser's solicitor to arrive on time for settlement: √ keys, or arrangements for their collection; √ signed disposition with draft; √ principal reports, certificates, guarantees, building control documentation etc; √ clear Form 11A Report; √ deliverable title deeds; signed letter of obligation with draft; √ letter of non-crystallisation (if applicable); √ charges search if seller is a company; √ any matrimonial home or family home declaration or consent (if applicable) √ receipted state for settlement and draft; √ discharge of any securities with draft and signed Form 2 with arrangements for paying the cost of registration; and √ signed Form 2 or Sasine Application Form (SAF) with arrangements for paying the cost of registration in respect of any burdens to be registered against the retained property. For a completion of commercial property, see the PSG checklist reproduced at the end of Chapter 11.		
	Confirm to purchaser's solicitor that the purchase funds have arrived and being held to order; ask whether your settlement items are in order and therefore whether funds can be released. Release keys. Telephone clients to confirm that the sale has been completed.		

No	Item	Due	Done
28	Repay bank loan once you have cleared funds. If sending a cheque in redemption of the loan, ensure that additional daily rate specified in the redemption statement is added for the time it will take the cheque to arrive in the post and clear. Over-estimate rather than under-estimate.		
29	Pay any other bills to come from the proceeds, eg estate agents.		
30	Pay your own fee and outlays from the proceeds.		
31	Send receipted invoices to client for accounts settled, with cheque for net free proceeds of the sale and statement of account. Payment can be made to the seller's bank account, if so directed or may be retained on interest-bearing account and applied to an onward purchase, if so instructed.		
32	Remind client to cancel any insurance policies or utilities in respect of the property. Notify Council of change of ownership if this has not been done before.		
33	Tidy up loose filing and close file once ledger is clear.		
34	Once discharge is received back from the Registers, this means the title has been registered. Write to purchaser's solicitors to ask for return of the letter of obligation.		

Appendix IV

Style letter to borrower's spouse

Dear [   ]

This letter confirms the advice that [I][we] gave you at our meeting [today] in respect of the proposals that your house known as [   ] (the Property) is to be mortgaged to [   ] (the Lender) to secure a loan from the Lender to [   ] (the Borrower).

The Lender requires that you are given this advice so that having signed the standard security (mortgage deed) [and related documents] you will not be able to claim afterwards that you are not legally bound by [it][them].

1   The property is owned [in your sole name][in the Borrower's sole name] [in the joint names of yourself and [   ]] and you [both] are required to sign [the standard security] [and related documents] in favour of the Lender.

2   Enclosed are copies of the standard security which you signed earlier today [and the mortgage conditions that are incorporated into it] [and related documents]. The following is a summary of the main provisions and implications, but does not cover everything.

3   The standard security is [initially] required to give the Lender security for a loan [of £[   ]][a loan facility of up to £[   ]] to be provided to the Borrower. [However, the mortgage will be on 'all sums due or to become due' terms and will also give the Lender security over the Property for:

   3.1   any further loan or increased facility that the Borrower (individually or jointly with you or anyone else) may in future obtain from the Lender while the standard security remains in existence, even if this is done without your knowledge or consent;

3.2 any existing loans from the Lender to the Borrower (individually or jointly with you or anyone else), even if you do not know about them;

3.3 any existing or future loans that you yourself may obtain (individually or jointly with anyone else) from the Lender while the standard security remains in existence;

3.4 any sums owing to the Lender, at any time while the standard security remains in existence, by any other person or company if you or the Borrower has already given, or in the future give, a guarantee for those sums to the Lender, and even if the Borrower has given or gives such a guarantee without your knowledge and consent;

3.5 interest on all such sums as charged by the Lender;

3.6 [anything else];

According to the terms of the loan the Lender can demand repayment at [any time], [on fixed dates], [by instalments], [set out repayment requirements].

4 During the subsistence of the mortgage, [you][the Borrower] must:

4.1 keep the Property insured in accordance with the Lender's requirements;

4.2 keep the Property in good repair;

4.3 not make any substantial alterations or changes of use without the Lender's consent;

4.4 not let the Property or take in lodgers without the Lender's consent;

4.5 comply with all conditions and restrictions affecting the Property as set out in the title deeds;

4.6 [anything else].

5 The standard security gives the Lender a [first] charge over the Property as security for all the sums mentioned in paragraph 3 above. You could lose the Property if the Borrower's business does not prosper, or if the

borrowing is increased unwisely. This is because, if any loan repayment or interest charge is not paid on time, the Lender would be entitled to call up the standard security and take court proceedings to evict you and any other occupiers from the Property and sell the Property in order to obtain repayment.

6   [The Lender reserves the right to transfer the benefit of the standard security to another lender.]

7   [In addition, the mortgage will contain an obligation by you to pay all sums falling within paragraph 3 above if the Borrower fails to pay them [up to a maximum of £[   ] plus interest charged by the Lender.] This means that [up to that level] you will be a guarantor for the liabilities of the Borrower to the Lender, you will be personally liable for those sums, you could be sued by the Lender for them and, if the value of the Property and your other assets is insufficient to meet those sums, you could be made bankrupt as well as losing the Property.]

8   [Any other feature of the facility needing comment?]

The above legal advice relates to the effect of the mortgage documents and the types of risks that arise. [However, [I am][we are] not qualified to assess the likelihood of those risks actually materialising. That depends largely on the financial standing and prospects of the Borrower [and his business], although you should also consider whether the sums secured could be repaid from the sale value of the Property and your other assets. You confirmed when we met that you were willing to sign [the mortgage documentation] without first assessing the risks by taking on those important financial aspects from a chartered accountant or other qualified professional financial adviser [independent of the Borrower].]

Please sign the acknowledgement at the end of the enclosed copy of this letter to acknowledge that you have been given, and you have understood, this advice, that you are willing to enter into the mortgage and that you will not required the Lender to vary any of the terms. [I][We] will retain the signed documentation in this office and will only release it to the Lender's solicitors on receipt of the signed duplicate letter.

Yours [   ]

ACKNOWLEDGEMENT

I confirm that I have read this letter and have received and understood the advice given in it. I confirm that I have decided, of my own free will, to enter into the mortgage, I do not require the Lender to vary any of the terms, [I do not require any further legal advice], and I agreed that the Lender may be told that I have received the advice in this letter.

Signed: Date:

Appendix V

Map of Scottish local government areas

Appendix VI

Map of registration counties

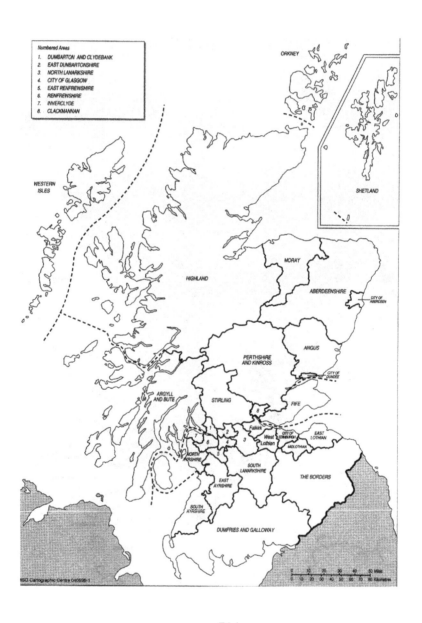

Numbered Areas
1. DUMBARTON AND CLYDEBANK
2. EAST DUNBARTONSHIRE
3. NORTH LANARKSHIRE
4. CITY OF GLASGOW
5. EAST RENFREWSHIRE
6. RENFREWSHIRE
7. INVERCLYDE
8. CLACKMANNAN

ORKNEY

SHETLAND

WESTERN ISLES

MORAY

HIGHLAND

ABERDEENSHIRE

CITY OF ABERDEEN

ANGUS

PERTHSHIRE AND KINROSS

CITY OF DUNDEE

ARGYLL AND BUTE

STIRLING

FIFE

Falkirk

West Lothian

CITY OF EDINBURGH

EAST LOTHIAN

MIDLOTHIAN

NORTH AYRSHIRE

SOUTH LANARKSHIRE

THE BORDERS

EAST AYRSHIRE

SOUTH AYRSHIRE

DUMFRIES AND GALLOWAY

HSO Cartographic Centre 040595-1

0   10   20   30   40   50 Miles
0   10   20   30   40   50   60   70   80 Kilometres

Index

References are to paragraph number